OPERATIONS
MANAGEMENT

Sustainability and Supply Chain Management

Jay Heizer • Barry Render • Chuck Munson

Operations Management
Sustainability and Supply Chain Management

Second Custom Edition for San Francisco State University

Taken from:
Operations Management: Sustainability and Supply Chain Management
by Jay Heizer, Barry Render, and Chuck Munson

Cover Art: Courtesy of Pearson Learning Solutions.

Taken from:

Operations Management: Sustainability and Supply Chain Management
by Jay Heizer, Barry Render, and Chuck Munson
Copyright © 2017, 2014, 2011 by Pearson Education, Inc.
New York, New York 10013

Pearson Education, Inc., 330 Hudson Street, New York, New York 10013
A Pearson Education Company
www.pearsoned.com

Printed in the United States of America

2   16

000200010272050423

ZS

ISBN 10: 1-323-50866-X
ISBN 13: 978-1-323-50866-4

To Karen Heizer Herrmann, all a sister could ever be

J.H.

To Donna, Charlie, and Jesse

B.R.

To Kim, Christopher, and Mark Munson for their unwavering support,
and to Bentonville High School teachers Velma Reed and Cheryl Gregory,
who instilled in me the importance of detail and a love of learning

C.M.

ABOUT THE AUTHORS

JAY HEIZER

Professor Emeritus, the Jesse H. Jones Chair of Business Administration, Texas Lutheran University, Seguin, Texas. He received his B.B.A. and M.B.A. from the University of North Texas and his Ph.D. in Management and Statistics from Arizona State University. He was previously a member of the faculty at the University of Memphis, the University of Oklahoma, Virginia Commonwealth University, and the University of Richmond. He has also held visiting positions at Boston University, George Mason University, the Czech Management Center, and the Otto-Von-Guericke University, Magdeburg.

Dr. Heizer's industrial experience is extensive. He learned the practical side of operations management as a machinist apprentice at Foringer and Company, as a production planner for Westinghouse Airbrake, and at General Dynamics, where he worked in engineering administration. In addition, he has been actively involved in consulting in the OM and MIS areas for a variety of organizations, including Philip Morris, Firestone, Dixie Container Corporation, Columbia Industries, and Tenneco. He holds the CPIM certification from APICS—the Association for Operations Management.

Professor Heizer has co-authored 5 books and has published more than 30 articles on a variety of management topics. His papers have appeared in the *Academy of Management Journal, Journal of Purchasing, Personnel Psychology, Production & Inventory Control Management, APICS—The Performance Advantage, Journal of Management History, IIE Solutions,* and *Engineering Management,* among others. He has taught operations management courses in undergraduate, graduate, and executive programs.

BARRY RENDER

Professor Emeritus, the Charles Harwood Professor of Operations Management, Crummer Graduate School of Business, Rollins College, Winter Park, Florida. He received his B.S. in Mathematics and Physics at Roosevelt University, and his M.S. in Operations Research and Ph.D. in Quantitative Analysis at the University of Cincinnati. He previously taught at George Washington University, University of New Orleans, Boston University, and George Mason University, where he held the Mason Foundation Professorship in Decision Sciences and was Chair of the Decision Sciences Department. Dr. Render has also worked in the aerospace industry for General Electric, McDonnell Douglas, and NASA.

Professor Render has co-authored 10 textbooks for Pearson, including *Managerial Decision Modeling with Spreadsheets, Quantitative Analysis for Management, Service Management, Introduction to Management Science,* and *Cases and Readings in Management Science. Quantitative Analysis for Management,* now in its 13th edition, is a leading text in that discipline in the United States and globally. Dr. Render's more than 100 articles on a variety of management topics have appeared in *Decision Sciences, Production and Operations Management, Interfaces, Information and Management, Journal of Management Information Systems, Socio-Economic Planning Sciences, IIE Solutions,* and *Operations Management Review,* among others.

Dr. Render has been honored as an AACSB Fellow and was twice named a Senior Fulbright Scholar. He was Vice President of the Decision Science Institute Southeast Region and served as Software Review Editor for *Decision Line* for six years and as Editor of the *New York Times* Operations Management special issues for five years. For nine years, Dr. Render was President of Management Service Associates of Virginia, Inc., whose technology clients included the FBI, NASA, the U.S. Navy, Fairfax County, Virginia, and C&P Telephone. He is currently Consulting Editor to *Pearson Press.*

Dr. Render has received Rollins College's Welsh Award as leading Professor and was selected by Roosevelt University as the recipient of the St. Claire Drake Award for Outstanding Scholarship. Dr. Render also received the Rollins College MBA Student Award for Best Overall Course, and was named Professor of the Year by full-time MBA students.

Professor of Operations Management, Carson College of Business, Washington State University, Pullman, Washington. He received his **BSBA** *summa cum laude* in finance, along with his MSBA and Ph.D. in operations management, from Washington University in St. Louis. For two years, he served as Associate Dean for Graduate Programs in Business at Washington State. He also worked for three years as a financial analyst for Contel Telephone Corporation.

Professor Munson serves as a senior editor for *Production and Operations Management*, and he serves on the editorial review board of four other journals. He has published more than 25 articles in such journals as *Production and Operations Management, IIE Transactions, Decision Sciences, Naval Research Logistics, European Journal of Operational Research, Journal of the Operational Research Society*, and *Annals of Operations Research*. He is editor of the book *The Supply Chain Management Casebook: Comprehensive Coverage and Best Practices in SCM*, and he has co-authored the research monograph *Quantity Discounts: An Overview and Practical Guide for Buyers and Sellers*. He is also coauthor of *Managerial Decision Modeling with Spreadsheets* (4th edition), published by Pearson.

Dr. Munson has taught operations management core and elective courses at the undergraduate, MBA, and Ph.D. levels at Washington State University. He has also conducted several teaching workshops at international conferences and for Ph.D. students at Washington State University. His major awards include being a Founding Board Member of the Washington State University President's Teaching Academy (2004); winning the WSU College of Business Outstanding Teaching Award (2001 and 2015), Research Award (2004), and Service Award (2009 and 2013); and being named the WSU MBA Professor of the Year (2000 and 2008).

CHUCK MUNSON

Brief Table of Contents

Table of Contents

PART TWO Designing Operations   *159*

PART FOUR   Business Analytics Modules

Module A   Decision-Making Tools   677

Module B   Linear Programming   699

Welcome to your operations management (OM) course. In this book, we present a state-of-the-art view of the operations function. Operations is an exciting area of management that has a profound effect on productivity. Indeed, few other activities have as much impact on the quality of our lives. The goal of this text is to present a broad introduction to the field of operations in a realistic, practical manner. Even if you are not planning on a career in the operations area, you will likely be working with people in operations. Therefore, having a solid understanding of the role of operations in an organization will be of substantial benefit to you. This book will also help you understand how OM affects society and your life. Certainly, you will better understand what goes on behind the scenes when you attend a concert or major sports event; purchase a bag of Frito-Lay potato chips; buy a meal at an Olive Garden or a Hard Rock Cafe; place an order through Amazon.com; board a flight on Alaska Airlines; or enter a hospital for medical care. More than one and a half million readers of our earlier editions seem to have endorsed this premise.

We welcome comments by email from our North American readers and from students using the International edition, the Indian edition, the Arabic edition, and our editions in Portuguese, Spanish, Turkish, Indonesian, and Chinese. Hopefully, you will find this material useful, interesting, and even exciting.

New to This Edition

We've made significant revisions to this edition, and want to share some of the changes with you.

Five New *Video Case Studies* Featuring Alaska Airlines

In this edition, we take you behind the scenes of Alaska Airlines, consistently rated as one of the top carriers in the country. This fascinating organization opened its doors—and planes—so we could examine leading edge OM in the airlines industry. We observe: the quality program at Alaska Air (Chapter 6); the process analysis behind the airline's 20-minute baggage retrieval guarantee (Chapter 7); how Alaska empowers its employees (Chapter 10); the airline's use of Lean, 5s, kaizen, and Gemba walks (Chapter 16); and the complexities of scheduling (Module B).

Our prior editions focused on integrated *Video Case Studies* for the Orlando Magic basketball team, Frito-Lay, Darden Restaurants, Hard Rock Cafe, Arnold Palmer Hospital, Wheeled Coach Ambulances, and Regal Marine. These *Video Case Studies* appear in this edition as well, along with the five new ones for Alaska Airlines. All of our videos are created by the authors, with the outstanding coauthorship of Beverly Amer at Northern Arizona University, to explicitly match with text content and terminology.

Alaska Airlines: 20-Minute Baggage Process—Guaranteed! Video Case

Alaska Airlines is unique among the nine major U.S. carriers not only for its extensive flight coverage of remote towns throughout Alaska (it also covers the U.S., Hawaii, and Mexico from its primary hub in Seattle). It is also one of the smallest independent airlines, with 10,300 employees, including 3,000 flight attendants and 1,500 pilots. What makes it really unique, though, is its ability to build state-of-the-art processes, using the latest technology, that yield high customer satisfaction. Indeed, J. D. Power and Associates has ranked Alaska Airlines highest in North America for seven years in a row for customer satisfaction.

Alaska Airlines was the first to sell tickets via the Internet, first to offer Web check-in and print boarding passes online, and first with kiosk check-in. As Wayne Newton, Director of System Operation Control, states, "We are passionate about our processes. If it's not measured, it's not managed."

One of the processes Alaska is most proud of is its baggage handling system. Passengers can check in at kiosks, tag their own bags with bar code stickers, and deliver them to a customer service agent at the carousel, which carries the bags through the vast underground system that eventually delivers the bags to a baggage handler. En route, each bag passes through TSA automated screening and is manually opened or inspected if it appears suspicious. With the help of bar code readers, conveyer belts automatically sort and transfer bags to their location (called a "pier") at the tarmac level. A baggage handler then loads the bags onto a cart and takes it to

Alaska Airlines

Creating Your Own Excel Spreadsheets

We continue to provide two free decision support software programs, Excel OM for Windows and Mac and POM for Windows, to help you and your students solve homework problems and case studies. These excellent packages are found in MyOMLab and at our text's Student Download Page.

Many instructors also encourage students to develop their own Excel spreadsheet models to tackle OM issues. With this edition, we provide numerous examples at chapter end on how to do so. "Creating Your Own Excel Spreadsheets" examples now appear in Chapters 1, 2, 4, 8, 12, and 13, Supplement 6, Supplement 7, and Modules A, B, and F. We hope these eleven samples will help expand students' spreadsheet capabilities.

Using Software for Productivity Analysis

This section presents three ways to solve productivity problems with computer software. First, you can create your own Excel spreadsheets to conduct productivity analysis. Second, you can use the Excel OM software that comes with this text. Third, POM for Windows is another program that is available with this text.

CREATING YOUR OWN EXCEL SPREADSHEETS

Program 1.1 illustrates how to build an Excel spreadsheet for the data in Example 2.

	A	B	C	D	E
1	Collins Title Insurance Ltd.		Enter the values for the old system in		
2	Productivity Increase Computations		column B and the new system in Column C.		
3					
4	Parameters		Old System	New System	
5	Length of Workday (hours)		8	8	
6	Number of Workers		4	4	
7	Labor Hours per Day		32	32	=C5*C6
8	Payroll Cost per Day		$640	$640	
9	Overhead Expenses		$400	$800	
10	Output (Titles per Day)		8	14	
11		=B10/B7		Productivity = Output/Input	
12					
13	Solutions		Old System	New System	% Increase
14	Labor Productivity (Titles per Labor-Hour)		0.25	0.4375	75.00%
15	Multifactor Productivity (Titles per Dollar)		0.0077	0.0097	26.39%
16		=C10/(C8+C9)		=(C14-B14)/B14	

Actions
Copy C7 to B7, Copy B14 to C14, Copy C15 to B15, and Copy D14 to D15

Create a row for each of the inputs used for the productivity measure. Put the output in the last row.

Program **1.1**

✕ USING EXCEL OM

Excel OM is an Excel "add-in" with 24 Operations Management decision support "Templates." To access the templates, double-click on the *Excel OM* tab at the top of the page, then in the menu bar choose the appropriate chapter (in this case Chapter 1), from either the "Chapter" or "Alphabetic" tab on the left. Each of Excel OM's 24 modules includes instructions for that particular module. The instructions can be turned on or off via the "instruction" tab in the menu bar.

P USING POM FOR WINDOWS

POM for Windows is decision support software that includes 24 Operations Management modules. The modules are accessed by double-clicking on *Module* in the menu bar, and then double-clicking on the appropriate (in this case *Productivity*) item. Instructions are provided for each module just below the menu bar.

Expanding and Reordering Our Set of Homework Problems

We believe that a vast selection of quality homework problems, ranging from easy to challenging (denoted by one to four dots), is critical for both instructors and students. Instructors need a broad selection of problems to choose from for homework, quizzes, and exams—without reusing the same set from semester to semester. We take pride in having more problems—by far, with 807—than any other OM text. We added dozens of new problems this edition. The following table illustrates the selection by chapter.

Chapter	Number of Problems	Chapter	Number of Problems	Chapter	Number of Problems
1	18	Supplement 7	45	15	27
2	12	8	34	16	12
3	33	9	27	17	24
4	59	10	46	Module A	32
5	28	11	8	Module B	42
Supplement 5	19	Supplement 11	20	Module C	18
6	21	12	53	Module D	39
Supplement 6	55	13	26	Module E	33
7	17	14	32	Module F	25

Further, with the majority of our adopters now using the MyOMLab learning system in their classes, we have reorganized all the homework problems—both those appearing in the printed text, as well as the Additional Homework Problems that are available in MyOMLab—by topic heading. We are identifying all problems by topic (see the following example).

The list of all problems by topic also appears at the end of each boxed example, as well as in the Rapid Review that closes each chapter. These handy references should make it easier to assign problems for homework, quizzes, and exams. A rich set of assignable problems and cases makes the learning experience more complete and pedagogically sound.

CHAPTER 5 | DESIGN OF GOODS AND SERVICES **187**

Problem **5.3** *is available in* MyOMLab.

Problems 5.4–5.8 relate to Product Development

•• **5.4** Construct a house of quality matrix for a wristwatch. Be sure to indicate specific customer wants that you think the general public desires. Then complete the matrix to show how an operations manager might identify specific attributes that can be measured and controlled to meet those customer desires.

•• **5.5** Using the house of quality, pick a real product (a good or service) and analyze how an existing organization satisfies customer requirements.

•• **5.6** Prepare a house of quality for a mousetrap.

•• **5.7** Conduct an interview with a prospective purchaser of a new bicycle and translate the customer's *wants* into the specific *hows* of the firm.

•••• **5.8** Using the house of quality sequence, as described in Figure 5.4 on page 169, determine how you might deploy resources to achieve the desired quality for a product or service whose production process you understand.

Problems 5.9–5.17 relate to Defining a Product

•• **5.9** Prepare a bill of material for (a) a pair of eyeglasses and its case or (b) a fast-food sandwich (visit a local sandwich

Problems 5.21–5.28 relate to the Application of Decision Trees to Product Design

•• **5.21** The product design group of Iyengar Electric Supplies, Inc., has determined that it needs to design a new series of switches. It must decide on one of three design strategies. The market forecast is for 200,000 units. The better and more sophisticated the design strategy and the more time spent on value engineering, the less will be the variable cost. The chief of engineering design, Dr. W. L. Berry, has decided that the following costs are a good estimate of the initial and variable costs connected with each of the three strategies:

a) *Low-tech:* A low-technology, low-cost process consisting of hiring several new junior engineers. This option has a fixed cost of $45,000 and variable-cost probabilities of .3 for $.55 each, .4 for $.50, and .3 for $.45.

b) *Subcontract:* A medium-cost approach using a good outside design staff. This approach would have a fixed cost of $65,000 and variable-cost probabilities of .7 of $.45, .2 of $.40, and .1 of $.35.

c) *High-tech:* A high-technology approach using the very best of the inside staff and the latest computer-aided design technology. This approach has a fixed cost of $75,000 and variable-cost probabilities of .9 of $.40 and .1 of $.35.

What is the best decision based on an expected monetary value (EMV) criterion? (*Note:* We want the lowest EMV, as we are dealing with costs in this problem.) Px

•• **5.22** MacDonald Products, Inc., of Clarkson, New York, has the option of (a) proceeding immediately with production of

Jay, Barry, and Chuck's OM Blog

As a complement to this text, we have created a companion blog, with coordinated features to help teach the OM course. There are teaching tips, highlights of OM items in the news (along with class discussion questions and links), video tips, guest posts by instructors using our text, sample OM syllabi from dozens of colleges, and much more—all arranged by chapter. To learn more about any chapter topics, visit *www.heizerrenderOM.wordpress.com*. As you prepare your lectures and syllabus, scan our blog for discussion ideas, teaching tips, and classroom exercises.

Lean Operations

In previous editions, we sought to explicitly differentiate the concepts of just-in-time, Lean, and Toyota Production System in Chapter 16. However, there is significant overlap and interchangeability among those three concepts, so we have revised Chapter 16 to incorporate the three concepts into an overall concept of "Lean." The chapter suggests that students view Lean as a comprehensive integrated operations strategy that sustains competitive advantage and results in increased returns to all stakeholders.

Chapter-by-Chapter Changes

To highlight the extent of the revisions in this edition, here are a few of the changes, on a chapter-by-chapter basis.

Chapter 1: Operations and Productivity

We updated Table 1.4 to reflect employment in various sectors and expanded our discussion of Lean operations. Our new case, Uber Technologies, introduces productivity by discussing the disruptive nature of the Uber business model. In addition, there is a new "Creating Your Own Excel Spreadsheets" example for both labor productivity and multifactor productivity.

Chapter 2: Operations Strategy in a Global Environment

We have updated Figure 2.1 to better reflect changes in the growth of world trade and Figure 2.5 to reflect product life cycle changes. The Minute Lube case has been revised as Rapid Lube. Example 1 (National Architects) has been expanded to clarify factor rating calculations and is also demonstrated with a "Creating Your Own Excel Spreadsheets" presentation.

Chapter 3: Project Management

We rewrote and updated the Bechtel Global Company Profile and added a new section on well-defined projects with the "agile" and "waterfall" approaches. There are two new OM in Action boxes: "Agile Project Management at Mastek," and "Behind the Tour de France."

Chapter 4: Forecasting

We created a new table comparing the MAD, MSE, and MAPE forecasting error measures. There is also a new OM in Action box called "NYC's Potholes and Regression Analysis."

Chapter 5: Design of Goods and Services

We expanded our treatment of *concurrent engineering* and added two new discussion questions. Solved Problem 5.1 has been revised.

Supplement 5: Sustainability in the Supply Chain

We wrote a new introductory section on Corporate Social Responsibility. There is also a new OM in Action box called "Blue Jeans and Sustainability" and 10 new homework problems.

Chapter 6: Managing Quality

We added new material to expand our discussion of Taguchi's quality loss function. There is a new section on SERVQUAL, and a new video case study, "Quality Counts at Alaska Airlines," appears here.

Supplement 6: Statistical Process Control

We added a figure on the relationship between sample size and sampling distribution. We also added raw data to Examples S2 and S3 to illustrate how ranges are computed. There is a new Excel spreadsheet to show students how to make their own *c*-chart, and we have added three new homework problems.

Chapter 7: Process Strategy

We wrote a new section on machine technology and additive manufacturing. There are two new discussion questions and three new homework problems. Our second new video case study is called "Alaska Airlines: 20-Minute Baggage Process—Guaranteed!"

Supplement 7: Capacity and Constraint Management

We added a new Table S7.1, which compares and clarifies three capacity measurements, with an example of each. There is a new treatment of expected output and actual output in Example S2. The discussion of bottleneck time versus throughput time has also been expanded. Example S3, capacity analysis with parallel processes, has been revised. We have also added a new "Creating Your Own Excel Spreadsheets" example for a break-even model. Finally, we updated the Arnold Palmer Hospital capacity planning case with recent data.

Chapter 8: Location Strategies

We added two new OM in Action boxes: "Iowa—Home of Corn and Facebook" and "Denmark's Meat Cluster." We changed the notation for the center-of-gravity model to simplify the equation and provided a new "Creating Your Own Excel Spreadsheets" presentation for the center-of-gravity example.

Chapter 9: Layout Strategies

We created a new Muther grid for office relationship charting and added a spread of five layouts showing how offices have evolved over time. There is a new OM in Action box called "Amazon Lets Loose the Robots," and there is a new graphic example of Proplanner's Flow Path Calculator. We have included a formula for idle time as a second measure of balance assignment efficiency and added new technology issues to the Arnold Palmer Hospital video case.

Chapter 10: Human Resources, Job Design, and Work Measurement

We added a new OM in Action box, "The Missing Perfect Chair," and revised the Operations Chart as a service example. Our third new video case study is "The 'People' Focus: Human Resources at Alaska Airlines."

Chapter 11: Supply Chain Management

We added "outsourcing" as a supply chain risk in Table 11.3.

Supplement 11: Supply Chain Management Analytics

We added a major section on the topic of Warehouse Storage, with a new model for allocating inventory to storage locations. There is a new discussion question and three new homework problems.

Chapter 12: Inventory Management

New Programs 12.1 and 12.2 illustrate "Creating Your Own Excel Spreadsheets" for both the production run model and the single-period inventory model. The Excel function NORMSINV is introduced throughout the chapter. The Quantity Discount Model section is totally rewritten to illustrate the *feasible solution* shortcut. Solved Problem 12.5 is likewise redone with the new approach.

Chapter 13: Aggregate Planning and S&OP

We added a new OM in Action box, "Revenue Management Makes Disney the 'King' of the Broadway Jungle." We also provided a new "Creating Your Own Excel Spreadsheets" example for the transportation method for aggregate planning, using the Solver approach.

Chapter 14: Material Requirements Planning (MRP) and ERP

The MRP II example now includes greenhouse gasses.

Chapter 15: Short-Term Scheduling

We begin this chapter with a new Global Company Profile featuring Alaska Airlines and the scheduling issues it faces in its northern climate. We have added two new graphics to help illustrate Forward and Backward Scheduling. There is also a new section called Performance Criteria, detailing how the choice of priority rule depends on four quantifiable criteria. We now explicitly define the performance criteria for sequencing jobs as separate numbered equations. Also, we provide an explicit formula for job lateness. There is a new OM in Action box called "Starbucks' Controversial Scheduling Software."

Chapter 16: Lean Operations

This chapter saw a major reorganization and rewrite with an enhanced focus on Lean operations. There is more material on supplier partnerships and building lean organizations. A new OM in Action box describes the use of kaizen at San Francisco General Hospital, and we have added a new video case study called "Lean Operations at Alaska Airlines."

Chapter 17: Maintenance and Reliability

There are no major changes in this chapter.

Module A: Decision-Making Tools

We added a discussion of "big data" and a new "Creating Your Own Excel Spreadsheets" example on how to evaluate a decision table.

Module B: Linear Programming

There is a new section on integer and binary programming, two new homework problems, and a new video case study called "Using LP to Meet Scheduling Challenges at Alaska Airlines." The corner point method is now covered *before* the iso-profit line approach.

Module C: Transportation Models

There are no major changes to Module C.

Module D: Waiting-Line Models

The limited population model (Model D) has been replaced by the finite population model, M/M/1 with finite source. This standardizes the queuing notation to match the M/M/1, M/M/s, and M/D/1. We have also expanded the coverage of Little's Law and added six new homework problems.

Module E: Learning Curves

There are no major changes to Module E.

Module F: Simulation

We added a new "Creating Your Own Excel Spreadsheets" example for a simulation problem.

Student Resources

To liven up the course and help students learn the content material, we have made available the following resources:

- *Forty-one exciting Video Case Studies (videos located at* MyOMLab*):* These *Video Case Studies* feature real companies (Alaska Airlines, The Orlando Magic, Frito-Lay, Darden Restaurants, Regal Marine, Hard Rock Cafe, Ritz-Carlton, Wheeled Coach, and Arnold Palmer Hospital) and allow students to watch short videos, read about the key topics, and answer questions. These case studies can also be assigned without using class time to show the videos. Each of them was developed and written by the text authors to specifically supplement the book's content. Instructors who wish to use these in class, and who don't have access to MyOMLab, should contact their Pearson Publishing Representative for access to the MyOMLab materials.

- *POM for Windows software (located at* MyOMLab *and at the Student Download Page, www .pearsonhighered.com/heizer):* POM for Windows is a powerful tool for easily solving OM problems. Its 24 modules can be used to solve most of the homework problems in the text.

- *Excel OM problem-solving software (located at* MyOMLab *and at the Student Download Page, www.pearsonhighered.com/heizer):* Excel OM is our exclusive user-friendly Excel add-in. Excel OM automatically creates worksheets to model and solve problems. Users select a topic from the pull-down menu and fill in the data, and then Excel will display and graph (where appropriate) the results. This software is great for student homework, what-if analysis, and classroom demonstrations. This edition includes a new version of Excel OM that is compatible with Microsoft Excel 2013 for Windows, Excel 2011 and 2016 for Mac, and earlier versions of Excel. Professor Howard Weiss, Temple University, developed both Excel OM for Windows and Mac, and POM for Windows to accompany our text and its problem set.

- *Excel OM data files (located at* MyOMLab *and at the Student Download Page, www .pearsonhighered.com/heizer):* These data files are prepared for specific examples and allow users to solve all the marked text examples without reentering any data.

- *Active Models (located at* MyOMLab *and at the Student Download Page, www.pearsonhighered .com/heizer):* These 28 Active Models are Excel-based OM simulations, designed to help students understand the quantitative methods shown in the textbook examples. Students may change the data in order to see how the changes affect the answers.

- *Virtual tours (located at* MyOMLab*):* These company tours provide direct links to companies—ranging from a hospital to an auto manufacturer—that practice key OM concepts. After touring each Web site, students are asked questions directly related to the concepts discussed in the chapter.

- *Online Tutorial Chapters (located at* MyOMLab *and at the Student Download Page, www .pearsonhighered.com/heizer):* "Statistical Tools for Managers," "Acceptance Sampling," "The Simplex Method of Linear Programming," "The MODI and VAM Methods of Solving Transportation Problems," and "Vehicle Routing and Scheduling" are provided as additional material.

- *Additional practice problems (located at* MyOMLab*):* These problems provide problem-solving experience. They supplement the examples and solved problems found in each chapter.

- *Additional case studies (located at* MyOMLab *and at the Student Download Page, www .pearsonhighered.com/heizer):* Over two dozen additional case studies supplement the ones in the text. Detailed solutions appear in the Solutions Manual.

- *Virtual office hours (located at* MyOMLab*):* Professors Heizer, Render, and Munson walk students through all 89 Solved Problems in a series of 5- to 20-minute explanations. These have been updated with this new edition.

Instructor Resources

At the Instructor Resource Center, *www.pearsonhighered.com/irc*, instructors can easily register to gain access to a variety of instructor resources available with this text in downloadable format. If assistance is needed, our dedicated technical support team is ready to help with the media supplements that accompany this text. Visit *http://247.pearsoned.com* for answers to frequently asked questions and toll-free user support phone numbers.

The following supplements are available with this text:

Instructor's Resource Manual

The Instructor's Resource Manual, updated by co-author Chuck Munson, contains many useful resources for instructors—PowerPoint presentations with annotated notes, course outlines, video notes, blog highlights, learning techniques, Internet exercises and sample answers, case analysis ideas, additional teaching resources, and faculty notes.

Instructor's Solutions Manual

The Instructor's Solutions Manual, written by the authors, contains the answers to all of the discussion questions, *Ethical Dilemmas*, Active Models, and cases in the text, as well as worked-out solutions to all the end-of-chapter problems, additional homework problems, and additional case studies.

PowerPoint Presentations

An extensive set of PowerPoint presentations, created by Professor Jeff Heyl of Lincoln University, is available for each chapter. With well over 2,000 slides, this set has excellent color and clarity.

Test Bank / TestGen® Computerized Test Bank

The test bank, updated by James Roh, contains a variety of true/false, multiple-choice, short-answer, and essay questions, along with a selection of written problems, for each chapter. Test questions are annotated with the following information:

- Difficulty level
- Type: multiple-choice, true/false, short-answer, essay, problem
- Learning objective
- AACSB (see the description that follows)

TestGen®, Pearson Education's test-generating software, is PC/MAC compatible and preloaded with all the test bank questions. The test program permits instructors to edit, add, and delete questions from the test bank to create customized tests.

AACSB

The Association to Advance Collegiate Schools of Business (AACSB)

The test bank has connected select questions to the general knowledge and skill guidelines found in the AACSB Assurance of Learning standards.

AACSB is a not-for-profit corporation of educational institutions, corporations, and other organizations devoted to the promotion and improvement of higher education in business administration and accounting. A collegiate institution offering degrees in business administration or accounting may volunteer for AACSB accreditation review. The AACSB makes initial accreditation decisions and conducts periodic reviews to promote continuous quality improvement in management education. Pearson Education is a proud member of the AACSB and is pleased to provide advice to help you apply AACSB assurance of learning standards.

What are AACSB assurance of learning standards? One of the criteria for AACSB accreditation is quality of the curricula. Although no specific courses are required, the AACSB expects a curriculum to include learning experiences in the following areas:

- Written and oral communication
- Ethical understanding and reasoning
- Analytical thinking
- Information technology
- Interpersonal relations and teamwork
- Diverse and multicultural work environments
- Reflective thinking
- Application of knowledge

Questions that test skills relevant to these guidelines are appropriately tagged. For example, a question regarding clothing manufactured for U.S. firms by 10-year olds in Asia would receive the Ethical understanding and reasoning tag.

Tagged questions help you measure whether students are grasping the course content that aligns with the AACSB guidelines noted. In addition, the tagged questions may help instructors identify potential applications of these skills. This in turn may suggest enrichment activities or other educational experiences to help students achieve these skills.

Video Package

Designed and created by the authors specifically for their Heizer/Render/Munson texts, the video package contains the following 41 videos:

- Frito-Lay: Operations Management in Manufacturing (Chapter 1)
- Hard Rock Cafe: Operations Management in Services (Chapter 1)
- Strategy at Regal Marine (Chapter 2)
- Hard Rock Cafe's Global Strategy (Chapter 2)
- Outsourcing Offshore at Darden (Chapter 2)
- Project Management at Arnold Palmer Hospital (Chapter 3)
- Managing Hard Rock's Rockfest (Chapter 3)
- Forecasting Ticket Revenue for Orlando Magic Basketball Games (Chapter 4)
- Forecasting at Hard Rock Cafe (Chapter 4)
- Product Design at Regal Marine (Chapter 5)
- Building Sustainability at the Orlando Magic's Amway Center (Supplement 5)
- Green Manufacturing and Sustainability at Frito-Lay (Supplement 5)
- Quality Counts at Alaska Airlines (Chapter 6)
- The Culture of Quality at Arnold Palmer Hospital (Chapter 6)
- Quality at the Ritz-Carlton Hotel Company (Chapter 6)
- Frito-Lay's Quality-Controlled Potato Chips (Supplement 6)
- Farm to Fork: Quality at Darden Restaurants (Supplement 6)
- Alaska Airlines: 20-Minute Baggage Process—Guaranteed! (Chapter 7)
- Process Strategy at Wheeled Coach (Chapter 7)
- Process Analysis at Arnold Palmer Hospital (Chapter 7)
- Capacity Planning at Arnold Palmer Hospital (Supplement 7)
- Locating the Next Red Lobster Restaurant (Chapter 8)
- Where to Place the Hard Rock Cafe (Chapter 8)
- Facility Layout at Wheeled Coach (Chapter 9)
- Laying Out Arnold Palmer Hospital's New Facility (Chapter 9)
- The "People" Focus: Human Resources at Alaska Airlines (Chapter 10)
- Hard Rock's Human Resource Strategy (Chapter 10)
- Darden's Global Supply Chains (Chapter 11)
- Supply Chain Management at Regal Marine (Chapter 11)
- Arnold Palmer Hospital's Supply Chain (Chapter 11)
- Managing Inventory at Frito-Lay (Chapter 12)
- Inventory Control at Wheeled Coach (Chapter 12)
- Using Revenue Management to Set Orlando Magic Ticket Prices (Chapter 13)
- When 18,500 Orlando Magic Fans Come to Dinner (Chapter 14)
- MRP at Wheeled Coach (Chapter 14)
- From the Eagles to the Magic: Converting the Amway Center (Chapter 15)
- Scheduling at Hard Rock Cafe (Chapter 15)
- Lean Operations at Alaska Airlines (Chapter 16)
- JIT at Arnold Palmer Hospital (Chapter 16)
- Maintenance Drives Profits at Frito-Lay (Chapter 17)
- Scheduling Challenges at Alaska Airlines (Module B)

Acknowledgments

We thank the many individuals who were kind enough to assist us in this endeavor. The following professors provided insights that guided us in this edition (their names are in bold) and in prior editions:

ALABAMA

John Mittenthal
University of Alabama

Philip F. Musa
University of Alabama at Birmingham

William Petty
University of Alabama

Doug Turner
Auburn University

ALASKA

Paul Jordan
University of Alaska

ARIZONA

Susan K. Norman
Northern Arizona University

Scott Roberts
Northern Arizona University

Vicki L. Smith-Daniels
Arizona State University

Susan K. Williams
Northern Arizona University

CALIFORNIA

Jean-Pierre Amor
University of San Diego

Moshen Attaran
California State University–Bakersfield

Ali Behnezhad
California State University–Northridge

Joe Biggs
California Polytechnic State University

Lesley Buehler
Ohlone College

Rick Hesse
Pepperdine

Ravi Kathuria
Chapman University

Richard Martin
California State University–Long Beach

Ozgur Ozluk
San Francisco State University

Zinovy Radovilsky
California State University–Hayward

Robert J. Schlesinger
San Diego State University

V. Udayabhanu
San Francisco State University

Rick Wing
San Francisco State University

COLORADO

Peter Billington
Colorado State University–Pueblo

Gregory Stock
University of Colorado at Colorado Springs

CONNECTICUT

David Cadden
Quinnipiac University

Larry A. Flick
Norwalk Community Technical College

FLORIDA

Joseph P. Geunes
University of Florida

Rita Gibson
Embry-Riddle Aeronautical University

Jim Gilbert
Rollins College

Donald Hammond
University of South Florida

Wende Huehn-Brown
St. Petersburg College

Adam Munson
University of Florida

Ronald K. Satterfield
University of South Florida

Theresa A. Shotwell
Florida A&M University

Jeff Smith
Florida State University

GEORGIA

John H. Blackstone
University of Georgia

Johnny Ho
Columbus State University

John Hoft
Columbus State University

John Miller
Mercer University

Nikolay Osadchiy
Emory University

Spyros Reveliotis
Georgia Institute of Technology

ILLINOIS

Suad Alwan
Chicago State University

Lori Cook
DePaul University

Matt Liontine
University of Illinois–Chicago

Zafar Malik
Governors State University

INDIANA

Barbara Flynn
Indiana University

B.P. Lingeraj
Indiana University

Frank Pianki
Anderson University

Stan Stockton
Indiana University

Jerry Wei
University of Notre Dame

Jianghua Wu
Purdue University

Xin Zhai
Purdue University

IOWA

Debra Bishop
Drake University

Kevin Watson
Iowa State University

Lifang Wu
University of Iowa

KANSAS

William Barnes
Emporia State University

George Heinrich
Wichita State University

Sue Helms
Wichita State University

Hugh Leach
Washburn University

M.J. Riley
Kansas State University

Teresita S. Salinas
Washburn University

Avanti P. Sethi
Wichita State University

KENTUCKY

Wade Ferguson
Western Kentucky University

Kambiz Tabibzadeh
Eastern Kentucky University

LOUISIANA

Roy Clinton
University of Louisiana at Monroe

L. Wayne Shell (retired)
Nicholls State University

MARYLAND

Eugene Hahn
Salisbury University

Samuel Y. Smith, Jr.
University of Baltimore

MASSACHUSETTS

Peter Ittig
University of Massachusetts

Jean Pierre Kuilboer
University of Massachusetts–Boston

Dave Lewis
University of Massachusetts–Lowell

Mike Maggard (retired)
Northeastern University

Peter Rourke
Wentworth Institute of Technology

Daniel Shimshak
University of Massachusetts–Boston

Ernest Silver
Curry College

Yu Amy Xia
Northeastern University

MICHIGAN

Darlene Burk
Western Michigan University

Damodar Golhar
Western Michigan University

Dana Johnson
Michigan Technological University

Doug Moodie
Michigan Technological University

MINNESOTA

Rick Carlson
Metropolitan State University

John Nicolay
University of Minnesota

Michael Pesch
St. Cloud State University

Manus Rungtusanatham
University of Minnesota

Kingshuk Sinha
University of Minnesota

Peter Southard
University of St. Thomas

MISSOURI

Shahid Ali
Rockhurst University

Stephen Allen
Truman State University

Sema Alptekin
University of Missouri–Rolla

Gregory L. Bier
University of Missouri–Columbia

James Campbell
University of Missouri–St. Louis

Wooseung Jang
University of Missouri–Columbia

Mary Marrs
University of Missouri–Columbia

A. Lawrence Summers
University of Missouri

NEBRASKA

Zialu Hug
University of Nebraska–Omaha

NEVADA

Joel D. Wisner
University of Nevada, Las Vegas

NEW JERSEY

Daniel Ball
Monmouth University

Leon Bazil
Stevens Institute of Technology

Mark Berenson
Montclair State University

Grace Greenberg
Rider University

Joao Neves
The College of New Jersey

Leonard Presby
William Paterson University

Faye Zhu
Rowan University

NEW MEXICO

William Kime
University of New Mexico

NEW YORK

Theodore Boreki
Hofstra University

John Drabouski
DeVry University

Richard E. Dulski
Daemen College

Jonatan Jelen
Baruch College

Beate Klingenberg
Marist College

Donna Mosier
SUNY Potsdam

Elizabeth Perry
SUNY Binghamton

William Reisel
St. John's University

Kaushik Sengupta
Hofstra University

Girish Shambu
Canisius College

Rajendra Tibrewala
New York Institute of Technology

NORTH CAROLINA

Coleman R. Rich
Elon University

Ray Walters
Fayetteville Technical Community College

OHIO

Victor Berardi
Kent State University

Andrew R. Thomas
University of Akron

OKLAHOMA

Wen-Chyuan Chiang
University of Tulsa

OREGON

Anne Deidrich
Warner Pacific College

Gordon Miller
Portland State University

John Sloan
Oregon State University

PENNSYLVANIA

Henry Crouch
Pittsburgh State University

Jeffrey D. Heim
Pennsylvania State University

James F. Kimpel
University of Pittsburgh

Ian M. Langella
Shippensburg University

Prafulla Oglekar
LaSalle University

David Pentico
Duquesne University

Stanford Rosenberg
LaRoche College

Edward Rosenthal
Temple University

Susan Sherer
Lehigh University

Howard Weiss
Temple University

RHODE ISLAND

Laurie E. Macdonald
Bryant College

John Swearingen
Bryant College

Susan Sweeney
Providence College

SOUTH CAROLINA

Jerry K. Bilbrey
Anderson University

Larry LaForge
Clemson University

Emma Jane Riddle
Winthrop University

TENNESSEE

Joseph Blackburn
Vanderbilt University

Hugh Daniel
Lipscomb University

Cliff Welborn
Middle Tennessee State University

TEXAS

Warren W. Fisher
Stephen F. Austin State University

Garland Hunnicutt
Texas State University

Gregg Lattier
Lee College

Henry S. Maddux III
Sam Houston State University

Arunachalam Narayanan
Texas A&M University

Ranga V. Ramasesh
Texas Christian University

Victor Sower
San Houston State University

Cecelia Temponi
Texas State University

John Visich-Disc
University of Houston

Dwayne Whitten
Texas A&M University

Bruce M. Woodworth
University of Texas–El Paso

UTAH

William Christensen
Dixie State College of Utah

Shane J. Schvaneveldt
Weber State University

Madeline Thimmes (retired)
Utah State University

VIRGINIA

Andy Litteral
University of Richmond

Arthur C. Meiners, Jr.
Marymount University

Michael Plumb
Tidewater Community College

WASHINGTON

Mark McKay
University of Washington

Chris Sandvig
Western Washington University

John Stec
Oregon Institute of Technology

WASHINGTON, DC

Narendrea K. Rustagi
Howard University

WEST VIRGINIA

Charles Englehardt
Salem International University

Daesung Ha
Marshall University

John Harpell
West Virginia University

James S. Hawkes
University of Charleston

WISCONSIN

James R. Gross
University of Wisconsin–Oshkosh

Marilyn K. Hart (retired)
University of Wisconsin–Oshkosh

Niranjan Pati
University of Wisconsin–La Crosse

X. M. Safford
Milwaukee Area Technical College

Rao J. Taikonda
University of Wisconsin–Oshkosh

WYOMING

Cliff Asay
University of Wyoming

INTERNATIONAL

Steven Harrod
Technical University of Denmark

Robert D. Klassen
University of Western Ontario

Ronald Lau
Hong Kong University of Science and Technology

In addition, we appreciate the wonderful people at Pearson Education who provided both help and advice: Stephanie Wall, our superb editor-in-chief; Lenny Ann Kucenski, our dynamo marketing manager; Linda Albelli, our editorial assistant; Courtney Kamauf and Andra Skaalrud for their fantastic and dedicated work on MyOMLab; Jeff Holcomb, our project manager team lead; Claudia Fernandes, our program manager; Jacqueline Martin, our senior project manager; and Heidi Allgair, our project manager at Cenveo® Publisher Services. We are truly blessed to have such a fantastic team of experts directing, guiding, and assisting us.

In this edition, we were thrilled to be able to include one of the country's premier airlines, Alaska Airlines, in our ongoing Video Case Study series. This was possible because of the wonderful efforts of COO/EVP-Operations Ben Minicucci, and his superb management team. This included John Ladner (Managing Director, Seattle Station Operations), Wayne Newton (Managing Director, Station Operations Control), Mike McQueen (Director, Schedule Planning), Chad Koehnke (Director, Planning and Resource Allocation), Cheryl Schulz (Executive Assistant to EVP Minicucci), Jeffrey Butler (V.P. Airport Operations & Customer Service), Dan Audette (Manager of Operations Research and Analysis), Allison Fletcher (Process Improvement Manager), Carlos Zendejas (Manager Line-Flying Operations, Pilots), Robyn Garner (Flight Attendant Trainer), and Nikki Meier and Sara Starbuck (Process Improvement Facilitators). We are grateful to all of these fine people, as well as the many others that participated in the development of the videos and cases during our trips to the Seattle headquarters.

We also appreciate the efforts of colleagues who have helped to shape the entire learning package that accompanies this text. Professor Howard Weiss (Temple University) developed the Active Models, Excel OM, and POM for Windows software; Professor Jeff Heyl (Lincoln University) created the PowerPoint presentations; and Professor James Roh (Rowan University) updated the test bank. Beverly Amer (Northern Arizona University) produced and directed the video series; Professors Keith Willoughby (Bucknell University) and Ken Klassen (Brock University) contributed the two Excel-based simulation games; and Professor Gary LaPoint (Syracuse University) developed the Microsoft Project crashing exercise and the dice game for SPC. We have been fortunate to have been able to work with all these people.

We wish you a pleasant and productive introduction to operations management.

JAY HEIZER
Texas Lutheran University
1000 W. Court Street
Seguin, TX 78155
Email: jheizer@tlu.edu

BARRY RENDER
Graduate School of Business
Rollins College
Winter Park, FL 32789
Email: brender@rollins.edu

CHUCK MUNSON
Carson College of Business
Washington State University
Pullman, WA 99164-4746
Email: munson@wsu.edu

TWO VERSIONS ARE AVAILABLE

This text is available in two versions: *Operations Management*, 12th edition, a hardcover, and *Principles of Operations Management*, 10th edition, a paperback. Both books include the identical core Chapters 1–17. However, *Operations Management*, 12th edition also includes six business analytics modules in Part IV.

OPERATIONS MANAGEMENT, 12TH EDITION
ISBN: 0-13-413042-1

PART I INTRODUCTION TO OPERATIONS MANAGEMENT
1. Operations and Productivity
2. Operations Strategy in a Global Environment
3. Project Management
4. Forecasting

PART II DESIGNING OPERATIONS
5. Design of Goods and Services
S5. Sustainability in the Supply Chain
6. Managing Quality
S6. Statistical Process Control
7. Process Strategy
S7. Capacity and Constraint Management
8. Location Strategies
9. Layout Strategies
10. Human Resources, Job Design, and Work Measurement

PART III MANAGING OPERATIONS
11. Supply Chain Management
S11. Supply Chain Management Analytics
12. Inventory Management
13. Aggregate Planning and S&OP
14. Material Requirements Planning (MRP) and ERP
15. Short-Term Scheduling
16. Lean Operations
17. Maintenance and Reliability

PART IV BUSINESS ANALYTICS MODULES
A. Decision-Making Tools
B. Linear Programming
C. Transportation Models
D. Waiting-Line Models
E. Learning Curves
F. Simulation

ONLINE TUTORIALS
1. Statistical Tools for Managers
2. Acceptance Sampling
3. The Simplex Method of Linear Programming
4. The MODI and VAM Methods of Solving Transportation Problems
5. Vehicle Routing and Scheduling

PRINCIPLES OF OPERATIONS MANAGEMENT, 10TH EDITION
ISBN: 0-13-418198-0

PART I INTRODUCTION TO OPERATIONS MANAGEMENT
1. Operations and Productivity
2. Operations Strategy in a Global Environment
3. Project Management
4. Forecasting

PART II DESIGNING OPERATIONS
5. Design of Goods and Services
S5. Sustainability in the Supply Chain
6. Managing Quality
S6. Statistical Process Control
7. Process Strategy
S7. Capacity and Constraint Management
8. Location Strategies
9. Layout Strategies
10. Human Resources, Job Design, and Work Measurement

PART III MANAGING OPERATIONS
11. Supply Chain Management
S11. Supply Chain Management Analytics
12. Inventory Management
13. Aggregate Planning and S&OP
14. Material Requirements Planning (MRP) and ERP
15. Short-Term Scheduling
16. Lean Operations
17. Maintenance and Reliability

ONLINE TUTORIALS
1. Statistical Tools for Managers
2. Acceptance Sampling
3. The Simplex Method of Linear Programming
4. The MODI and VAM Methods of Solving Transportation Problems
5. Vehicle Routing and Scheduling

OPERATIONS MANAGEMENT

Sustainability and Supply Chain Management

Operations and Productivity

CHAPTER OUTLINE

Alaska Airlines

10 OM STRATEGY DECISIONS

- Design of Goods and Services
- Managing Quality
- Process Strategy
- Location Strategies
- Layout Strategies
- Human Resources
- Supply-Chain Management
- Inventory Management
- Scheduling
- Maintenance

Operations Management at Hard Rock Cafe

Operations managers throughout the world are producing products every day to provide for the well-being of society. These products take on a multitude of forms. They may be washing machines at Whirlpool, motion pictures at DreamWorks, rides at Disney World, or food at Hard Rock Cafe. These firms produce thousands of complex products every day—to be delivered as the customer ordered them, when the customer wants them, and where the customer wants them. Hard Rock does this for over 35 million guests worldwide every year. This is a challenging task, and the operations manager's job, whether at Whirlpool, DreamWorks, Disney, or Hard Rock, is demanding.

Hard Rock Cafe in Orlando, Florida, prepares over 3,500 meals each day. Seating more than 1,500 people, it is one of the largest restaurants in the world. But Hard Rock's operations managers serve the hot food hot and the cold food cold.

Andre Jenny/Alamy

Operations managers are interested in the attractiveness of the layout, but they must be sure that the facility contributes to the efficient movement of people and material with the necessary controls to ensure that proper portions are served.

Demetrio Carrasco/Rough Guides/Dorling Kindersley, Ltd.

Presselect/Alamy

Lots of work goes into designing, testing, and costing meals. Then suppliers deliver quality products on time, every time, for well-trained cooks to prepare quality meals. But none of that matters unless an enthusiastic waitstaff, such as the one shown here, holding guitars previously owned by members of U2, is doing its job.

Efficient kitchen layouts, motivated personnel, tight schedules, and the right ingredients at the right place at the right time are required to delight the customer.

Jack Picone/Alamy

Orlando-based Hard Rock Cafe opened its first restaurant in London in 1971, making it over 45 years old and the granddaddy of theme restaurants. Although other theme restaurants have come and gone, Hard Rock is still going strong, with 150 restaurants in more than 53 countries—and new restaurants opening each year. Hard Rock made its name with rock music memorabilia, having started when Eric Clapton, a regular customer, marked his favorite bar stool by hanging his guitar on the wall in the London cafe. Now Hard Rock has 70,000 items and millions of dollars invested in memorabilia. To keep customers coming back time and again, Hard Rock creates value in the form of good food and entertainment.

The operations managers at Hard Rock Cafe at Universal Studios in Orlando provide more than 3,500 custom products—in this case meals—every day. These products are designed, tested, and then analyzed for cost of ingredients, labor requirements, and customer satisfaction. On approval, menu items are put into production—and then only if the ingredients are available from qualified suppliers. The production process, from receiving, to cold storage, to grilling or baking or frying, and a dozen other steps, is designed and maintained to yield a quality meal. Operations managers, using the best people they can recruit and train, also prepare effective employee schedules and design efficient layouts.

Managers who successfully design and deliver goods and services throughout the world understand operations. In this text, we look not only at how Hard Rock's managers create value but also how operations managers in other services, as well as in manufacturing, do so. Operations management is demanding, challenging, and exciting. It affects our lives every day. Ultimately, operations managers determine how well we live. ◄

STUDENT TIP ◆
Let's begin by defining what this course is about.

What Is Operations Management?

LO 1.1 *Define* operations management

Operations management (OM) is a discipline that applies to restaurants like Hard Rock Cafe as well as to factories like Ford and Whirlpool. The techniques of OM apply throughout the world to virtually all productive enterprises. It doesn't matter if the application is in an office, a hospital, a restaurant, a department store, or a factory—the production of goods and services requires operations management. And the *efficient* production of goods and services requires effective applications of the concepts, tools, and techniques of OM that we introduce in this book.

As we progress through this text, we will discover how to manage operations in an economy in which both customers and suppliers are located throughout the world. An array of informative examples, charts, text discussions, and pictures illustrates concepts and provides information. We will see how operations managers create the goods and services that enrich our lives.

In this chapter, we first define *operations management*, explaining its heritage and exploring the exciting role operations managers play in a huge variety of organizations. Then we discuss production and productivity in both goods- and service-producing firms. This is followed by a discussion of operations in the service sector and the challenge of managing an effective and efficient production system.

Production is the creation of goods and services. Operations management (OM) is the set of activities that creates value in the form of goods and services by transforming inputs into outputs. Activities creating goods and services take place in all organizations. In manufacturing firms, the production activities that create goods are usually quite obvious. In them, we can see the creation of a tangible product such as a Sony TV or a Harley-Davidson motorcycle.

In an organization that does not create a tangible good or product, the production function may be less obvious. We often call these activities *services*. The services may be "hidden" from the public and even from the customer. The product may take such forms as the transfer of funds from a savings account to a checking account, the transplant of a liver, the filling of an empty seat on an airplane, or the education of a student. Regardless of whether the end product is a good or service, the production activities that go on in the organization are often referred to as operations, or *operations management*.

VIDEO 1.1
Operations Management at Hard Rock

VIDEO 1.2
Operations Management at Frito-Lay

Production
The creation of goods and services.

Operations management (OM)
Activities that relate to the creation of goods and services through the transformation of inputs to outputs.

STUDENT TIP ◆
Operations is one of the three functions that every organization performs.

Organizing to Produce Goods and Services

To create goods and services, all organizations perform three functions (see Figure 1.1). These functions are the necessary ingredients not only for production but also for an organization's survival. They are:

1. *Marketing*, which generates the demand, or at least takes the order for a product or service (nothing happens until there is a sale).
2. *Production/operations*, which creates, produces, and delivers the product.
3. *Finance/accounting*, which tracks how well the organization is doing, pays the bills, and collects the money.

Universities, churches or synagogues, and businesses all perform these functions. Even a volunteer group such as the Boy Scouts of America is organized to perform these three basic

(A)

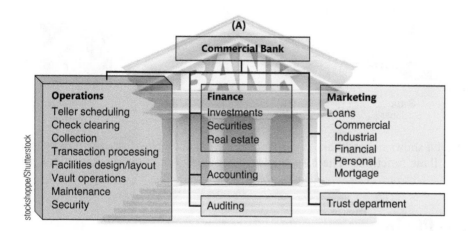

Commercial Bank

Operations
Teller scheduling
Check clearing
Collection
Transaction processing
Facilities design/layout
Vault operations
Maintenance
Security

Finance
Investments
Securities
Real estate

Accounting

Auditing

Marketing
Loans
 Commercial
 Industrial
 Financial
 Personal
 Mortgage

Trust department

stockshoppe/Shutterstock

Figure **1.1**

Organization Charts for Two Service Organizations and One Manufacturing Organization

(A) a bank, (B) an airline, and (C) a manufacturing organization. The blue areas are OM activities.

◆ **STUDENT TIP**

The areas in blue indicate the significant role that OM plays in both manufacturing and service firms.

(B)

Airline

Operations
Ground support equipment
Maintenance
Ground operations
 Facility maintenance
 Catering
Flight operations
 Crew scheduling
 Flying
 Communications
 Dispatching
Management science

Finance/accounting
Accounting
 Accounts payable
 Accounts receivable
 General ledger
Finance
 Cash control
 International
  exchange

Marketing
Traffic administration
 Reservations
 Schedules
 Tariffs (pricing)
Sales
Advertising

Sergiy Serdyuk/Fotolia

(C)

Manufacturing

Operations
Facilities
 Construction; maintenance
Production and inventory control
 Scheduling; materials control
Quality assurance and control
Supply-chain management
Manufacturing
 Tooling; fabrication; assembly
Design
 Product development and design
 Detailed product specifications
Industrial engineering
 Efficient use of machines, space,
 and personnel
Process analysis
 Development and installation of
 production tools and equipment

Finance/accounting
Disbursements/credits
 Accounts receivable
 Accounts payable
 General ledger
Funds management
 Money market
 International exchange
Capital requirements
 Stock issue
 Bond issue and recall

Marketing
Sales promotion
Advertising
Sales
Market research

Alexzel/Shutterstock

| Farmer | Syrup producer | Bottler | Distributor | Retailer |

functions. Figure 1.1 shows how a bank, an airline, and a manufacturing firm organize themselves to perform these functions. The blue-shaded areas show the operations functions in these firms.

The Supply Chain

Through the three functions—marketing, operations, and finance—value for the customer is created. However, firms seldom create this value by themselves. Instead, they rely on a variety of suppliers who provide everything from raw materials to accounting services. These suppliers, when taken together, can be thought of as a *supply chain*. A supply chain (see Figure 1.2) is a global network of organizations and activities that supply a firm with goods and services.

Supply chain
A global network of organizations and activities that supplies a firm with goods and services.

As our society becomes more technologically oriented, we see increasing specialization. Specialized expert knowledge, instant communication, and cheaper transportation also foster specialization and worldwide supply chains. It just does not pay for a firm to try to do everything itself. The expertise that comes with specialization exists up and down the supply chain, adding value at each step. When members of the supply chain collaborate to achieve high levels of customer satisfaction, we have a tremendous force for efficiency and competitive advantage. Competition in the 21st century is not between companies; it is between *supply chains*.

Why Study OM?

We study OM for four reasons:

1. OM is one of the three major functions of any organization, and it is integrally related to all the other business functions. All organizations market (sell), finance (account), and produce (operate), and it is important to know how the OM activity functions. Therefore, we study *how people organize themselves for productive enterprise*.
2. We study OM because we want to know *how goods and services are produced*. The production function is the segment of our society that creates the products and services we use.
3. We study OM to *understand what operations managers do*. Regardless of your job in an organization, you can perform better if you understand what operations managers do. In addition, understanding OM will help you explore the numerous and lucrative career opportunities in the field.
4. We study OM *because it is such a costly part of an organization*. A large percentage of the revenue of most firms is spent in the OM function. Indeed, OM provides a major opportunity for an organization to improve its profitability and enhance its service to society. Example 1 considers how a firm might increase its profitability via the production function.

Example 1 | EXAMINING THE OPTIONS FOR INCREASING CONTRIBUTION

Fisher Technologies is a small firm that must double its dollar contribution to fixed cost and profit in order to be profitable enough to purchase the next generation of production equipment. Management has determined that if the firm fails to increase contribution, its bank will not make the loan and the equipment cannot be purchased. If the firm cannot purchase the equipment, the limitations of the old equipment will force Fisher to go out of business and, in doing so, put its employees out of work and discontinue producing goods and services for its customers.

APPROACH ▶ Table 1.1 shows a simple profit-and-loss statement and three strategic options (marketing, finance/accounting, and operations) for the firm. The first option is a *marketing option*, where excellent marketing management may increase sales by 50%. By increasing sales by 50%, contribution will in turn increase 71%. But increasing sales 50% may be difficult; it may even be impossible.

TABLE 1.1	Options for Increasing Contribution			
		MARKETING OPTION[a]	FINANCE/ ACCOUNTING OPTION[b]	OM OPTION[c]
	CURRENT	INCREASE SALES REVENUE 50%	REDUCE FINANCE COSTS 50%	REDUCE PRODUCTION COSTS 20%
Sales	$100,000	$150,000	$100,000	$100,000
Costs of goods	−80,000	−120,000	−80,000	−64,000
Gross margin	20,000	30,000	20,000	36,000
Finance costs	−6,000	−6,000	−3,000	−6,000
Subtotal	14,000	24,000	17,000	30,000
Taxes at 25%	−3,500	−6,000	−4,250	−7,500
Contribution[d]	$ 10,500	$ 18,000	$ 12,750	$ 22,500

[a]Increasing sales 50% increases contribution by $7,500, or 71% (7,500/10,500).
[b]Reducing finance costs 50% increases contribution by $2,250, or 21% (2,250/10,500).
[c]Reducing production costs 20% increases contribution by $12,000, or 114% (12,000/10,500).
[d]Contribution to fixed cost (excluding finance costs) and profit.

The second option is a *finance/accounting option*, where finance costs are cut in half through good financial management. But even a reduction of 50% is still inadequate for generating the necessary increase in contribution. Contribution is increased by only 21%.

The third option is an *OM option*, where management reduces production costs by 20% and increases contribution by 114%.

SOLUTION ▶ Given the conditions of our brief example, Fisher Technologies has increased contribution from $10,500 to $22,500. It may now have a bank willing to lend it additional funds.

INSIGHT ▶ The OM option not only yields the greatest improvement in contribution but also may be the only feasible option. Increasing sales by 50% and decreasing finance cost by 50% may both be virtually impossible. Reducing operations cost by 20% may be difficult but feasible.

LEARNING EXERCISE ▶ What is the impact of only a 15% decrease in costs in the OM option? [Answer: A $19,500 contribution; an 86% increase.]

Example 1 underscores the importance of the effective operations activity of a firm. Development of increasingly effective operations is the approach taken by many companies as they face growing global competition.

What Operations Managers Do

All good managers perform the basic functions of the management process. The management process consists of *planning*, *organizing*, *staffing*, *leading*, and *controlling*. Operations managers apply this management process to the decisions they make in the OM function. The 10 strategic OM decisions are introduced in Table 1.2. Successfully addressing each of these decisions requires planning, organizing, staffing, leading, and controlling.

Where Are the OM Jobs? How does one get started on a career in operations? The 10 strategic OM decisions identified in Table 1.2 are made by individuals who work in the disciplines shown in the blue areas of Figure 1.1. Business students who know their accounting,

10 Strategic OM Decisions
Design of goods and services
Managing quality
Process strategy
Location strategies
Layout strategies
Human resources
Supply-chain management
Inventory management
Scheduling
Maintenance

STUDENT TIP ◈

An operations manager must successfully address the 10 decisions around which this text is organized.

TABLE 1.2	Ten Strategic Operations Management Decisions	
DECISION		**CHAPTER(S)**
1. *Design of goods and services:* Defines much of what is required of operations in each of the other OM decisions. For instance, product design usually determines the lower limits of cost and the upper limits of quality, as well as major implications for sustainability and the human resources required.		5, Supplement 5
2. *Managing quality:* Determines the customer's quality expectations and establishes policies and procedures to identify and achieve that quality.		6, Supplement 6
3. *Process and capacity strategy:* Determines how a good or service is produced (i.e., the process for production) and commits management to specific technology, quality, human resources, and capital investments that determine much of the firm's basic cost structure.		7, Supplement 7
4. *Location strategy:* Requires judgments regarding nearness to customers, suppliers, and talent, while considering costs, infrastructure, logistics, and government.		8
5. *Layout strategy:* Requires integrating capacity needs, personnel levels, technology, and inventory requirements to determine the efficient flow of materials, people, and information.		9
6. *Human resources and job design:* Determines how to recruit, motivate, and retain personnel with the required talent and skills. People are an integral and expensive part of the total system design.		10
7. *Supply chain management:* Decides how to integrate the supply chain into the firm's strategy, including decisions that determine what is to be purchased, from whom, and under what conditions.		11, Supplement 11
8. *Inventory management:* Considers inventory ordering and holding decisions and how to optimize them as customer satisfaction, supplier capability, and production schedules are considered.		12, 14, 16
9. *Scheduling:* Determines and implements intermediate- and short-term schedules that effectively and efficiently utilize both personnel and facilities while meeting customer demands.		13, 15
10. *Maintenance:* Requires decisions that consider facility capacity, production demands, and personnel necessary to maintain a reliable and stable process.		17

statistics, finance, and OM have an opportunity to assume entry-level positions in all of these areas. As you read this text, identify disciplines that can assist you in making these decisions. Then take courses in those areas. The more background an OM student has in accounting, statistics, information systems, and mathematics, the more job opportunities will be available. About 40% of *all* jobs are in OM.

The following professional organizations provide various certifications that may enhance your education and be of help in your career:

◆ APICS, the Association for Operations Management (www.apics.org)
◆ American Society for Quality (ASQ) (www.asq.org)
◆ Institute for Supply Management (ISM) (www.ism.ws)
◆ Project Management Institute (PMI) (www.pmi.org)
◆ Council of Supply Chain Management Professionals (www.cscmp.org)

Figure 1.3 shows some recent job opportunities.

The Heritage of Operations Management

The field of OM is relatively young, but its history is rich and interesting. Our lives and the OM discipline have been enhanced by the innovations and contributions of numerous individuals. We now introduce a few of these people, and we provide a summary of significant events in operations management in Figure 1.4.

Operations Management Positions

SEARCH JOBS

| Date | | Job Title |

| 1/15 | **Plant Manager** |

Division of Fortune 1000 company seeks plant manager for plant located in the upper Hudson Valley area. This plant manufactures loading dock equipment for commercial markets. The candidate must be experienced in plant management including expertise in production planning, purchasing, and inventory management. Good written and oral communication skills are a must, along with excellent application of skills in managing people.

| 2/23 | **Operations Analyst** |

Expanding national coffee shop: top 10 "Best Places to Work" wants junior level systems analyst to join our excellent store improvement team. Business or I.E. degree, work methods, labor standards, ergonomics, cost accounting knowledge a plus. This is a hands-on job and excellent opportunity for a team player with good people skills. West Coast location. Some travel required.

| 3/18 | **Quality Manager** |

Several openings exist in our small package processing facilities in the Northeast, Florida, and Southern California for quality managers. These highly visible positions require extensive use of statistical tools to monitor all aspects of service, timeliness, and workload measurement. The work involves (1) a combination of hands-on applications and detailed analysis using databases and spreadsheets, (2) processing of audits to identify areas for improvement, and (3) management of implementation of changes. Positions involve night hours and weekends.

| 4/6 | **Supply-Chain Manager and Planner** |

Responsibilities entail negotiating contracts and establishing long-term relationships with suppliers. We will rely on the selected candidate to maintain accuracy in the purchasing system, invoices, and product returns. A bachelor's degree and up to 2 years related experience are required. Working knowledge of MRP, ability to use feedback to master scheduling and suppliers and consolidate orders for best price and delivery are necessary. Proficiency in all PC Windows applications, particularly Excel and Word, is essential. Effective verbal and written communication skills are essential.

| 5/14 | **Process Improvement Consultants** |

An expanding consulting firm is seeking consultants to design and implement lean production and cycle time reduction plans in both service and manufacturing processes. Our firm is currently working with an international bank to improve its back office operations, as well as with several manufacturing firms. A business degree required; APICS certification a plus.

Figure **1.3**

Many Opportunities Exist for Operations Managers

Eli Whitney (1800) is credited for the early popularization of interchangeable parts, which was achieved through standardization and quality control. Through a contract he signed with the U.S. government for 10,000 muskets, he was able to command a premium price because of their interchangeable parts.

Frederick W. Taylor (1881), known as the father of scientific management, contributed to personnel selection, planning and scheduling, motion study, and the now popular field of ergonomics. One of his major contributions was his belief that management should be much more resourceful and aggressive in the improvement of work methods. Taylor and his colleagues, Henry L. Gantt and Frank and Lillian Gilbreth, were among the first to systematically seek the best way to produce.

Another of Taylor's contributions was the belief that management should assume more responsibility for:

1. Matching employees to the right job.
2. Providing the proper training.
3. Providing proper work methods and tools.
4. Establishing legitimate incentives for work to be accomplished.

Everett Collection/Newscom

Cost Focus		Quality Focus	Customization Focus	Globalization Focus
Early Concepts 1776–1880 Labor Specialization (Smith, Babbage) Standardized Parts (Whitney) **Scientific Management Era 1880–1910** Gantt Charts (Gantt) Motion & Time Studies (Gilbreth) Process Analysis (Taylor) Queuing Theory (Erlang)	**Mass Production Era 1910–1980** Moving Assembly Line (Ford/Sorensen) Statistical Sampling (Shewhart) Economic Order Quantity (Harris) Linear Programming PERT/CPM (DuPont) Material Requirements Planning (MRP)	**Lean Production Era 1980–1995** Just-in-Time (JIT) Computer-Aided Design (CAD) Electronic Data Interchange (EDI) Total Quality Management (TQM) Baldrige Award Empowerment Kanbans	**Mass Customization Era 1995–2005** Internet/E-Commerce Enterprise Resource Planning International Quality Standards (ISO) Finite Scheduling Supply Chain Management Mass Customization Build-to-Order Radio Frequency Identification (RFID)	**Globalization Era 2005–2020** Global Supply Chains Growth of Transnational Organizations Instant Communications Sustainability Ethics in a Global Workforce Logistics

Figure **1.4**

Significant Events in Operations Management

By 1913, Henry Ford and Charles Sorensen combined what they knew about standardized parts with the quasi-assembly lines of the meatpacking and mail-order industries and added the revolutionary concept of the assembly line, where men stood still and material moved.

Quality control is another historically significant contribution to the field of OM. Walter Shewhart (1924) combined his knowledge of statistics with the need for quality control and provided the foundations for statistical sampling in quality control. W. Edwards Deming (1950) believed, as did Frederick Taylor, that management must do more to improve the work environment and processes so that quality can be improved.

Operations management will continue to progress as contributions from other disciplines, including *industrial engineering, statistics, management,* and *economics,* improve decision making.

Innovations from the *physical sciences* (biology, anatomy, chemistry, physics) have also contributed to advances in OM. These innovations include new adhesives, faster integrated circuits, gamma rays to sanitize food products, and specialized glass for iPhones and plasma TVs. Innovation in products and processes often depends on advances in the physical sciences.

Especially important contributions to OM have come from *information technology,* which we define as the systematic processing of data to yield information. Information technology—with wireless links, Internet, and e-commerce—is reducing costs and accelerating communication.

Decisions in operations management require individuals who are well versed in analytical tools, in information technology, and often in one of the biological or physical sciences. In this textbook, we look at the diverse ways a student can prepare for a career in operations management.

Operations for Goods and Services

Manufacturers produce a tangible product, while service products are often intangible. But many products are a combination of a good and a service, which complicates the definition of a service. Even the U.S. government has trouble generating a consistent definition. Because definitions vary, much of the data and statistics generated about the service sector are inconsistent. However, we define services as including repair and maintenance, government, food and lodging, transportation, insurance, trade, financial, real estate, education, legal, medical, entertainment, and other professional occupations.

The operation activities for both goods and services are often very similar. For instance, both have quality standards, are designed and produced on a schedule that meets customer demand, and are made in a facility where people are employed. However, some major differences *do* exist between goods and services. These are presented in Table 1.3.

We should point out that in many cases, the distinction between goods and services is not clear-cut. In reality, almost all services and almost all goods are a mixture of a service and a tangible product. Even services such as consulting may require a tangible report. Similarly, the sale of most goods includes a service. For instance, many products have the service components of financing and delivery (e.g., automobile sales). Many also require after-sale training and maintenance (e.g., office copiers and machinery). "Service" activities may also be an integral part of production. Human resource activities, logistics, accounting, training, field service, and repair are all service activities, but they take place within a manufacturing organization. Very few services are "pure," meaning they have no tangible component. Counseling may be one of the exceptions.

Growth of Services

Services constitute the largest economic sector in postindustrial societies. Until about 1900, most Americans were employed in agriculture. Increased agricultural productivity allowed people to leave the farm and seek employment in the city. Similarly, manufacturing employment has decreased for the past 60 years. The changes in agriculture, manufacturing, and service employment as a percentage of the workforce are shown in Figure 1.5. Although the *number* of people employed in manufacturing has decreased since 1950, each person is now producing almost 20 times more than in 1950. Services became the dominant

STUDENT TIP
Services are especially important because almost 80% of all jobs are in service firms.

Services
Economic activities that typically produce an intangible product (such as education, entertainment, lodging, government, financial, and health services).

LO 1.2 *Explain* the distinction between goods and services

TABLE 1.3 Differences Between Goods and Services

CHARACTERISTICS OF SERVICES	CHARACTERISTICS OF GOODS
Intangible: Ride in an airline seat	Tangible: The seat itself
Produced and consumed simultaneously: Beauty salon produces a haircut that is consumed as it is produced	Product can usually be kept in inventory (beauty care products)
Unique: Your investments and medical care are unique	Similar products produced (iPods)
High customer interaction: Often what the customer is paying for (consulting, education)	Limited customer involvement in production
Inconsistent product definition: Auto insurance changes with age and type of car	Product standardized (iPhone)
Often knowledge based: Legal, education, and medical services are hard to automate	Standard tangible product tends to make automation feasible
Services dispersed: Service may occur at retail store, local office, house call, or via Internet.	Product typically produced at a fixed facility
Quality may be hard to evaluate: Consulting, education, and medical services	Many aspects of quality for tangible products are easy to evaluate (strength of a bolt)
Reselling is unusual: Musical concert or medical care	Product often has some residual value

U.S. Agriculture, Manufacturing, and Service Employment

Source: U.S. Bureau of Labor Statistics.

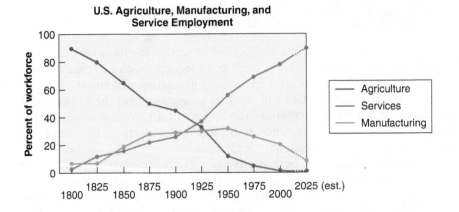

Service sector

The segment of the economy that includes trade, financial, lodging, education, legal, medical, and other professional occupations.

employer in the early 1920s, with manufacturing employment peaking at about 32% in 1950. The huge productivity increases in agriculture and manufacturing have allowed more of our economic resources to be devoted to services. Consequently, much of the world can now enjoy the pleasures of education, health services, entertainment, and myriad other things that we call services. Examples of firms and percentage of employment in the U.S. service sector are shown in Table 1.4. Table 1.4 also provides employment percentages for the nonservice sectors of manufacturing, construction, agriculture, and mining on the bottom four lines.

Service Pay

Although there is a common perception that service industries are low paying, in fact, many service jobs pay very well. Operations managers in the maintenance facility of an airline are very well paid, as are the operations managers who supervise computer services to the financial community. About 42% of all service workers receive wages above the national average. However, the service-sector average is driven down because 14 of the U.S. Department of

TABLE 1.4	Examples of Organizations in Each Sector	
SECTOR	**EXAMPLE**	**PERCENT OF ALL JOBS**
Service Sector		
Education, Medical, Other	San Diego State University, Arnold Palmer Hospital	15.3
Trade (retail, wholesale), Transportation	Walgreen's, Walmart, Nordstrom, Alaska Airlines	15.8
Information, Publishers, Broadcast	IBM, Bloomberg, Pearson, ESPN	1.9
Professional, Legal, Business Services, Associations	Snelling and Snelling, Waste Management, American Medical Association, Ernst & Young	13.6 / 85.2
Finance, Insurance, Real Estate	Citicorp, American Express, Prudential, Aetna	9.6
Leisure, Lodging, Entertainment	Olive Garden, Motel 6, Walt Disney	10.4
Government (Fed, State, Local)	U.S., State of Alabama, Cook County	15.6
Manufacturing Sector	General Electric, Ford, U.S. Steel, Intel	8.6
Construction Sector	Bechtel, McDermott	4.3
Agriculture	King Ranch	1.4
Mining Sector	Homestake Mining	.5
Grand Total		100.0

Source: Bureau of Labor Statistics, 2015.

Commerce categories of the 33 service industries do indeed pay below the all-private industry average. Of these, retail trade, which pays only 61% of the national private industry average, is large. But even considering the retail sector, the average wage of all service workers is about 96% of the average of all private industries.

The Productivity Challenge

The creation of goods and services requires changing resources into goods and services. The more efficiently we make this change, the more productive we are and the more value is added to the good or service provided. Productivity is the ratio of outputs (goods and services) divided by the inputs (resources, such as labor and capital) (see Figure 1.6). The operations manager's job is to enhance (improve) this ratio of outputs to inputs. Improving productivity means improving efficiency.[1]

This improvement can be achieved in two ways: reducing inputs while keeping output constant or increasing output while keeping inputs constant. Both represent an improvement in productivity. In an economic sense, inputs are labor, capital, and management, which are integrated into a production system. Management creates this production system, which provides the conversion of inputs to outputs. Outputs are goods and services, including such diverse items as guns, butter, education, improved judicial systems, and ski resorts. *Production* is the making of goods and services. High production may imply only that more people are working and that employment levels are high (low unemployment), but it does not imply high *productivity*.

Measurement of productivity is an excellent way to evaluate a country's ability to provide an improving standard of living for its people. *Only through increases in productivity can the standard of living improve.* Moreover, only through increases in productivity can labor, capital, and management receive additional payments. If returns to labor, capital, or management are increased without increased productivity, prices rise. On the other hand, downward pressure is placed on prices when productivity increases because more is being produced with the same resources.

The benefits of increased productivity are illustrated in the *OM in Action* box "Improving Productivity at Starbucks."

For well over a century (from about 1869), the U.S. has been able to increase productivity at an average rate of almost 2.5% per year. Such growth has doubled U.S. wealth every 30 years. The manufacturing sector, although a decreasing portion of the U.S. economy, has on occasion seen annual productivity increases exceeding 4%, and service sector increases of almost 1%. However, U.S. annual productivity growth in the early part of the 21st century is slightly below the 2.5% range for the economy as a whole and in recent years has been trending down.[2]

In this text, we examine how to improve productivity through operations management. Productivity is a significant issue for the world and one that the operations manager is uniquely qualified to address.

Productivity

The ratio of outputs (goods and services) divided by one or more inputs (such as labor, capital, or management).

LO 1.3 *Explain* the difference between production and productivity

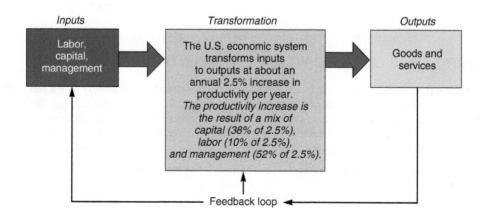

Inputs	Transformation	Outputs
Labor, capital, management	The U.S. economic system transforms inputs to outputs at about an annual 2.5% increase in productivity per year. *The productivity increase is the result of a mix of capital (38% of 2.5%), labor (10% of 2.5%), and management (52% of 2.5%).*	Goods and services

— Feedback loop ◀—

Figure **1.6**

The Economic System Adds Value by Transforming Inputs to Outputs

An effective feedback loop evaluates performance against a strategy or standard. It also evaluates customer satisfaction and sends signals to managers controlling the inputs and transformation process.

OM in Action | Improving Productivity at Starbucks

"This is a game of seconds ..." says Silva Peterson, whom Starbucks has put in charge of saving seconds. Her team of 10 analysts is constantly asking themselves: "How can we shave time off this?"

Peterson's analysis suggested that there were some obvious opportunities. First, stop requiring signatures on credit-card purchases under $25. This sliced 8 seconds off the transaction time at the cash register.

Then analysts noticed that Starbucks' largest cold beverage, the Venti size, required two bending and digging motions to scoop up enough ice. The scoop was too small. Redesign of the scoop provided the proper amount in one motion and cut 14 seconds off the average time of 1 minute.

Third were new espresso machines; with the push of a button, the machines grind coffee beans and brew. This allowed the server, called a "barista" in Starbucks's vocabulary, to do other things. The savings: about 12 seconds per espresso shot.

As a result, operations improvements at Starbucks outlets have increased the average transactions per hour to 11.7—a 46% increase—and yearly volume by $250,000, to about $1 million. The result: a 27% improvement in overall productivity—about 4.5% per year. In the service industry, a 4.5% per year increase is very tasty.

Sources: BusinessWeek (August 23–30, 2012) and The Wall Street Journal (October 13, 2010 and August 4, 2009).

Kondor83/Shutterstock

Productivity Measurement

LO 1.4 *Compute single-factor productivity*

The measurement of productivity can be quite direct. Such is the case when productivity is measured by labor-hours per ton of a specific type of steel. Although labor-hours is a common measure of input, other measures such as capital (dollars invested), materials (tons of ore), or energy (kilowatts of electricity) can be used.[3] An example of this can be summarized in the following equation:

$$\text{Productivity} = \frac{\text{Units produced}}{\text{Input used}} \tag{1-1}$$

For example, if units produced = 1,000 and labor-hours used is 250, then:

$$\text{Single-factor productivity} = \frac{\text{Units produced}}{\text{Labor-hours used}} = \frac{1,000}{250} = 4 \text{ units per labor-hour}$$

Single-factor productivity

Indicates the ratio of goods and services produced (outputs) to one resource (input).

Multifactor productivity

Indicates the ratio of goods and services produced (outputs) to many or all resources (inputs).

The use of just one resource input to measure productivity, as shown in Equation (1-1), is known as single-factor productivity. However, a broader view of productivity is multifactor productivity, which includes all inputs (e.g., capital, labor, material, energy). Multifactor productivity is also known as *total factor productivity*. Multifactor productivity is calculated by combining the input units as shown here:

$$\text{Multifactor productivity} = \frac{\text{Output}}{\text{Labor} + \text{Material} + \text{Energy} + \text{Capital} + \text{Miscellaneous}} \tag{1-2}$$

To aid in the computation of multifactor productivity, the individual inputs (the denominator) can be expressed in dollars and summed as shown in Example 2.

Example 2 | COMPUTING SINGLE-FACTOR AND MULTIFACTOR GAINS IN PRODUCTIVITY

Collins Title Insurance Ltd. wants to evaluate its labor and multifactor productivity with a new computerized title-search system. The company has a staff of four, each working 8 hours per day (for a payroll cost of $640/day) and overhead expenses of $400 per day. Collins processes and closes on 8 titles each day. The new computerized title-search system will allow the processing of 14 titles per day. Although the staff, their work hours, and pay are the same, the overhead expenses are now $800 per day.

APPROACH ▶ Collins uses Equation (1-1) to compute labor productivity and Equation (1-2) to compute multifactor productivity.

SOLUTION ▶

LO 1.5 *Compute multifactor productivity*

Labor productivity with the old system: $\dfrac{8 \text{ titles per day}}{32 \text{ labor-hours}} = .25$ titles per labor-hour

Labor productivity with the new system: $\dfrac{14 \text{ titles per day}}{32 \text{ labor-hours}} = .4375$ titles per labor-hour

Multifactor productivity with the old system: $\dfrac{8 \text{ titles per day}}{\$640 + 400} = .0077$ titles per dollar

Multifactor productivity with the new system: $\dfrac{14 \text{ titles per day}}{\$640 + 800} = .0097$ titles per dollar

Labor productivity has increased from .25 to .4375. The change is $(.4375 - .25)/.25 = 0.75$, or a 75% increase in labor productivity. Multifactor productivity has increased from .0077 to .0097. This change is $(.0097 - .0077)/.0077 = 0.26$, or a 26% increase in multifactor productivity.

INSIGHT ▶ Both the labor (single-factor) and multifactor productivity measures show an increase in productivity. However, the multifactor measure provides a better picture of the increase because it includes all the costs connected with the increase in output.

LEARNING EXERCISE ▶ If the overhead goes to $960 (rather than $800), what is the multifactor productivity? [Answer: .00875.]

RELATED PROBLEMS ▶ 1.1, 1.2, 1.4, 1.5, 1.6, 1.7, 1.8, 1.9, 1.10, 1.11, 1.13, 1.14, 1.17

Use of productivity measures aids managers in determining how well they are doing. But results from the two measures can be expected to vary. If labor productivity growth is entirely the result of capital spending, measuring just labor distorts the results. Multifactor productivity is usually better, but more complicated. Labor productivity is the more popular measure. The multifactor-productivity measures provide better information about the trade-offs among factors, but substantial measurement problems remain. Some of these measurement problems are:

1. *Quality* may change while the quantity of inputs and outputs remains constant. Compare an HDTV of this decade with a black-and-white TV of the 1950s. Both are TVs, but few people would deny that the quality has improved. The unit of measure—a TV—is the same, but the quality has changed.
2. *External elements* may cause an increase or a decrease in productivity for which the system under study may not be directly responsible. A more reliable electric power service may greatly improve production, thereby improving the firm's productivity because of this support system rather than because of managerial decisions made within the firm.
3. *Precise units of measure* may be lacking. Not all automobiles require the same inputs: Some cars are subcompacts, others are 911 Turbo Porsches.

Productivity measurement is particularly difficult in the service sector, where the end product can be hard to define. For example, economic statistics ignore the quality of your haircut, the outcome of a court case, or the service at a retail store. In some cases, adjustments are made for the quality of the product sold but *not* the quality of the sales presentation or the advantage of a broader product selection. Productivity measurements require specific inputs and outputs, but a free economy is producing worth—what people want—which includes convenience, speed, and safety. Traditional measures of outputs may be a very poor measure of these other measures of worth. Note the quality-measurement problems in a law office, where each case is different, altering the accuracy of the measure "cases per labor-hour" or "cases per employee."

Productivity Variables

As we saw in Figure 1.6, productivity increases are dependent on three productivity variables:

1. *Labor,* which contributes about 10% of the annual increase.
2. *Capital,* which contributes about 38% of the annual increase.
3. *Management,* which contributes about 52% of the annual increase.

These three factors are critical to improved productivity. They represent the broad areas in which managers can take action to improve productivity.

Productivity variables

The three factors critical to productivity improvement—labor, capital, and the art and science of management.

Figure **1.7**

About Half of the 17-Year-Olds in the U.S. Cannot Correctly Answer Questions of This Type

LO 1.6 *Identify* the critical variables in enhancing productivity

Labor Improvement in the contribution of labor to productivity is the result of a healthier, better-educated, and better-nourished labor force. Some increase may also be attributed to a shorter workweek. Historically, about 10% of the annual improvement in productivity is attributed to improvement in the quality of labor. Three key variables for improved labor productivity are:

1. Basic education appropriate for an effective labor force.
2. Diet of the labor force.
3. Social overhead that makes labor available, such as transportation and sanitation.

Illiteracy and poor diets are a major impediment to productivity, costing countries up to 20% of their productivity. Infrastructure that yields clean drinking water and sanitation is also an opportunity for improved productivity, as well as an opportunity for better health, in much of the world.

In developed nations, the challenge becomes *maintaining and enhancing the skills of labor* in the midst of rapidly expanding technology and knowledge. Recent data suggest that the average American 17-year-old knows significantly less mathematics than the average Japanese at the same age, and about half cannot answer the questions in Figure 1.7. Moreover, about one-third of American job applicants tested for basic skills were deficient in reading, writing, or math.

Overcoming shortcomings in the quality of labor while other countries have a better labor force is a major challenge. Perhaps improvements can be found not only through increasing competence of labor but also via *better utilized labor with a stronger commitment*. Training, motivation, team building, and the human resource strategies discussed in Chapter 10, as well as improved education, may be among the many techniques that will contribute to increased labor productivity. Improvements in labor productivity are possible; however, they can be expected to be increasingly difficult and expensive.

Capital Human beings are tool-using animals. Capital investment provides those tools. Capital investment has increased in the U.S. every year except during a few very severe recession periods. Annual capital investment in the U.S. has increased at an annual rate of 1.5% after allowances for depreciation.

Inflation and taxes increase the cost of capital, making capital investment increasingly expensive. When the capital invested per employee drops, we can expect a drop in productivity. Using labor rather than capital may reduce unemployment in the short run, but it also makes economies less productive and therefore lowers wages in the long run. Capital investment is often a necessary, but seldom a sufficient, ingredient in the battle for increased productivity.

The trade-off between capital and labor is continually in flux. The higher the cost of capital or perceived risk, the more projects requiring capital are "squeezed out": they are not pursued because the potential return on investment for a given risk has been reduced. Managers adjust their investment plans to changes in capital cost and risk.

Management Management is a factor of production and an economic resource. Management is responsible for ensuring that labor and capital are effectively used to increase productivity. Management accounts for over half of the annual increase in productivity. This increase includes improvements made through the use of knowledge and the application of technology.

Knowledge society

A society in which much of the labor force has migrated from manual work to work based on knowledge.

Using knowledge and technology is critical in postindustrial societies. Consequently, postindustrial societies are also known as knowledge societies. Knowledge societies are those in which much of the labor force has migrated from manual work to technical and information-processing

The effective use of capital often means finding the proper trade-off between investment in capital assets (automation, left) and human assets (a manual process, right). While there are risks connected with any investment, the cost of capital and physical investments is fairly clear-cut, but the cost of employees has many hidden costs including fringe benefits, social insurance, and legal constraints on hiring, employment, and termination.

tasks requiring ongoing education. The required education and training are important high-cost items that are the responsibility of operations managers as they build organizations and workforces. The expanding knowledge base of contemporary society requires that managers use *technology and knowledge effectively.*

More effective use of capital also contributes to productivity. It falls to the operations manager, as a productivity catalyst, to select the best new capital investments as well as to improve the productivity of existing investments.

The productivity challenge is difficult. A country cannot be a world-class competitor with second-class inputs. Poorly educated labor, inadequate capital, and dated technology are second-class inputs. High productivity and high-quality outputs require high-quality inputs, including good operations managers.

Productivity and the Service Sector

The service sector provides a special challenge to the accurate measurement of productivity and productivity improvement. The traditional analytical framework of economic theory is based primarily on goods-producing activities. Consequently, most published economic data relate to goods production. But the data do indicate that, as our contemporary service economy has increased in size, we have had slower growth in productivity.

Siemens, a multi-billion-dollar German conglomerate, has long been known for its apprentice programs in its home country. Because education is often the key to efficient operations in a technological society, Siemens has spread its apprentice-training programs to its U.S. plants. These programs are laying the foundation for the highly skilled workforce that is essential for global competitiveness.

OM in Action — Taco Bell Improves Productivity and Goes Green to Lower Costs

Founded in 1962 by Glenn Bell, Taco Bell seeks competitive advantage via low cost. Like many other services, Taco Bell relies on its operations management to improve productivity and reduce cost.

Its menu and meals are designed to be easy to prepare. Taco Bell has shifted a substantial portion of food preparation to suppliers who could perform food processing more efficiently than a stand-alone restaurant. Ground beef is precooked prior to arrival and then reheated, as are many dishes that arrive in plastic boil bags for easy sanitary reheating. Similarly, tortillas arrive already fried and onions prediced. Efficient layout and automation has cut to 8 seconds the time needed to prepare tacos and burritos and has cut time in the drive-through lines by 1 minute. These advances have been combined with training and empowerment to increase the span of management from one supervisor for 5 restaurants to one supervisor for 30 or more.

Operations managers at Taco Bell have cut in-store labor by 15 hours per day and reduced floor space by more than 50%. The result is a store that can average 164 seconds for each customer, from drive-up to pull-out.

In 2010, Taco Bell completed the rollout of its new Grill-to-Order kitchens by installing water- and energy-saving grills that conserve 300 million gallons of water and 200 million kilowatt hours of electricity each year. This "green"-inspired cooking method also saves the company's 5,800 restaurants $17 million per year.

Effective operations management has resulted in productivity increases that support Taco Bell's low-cost strategy. Taco Bell is now the fast-food low-cost leader with a 58% share of the Mexican fast-food market.

Bob Pardue-Signs/Alamy

Sources: Business Week (May 5, 2011); *Harvard Business Review* (July/August 2008); and J. Hueter and W. Swart, *Interfaces* (Vol. 28; issue 1).

Productivity of the service sector has proven difficult to improve because service-sector work is:

1. Typically labor intensive (e.g., counseling, teaching).
2. Frequently focused on unique individual attributes or desires (e.g., investment advice).
3. Often an intellectual task performed by professionals (e.g., medical diagnosis).
4. Often difficult to mechanize and automate (e.g., a haircut).
5. Often difficult to evaluate for quality (e.g., performance of a law firm).

The more intellectual and personal the task, the more difficult it is to achieve increases in productivity. Low-productivity improvement in the service sector is also attributable to the growth of low-productivity activities in the service sector. These include activities not previously a part of the measured economy, such as child care, food preparation, house cleaning, and laundry service. These activities have moved out of the home and into the measured economy as more and more women have joined the workforce. Inclusion of these activities has probably resulted in lower measured productivity for the service sector, although, in fact, actual productivity has probably increased because these activities are now more efficiently produced than previously.

However, despite the difficulty of improving productivity in the service sector, improvements are being made. And this text presents a multitude of ways to make these improvements. Indeed, what can be done when management pays attention to how work actually gets done is astonishing!

Although the evidence indicates that all industrialized countries have the same problem with service productivity, the U.S. remains the world leader in overall productivity *and* service productivity. Retailing is twice as productive in the U.S. as in Japan, where laws protect shopkeepers from discount chains. The U.S. telephone industry is at least twice as productive as Germany's. The U.S. banking system is also 33% more efficient than Germany's banking oligopolies. However, because productivity is central to the operations manager's job and because the service sector is so large, we take special note in this text of how to improve productivity in the service sector. (See, for instance, the *OM in Action* box "Taco Bell Improves Productivity and Goes Green to Lower Costs.")

Current Challenges in Operations Management

Operations managers work in an exciting and dynamic environment. This environment is the result of a variety of challenging forces, from globalization of world trade to the transfer of ideas, products, and money at electronic speeds. Let's look at some of these challenges:

◆ *Globalization:* The rapid decline in the cost of communication and transportation has made markets global. Similarly, resources in the form of capital, materials, talent, and labor are also now global. As a result, countries throughout the world are contributing to globalization as they vie for economic growth. Operations managers are rapidly seeking creative designs, efficient production, and high-quality goods via international collaboration.

◆ *Supply-chain partnering:* Shorter product life cycles, demanding customers, and fast changes in technology, materials, and processes require supply-chain partners to be in tune with the needs of end users. And because suppliers may be able to contribute unique expertise, operations managers are outsourcing and building long-term partnerships with critical players in the supply chain.

◆ *Sustainability:* Operations managers' continuing battle to improve productivity is concerned with designing products and processes that are ecologically sustainable. This means designing green products and packaging that minimize resource use, can be recycled or re-used, and are generally environmentally friendly.

◆ *Rapid product development:* Technology combined with rapid international communication of news, entertainment, and lifestyles is dramatically chopping away at the life span of products. OM is answering with new management structures, enhanced collaboration, digital technology, and creative alliances that are more responsive and effective.

◆ *Mass customization:* Once managers recognize the *world* as the marketplace, the cultural and individual differences become quite obvious. In a world where consumers are increasingly aware of innovation and options, substantial pressure is placed on firms to respond in a creative way. And OM must rapidly respond with product designs and flexible production processes that cater to the individual whims of consumers. The goal is to produce customized products, whenever and wherever needed.

◆ *Lean operations:* Lean is the management model sweeping the world and providing the standard against which operations managers must compete. Lean can be thought of as the driving force in a well-run operation, where the customer is satisfied, employees are respected, and waste does not exist. The theme of this text is to build organizations that are more efficient, where management creates enriched jobs that help employees engage in continuous improvement, and where goods and services are produced and delivered when and where the customer desires them. These ideas are also captured in the phrase *Lean*.

These challenges must be successfully addressed by today's operations managers. This text will provide you with the foundations necessary to meet those challenges.

Ethics, Social Responsibility, and Sustainability

The systems that operations managers build to convert resources into goods and services are complex. And they function in a world where the physical and social environment is evolving, as are laws and values. These dynamics present a variety of challenges that come from the conflicting perspectives of stakeholders, such as customers, distributors, suppliers, owners, lenders, employees, and community. Stakeholders, as well as government agencies at various levels, require constant monitoring and thoughtful responses.

Identifying ethical and socially responsible responses while developing sustainable processes that are also effective and efficient productive systems is not easy. Managers are also challenged to:

◆ Develop and produce safe, high-quality green products
◆ Train, retain, and motivate employees in a safe workplace
◆ Honor stakeholder commitments

Managers must do all this while meeting the demands of a very competitive and dynamic world marketplace. If operations managers have a *moral awareness and focus on increasing productivity in this system*, then many of the ethical challenges will be successfully addressed. The organization will use fewer resources, the employees will be committed, the market will be satisfied, and the ethical climate will be enhanced. Throughout this text, we note ways in which operations managers can take ethical and socially responsible actions while successfully addressing these challenges of the market. We also conclude each chapter with an *Ethical Dilemma* exercise.

Stakeholders

Those with a vested interest in an organization, including customers, distributors, suppliers, owners, lenders, employees, and community members.

Summary

Operations, marketing, and finance/accounting are the three functions basic to all organizations. The operations function creates goods and services. Much of the progress of operations management has been made in the twentieth century, but since the beginning of time, humankind has been attempting to improve its material well-being. Operations managers are key players in the battle to improve productivity.

As societies become increasingly affluent, more of their resources are devoted to services. In the U.S., more than 85% of the workforce is employed in the service sector. Productivity improvements and a sustainable environment are difficult to achieve, but operations managers are the primary vehicle for making improvements.

Key Terms

Production (p. 4)
Operations management (OM) (p. 4)
Supply chain (p. 6)
10 strategic OM decisions (p. 7)

Services (p. 11)
Service sector (p. 12)
Productivity (p. 13)
Single-factor productivity (p. 14)

Multifactor productivity (p. 14)
Productivity variables (p. 15)
Knowledge society (p. 16)
Stakeholders (p. 19)

Ethical Dilemma

The American car battery industry boasts that its recycling rate now exceeds 95%, the highest rate for any commodity. However, with changes brought about by specialization and globalization, parts of the recycling system are moving offshore. This is particularly true of automobile batteries, which contain lead. The Environmental Protection Agency (EPA) is contributing to the offshore flow with newly implemented standards that make domestic battery recycling increasingly difficult and expensive. The result is a major increase in used batteries going to Mexico, where environmental standards and control are less demanding than they are in the U.S. One in five batteries is now exported to Mexico. There is seldom difficulty finding buyers because lead is expensive and in worldwide demand. While U.S.

recyclers operate in sealed, mechanized plants, with smokestacks equipped with scrubbers and plant surroundings monitored for traces of lead, this is not the case in most Mexican plants. The harm from lead is legendary, with long-run residual effects. Health issues include high blood pressure, kidney damage, detrimental effects on fetuses during pregnancy, neurological problems, and arrested development in children.

Given the two scenarios below, what action do you take?

a) You own an independent auto repair shop and are trying to safely dispose of a few old batteries each week. (Your battery supplier is an auto parts supplier who refuses to take your old batteries.)

b) You are manager of a large retailer responsible for disposal of thousands of used batteries each day.

Discussion Questions

1. Why should one study operations management?
2. Identify four people who have contributed to the theory and techniques of operations management.
3. Briefly describe the contributions of the four individuals identified in the preceding question.
4. Figure 1.1 outlines the operations, finance/accounting, and marketing functions of three organizations. Prepare a chart similar to Figure 1.1 outlining the same functions for one of the following:
   a. a newspaper
   b. a drugstore
   c. a college library
   d. a summer camp
   e. a small costume-jewelry factory
5. Answer Question 4 for some other organization, perhaps an organization where you have worked.
6. What are the three basic functions of a firm?
7. Identify the 10 strategic operations management decisions.
8. Name four areas that are significant to improving labor productivity.

9. The U.S., and indeed much of the rest of the world, has been described as a "knowledge society." How does this affect productivity measurement and the comparison of productivity between the U.S. and other countries?
10. What are the measurement problems that occur when one attempts to measure productivity?
11. Mass customization and rapid product development were identified as challenges to modern manufacturing operations. What is the relationship, if any, between these challenges? Can you cite any examples?
12. What are the five reasons productivity is difficult to improve in the service sector?
13. Describe some of the actions taken by Taco Bell to increase productivity that have resulted in Taco Bell's ability to serve "twice the volume with half the labor."
14. As a library or Internet assignment, find the U.S. productivity rate (increase) last year for the (a) national economy, (b) manufacturing sector, and (c) service sector.

Using Software for Productivity Analysis

This section presents three ways to solve productivity problems with computer software. First, you can create your own Excel spreadsheets to conduct productivity analysis. Second, you can use the Excel OM software that comes with this text. Third, POM for Windows is another program that is available with this text.

CREATING YOUR OWN EXCEL SPREADSHEETS

Program 1.1 illustrates how to build an Excel spreadsheet for the data in Example 2.

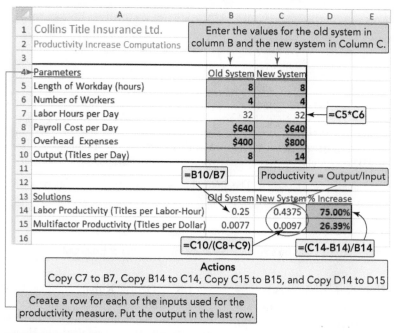

Program **1.1**

✗ USING EXCEL OM

Excel OM is an Excel "add-in" with 24 Operations Management decision support "Templates." To access the templates, double-click on the *Excel OM* tab at the top of the page, then in the menu bar choose the appropriate chapter (in this case Chapter 1), from either the "Chapter" or "Alphabetic" tab on the left. Each of Excel OM's 24 modules includes instructions for that particular module. The instructions can be turned on or off via the "instruction" tab in the menu bar.

P USING POM FOR WINDOWS

POM for Windows is decision support software that includes 24 Operations Management modules. The modules are accessed by double-clicking on *Module* in the menu bar, and then double-clicking on the appropriate (in this case *Productivity*) item. Instructions are provided for each module just below the menu bar.

Solved Problems   Virtual Office Hours help is available in MyOMLab.

SOLVED PROBLEM 1.1

Productivity can be measured in a variety of ways, such as by labor, capital, energy, material usage, and so on. At Modern Lumber, Inc., Art Binley, president and producer of apple crates sold to growers, has been able, with his current equipment, to produce 240 crates per 100 logs. He currently purchases 100 logs per day, and each log requires 3 labor-hours to process. He believes that he can hire a professional buyer who can buy a better-quality log at the same cost. If this is the case, he can increase his production to 260 crates per 100 logs. His labor-hours will increase by 8 hours per day.

What will be the impact on productivity (measured in crates per labor-hour) if the buyer is hired?

SOLUTION

(a) Current labor productivity $= \dfrac{240 \text{ crates}}{100 \text{ logs} \times 3 \text{ hours/log}}$

$= \dfrac{240}{300}$

$= .8$ crates per labor-hour

(b) Labor productivity with buyer $= \dfrac{260 \text{ crates}}{(100 \text{ logs} \times 3 \text{ hours/log}) + 8 \text{ hours}}$

$= \dfrac{260}{308}$

$= .844$ crates per labor-hour

Using current productivity (.80 from [a]) as a base, the increase will be 5.5% (.844/.8 = 1.055, or a 5.5% increase).

SOLVED PROBLEM 1.2

Art Binley has decided to look at his productivity from a multi-factor (total factor productivity) perspective (refer to Solved Problem 1.1). To do so, he has determined his labor, capital, energy, and material usage and decided to use dollars as the common denominator. His total labor-hours are now 300 per day and will increase to 308 per day. His capital and energy costs will remain constant at $350 and $150 per day, respectively. Material costs for the 100 logs per day are $1,000 and will remain the same. Because he pays an average of $10 per hour (with fringes), Binley determines his productivity increase as follows:

SOLUTION

CURRENT SYSTEM	
Labor:	300 hrs. @10 = 3,000
Material:	100 logs/day 1,000
Capital:	350
Energy:	150
Total Cost:	$4,500

SYSTEM WITH PROFESSIONAL BUYER	
308 hrs. @10 =	$3,080
	1,000
	350
	150
	$4,580

Multifactor productivity of current system:
= 240 crates/$4,500 = .0533 crates/dollar

Multifactor productivity of proposed system:
= 260 crates/$4,580 = .0568 crates/dollar

Using current productivity (.0533) as a base, the increase will be .066. That is, .0568/.0533 = 1.066, or a 6.6% increase.

Problems   *Note:* **Px** means the problem may be solved with POM for Windows and/or Excel OM.

Problems 1.1 to 1.17 relate to The Productivity Challenge

• **1.1**   Chuck Sox makes wooden boxes in which to ship motorcycles. Chuck and his three employees invest a total of 40 hours per day making the 120 boxes.
a) What is their productivity?
b) Chuck and his employees have discussed redesigning the process to improve efficiency. If they can increase the rate to 125 per day, what will be their new productivity?
c) What will be their unit *increase* in productivity per hour?
d) What will be their percentage change in productivity? **Px**

• **1.2**   Carbondale Casting produces cast bronze valves on a 10-person assembly line. On a recent day, 160 valves were produced during an 8-hour shift.
a) Calculate the labor productivity of the line.
b) John Goodale, the manager at Carbondale, changed the layout and was able to increase production to 180 units per 8-hour shift. What is the new labor productivity per labor-hour?
c) What is the percentage of productivity increase? **Px**

• **1.3**   This year, Druehl, Inc., will produce 57,600 hot water heaters at its plant in Delaware, in order to meet expected global demand. To accomplish this, each laborer at the plant will work 160 hours per month. If the labor productivity at the plant is 0.15 hot water heaters per labor-hour, how many laborers are employed at the plant?

• **1.4**   Lori Cook produces "Final Exam Care Packages" for resale by her sorority. She is currently working a total of 5 hours per day to produce 100 care packages.
a) What is Lori's productivity?
b) Lori thinks that by redesigning the package, she can increase her total productivity to 133 care packages per day. What will be her new productivity?
c) What will be the percentage increase in productivity if Lori makes the change? **Px**

•• **1.5**   George Kyparisis makes bowling balls in his Miami plant. With recent increases in his costs, he has a newfound interest in efficiency. George is interested in determining the productivity of his organization. He would like to know if his organization is maintaining the manufacturing average of 3% increase in productivity per year? He has the following data representing a month from last year and an equivalent month this year:

	LAST YEAR	NOW
Units produced	1,000	1,000
Labor (hours)	300	275
Resin (pounds)	50	45
Capital invested ($)	10,000	11,000
Energy (BTU)	3,000	2,850

Show the productivity percentage change for each category and then determine the improvement for labor-hours, the typical standard for comparison. **Px**

•• **1.6**   George Kyparisis (using data from Problem 1.5) determines his costs to be as follows:

♦ *Labor:* $10 per hour
♦ *Resin:* $5 per pound
♦ *Capital expense:* 1% per month of investment
♦ *Energy:* $0.50 per BTU

Show the percent change in productivity for one month last year versus one month this year, on a multifactor basis with dollars as the common denominator. **Px**

• **1.7** Hokey Min's Kleen Karpet cleaned 65 rugs in October, consuming the following resources:

Labor:	520 hours at $13 per hour
Solvent:	100 gallons at $5 per gallon
Machine rental:	20 days at $50 per day

a) What is the labor productivity per dollar?
b) What is the multifactor productivity? **Px**

•• **1.8** Lillian Fok is president of Lakefront Manufacturing, a producer of bicycle tires. Fok makes 1,000 tires per day with the following resources:

Labor:	400 hours per day @ $12.50 per hour
Raw material:	20,000 pounds per day @ $1 per pound
Energy:	$5,000 per day
Capital costs:	$10,000 per day

a) What is the labor productivity per labor-hour for these tires at Lakefront Manufacturing?
b) What is the multifactor productivity for these tires at Lakefront Manufacturing?
c) What is the percent change in multifactor productivity if Fok can reduce the energy bill by $1,000 per day without cutting production or changing any other inputs? **Px**

••• **1.9** Brown's, a local bakery, is worried about increased costs—particularly energy. Last year's records can provide a fairly good estimate of the parameters for this year. Wende Brown, the owner, does not believe things have changed much, but she did invest an additional $3,000 for modifications to the bakery's ovens to make them more energy efficient. The modifications were supposed to make the ovens at least 15% more efficient. Brown has asked you to check the energy savings of the new ovens and also to look over other measures of the bakery's productivity to see if the modifications were beneficial. You have the following data to work with:

	LAST YEAR	NOW
Production (dozen)	1,500	1,500
Labor (hours)	350	325
Capital investment ($)	15,000	18,000
Energy (BTU)	3,000	2,750

Px

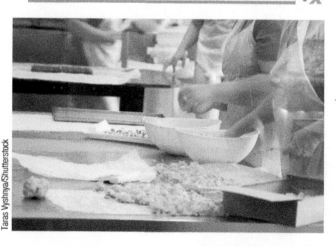

•• **1.10** Munson Performance Auto, Inc., modifies 375 autos per year. The manager, Adam Munson, is interested in obtaining a measure of overall performance. He has asked you to provide him with a multifactor measure of last year's performance as a benchmark for future comparison. You have assembled the following data. Resource inputs were labor, 10,000 hours; 500 suspension and engine modification kits; and energy, 100,000 kilowatt-hours. Average labor cost last year was $20 per hour, kits cost $1,000 each, and energy costs were $3 per kilowatt-hour. What do you tell Mr. Munson? **Px**

•• **1.11** Lake Charles Seafood makes 500 wooden packing boxes for fresh seafood per day, working in two 10-hour shifts. Due to increased demand, plant managers have decided to operate three 8-hour shifts instead. The plant is now able to produce 650 boxes per day.
a) Calculate the company's productivity before the change in work rules and after the change.
b) What is the percentage increase in productivity?
c) If production is increased to 700 boxes per day, what is the new productivity? **Px**

••• **1.12** Charles Lackey operates a bakery in Idaho Falls, Idaho. Because of its excellent product and excellent location, demand has increased by 25% in the last year. On far too many occasions, customers have not been able to purchase the bread of their choice. Because of the size of the store, no new ovens can be added. At a staff meeting, one employee suggested ways to load the ovens differently so that more loaves of bread can be baked at one time. This new process will require that the ovens be loaded by hand, requiring additional manpower. This is the only thing to be changed. If the bakery makes 1,500 loaves per month with a labor productivity of 2.344 loaves per labor-hour, how many workers will Lackey need to *add*? (*Hint:* Each worker works 160 hours per month.)

•• **1.13** Refer to Problem 1.12. The pay will be $8 per hour for employees. Charles Lackey can also improve the yield by purchasing a new blender. The new blender will mean an increase in his investment. This added investment has a cost of $100 per month, but he will achieve the same output (an increase to 1,875) as the change in labor-hours. Which is the better decision?
a) Show the productivity change, in loaves per dollar, with an increase in labor cost (from 640 to 800 hours).
b) Show the new productivity, in loaves per dollar, with only an increase in investment ($100 per month more).
c) Show the percent productivity change for labor and investment.

••• **1.14** Refer to Problems 1.12 and 1.13. If Charles Lackey's utility costs remain constant at $500 per month, labor at $8 per hour, and cost of ingredients at $0.35 per loaf, but Charles does not purchase the blender suggested in Problem 1.13, what will the productivity of the bakery be? What will be the percent increase or decrease?

•• **1.15** In December, General Motors produced 6,600 customized vans at its plant in Detroit. The labor productivity at this plant is known to have been 0.10 vans per labor-hour during that month. 300 laborers were employed at the plant that month.
a) How many hours did the average laborer work that month?
b) If productivity can be increased to 0.11 vans per labor-hour, how many hours would the average laborer work that month?

•• **1.16**   Susan Williams runs a small Flagstaff job shop where garments are made. The job shop employs eight workers. Each worker is paid $10 per hour. During the first week of March, each worker worked 45 hours. Together, they produced a batch of 132 garments. Of these garments, 52 were "seconds" (meaning that they were flawed). The seconds were sold for $90 each at a factory outlet store. The remaining 80 garments were sold to retail outlets at a price of $198 per garment. What was the labor productivity, in dollars per labor-hour, at this job shop during the first week of March?

••• **1.17**   As part of a study for the Department of Labor Statistics, you are assigned the task of evaluating the improvement in productivity of small businesses. Data for one of the small businesses you are to evaluate are shown at right. The data are the monthly average of last year and the monthly average this year. Determine the multifactor productivity with dollars as the common denominator for:

a) Last year.
b) This year.
c) Then determine the percent change in productivity for the monthly average last year versus the monthly average this year on a multifactor basis.

◆ *Labor:* $8 per hour

◆ *Capital:* 0.83% per month of investment

◆ *Energy:* $0.60 per BTU

	LAST YEAR	THIS YEAR
Production (dozen)	1,500	1,500
Labor (hours)	350	325
Capital investment ($)	15,000	18,000
Energy (BTU)	3,000	2,700

CASE STUDIES

Uber Technologies, Inc.

The $41 billion dollar firm Uber Technology, Inc., is unsettling the traditional taxi business. In over 40 countries and 240 markets around the world, Uber and similar companies are challenging the existing taxi business model. Uber and its growing list of competitors, Lyft, Sidecar, and Flywheel in America, and fledging rivals in Europe, Asia, and India, think their smart phone apps can provide a new and improved way to call a taxi. This disruptive business model uses an app to arrange rides between riders and cars, theoretically a nearby car, which is tracked by the app. The Uber system also provides a history of rides, routes, and fees as well as automatic billing. In addition, driver and rider are also allowed to evaluate each other. The services are increasingly popular, worrying established taxi services in cities from New York to Berlin, and from Rio de Janeiro to Bangkok. In many markets, Uber has proven to be the best, fastest, and most reliable way to find a ride. Consumers worldwide are endorsing the system as a replacement for the usual taxi ride. As the most established competitor in the field, Uber is putting more cars on the road, meaning faster pickup times, which should attract even more riders, which in turn attracts even more drivers, and so on. This growth cycle may speed the demise of the existing taxi businesses as well as provide substantial competition for firms with a technology-oriented model similar to Uber's.

The Uber business model initially attempts to bypass a number of regulations and at the same time offer better service and lower fees than traditional taxis. However, the traditional taxi industry is fighting back, and regulations are mounting. The regulations vary by country and city, but increasingly special licensing, testing, and inspections are being imposed. Part of the fee charged to riders does not go to the driver, but to Uber, as there are real overhead costs. Uber's costs, depending on the locale, may include insurance, background checks for drivers, vetting of vehicles, software development and maintenance, and centralized billing. How these overhead costs compare to traditional taxi costs is yet to be determined. Therefore, improved efficiency may not be immediately obvious, and contract provisions are significant (see www.uber.com/legal/usa/terms).

In addition to growing regulations, a complicating factor in the model is finding volunteer drivers at inopportune times. A sober driver and a clean car at 1:00 a.m. New Year's Eve does cost more. Consequently, Uber has introduced "surge" pricing. Surge pricing means a higher price, sometimes much higher, than normal. Surge pricing has proven necessary to ensure that cars and drivers are available at unusual times. These higher surge prices can be a shock to riders, making the "surge price" a contentious issue.

Discussion Questions

1. The market has decided that Uber and its immediate competitors are adding efficiency to our society. How is Uber providing that added efficiency?

2. Do you think the Uber model will work in the trucking industry?

3. In what other areas/industries might the Uber model be used?

Sources: Wall Street Journal (January 2, 2015), B3, and (Dec. 18, 2014), D1; and www.bloombergview.com/articles/2014-12-11/can-uber-rule-the-world.

Frito-Lay: Operations Management in Manufacturing

Video Case

Frito-Lay, the massive Dallas-based subsidiary of PepsiCo, has 38 plants and 48,000 employees in North America. Seven of Frito-Lay's 41 brands exceed $1 billion in sales: Fritos, Lay's, Cheetos, Ruffles, Tostitos, Doritos, and Walker's Potato Chips. Operations is the focus of the firm—from designing products for new markets, to meeting changing consumer preferences, to adjusting to rising commodity costs, to subtle issues involving flavors and preservatives—OM is under constant cost, time, quality, and market pressure. Here is a look at how the 10 decisions of OM are applied at this food processor.

In the food industry, product development kitchens experiment with new products, submit them to focus groups, and perform test marketing. Once the product specifications have been set, processes capable of meeting those specifications and the necessary quality standards are created. At Frito-Lay, quality begins at the farm, with onsite inspection of the potatoes used in Ruffles and the corn used in Fritos. Quality continues throughout the manufacturing process, with visual inspections and with statistical process control of product variables such as oil, moisture, seasoning, salt, thickness, and weight. Additional quality evaluations are conducted throughout shipment, receipt, production, packaging, and delivery.

The production process at Frito-Lay is designed for large volumes and small variety, using expensive special-purpose equipment, and with swift movement of material through the facility. Product-focused facilities, such as Frito-Lay's, typically have high capital costs, tight schedules, and rapid processing. Frito-Lay's facilities are located regionally to aid in the rapid delivery of products because freshness is a critical issue. Sanitary issues and necessarily fast processing of products put a premium on an efficient layout. Production lines are designed for balanced throughput and high utilization. Cross-trained workers, who handle a variety of production lines, have promotion paths identified for their particular skill set. The company rewards employees with medical, retirement, and education plans. Its turnover is very low.

The supply chain is integral to success in the food industry; vendors must be chosen with great care. Moreover, the finished food product is highly dependent on perishable raw materials. Consequently, the supply chain brings raw material (potatoes, corn, etc.) to the plant securely and rapidly to meet tight production schedules. For instance, from the time that potatoes are picked in St. Augustine, Florida, until they are unloaded at the Orlando plant, processed, packaged, and shipped from the plant is under 12 hours. The requirement for fresh product requires on-time, just-in-time deliveries combined with both low raw material and finished goods inventories. The continuous-flow nature of the specialized equipment in the production process permits little work-in-process inventory. The plants usually run 24/7. This means that there are four shifts of employees each week.

Tight scheduling to ensure the proper mix of fresh finished goods on automated equipment requires reliable systems and effective maintenance. Frito-Lay's workforce is trained to recognize problems early, and professional maintenance personnel are available on every shift. Downtime is very costly and can lead to late deliveries, making maintenance a high priority.

Discussion Questions*

1. From your knowledge of production processes and from the case and the video, identify how each of the 10 decisions of OM is applied at Frito-Lay.
2. How would you determine the productivity of the production process at Frito-Lay?
3. How are the 10 decisions of OM different when applied by the operations manager of a production process such as Frito-Lay versus a service organization such as Hard Rock Cafe (see the Hard Rock Cafe video case below)?

*You may wish to view the video that accompanies this case before addressing these questions.

Hard Rock Cafe: Operations Management in Services

Video Case

In its 45 years of existence, Hard Rock has grown from a modest London pub to a global power managing 150 cafes, 13 hotels/casinos, and live music venues. This puts Hard Rock firmly in the service industry—a sector that employs over 75% of the people in the U.S. Hard Rock moved its world headquarters to Orlando, Florida, in 1988 and has expanded to more than 40 locations throughout the U.S., serving over 100,000 meals each day. Hard Rock chefs are modifying the menu from classic American—burgers and chicken wings—to include higher-end items such as stuffed veal chops and lobster tails. Just as taste in music changes over time, so does Hard Rock Cafe, with new menus, layouts, memorabilia, services, and strategies.

At Orlando's Universal Studios, a traditional tourist destination, Hard Rock Cafe serves over 3,500 meals each day. The cafe employs about 400 people. Most are employed in the restaurant, but some work in the retail shop. Retail is now a standard and increasingly prominent feature in Hard Rock Cafes (since close to 48% of revenue comes from this source).

Cafe employees include kitchen and waitstaff, hostesses, and bartenders. Hard Rock employees are not only competent in their job skills but are also passionate about music and have engaging personalities. Cafe staff is scheduled down to 15-minute intervals to meet seasonal and daily demand changes in the tourist environment of Orlando. Surveys are done on a regular basis to evaluate quality of food and service at the cafe. Scores are rated on a 1-to-7 scale, and if the score is not a 7, the food or service is a failure.

Hard Rock is adding a new emphasis on live music and is redesigning its restaurants to accommodate the changing tastes. Since Eric Clapton hung his guitar on the wall to mark his favorite bar stool, Hard Rock has become the world's leading collector and exhibitor of rock 'n' roll memorabilia, with changing exhibits at its cafes throughout the world. The collection includes 70,000 pieces, valued at $40 million. In keeping with the times, Hard Rock also maintains a Web site, www.hardrock.com, which receives over 100,000 hits per week, and a weekly cable television program on VH1. Hard Rock's brand recognition, at 92%, is one of the highest in the world.

Discussion Questions*

1. From your knowledge of restaurants, from the video, from the *Global Company Profile* that opens this chapter, and from the case itself, identify how each of the 10 OM strategy decisions is applied at Hard Rock Cafe.

2. How would you determine the productivity of the kitchen staff and waitstaff at Hard Rock?

3. How are the 10 OM strategy decisions different when applied to the operations manager of a service operation such as Hard Rock versus an automobile company such as Ford Motor Company?

*You may wish to view the video that accompanies this case before addressing these questions.

- **Additional Case Study:** Visit MyOMLab for these case studies:
  National Air Express: Introduces the issue of productivity, productivity improvement, and measuring productivity.
  Zychol Chemicals Corp.: The production manager must prepare a productivity report, which includes multifactor analysis.

Endnotes

1. *Efficiency* means doing the job well—with a minimum of resources and waste. Note the distinction between being *efficient*, which implies doing the job well, and *effective*, which means doing the right thing. A job well done—say, by applying the 10 strategic decisions of operations management—helps us be *efficient*; developing and using the correct strategy helps us be *effective*.

2. U.S. Dept. of Labor, 2015: www.bls.gov/lpc/

3. The quality and time period are assumed to remain constant.

Chapter 1 *Rapid* Review

Main Heading	Review Material	MyOMLab
WHAT IS OPERATIONS MANAGEMENT? (p. 4)	▪ **Production**—The creation of goods and services ▪ **Operations management (OM)**—Activities that relate to the creation of goods and services through the transformation of inputs to outputs	Concept Questions: 1.1–1.4 **VIDEOS 1.1 and 1.2** OM at Hard Rock OM at Frito-Lay
ORGANIZING TO PRODUCE GOODS AND SERVICES (pp. 4–6)	All organizations perform three functions to create goods and services: 1. *Marketing*, which generates demand 2. *Production/operations*, which creates the product 3. *Finance/accounting*, which tracks how well the organization is doing, pays the bills, and collects the money	Concept Questions: 2.1–2.4
THE SUPPLY CHAIN (p. 6)	▪ **Supply chain**—A global network of organizations and activities that supply a firm with goods and services	Concept Questions: 3.1–3.4
WHY STUDY OM? (pp. 6–7)	We study OM for four reasons: 1. To learn how people organize themselves for productive enterprise 2. To learn how goods and services are produced 3. To understand what operations managers do 4. Because OM is a costly part of an organization	Concept Questions: 4.1–4.2
WHAT OPERATIONS MANAGERS DO (pp. 7–8)	Ten **OM strategic decisions** are required of operations managers: 1. Design of goods and services 2. Managing quality 3. Process strategy 4. Location strategies 5. Layout strategies 6. Human resources 7. Supply chain management 8. Inventory management 9. Scheduling 10. Maintenance About 40% of *all* jobs are in OM. Operations managers possess job titles such as plant manager, quality manager, process improvement consultant, and operations analyst.	Concept Questions: 5.1–5.4
THE HERITAGE OF OPERATIONS MANAGEMENT (pp. 8–10)	Significant events in modern OM can be classified into six eras: 1. Early concepts (1776–1880)—Labor specialization (Smith, Babbage), standardized parts (Whitney) 2. Scientific management (1880–1910)—Gantt charts (Gantt), motion and time studies (Gilbreth), process analysis (Taylor), queuing theory (Erlang) 3. Mass production (1910–1980)—Assembly line (Ford/Sorensen), statistical sampling (Shewhart), economic order quantity (Harris), linear programming (Dantzig), PERT/CPM (DuPont), material requirements planning 4. Lean production (1980–1995)—Just-in-time, computer-aided design, electronic data interchange, total quality management, Baldrige Award, empowerment, kanbans 5. Mass customization (1995–2005)—Internet/e-commerce, enterprise resource planning, international quality standards, finite scheduling, supply-chain management, mass customization, build-to-order, radio frequency identification (RFID) 6. Globalization era (2005–2020)—Global supply chains, growth of transnational organizations, instant communications, sustainability, ethics in a global work force, logistics and shipping	Concept Questions: 6.1–6.4
OPERATIONS FOR GOODS AND SERVICES (pp. 11–13)	▪ **Services**—Economic activities that typically produce an intangible product (such as education, entertainment, lodging, government, financial, and health services). Almost all services and almost all goods are a mixture of a service and a tangible product. ▪ **Service sector**—The segment of the economy that includes trade, financial, lodging, education, legal, medical, and other professional occupations. Services now constitute the largest economic sector in postindustrial societies. The huge productivity increases in agriculture and manufacturing have allowed more of our economic resources to be devoted to services. Many service jobs pay very well.	Concept Questions: 7.1–7.4

Rapid Review

MyOMLab

Main Heading	Review Material	
THE PRODUCTIVITY CHALLENGE (pp. 13–18)	■ **Productivity**—The ratio of outputs (goods and services) divided by one or more inputs (such as labor, capital, or management) High production means producing many units, while high productivity means producing units efficiently. Only through increases in productivity can the standard of living of a country improve. U.S. productivity has averaged a 2.5% increase per year for over a century. $$\text{Single-factor productivity} = \frac{\text{Units produced}}{\text{Input used}} \qquad (1\text{-}1)$$ ■ **Single-factor productivity**—Indicates the ratio of goods and services produced (outputs) to one resource (input). ■ **Multifactor productivity**—Indicates the ratio of goods and services produced (outputs) to many or all resources (inputs). Multifactor productivity $$= \frac{\text{Output}}{\text{Labor + Material + Energy + Capital + Miscellaneous}} \qquad (1\text{-}2)$$ Measurement problems with productivity include: (1) the quality may change, (2) external elements may interfere, and (3) precise units of measure may be lacking. ■ **Productivity variables**—The three factors critical to productivity improvement are labor (10%), capital (38%), and management (52%). ■ **Knowledge society**—A society in which much of the labor force has migrated from manual work to work based on knowledge	Concept Questions: 8.1–8.4 Problems: 1.1–1.17 Virtual Office Hours for Solved Problems: 1.1, 1.2
CURRENT CHALLENGES IN OPERATIONS MANAGEMENT (pp. 18–19)	Some of the current challenges for operations managers include: ■ Global focus; international collaboration ■ Supply chain partnering; joint ventures; alliances ■ Sustainability; green products; recycle, reuse ■ Rapid product development; design collaboration ■ Mass customization; customized products ■ Lean operations; continuous improvement and elimination of waste	Concept Questions: 9.1–9.4
ETHICS, SOCIAL RESPONSIBILITY, AND SUSTAINABILITY (p. 19)	Among the many ethical challenges facing operations managers are (1) efficiently developing and producing safe, quality products; (2) maintaining a clean environment; (3) providing a safe workplace; and (4) honoring stakeholder commitments. ■ **Stakeholders**—Those with a vested interest in an organization	Concept Question: 10.1

Self Test

■ **Before taking the self-test,** refer to the learning objectives listed at the beginning of the chapter and the key terms listed at the end of the chapter.

LO 1.1 Productivity increases when:
a) inputs increase while outputs remain the same.
b) inputs decrease while outputs remain the same.
c) outputs decrease while inputs remain the same.
d) inputs and outputs increase proportionately.
e) inputs increase at the same rate as outputs.

LO 1.2 Services often:
a) are tangible.
b) are standardized.
c) are knowledge based.
d) are low in customer interaction.
e) have consistent product definition.

LO 1.3 Productivity:
a) can use many factors as the numerator.
b) is the same thing as production.
c) increases at about 0.5% per year.
d) is dependent upon labor, management, and capital.
e) is the same thing as effectiveness.

LO 1.4 Single-factor productivity:
a) remains constant.
b) is never constant.
c) usually uses labor as a factor.
d) seldom uses labor as a factor.
e) uses management as a factor.

LO 1.5 Multifactor productivity:
a) remains constant.
b) is never constant.
c) usually uses substitutes as common variables for the factors of production.
d) seldom uses labor as a factor.
e) always uses management as a factor.

LO 1.6 Productivity increases each year in the U.S. are a result of three factors:
a) labor, capital, management
b) engineering, labor, capital
c) engineering, capital, quality control
d) engineering, labor, data processing
e) engineering, capital, data processing

Answers: LO 1.1. b; LO 1.2. c; LO 1.3. d; LO 1.4. c; LO 1.5. c; LO 1.6. a.

Operations Strategy in a Global Environment

CHAPTER OUTLINE

Alaska Airlines

Boeing's Global Supply-Chain Strategy Yields Competitive Advantage

Boeing's strategy for its 787 Dreamliner is unique for its technologically advanced product design and vast global supply chain.

The Dreamliner incorporates the latest in a wide range of aerospace technologies, from airframe and engine design to super-lightweight titanium-graphite laminate and carbon-fiber composites. The electronic monitoring system that allows the airplane to report maintenance

With the 787's state-of-the-art design, more spacious interior, and global suppliers, Boeing has garnered record sales worldwide.

Some of the International Suppliers of Boeing 787 Components

SUPPLIER	HQ COUNTRY	COMPONENT
Latecoere	France	Passenger doors
Labinel	France	Wiring
Dassault	France	Design and product life cycle management software
Messier-Bugatti	France	Electric brakes
Thales	France	Electrical power conversion system
Messier-Dowty	France	Landing gear structure
Diehl	Germany	Interior lighting
Cobham	UK	Fuel pumps and valves
Rolls-Royce	UK	Engines
Smiths Aerospace	UK	Central computer system
BAE Systems	UK	Electronics
Alenia Aeronautica	Italy	Upper center fuselage
Toray Industries	Japan	Carbon fiber for wing and tail units
Fuji Heavy Industries	Japan	Center wing box
Kawasaki Heavy Ind.	Japan	Forward fuselage, fixed sections of wing
Teijin Seiki	Japan	Hydraulic actuators
Mitsubishi Heavy Ind.	Japan	Wing box
Chengdu Aircraft	China	Rudder
Hafei Aviation	China	Parts
Korean Airlines	South Korea	Wingtips
Saab	Sweden	Cargo and access doors

requirements in real time to ground-based computer systems is another product innovation. Boeing's collaboration with General Electric and Rolls-Royce has resulted in the development of more efficient engines and an emissions reduction of 20%. The advances in engine technology contribute as much as 8% of the increased fuel/payload efficiency of the new airplane, representing a nearly two-generation jump in technology.

Boeing's design group at its Everett, Washington, facility led an international team of aerospace companies in development of this state-of-the-art plane. Technologically advanced design, new manufacturing processes, and a committed international supply chain have helped Boeing and its partners achieve unprecedented levels of performance in design and manufacture.

State-of-the-art composite sections of the 787 are built around the world and shipped to Boeing for final assembly.

Components from Boeing's worldwide supply chain come together on assembly lines in Everett, Washington, and Charleston, South Carolina. Although components come from throughout the world, about 35% of the 787 structure comes from Japanese companies.

The 787 is global not only because it has a range of 8,300 miles, but also because it is built all over the world. With a huge financial commitment of over $5 billion, Boeing needed partners. The global nature of both the technology and the aircraft market meant finding exceptional engineering talent and suppliers, wherever they might be. It also meant developing a culture of collaboration and integration with firms willing to step up to the risk associated with this revolutionary and very expensive new product.

State-of-the-art technology, multinational aircraft certifications, the cross-culture nature of the communications, and logistical challenges all added to the supply chain risk. In the end, Boeing accepted the challenge of teaming with more than 300 suppliers in over a dozen countries. Twenty of these suppliers developed technologies, design concepts, and major systems for the 787. Some of them are shown in the table. The partners brought commitment to the table. The expectation is that countries that have a stake in the Dreamliner are more likely to buy from Boeing than from its European competitor, Airbus.

Japanese companies are producing over 35% of the project, and Italy's Alenia Aeronautica is building an additional 10% of the plane.

The innovative Dreamliner, with its global range and worldwide supply chain, is setting new levels of operational efficiency. As a result, it is the fastest-selling commercial jet in history with over 1,100 planes sold. Boeing's Dreamliner reflects the global nature of business in the 21st century.

Boeing's collaborative technology enables a "virtual workspace" that allows Everett, Washington-based engineers, as well as partners in Australia, Japan, Italy, Canada, and across the United States, to make concurrent design changes to the airplane in real time. Digitally designing, building, and testing before production not only reduces design time and errors, but also improves efficiencies in component manufacturing and assembly.

A Global View of Operations and Supply Chains

Today's successful operations manager has a global view of operations strategy. Since the early 1990s, nearly 3 billion people in developing countries have overcome the cultural, religious, ethnic, and political barriers that constrain productivity. And now they are all players on the global economic stage. As these barriers disappear, simultaneous advances are being made in technology, reliable shipping, and inexpensive communication. These changes mean that, increasingly, firms find their customers and suppliers located around the world. The unsurprising result is the growth of world trade (see Figure 2.1), global capital markets, and the international movement of people. This means increasing economic integration and interdependence of countries—in a word, globalization. In response, organizations are hastily extending their distribution channels and supply chains globally. The result is innovative strategies where firms compete not just with their own expertise but with the talent in their entire global supply chain. For instance:

◆ Boeing is competitive because both its sales and supply chain are worldwide.

◆ Italy's Benetton moves inventory to stores around the world faster than its competition with rapid communication and by building exceptional flexibility into design, production, and distribution.

◆ Sony purchases components from a supply chain that extends to Thailand, Malaysia, and elsewhere around the world for assembly of its electronic products, which in turn are distributed around the world.

◆ Volvo, considered a Swedish company, was purchased by a Chinese company, Geely. But the current Volvo S40 is assembled in Belgium, South Africa, Malaysia, and China, on a platform shared with the Mazda 3 (built in Japan) and the Ford Focus (built in Europe).

◆ China's Haier (pronounced "higher") is now producing compact refrigerators (it has one-third of the U.S. market) and refrigerated wine cabinets (it has half of the U.S. market) in South Carolina.

Figure **2.1**

Growth of World Trade as a Percent of World GDP
Sources: World Bank; World Trade Organization; and IMF.

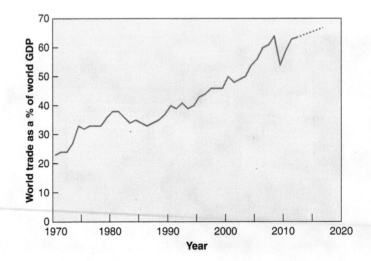

Globalization means customers, talent, and suppliers are worldwide. The new standards of global competitiveness impact quality, variety, customization, convenience, timeliness, and cost. Globalization strategies contribute efficiency, adding value to products and services, but they also complicate the operations manager's job. Complexity, risk, and competition are intensified, forcing companies to adjust for a shrinking world.

We have identified six reasons domestic business operations decide to change to some form of international operation. They are:

1. Improve the supply chain.
2. Reduce costs and exchange rate risk.
3. Improve operations.
4. Understand markets.
5. Improve products.
6. Attract and retain global talent.

Let us examine, in turn, each of the six reasons.

Improve the Supply Chain   The supply chain can often be improved by locating facilities in countries where unique resources are available. These resources may be human resource expertise, low-cost labor, or raw material. For example, auto-styling studios from throughout the world have migrated to the auto mecca of southern California to ensure the necessary expertise in contemporary auto design. Similarly, world athletic shoe production has migrated from South Korea to Guangzhou, China; this location takes advantage of the low-cost labor and production competence in a city where 40,000 people work making athletic shoes for the world. And a perfume manufacturer wants a presence in Grasse, France, where much of the world's perfume essences are prepared from the flowers of the Mediterranean.

Reduce Costs and Exchange Rate Risk   Many international operations seek to reduce risks associated with changing currency values (exchange rates) as well as take advantage of the tangible opportunities to reduce their direct costs. (See the *OM in Action* box "U.S. Cartoon Production at Home in Manila.") Less stringent government regulations on a wide variety of operations practices (e.g., environmental control, health and safety) can also reduce indirect costs.

Shifting low-skilled jobs to another country has several potential advantages. First, and most obviously, the firm may reduce costs. Second, moving the lower-skilled jobs to a lower-cost location frees higher-cost workers for more valuable tasks. Third, reducing wage costs allows the savings to be invested in improved products and facilities (and the retraining of existing workers, if necessary) at the home location. Finally, having facilities in countries with different currencies can allow firms to finesse currency risk (and related costs) as economic conditions dictate.

OM in Action   U.S. Cartoon Production at Home in Manila

Fred Flintstone is not from Bedrock. He is actually from Manila, capital of the Philippines. So are Tom and Jerry, Aladdin, and Donald Duck. More than 90% of American television cartoons are produced in Asia and India, with the Philippines leading the way. With their natural advantage of English as an official language and a strong familiarity with U.S. culture, animation companies in Manila now employ more than 1,700 people. Filipinos understand Western culture, and "you need to have a group of artists that can understand the humor that goes with it," says Bill Dennis, a Hanna-Barbera executive.

Major studios like Disney, Marvel, Warner Brothers, and Hanna-Barbera send *storyboards*—cartoon action outlines—and voice tracks to the Philippines.

Artists there draw, paint, and film about 20,000 sketches for a 30-minute episode. The cost of $130,000 to produce an episode in the Philippines compares with $160,000 in Korea and $500,000 in the United States.

Sources: Animation Insider (March 30, 2011); *The New York Times* (February 26, 2004): and *The Wall Street Journal* (August 9, 2005).

artisticco/Fotolia

Maquiladoras
Mexican factories located along the U.S.–Mexico border that receive preferential tariff treatment.

World Trade Organization (WTO)
An international organization that promotes world trade by lowering barriers to the free flow of goods across borders.

North American Free Trade Agreement (NAFTA)
A free trade agreement between Canada, Mexico, and the United States.

European Union (EU)
A European trade group that has 28 member states.

The United States and Mexico have created maquiladoras (free trade zones) that allow manufacturers to cut their costs by paying only for the value added by Mexican workers. If a U.S. manufacturer, such as Caterpillar, brings a $1,000 engine to a maquiladora operation for assembly work costing $200, tariff duties will be charged only on the $200 of work performed in Mexico.

Trade agreements also help reduce tariffs and thereby reduce the cost of operating facilities in foreign countries. The World Trade Organization (WTO) has helped reduce tariffs from 40% in 1940 to less than 3% today. Another important trade agreement is the North American Free Trade Agreement (NAFTA). NAFTA seeks to phase out all trade and tariff barriers among Canada, Mexico, and the U.S. Other trade agreements that are accelerating global trade include APEC (the Pacific Rim countries), SEATO (Australia, New Zealand, Japan, Hong Kong, South Korea, New Guinea, and Chile), MERCOSUR (Argentina, Brazil, Paraguay, and Uruguay), and CAFTA (Central America, Dominican Republic, and United States).

Another trading group is the European Union (EU).[1] The European Union has reduced trade barriers among the participating European nations through standardization and a common currency, the euro. However, this major U.S. trading partner, with over 500 million people, is also placing some of the world's most restrictive conditions on products sold in the EU. Everything from recycling standards to automobile bumpers to hormone-free farm products must meet EU standards, complicating international trade.

Improve Operations Operations learn from better understanding of management innovations in different countries. For instance, the Japanese have improved inventory management, the Germans are aggressively using robots, and the Scandinavians have contributed to improved ergonomics throughout the world.

Another reason to have international operations is to reduce response time to meet customers' changing product and service requirements. Customers who purchase goods and services from U.S. firms are increasingly located in foreign countries. Providing them with quick and adequate service is often improved by locating facilities in their home countries.

Understand Markets Because international operations require interaction with foreign customers, suppliers, and other competitive businesses, international firms inevitably learn about opportunities for new products and services. Europe led the way with cell phone innovations, and then the Japanese and Indians led with cell phone fads. Knowledge of markets not only helps firms understand where the market is going but also helps firms diversify their customer base, add production flexibility, and smooth the business cycle.

Another reason to go into foreign markets is the opportunity to expand the *life cycle* (i.e., stages a product goes through; see Chapter 5) of an existing product. While some products in the U.S. are in a "mature" stage of their product life cycle, they may represent state-of-the-art products in less-developed countries.

Improve Products Learning does not take place in isolation. Firms serve themselves and their customers well when they remain open to the free flow of ideas. For example, Toyota and BMW will manage joint research and share development costs on battery research for the next generation of green cars. Their relationship also provides Toyota with BMW's highly regarded diesel engines for its European market, where diesel-powered vehicles make up more than half of the market. The payoff is reduced risk in battery development for both, a state-of-the-art diesel engine for Toyota in Europe, and lower per-unit diesel engine cost for BMW. Similarly, international learning in operations is taking place as South Korea's Samsung and Germany's Robert Bosch join to produce lithium-ion batteries to the benefit of both.

Attract and Retain Global Talent Global organizations can attract and retain better employees by offering more employment opportunities. They need people in all functional areas and areas of expertise worldwide. Global firms can recruit and retain good employees because they provide both greater growth opportunities and insulation against

A worldwide strategy places added burdens on operations management. Because of economic and lifestyle differences, designers must target products to each market. For instance, clothes washers sold in northern countries must spin-dry clothes much better than those in warmer climates, where consumers are likely to line-dry them. Similarly, as shown here, Whirlpool refrigerators sold in Bangkok are manufactured in bright colors because they are often put in living rooms.

Kraipit Phanvut/Sipa Press

unemployment during times of economic downturn. During economic downturns in one country or continent, a global firm has the means to relocate unneeded personnel to more prosperous locations.

So, to recap, successfully achieving a competitive advantage in our shrinking world means maximizing all the possible opportunities, from tangible to intangible, that international operations can offer.

Cultural and Ethical Issues

While there are great forces driving firms toward globalization, many challenges remain. One of these challenges is reconciling differences in social and cultural behavior. With issues ranging from bribery, to child labor, to the environment, managers sometimes do not know how to respond when operating in a different culture. What one country's culture deems acceptable may be considered unacceptable or illegal in another. It is not by chance that there are fewer female managers in the Middle East than in India.

In the last decade, changes in international laws, agreements, and codes of conduct have been applied to define ethical behavior among managers around the world. The WTO, for example, helps to make uniform the protection of both governments and industries from foreign firms that engage in unethical conduct. Even on issues where significant differences between cultures exist, as in the area of bribery or the protection of intellectual property, global uniformity is slowly being accepted by most nations.

Despite cultural and ethical differences, we live in a period of extraordinary mobility of capital, information, goods, and even people. We can expect this to continue. The financial sector, the telecommunications sector, and the logistics infrastructure of the world are healthy institutions that foster efficient and effective use of capital, information, and goods. Globalization, with all its opportunities and risks, is here. It must be embraced as managers develop their missions and strategies.

Developing Missions and Strategies

STUDENT TIP
Getting an education and managing an organization both require a mission and strategy.

An effective operations management effort must have a *mission* so it knows where it is going and a *strategy* so it knows how to get there. This is the case for a small domestic organization as well as a large international organization.

Mission

Mission
The purpose or rationale for an organization's existence.

LO 2.1 *Define* mission and strategy

Economic success, indeed survival, is the result of identifying missions to satisfy a customer's needs and wants. We define the organization's mission as its purpose—what it will contribute to society. Mission statements provide boundaries and focus for organizations and the concept around which the firm can rally. The mission states the rationale for the organization's existence. Developing a good strategy is difficult, but it is much easier if the mission has been well defined. Figure 2.2 provides examples of mission statements.

Once an organization's mission has been decided, each functional area within the firm determines its supporting mission. By *functional area* we mean the major disciplines required by the firm, such as marketing, finance/accounting, and production/operations. Missions for each function are developed to support the firm's overall mission. Then within that function lower-level supporting missions are established for the OM functions. Figure 2.3 provides such a hierarchy of sample missions.

Strategy

Strategy
How an organization expects to achieve its missions and goals.

LO 2.2 *Identify* and explain three strategic approaches to competitive advantage

With the mission established, strategy and its implementation can begin. Strategy is an organization's action plan to achieve the mission. Each functional area has a strategy for achieving its mission and for helping the organization reach the overall mission. These strategies exploit opportunities and strengths, neutralize threats, and avoid weaknesses. In the following sections, we will describe how strategies are developed and implemented.

Firms achieve missions in three conceptual ways: (1) differentiation, (2) cost leadership, and (3) response. This means operations managers are called on to deliver goods and services that are (1) *better*, or at least different, (2) *cheaper*, and (3) more *responsive*. Operations managers translate these *strategic concepts* into tangible tasks to be accomplished. Any one or combination of these three strategic concepts can generate a system that has a unique advantage over competitors.

VIDEO 2.1
Operations Strategy at Regal Marine

Achieving Competitive Advantage Through Operations

Competitive advantage
The creation of a unique advantage over competitors.

Each of the three strategies provides an opportunity for operations managers to achieve competitive advantage. Competitive advantage implies the creation of a system that has a unique advantage over competitors. The idea is to create customer value in an efficient and sustainable way. Pure forms of these strategies may exist, but operations managers will more likely

Figure 2.2

Mission Statements for Three Organizations
Source: Mission statement from Merck. Copyright © by Merck & Co., Inc. Reprinted with permission.

Merck
The mission of Merck is to provide society with superior products and services—innovations and solutions that improve the quality of life and satisfy customer needs—to provide employees with meaningful work and advancement opportunities and investors with a superior rate of return.
PepsiCo
Our mission is to be the world's premier consumer products company focused on convenient foods and beverages. We seek to produce financial rewards to investors as we provide opportunities for growth and enrichment to our employees, our business partners and the communities in which we operate. And in everything we do, we strive for honesty, fairness and integrity.
Arnold Palmer Hospital
Arnold Palmer Hospital for Children provides state of the art, family-centered healthcare focused on restoring the joy of childhood in an environment of compassion, healing, and hope.

Figure 2.3

Sample Missions for a Company, the Operations Function, and Major OM Departments

Sample Company Mission	
To manufacture and service an innovative, growing, and profitable worldwide microwave communications business that exceeds our customers' expectations.	
Sample Operations Management Mission	
To produce products consistent with the company's mission as the worldwide low-cost manufacturer.	
Sample OM Department Missions	
Product design	To design and produce products and services with outstanding quality and inherent customer value.
Quality management	To attain the exceptional value that is consistent with our company mission and marketing objectives by close attention to design, supply chain, production, and field service opportunities.
Process design	To determine, design, and develop the production process and equipment that will be compatible with low-cost product, high quality, and a good quality of work life.
Location	To locate, design, and build efficient and economical facilities that will yield high value to the company, its employees, and the community.
Layout design	To achieve, through skill, imagination, and resourcefulness in layout and work methods, production effectiveness and efficiency while supporting a high quality of work life.
Human resources	To provide a good quality of work life, with well-designed, safe, rewarding jobs, stable employment, and equitable pay, in exchange for outstanding individual contribution from employees at all levels.
Supply-chain management	To collaborate with suppliers to develop innovative products from stable, effective, and efficient sources of supply.
Inventory	To achieve low investment in inventory consistent with high customer service levels and high facility utilization.
Scheduling	To achieve high levels of throughput and timely customer delivery through effective scheduling.
Maintenance	To achieve high utilization of facilities and equipment by effective preventive maintenance and prompt repair of facilities and equipment.

be called on to implement some combination of them. Let us briefly look at how managers achieve competitive advantage via *differentiation*, *low cost*, and *response*.

Competing on Differentiation

Safeskin Corporation is number one in latex exam gloves because it has differentiated itself and its products. It did so by producing gloves that were designed to prevent allergic reactions about which doctors were complaining. When other glove makers caught up, Safeskin developed hypoallergenic gloves. Then it added texture to its gloves. Then it developed a synthetic disposable glove for those allergic to latex—always staying ahead of the competition. Safeskin's strategy is to develop a reputation for designing and producing reliable state-of-the-art gloves, thereby differentiating itself.

Differentiation is concerned with providing *uniqueness*. A firm's opportunities for creating uniqueness are not located within a particular function or activity but can arise in virtually everything the firm does. Moreover, because most products include some service, and most services

Differentiation

Distinguishing the offerings of an organization in a way that the customer perceives as adding value.

include some product, the opportunities for creating this uniqueness are limited only by imagination. Indeed, differentiation should be thought of as going beyond both physical characteristics and service attributes to encompass everything about the product or service that influences the value that the customers derive from it. Therefore, effective operations managers assist in defining everything about a product or service that will influence the potential value to the customer. This may be the convenience of a broad product line, product features, or a service related to the product. Such services can manifest themselves through convenience (location of distribution centers, stores, or branches), training, product delivery and installation, or repair and maintenance services.

In the service sector, one option for extending product differentiation is through an *experience*. Differentiation by experience in services is a manifestation of the growing "experience economy." The idea of experience differentiation is to engage the customer—to use people's five senses so they become immersed, or even an active participant, in the product. Disney does this with the Magic Kingdom. People no longer just go on a ride; they are immersed in the Magic Kingdom—surrounded by dynamic visual and sound experiences that complement the physical ride. Some rides further engage the customer with changing air flow and smells, as well as having them steer the ride or shoot at targets or villains. Even movie theaters are moving in this direction with surround sound, moving seats, changing "smells," and mists of "rain," as well as multimedia inputs to story development.

Experience differentiation

Engaging a customer with a product through imaginative use of the five senses, so the customer "experiences" the product.

Theme restaurants, such as Hard Rock Cafe, likewise differentiate themselves by providing an "experience." Hard Rock engages the customer with classic rock music, big-screen rock videos, memorabilia, and staff who can tell stories. In many instances, a full-time guide is available to explain the displays, and there is always a convenient retail store so the guest can take home a tangible part of the experience. The result is a "dining experience" rather than just a meal. In a less dramatic way, both Starbucks and your local supermarket deliver an experience when they provide music and the aroma of fresh coffee or freshly baked bread.

VIDEO 2.2
Hard Rock's Global Strategy

Competing on Cost

Southwest Airlines has been a consistent moneymaker while other U.S. airlines have lost billions. Southwest has done this by fulfilling a need for low-cost and short-hop flights. Its operations strategy has included use of secondary airports and terminals, first-come, first-served seating, few fare options, smaller crews flying more hours, snacks-only or no-meal flights, and no downtown ticket offices.

In addition, and less obviously, Southwest has very effectively matched capacity to demand and effectively utilized this capacity. It has done this by designing a route structure that matches the capacity of its Boeing 737, the only plane in its fleet. Second, it achieves more air miles than other airlines through faster turnarounds—its planes are on the ground less.

One driver of a low-cost strategy is a facility that is effectively utilized. Southwest and others with low-cost strategies understand this and use financial resources effectively. Identifying the optimum size (and investment) allows firms to spread overhead costs, providing a cost advantage. For instance, Walmart continues to pursue its low-cost strategy with superstores, open 24 hours a day. For 20 years, it has successfully grabbed market share. Walmart has driven down store overhead costs, shrinkage, and distribution costs. Its rapid transportation of goods, reduced warehousing costs, and direct shipment from manufacturers have resulted in high inventory turnover and made it a low-cost leader.

Likewise, Franz Colruyt, a Belgian discount food retailer, is also an aggressive cost cutter. Colruyt cuts overhead by using converted factory warehouses, movie theaters, and garages as outlets. Customers find no background music, shopping bags, or bright lights: all have been eliminated to cut costs. Walmart and Colruyt are winning with a low-cost strategy.

Low-cost leadership

Achieving maximum value, as perceived by the customer.

Low-cost leadership entails achieving maximum *value* as defined by your customer. It requires examining each of the 10 OM decisions in a relentless effort to drive down costs while meeting customer expectations of value. A low-cost strategy does *not* imply low value or low quality.

Competing on Response

The third strategy option is response. Response is often thought of as *flexible* response, but it also refers to *reliable* and *quick* response. Indeed, we define response as including the entire range of values related to timely product development and delivery, as well as reliable scheduling and flexible performance.

Response

A set of values related to rapid, flexible, and reliable performance.

Flexible response may be thought of as the ability to match changes in a marketplace where design innovations and volumes fluctuate substantially.

Hewlett-Packard is an exceptional example of a firm that has demonstrated flexibility in both design and volume changes in the volatile world of personal computers. HP's products often have a life cycle of months, and volume and cost changes during that brief life cycle are dramatic. However, HP has been successful at institutionalizing the ability to change products and volume to respond to dramatic changes in product design and costs—thus building a *sustainable competitive advantage*.

The second aspect of response is the *reliability* of scheduling. One way the German machine industry has maintained its competitiveness despite having the world's highest labor costs is through reliable response. This response manifests itself in reliable scheduling. German machine firms have meaningful schedules—and they perform to these schedules. Moreover, the results of these schedules are communicated to the customer, and the customer can, in turn, rely on them. Consequently, the competitive advantage generated through reliable response has value to the end customer.

The third aspect of response is *quickness*. Johnson Electric Holdings, Ltd., with headquarters in Hong Kong, makes 83 million tiny motors each month. The motors go in cordless tools, household appliances, and personal care items such as hair dryers; dozens are found in each automobile. Johnson's major competitive advantage is speed: speed in product development, speed in production, and speed in delivery.

Whether it is a production system at Johnson Electric or a pizza delivered in 5 minutes by Pizza Hut, the operations manager who develops systems that respond quickly can have a competitive advantage.

In practice, differentiation, low cost, and response can increase productivity and generate a sustainable competitive advantage. Proper implementation of the ten decisions by operations managers (see Figure 2.4) will allow these advantages to be achieved.

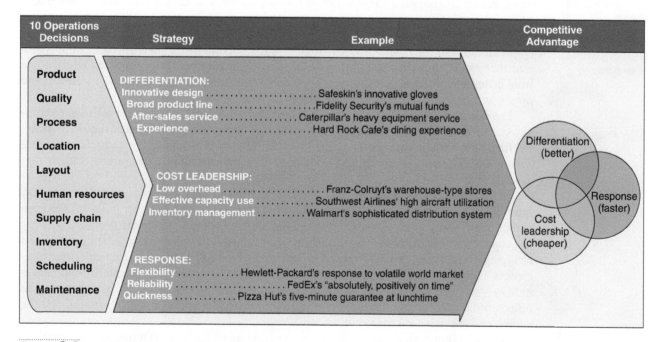

Figure 2.4

Achieving Competitive Advantage Through Operations

Response strategy wins orders at Super Fast Pizza. Using a wireless connection, orders are transmitted to $20,000 kitchens in vans. The driver, who works solo, receives a printed order, goes to the kitchen area, pulls premade pizzas from the cooler, and places them in the oven—it takes about 1 minute. The driver then delivers the pizza—sometimes even arriving before the pizza is ready.

Darren Hauck/AP Images

Issues in Operations Strategy

Whether the OM strategy is differentiation, cost, or response (as shown in Figure 2.4), OM is a critical player. Therefore, prior to establishing and attempting to implement a strategy, some alternate perspectives may be helpful. One perspective is to take a resources view. This means thinking in terms of the financial, physical, human, and technological resources available and ensuring that the potential strategy is compatible with those resources. Another perspective is Porter's value-chain analysis.[2] Value-chain analysis is used to identify activities that represent strengths, or potential strengths, and may be opportunities for developing competitive advantage. These are areas where the firm adds its unique *value* through product research, design, human resources, supply-chain management, process innovation, or quality management. Porter also suggests analysis of competitors via what he calls his five forces model.[3] These potential competing forces are immediate rivals, potential entrants, customers, suppliers, and substitute products.

In addition to the competitive environment, the operations manager needs to understand that the firm is operating in a system with many other external factors. These factors range from economic, to legal, to cultural. They influence strategy development and execution and require constant scanning of the environment.

The firm itself is also undergoing constant change. Everything from resources, to technology, to product life cycles is in flux. Consider the significant changes required within the firm as its products move from introduction, to growth, to maturity, and to decline (see Figure 2.5). These internal changes, combined with external changes, require strategies that are dynamic.

In this chapter's *Global Company Profile*, Boeing provides an example of how strategy must change as technology and the environment change. Boeing can now build planes from carbon fiber, using a global supply chain. Like many other OM strategies, Boeing's strategy has changed with technology and globalization. Microsoft has also had to adapt quickly to a changing environment. Faster processors, new computer languages, changing customer preferences, increased security issues, the Internet, the cloud, and Google have all driven changes at Microsoft. These forces have moved Microsoft's product strategy from operating systems to office products, to Internet service provider, and now to integrator of computers, cell phones, games, and television via the cloud.

The more thorough the analysis and understanding of both the external and internal factors, the more likely that a firm can find the optimum use of its resources. Once a firm understands itself and the environment, a SWOT analysis, which we discuss next, is in order.

Resources view

A method managers use to evaluate the resources at their disposal and manage or alter them to achieve competitive advantage.

Value-chain analysis

A way to identify those elements in the product/service chain that uniquely add value.

Five forces model

A method of analyzing the five forces in the competitive environment.

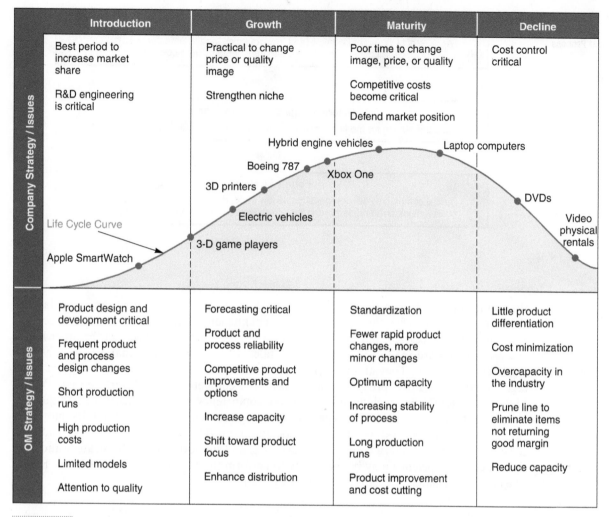

	Introduction	Growth	Maturity	Decline
Company Strategy / Issues	Best period to increase market share R&D engineering is critical	Practical to change price or quality image Strengthen niche	Poor time to change image, price, or quality Competitive costs become critical Defend market position	Cost control critical
OM Strategy / Issues	Product design and development critical Frequent product and process design changes Short production runs High production costs Limited models Attention to quality	Forecasting critical Product and process reliability Competitive product improvements and options Increase capacity Shift toward product focus Enhance distribution	Standardization Fewer rapid product changes, more minor changes Optimum capacity Increasing stability of process Long production runs Product improvement and cost cutting	Little product differentiation Cost minimization Overcapacity in the industry Prune line to eliminate items not returning good margin Reduce capacity

Within the life cycle curve: Apple SmartWatch, 3-D game players, Electric vehicles, 3D printers, Boeing 787, Hybrid engine vehicles, Xbox One, Laptop computers, DVDs, Video physical rentals. Life Cycle Curve.

Figure 2.5

Strategy and Issues During a Product's Life

Strategy Development and Implementation

A SWOT analysis is a formal review of internal strengths and weaknesses and external opportunities and threats. Beginning with SWOT analyses, organizations position themselves, through their strategy, to have a competitive advantage. A firm may have excellent design skills or great talent at identifying outstanding locations. However, it may recognize limitations of its manufacturing process or in finding good suppliers. The idea is to maximize opportunities and minimize threats in the environment while maximizing the advantages of the organization's strengths and minimizing the weaknesses. Any preconceived ideas about mission are then reevaluated to ensure they are consistent with the SWOT analysis. Subsequently, a strategy for achieving the mission is developed. This strategy is continually evaluated against the value provided customers and competitive realities. The process is shown in Figure 2.6. From this process, key success factors are identified.

Key Success Factors and Core Competencies

Because no firm does everything exceptionally well, a successful strategy requires determining the firm's key success factors and core competencies. Key success factors (KSFs) are those activities that are necessary for a firm to achieve its goals. Key success factors can be so significant

Figure **2.6**

Strategy Development Process

> **Analyze the Environment**
> Identify strengths, weaknesses, opportunities, and threats.
> Understand the environment, customers, industry, and competitors.

> **Determine the Corporate Mission**
> State the reason for the firm's existence and identify the value it wishes to create.

> **Form a Strategy**
> Build a competitive advantage, such as low price, design or volume flexibility,
> quality, quick delivery, dependability, after-sale services, or broad product lines.

Core competencies
A set of skills, talents, and capabilities in which a firm is particularly strong.

that a firm must get them right to survive. A KSF for McDonald's, for example, is layout. Without an effective drive-through and an efficient kitchen, McDonald's cannot be successful. KSFs are often necessary, but not sufficient for competitive advantage. On the other hand, core competencies are the set of unique skills, talents, and capabilities that a firm does at a world-class standard. They allow a firm to set itself apart and develop a competitive advantage. Organizations that prosper identify their core competencies and nurture them. While McDonald's KSFs may include layout, its core competency may be consistency and quality. Honda Motors' core competence is gas-powered engines—engines for automobiles, motorcycles, lawn mowers, generators, snow blowers, and more. The idea is to build KSFs and core competencies that provide a competitive advantage and support a successful strategy and mission. A core competency may be the ability to perform the KSFs or a combination of KSFs. The operations manager begins this inquiry by asking:

LO 2.3 *Understand* the significance of key success factors and core competencies

- ◆ "What tasks must be done particularly well for a given strategy to succeed?"
- ◆ "Which activities provide a competitive advantage?"
- ◆ "Which elements contain the highest likelihood of failure, and which require additional commitment of managerial, monetary, technological, and human resources?"

Only by identifying and strengthening key success factors and core competencies can an organization achieve sustainable competitive advantage. In this text we focus on the 10 strategic OM decisions that typically include the KSFs. These decisions, plus major decision areas for marketing and finance, are shown in Figure 2.7.

Honda's core competence is the design and manufacture of gas-powered engines. This competence has allowed Honda to become a leader in the design and manufacture of a wide range of gas-powered products. Tens of millions of these products are produced and shipped around the world.

Automobiles — Julie Lucht/Shutterstock

Generators — American Honda Motor Co., Inc.

Motorcycles — Courtesy of www. HondaNews.com

Water Pumps — American Honda Motor Co., Inc.

Marine Motors — American Honda Motor Co., Inc.

Race Cars — American Honda Motor Co., Inc.

4-Wheel Scooters — American Honda Motor Co., Inc.

Snow Blowers — American Honda Motor Co., Inc.

Figure **2.7**

Implement Strategy by Identifying and Executing Key Success Factors That Support Core Competencies

> **STUDENT TIP**
> These 10 decisions are used to implement a specific strategy and yield a competitive advantage.

Integrating OM with Other Activities

Whatever the KSFs and core competencies, they must be supported by the related activities. One approach to identifying the activities is an activity map, which links competitive advantage, KSFs, and supporting activities. For example, Figure 2.8 shows how Southwest Airlines, whose core competency is operations, built a set of integrated activities to support its low-cost competitive advantage. Notice how the KSFs support operations and in turn are supported by other activities. The activities fit together and reinforce each other. In this way, all of the areas support the company's objectives. For example, short-term scheduling in the airline industry is dominated by volatile customer travel patterns. Day-of-week preference, holidays, seasonality, college schedules, and so on all play roles in changing flight schedules. Consequently, airline scheduling, although an OM activity, is tied to marketing. Effective scheduling in the trucking industry is reflected in the amount of time trucks travel loaded. But maximizing the time trucks travel loaded requires the integration of information from deliveries completed, pickups pending, driver availability, truck maintenance, and customer priority. Success requires integration of all of these activities.

Activity map
A graphical link of competitive advantage, KSFs, and supporting activities.

The better the activities are integrated and reinforce each other, the more sustainable the competitive advantage. By focusing on enhancing its core competence and KSFs with a supporting set of activities, firms such as Southwest Airlines have built successful strategies.

Building and Staffing the Organization

Once a strategy, KSFs, and the necessary integration have been identified, the second step is to group the necessary activities into an organizational structure. Then, managers must staff the organization with personnel who will get the job done. The manager works with subordinate managers to build plans, budgets, and programs that will successfully implement strategies that achieve missions. Firms tackle this organization of the operations function in a variety of

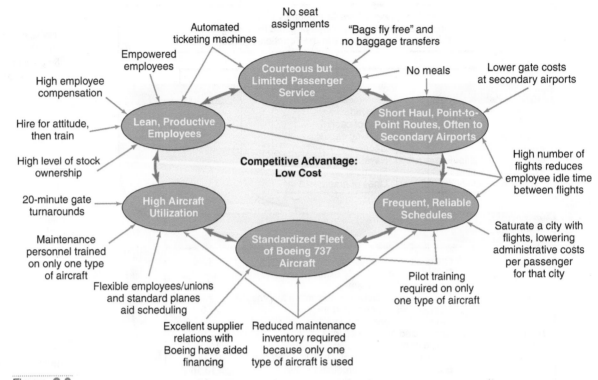

Figure **2.8**

Activity Mapping of Southwest Airlines' Low-Cost Competitive Advantage

To achieve a low-cost competitive advantage, Southwest has identified a number of key success factors (connected by red arrows) and support activities (shown by blue arrows). As this figure indicates, Southwest's low-cost strategy is highly dependent on a very well-run operations function.

ways. The organization charts shown in Chapter 1 (Figure 1.1) indicate the way some firms have organized to perform the required activities. *The operations manager's job is to implement an OM strategy, provide competitive advantage, and increase productivity.*

Implementing the 10 Strategic OM Decisions

As mentioned earlier, the implementation of the 10 strategic OM decisions is influenced by a variety of issues—from missions and strategy to key success factors and core competencies—while addressing such issues as product mix, product life cycle, and competitive environment. Because each product brings its own mix of attributes, the importance and method of implementation of the 10 strategic OM decisions will vary. Throughout this text, we discuss how these decisions are implemented in ways that provide competitive advantage. How this might be done for two drug companies, one seeking competitive advantage via differentiation and the other via low cost, is shown in Table 2.1.

Strategic Planning, Core Competencies, and Outsourcing

As organizations develop missions, goals, and strategies, they identify their strengths—what they do as well as or better than their competitors—as their *core competencies*. By contrast, *non-core activities*, which can be a sizable portion of an organization's total business, are good candidates for outsourcing. Outsourcing is transferring activities that have traditionally been internal to external suppliers.

Outsourcing is not a new concept, but it does add complexity and risk to the supply chain. Because of its potential, outsourcing continues to expand. The expansion is accelerating due to

Outsourcing

Transferring a firm's activities that have traditionally been internal to external suppliers.

TABLE 2.1	Operations Strategies of Two Drug Companies*	
COMPETITIVE ADVANTAGE	BRAND NAME DRUGS, INC.	GENERIC DRUG CORP.
	PRODUCT DIFFERENTIATION STRATEGY	LOW-COST STRATEGY
Product selection and design	Heavy R&D investment; extensive labs; focus on development in a broad range of drug categories	Low R&D investment; focus on development of generic drugs
Quality	Quality is major priority, standards exceed regulatory requirements	Meets regulatory requirements on a country-by-country basis, as necessary
Process	Product and modular production process; tries to have long product runs in specialized facilities; builds capacity ahead of demand	Process focused; general production processes; "job shop" approach, short-run production; focus on high utilization
Location	Still located in city where it was founded	Recently moved to low-tax, low-labor-cost environment
Layout	Layout supports automated product-focused production	Layout supports process-focused "job shop" practices
Human resources	Hire the best; nationwide searches	Very experienced top executives hired to provide direction; other personnel paid below industry average
Supply chain	Long-term supplier relationships	Tends to purchase competitively to find bargains
Inventory	Maintains high finished goods inventory primarily to ensure all demands are met	Process focus drives up work-in-process inventory; finished goods inventory tends to be low
Scheduling	Centralized production planning	Many short-run products complicate scheduling
Maintenance	Highly trained staff; extensive parts inventory	Highly trained staff to meet changing demands

*Notice how the 10 decisions are altered to build two distinct strategies in the same industry.

three global trends: (1) increased technological expertise, (2) more reliable and cheaper transportation, and (3) the rapid development and deployment of advancements in telecommunications and computers. This rich combination of economic advances is contributing to both lower cost and more specialization. As a result more firms are candidates for outsourcing of non-core activities.

Outsourcing implies an agreement (typically a legally binding contract) with an external organization. The classic make-or-buy decision, concerning which products to make and which to buy, is the basis of outsourcing. When firms such as Apple find that their core competency is in creativity, innovation, and product design, they may want to outsource manufacturing.

VIDEO 2.3
Outsourcing Offshore at Darden

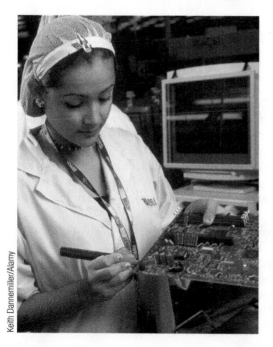

Keith Dannemiller/Alamy

Contract manufacturers such as Flextronics provide outsourcing service to IBM, Cisco Systems, HP, Microsoft, Sony, Nortel, Ericsson, and Sun, among many others. Flextronics is a high-quality producer that has won over 450 awards, including the Malcolm Baldrige Award. One of the side benefits of outsourcing is that client firms such as IBM can actually improve their performance by using the competencies of an outstanding firm like Flextronics. But there are risks involved in outsourcing.

Outsourcing manufacturing is an extension of the long-standing practice of *subcontracting* production activities, which when done on a continuing basis is known as *contract manufacturing*. Contract manufacturing is becoming standard practice in many industries, from computers to automobiles. For instance, Johnson & Johnson, like many other big drug companies whose core competency is research and development, often farms out manufacturing to contractors. On the other hand, Sony's core competency is electromechanical design of chips. This is its core competency, but Sony is also one of the best in the world when it comes to rapid response and specialized production of these chips. Therefore, Sony finds that it wants to be its own *manufacturer*, while specialized providers come up with major innovations in such areas as software, human resources, and distribution. These areas are the providers' business, not Sony's, and the provider may very well be better at it than Sony.

Other examples of outsourcing non-core activities include:

- DuPont's legal services routed to the Philippines
- IBM's handing of travel services and payroll and Hewlett-Packard's provision of IT services to P&G
- Production of the Audi A4 convertible and Mercedes CLK convertible by Wilheim Karmann in Osnabruck, Germany
- Blue Cross sending hip resurfacing surgery patients to India

Managers evaluate their strategies and core competencies and ask themselves how to use the assets entrusted to them. Do they want to be the company that does low-margin work at 3%–4% or the innovative firm that makes a 30%–40% margin? PC and iPad contract manufacturers in China and Taiwan earn 3%–4%, but Apple, which innovates, designs, and sells, has a margin 10 times as large.

The Theory of Comparative Advantage

Theory of comparative advantage

A theory which states that countries benefit from specializing in (and exporting) goods and services in which they have relative advantage, and they benefit from importing goods and services in which they have a relative disadvantage.

The motivation for international outsourcing comes from the theory of comparative advantage. This theory focuses on the economic concept of relative advantage. According to the theory, if an external provider, regardless of its geographic location, can perform activities more productively than the purchasing firm, then the external provider should do the work. This allows the purchasing firm to focus on what it does best—its core competencies. Consistent with the theory of comparative advantage, outsourcing continues to grow. But outsourcing the wrong activities can be a disaster. And even outsourcing non-core activities has risks.

STUDENT TIP ◆

The substantial risk of outsourcing requires managers to invest in the effort to make sure they do it right.

Risks of Outsourcing

Risk management starts with a realistic analysis of uncertainty and results in a strategy that minimizes the impact of these uncertainties. Indeed, outsourcing *is* risky, with roughly half of all outsourcing agreements failing because of inadequate planning and analysis. Timely delivery and quality standards can be major problems, as can underestimating increases in inventory and logistics costs. Some potential advantages and disadvantages of outsourcing are shown in Table 2.2. A survey of North American companies found that, as a group, those that outsourced customer service saw a drop in their score on the American Consumer Satisfaction Index. The declines were roughly the same whether companies outsourced domestically or overseas.[4]

However, when outsourcing is overseas, additional issues must be considered. These issues include financial attractiveness, people skills and availability, and the general business environment. Another risk of outsourcing overseas is the political backlash that results from moving jobs to foreign countries. The perceived loss of jobs has fueled anti-outsourcing rhetoric. This rhetoric is contributing to a process known as *reshoring*, the return of business activity to the originating country. (See the *OM in Action* box "Reshoring to Small-Town U.S.A.")

TABLE 2.2	Potential Advantages and Disadvantages of Outsourcing	
ADVANTAGES	**DISADVANTAGES**	
Cost savings	Increased logistics and inventory costs	
Gaining outside expertise that comes with specialization	Loss of control (quality, delivery, etc.)	
Improving operations and service	Potential creation of future competition	
Maintaining a focus on core competencies	Negative impact on employees	
Accessing outside technology	Risks may not manifest themselves for years	

In addition to the external risks, operations managers must deal with other issues that outsourcing brings. These include: (1) reduced employment levels, (2) changes in facility requirements, (3) potential adjustments to quality control systems and manufacturing processes, and (4) expanded logistics issues, including insurance, tariffs, customs, and timing.

To summarize, managers can find substantial efficiencies in outsourcing non-core activities, but they must be cautious in outsourcing those elements of the product or service that provide a competitive advantage. The next section provides a methodology that helps analyze the outsourcing decision process.

Rating Outsource Providers

Research indicates that the most common reason for the failure of outsourcing agreements is that the decisions are made without sufficient analysis. The *factor-rating method* provides an objective way to evaluate outsource providers. We assign points for each factor to each provider and then importance weights to each of the factors. We now apply the technique in Example 1 to compare outsourcing providers being considered by a firm.

LO 2.4 *Use* factor rating to evaluate both country and outsource providers

---

OM in Action   Reshoring to Small-Town U.S.A.

U.S. companies continue their global search for efficiency by outsourcing call centers and back-office operations, but many find they need to look no farther than a place like Dubuque, Iowa.

To U.S. firms facing quality problems with their outsourcing operations overseas and bad publicity at home, small-town America is emerging as a pleasant alternative. Dubuque (population 57,313), Nacogdoches, Texas (population 29,914), or Twin Falls, Idaho (population 34,469), may be the perfect call center location. Even though the pay is low, the jobs are some of the best available to small-town residents.

By moving out of big cities to the cheaper labor and real estate of small towns, companies can save millions and still increase productivity. A call center in a town that just lost its major manufacturing plant finds the jobs easy to fill.

IBM, which has been criticized in the past for moving jobs to India and other offshore locations, picked Dubuque for its new remote computer-services center with 1,300 jobs.

Taking advantage of even cheaper wages in other countries will not stop soon, though. Is India the unstoppable overseas call center capital that people think it is? Not at all. Despite its population of 1.3 billion, only a small percentage of its workers have the language skills and technical education to work in Western-style industries. Already, India has been warned that if call centers can't recruit at reasonable wages, its jobs will move to the Philippines, South Africa, and Ghana. And indeed, Dell, Apple, and Britain's Powergen are reshoring from Indian call centers, claiming their costs had become too high.

Sources: Industry Week (August 5, 2014) and The Wall Street Journal, (November 27, 2013).

Keith Dannemiller/Alamy

Example 1

RATING PROVIDER SELECTION CRITERIA

National Architects, Inc., a San Francisco–based designer of high-rise office buildings, has decided to outsource its information technology (IT) function. Three outsourcing providers are being actively considered: one in the U.S., one in India, and one in Israel.

APPROACH ▶   National's VP–Operations, Susan Cholette, has made a list of seven criteria she considers critical. After putting together a committee of four other VPs, she has rated each firm (boldface type, on a 1–5 scale, with 5 being highest) and has also placed an importance weight on each of the factors, as shown in Table 2.3.

TABLE 2.3	Factor Ratings Applied to National Architects' Potential IT Outsourcing Providers			
		OUTSOURCE PROVIDERS		
FACTOR (CRITERION)*	**IMPORTANCE WEIGHT**	**BIM (U.S.)**	**S.P.C. (INDIA)**	**TELCO (ISRAEL)**
1. Can reduce operating costs	.2	.2 × 3 = .6	.2 × 3 = .6	.2 × 5 = 1.0
2. Can reduce capital investment	.2	.2 × 4 = .8	.2 × 3 = .6	.2 × 3 = .6
3. Skilled personnel	.2	.2 × 5 = 1.0	.2 × 4 = .8	.2 × 3 = .6
4. Can improve quality	.1	.1 × 4 = .4	.1 × 5 = .5	.1 × 2 = .2
5. Can gain access to technology not in company	.1	.1 × 5 = .5	.1 × 3 = .3	.1 × 5 = .5
6. Can create additional capacity	.1	.1 × 4 = .4	.1 × 2 = .2	.1 × 4 = .4
7. Aligns with policy/philosophy/culture	.1	.1 × 2 = .2	.1 × 3 = .3	.1 × 5 = .5
Total Weighted Score		3.9	3.3	3.8

*These seven major criteria are based on a survey of 165 procurement executives, as reported in J. Schildhouse, *Inside Supply Management* (December 2005): 22–29.

SOLUTION ▶   Susan multiplies each rating by the weight and sums the products in each column to generate a total score for each outsourcing provider. She selects BIM, which has the highest overall rating.

INSIGHT ▶   When the total scores are as close (3.9 vs. 3.8) as they are in this case, it is important to examine the sensitivity of the results to inputs. For example, if one of the importance weights or factor scores changes even marginally, the final selection may change. Management preference may also play a role here.

LEARNING EXERCISE ▶   Susan decides that "Skilled personnel" should instead get a weight of 0.1 and "Aligns with policy/philosophy/culture" should increase to 0.2. How do the total scores change? [Answer: BIM = 3.6, S.P.C. = 3.2, and Telco = 4.0, so Telco would be selected.]

RELATED PROBLEMS ▶   2.8–2.12

EXCEL **OM** Data File **Ch02Ex1.xls** can be found in MyOMLab.

Most U.S. toy companies now outsource their production to Chinese manufacturers. Cost savings are significant, but there are several downsides, including loss of control over such issues as quality. A few years ago, Mattel had to recall 10.5 million Elmos, Big Birds, and SpongeBobs. These made-in-China toys contained excessive levels of lead in their paint. More recently, quality issues have dealt with poisonous pet food, tainted milk products, and contaminated sheetrock.

A. Ramey/PhotoEdit, Inc.

Global Operations Strategy Options

As we suggested early in this chapter, many operations strategies now require an international dimension. An international business is any firm that engages in international trade or investment. A multinational corporation (MNC) is a firm with *extensive* international business involvement. MNCs buy resources, create goods or services, and sell goods or services in a variety of countries. The term *multinational corporation* applies to most of the world's large, well-known businesses. Certainly IBM is a good example of an MNC. It imports electronics components to the U.S. from over 50 countries, exports to over 130 countries, has facilities in 45 countries, and earns more than half its sales and profits abroad.

Operations managers of international and multinational firms approach global opportunities with one of four strategies: *international, multidomestic, global,* or *transnational* (see Figure 2.9). The matrix of Figure 2.9 has a vertical axis of cost reduction and a horizontal axis of local responsiveness. Local responsiveness implies quick response and/or the differentiation necessary for the local market. The operations manager must know how to position the firm in this matrix. Let us briefly examine each of the four strategies.

An international strategy uses exports and licenses to penetrate the global arena. This strategy is the least advantageous, with little local responsiveness and little cost advantage. But an international strategy is often the easiest, as exports can require little change in existing operations, and licensing agreements often leave much of the risk to the licensee.

The multidomestic strategy has decentralized authority with substantial autonomy at each business. These are typically subsidiaries, franchises, or joint ventures with substantial independence. The advantage of this strategy is maximizing a competitive response for the local market; however, the strategy has little or no cost advantage. Many food producers, such as Heinz, use a multidomestic strategy to accommodate local tastes because global integration of the production process is not critical. The concept is one of "we were successful in the home market; let's export the management talent and processes, not necessarily the product, to accommodate another market."

A global strategy has a high degree of centralization, with headquarters coordinating the organization to seek out standardization and learning between plants, thus generating economies of scale. This strategy is appropriate when the strategic focus is cost reduction but has little to recommend it when the demand for local responsiveness is high. Caterpillar, the world leader in earth-moving equipment, and Texas Instruments, a world leader in semiconductors, pursue global strategies. Caterpillar and Texas Instruments find this strategy advantageous because the end products are similar throughout the world. Earth-moving equipment is the same in Nigeria as in Iowa.

International business
A firm that engages in cross-border transactions.

Multinational corporation (MNC)
A firm that has extensive involvement in international business, owning or controlling facilities in more than one country.

International strategy
A strategy in which global markets are penetrated using exports and licenses.

Multidomestic strategy
A strategy in which operating decisions are decentralized to each country to enhance local responsiveness.

Global strategy
A strategy in which operating decisions are centralized and headquarters coordinates the standardization and learning between facilities.

LO 2.5 *Identify* and explain four global operations strategy options

Figure **2.9**

Four International Operations Strategies

Source: See a similar presentation in M. Hitt, R. D. Ireland, and R. E. Hoskisson, *Strategic Management: Concepts, Competitiveness, and Globalization,* 8th ed. (Cincinnati: Southwestern College Publishing).

In a continuing fierce worldwide battle, both Komatsu and Caterpillar seek global advantage in the heavy equipment market. As Komatsu (left) moved west to the UK, Caterpillar (right) moved east, with 13 facilities and joint ventures in China. Both firms are building equipment throughout the world as cost and logistics dictate. Their global strategies allow production to move as markets, risk, and exchange rates suggest.

Transnational strategy

A strategy that combines the benefits of global-scale efficiencies with the benefits of local responsiveness.

A transnational strategy exploits the economies of scale and learning, as well as pressure for responsiveness, by recognizing that core competence does not reside in just the "home" country but can exist anywhere in the organization. *Transnational* describes a condition in which material, people, and ideas cross—or *transgress*—national boundaries. These firms have the potential to pursue all three operations strategies (i.e., differentiation, low cost, and response). Such firms can be thought of as "world companies" whose country identity is not as important as their interdependent network of worldwide operations. Nestlé is a good example of such a company. Although it is legally Swiss, 95% of its assets are held and 98% of its sales are made outside Switzerland. Fewer than 10% of its workers are Swiss.

Summary

Global operations provide an increase in both the challenges and opportunities for operations managers. Although the task is difficult, operations managers can and do improve productivity. They build and manage global OM functions and supply chains that contribute in a significant way to competitiveness. Organizations identify their strengths and weaknesses. They then develop effective missions and strategies that account for these strengths and weaknesses and complement the opportunities and threats in the environment. If this procedure is performed well, the organization can have competitive advantage through some combination of product differentiation, low cost, and response.

Increasing specialization provides economic pressure to build organizations that focus on core competencies and to outsource the rest. But there is also a need for planning outsourcing to make it beneficial to all participants. In this increasingly global world, competitive advantage is often achieved via a move to international, multidomestic, global, or transnational strategies.

Effective use of resources, whether domestic or international, is the responsibility of the professional manager, and professional managers are among the few in our society who *can* achieve this performance. The challenge is great, and the rewards to the manager and to society are substantial.

Key Terms

Maquiladoras (p. 34)
World Trade Organization (WTO) (p. 34)
North American Free Trade Agreement (NAFTA) (p. 34)
European Union (EU) (p. 34)
Mission (p. 36)
Strategy (p. 36)
Competitive advantage (p. 36)
Differentiation (p. 38)

Experience differentiation (p. 38)
Low-cost leadership (p. 38)
Response (p. 39)
Resources view (p. 40)
Value-chain analysis (p. 40)
Five forces model (p. 40)
SWOT analysis (p. 41)
Key success factors (KSFs) (p. 41)
Core competencies (p. 42)

Activity map (p. 43)
Outsourcing (p. 44)
Theory of comparative advantage (p. 46)
International business (p. 49)
Multinational corporation (MNC) (p. 49)
International strategy (p. 49)
Multidomestic strategy (p. 49)
Global strategy (p. 49)
Transnational strategy (p. 50)

Ethical Dilemma

As a manufacturer of athletic shoes whose image—indeed performance—is widely regarded as socially responsible, you find your costs increasing. Traditionally, your athletic shoes have been made in Indonesia and South Korea. Although the ease of doing business in those countries has been improving, wage rates have also been increasing. The labor-cost differential between your current suppliers and a contractor who will get the shoes made in China now exceeds $1 per pair. Your sales next year are projected to be 10 million pairs, and your analysis suggests that this cost differential is not offset by any other tangible costs; you face only the political risk and potential damage to your commitment to social responsibility. Thus, this $1 per pair savings should flow directly to your bottom line. There is no doubt that the Chinese government engages in censorship, remains repressive, and is a long way from a democracy. Moreover, you will have little or no control over working conditions, sexual harassment, and pollution. What do you do, and on what basis do you make your decision?

Michael S. Yamashita/Corbis

Discussion Questions

1. Based on the descriptions and analyses in this chapter, would Boeing be better described as a global firm or a transnational firm? Discuss.
2. List six reasons to internationalize operations.
3. Coca-Cola is called a global product. Does this mean that Coca-Cola is formulated in the same way throughout the world? Discuss.
4. Define *mission*.
5. Define *strategy*.
6. Describe how an organization's *mission* and *strategy* have different purposes.
7. Identify the mission and strategy of your automobile repair garage. What are the manifestations of the 10 strategic OM decisions at the garage? That is, how is each of the 10 decisions accomplished?
8. As a library or Internet assignment, identify the mission of a firm and the strategy that supports that mission.
9. How does an OM strategy change during a product's life cycle?
10. There are three primary ways to achieve competitive advantage. Provide an example, not included in the text, of each. Support your choices.
11. Given the discussion of Southwest Airlines in the text, define an *operations* strategy for that firm now that it has purchased AirTran.
12. How must an operations strategy integrate with marketing and accounting?
13. How would you summarize outsourcing trends?
14. What potential cost-saving advantages might firms experience by using outsourcing?
15. What internal issues must managers address when outsourcing?
16. How should a company select an outsourcing provider?
17. What are some of the possible consequences of poor outsourcing?
18. What global operations strategy is most descriptive of McDonald's?

Using Software to Solve Outsourcing Problems

Excel, Excel OM, and POM for Windows may be used to solve many of the problems in this chapter.

CREATING YOUR OWN EXCEL SPREADSHEETS

Program 2.1 illustrates how to build an Excel spreadsheet for the data in Example 1. In this example the factor rating method is used to compare National Architects' three potential outsourcing providers.

This program provides the data inputs for seven important factors, including their weights (0.0–1.0) and ratings (1–5 scale where 5 is the highest rating) for each country. As we see, BIM is most highly rated, with a 3.9 score, versus 3.3 for S.P.C. and 3.8 for Telco.

✗ USING EXCEL OM

Excel OM (free with your text and also found in MyOMLab) may be used to solve Example 1 (with the Factor Rating module).

P USING POM FOR WINDOWS

POM for Windows also includes a factor rating module. For details, refer to Appendix IV. POM for Windows is also found in MyOMLab and can solve all problems labeled with a P.

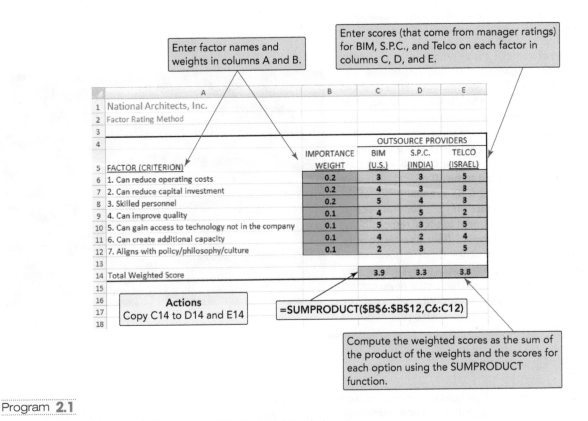

Enter factor names and weights in columns A and B.

Enter scores (that come from manager ratings) for BIM, S.P.C., and Telco on each factor in columns C, D, and E.

	A	B	C	D	E
1	National Architects, Inc.				
2	Factor Rating Method				
3					
4				OUTSOURCE PROVIDERS	
5	FACTOR (CRITERION)	IMPORTANCE WEIGHT	BIM (U.S.)	S.P.C. (INDIA)	TELCO (ISRAEL)
6	1. Can reduce operating costs	0.2	3	3	5
7	2. Can reduce capital investment	0.2	4	3	3
8	3. Skilled personnel	0.2	5	4	3
9	4. Can improve quality	0.1	4	5	2
10	5. Can gain access to technology not in the company	0.1	5	3	5
11	6. Can create additional capacity	0.1	4	2	4
12	7. Aligns with policy/philosophy/culture	0.1	2	3	5
13					
14	Total Weighted Score		3.9	3.3	3.8
15					
16	**Actions**				
17	Copy C14 to D14 and E14				
18					

=SUMPRODUCT($B$6:$B$12,C6:C12)

Compute the weighted scores as the sum of the product of the weights and the scores for each option using the SUMPRODUCT function.

Program **2.1**

Using Excel to Develop a Factor Rating Analysis, With Data from Example 1.

Solved Problems   Virtual Office Hours help is available in MyOMLab.

SOLVED PROBLEM 2.1

The global tire industry continues to consolidate. Michelin buys Goodrich and Uniroyal and builds plants throughout the world. Bridgestone buys Firestone, expands its research budget, and focuses on world markets. Goodyear spends almost 4% of its sales revenue on research. These three aggressive firms have come to dominate the world tire market, with total market share approaching 60%. And the German tire maker Continental AG has strengthened its position as fourth in the world, with a dominant presence in Germany and a research budget of 6%. Against this formidable array, the old-line Italian tire company Pirelli SpA is challenged to respond effectively. Although Pirelli still has almost 5% of the market, it is a relatively small player in a tough, competitive business.

And although the business is reliable even in recessions, as motorists still need replacement tires, the competition is getting stronger. The business rewards companies that have large market shares and long production runs. Pirelli, with its small market share and 1,200 specialty tires, has neither. However, Pirelli has some strengths: an outstanding reputation for tire research and excellent high-performance tires, including supplying specially engineered tires for performance automobiles, Ducati motorcycles, and Formula 1 racing teams. In addition, Pirelli's operations managers complement the creative engineering with world-class innovative manufacturing processes that allow rapid changeover to different models and sizes of tires.

Use a SWOT analysis to establish a feasible strategy for Pirelli.

SOLUTION

First, find an opportunity in the world tire market that avoids the threat of the mass-market onslaught by the big-three tire makers. Second, use the internal marketing strength represented by Pirelli's strong brand name supplying Formula 1 racing and a history of winning World Rally Championships. Third, maximize the innovative capabilities of an outstanding operations function. This is a classic differentiation strategy, supported by activity mapping that ties Pirelli's marketing strength to research and its innovative operations function.

To implement this strategy, Pirelli is differentiating itself with a focus on higher-margin performance tires and away from the low-margin standard tire business. Pirelli has established deals with luxury brands Jaguar, BMW, Maserati, Ferrari, Bentley, and Lotus Elise and established itself as a provider of a large share of the tires on new Porsches and S-class Mercedes. Pirelli also made a strategic decision to divest itself of other businesses. As a result, the vast majority of the company's tire production is now high-performance tires. People are willing to pay a premium for Pirellis.

The operations function continued to focus its design efforts on performance tires and developing a system of modular tire manufacture that allows much faster switching between models. This modular system, combined with billions of dollars in new manufacturing investment, has driven batch sizes down to as small as 150 to 200, making small-lot performance tires economically feasible. Manufacturing innovations at Pirelli have streamlined the production process, moving it from a 14-step process to a 3-step process.

Pirelli still faces a threat from the big three going after the performance market, but the company has bypassed its weakness of having a small market share with a substantial research budget and an innovative operations function. The firm now

has 19 plants in 13 countries and a presence in more than 160 countries, with sales approaching $8 billion.

Sources: Based on *The Economist* (January 8, 2011): 65; **www.pirelli.com**; and **RubberNews.com**.

SOLVED PROBLEM 2.2

DeHoratius Electronics, Inc., is evaluating several options for sourcing a critical processor for its new modem. Three sources are being considered: Hi-Tech in Canada, Zia in Hong Kong, and Zaragoza in Spain. The owner, Nicole DeHoratius, has determined that only three criteria are critical. She has rated each firm on a 1–5 scale (with 5 being highest) and has also placed an importance weight on each of the factors, as shown below:

FACTOR (CRITERION)	IMPORTANCE WEIGHT	HI-TECH (CANADA)		ZIA (HONG KONG)		ZARAGOZA (SPAIN)	
		Rating	Wtd. Score	Rating	Wtd.score	Rating	Wtd. Score
1. Cost	.5	3	1.5	3	1.5	5	2.5
2. Reliability	.2	4	.8	3	.6	3	.6
3. Competence	.3	5	1.5	4	1.2	3	.9
Totals	1.0		3.8		3.3		4.0

SOLUTION

Nicole multiplies each rating by the weight and sums the products in each column to generate a total score for each outsourcing provider. For example the weighted score for Hi-Tech equals $(.5 \times 3) + (.2 \times 4) + (.3 \times 5) = 1.5 + .8 + 1.5 = 3.8$. She selects Zaragoza, which has the highest overall rating.

Problems   *Note:* **Px** means the problem may be solved with POM for Windows and/or Excel OM.

Problems 2.1–2.3 relate to A Global View of Operations and Supply Chains

•• **2.1** Match the product with the proper parent company and country in the table below:

PRODUCT	PARENT COMPANY	COUNTRY
Arrow Shirts	a. Volkswagen	1. France
Braun Household Appliances	b. Bidermann International	2. Great Britain
Volvo Autos	c. Bridgestone	3. Germany
Firestone Tires	d. Campbell Soup	4. Japan
Godiva Chocolate	e. Credit Lyonnais	5. U.S.
Häagen-Dazs Ice Cream (USA)	f. Tata	6. Switzerland
Jaguar Autos	g. Procter & Gamble	7. China
MGM Movies	h. Michelin	8. India
Lamborghini Autos	i. Nestlé	
Goodrich Tires	j. Geely	
Alpo Pet Foods		

•• **2.2** Based on the corruption perception index developed by Transparency International (**www.transparency.org**), rank the following countries from most corrupt to least: Venezuela, Denmark, the U.S., Switzerland, and China.

•• **2.3** Based on the competitiveness ranking developed by the Global Competitiveness Index (**www.weforum.org**), rank the following countries from most competitive to least: Mexico, Switzerland, the U.S., and China.

Problems 2.4 and 2.5 relate to Achieving Competitive Advantage Through Operations

• **2.4** The text provides three primary strategic approaches (differentiation, cost, and response) for achieving competitive advantage. Provide an example of each not given in the text. Support your choices. (*Hint:* Note the examples provided in the text.)

•• **2.5** Within the food service industry (restaurants that serve meals to customers, but not just fast food), find examples of firms that have sustained competitive advantage by competing on the basis of (1) cost leadership, (2) response, and (3) differentiation. Cite one example in each category; provide a sentence or two in support of each choice. Do not use fast-food chains for all categories. (*Hint:* A "99¢ menu" is very easily copied and is not a good source of sustained advantage.)

Problem 2.6 relates to Issues in Operations Strategy

•••**2.6** Identify how changes within an organization affect the OM strategy for a company. For instance, discuss what impact the following internal factors might have on OM strategy:
a) Maturing of a product.
b) Technology innovation in the manufacturing process.
c) Changes in laptop computer design that builds in wireless technology.

Problem 2.7 relates to Strategy Development and Implementation

•••**2.7** Identify how changes in the external environment affect the OM strategy for a company. For instance, discuss what impact the following external factors might have on OM strategy:
a) Major increases in oil prices.
b) Water- and air-quality legislation.

c) Fewer young prospective employees entering the labor market.

d) Inflation versus stable prices.

e) Legislation moving health insurance from a pretax benefit to taxable income.

Problems 2.8–2.12 relate to Strategic Planning, Core Competencies, and Outsourcing

•• **2.8** Claudia Pragram Technologies, Inc., has narrowed its choice of outsourcing provider to two firms located in different countries. Pragram wants to decide which one of the two countries is the better choice, based on risk-avoidance criteria. She has polled her executives and established four criteria. The resulting ratings for the two countries are presented in the table below, where 1 is a lower risk and 3 is a higher risk.

SELECTION CRITERION	ENGLAND	CANADA
Price of service from outsourcer	2	3
Nearness of facilities to client	3	1
Level of technology	1	3
History of successful outsourcing	1	2

The executives have determined four criteria weightings: Price, with a weight of 0.1; Nearness, with 0.6; Technology, with 0.2; and History, with 0.1.

a) Using the factor-rating method, which country would you select?

b) Double each of the weights used in part (a) (to 0.2, 1.2, 0.4, and 0.2, respectively). What effect does this have on your answer? Why? **Px**

•• **2.9** Ranga Ramasesh is the operations manager for a firm that is trying to decide which one of four countries it should research for possible outsourcing providers. The first step is to select a country based on cultural risk factors, which are critical to eventual business success with the provider. Ranga has reviewed outsourcing provider directories and found that the four countries in the table that follows have an ample number of providers from which they can choose. To aid in the country selection step, he has enlisted the aid of a cultural expert, John Wang, who has provided ratings of the various criteria in the table. The resulting ratings are on a 1 to 10 scale, where 1 is a low risk and 10 is a high risk.

John has also determined six criteria weightings: Trust, with a weight of 0.4; Quality, with 0.2; Religious, with 0.1; Individualism, with 0.1; Time, with 0.1; and Uncertainty, with 0.1. Using the factor-rating method, which country should Ranga select? **Px**

CULTURE SELECTION CRITERION	MEXICO	PANAMA	COSTA RICA	PERU
Trust	1	2	2	1
Society value of quality work	7	10	9	10
Religious attitudes	3	3	3	5
Individualism attitudes	5	2	4	8
Time orientation attitudes	4	6	7	3
Uncertainty avoidance attitudes	3	2	4	2

•• **2.10** Fernando Garza's firm wishes to use factor rating to help select an outsourcing provider of logistics services.

a) With weights from 1–5 (5 highest) and ratings 1–100 (100 highest), use the following table to help Garza make his decision:

		RATING OF LOGISTICS PROVIDERS		
CRITERION	WEIGHT	OVERNIGHT SHIPPING	WORLDWIDE DELIVERY	UNITED FREIGHT
Quality	5	90	80	75
Delivery	3	70	85	70
Cost	2	70	80	95

b) Garza decides to increase the weights for quality, delivery, and cost to 10, 6, and 4, respectively. How does this change your conclusions? Why?

c) If Overnight Shipping's ratings for each of the factors increase by 10%, what are the new results? **Px**

••• **2.11** Walker Accounting Software is marketed to small accounting firms throughout the U.S. and Canada. Owner George Walker has decided to outsource the company's help desk and is considering three providers: Manila Call Center (Philippines), Delhi Services (India), and Moscow Bell (Russia). The following table summarizes the data Walker has assembled. Which outsourcing firm has the best rating? (Higher weights imply higher importance and higher ratings imply more desirable providers.) **Px**

		PROVIDER RATINGS		
CRITERION	IMPORTANCE WEIGHT	MANILA	DELHI	MOSCOW
Flexibility	0.5	5	1	9
Trustworthiness	0.1	5	5	2
Price	0.2	4	3	6
Delivery	0.2	5	6	6

•••• **2.12** Rao Technologies, a California-based high-tech manufacturer, is considering outsourcing some of its electronics production. Four firms have responded to its request for bids, and CEO Mohan Rao has started to perform an analysis on the scores his OM team has entered in the table below.

		RATINGS OF OUTSOURCE PROVIDERS			
FACTOR	WEIGHT	A	B	C	D
Labor	w	5	4	3	5
Quality procedures	30	2	3	5	1
Logistics system	5	3	4	3	5
Price	25	5	3	4	4
Trustworthiness	5	3	2	3	5
Technology in place	15	2	5	4	4
Management team	15	5	5	4	1

Weights are on a scale from 1 through 30, and the outsourcing provider scores are on a scale of 1 through 5. The weight for the labor factor is shown as a w because Rao's OM team cannot agree on a value for this weight. For what range of values of w, if any, is company C a recommended outsourcing provider, according to the factor-rating method?

Problem 2.13 relates to Global Operations Strategy Options

•• **2.13** Does Boeing practice a multinational operations strategy, a global operations strategy, or a transnational operations strategy? Support your choice with specific references to Boeing's operations and the characteristics of each type of organization.

CASE STUDIES

Rapid-Lube

A huge market exists for automobile tune-ups, oil changes, and lubrication service for more than 250 million vehicles on U.S. roads. Some of this demand is filled by full-service auto dealerships, some by Walmart and Firestone, and some by other tire/service dealers. However, Rapid-Lube, Mobil-Lube, Jiffy-Lube and others have also developed strategies to accommodate this opportunity.

Rapid-Lube stations perform oil changes, lubrication, and interior cleaning in a spotless environment. The buildings are clean, usually painted white, and often surrounded by neatly trimmed landscaping. To facilitate fast service, cars can be driven through three abreast. At Rapid-Lube, the customer is greeted by service representatives who are graduates of Rapid-Lube U. The Rapid-Lube school is not unlike McDonald's Hamburger University near Chicago or Holiday Inn's training school in Memphis. The greeter takes the order, which typically includes fluid checks (oil, water, brake fluid, transmission fluid, differential grease) and the necessary lubrication, as well as filter changes for air and oil. Service personnel in neat uniforms then move into action. The standard three-person team has one person checking fluid levels under the hood, another assigned interior vacuuming and window cleaning, and the third in the garage pit, removing the oil filter, draining the oil, checking the differential and transmission, and lubricating as necessary. Precise task assignments and good training are designed to move the car into and out of the bay in 10 minutes. The business model is to charge no more, and hopefully less, than gas stations, automotive repair chains, and auto dealers, while providing better and faster service.

Discussion Questions

1. What constitutes the mission of Rapid-Lube?
2. How does the Rapid-Lube operations strategy provide competitive advantage? (*Hint:* Evaluate how Rapid-Lube's traditional competitors perform the 10 decisions of operations management vs. how Rapid-Lube performs them.)
3. Is it likely that Rapid-Lube has increased productivity over its more traditional competitors? Why? How would we measure productivity in this industry?

Strategy at Regal Marine Video Case

Regal Marine, one of the U.S.'s 10 largest power-boat manufacturers, achieves its mission—providing luxury performance boats to customers worldwide—using the strategy of differentiation. It differentiates its products through constant innovation, unique features, and high quality. Increasing sales at the Orlando, Florida, family-owned firm suggest that the strategy is working.

As a quality boat manufacturer, Regal Marine starts with continuous innovation, as reflected in computer-aided design (CAD), high-quality molds, and close tolerances that are controlled through both defect charts and rigorous visual inspection. In-house quality is not enough, however. Because a product is only as good as the parts put into it, Regal has established close ties with a large number of its suppliers to ensure both flexibility and perfect parts. With the help of these suppliers, Regal can profitably produce a product line of 22 boats, ranging from the $14,000 19-foot boat to the $500,000 44-foot Commodore yacht.

"We build boats," says VP Tim Kuck, "but we're really in the 'fun' business. Our competition includes not only 300 other boat, canoe, and yacht manufacturers in our $17 billion industry, but home theaters, the Internet, and all kinds of alternative family entertainment." Fortunately Regal has been paying down debt and increasing market share.

Regal has also joined with scores of other independent boat makers in the American Boat Builders Association. Through economies of scale in procurement, Regal is able to navigate against billion-dollar competitor Brunswick (makers of the Sea Ray and Bayliner brands). The *Global Company Profile* featuring Regal Marine (which opens Chapter 5) provides further background on Regal and its strategy.

Discussion Questions*

1. State Regal Marine's mission in your own words.
2. Identify the strengths, weaknesses, opportunities, and threats that are relevant to the strategy of Regal Marine.
3. How would you define Regal's strategy?
4. How would each of the 10 operations management decisions apply to operations decision making at Regal Marine?

*You may wish to view the video that accompanies the case before addressing these questions.

Hard Rock Cafe's Global Strategy Video Case

Hard Rock brings the concept of the "experience economy" to its cafe operation. The strategy incorporates a unique "experience" into its operations. This innovation is somewhat akin to mass customization in manufacturing. At Hard Rock, the experience concept is to provide not only a custom meal from the menu but a dining event that includes a unique visual and sound experience not duplicated anywhere else in the world. This strategy is succeeding. Other theme restaurants have come and gone while Hard Rock continues to grow. As Professor C. Markides of the London Business School says, "The trick is not to play the game better than the competition, but to develop and play an altogether different game."* At Hard Rock, the different game is the experience game.

From the opening of its first cafe in London in 1971, during the British rock music explosion, Hard Rock has been serving food and rock music with equal enthusiasm. Hard Rock Cafe has 40 U.S. locations, about a dozen in Europe, and the remainder

*Constantinos Markides, "Strategic Innovation," *MIT Sloan Management Review* 38, no. 3: 9.

scattered throughout the world, from Bangkok and Beijing to Beirut. New construction, leases, and investment in remodeling are long term; so a global strategy means special consideration of political risk, currency risk, and social norms in a context of a brand fit. Although Hard Rock is one of the most recognized brands in the world, this does not mean its cafe is a natural everywhere. Special consideration must be given to the supply chain for the restaurant and its accompanying retail store. About 48% of a typical cafe's sales are from merchandise.

The Hard Rock Cafe business model is well defined, but because of various risk factors and differences in business practices and employment law, Hard Rock elects to franchise about half of its cafes. Social norms and preferences often suggest some tweaking of menus for local taste. For instance, Hard Rock focuses less on hamburgers and beef and more on fish and lobster in its British cafes.

Because 70% of Hard Rock's guests are tourists, recent years have found it expanding to "destination" cities. While this has been a winning strategy for decades, allowing the firm to grow from one London cafe to 145 facilities in 60 countries, it has made Hard Rock susceptible to economic fluctuations that hit the tourist business hardest. So Hard Rock is signing a long-term lease for a new location in Nottingham, England, to join recently opened cafes in Manchester and Birmingham—cities that are not standard tourist destinations. At the same time, menus are being upgraded. Hopefully, repeat business from locals in these cities will smooth demand and make Hard Rock less dependent on tourists.

Discussion Questions*

1. Identify the strategy changes that have taken place at Hard Rock Cafe since its founding in 1971.
2. As Hard Rock Cafe has changed its strategy, how has its responses to some of the 10 decisions of OM changed?
3. Where does Hard Rock fit in the four international operations strategies outlined in Figure 2.9? Explain your answer.

*You may wish to view the video that accompanies the case before addressing these questions.

Outsourcing Offshore at Darden

Video Case

Darden Restaurants, owner of popular brands such as Olive Garden, Bahama Breeze, and Longhorn Grill, serves more than 320 million meals annually in over 1,500 restaurants across the U.S. and Canada. To achieve competitive advantage via its supply chain, Darden must achieve excellence at each step. With purchases from 35 countries, and seafood products with a shelf life as short as 4 days, this is a complex and challenging task.

Those 320 million meals annually mean 40 million pounds of shrimp and huge quantities of tilapia, swordfish, and other fresh purchases. Fresh seafood is typically flown to the U.S. and monitored each step of the way to ensure that 34°F is maintained.

Darden's purchasing agents travel the world to find competitive advantage in the supply chain. Darden personnel from supply chain and development, quality assurance, and environmental relations contribute to developing, evaluating, and checking suppliers. Darden also has seven native-speaking representatives living on other continents to provide continuing support and evaluation of suppliers. All suppliers must abide by Darden's food standards, which typically exceed FDA and other industry standards. Darden expects continuous improvement in durable relationships that increase quality and reduce cost.

Darden's aggressiveness and development of a sophisticated supply chain provide an opportunity for outsourcing. Much food preparation is labor intensive and is often more efficient when handled in bulk. This is particularly true where large volumes may justify capital investment. For instance, Tyson and Iowa Beef prepare meats to Darden's specifications much more economically than can individual restaurants. Similarly, Darden has found that it can outsource both the cutting of salmon to the proper portion size and the cracking/peeling of shrimp more cost-effectively offshore than in U.S. distribution centers or individual restaurants.

Discussion Questions*

1. What are some outsourcing opportunities in a restaurant?
2. What supply chain issues are unique to a firm sourcing from 35 countries?
3. Examine how other firms or industries develop international supply chains as compared to Darden.
4. Why does Darden outsource harvesting and preparation of much of its seafood?

*You may wish to view the video that accompanies this case study before answering these questions.

- **Additional Case Study:** Visit MyOMLab for this free case study:
  Outsourcing to Tata: The Indian outsourcing firm is hired by New Mexico.

Endnotes

1. The 28 members of the European Union (EU) as of 2015 were Austria, Belgium, Bulgaria, Cyprus, Croatia, Czech Republic, Denmark, Estonia, Finland, France, Germany, Greece, Hungary, Ireland, Italy, Latvia, Lithuania, Luxembourg, Malta, the Netherlands, Poland, Portugal, Romania, Slovakia, Slovenia, Spain, Sweden, and United Kingdom. Not all have adopted the euro. In addition, Iceland, Macedonia, Montenegro, and Turkey are candidates for entry into the European Union.

2. M. E. Porter, *Competitive Advantage: Creating and Sustaining Superior Performance.* New York: The Free Press, 1985.
3. M. E. Porter, *Competitive Strategy: Techniques for Analyzing Industries and Competitors.* New York: The Free Press, 1980, 1998.
4. J. Whitaker, M. S. Krishnan, and C. Fornell. "How Offshore Outsourcing Affects Customer Satisfaction." *The Wall Street Journal* (July 7, 2008): R4.

Chapter 2 *Rapid* Review

Main Heading	Review Material	MyOMLab
A GLOBAL VIEW OF OPERATIONS AND SUPPLY CHAINS (pp. 32–35)	Domestic business operations decide to change to some form of international operations for six main reasons: 1. Improve supply chain 2. Reduce costs and exchange rate risks 3. Improve operations 4. Understand markets 5. Improve products 6. Attract and retain global talent ■ **Maquiladoras**—Mexican factories located along the U.S.–Mexico border that receive preferential tariff treatment. ■ **World Trade Organization (WTO)**—An international organization that promotes world trade by lowering barriers to the free flow of goods across borders. ■ **NAFTA**—A free trade agreement between Canada, Mexico, and the United States. ■ **European Union (EU)**—A European trade group that has 28 member states.	Concept Questions: 1.1–1.4 Problems: 2.1–2.3
DEVELOPING MISSIONS AND STRATEGIES (pp. 35–36)	An effective operations management effort must have a *mission* so it knows where it is going and a *strategy* so it knows how to get there. ■ **Mission**—The purpose or rationale for an organization's existence. ■ **Strategy**—How an organization expects to achieve its missions and goals. The three strategic approaches to competitive advantage are: 1. Differentiation 2. Cost leadership 3. Response	Concept Questions: 2.1–2.4 **VIDEO 2.1** Operations Strategy at Regal Marine
ACHIEVING COMPETITIVE ADVANTAGE THROUGH OPERATIONS (pp. 36–40)	■ **Competitive advantage**—The creation of a unique advantage over competitors. ■ **Differentiation**—Distinguishing the offerings of an organization in a way that the customer perceives as adding value. ■ **Experience differentiation**—Engaging the customer with a product through imaginative use of the five senses, so the customer "experiences" the product. ■ **Low-cost leadership**—Achieving maximum value, as perceived by the customer. ■ **Response**—A set of values related to rapid, flexible, and reliable performance.	Concept Questions: 3.1–3.4 Problems: 2.4–2.5 **VIDEO 2.2** Hard Rock's Global Strategy
ISSUES IN OPERATIONS STRATEGY (pp. 40–41)	■ **Resources view**—A view in which managers evaluate the resources at their disposal and manage or alter them to achieve competitive advantage. ■ **Value-chain analysis**—A way to identify the elements in the product/service chain that uniquely add value. ■ **Five forces model**—A way to analyze the five forces in the competitive environment. Forces in Porter's five forces model are (1) immediate rivals, (2) potential entrants, (3) customers, (4) suppliers, and (5) substitute products. Different issues are emphasized during different stages of the product life cycle: ■ *Introduction*—Company strategy: Best period to increase market share, R&D engineering is critical. OM strategy: Product design and development critical, frequent product and process design changes, short production runs, high production costs, limited models, attention to quality. ■ *Growth*—Company strategy: Practical to change price or quality image, strengthen niche. OM strategy: Forecasting critical, product and process reliability, competitive product improvements and options, increase capacity, shift toward product focus, enhance distribution. ■ *Maturity*—Company strategy: Poor time to change image or price or quality, competitive costs become critical, defend market position. OM strategy: Standardization, less rapid product changes (more minor changes), optimum capacity, increasing stability of process, long production runs, product improvement and cost cutting. ■ *Decline*—Company strategy: Cost control critical. OM strategy: Little product differentiation, cost minimization, overcapacity in the industry, prune line to eliminate items not returning good margin, reduce capacity.	Concept Questions: 4.1–4.4 Problem: 2.6

Main Heading	Review Material	
STRATEGY DEVELOPMENT AND IMPLEMENTATION (pp. 41–44)	▪ **SWOT analysis**—A method of determining internal strengths and weaknesses and external opportunities and threats. ▪ **Key success factors (KSFs)**—Activities or factors that are key to achieving competitive advantage. ▪ **Core competencies**—A set of unique skills, talents, and activities that a firm does particularly well. A core competence may be a combination of KSFs. ▪ **Activity map**—A graphical link of competitive advantage, KSFs, and supporting activities.	Concept Questions: 5.1–5.4 Problem: 2.7 Virtual Office Hours for Solved Problem: 2.1
STRATEGIC PLANNING, CORE COMPETENCIES, AND OUTSOURCING (pp. 44–48)	▪ **Outsourcing**—Procuring from external sources services or products that are normally part of an organization. ▪ **Theory of comparative advantage**—The theory which states that countries benefit from specializing in (and exporting) products and services in which they have relative advantage and importing goods in which they have a relative disadvantage. Perhaps half of all outsourcing agreements fail because of inappropriate planning and analysis. Potential risks of outsourcing include: ▪ A drop in quality or customer service ▪ Political backlash that results from outsourcing to foreign countries ▪ Negative impact on employees ▪ Potential future competition ▪ Increased logistics and inventory costs The most common reason given for outsourcing failure is that the decision was made without sufficient understanding and analysis. The factor-rating method is an excellent tool for dealing with both country risk assessment and provider selection problems.	Concept Questions: 6.1–6.4 Problems: 2.8–2.12 Virtual Office Hours for Solved Problem: 2.2 **VIDEO 2.3** Outsourcing Offshore at Darden
GLOBAL OPERATIONS STRATEGY OPTIONS (pp. 49–50)	▪ **International business**—A firm that engages in cross-border transactions. ▪ **Multinational corporation (MNC)**—A firm that has extensive involvement in international business, owning or controlling facilities in more than one country. The four operations strategies for approaching global opportunities can be classified according to local responsiveness and cost reduction: ▪ **International strategy**—A strategy in which global markets are penetrated using exports and licenses with little local responsiveness. ▪ **Multidomestic strategy**—A strategy in which operating decisions are decentralized to each country to enhance local responsiveness. ▪ **Global strategy**—A strategy in which operating decisions are centralized and headquarters coordinates the standardization and learning between facilities. ▪ **Transnational strategy**—A strategy that combines the benefits of global-scale efficiencies with the benefits of local responsiveness. These firms transgress national boundaries.	Concept Questions: 7.1–7.4 Problem 2.13

Self Test

▪ Before taking the self-test, refer to the learning objectives listed at the beginning of the chapter and the key terms listed at the end of the chapter.

LO 2.1 A mission statement is beneficial to an organization because it:
  a) is a statement of the organization's purpose.
  b) provides a basis for the organization's culture.
  c) identifies important constituencies.
  d) details specific income goals.
  e) ensures profitability.

LO 2.2 The three strategic approaches to competitive advantage are ____, ____, and ____.

LO 2.3 Core competencies are those strengths in a firm that include:
  a) specialized skills.
  b) unique production methods.
  c) proprietary information/knowledge.
  d) things a company does better than others.
  e) all of the above.

LO 2.4 Evaluating outsourcing providers by comparing their weighted average scores involves:
  a) factor-rating analysis.
  b) cost-volume analysis.
  c) transportation model analysis.
  d) linear regression analysis.
  e) crossover analysis.

LO 2.5 A company that is organized across international boundaries, with decentralized authority and substantial autonomy at each business via subsidiaries, franchises, or joint ventures, has:
  a) a global strategy.
  b) a transnational strategy.
  c) an international strategy.
  d) a multidomestic strategy.

Answers: LO 2.1. a; LO 2.2. differentiation, cost leadership, response; LO 2.3. e; LO 2.4. a; LO 2.5. c.

Project Management

CHAPTER OUTLINE

Alaska Airlines

Project Management Provides a Competitive Advantage for Bechtel

Over a century old, the San Francisco–based Bechtel Group (www.bechtel.com) is the world's premier manager of massive construction and engineering projects. Known for billion-dollar projects, Bechtel is famous for its construction feats on the Hoover Dam, the Boston Central Artery/Tunnel project, the Riyadh, Saudi Arabia Metro, and over 25,000 other projects in 160 countries. With 53,000 employees and revenues over $39 billion, Bechtel is the U.S.'s largest project manager.

Philipus/Alamy

A massive dredge hired by Bechtel removes silt from Iraq's port at Umm Qasr. This paved the way for large-scale deliveries of U.S. food and the return of commercial shipping.

Steve Hebert/Bechtel National, Inc./PRN/Newscom

In addition to major construction projects, Bechtel used its project management skills to provide emergency response to major catastrophes as it did here in the wake of Hurricane Katrina.

Conditions weren't what Bechtel expected when it won a series of billion-dollar contracts from the U.S. government to help reconstruct war-torn Iraq in the last decade. That country's defeat by Allied forces hadn't caused much war damage. Instead, what Bechtel found was a nation that had been crumbling for years. None of the sewage plants in Baghdad worked. Power flicked on and off. Towns and cities had been left to decay. And scavengers were stealing everything from museum artifacts to electric power lines. Bechtel's job was to oversee electric power, sewage, transportation, and airport repairs.

Bechtel's crews travelled under armed escort and slept in trailers surrounded by razor wire. But the company's efforts have paid off. Iraq's main seaport, Umm Qasr, has opened. Electrical generation is back to prewar levels, and Bechtel has refurbished more than 1,200 schools.

With a global procurement program, Bechtel easily tapped the company's network of suppliers and buyers worldwide to help rebuild Iraq's infrastructure.

Courtesy of Bechtel Corporation

Managing massive construction projects such as this is the strength of Bechtel. With large penalties for late completion and incentives for early completion, a good project manager is worth his or her weight in gold.

Other interesting recent Bechtel projects include:

- Constructing 30 high-security data centers worldwide for Equinix, Inc. ($1.2 billion).
- Building and running a rail line between London and the Channel Tunnel ($4.6 billion).
- Developing an oil pipeline from the Caspian Sea region to Russia ($850 million).
- Expanding the Dubai Airport in the United Arab Emirates ($600 million) and the Miami International Airport ($2 billion).
- Building liquefied natural gas plants in Trinidad, West Indies ($1 billion).

- Building a new subway for Athens, Greece ($2.6 billion).
- Constructing a natural gas pipeline in Thailand ($700 million).
- Building 30 plants for iMotors.com, a company that sells refurbished autos online ($300 million).
- Building a highway to link the north and south of Croatia ($303 million).

When companies or countries seek out firms to manage massive projects, they go to Bechtel, which, again and again, through outstanding project management, has demonstrated its competitive advantage.

Thomas Hartwell/U.S. Agency for International Development (USAID)

Reconstructed terminal at Baghdad International Airport.

Joe Cavaretta/AP Images

Bechtel was the construction contractor for the Hoover Dam. This dam, on the Colorado River, is the highest in the Western Hemisphere.

The Importance of Project Management

When Bechtel, the subject of the opening Global Company Profile, begins a project, it quickly has to mobilize substantial resources, often consisting of manual workers, construction professionals, cooks, medical personnel, and even security forces. Its project management team develops a supply chain to access materials to build everything from ports to bridges, dams, and monorails. Bechtel is just one example of a firm that faces modern phenomena: growing project complexity and collapsing product/service life cycles. This change stems from awareness of the strategic value of time-based competition and a quality mandate for continuous improvement. Each new product/service introduction is a unique event—a project. In addition, projects are a common part of our everyday life. We may be planning a wedding or a surprise birthday party, remodeling a house, or preparing a semester-long class project.

Scheduling projects can be a difficult challenge for operations managers. The stakes in project management are high. Cost overruns and unnecessary delays occur due to poor scheduling and poor controls.

Projects that take months or years to complete are usually developed outside the normal production system. Project organizations within the firm may be set up to handle such jobs and are often disbanded when the project is complete. On other occasions, managers find projects just a part of their job. The management of projects involves three phases (see Figure 3.1):

1. *Planning:* This phase includes goal setting, defining the project, and team organization.
2. *Scheduling:* This phase relates people, money, and supplies to specific activities and relates activities to each other.
3. *Controlling:* Here the firm monitors resources, costs, quality, and budgets. It also revises or changes plans and shifts resources to meet time and cost demands.

We begin this chapter with a brief overview of these functions. Three popular techniques to allow managers to plan, schedule, and control—Gantt charts, PERT, and CPM—are also described.

Project Planning

Projects can be defined as a series of related tasks directed toward a major output. In some firms a project organization is developed to make sure existing programs continue to run smoothly on a day-to-day basis while new projects are successfully completed.

For companies with multiple large projects, such as a construction firm, a project organization is an effective way of assigning the people and physical resources needed. It is a temporary organization structure designed to achieve results by using specialists from throughout the firm.

The project organization may be most helpful when:

1. Work tasks can be defined with a specific goal and deadline.
2. The job is unique or somewhat unfamiliar to the existing organization.
3. The work contains complex interrelated tasks requiring specialized skills.

Project organization
An organization formed to ensure that programs (projects) receive the proper management and attention.

Planning the Project (Before project)

Performance
Set the goals   Define the project   Develop work breakdown structure   Identify team/resources

Figure **3.1**

Project Planning, Scheduling, and Controlling

Scheduling the Project

Sequence activities   Assign people   Schedule deliverables   Schedule resources

⊕ STUDENT TIP

Managers must "make the plan and then work the plan."

Controlling the Project (During project)

Monitor resources, costs, quality   Revise and change plans   Shift resources

4. The project is temporary but critical to the organization.
5. The project cuts across organizational lines.

The Project Manager

An example of a project organization is shown in Figure 3.2. Project team members are temporarily assigned to a project and report to the project manager. The manager heading the project coordinates activities with other departments and reports directly to top management. Project managers receive high visibility in a firm and are responsible for making sure that (1) all necessary activities are finished in proper sequence and on time; (2) the project comes in within budget; (3) the project meets its quality goals; and (4) the people assigned to the project receive the motivation, direction, and information needed to do their jobs. This means that project managers should be good coaches and communicators, and be able to organize activities from a variety of disciplines.

Figure **3.2**

A Sample Project Organization

⊕ STUDENT TIP

Project organizations can be temporary or permanent. A permanent organization is usually called a *matrix organization*.

Ethical Issues Faced in Project Management Project managers not only have high visibility but they also face ethical decisions on a daily basis. How they act establishes the code of conduct for the project. Project managers often deal with (1) offers of gifts from contractors, (2) pressure to alter status reports to mask the reality of delays, (3) false reports for charges of time and expenses, and (4) pressures to compromise quality to meet bonuses or avoid penalties related to schedules.

Using the Project Management Institute's (**www.pmi.org**) ethical codes is one means of trying to establish standards. These codes need to be accompanied by good leadership and a strong organizational culture, with its ingrained ethical standards and values.

Work Breakdown Structure

Work breakdown structure (WBS)

A hierarchical description of a project into more and more detailed components.

The project management team begins its task well in advance of project execution so that a plan can be developed. One of its first steps is to carefully establish the project's objectives, then break the project down into manageable parts. This work breakdown structure (WBS) defines the project by dividing it into its major subcomponents (or tasks), which are then subdivided into more detailed components, and finally into a set of activities and their related costs. The division of the project into smaller and smaller tasks can be difficult, but is critical to managing the project and to scheduling success. Gross requirements for people, supplies, and equipment are also estimated in this planning phase.

The work breakdown structure typically decreases in size from top to bottom and is indented like this:

Level
1. Project
2.   Major tasks in the project
3.   Subtasks in major tasks
4.   Activities (or "work packages") to be completed

This hierarchical framework can be illustrated with the development of Microsoft's operating system Windows 8. As we see in Figure 3.3, the project, creating a new operating system, is labeled 1.0. The first step is to identify the major tasks in the project (level 2). Three examples would be software design (1.1), cost management plan (1.2), and system testing (1.3). Two major subtasks for 1.1 are development of graphical user interfaces (GUIs) (1.1.1) and creating compatibility with previous versions of Windows (1.1.2). The major subtasks for 1.1.2 are level-4 activities, such as creating a team to handle compatibility with Windows 7 (1.1.2.1),

Figure 3.3

Work Breakdown Structure

creating a team for Windows Vista (1.1.2.2), and creating a team for Windows XP (1.1.2.3). There are usually many level-4 activities.

Project Scheduling

Project scheduling involves sequencing and allotting time to all project activities. At this stage, managers decide how long each activity will take and compute the resources needed at each stage of production. Managers may also chart separate schedules for personnel needs by type of skill (management, engineering, or pouring concrete, for example) and material needs.

One popular project scheduling approach is the Gantt chart. Gantt charts are low-cost means of helping managers make sure that (1) activities are planned, (2) order of performance is documented, (3) activity time estimates are recorded, and (4) overall project time is developed. As Figure 3.4 shows, Gantt charts are easy to understand. Horizontal bars are drawn for each project activity along a time line. This illustration of a routine servicing of a Delta jetliner during a 40-minute layover shows that Gantt charts also can be used for scheduling repetitive operations. In this case, the chart helps point out potential delays. The *OM in Action* box on Delta provides additional insights.

On simple projects, scheduling charts such as these permit managers to observe the progress of each activity and to spot and tackle problem areas. Gantt charts, though, do not adequately illustrate the interrelationships between the activities and the resources.

PERT and CPM, the two widely used network techniques that we shall discuss shortly, *do* have the ability to consider precedence relationships and interdependency of activities. On complex projects, the scheduling of which is almost always computerized, PERT and CPM thus have an edge over the simpler Gantt charts. Even on huge projects, though, Gantt charts can be used as summaries of project status and may complement the other network approaches.

To summarize, whatever the approach taken by a project manager, project scheduling serves several purposes:

1. It shows the relationship of each activity to others and to the whole project.
2. It identifies the precedence relationships among activities.
3. It encourages the setting of realistic time and cost estimates for each activity.
4. It helps make better use of people, money, and material resources by identifying critical bottlenecks in the project.

Gantt charts
Planning charts used to schedule resources and allocate time.

LO 3.1 *Use* a Gantt chart for scheduling

Passengers	Deplaning					
	Baggage claim					
Baggage	Container offload					
Fueling	Pumping					
	Engine injection water					
Cargo and mail	Container offload					
Galley servicing	Main cabin door					
	Aft cabin door					
Lavatory servicing	Aft, center, forward					
Drinking water	Loading					
Cabin cleaning	First-class section					
	Economy section					
Cargo and mail	Container/bulk loading					
Flight service	Galley/cabin check					
	Receive passengers					
Operating crew	Aircraft check					
Baggage	Loading					
Passengers	Boarding					

                    0   10   20   30   40
                              Time, minutes

Figure 3.4

Gantt Chart of Service Activities for a Delta Jet during a 40-Minute Layover

Delta saves $50 million a year with this turnaround time, which is a reduction from its traditional 60-minute routine.

OM in Action | **Delta's Ground Crew Orchestrates a Smooth Takeoff**

Flight 574's engines screech its arrival as the jet lumbers down Richmond's taxiway with 140 passengers arriving from Atlanta. In 40 minutes, the plane is to be airborne again.

However, before this jet can depart, there is business to attend to: passengers, luggage, and cargo to unload and load; thousands of gallons of jet fuel and countless drinks to restock; cabin and restrooms to clean; toilet holding tanks to drain; and engines, wings, and landing gear to inspect.

The 10-person ground crew knows that a miscue anywhere—a broken cargo loader, lost baggage, misdirected passengers—can mean a late departure and trigger a chain reaction of headaches from Richmond to Atlanta to every destination of a connecting flight.

Carla Sutera, the operations manager for Delta's Richmond International Airport, views the turnaround operation like a pit boss awaiting a race car. Trained crews are in place for Flight 574 with baggage carts and tractors, hydraulic cargo loaders, a truck to load food and drinks, another to lift the cleanup crew, another to put fuel on, and a fourth to take water off. The "pit crew" usually performs so smoothly that most passengers never suspect the proportions of the effort. Gantt charts, such as the one in Figure 3.4, aid Delta and other airlines with the staffing and scheduling that are needed for this task.

Sources: Knight Ridder Tribune Business News (July 16, 2005) and (November 21, 2002).

Jeff Topping/Getty Images

Project Controlling

VIDEO 3.2
Project Management at Arnold Palmer Hospital

The control of projects, like the control of any management system, involves close monitoring of resources, costs, quality, and budgets. Control also means using a feedback loop to revise the project plan and having the ability to shift resources to where they are needed most. Computerized PERT/CPM reports and charts are widely available today from scores of competing software firms. Some of the more popular of these programs are Oracle Primavera (by Oracle), MindView (by Match Ware), HP Project (by Hewlett-Packard), Fast Track (by AEC Software), and Microsoft Project (by Microsoft Corp.), which we illustrate in this chapter.

STUDENT TIP

To use project management software, you first need to understand the next two sections in this chapter.

These programs produce a broad variety of reports, including (1) detailed cost breakdowns, (2) labor requirements, (3) cost and hour summaries, (4) raw material and expenditure forecasts, (5) variance reports, (6) time analysis reports, and (7) work status reports.

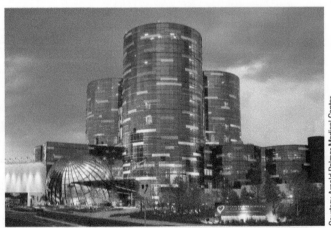

Construction of the new 11-story building at Arnold Palmer Hospital in Orlando, Florida, was an enormous project for the hospital administration. The photo on the left shows the first six floors under construction. The photo on the right shows the building as completed two years later. Prior to beginning actual construction, regulatory and funding issues added, as they do with most projects, substantial time to the overall project. Cities have zoning and parking issues; the EPA has drainage and waste issues; and regulatory authorities have their own requirements, as do issuers of bonds. The $100 million, 4-year project at Arnold Palmer Hospital is discussed in the Video Case Study at the end of this chapter.

Courtesy Arnold Palmer Medical Center

Courtesy Arnold Palmer Medical Center

OM in Action	Agile Project Management at Mastek

Agile project management has changed the way that Mastek Corp., in Mumbai, India, develops its educational software products. On a traditional well-defined project, managers are actively involved in directing work and telling their team what needs to be done—a style often referred to as a step-by-step *waterfall* style of project management.

Agile project management is different. In the early stages, the project manager creates a high-level plan, based on outline requirements and a high-level view of the solution. From that point, the end project is created iteratively and incrementally, with each increment building on the output of steps preceding it.

The principles of agile are essentially communication and transparency. Instead of waiting for something to be delivered, with limited understanding of the desired end result, there are numerous checkpoints and feedback loops to track progress.

Agile provides Mastek the ability to keep costs under control. Without agile, the cost of quality increases. "It's much harder to correct mistakes when a software product is nearing its final phase of development," says a company executive. "It's much better to develop it as you go along. I think agile project management would help any software developer."

Sources: AMPG International (2015) and **www.cprime.com** (2012).

Controlling projects can be difficult. The stakes are high; cost overruns and unnecessary delays can occur due to poor planning, scheduling, and controls. Some projects are "well-defined," whereas others may be "ill-defined." Projects typically only become well-defined after detailed extensive initial planning and careful definition of required inputs, resources, processes, and outputs. Well-established projects where constraints are known (e.g., buildings and roads) and engineered products (e.g., airplanes and cars) with well-defined specifications and drawings may fall into this category. Well-defined projects are assumed to have changes small enough to be managed without substantially revising plans. They use what is called a *waterfall* approach, where the project progresses smoothly, in a step-by-step manner, through each phase to completion.

But many projects, such as software development (e.g., 3-D games) and new technology (e.g., landing the Mars land rover) are ill-defined. These projects require what is known as an *agile* style of management with collaboration and constant feedback to adjust to the many unknowns of the evolving technology and project specifications. The *OM in Action* box "Agile Project Management at Mastek" provides such an example. Most projects fall somewhere between waterfall and agile.

Project Management Techniques: PERT and CPM

Program evaluation and review technique (PERT) and the critical path method (CPM) were both developed in the 1950s to help managers schedule, monitor, and control large and complex projects. CPM arrived first, as a tool developed to assist in the building and maintenance of chemical plants at duPont. Independently, PERT was developed in 1958 for the U.S. Navy.

Program evaluation and review technique (PERT)
A project management technique that employs three time estimates for each activity.

Critical path method (CPM)
A project management technique that uses only one time factor per activity.

The Framework of PERT and CPM

PERT and CPM both follow six basic steps:

1. Define the project and prepare the work breakdown structure.
2. Develop the relationships among the activities. Decide which activities must precede and which must follow others.
3. Draw the network connecting all the activities.
4. Assign time and/or cost estimates to each activity.
5. Compute the *longest* time path through the network. This is called the critical path.
6. Use the network to help plan, schedule, monitor, and control the project.

Critical path
The computed *longest* time path(s) through a network.

Step 5, finding the critical path, is a major part of controlling a project. The activities on the critical path represent tasks that will delay the entire project if they are not completed on time. Managers can gain the flexibility needed to complete critical tasks by identifying noncritical activities and replanning, rescheduling, and reallocating labor and financial resources.

Although PERT and CPM differ to some extent in terminology and in the construction of the network, their objectives are the same. Furthermore, the analysis used in both techniques is very similar. The major difference is that PERT employs three time estimates for each activity. These time estimates are used to compute expected values and standard deviations for the activity. CPM makes the assumption that activity times are known with certainty and hence requires only one time factor for each activity.

For purposes of illustration, the rest of this section concentrates on a discussion of PERT. Most of the comments and procedures described, however, apply just as well to CPM.

PERT and CPM are important because they can help answer questions such as the following about projects with thousands of activities:

1. When will the entire project be completed?
2. What are the critical activities or tasks in the project—that is, which activities will delay the entire project if they are late?
3. Which are the noncritical activities—the ones that can run late without delaying the whole project's completion?
4. What is the probability that the project will be completed by a specific date?
5. At any particular date, is the project on schedule, behind schedule, or ahead of schedule?
6. On any given date, is the money spent equal to, less than, or greater than the budgeted amount?
7. Are there enough resources available to finish the project on time?
8. If the project is to be finished in a shorter amount of time, what is the best way to accomplish this goal at the least cost?

Network Diagrams and Approaches

The first step in a PERT or CPM network is to divide the entire project into significant activities in accordance with the work breakdown structure. There are two approaches for drawing a project network: activity on node (AON) and activity on arrow (AOA). Under the AON convention, *nodes* designate activities. Under AOA, *arrows* represent activities. Activities consume time and resources. The basic difference between AON and AOA is that the nodes in an AON diagram represent activities. In an AOA network, the nodes represent the starting and finishing times of an activity and are also called *events*. So nodes in AOA consume neither time nor resources.

Although both AON and AOA are popular in practice, many of the project management software packages, including Microsoft Project, use AON networks. For this reason, although we illustrate both types of networks in the next examples, we focus on AON networks in subsequent discussions in this chapter.

Activity-on-node (AON)
A network diagram in which nodes designate activities.

Activity-on-arrow (AOA)
A network diagram in which arrows designate activities.

Example 1 | PREDECESSOR RELATIONSHIPS FOR POLLUTION CONTROL AT MILWAUKEE PAPER

Milwaukee Paper Manufacturing had long delayed the expense of installing advanced computerized air pollution control equipment in its facility. But when the board of directors adopted a new proactive policy on sustainability, it did not just *authorize* the budget for the state-of-the-art equipment. It directed the plant manager, Julie Ann Williams, to complete the installation in time for a major announcement of the policy, on Earth Day, exactly 16 weeks away! Under strict deadline from her bosses, Williams needs to be sure that installation of the filtering system progresses smoothly and on time.

Given the following information, develop a table showing activity precedence relationships.

APPROACH ▶ Milwaukee Paper has identified the eight activities that need to be performed in order for the project to be completed. When the project begins, two activities can be simultaneously started: building the internal components for the device (activity A) and the modifications necessary for the floor and roof (activity B). The construction of the collection stack (activity C) can begin when the internal components are completed. Pouring the concrete floor and installation of the frame (activity D) can be started as soon as the internal components are completed and the roof and floor have been modified.

After the collection stack has been constructed, two activities can begin: building the high-temperature burner (activity E) and installing the pollution control system (activity F). The air pollution device can be installed (activity G) after the concrete floor has been poured, the frame has been installed, and the high-temperature burner has been built. Finally, after the control system and pollution device have been installed, the system can be inspected and tested (activity H).

SOLUTION ▶   Activities and precedence relationships may seem rather confusing when they are presented in this descriptive form. It is therefore convenient to list all the activity information in a table, as shown in Table 3.1. We see in the table that activity A is listed as an *immediate predecessor* of activity C. Likewise, both activities D and E must be performed prior to starting activity G.

TABLE 3.1	Milwaukee Paper Manufacturing's Activities and Predecessors	
ACTIVITY	**DESCRIPTION**	**IMMEDIATE PREDECESSORS**
A	Build internal components	—
B	Modify roof and floor	—
C	Construct collection stack	A
D	Pour concrete and install frame	A, B
E	Build high-temperature burner	C
F	Install pollution control system	C
G	Install air pollution device	D, E
H	Inspect and test	F, G

INSIGHT ▶   To complete a network, all predecessors must be clearly defined.

LEARNING EXERCISE ▶   What is the impact on this sequence of activities if Environmental Protection Agency (EPA) approval is required after *Inspect and Test*? [Answer: The immediate predecessor for the new activity would be H, *Inspect and Test*, with *EPA approval* as the last activity.]

Activity-on-Node Example

Note that in Example 1, we only list the *immediate* predecessors for each activity. For instance, in Table 3.1, because activity A precedes activity C, and activity C precedes activity E, the fact that activity A precedes activity E is *implicit*. This relationship need not be explicitly shown in the activity precedence relationships.

When there are many activities in a project with fairly complicated precedence relationships, it is difficult for an individual to comprehend the complexity of the project from just the tabular information. In such cases, a visual representation of the project, using a *project network*, is convenient and useful. A project network is a diagram of all the activities and the precedence relationships that exist between these activities in a project. Example 2 illustrates how to construct an AON project network for Milwaukee Paper Manufacturing.

LO 3.2 *Draw* AOA and AON networks

It is convenient to have the project network start and finish with a unique node. In the Milwaukee Paper example, it turns out that a unique activity, H, is the last activity in the project. We therefore automatically have a unique ending node.

In situations in which a project has multiple ending activities, we include a "dummy" ending activity. We illustrate this type of situation in Solved Problem 3.1 at the end of this chapter.

Example 2

AON GRAPH FOR MILWAUKEE PAPER

Draw the AON network for Milwaukee Paper, using the data in Example 1.

APPROACH ▶ In the AON approach, we denote each activity by a node. The lines, or arrows, represent the precedence relationships between the activities.

SOLUTION ▶ In this example, there are two activities (A and B) that do not have any predecessors. We draw separate nodes for each of these activities, as shown in Figure 3.5. Although not required, it is usually convenient to have a unique starting activity for a project. We have therefore included a *dummy activity* called *Start* in Figure 3.5. This dummy activity does not really exist and takes up zero time and resources. Activity *Start* is an immediate predecessor for both activities A and B, and it serves as the unique starting activity for the entire project.

Dummy activity

An activity having no time that is inserted into a network to maintain the logic of the network.

Figure 3.5

Beginning AON Network for Milwaukee Paper

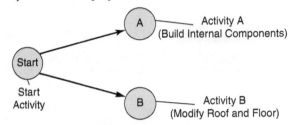

We now show the precedence relationships using lines with arrow symbols. For example, an arrow from activity Start to activity A indicates that Start is a predecessor for activity A. In a similar fashion, we draw an arrow from Start to B.

Next, we add a new node for activity C. Because activity A precedes activity C, we draw an arrow from node A to node C (see Figure 3.6). Likewise, we first draw a node to represent activity D. Then, because activities A and B both precede activity D, we draw arrows from A to D and from B to D (see Figure 3.6).

Figure 3.6

Intermediate AON Network for Milwaukee Paper

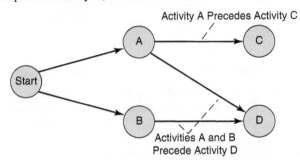

We proceed in this fashion, adding a separate node for each activity and a separate line for each precedence relationship that exists. The complete AON project network for the Milwaukee Paper Manufacturing project is shown in Figure 3.7.

Figure 3.7

Complete AON Network for Milwaukee Paper

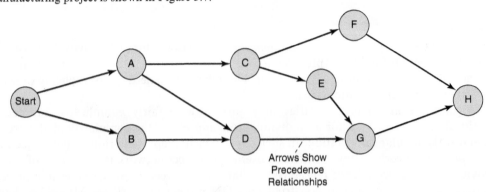

INSIGHT ▶ Drawing a project network properly takes some time and experience. We would like the lines to be straight and arrows to move to the right when possible.

LEARNING EXERCISE ▶ If *EPA Approval* occurs after *Inspect and Test*, what is the impact on the graph? [Answer: A straight line is extended to the right beyond H (with a node I added) to reflect the additional activity.]

RELATED PROBLEMS ▶ 3.4a, 3.5, 3.8, 3.9, 3.10, 3.11a, 3.12 (3.13–3.14 are available in MyOMLab)

Activity-on-Arrow Example

In an AOA project network we can represent activities by arrows. A node represents an *event*, which marks the start or completion time of an activity. We usually identify an event (node) by a number.

Example 3

ACTIVITY-ON-ARROW FOR MILWAUKEE PAPER

Draw the complete AOA project network for Milwaukee Paper's problem.

APPROACH ▶ Using the data from Table 3.1 in Example 1, draw one activity at a time, starting with A.

SOLUTION ▶ We see that activity A starts at event 1 and ends at event 2. Likewise, activity B starts at event 1 and ends at event 3. Activity C, whose only immediate predecessor is activity A, starts at node 2 and ends at node 4. Activity D, however, has two predecessors (i.e., A and B). Hence, we need both activities A and B to end at event 3, so that activity D can start at that event. However, we cannot have multiple activities with common starting and ending nodes in an AOA network. To overcome this difficulty, in such cases, we may need to add a dummy line (activity) to enforce the precedence relationship. The dummy activity, shown in Figure 3.8 as a dashed line, is inserted between events 2 and 3 to make the diagram reflect the precedence between A and D. The remainder of the AOA project network for Milwaukee Paper's example is also shown.

Figure 3.8

Complete AOA Network (with Dummy Activity) for Milwaukee Paper

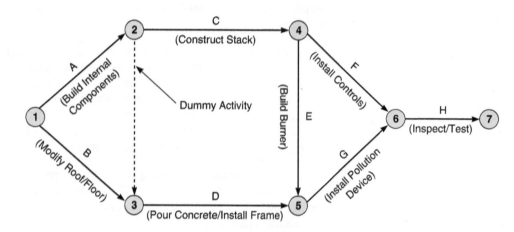

STUDENT TIP ◉
The dummy activity consumes no time, but note how it changes precedence. Now activity D cannot begin until *both* B and the dummy are complete.

INSIGHT ▶ Dummy activities are common in AOA networks. They do not really exist in the project and take zero time.

LEARNING EXERCISE ▶ A new activity, *EPA Approval*, follows activity H. Add it to Figure 3.8. [Answer: Insert an arrowed line from node 7, which ends at a new node 8, and is labeled I (EPA Approval).]

RELATED PROBLEMS ▶ 3.4b, 3.6, 3.7

Determining the Project Schedule

Look back at Figure 3.7 (in Example 2) for a moment to see Milwaukee Paper's completed AON project network. Once this project network has been drawn to show all the activities and their precedence relationships, the next step is to determine the project schedule. That is, we need to identify the planned starting and ending time for each activity.

Let us assume Milwaukee Paper estimates the time required for each activity, in weeks, as shown in Table 3.2. The table indicates that the total time for all eight of the company's activities is 25 weeks. However, because several activities can take place simultaneously, it is clear that the total project completion time may be less than 25 weeks. To find out just how long the project will take, we perform the critical path analysis for the network.

Critical path analysis
A process that helps determine a project schedule.

TABLE 3.2	Time Estimates for Milwaukee Paper Manufacturing	
ACTIVITY	DESCRIPTION	TIME (WEEKS)
A	Build internal components	2
B	Modify roof and floor	3
C	Construct collection stack	2
D	Pour concrete and install frame	4
E	Build high-temperature burner	4
F	Install pollution control system	3
G	Install air pollution device	5
H	Inspect and test	2
	Total time (weeks)	25

STUDENT TIP ◆

Does this mean the project will take 25 weeks to complete? No. Don't forget that several of the activities are being performed at the same time. It would take 25 weeks if they were done sequentially.

As mentioned earlier, the critical path is the *longest* time path through the network. To find the critical path, we calculate two distinct starting and ending times for each activity. These are defined as follows:

Earliest start (ES) = earliest time at which an activity can start, assuming all predecessors have been completed
Earliest finish (EF) = earliest time at which an activity can be finished
Latest start (LS) = latest time at which an activity can start so as to not delay the completion time of the entire project
Latest finish (LF) = latest time by which an activity has to finish so as to not delay the completion time of the entire project

We use a two-pass process, consisting of a forward pass and a backward pass, to determine these time schedules for each activity. The early start and finish times (ES and EF) are determined during the forward pass. The late start and finish times (LS and LF) are determined during the backward pass.

Forward pass

A process that identifies all the early times.

LO 3.3 *Complete forward and backward passes for a project*

Forward Pass

To clearly show the activity schedules on the project network, we use the notation shown in Figure 3.9. The ES of an activity is shown in the top left corner of the node denoting that activity. The EF is shown in the top right corner. The latest times, LS and LF, are shown in the bottom-left and bottom-right corners, respectively.

Figure 3.9

Notation Used in Nodes for Forward and Backward Pass

Earliest Start Time Rule   Before an activity can start, *all* its immediate predecessors must be finished:

◆ If an activity has only a single immediate predecessor, its ES equals the EF of the predecessor.

◆ If an activity has multiple immediate predecessors, its ES is the maximum of all EF values of its predecessors. That is:

$$ES = Max \{EF \text{ of all immediate predecessors}\} \qquad (3\text{-}1)$$

◑ STUDENT TIP

All predecessor activities must be completed before an acitivity can begin.

Earliest Finish Time Rule   The earliest finish time (EF) of an activity is the sum of its earliest start time (ES) and its activity time. That is:

$$EF = ES + \text{Activity time} \qquad (3\text{-}2)$$

Example 4 | COMPUTING EARLIEST START AND FINISH TIMES FOR MILWAUKEE PAPER

Calculate the earliest start and finish times for the activities in the Milwaukee Paper Manufacturing project.

APPROACH ▶   Use Table 3.2, which contains the activity times. Complete the project network for the company's project, along with the ES and EF values for all activities.

SOLUTION ▶   With the help of Figure 3.10, we describe how these values are calculated.

Because activity Start has no predecessors, we begin by setting its ES to 0. That is, activity Start can begin at time 0, which is the same as the beginning of week 1. If activity Start has an ES of 0, its EF is also 0, since its activity time is 0.

Next, we consider activities A and B, both of which have only Start as an immediate predecessor. Using the earliest start time rule, the ES for both activities A and B equals zero, which is the EF of activity Start. Now, using the earliest finish time rule, the EF for A is 2 (= 0 + 2), and the EF for B is 3 (= 0 + 3).

Since activity A precedes activity C, the ES of C equals the EF of A (= 2). The EF of C is therefore 4 (= 2 + 2).

We now come to activity D. Both activities A and B are immediate predecessors for D. Whereas A has an EF of 2, activity B has an EF of 3. Using the earliest start time rule, we compute the ES of activity D as follows:

$$ES \text{ of } D = Max\{EF \text{ of } A, EF \text{ of } B\} = Max (2, 3) = 3$$

The EF of D equals 7 (= 3 + 4). Next, both activities E and F have activity C as their only immediate predecessor. Therefore, the ES for both E and F equals 4 (= EF of C). The EF of E is 8 (= 4 + 4), and the EF of F is 7 (= 4 + 3).

Activity G has both activities D and E as predecessors. Using the earliest start time rule, its ES is therefore the maximum of the EF of D and the EF of E. Hence, the ES of activity G equals 8 (= maximum of 7 and 8), and its EF equals 13 (= 8 + 5).

Finally, we come to activity H. Because it also has two predecessors, F and G, the ES of H is the maximum EF of these two activities. That is, the ES of H equals 13 (= maximum of 13 and 7). This implies that the EF of H is 15 (= 13 + 2). Because H is the last activity in the project, this also implies that the earliest time in which the entire project can be completed is 15 weeks.

INSIGHT ▶   The ES of an activity that has only one predecessor is simply the EF of that predecessor. For an activity with more than one predecessor, we must carefully examine the EFs of all immediate predecessors and choose the largest one.

LEARNING EXERCISE ▶   A new activity I, *EPA Approval*, takes 1 week. Its predecessor is activity H. What are I's ES and EF? [Answer: 15, 16]

RELATED PROBLEMS ▶   3.15, 3.16, 3.19c

EXCEL **OM** Data File **Ch03Ex4.xls** can be found in MyOMLab.

Although the forward pass allows us to determine the earliest project completion time, it does not identify the critical path. To identify this path, we need to now conduct the backward pass to determine the LS and LF values for all activities.

Figure 3.10   **Earliest Start and Earliest Finish Times for Milwaukee Paper**

Backward Pass

Backward pass

An activity that finds all the late start and late finish times.

Just as the forward pass began with the first activity in the project, the backward pass begins with the last activity in the project. For each activity, we first determine its LF value, followed by its LS value. The following two rules are used in this process.

Latest Finish Time Rule   This rule is again based on the fact that before an activity can start, all its immediate predecessors must be finished:

- If an activity is an immediate predecessor for just a single activity, its LF equals the LS of the activity that immediately follows it.
- If an activity is an immediate predecessor to more than one activity, its LF is the minimum of all LS values of all activities that immediately follow it. That is:

$$\text{LF} = \text{Min\{LS of all immediate following activities\}} \qquad (3\text{-}3)$$

Latest Start Time Rule   The latest start time (LS) of an activity is the difference of its latest finish time (LF) and its activity time. That is:

$$\text{LS} = \text{LF} - \text{Activity time} \qquad (3\text{-}4)$$

Example 5 | **COMPUTING LATEST START AND FINISH TIMES FOR MILWAUKEE PAPER**

Calculate the latest start and finish times for each activity in Milwaukee Paper's pollution project.

APPROACH ▶ Use Figure 3.10 as a beginning point. Overlay 1 of Figure 3.10 shows the complete project network for Milwaukee Paper, along with added LS and LF values for all activities. In what follows, we see how these values were calculated.

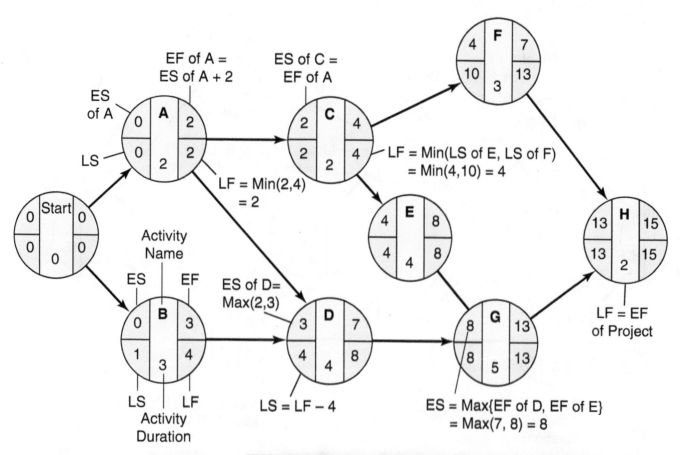

ES of A
EF of A = ES of A + 2
ES of C = EF of A

LS

LF = Min(2,4) = 2

Activity Name

ES   EF

ES of D= Max(2,3)

LS   LF
Activity Duration

LF = Min(LS of E, LS of F) = Min(4,10) = 4

LS = LF − 4

ES = Max{EF of D, EF of E} = Max(7, 8) = 8

LF = EF of Project

Figure **3.10**   Overlay 1: Latest Start and Finish Times Are Now Added.

1

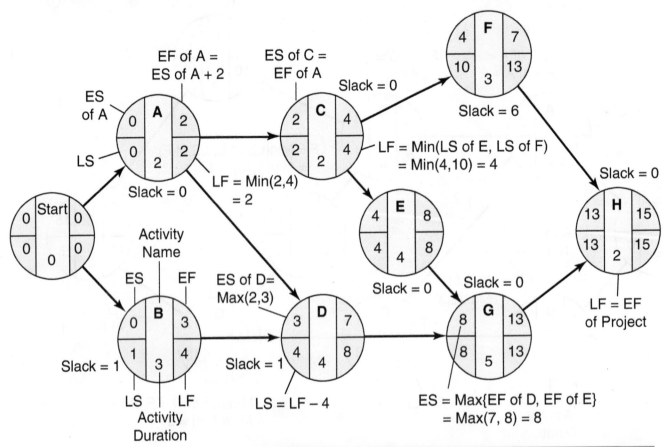

Figure **3.10**   Overlay 2: Slack Times Are Now Computed and Added.

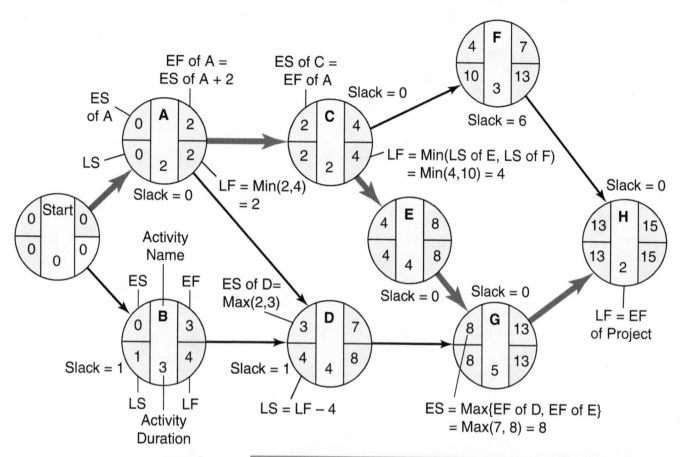

Figure **3.10** | Overlay 3: The Critical Path Is Now Shown in Five Thick Blue Lines.

3

SOLUTION ▶ We begin by assigning an LF value of 15 weeks for activity H. That is, we specify that the latest finish time for the entire project is the same as its earliest finish time. Using the latest start time rule, the LS of activity H is equal to 13 (= 15 − 2).

Because activity H is the lone succeeding activity for both activities F and G, the LF for both F and G equals 13. This implies that the LS of G is 8 (= 13 − 5), and the LS of F is 10 (= 13 − 3).

Proceeding in this fashion, we see that the LF of E is 8 (= LS of G), and its LS is 4 (= 8 − 4). Likewise, the LF of D is 8 (= LS of G), and its LS is 4 (= 8 − 4).

We now consider activity C, which is an immediate predecessor to two activities: E and F. Using the latest finish time rule, we compute the LF of activity C as follows:

$$\text{LF of C} = \text{Min}\{\text{LS of E, LS of F}\} = \text{Min}(4, 10) = 4$$

The LS of C is computed as 2 (= 4 − 2). Next, we compute the LF of B as 4 (= LS of D) and its LS as 1 (= 4 − 3).

We now consider activity A. We compute its LF as 2 (= minimum of LS of C and LS of D). Hence, the LS of activity A is 0 (= 2 − 2). Finally, both the LF and LS of activity Start are equal to 0.

INSIGHT ▶ The LF of an activity that is the predecessor of only one activity is just the LS of that following activity. If the activity is the predecessor to more than one activity, its LF is the smallest LS value of all activities that follow immediately.

LEARNING EXERCISE ▶ A new activity I, *EPA Approval*, takes 1 week. Its predecessor is activity H. What are I's LS and LF? [Answer: 15, 16]

RELATED PROBLEMS ▶ 3.15, 3.19c

Calculating Slack Time and Identifying the Critical Path(s)

After we have computed the earliest and latest times for all activities, it is a simple matter to find the amount of slack time that each activity has. Slack is the length of time an activity can be delayed without delaying the entire project. Mathematically:

$$\text{Slack} = \text{LS} − \text{ES} \quad \text{or} \quad \text{Slack} = \text{LF} − \text{EF} \tag{3-5}$$

Slack time
Free time for an activity. Also referred to as free float or free slack.

Example 6

CALCULATING SLACK TIMES FOR MILWAUKEE PAPER

Calculate the slack for the activities in the Milwaukee Paper project.

APPROACH ▶ Start with the data in Overlay 1 of Figure 3.10 in Example 5 and develop Table 3.3 one line at a time.

SOLUTION ▶ Table 3.3 summarizes the ES, EF, LS, LF, and slack time for all of the firm's activities. Activity B, for example, has 1 week of slack time because its LS is 1 and its ES is 0 (alternatively, its LF is 4 and its EF is 3). This means that activity B can be delayed by up to 1 week, and the whole project can still be finished in 15 weeks.

On the other hand, activities A, C, E, G, and H have *no* slack time. This means that none of them can be delayed without delaying the entire project. Conversely, if plant manager Julie Ann Williams wants to reduce the total project times, she will have to reduce the length of one of these activities.

Overlay 2 of Figure 3.10 shows the slack computed for each activity.

INSIGHT ▶ Slack may be computed from either early/late starts or early/late finishes. The key is to find which activities have zero slack.

TABLE 3.3		Milwaukee Paper's Schedule and Slack Times					
ACTIVITY	ACTIVITY TIME	EARLIEST START ES	EARLIEST FINISH EF	LATEST START LS	LATEST FINISH LF	SLACK LS – ES	ON CRITICAL PATH
A	2	0	2	0	2	0	Yes
B	3	0	3	1	4	1	No
C	2	2	4	2	4	0	Yes
D	4	3	7	4	8	1	No
E	4	4	8	4	8	0	Yes
F	3	4	7	10	13	6	No
G	5	8	13	8	13	0	Yes
H	2	13	15	13	15	0	Yes

LEARNING EXERCISE ▶ A new activity I, *EPA Approval*, follows activity H and takes 1 week. Is it on the critical path? [Answer: Yes, it's LS – ES = 0]

RELATED PROBLEMS ▶ 3.8d, 3.15d, 3.19c

ACTIVE **MODEL** 3.1 This example is further illustrated in Active Model 3.1 in MyOMLab.

LO 3.4 *Determine a critical path*

The activities with zero slack are called *critical activities* and are said to be on the critical path. The critical path is a continuous path through the project network that:

- Starts at the first activity in the project (Start in our example).
- Terminates at the last activity in the project (H in our example).
- Includes only critical activities (i.e., activities with no slack time).

Example 7

SHOWING CRITICAL PATH WITH BLUE ARROWS

Show Milwaukee Paper's critical path and find the project completion time.

APPROACH ▶ We use Table 3.3 and Overlay 3 of Figure 3.10. Overlay 3 of Figure 3.10 indicates that the total project completion time of 15 weeks corresponds to the longest path in the network. That path is Start-A-C-E-G-H in network form. It is shown with thick blue arrows.

INSIGHT ▶ The critical path follows the activities with slack = 0. This is considered the longest path through the network.

LEARNING EXERCISE ▶ Why are activities B, D, and F not on the path with the thick blue line? [Answer: They are not critical and have slack values of 1, 1, and 6 weeks, respectively.]

RELATED PROBLEMS ▶ 3.5–3.11, 3.16, 3.19b, 3.21a

Total Slack Time Look again at the project network in Overlay 3 of Figure 3.10. Consider activities B and D, which have slack of 1 week each. Does it mean that we can delay *each* activity by 1 week, and still complete the project in 15 weeks? The answer is no.

Let's assume that activity B is delayed by 1 week. It has used up its slack of 1 week and now has an EF of 4. This implies that activity D now has an ES of 4 and an EF of 8. Note that these are also its LS and LF values, respectively. That is, activity D also has no slack time now. Essentially, the slack of 1 week that activities B and D had is, for that path, *shared* between them. Delaying either activity by 1 week causes not only that activity, but also the other activity, to lose its slack. This type of a slack time is referred to as *total slack*. Typically, when two or more noncritical activities appear successively in a path, they share total slack.

To plan, monitor, and control the huge number of details involved in sponsoring a rock festival attended by more than 100,000 fans, managers use Microsoft Project and the tools discussed in this chapter. The *Video Case Study* "Managing Hard Rock's Rockfest," at the end of the chapter, provides more details of the management task.

Variability in Activity Times

In identifying all earliest and latest times so far, and the associated critical path(s), we have adopted the CPM approach of assuming that all activity times are known and fixed constants. That is, there is no variability in activity times. However, in practice, it is likely that activity completion times vary depending on various factors.

For example, building internal components (activity A) for Milwaukee Paper Manufacturing is estimated to finish in 2 weeks. Clearly, supply-chain issues such as late arrival of materials, absence of key personnel, and so on could delay this activity. Suppose activity A actually ends up taking 3 weeks. Because A is on the critical path, the entire project will now be delayed by 1 week to 16 weeks. If we had anticipated completion of this project in 15 weeks, we would obviously miss our Earth Day deadline.

Although some activities may be relatively less prone to delays, others could be extremely susceptible to delays. For example, activity B (modify roof and floor) could be heavily dependent on weather conditions. A spell of bad weather could significantly affect its completion time.

This means that we cannot ignore the impact of variability in activity times when deciding the schedule for a project. PERT addresses this issue.

Three Time Estimates in PERT

In PERT, we employ a probability distribution based on three time estimates for each activity, as follows:

Optimistic time (a) = time an activity will take if everything goes as planned. In estimating this value, there should be only a small probability (say, 1/100) that the activity time will be $< a$.

Pessimistic time (b) = time an activity will take assuming very unfavorable conditions. In estimating this value, there should also be only a small probability (also 1/100) that the activity time will be $> b$.

Most likely time (m) = most realistic estimate of the time required to complete an activity.

When using PERT, we often assume that activity time estimates follow the beta probability distribution (see Figure 3.11). This continuous distribution is often appropriate for determining the expected value and variance for activity completion times.

♦ STUDENT TIP

PERT's ability to handle three time estimates for each activity enables us to compute the probability that we can complete the project by a target date.

Optimistic time
The "best" activity completion time that could be obtained in a PERT network.

Pessimistic time
The "worst" activity time that could be expected in a PERT network.

Most likely time
The most probable time to complete an activity in a PERT network.

Figure 3.11

Beta Probability Distribution with Three Time Estimates

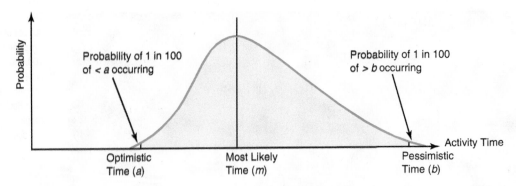

To find the *expected activity time*, *t*, the beta distribution weights the three time estimates as follows:

$$t = (a + 4m + b)/6 \qquad (3\text{-}6)$$

That is, the most likely time (*m*) is given four times the weight as the optimistic time (*a*) and pessimistic time (*b*). The time estimate *t* computed using Equation (3-6) for each activity is used in the project network to compute all earliest and latest times.

To compute the *dispersion* or *variance of activity completion time*, we use the formula:[1]

$$\text{Variance} = [(b - a)/6]^2 \qquad (3\text{-}7)$$

Example 8

EXPECTED TIMES AND VARIANCES FOR MILWAUKEE PAPER

Julie Ann Williams and the project management team at Milwaukee Paper want an expected time and variance for Activity F (Installing the Pollution Control System) where:

$$a = 1 \text{ week}, m = 2 \text{ weeks}, b = 9 \text{ weeks}$$

APPROACH ▶   Use Equations (3–6) and (3–7) to compute the expected time and variance for F.

SOLUTION ▶   The expected time for Activity F is:

$$t = \frac{a + 4m + b}{6} = \frac{1 + 4(2) + 9}{6} = \frac{18}{6} = 3 \text{ weeks}$$

LO 3.5 *Calculate* the variance of activity times

The variance for Activity F is:

$$\text{Variance} = \left[\frac{(b - a)}{6}\right]^2 = \left[\frac{(9 - 1)}{6}\right]^2 = \left(\frac{8}{6}\right)^2 = \frac{64}{36} = 1.78$$

INSIGHT ▶   Williams now has information that allows her to understand and manage Activity F. The expected time is, in fact, the activity time used in our earlier computation and identification of the critical path.

LEARNING EXERCISE ▶   Review the expected times and variances for all of the other activities in the project. These are shown in Table 3.4.

TABLE 3.4   **Time Estimates (in weeks) for Milwaukee Paper's Project**

ACTIVITY	OPTIMISTIC a	MOST LIKELY m	PESSIMISTIC b	EXPECTED TIME $t = (a + 4m + b)/6$	VARIANCE $[(b - a)/6]^2$
A	1	2	3	2	$[(3 - 1)/6]^2 = 4/36 = .11$
B	2	3	4	3	$[(4 - 2)/6]^2 = 4/36 = .11$
C	1	2	3	2	$[(3 - 1)/6]^2 = 4/36 = .11$
D	2	4	6	4	$[(6 - 2)/6]^2 = 16/36 = .44$
E	1	4	7	4	$[(7 - 1)/6]^2 = 36/36 = 1.00$
F	1	2	9	3	$[(9 - 1)/6]^2 = 64/36 = 1.78$
G	3	4	11	5	$[(11 - 3)/6]^2 = 64/36 = 1.78$
H	1	2	3	2	$[(3 - 1)/6]^2 = 4/36 = .11$

RELATED PROBLEMS ▶   3.17a, b, 3.18, 3.19a, 3.20a (3.26b, 3.27 are available in MyOMLab)

EXCEL **OM** Data File **Ch03Ex8.xls** can be found in MyOMLab.

Kim Hong-Ji/Reuters

Here we see a ship being built at the Hyundai shipyard, Asia's largest shipbuilder, in Korea. Managing this project uses the same techniques as managing the remodeling of a store, installing a new production line, or implementing a new computer system.

Probability of Project Completion

The critical path analysis helped us determine that Milwaukee Paper's expected project completion time is 15 weeks. Julie Ann Williams knows, however, that there is significant variation in the time estimates for several activities. Variation in activities that are on the critical path can affect the overall project completion time—possibly delaying it. This is one occurrence that worries the plant manager considerably.

PERT uses the variance of critical path activities to help determine the variance of the overall project. Project variance is computed by summing variances of *critical* activities:

$$\sigma_p^2 = \text{Project variance} = \Sigma(\text{variances of activities on critical path}) \qquad (3\text{-}8)$$

Example 9

COMPUTING PROJECT VARIANCE AND STANDARD DEVIATION FOR MILWAUKEE PAPER

Milwaukee Paper's managers now wish to know the project's variance and standard deviation.

APPROACH ▶   Because the activities are independent, we can add the variances of the activities on the critical path and then take the square root to determine the project's standard deviation.

SOLUTION ▶   From Example 8 (Table 3.4), we have the variances of all of the activities on the critical path. Specifically, we know that the variance of activity A is 0.11, variance of activity C is 0.11, variance of activity E is 1.00, variance of activity G is 1.78, and variance of activity H is 0.11.

Compute the total project variance and project standard deviation:

$$\text{Project variance}\,(\sigma_p^2) = 0.11 + 0.11 + 1.00 + 1.78 + 0.11 = 3.11$$

which implies:

$$\text{Project standard deviation}\,(\sigma_p) = \sqrt{\text{Project variance}} = \sqrt{3.11} = 1.76 \text{ weeks}$$

INSIGHT ▶   Management now has an estimate not only of expected completion time for the project but also of the standard deviation of that estimate.

LEARNING EXERCISE ▶   If the variance for activity A is actually 0.30 (instead of 0.11), what is the new project standard deviation? [Answer: 1.817.]

RELATED PROBLEMS ▶   3.17e (3.24 is available in MyOMLab)

Figure **3.12**

Probability Distribution for Project Completion Times at Milwaukee Paper

How can this information be used to help answer questions regarding the probability of finishing the project on time? PERT makes two more assumptions: (1) total project completion times follow a normal probability distribution, and (2) activity times are statistically independent. With these assumptions, the bell-shaped normal curve shown in Figure 3.12 can be used to represent project completion dates. This normal curve implies that there is a 50% chance that the manufacturer's project completion time will be less than 15 weeks and a 50% chance that it will exceed 15 weeks.

Example 10

PROBABILITY OF COMPLETING A PROJECT ON TIME

Julie Ann Williams would like to find the probability that her project will be finished on or before the 16-week Earth Day deadline.

APPROACH ▶ To do so, she needs to determine the appropriate area under the normal curve. This is the area to the left of the 16th week.

SOLUTION ▶ The standard normal equation can be applied as follows:

$$Z = (\text{Due date} - \text{Expected date of completion})/\sigma_p$$
$$= (16 \text{ weeks} - 15 \text{ weeks})/1.76 \text{ weeks} = 0.57 \tag{3-9}$$

> **STUDENT TIP** ◀
>
> Here is a chance to review your statistical skills and use of a normal distribution table (Appendix I).

where Z is the number of standard deviations the due date or target date lies from the mean or expected date.

Referring to the Normal Table in Appendix I (alternatively using the Excel formula =NORMSDIST(0.57)), we find a Z-value of 0.57 to the right of the mean indicates a probability of 0.7157. Thus, there is a 71.57% chance that the pollution control equipment can be put in place in 16 weeks or less. This is shown in Figure 3.13.

Figure **3.13**

Probability That Milwaukee Paper Will Meet the 16-Week Deadline

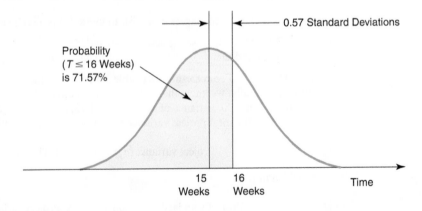

INSIGHT ▶ The shaded area to the left of the 16th week (71.57%) represents the probability that the project will be completed in less than 16 weeks.

LEARNING EXERCISE ▶ What is the probability that the project will be completed on or before the 17th week? [Answer: About 87.2%.]

RELATED PROBLEMS ▶ 3.17f, 3.19d, 3.20d, 3.21b, 3.23 (3.25, 3.26e,f,g are available in MyOMLab)

Determining Project Completion Time for a Given Confidence Level Let's say Julie Ann Williams is worried that there is only a 71.57% chance that the pollution control equipment can be put in place in 16 weeks or less. She thinks that it may be possible to plead with the board of directors for more time. However, before she approaches the board, she wants to arm herself with sufficient information about the project. Specifically, she wants to find the deadline by which she has a 99% chance of completing the project. She hopes to use her analysis to convince the board to agree to this extended deadline, even though she is aware of the public relations damage the delay will cause.

Clearly, this due date would be greater than 16 weeks. However, what is the exact value of this new due date? To answer this question, we again use the assumption that Milwaukee Paper's project completion time follows a normal probability distribution with a mean of 15 weeks and a standard deviation of 1.76 weeks.

Example 11

COMPUTING PROBABILITY FOR ANY COMPLETION DATE

Julie Ann Williams wants to find the due date that gives her company's project a 99% chance of *on-time* completion.

APPROACH ▶ She first needs to compute the Z-value corresponding to 99%, as shown in Figure 3.14. Mathematically, this is similar to Example 10, except the unknown is now the due date rather than Z.

Figure **3.14**

Z-Value for 99% Probability of Project Completion at Milwaukee Paper

SOLUTION ▶ Referring again to the Normal Table in Appendix I (alternatively using the Excel formula =NORMSINV(0.99)), we identify a Z-value of 2.33 as being closest to the probability of 0.99. That is, Julie Ann Williams's due date should be 2.33 standard deviations above the mean project completion time. Starting with the standard normal equation [see Equation (3-9)], we can solve for the due date and rewrite the equation as:

$$\text{Due date} = \text{Expected completion time} + (Z \times \sigma_p)$$
$$= 15 + (2.33 \times 1.76) = 19.1 \text{ weeks} \qquad (3\text{-}10)$$

INSIGHT ▶ If Williams can get the board to agree to give her a new deadline of 19.1 weeks (or more), she can be 99% sure of finishing the project by that new target date.

LEARNING EXERCISE ▶ What due date gives the project a 95% chance of on-time completion? [Answer: About 17.9 weeks.]

RELATED PROBLEMS ▶ 3.21c, 3.23e

Variability in Completion Time of Noncritical Paths In our discussion so far, we have focused exclusively on the variability in the completion times of activities on the critical path. This seems logical because these activities are, by definition, the more important activities in a project network. However, when there is variability in activity times, it is important that we also investigate the variability in the completion times of activities on *noncritical* paths.

Consider, for example, activity D in Milwaukee Paper's project. Recall from Overlay 3 in Figure 3.10 (in Example 7) that this is a noncritical activity, with a slack time of 1 week. We have therefore not considered the variability in D's time in computing the probabilities of project completion times. We observe, however, that D has a variance of 0.44 (see Table 3.4 in

Example 8). In fact, the pessimistic completion time for D is 6 weeks. This means that if D ends up taking its pessimistic time to finish, the project will not finish in 15 weeks, even though D is not a critical activity.

For this reason, when we find probabilities of project completion times, it may be necessary for us to not focus only on the critical path(s). Indeed, some research has suggested that expending project resources to reduce the variability of activities not on the critical path can be an effective element in project management. We may need also to compute these probabilities for noncritical paths, especially those that have relatively large variances. It is possible for a noncritical path to have a smaller probability of completion within a due date, when compared with the critical path. Determining the variance and probability of completion for a noncritical path is done in the same manner as Examples 9 and 10.

What Project Management Has Provided So Far Project management techniques have thus far been able to provide Julie Ann Williams with several valuable pieces of management information:

1. The project's expected completion date is 15 weeks.
2. There is a 71.57% chance that the equipment will be in place within the 16-week deadline. PERT analysis can easily find the probability of finishing by any date Williams is interested in.
3. Five activities (A, C, E, G, and H) are on the critical path. If any one of these is delayed for any reason, the entire project will be delayed.
4. Three activities (B, D, F) are not critical and have some slack time built in. This means that Williams can borrow from their resources, and, if necessary, she may be able to speed up the whole project.
5. A detailed schedule of activity starting and ending dates, slack, and critical path activities has been made available (see Table 3.3 in Example 6).

Cost-Time Trade-Offs and Project Crashing

While managing a project, it is not uncommon for a project manager to be faced with either (or both) of the following situations: (1) the project is behind schedule, and (2) the scheduled project completion time has been moved forward. In either situation, some or all of the remaining activities need to be speeded up (usually by adding resources) to finish the project by the desired due date. The process by which we shorten the duration of a project in the cheapest manner possible is called project crashing.

Crashing

Shortening activity time in a network to reduce time on the critical path so total completion time is reduced.

CPM is a technique in which each activity has a *normal* or *standard* time that we use in our computations. Associated with this normal time is the *normal* cost of the activity. However, another time in project management is the *crash time*, which is defined as the shortest duration required to complete an activity. Associated with this crash time is the *crash cost* of the activity. Usually, we can shorten an activity by adding extra resources (e.g., equipment, people) to it. Hence, it is logical for the crash cost of an activity to be higher than its normal cost.

The amount by which an activity can be shortened (i.e., the difference between its normal time and crash time) depends on the activity in question. We may not be able to shorten some activities at all. For example, if a casting needs to be heat-treated in the furnace for 48 hours, adding more resources does not help shorten the time. In contrast, we may be able to shorten some activities significantly (e.g., frame a house in 3 days instead of 10 days by using three times as many workers).

Likewise, the cost of crashing (or shortening) an activity depends on the nature of the activity. Managers are usually interested in speeding up a project at the least additional cost. Hence, when choosing which activities to crash, and by how much, we need to ensure the following:

- The amount by which an activity is crashed is, in fact, permissible
- Taken together, the shortened activity durations will enable us to finish the project by the due date
- The total cost of crashing is as small as possible

Crashing a project involves four steps:

LO 3.6 *Crash* a project

STEP 1: Compute the crash cost per week (or other time period) for each activity in the network. If crash costs are linear over time, the following formula can be used:

$$\text{Crash cost per period} = \frac{(\text{Crash cost} - \text{Normal cost})}{(\text{Normal time} - \text{Crash time})} \qquad (3\text{-}11)$$

STEP 2: Using the current activity times, find the critical path(s) in the project network. Identify the critical activities.

STEP 3: If there is only one critical path, then select the activity on this critical path that (a) can still be crashed and (b) has the smallest crash cost per period. Crash this activity by one period.

   If there is more than one critical path, then select one activity from each critical path such that (a) each selected activity can still be crashed and (b) the total crash cost per period of *all* selected activities is the smallest. Crash each activity by one period. Note that the same activity may be common to more than one critical path.

STEP 4: Update all activity times. If the desired due date has been reached, stop. If not, return to Step 2.

We illustrate project crashing in Example 12.

Example 12

PROJECT CRASHING TO MEET A DEADLINE AT MILWAUKEE PAPER

Suppose the plant manager at Milwaukee Paper Manufacturing has been given only 13 weeks (instead of 16 weeks) to install the new pollution control equipment. As you recall, the length of Julie Ann Williams's critical path was 15 weeks, but she must now complete the project in 13 weeks.

APPROACH ▶ Williams needs to determine which activities to crash, and by how much, to meet this 13-week due date. Naturally, Williams is interested in speeding up the project by 2 weeks, at the least additional cost.

SOLUTION ▶ The company's normal and crash times, and normal and crash costs, are shown in Table 3.5. Note, for example, that activity B's normal time is 3 weeks (the estimate used in computing the critical path), and its crash time is 1 week. This means that activity B can be shortened by up to 2 weeks if extra resources are provided. The cost of these additional resources is $4,000 (= difference between the crash cost of $34,000 and the normal cost of $30,000). If we assume that the crashing cost is linear over time (i.e., the cost is the same each week), activity B's crash cost per week is $2,000 (= $4,000/2).

TABLE 3.5   **Normal and Crash Data for Milwaukee Paper Manufacturing**

ACTIVITY	TIME (WEEKS) NORMAL	TIME (WEEKS) CRASH	COST ($) NORMAL	COST ($) CRASH	CRASH COST PER WEEK ($)	CRITICAL PATH?
A	2	1	22,000	22,750	750	Yes
B	3	1	30,000	34,000	2,000	No
C	2	1	26,000	27,000	1,000	Yes
D	4	3	48,000	49,000	1,000	No
E	4	2	56,000	58,000	1,000	Yes
F	3	2	30,000	30,500	500	No
G	5	2	80,000	84,500	1,500	Yes
H	2	1	16,000	19,000	3,000	Yes

This calculation for Activity B is shown in Figure 3.15. Crash costs for all other activities can be computed in a similar fashion.

Figure **3.15**

Crash and Normal Times and Costs for Activity B

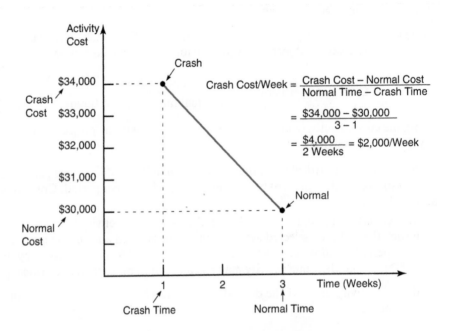

Figure **3.15**

Crash and Normal Times and Costs for Activity B

Steps 2, 3, and 4 can now be applied to reduce Milwaukee Paper's project completion time at a minimum cost. We show the project network for Milwaukee Paper again in Figure 3.16.

Figure **3.16**

Critical Path and Slack Times for Milwaukee Paper

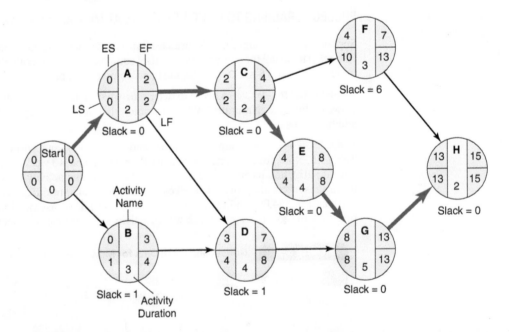

The current critical path (using normal times) is Start–A–C–E–G–H, in which Start is just a dummy starting activity. Of these critical activities, activity A has the lowest crash cost per week of $750. Julie Ann Williams should therefore crash activity A by 1 week to reduce the project completion time to 14 weeks. The cost is an additional $750. Note that activity A cannot be crashed any further, since it has reached its crash limit of 1 week.

At this stage, the original path Start–A–C–E–G–H remains critical with a completion time of 14 weeks. However, a new path Start–B–D–G–H is also critical now, with a completion time of 14 weeks. Hence, any further crashing must be done to both critical paths.

On each of these critical paths, we need to identify one activity that can still be crashed. We also want the total cost of crashing an activity on each path to be the smallest. We might be tempted to simply pick the activities with the smallest crash cost per period in each path. If we did this, we would select activity C from the first path and activity D from the second path. The total crash cost would then be $2,000 (= $1,000 + $1,000).

But we spot that activity G is common to both paths. That is, by crashing activity G, we will simultaneously reduce the completion time of both paths. Even though the $1,500 crash cost for activity G is higher than that for activities C and D, we would still prefer crashing G because the total crashing cost will now be only $1,500 (compared with the $2,000 if we crash C and D).

INSIGHT ▶ To crash the project down to 13 weeks, Williams should crash activity A by 1 week and activity G by 1 week. The total additional cost will be $2,250 (= $750 + $1,500). This is important because many contracts for projects include bonuses or penalties for early or late finishes.

LEARNING EXERCISE ▶ Say the crash cost for activity B is $31,000 instead of $34,000. How does this change the answer? [Answer: no change.]

RELATED PROBLEMS ▶ 3.28–3.32 (3.33 is available in MyOMLab)

EXCEL **OM** Data File **Ch03Ex12.xls** can be found in MyOMLab.

A Critique of PERT and CPM

As a critique of our discussions of PERT, here are some of its features about which operations managers need to be aware:

Advantages

1. Especially useful when scheduling and controlling large projects.
2. Straightforward concept and not mathematically complex.
3. Graphical networks help highlight relationships among project activities.
4. Critical path and slack time analyses help pinpoint activities that need to be closely watched.
5. Project documentation and graphs point out who is responsible for various activities.
6. Applicable to a wide variety of projects.
7. Useful in monitoring not only schedules but costs as well.

OM in Action   Behind the Tour de France

The large behind-the-scenes operations that support a football World Cup or Formula One racing team are well-known, but a Tour de France team also needs major support. "A Tour de France team is like a large traveling circus," says the coach of the Belkin team. "The public only sees the riders, but they could not function without the unseen support staff." The base to the team's cycling pyramid includes everything from osteopaths to mechanics, from logistics staff to PR people. Their project management skills require substantial know-how, as well as the ability to guarantee that riders are in peak physical, nutritional, and psychological condition. This can mean deciding which snack bars to give the cyclists before, during, and after race stages, while ensuring there are scientifically based cooling regimens in place for the riders. The team's huge truck, coach, three vans, and five cars resemble the sort of traveling convoy more associated with an international music act. Here are just some of the supplies the project management team for Belkin handles:

◆ 11 mattresses
◆ 36 aero suits, 45 bib shorts, 54 race jerseys, 250 podium caps
◆ 63 bikes
◆ 140 wheels, 220 tires
◆ 250 feeding bags, 3,000 water bottles
◆ 2,190 nutrition gels, 3,800 nutrition bars

Marc Pagani Photography/Shutterstock

◆ 10 jars of peanut butter, 10 boxes of chocolate sprinkles, 20 bags of wine gums, 20 jars of jam
◆ 80 kg of nuts, raisins, apricots, and figs, plus 50 kg of cereals

The project management behind a world-tour team is complex: These top teams often compete in two to three races simultaneously, in different countries and sometimes on different continents. Each team has 25–35 riders (9 compete in any single race), coming from different parts of the world, going to different races at different times, each with his own physique and strengths. They have customized bikes, uniforms, and food preferences. The support staff can include another 30 people.

Sources: BBC News (July 6, 2014) and *The Operations Room* (June 24, 2013).

Limitations

1. Project activities have to be clearly defined, independent, and stable in their relationships.
2. Precedence relationships must be specified and networked together.
3. Time estimates tend to be subjective and are subject to fudging by managers who fear the dangers of being overly optimistic or not pessimistic enough.
4. There is the inherent danger of placing too much emphasis on the longest, or critical, path. Near-critical paths need to be monitored closely as well.

Using Microsoft Project to Manage Projects

The approaches discussed so far are effective for managing small projects. However, for large or complex projects, specialized project management software is much preferred. In this section, we provide a brief introduction to the most popular example of such specialized software, Microsoft Project. A time-limited version of Microsoft Project may be requested with this text.

Microsoft Project is extremely useful in drawing project networks, identifying the project schedule, and managing project costs and other resources.

Entering Data   Let us again consider the Milwaukee Paper Manufacturing project. Recall that this project has eight activities (repeated in the margin). The first step is to define the activities and their precedence relationships. To do so, we select File|New to open a blank project. We type the project start date (as July 1), then enter all activity information (see Program 3.1). For each activity (or task, as Microsoft Project calls it), we fill in the name and duration. The description of the activity is also placed in the *Task Name* column in Program 3.1. As we enter activities and durations, the software automatically inserts start and finish dates.

The next step is to define precedence relationships between these activities. To do so, we enter the relevant activity numbers (e.g., 1, 2) in the *Predecessors* column.

Viewing the Project Schedule   When all links have been defined, the complete project schedule can be viewed as a Gantt chart. We can also select View|Network Diagram to view the schedule as a project network (shown in Program 3.2). The critical path is shown in red on the

Milwaukee Paper Co. Activities

ACTIVITY	TIME (WKS)	PREDE-CESSORS
A	2	—
B	3	—
C	2	A
D	4	A, B
E	4	C
F	3	C
G	5	D, E
H	2	F, G

Program **3.1**

Gantt Chart in Microsoft Project for Milwaukee Paper Manufacturing

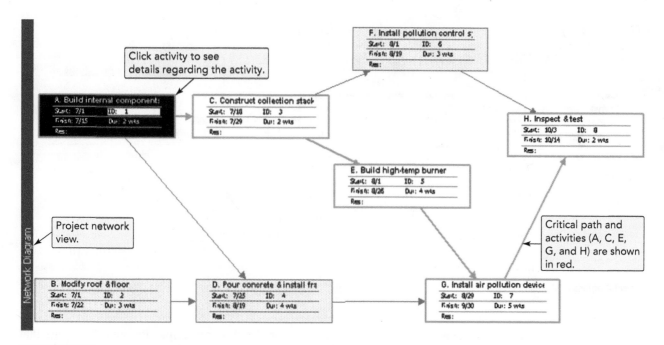

Program **3.2**

Project Network in Microsoft Project for Milwaukee Paper Manufacturing

screen in the network diagram. We can click on any of the activities in the project network to view details of the activities. Likewise, we can easily add or remove activities from the project network. Each time we do so, Microsoft Project automatically updates all start dates, finish dates, and the critical path(s). If desired, we can manually change the layout of the network (e.g., reposition activities) by changing the options in Format|Layout.

Programs 3.1 and 3.2 show that if Milwaukee Paper's project starts July 1, it can be finished on October 14. The start and finish dates for all activities are also clearly identified. Project management software, we see, can greatly simplify the scheduling procedures discussed earlier in this chapter.

PERT Analysis Microsoft Project does not perform the PERT probability calculations discussed in Examples 10 and 11. However, by clicking View|Toolbars|PERT Analysis, we can get Microsoft Project to allow us to enter optimistic, most likely, and pessimistic times for each activity. We can then choose to view Gantt charts based on any of these three times for each activity.

Tracking the Time Status of a Project Perhaps the biggest advantage of using software to manage projects is that it can track the progress of the project. In this regard, Microsoft Project has many features available to track individual activities in terms of time, cost, resource usage, and so on.

An easy way to track the time progress of tasks is to enter the percent of work completed for each task. One way to do so is to double-click on any activity in the *Task Name* column in Program 3.1. A window is displayed that allows us to enter the percent of work completed for each task.

The table in the margin provides data regarding the percent of each of Milwaukee Paper's activities that are completed as of today. (Assume that today is Friday, August 12, i.e., the end of the sixth week of the project schedule.)

As shown in Program 3.3, the Gantt chart immediately reflects this updated information by drawing a thick line within each activity's bar. The length of this line is proportional to the percent of that activity's work that has been completed.

How do we know if we are on schedule? Notice that there is a vertical line shown on the Gantt chart corresponding to today's date. Microsoft Project will automatically move this line to correspond with the current date. If the project is on schedule, we should see all bars to the *left*

Pollution Project Percentage Completed on Aug. 12	
ACTIVITY	COMPLETED
A	100
B	100
C	100
D	10
E	20
F	20
G	0
H	0

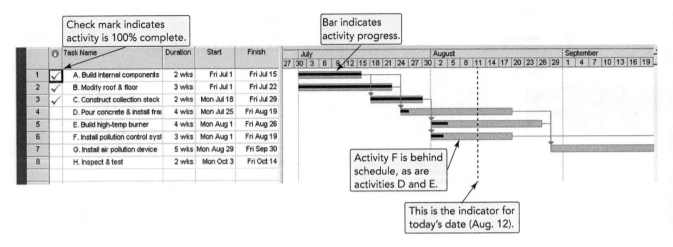

Program **3.3**

Tracking Project Progress in Microsoft Project

of today's line indicate that they have been completed. For example, Program 3.3 shows that activities A, B, and C are on schedule. In contrast, activities D, E, and F appear to be behind schedule. These activities need to be investigated further to determine the reason for the delay. This type of easy *visual* information is what makes such software so useful in practice for project management.

We encourage you to load the copy of Microsoft Project that may be ordered with your text and to create a project network for work you are currently doing.

Summary

PERT, CPM, and other scheduling techniques have proven to be valuable tools in controlling large and complex projects. Managers use such techniques to segment projects into discrete activities (work breakdown structures), indentifying specific resources and time requirements for each. With PERT and CPM, managers can understand the status of each activity, including its earliest start, latest start, earliest finish, and latest finish (ES, LS, EF, and LF) times. By controlling the trade-off between ES and LS, managers can identify the activities that have slack and can address resource allocation, perhaps by smoothing resources. Effective project management also allows managers to focus on the activities that are critical to timely project completion. By understanding the project's critical path, they know where crashing makes the most economic sense.

Good project management also allows firms to efficiently create products and services for global markets and to respond effectively to global competition. Microsoft Project, illustrated in this chapter, is one of a wide variety of software packages available to help managers handle network modeling problems.

The models described in this chapter require good management practices, detailed work breakdown structures, clear responsibilities assigned to activities, and straightforward and timely reporting systems. All are critical parts of project management.

Key Terms

Project organization (p. 62)
Work breakdown structure (WBS) (p. 64)
Gantt charts (p. 65)
Program evaluation and review technique (PERT) (p. 67)
Critical path method (CPM) (p. 67)

Critical path (p. 67)
Activity-on-node (AON) (p. 68)
Activity-on-arrow (AOA) (p. 68)
Dummy activity (p. 70)
Critical path analysis (p. 71)
Forward pass (p. 72)

Backward pass (p. 74)
Slack time (p. 75)
Optimistic time (p. 77)
Pessimistic time (p. 77)
Most likely time (p. 77)
Crashing (p. 82)

Ethical Dilemma

Two examples of massively mismanaged projects are TAURUS and the "Big Dig." The first, formally called the London Stock Exchange Automation Project, cost $575 million before it was finally abandoned. Although most IT projects have a reputation for cost overruns, delays, and underperformance, TAURUS set a new standard.

But even TAURUS paled next to the biggest, most expensive public works project in U.S. history—Boston's 15-year-long Central Artery/Tunnel Project. Called the Big Dig, this was perhaps the poorest and most felonious case of project mismanagement in decades. From a starting $2 billion budget to a final price tag of $15 billion, the Big Dig cost more than the Panama Canal, Hoover Dam, or Interstate 95, the 1,919-mile highway between Maine and Florida.

Read about one of these two projects (or another of your choice) and explain why it faced such problems. How and why do project managers allow such massive endeavors to fall into such a state? What do you think are the causes?

Discussion Questions

1. Give an example of a situation in which project management is needed.
2. Explain the purpose of project organization.
3. What are the three phases involved in the management of a large project?
4. What are some of the questions that can be answered with PERT and CPM?
5. Define *work breakdown structure*. How is it used?
6. What is the use of Gantt charts in project management?
7. What is the difference between an activity-on-arrow (AOA) network and an activity-on-node (AON) network? Which is primarily used in this chapter?
8. What is the significance of the critical path?
9. What would a project manager have to do to crash an activity?
10. Describe how expected activity times and variances can be computed in a PERT network.
11. Define *earliest start, earliest finish, latest finish*, and *latest start* times.
12. Students are sometimes confused by the concept of critical path, and want to believe that it is the *shortest* path through a network. Convincingly explain why this is not so.
13. What are dummy activities? Why are they used in activity-on-arrow (AOA) project networks?
14. What are the three time estimates used with PERT?
15. Would a project manager ever consider crashing a noncritical activity in a project network? Explain convincingly.
16. How is the variance of the total project computed in PERT?
17. Describe the meaning of slack, and discuss how it can be determined.
18. How can we determine the probability that a project will be completed by a certain date? What assumptions are made in this computation?
19. Name some of the widely used project management software programs.
20. What is the difference between the *waterfall* approach and *agile* project management?

Using Software to Solve Project Management Problems

In addition to the Microsoft Project software illustrated earlier, both Excel OM and POM for Windows are available to readers of this text as project management tools.

✘ USING EXCEL OM

Excel OM has a Project Scheduling module. Program 3.4 uses the data from the Milwaukee Paper Manufacturing example in this chapter (see Examples 4 and 5). The PERT/CPM analysis also handles activities with three time estimates.

P USING POM FOR WINDOWS

POM for Window's Project Scheduling module can also find the expected project completion time for a CPM and PERT network with either one or three time estimates. POM for Windows also performs project crashing. For further details refer to Appendix IV.

Program **3.4**

Excel OM's Use of Milwaukee Paper Manufacturing's Data from Examples 4 and 5

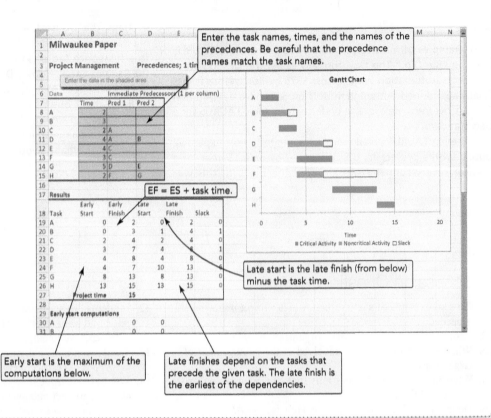

Enter the task names, times, and the names of the precedences. Be careful that the precedence names match the task names.

EF = ES + task time.

Late start is the late finish (from below) minus the task time.

Early start is the maximum of the computations below.

Late finishes depend on the tasks that precede the given task. The late finish is the earliest of the dependencies.

Solved Problems   Virtual Office Hours help is available in MyOMLab.

SOLVED PROBLEM 3.1

Construct an AON network based on the following:

ACTIVITY	IMMEDIATE PREDECESSOR(S)
A	—
B	—
C	—
D	A, B
E	C

SOLUTION

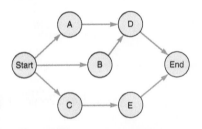

SOLVED PROBLEM 3.2

Insert a dummy activity and event to correct the following AOA network:

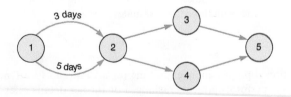

SOLUTION

Because we cannot have two activities starting and ending at the same node, we add the following dummy activity and dummy event to obtain the correct AOA network:

SOLVED PROBLEM 3.3

Calculate the critical path, project completion time T, and project variance σ_p^2, based on the following AON network information:

ACTIVITY	TIME	VARIANCE	ES	EF	LS	LF	SLACK
A	2	$\frac{2}{6}$	0	2	0	2	0
B	3	$\frac{2}{6}$	0	3	1	4	1
C	2	$\frac{4}{6}$	2	4	2	4	0
D	4	$\frac{4}{6}$	3	7	4	8	1
E	4	$\frac{2}{6}$	4	8	4	8	0
F	3	$\frac{1}{6}$	4	7	10	13	6
G	5	$\frac{1}{6}$	8	13	8	13	0

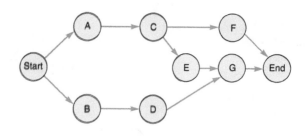

SOLUTION

We conclude that the critical path is Start–A–C–E–G–End:

$$\text{Total project time} = T = 2 + 2 + 4 + 5 = 13$$

and

$$\sigma_p^2 = \Sigma \text{ Variances on the critical path}$$
$$= \frac{2}{6} + \frac{4}{6} + \frac{2}{6} + \frac{1}{6} = \frac{9}{6} = 1.5$$

SOLVED PROBLEM 3.4

To complete the wing assembly for an experimental aircraft, Jim Gilbert has laid out the seven major activities involved. These activities have been labeled A through G in the following table, which also shows their estimated completion times (in weeks) and immediate predecessors. Determine the expected time and variance for each activity.

ACTIVITY	a	m	b	IMMEDIATE PREDECESSORS
A	1	2	3	—
B	2	3	4	—
C	4	5	6	A
D	8	9	10	B
E	2	5	8	C, D
F	4	5	6	D
G	1	2	3	E

SOLUTION

Expected times and variances can be computed using Equations (3–6) and (3–7) presented on page 78 in this chapter. The results are summarized in the following table:

ACTIVITY	EXPECTED TIME (IN WEEKS)	VARIANCE
A	2	$\frac{1}{9}$
B	3	$\frac{1}{9}$
C	5	$\frac{1}{9}$
D	9	$\frac{1}{9}$
E	5	1
F	5	$\frac{1}{9}$
G	2	$\frac{1}{9}$

SOLVED PROBLEM 3.5

Referring to Solved Problem 3.4, now Jim Gilbert would like to determine the critical path for the entire wing assembly project as well as the expected completion time for the total project. In addition, he would like to determine the earliest and latest start and finish times for all activities.

SOLUTION

The AON network for Gilbert's project is shown in Figure 3.17. Note that this project has multiple activities (A and B) with no immediate predecessors, and multiple activities (F and G) with no successors. Hence, in addition to a unique starting activity (Start), we have included a unique finishing activity (End) for the project.

Figure 3.17 shows the earliest and latest times for all activities. The results are also summarized in the following table:

ACTIVITY	ACTIVITY TIME				SLACK
	ES	EF	LS	LF	
A	0	2	5	7	5
B	0	3	0	3	0
C	2	7	7	12	5
D	3	12	3	12	0
E	12	17	12	17	0
F	12	17	14	19	2
G	17	19	17	19	0

Expected project length = 19 weeks
Variance of the critical path = 1.333
Standard deviation of the critical path = 1.155 weeks

The activities along the critical path are B, D, E, and G. These activities have zero slack as shown in the table.

Figure **3.17**

Critical Path for Solved Problem 3.5

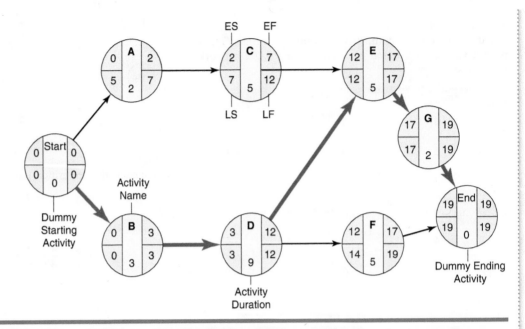

SOLVED PROBLEM 3.6

The following information has been computed from a project:

$$\text{Expected total project time} = T = 62 \text{ weeks}$$
$$\text{Project variance } (\sigma_p^2) = 81$$

What is the probability that the project will be completed 18 weeks *before* its expected completion date?

SOLUTION

The desired completion date is 18 weeks before the expected completion date, 62 weeks. The desired completion date is 44 (or 62–18) weeks:

$$\sigma_p = \sqrt{\text{Project variance}}$$

$$Z = \frac{\text{Due date} - \text{Expected completion date}}{\sigma_p}$$

$$= \frac{44 - 62}{9} = \frac{-18}{9} = -2.0$$

The normal curve appears as follows:

Due date = 44 $T = 62$

Because the normal curve is symmetrical and table values are calculated for positive values of Z, the area desired is equal to 1−(table value). For $Z = +2.0$ the area from the table is .97725. Thus, the area corresponding to a Z-value of −2.0 is .02275 (or 1 − .97725). Hence, the probability of completing the project 18 weeks before the expected completion date is approximately .023, or 2.3%.

SOLVED PROBLEM 3.7

Determine the least cost of reducing the project completion date by 3 months based on the following information:

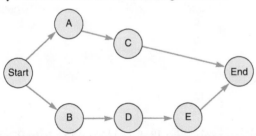

ACTIVITY	NORMAL TIME (MONTHS)	CRASH TIME (MONTHS)	NORMAL COST	CRASH COST
A	6	4	$2,000	$2,400
B	7	5	3,000	3,500
C	7	6	1,000	1,300
D	6	4	2,000	2,600
E	9	8	8,800	9,000

SOLUTION

The first step in this problem is to compute ES, EF, LS, LF, and slack for each activity.

ACTIVITY	ES	EF	LS	LF	SLACK
A	0	6	9	15	9
B	0	7	0	7	0
C	6	13	15	22	9
D	7	13	7	13	0
E	13	22	13	22	0

The critical path consists of activities B, D, and E.

Next, crash cost/month must be computed for each activity:

ACTIVITY	NORMAL TIME–CRASH TIME	CRASH COST–NORMAL COST	CRASH COST/ MONTH	CRITICAL PATH?
A	2	$400	$200/month	No
B	2	500	250/month	Yes
C	1	300	300/month	No
D	2	600	300/month	Yes
E	1	200	200/month	Yes

Finally, we will select that activity on the critical path with the smallest crash cost/month. This is activity E. Thus, we can reduce the total project completion date by 1 month for an

additional cost of $200. We still need to reduce the project completion date by 2 more months. This reduction can be achieved at least cost along the critical path by reducing activity B by 2 months for an additional cost of $500. Neither reduction has an effect on noncritical activities. This solution is summarized in the following table:

ACTIVITY	MONTHS REDUCED	COST
E	1	$200
B	2	500
		Total: $700

Problems

Note: **Px** means the problem may be solved with POM for Windows and/or Excel OM.

Problems 3.1–3.2 relate to Project Planning

• **3.1** The work breakdown structure (WBS) for building a house (levels 1 and 2) is shown below:

a) Add two level-3 activities to each of the level-2 activities to provide more detail to the WBS.
b) Select one of your level-3 activities and add two level-4 activities below it.

•• **3.2** James Lawson has decided to run for a seat as Congressman from the House of Representatives, District 34, in Florida. He views his 8-month campaign for office as a major project and wishes to create a work breakdown structure (WBS) to help control the detailed scheduling. So far, he has developed the following pieces of the WBS:

LEVEL	LEVEL ID NO.	ACTIVITY
1	1.0	Develop political campaign
2	1.1	Fund-raising plan
3	1.1.1	_____
3	1.1.2	_____
3	1.1.3	_____
2	1.2	Develop a position on major issues
3	1.2.1	_____
3	1.2.2	_____
3	1.2.3	_____
2	1.3	Staffing for campaign
3	1.3.1	_____
3	1.3.2	_____
3	1.3.3	_____
3	1.3.4	_____
2	1.4	Paperwork compliance for candidacy
3	1.4.1	_____
3	1.4.2	_____
2	1.5	Ethical plan/issues
3	1.5.1	_____

Help Lawson by providing details where the blank lines appear. Are there any other major (level-2) activities to create? If so, add an ID no. 1.6 and insert them.

Problem 3.3 relates to Project Scheduling

•• **3.3** The City Commission of Nashville has decided to build a botanical garden and picnic area in the heart of the city for the recreation of its citizens. The precedence table for all the activities required to construct this area successfully is given. Draw the Gantt chart for the whole construction activity.

CODE	ACTIVITY	DESCRIPTION	TIME (IN HOURS)	IMMEDIATE PREDECESSOR(S)
A	Planning	Find location; determine resource requirements	20	None
B	Purchasing	Requisition of lumber and sand	60	Planning
C	Excavation	Dig and grade	100	Planning
D	Sawing	Saw lumber into appropriate sizes	30	Purchasing
E	Placement	Position lumber in correct locations	20	Sawing, excavation
F	Assembly	Nail lumber together	10	Placement
G	Infill	Put sand in and under the equipment	20	Assembly
H	Outfill	Put dirt around the equipment	10	Assembly
I	Decoration	Put grass all over the garden, landscape, paint	30	Infill, outfill

Problems 3.4–3.14 relate to Project Management Techniques

•• **3.4** Refer to the table in Problem 3.3.
a) Draw the AON network for the construction activity.
b) Draw the AOA network for the construction activity.

• **3.5** Draw the activity-on-node (AON) project network associated with the following activities for Carl Betterton's construction project. How long should it take Carl and his team to complete this project? What are the critical path activities?

ACTIVITY	IMMEDIATE PREDECESSOR(S)	TIME (DAYS)
A	—	3
B	A	4
C	A	6
D	B	6
E	B	4
F	C	4
G	D	6
H	E, F	8

• **3.6** Given the activities whose sequence is described by the following table, draw the appropriate activity-on-arrow (AOA) network diagram.
a) Which activities are on the critical path?
b) What is the length of the critical path?

ACTIVITY	IMMEDIATE PREDECESSOR(S)	TIME (DAYS)
A	—	5
B	A	2
C	A	4
D	B	5
E	B	5
F	C	5
G	E, F	2
H	D	3
I	G, H	5

• **3.7** Using AOA, diagram the network described below for Lillian Fok's construction project. Calculate its critical path. How long is the minimum duration of this network?

ACTIVITY	NODES	TIME (WEEKS)	ACTIVITY	NODES	TIME (WEEKS)
J	1–2	10	N	3–4	2
K	1–3	8	O	4–5	7
L	2–4	6	P	3–5	5
M	2–3	3			

•• **3.8** Roger Ginde is developing a program in supply chain management certification for managers. Ginde has listed a number of activities that must be completed before a training program of this nature could be conducted. The activities, immediate predecessors, and times appear in the accompanying table:

ACTIVITY	IMMEDIATE PREDECESSOR(S)	TIME (DAYS)
A	—	2
B	—	5
C	—	1
D	B	10
E	A, D	3
F	C	6
G	E, F	8

a) Develop an AON network for this problem.
b) What is the critical path?
c) What is the total project completion time?
d) What is the slack time for each individual activity? **Px**

•• **3.9** Task time estimates for the modification of an assembly line at Jim Goodale's Carbondale, Illinois, factory are as follows:

ACTIVITY	TIME (IN HOURS)	IMMEDIATE PREDECESSORS
A	6.0	—
B	7.2	—
C	5.0	A
D	6.0	B, C
E	4.5	B, C
F	7.7	D
G	4.0	E, F

a) Draw the project network using AON.
b) Identify the critical path.
c) What is the expected project length?
d) Draw a Gantt chart for the project. **Px**

• **3.10** The activities described by the following table are given for the Howard Corporation in Kansas:

ACTIVITY	IMMEDIATE PREDECESSOR(S)	TIME
A	—	9
B	A	7
C	A	3
D	B	6
E	B	9
F	C	4
G	E, F	6
H	D	5
I	G, H	3

a) Draw the appropriate AON PERT diagram for J.C. Howard's management team.
b) Find the critical path.
c) What is the project completion time? **Px**

•• **3.11** The following is a table of activities associated with a project at Rafay Ishfaq's software firm in Chicago, their durations, and what activities each must precede:

ACTIVITY	DURATION (WEEKS)	PRECEDES
A (start)	1	B, C
B	1	E
C	4	F
E	2	F
F (end)	2	—

a) Draw an AON diagram of the project, including activity durations.
b) Define the critical path, listing all critical activities in chronological order.
c) What is the project duration (in weeks)?
d) What is the slack (in weeks) associated with any and all non-critical paths through the project?

• **3.12** The activities needed to build a prototype laser scanning machine at Dave Fletcher Corp. are listed in the following table. Construct an AON network for these activities.

ACTIVITY	IMMEDIATE PREDECESSOR(S)	ACTIVITY	IMMEDIATE PREDECESSOR(S)
A	—	E	B
B	—	F	B
C	A	G	C, E
D	A	H	D, F

Additional problems 3.13–3.14 are available in MyOMLab.

Problems 3.15–3.16 relate to Determining the Project Schedule

• **3.15** Dave Fletcher (see Problem 3.12) was able to determine the activity times for constructing his laser scanning machine. Fletcher would like to determine ES, EF, LS, LF, and slack for each activity. The total project completion time and the critical path should also be determined. Here are the activity times:

ACTIVITY	TIME (WEEKS)	ACTIVITY	TIME (WEEKS)
A	6	E	4
B	7	F	6
C	3	G	10
D	2	H	7

••• **3.16** The Rover 6 is a new custom-designed sports car. An analysis of the task of building the Rover 6 reveals the following list of relevant activities, their immediate predecessors, and their duration:[2]

JOB LETTER	DESCRIPTION	IMMEDIATE PREDECESSOR(S)	NORMAL TIME (DAYS)
A	Start	—	0
B	Design	A	8
C	Order special accessories	B	0.1
D	Build frame	B	1
E	Build doors	B	1
F	Attach axles, wheels, gas tank	D	1
G	Build body shell	B	2
H	Build transmission and drivetrain	B	3
I	Fit doors to body shell	G, E	1
J	Build engine	B	4
K	Bench-test engine	J	2
L	Assemble chassis	F, H, K	1
M	Road-test chassis	L	0.5
N	Paint body	I	2
O	Install wiring	N	1
P	Install interior	N	1.5
Q	Accept delivery of special accessories	C	5
R	Mount body and accessories on chassis	M, O, P, Q	1
S	Road test car	R	0.5
T	Attach exterior trim	S	1
U	Finish	T	0

a) Draw a network diagram for the project.
b) Mark the critical path and state its length.
c) If the Rover 6 had to be completed 2 days earlier, would it help to:
   i) Buy preassembled transmissions and drivetrains?
   ii) Install robots to halve engine-building time?
   iii) Speed delivery of special accessories by 3 days?
d) How might resources be borrowed from activities on the non-critical path to speed activities on the critical path? **Px**

•••**3.17** Ross Hopkins, president of Hopkins Hospitality, has developed the tasks, durations, and predecessor relationships in the following table for building new motels. Draw the AON network and answer the questions that follow.

ACTIVITY	IMMEDIATE PREDECESSOR(S)	TIME ESTIMATES (IN WEEKS)		
		OPTIMISTIC	MOST LIKELY	PESSIMISTIC
A	—	4	8	10
B	A	2	8	24
C	A	8	12	16
D	A	4	6	10
E	B	1	2	3
F	E, C	6	8	20
G	E, C	2	3	4
H	F	2	2	2
I	F	6	6	6
J	D, G, H	4	6	12
K	I, J	2	2	3

a) What is the expected (estimated) time for activity C?
b) What is the variance for activity C?
c) Based on the calculation of estimated times, what is the critical path?
d) What is the estimated time of the critical path?
e) What is the activity variance along the critical path?
f) What is the probability of completion of the project before week 36? **Px**

• **3.18** A renovation of the gift shop at Orlando Amway Center has six activities (in hours). For the following estimates of *a*, *m*, and *b*, calculate the expected time and the standard deviation for each activity:

ACTIVITY	a	m	b
A	11	15	19
B	27	31	41
C	18	18	18
D	8	13	19
E	17	18	20
F	16	19	22

Px

••**3.19** Kelle Carpet and Trim installs carpet in commercial offices. Peter Kelle has been very concerned with the amount of time it took to complete several recent jobs. Some of his workers are very unreliable. A list of activities and their optimistic completion time, the most likely completion time, and the pessimistic completion time (all in days) for a new contract are given in the following table:

ACTIVITY	TIME (DAYS)			IMMEDIATE PREDECESSOR(S)
	a	m	b	
A	3	6	8	—
B	2	4	4	—
C	1	2	3	—
D	6	7	8	C
E	2	4	6	B, D
F	6	10	14	A, E
G	1	2	4	A, E
H	3	6	9	F
I	10	11	12	G
J	14	16	20	C
K	2	8	10	H, I

a) Determine the expected completion time and variance for each activity.
b) Determine the total project completion time and the critical path for the project.
c) Determine ES, EF, LS, LF, and slack for each activity.
d) What is the probability that Kelle Carpet and Trim will finish the project in 40 days or less? **Px**

•••**3.20** The estimated times and immediate predecessors for the activities in a project at George Kyparis's retinal scanning company are given in the following table. Assume that the activity times are independent.

ACTIVITY	IMMEDIATE PREDECESSOR	TIME (WEEKS)		
		a	m	b
A	—	9	10	11
B	—	4	10	16
C	A	9	10	11
D	B	5	8	11

a) Calculate the expected time and variance for each activity.
b) What is the expected completion time of the critical path? What is the expected completion time of the other path in the network?
c) What is the variance of the critical path? What is the variance of the other path in the network?
d) If the time to complete path A–C is normally distributed, what is the probability that this path will be finished in 22 weeks or less?
e) If the time to complete path B–D is normally distributed, what is the probability that this path will be finished in 22 weeks or less?
f) Explain why the probability that the *critical path* will be finished in 22 weeks or less is not necessarily the probability that the *project* will be finished in 22 weeks or less. **Px**

• • • **3.21** Rich Cole Control Devices, Inc., produces custom-built relay devices for auto makers. The most recent project undertaken by Cole requires 14 different activities. Cole's managers would like to determine the total project completion time (in days) and those activities that lie along the critical path. The appropriate data are shown in the following table.
a) What is the probability of being done in 53 days?
b) What date results in a 99% probability of completion?

ACTIVITY	IMMEDIATE PREDECESSOR(S)	OPTIMISTIC TIME	MOST LIKELY TIME	PESSIMISTIC TIME
A	—	4	6	7
B	—	1	2	3
C	A	6	6	6
D	A	5	8	11
E	B, C	1	9	18
F	D	2	3	6
G	D	1	7	8
H	E, F	4	4	6
I	G, H	1	6	8
J	I	2	5	7
K	I	8	9	11
L	J	2	4	6
M	K	1	2	3
N	L, M	6	8	10

Px

• • • **3.22** Four Squares Productions, a firm hired to coordinate the release of the movie *Pirates of the Caribbean: On Stranger Tides* (starring Johnny Depp), identified 16 activities to be completed before the release of the film.
a) How many weeks in advance of the film release should Four Squares have started its marketing campaign? What is the critical path? The tasks (in time units of weeks) are as follows:

ACTIVITY	IMMEDIATE PREDECESSOR(S)	OPTIMISTIC TIME	MOST LIKELY TIME	PESSIMISTIC TIME
A	—	1	2	4
B	—	3	3.5	4
C	—	10	12	13
D	—	4	5	7
E	—	2	4	5
F	A	6	7	8
G	B	2	4	5.5
H	C	5	7.7	9
I	C	9.9	10	12
J	C	2	4	5
K	D	2	4	6
L	E	2	4	6
M	F, G, H	5	6	6.5
N	J, K, L	1	1.1	2
O	I, M	5	7	8
P	N	5	7	9

b) What is the probability of completing the marketing campaign in the time (in weeks) noted in part a?
c) If activities I and J were not necessary, what impact would this have on the critical path and the number of weeks needed to complete the marketing campaign? **Px**

Tracy Whiteside/Shutterstock

• • **3.23** Using PERT, Adam Munson was able to determine that the expected project completion time for the construction of a pleasure yacht is 21 months, and the project variance is 4.
a) What is the probability that the project will be completed in 17 months?
b) What is the probability that the project will be completed in 20 months?
c) What is the probability that the project will be completed in 23 months?
d) What is the probability that the project will be completed in 25 months?
e) What is the due date that yields a 95% chance of completion? **Px**

Additional problems **3.24–3.27** are available in MyOMLab.

Problems 3.28–3.33 relate to Cost-Time Trade-Offs and Project Crashing

•• **3.28** Assume that the activities in Problem 3.11 have the following costs to shorten: A, \$300/week; B, \$100/week; C, \$200/week; E, \$100/week; and F, \$400/week. Assume also that you can crash an activity down to 0 weeks in duration and that every week you can shorten the project is worth \$250 to you. What activities would you crash? What is the total crashing cost?

••• **3.29** What is the minimum cost of crashing the following project that Roger Solano manages at Slippery Rock University by 4 days?

ACTIVITY	NORMAL TIME (DAYS)	CRASH TIME (DAYS)	NORMAL COST	CRASH COST	IMMEDIATE PREDECESSOR(S)
A	6	5	\$ 900	\$1,000	—
B	8	6	300	400	—
C	4	3	500	600	—
D	5	3	900	1,200	A
E	8	5	1,000	1,600	C

PX

•• **3.30** Three activities are candidates for crashing on a project network for a large computer installation (all are, of course, critical). Activity details are in the following table:

ACTIVITY	PREDE-CESSOR	NORMAL TIME	NORMAL COST	CRASH TIME	CRASH COST
A	—	7 days	\$6,000	6 days	\$6,600
B	A	4 days	1,200	2 days	3,000
C	B	11 days	4,000	9 days	6,000

a) What action would you take to reduce the critical path by 1 day?
b) Assuming no other paths become critical, what action would you take to reduce the critical path one additional day?
c) What is the total cost of the 2-day reduction? PX

••• **3.31** Development of Version 2.0 of a particular accounting software product is being considered by Jose Noguera's technology firm in Baton Rouge. The activities necessary for the completion of this project are listed in the following table:

ACTIVITY	NORMAL TIME (WEEKS)	CRASH TIME (WEEKS)	NORMAL COST	CRASH COST	IMMEDIATE PREDECESSOR(S)
A	4	3	\$2,000	\$2,600	—
B	2	1	2,200	2,800	—
C	3	3	500	500	—
D	8	4	2,300	2,600	A
E	6	3	900	1,200	B
F	3	2	3,000	4,200	C
G	4	2	1,400	2,000	D, E

a) What is the project completion date?
b) What is the total cost required for completing this project on normal time?
c) If you wish to reduce the time required to complete this project by 1 week, which activity should be crashed, and how much will this increase the total cost?
d) What is the maximum time that can be crashed? How much would costs increase? PX

••• **3.32** Kimpel Products makes pizza ovens for commercial use. James Kimpel, CEO, is contemplating producing smaller ovens for use in high school and college kitchens. The activities necessary to build an experimental model and related data are given in the following table:

ACTIVITY	NORMAL TIME (WEEKS)	CRASH TIME (WEEKS)	NORMAL COST (\$)	CRASH COST (\$)	IMMEDIATE PREDECESSOR(S)
A	3	2	1,000	1,600	—
B	2	1	2,000	2,700	—
C	1	1	300	300	—
D	7	3	1,300	1,600	A
E	6	3	850	1,000	B
F	2	1	4,000	5,000	C
G	4	2	1,500	2,000	D, E

a) What is the project completion date?
b) Crash this project to 10 weeks at the least cost.
c) Crash this project to 7 weeks (which is the maximum it can be crashed) at the least cost. PX

Additional problem **3.33** is available in MyOMLab.

CASE STUDIES

Southwestern University: (A)*

Southwestern University (SWU), a large state college in Stephenville, Texas, 30 miles southwest of the Dallas/Fort Worth metroplex, enrolls close to 20,000 students. In a typical town–gown relationship, the school is a dominant force in the small city, with more students during fall and spring than permanent residents.

A longtime football powerhouse, SWU is a member of the Big Eleven conference and is usually in the top 20 in college football rankings. To bolster its chances of reaching the elusive and long-desired number-one ranking, in 2009, SWU hired the legendary Phil Flamm as its head coach.

*This integrated study runs throughout the text. Other issues facing Southwestern's football expansion include (B) forecasting game attendance (Chapter 4); (C) quality of facilities (Chapter 6); (D) break-even analysis for food services (Supplement 7); (E) location of the new stadium (Chapter 8); (F) inventory planning of football programs (Chapter 12); and (G) scheduling of campus security officers/staff for game days (Chapter 13).

TABLE 3.6	Southwestern University Project						
				TIME ESTIMATES (DAYS)			
ACTIVITY	DESCRIPTION	PREDECESSOR(S)	OPTIMISTIC	MOST LIKELY	PESSIMISTIC	CRASH COST/DAY	
A	Bonding, insurance, tax structuring	—	20	30	40	$1,500	
B	Foundation, concrete footings for boxes	A	20	65	80	3,500	
C	Upgrading skybox stadium seating	A	50	60	100	4,000	
D	Upgrading walkways, stairwells, elevators	C	30	50	100	1,900	
E	Interior wiring, lathes	B	25	30	35	9,500	
F	Inspection approvals	E	0.1	0.1	0.1	0	
G	Plumbing	D, F	25	30	35	2,500	
H	Painting	G	10	20	30	2,000	
I	Hardware/AC/metal workings	H	20	25	60	2,000	
J	Tile/carpet/windows	H	8	10	12	6,000	
K	Inspection	J	0.1	0.1	0.1	0	
L	Final detail work/cleanup	I, K	20	25	60	4,500	

One of Flamm's demands on joining SWU had been a new stadium. With attendance increasing, SWU administrators began to face the issue head-on. After 6 months of study, much political arm wrestling, and some serious financial analysis, Dr. Joel Wisner, president of Southwestern University, had reached a decision to expand the capacity at its on-campus stadium.

Adding thousands of seats, including dozens of luxury skyboxes, would not please everyone. The influential Flamm had argued the need for a first-class stadium, one with built-in dormitory rooms for his players and a palatial office appropriate for the coach of a future NCAA champion team. But the decision was made, and *everyone*, including the coach, would learn to live with it.

The job now was to get construction going immediately after the 2015 season ended. This would allow exactly 270 days until the 2016 season opening game. The contractor, Hill Construction (Bob Hill being an alumnus, of course), signed his contract. Bob Hill looked at the tasks his engineers had outlined and looked President Wisner in the eye. "I guarantee the team will be able to take the field on schedule next year," he said with a sense of confidence. "I sure hope so," replied Wisner. "The contract penalty of $10,000 per day for running late is nothing compared to what Coach Flamm will do to you if our opening game with Penn State is delayed or canceled." Hill, sweating slightly, did not need to respond. In football-crazy Texas, Hill Construction would be *mud* if the 270-day target was missed.

Back in his office, Hill again reviewed the data (see Table 3.6) and noted that optimistic time estimates can be used as crash times. He then gathered his foremen. "Folks, if we're not 75% sure we'll finish this stadium in less than 270 days, I want this project crashed! Give me the cost figures for a target date of 250 days—also for 240 days. I want to be *early*, not just on time!"

Discussion Questions

1. Develop a network drawing for Hill Construction and determine the critical path. How long is the project expected to take?

2. What is the probability of finishing in 270 days?

3. If it is necessary to crash to 250 or 240 days, how would Hill do so, and at what costs? As noted in the case, assume that optimistic time estimates can be used as crash times.

Project Management at Arnold Palmer Hospital

Video Case

The equivalent of a new kindergarten class is born every day at Orlando's Arnold Palmer Hospital. With more than 13,000 births in the mid-2000s in a hospital that was designed 15 years earlier for a capacity of 6,500 births a year, the newborn intensive care unit was stretched to the limit. Moreover, with continuing strong population growth in central Florida, the hospital was often full. It was clear that new facilities were needed. After much analysis, forecasting, and discussion, the management team decided to build a new 273-bed building across the street from the existing hospital. But the facility had to be built in accordance with the hospital's Guiding Principles and its uniqueness as a health center dedicated to the specialized needs of women and infants. Those Guiding Principles are: *Family-centered focus, a healing environment where privacy and dignity are respected, sanctuary of caring that includes warm, serene surroundings with natural lighting, sincere and dedicated staff providing the highest quality care, and patient-centered flow and function.*

The vice president of business development, Karl Hodges, wanted a hospital that was designed from the inside out by the people who understood the Guiding Principles, who knew most about the current system, and who were going to use the new system, namely, the doctors and nurses. Hodges and his staff spent 13 months discussing expansion needs with this group, as well as with patients and the community, before developing a proposal

TABLE 3.7	Expansion Planning and Arnold Palmer Hospital Construction Activities and Times[a]	
ACTIVITY	**SCHEDULED TIME**	**PRECEDENCE ACTIVITY(IES)**
1. Proposal and review	1 month	—
2. Establish master schedule	2 weeks	1
3. Architect selection process	5 weeks	1
4. Survey whole campus and its needs	1 month	1
5. Conceptual architect's plans	6 weeks	3
6. Cost estimating	2 months	2, 4, 5
7. Deliver plans to board for consideration/decision	1 month	6
8. Surveys/regulatory review	6 weeks	6
9. Construction manager selection	9 weeks	6
10. State review of need for more hospital beds ("Certificate of Need")	3.5 months	7, 8
11. Design drawings	4 months	10
12. Construction documents	5 months	9, 11
13. Site preparation/demolish existing building	9 weeks	11
14. Construction start/building pad	2 months	12, 13
15. Relocate utilities	6 weeks	12
16. Deep foundations	2 months	14
17. Building structure in place	9 months	16
18. Exterior skin/roofing	4 months	17
19. Interior buildout	12 months	17
20. Building inspections	5 weeks	15, 19
21. Occupancy	1 month	20

[a]This list of activities is abbreviated for purposes of this case study. For simplification, assume each week = .25 months (i.e., 2 weeks = .5 month, 6 weeks = 1.5 months, etc.).

for the new facility. An administrative team created 35 user groups, which held over 1,000 planning meetings (lasting from 45 minutes to a whole day). They even created a "Supreme Court" to deal with conflicting views on the multifaceted issues facing the new hospital.

Funding and regulatory issues added substantial complexity to this major expansion, and Hodges was very concerned that the project stay on time and within budget. Tom Hyatt, director of facility development, was given the task of onsite manager of the $100 million project, in addition to overseeing ongoing renovations, expansions, and other projects. The activities in the multiyear project for the new building at Arnold Palmer are shown in Table 3.7.

Discussion Questions*

1. Develop the network for planning and construction of the new hospital at Arnold Palmer.
2. What is the critical path, and how long is the project expected to take?
3. Why is the construction of this 11-story building any more complex than construction of an equivalent office building?
4. What percent of the whole project duration was spent in planning that occurred prior to the proposal and reviews? Prior to the actual building construction? Why?

*You may wish to view the video accompanying this case before addressing these questions.

Managing Hard Rock's Rockfest

Video Case

At the Hard Rock Cafe, like many organizations, project management is a key planning tool. With Hard Rock's constant growth in hotels and cafes, remodeling of existing cafes, scheduling for Hard Rock Live concert and event venues, and planning the annual Rockfest, managers rely on project management techniques and software to maintain schedule and budget performance.

"Without Microsoft Project," says Hard Rock Vice-President Chris Tomasso, "there is no way to keep so many people on the same page." Tomasso is in charge of the Rockfest event, which is attended by well over 100,000 enthusiastic fans. The challenge is pulling it off within a tight 9-month planning horizon. As the event approaches, Tomasso devotes greater energy to its activities. For the first 3 months, Tomasso updates his Microsoft Project charts monthly. Then at the 6-month mark, he updates his progress weekly. At the 9-month mark, he checks and corrects his schedule twice a week.

Early in the project management process, Tomasso identifies 10 major tasks (called level-2 activities in a work breakdown structure, or WBS):[†] talent booking, ticketing, marketing/PR, online promotion, television, show production, travel, sponsorships, operations, and merchandising. Using a WBS, each of these is further divided into a series of subtasks. Table 3.8 identifies 26 of the major activities and subactivities, their immediate predecessors, and time estimates. Tomasso enters all these into the Microsoft Project software.[‡] Tomasso alters the Microsoft Project document and the time line as the

project progresses. "It's okay to change it as long as you keep on track," he states.

The day of the rock concert itself is not the end of the project planning. "It's nothing but surprises. A band not being able to get to the venue because of traffic jams is a surprise, but an 'anticipated' surprise. We had a helicopter on stand-by ready to fly the band in," says Tomasso.

On completion of Rockfest in July, Tomasso and his team have a 3-month reprieve before starting the project planning process again.

[†]The level-1 activity is the Rockfest concert itself.
[‡]There are actually 127 activities used by Tomasso; the list is abbreviated for this case study.

TABLE 3.8	Some of the Major Activities and Subactivities in the Rockfest Plan		
ACTIVITY	DESCRIPTION	PREDECESSOR(S)	TIME (WEEKS)
A	Finalize site and building contracts	—	7
B	Select local promoter	A	3
C	Hire production manager	A	3
D	Design promotional Web site	B	5
E	Set TV deal	D	6
F	Hire director	E	4
G	Plan for TV camera placement	F	2
H	Target headline entertainers	B	4
I	Target support entertainers	H	4
J	Travel accommodations for talent	I	10
K	Set venue capacity	C	2
L	Ticketmaster contract	D, K	3
M	On-site ticketing	L	8
N	Sound and staging	C	6
O	Passes and stage credentials	G, R	7
P	Travel accommodations for staff	B	20
Q	Hire sponsor coordinator	B	4
R	Finalize sponsors	Q	4
S	Define/place signage for sponsors	R, X	3
T	Hire operations manager	A	4
U	Develop site plan	T	6
V	Hire security director	T	7
W	Set police/fire security plan	V	4
X	Power, plumbing, AC, toilet services	U	8
Y	Secure merchandise deals	B	6
Z	Online merchandise sales	Y	6

Discussion Questions[§]

1. Identify the critical path and its activities for Rockfest. How long does the project take?

2. Which activities have a slack time of 8 weeks or more?

3. Identify five major challenges a project manager faces in events such as this one.

4. Why is a work breakdown structure useful in a project such as this? Take the 26 activities and break them into what you think should be level-2, level-3, and level-4 tasks.

[§]You may wish to view the video accompanying this case before addressing these questions.

- **Additional Case Study:** Visit MyOMLab for this free case study:
  Shale Oil Company: This oil refinery must shut down for maintenance of a major piece of equipment.

Endnotes

1. This formula is based on the statistical concept that from one end of the beta distribution to the other is 6 standard deviations (± 3 standard deviations from the mean). Because $(b - a)$ is 6 standard deviations, the variance is $[(b - a)/6]^2$.

2. *Source:* Adapted from James A. D. Stoner, *Management*, 6th ed. (Upper Saddle River, NJ: Pearson).

Chapter 3 *Rapid* Review

Main Heading	Review Material	MyOMLab
THE IMPORTANCE OF PROJECT MANAGEMENT (p. 62)	The management of projects involves three phases: 1. *Planning*—This phase includes goal setting, defining the project, and team organization. 2. *Scheduling*—This phase relates people, money, and supplies to specific activities and relates activities to each other. 3. *Controlling*—Here the firm monitors resources, costs, quality, and budgets. It also revises or changes plans and shifts resources to meet time and cost demands.	Concept Questions: 1.1–1.4 **VIDEO 3.1** Project Management at Hard Rock's Rockfest
PROJECT PLANNING (pp. 62–65)	Projects can be defined as a series of related tasks directed toward a major output. ■ **Project organization**—An organization formed to ensure that programs (projects) receive the proper management and attention. ■ **Work breakdown structure (WBS)**—Defines a project by dividing it into more and more detailed components.	Concept Questions: 2.1–2.4 Problems: 3.1–3.2
PROJECT SCHEDULING (pp. 65–66)	■ **Gantt charts**—Planning charts used to schedule resources and allocate time. Project scheduling serves several purposes: 1. It shows the relationship of each activity to others and to the whole project. 2. It identifies the precedence relationships among activities. 3. It encourages the setting of realistic time and cost estimates for each activity. 4. It helps make better use of people, money, and material resources by identifying critical bottlenecks in the project.	Concept Questions: 3.1–3.4 Problem: 3.3
PROJECT CONTROLLING (pp. 66–67)	Computerized programs produce a broad variety of PERT/CPM reports, including (1) detailed cost breakdowns for each task, (2) total program labor curves, (3) cost distribution tables, (4) functional cost and hour summaries, (5) raw material and expenditure forecasts, (6) variance reports, (7) time analysis reports, and (8) work status reports.	Concept Questions: 4.1–4.2 **VIDEO 3.2** Project Management at Arnold Palmer Hospital
PROJECT MANAGEMENT TECHNIQUES: PERT AND CPM (pp. 67–71)	■ **Program evaluation and review technique (PERT)**—A project management technique that employs three time estimates for each activity. ■ **Critical path method (CPM)**—A project management technique that uses only one estimate per activity. ■ **Critical path**—The computed *longest* time path(s) through a network. PERT and CPM both follow six basic steps. The activities on the critical path will delay the entire project if they are not completed on time. ■ **Activity-on-node (AON)**—A network diagram in which nodes designate activities. ■ **Activity-on-arrow (AOA)**—A network diagram in which arrows designate activities. In an AOA network, the nodes represent the starting and finishing times of an activity and are also called *events*. ■ **Dummy activity**—An activity having no time that is inserted into a network to maintain the logic of the network. A dummy ending activity can be added to the end of an AON diagram for a project that has multiple ending activities.	Concept Questions: 5.1–5.4 Problems: 3.4–3.14 Virtual Office Hours for Solved Problems: 3.1, 3.2
DETERMINING THE PROJECT SCHEDULE (pp. 71–77)	■ **Critical path analysis**—A process that helps determine a project schedule. To find the critical path, we calculate two distinct starting and ending times for each activity: ■ *Earliest start (ES)* = Earliest time at which an activity can start, assuming that all predecessors have been completed ■ *Earliest finish (EF)* = Earliest time at which an activity can be finished ■ *Latest start (LS)* = Latest time at which an activity can start, without delaying the completion time of the entire project ■ *Latest finish (LF)* = Latest time by which an activity has to finish so as to not delay the completion time of the entire project ■ **Forward pass**—A process that identifies all the early start and early finish times. $$ES = \text{Max \{EF of all immediate predecessors\}} \quad (3\text{-}1)$$ $$EF = ES + \text{Activity time} \quad (3\text{-}2)$$ ■ **Backward pass**—A process that identifies all the late start and late finish times. $$LF = \text{Min \{LS of all immediate following activities\}} \quad (3\text{-}3)$$ $$LS = LF - \text{Activity time} \quad (3\text{-}4)$$	Concept Questions: 6.1–6.4 Problems: 3.15, 3.16

Main Heading	Review Material	MyOMLab
	■ **Slack time**—Free time for an activity. $$\text{Slack} = \text{LS} - \text{ES} \quad \text{or} \quad \text{Slack} = \text{LF} - \text{EF} \qquad (3\text{-}5)$$ The activities with zero slack are called *critical activities* and are said to be on the critical path. The critical path is a continuous path through the project network that starts at the first activity in the project, terminates at the last activity in the project, and includes only critical activities.	Virtual Office Hours for Solved Problem: 3.3 ACTIVE MODEL 3.1
VARIABILITY IN ACTIVITY TIMES (pp. 77–82)	■ **Optimistic time** (a)—The "best" activity completion time that could be obtained in a PERT network. ■ **Pessimistic time** (b)—The "worst" activity time that could be expected in a PERT network. ■ **Most likely time** (m)—The most probable time to complete an activity in a PERT network. When using PERT, we often assume that activity time estimates follow the beta distribution. $$\text{Expected activity time } t = (a + 4m + b)/6 \qquad (3\text{-}6)$$ $$\text{Variance of activity completion time} = [(b - a)/6]^2 \qquad (3\text{-}7)$$ $$\sigma_p^2 = \text{Project variance} = \Sigma \text{ (variances of activities on critical path)} \qquad (3\text{-}8)$$ $$Z = (\text{Due date} - \text{Expected date of completion})/\sigma_p \qquad (3\text{-}9)$$ $$\text{Due date} = \text{Expected completion time} + (Z \times \sigma_p) \qquad (3\text{-}10)$$	Concept Questions: 7.1–7.4 Problems: 3.17–3.27 Virtual Office Hours for Solved Problems: 3.4, 3.5, 3.6
COST-TIME TRADE-OFFS AND PROJECT CRASHING (pp. 82–85)	■ **Crashing**—Shortening activity time in a network to reduce time on the critical path so total completion time is reduced. $$\text{Crash cost per period} = \frac{(\text{Crash cost} - \text{Normal cost})}{(\text{Normal time} - \text{Crash time})} \qquad (3\text{-}11)$$	Concept Questions: 8.1–8.4 Problems: 3.28–3.33 Virtual Office Hours for Solved Problem: 3.7
A CRITIQUE OF PERT AND CPM (pp. 85–86)	As with every technique for problem solving, PERT and CPM have a number of advantages as well as several limitations.	Concept Questions: 9.1–9.4
USING MICROSOFT PROJECT TO MANAGE PROJECTS (pp. 86–88)	Microsoft Project, the most popular example of specialized project management software, is extremely useful in drawing project networks, identifying the project schedule, and managing project costs and other resources.	Concept Questions: 10.1–10.4

Self Test

■ **Before taking the self-test,** refer to the learning objectives listed at the beginning of the chapter and the key terms listed at the end of the chapter.

LO 3.1 Which of the following statements regarding Gantt charts is true?
- a) Gantt charts give a timeline and precedence relationships for each activity of a project.
- b) Gantt charts use the four standard spines: Methods, Materials, Manpower, and Machinery.
- c) Gantt charts are visual devices that show the duration of activities in a project.
- d) Gantt charts are expensive.
- e) All of the above are true.

LO 3.2 Which of the following is true about AOA and AON networks?
- a) In AOA, arrows represent activities.
- b) In AON, nodes represent activities.
- c) Activities consume time and resources.
- d) Nodes are also called *events* in AOA.
- e) All of the above.

LO 3.3 Slack time equals:
- a) ES + t.
- b) LS − ES.
- c) zero.
- d) EF − ES.

LO 3.4 The critical path of a network is the:
- a) shortest-time path through the network.
- b) path with the fewest activities.
- c) path with the most activities.
- d) longest-time path through the network.

LO 3.5 PERT analysis computes the variance of the total project completion time as:
- a) the sum of the variances of all activities in the project.
- b) the sum of the variances of all activities on the critical path.
- c) the sum of the variances of all activities not on the critical path.
- d) the variance of the final activity of the project.

LO 3.6 The crash cost per period:
- a) is the difference in costs divided by the difference in times (crash and normal).
- b) is considered to be linear in the range between normal and crash.
- c) needs to be determined so that the smallest cost values on the critical path can be considered for time reduction first.
- d) all of the above.

Answers: LO 3.1. c; LO 3.2. e; LO 3.3. b; LO 3.4. d; LO 3.5. b; LO 3.6. d.

Forecasting

CHAPTER OUTLINE

Alaska Airlines

CHAPTER 4

Forecasting Provides a Competitive Advantage for Disney

Travelshots/Peter Phipp/Travelshots.com/Alamy

Donald Duck, Goofy, and Mickey Mouse provide the public image of Disney to the world. Forecasts drive the work schedules of 72,000 cast members working at Walt Disney World Resort near Orlando.

When it comes to the world's most respected global brands, Walt Disney Parks & Resorts is a visible leader. Although the monarch of this magic kingdom is no man but a mouse—Mickey Mouse—it's CEO Robert Iger who daily manages the entertainment giant.

Disney's global portfolio includes Shanghai Disney (2016), Hong Kong Disneyland (2005), Disneyland Paris (1992), and Tokyo Disneyland (1983). But it is Walt Disney World Resort (in Florida) and Disneyland Resort (in California) that drive profits in this $50 billion corporation, which is ranked in the top 100 in both the *Fortune* 500 and *Financial Times* Global 500.

Revenues at Disney are all about people—how many visit the parks and how they spend money while there. When Iger receives a daily report from his four theme parks and two water parks near Orlando, the report contains only two numbers: the *forecast* of yesterday's attendance at the parks (Magic Kingdom, Epcot, Disney's Animal Kingdom, Disney-Hollywood Studios, Typhoon Lagoon, and Blizzard Beach) and the *actual* attendance. An error close to zero is expected. Iger takes his forecasts very seriously.

The forecasting team at Walt Disney World Resort doesn't just do a daily prediction, however, and Iger is not its only customer. The team also provides daily, weekly, monthly, annual, and 5-year forecasts to the labor management, maintenance, operations, finance, and park scheduling departments. Forecasters use judgmental models, econometric models, moving-average models, and regression analysis.

The giant sphere is the symbol of Epcot, one of Disney's four Orlando parks, for which forecasts of meals, lodging, entertainment, and transportation must be made. This Disney monorail moves guests among parks and the 28 hotels on the massive 47-square-mile property (about the size of San Francisco and twice the size of Manhattan).

Nicolas Chan/Alamy

A daily forecast of attendance is made by adjusting Disney's annual operating plan for weather forecasts, the previous day's crowds, conventions, and seasonal variations. One of the two water parks at Walt Disney World Resort, Typhoon Lagoon, is shown here.

Kevin Fleming/Corbis

Melvyn Longhurst/Corbis

Cinderella's iconic castle is a focal point for meeting up with family and friends in the massive park. The statue of Walt Disney greets visitors to the open plaza.

With 20% of Walt Disney World Resort's customers coming from outside the United States, its economic model includes such variables as gross domestic product (GDP), cross-exchange rates, and arrivals into the U.S. Disney also uses 35 analysts and 70 field people to survey 1 million people each year. The surveys, administered to guests at the parks and its 20 hotels, to employees, and to travel industry professionals, examine future travel plans and experiences at the parks. This helps forecast not only attendance but also behavior at each ride (e.g., how long people will wait, how many times they will ride). Inputs to the monthly forecasting model include airline specials, speeches by the chair of the Federal Reserve, and Wall Street trends. Disney even monitors 3,000 school districts inside and outside the U.S. for holiday/vacation schedules. With this approach, Disney's 5-year attendance forecast yields just a 5% error on average. Its annual forecasts have a 0% to 3% error.

Attendance forecasts for the parks drive a whole slew of management decisions. For example, capacity on any day can be increased by opening at 8 A.M. instead of the usual 9 A.M., by opening more shows or rides, by adding more food/ beverage carts (9 million hamburgers and 50 million Cokes are sold per year!), and by bringing in more employees (called "cast members"). Cast members are scheduled in 15-minute intervals throughout the parks for flexibility. Demand can be managed by limiting the number of guests admitted to the

dmac/Alamy

Forecasts are critical to making sure rides are not overcrowded. Disney is good at "managing demand" with techniques such as adding more street activities to reduce long lines for rides. On slow days, Disney calls fewer cast members to work.

parks, with the "FAST PASS" reservation system, and by shifting crowds from rides to more street parades.

At Disney, forecasting is a key driver in the company's success and competitive advantage. ◣

What Is Forecasting?

Every day, managers like those at Disney make decisions without knowing what will happen in the future. They order inventory without knowing what sales will be, purchase new equipment despite uncertainty about demand for products, and make investments without knowing what profits will be. Managers are always trying to make better estimates of what will happen in the future in the face of uncertainty. Making good estimates is the main purpose of forecasting.

> **STUDENT TIP** ◆
> An increasingly complex world economy makes forecasting challenging.

In this chapter, we examine different types of forecasts and present a variety of forecasting models. Our purpose is to show that there are many ways for managers to forecast. We also provide an overview of business sales forecasting and describe how to prepare, monitor, and judge the accuracy of a forecast. Good forecasts are an *essential* part of efficient service and manufacturing operations.

> **Forecasting**
> The art and science of predicting future events.

Forecasting is the art and science of predicting future events. Forecasting may involve taking historical data (such as past sales) and projecting them into the future with a mathematical model. It may be a subjective or an intuitive prediction (e.g., "this is a great new product and will sell 20% more than the old one"). It may be based on demand-driven data, such as customer plans to purchase, and projecting them into the future. Or the forecast may involve a combination of these, that is, a mathematical model adjusted by a manager's good judgment.

As we introduce different forecasting techniques in this chapter, you will see that there is seldom one superior method. Forecasts may be influenced by a product's position in its life cycle—whether sales are in an introduction, growth, maturity, or decline stage. Other products can be influenced by the demand for a related product—for example, navigation systems may track with new car sales. Because there are limits to what can be expected from forecasts, we develop error measures. Preparing and monitoring forecasts can also be costly and time consuming.

Few businesses, however, can afford to avoid the process of forecasting by just waiting to see what happens and then taking their chances. Effective planning in both the short run and long run depends on a forecast of demand for the company's products.

Forecasting Time Horizons

> **LO 4.1** *Understand* the three time horizons and which models apply for each

A forecast is usually classified by the *future time horizon* that it covers. Time horizons fall into three categories:

1. *Short-range forecast:* This forecast has a time span of up to 1 year but is generally less than 3 months. It is used for planning purchasing, job scheduling, workforce levels, job assignments, and production levels.

2. *Medium-range forecast:* A medium-range, or intermediate, forecast generally spans from 3 months to 3 years. It is useful in sales planning, production planning and budgeting, cash budgeting, and analysis of various operating plans.

3. *Long-range forecast:* Generally 3 years or more in time span, long-range forecasts are used in planning for new products, capital expenditures, facility location or expansion, and research and development.

Medium- and long-range forecasts are distinguished from short-range forecasts by three features:

1. First, intermediate and long-range forecasts *deal with more comprehensive issues* supporting management decisions regarding planning and products, plants, and processes. Implementing some facility decisions, such as GM's decision to open a new Brazilian manufacturing plant, can take 5 to 8 years from inception to completion.
2. Second, short-term forecasting usually *employs different methodologies* than longer-term forecasting. Mathematical techniques, such as moving averages, exponential smoothing, and trend extrapolation (all of which we shall examine shortly), are common to short-run projections. Broader, *less* quantitative methods are useful in predicting such issues as whether a new product, like the optical disk recorder, should be introduced into a company's product line.
3. Finally, as you would expect, short-range forecasts *tend to be more accurate* than longer-range forecasts. Factors that influence demand change every day. Thus, as the time horizon lengthens, it is likely that forecast accuracy will diminish. It almost goes without saying, then, that sales forecasts must be updated regularly to maintain their value and integrity. After each sales period, forecasts should be reviewed and revised.

Types of Forecasts

Organizations use three major types of forecasts in planning future operations:

1. Economic forecasts address the business cycle by predicting inflation rates, money supplies, housing starts, and other planning indicators.
2. Technological forecasts are concerned with rates of technological progress, which can result in the birth of exciting new products, requiring new plants and equipment.
3. Demand forecasts are projections of demand for a company's products or services. Forecasts drive decisions, so managers need immediate and accurate information about real demand. They need *demand-driven forecasts*, where the focus is on rapidly identifying and tracking customer desires. These forecasts may use recent point-of-sale (POS) data, retailer-generated reports of customer preferences, and any other information that will help to forecast with the most current data possible. Demand-driven forecasts drive a company's production, capacity, and scheduling systems and serve as inputs to financial, marketing, and personnel planning. In addition, the payoff in reduced inventory and obsolescence can be huge.

Economic forecasts
Planning indicators that are valuable in helping organizations prepare medium- to long-range forecasts.

Technological forecasts
Long-term forecasts concerned with the rates of technological progress.

Demand forecasts
Projections of a company's sales for each time period in the planning horizon.

Economic and technological forecasting are specialized techniques that may fall outside the role of the operations manager. The emphasis in this chapter will therefore be on demand forecasting.

The Strategic Importance of Forecasting

Good forecasts are of critical importance in all aspects of a business: *The forecast is the only estimate of demand until actual demand becomes known.* Forecasts of demand therefore drive decisions in many areas. Let's look at the impact of product demand forecast on three activities: (1) supply-chain management, (2) human resources, and (3) capacity.

Supply-Chain Management

Good supplier relations and the ensuing advantages in product innovation, cost, and speed to market depend on accurate forecasts. Here are just three examples:

- Apple has built an effective global system where it controls nearly every piece of the supply chain, from product design to retail store. With rapid communication and accurate data shared up and down the supply chain, innovation is enhanced, inventory costs are reduced, and speed to market is improved. Once a product goes on sale, Apple tracks demand by the hour for each store and adjusts production forecasts daily. At Apple, forecasts for its supply chain are a strategic weapon.

♦ Toyota develops sophisticated car forecasts with input from a variety of sources, including dealers. But forecasting the demand for accessories such as navigation systems, custom wheels, spoilers, and so on is particularly difficult. And there are over 1,000 items that vary by model and color. As a result, Toyota not only reviews reams of data with regard to vehicles that have been built and wholesaled but also looks in detail at vehicle forecasts before it makes judgments about the future accessory demand. When this is done correctly, the result is an efficient supply chain and satisfied customers.

♦ Walmart collaborates with suppliers such as Sara Lee and Procter & Gamble to make sure the right item is available at the right time in the right place and at the right price. For instance, in hurricane season, Walmart's ability to analyze 700 million store–item combinations means it can forecast that not only flashlights but also Pop-Tarts and beer sell at seven times the normal demand rate. These forecasting systems are known as *collaborative planning, forecasting, and replenishment* (CPFR). They combine the intelligence of multiple supply-chain partners. The goal of CPFR is to create significantly more accurate information that can power the supply chain to greater sales and profits.

Human Resources

Hiring, training, and laying off workers all depend on anticipated demand. If the human resources department must hire additional workers without warning, the amount of training declines, and the quality of the workforce suffers. A large Louisiana chemical firm almost lost its biggest customer when a quick expansion to around-the-clock shifts led to a total breakdown in quality control on the second and third shifts.

Capacity

When capacity is inadequate, the resulting shortages can lead to loss of customers and market share. This is exactly what happened to Nabisco when it underestimated the huge demand for its new Snackwell Devil's Food Cookies. Even with production lines working overtime, Nabisco could not keep up with demand, and it lost customers. Nintendo faced this problem when its Wii was introduced and exceeded all forecasts for demand. Amazon made the same error with its Kindle. On the other hand, when excess capacity exists, costs can skyrocket.

Seven Steps in the Forecasting System

Forecasting follows seven basic steps. We use Disney World, the focus of this chapter's *Global Company Profile*, as an example of each step:

1. *Determine the use of the forecast:* Disney uses park attendance forecasts to drive decisions about staffing, opening times, ride availability, and food supplies.
2. *Select the items to be forecasted:* For Disney World, there are six main parks. A forecast of daily attendance at each is the main number that determines labor, maintenance, and scheduling.
3. *Determine the time horizon of the forecast:* Is it short, medium, or long term? Disney develops daily, weekly, monthly, annual, and 5-year forecasts.
4. *Select the forecasting model(s):* Disney uses a variety of statistical models that we shall discuss, including moving averages, econometrics, and regression analysis. It also employs judgmental, or nonquantitative, models.
5. *Gather the data needed to make the forecast:* Disney's forecasting team employs 35 analysts and 70 field personnel to survey 1 million people/businesses every year. Disney also uses a firm called Global Insights for travel industry forecasts and gathers data on exchange rates, arrivals into the U.S., airline specials, Wall Street trends, and school vacation schedules.

6. *Make the forecast.*
7. *Validate and implement the results:* At Disney, forecasts are reviewed daily at the highest levels to make sure that the model, assumptions, and data are valid. Error measures are applied; then the forecasts are used to schedule personnel down to 15-minute intervals.

These seven steps present a systematic way of initiating, designing, and implementing a forecasting system. When the system is to be used to generate forecasts regularly over time, data must be routinely collected. Then actual computations are usually made by computer.

Regardless of the system that firms like Disney use, each company faces several realities:

♦ Outside factors that we cannot predict or control often impact the forecast.

♦ Most forecasting techniques assume that there is some underlying stability in the system. Consequently, some firms automate their predictions using computerized forecasting software, then closely monitor only the product items whose demand is erratic.

♦ Both product family and aggregated forecasts are more accurate than individual product forecasts. Disney, for example, aggregates daily attendance forecasts by park. This approach helps balance the over- and underpredictions for each of the six attractions.

Forecasting Approaches

There are two general approaches to forecasting, just as there are two ways to tackle all decision modeling. One is a quantitative analysis; the other is a qualitative approach. Quantitative forecasts use a variety of mathematical models that rely on historical data and/or associative variables to forecast demand. Subjective or qualitative forecasts incorporate such factors as the decision maker's intuition, emotions, personal experiences, and value system in reaching a forecast. Some firms use one approach and some use the other. In practice, a combination of the two is usually most effective.

Overview of Qualitative Methods

In this section, we consider four different *qualitative* forecasting techniques:

1. Jury of executive opinion: Under this method, the opinions of a group of high-level experts or managers, often in combination with statistical models, are pooled to arrive at a group estimate of demand. Bristol-Myers Squibb Company, for example, uses 220 well-known research scientists as its jury of executive opinion to get a grasp on future trends in the world of medical research.

2. Delphi method: There are three different types of participants in the Delphi method: decision makers, staff personnel, and respondents. Decision makers usually consist of a group of 5 to 10 experts who will be making the actual forecast. Staff personnel assist decision makers by preparing, distributing, collecting, and summarizing a series of questionnaires and survey results. The respondents are a group of people, often located in different places, whose judgments are valued. This group provides inputs to the decision makers before the forecast is made.

   The state of Alaska, for example, has used the Delphi method to develop its long-range economic forecast. A large part of the state's budget is derived from the million-plus barrels of oil pumped daily through a pipeline at Prudhoe Bay. The large Delphi panel of experts had to represent all groups and opinions in the state and all geographic areas.

3. Sales force composite: In this approach, each salesperson estimates what sales will be in his or her region. These forecasts are then reviewed to ensure that they are realistic. Then they are combined at the district and national levels to reach an overall forecast. A variation of this approach occurs at Lexus, where every quarter Lexus dealers have a "make meeting." At this meeting, they talk about what is selling, in what colors, and with what options, so the factory knows what to build.

4. Market survey: This method solicits input from customers or potential customers regarding future purchasing plans. It can help not only in preparing a forecast but also in improving

Quantitative forecasts
Forecasts that employ mathematical modeling to forecast demand.

Qualitative forecasts
Forecasts that incorporate such factors as the decision maker's intuition, emotions, personal experiences, and value system.

Jury of executive opinion
A forecasting technique that uses the opinion of a small group of high-level managers to form a group estimate of demand.

Delphi method
A forecasting technique using a group process that allows experts to make forecasts.

LO 4.2 *Explain* when to use each of the four qualitative models

Sales force composite
A forecasting technique based on salespersons' estimates of expected sales.

Market survey
A forecasting method that solicits input from customers or potential customers regarding future purchasing plans.

product design and planning for new products. The consumer market survey and sales force composite methods can, however, suffer from overly optimistic forecasts that arise from customer input.

Overview of Quantitative Methods[1]

Five quantitative forecasting methods, all of which use historical data, are described in this chapter. They fall into two categories:

1. Naive approach
2. Moving averages   } **Time-series models**
3. Exponential smoothing
4. Trend projection
5. Linear regression   } **Associative model**

Time series
A forecasting technique that uses a series of past data points to make a forecast.

Time-Series Models Time-series models predict on the assumption that the future is a function of the past. In other words, they look at what has happened over a period of time and use a series of past data to make a forecast. If we are predicting sales of lawn mowers, we use the past sales for lawn mowers to make the forecasts.

Associative Models Associative models, such as linear regression, incorporate the variables or factors that might influence the quantity being forecast. For example, an associative model for lawn mower sales might use factors such as new housing starts, advertising budget, and competitors' prices.

STUDENT TIP◊
Here is the meat of this chapter. We now show you a wide variety of models that use time-series data.

Time-Series Forecasting

A time series is based on a sequence of evenly spaced (weekly, monthly, quarterly, and so on) data points. Examples include weekly sales of Nike Air Jordans, quarterly earnings reports of Microsoft stock, daily shipments of Coors beer, and annual consumer price indices. Forecasting time-series data implies that future values are predicted *only* from past values and that other variables, no matter how potentially valuable, may be ignored.

Decomposition of a Time Series

Analyzing time series means breaking down past data into components and then projecting them forward. A time series has four components:

1. *Trend* is the gradual upward or downward movement of the data over time. Changes in income, population, age distribution, or cultural views may account for movement in trend.

STUDENT TIP◊
The peak "seasons" for sales of Frito-Lay chips are the Super Bowl, Memorial Day, Labor Day, and the Fourth of July.

2. *Seasonality* is a data pattern that repeats itself after a period of days, weeks, months, or quarters. There are six common seasonality patterns:

PERIOD LENGTH	"SEASON" LENGTH	NUMBER OF "SEASONS" IN PATTERN
Week	Day	7
Month	Week	$4-4\frac{1}{2}$
Month	Day	28–31
Year	Quarter	4
Year	Month	12
Year	Week	52

Restaurants and barber shops, for example, experience weekly seasons, with Saturday being the peak of business. See the *OM in Action* box "Forecasting at Olive Garden." Beer distributors forecast yearly patterns, with monthly seasons. Three "seasons"—May, July, and September—each contain a big beer-drinking holiday.

OM in Action   Forecasting at Olive Garden

It's Friday night in the college town of Gainesville, Florida, and the local Olive Garden restaurant is humming. Customers may wait an average of 30 minutes for a table, but they can sample new wines and cheeses and admire scenic paintings of Italian villages on the Tuscan-style restaurant's walls. Then comes dinner with portions so huge that many people take home a doggie bag. The typical bill: under $15 per person.

Crowds flock to the Darden restaurant chain's Olive Garden, Seasons 52, and Bahama Breeze for value and consistency—*and* they get it.

Every night, Darden's computers crank out forecasts that tell store managers what demand to anticipate the next day. The forecasting software generates a total meal forecast and breaks that down into specific menu items. The system tells a manager, for instance, that if 625 meals will be served the next day, "you will serve these items in these quantities. So before you go home, pull 25 pounds of shrimp and 30 pounds of crab out, and tell your operations people to prepare 42 portion packs of chicken, 75 scampi dishes, 8 stuffed flounders, and so on." Managers often fine-tune the quantities based on local conditions, such as weather or a convention, but they know what their customers are going to order.

By relying on demand history, the forecasting system has cut millions of dollars of waste out of the system. The forecast also reduces labor costs by providing the necessary information for improved scheduling. Labor costs decreased almost a full percent in the first year, translating into additional millions in savings for the Darden chain. In the low-margin restaurant business, every dollar counts.

Sources: InformationWeek (April 1, 2014); *USA Today* (Oct. 13, 2014); and *FastCompany* (July-August 2009).

---

3. *Cycles* are patterns in the data that occur every several years. They are usually tied into the business cycle and are of major importance in short-term business analysis and planning. Predicting business cycles is difficult because they may be affected by political events or by international turmoil.
4. *Random variations* are "blips" in the data caused by chance and unusual situations. They follow no discernible pattern, so they cannot be predicted.

LO 4.3 *Apply* the naive, moving-average, exponential smoothing, and trend methods

Figure 4.1 illustrates a demand over a 4-year period. It shows the average, trend, seasonal components, and random variations around the demand curve. The average demand is the sum of the demand for each period divided by the number of data periods.

Naive Approach

The simplest way to forecast is to assume that demand in the next period will be equal to demand in the most recent period. In other words, if sales of a product—say, Nokia cell phones—were 68 units in January, we can forecast that February's sales will also be 68 phones.

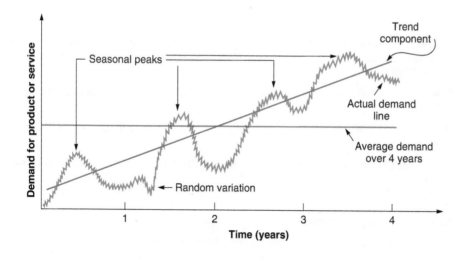

Figure **4.1**

Demand Charted over 4 Years, with a Growth Trend and Seasonality Indicated

◆ **STUDENT TIP**

Forecasting is easy when demand is stable. But with trend, seasonality, and cycles considered, the job is a lot more interesting.

Naive approach

A forecasting technique that assumes that demand in the next period is equal to demand in the most recent period.

Does this make any sense? It turns out that for some product lines, this naive approach is the most cost-effective and efficient objective forecasting model. At least it provides a starting point against which more sophisticated models that follow can be compared.

Moving Averages

Moving averages

A forecasting method that uses an average of the n most recent periods of data to forecast the next period.

A moving-average forecast uses a number of historical actual data values to generate a forecast. Moving averages are useful *if we can assume that market demands will stay fairly steady over time*. A 4-month moving average is found by simply summing the demand during the past 4 months and dividing by 4. With each passing month, the most recent month's data are added to the sum of the previous 3 months' data, and the earliest month is dropped. This practice tends to smooth out short-term irregularities in the data series.

Mathematically, the simple moving average (which serves as an estimate of the next period's demand) is expressed as:

$$\text{Moving average} = \frac{\Sigma \text{ demand in previous } n \text{ periods}}{n} \qquad (4\text{-}1)$$

where n is the number of periods in the moving average—for example, 4, 5, or 6 months, respectively, for a 4-, 5-, or 6-period moving average.

Example 1 shows how moving averages are calculated.

Example 1

DETERMINING THE MOVING AVERAGE

Donna's Garden Supply wants a 3-month moving-average forecast, including a forecast for next January, for shed sales.

APPROACH ▶ Storage shed sales are shown in the middle column of the following table. A 3-month moving average appears on the right.

MONTH	ACTUAL SHED SALES	3-MONTH MOVING AVERAGE
January	10	
February	12	
March	13	
April	16	$(10 + 12 + 13)/3 = 11\frac{2}{3}$
May	19	$(12 + 13 + 16)/3 = 13\frac{2}{3}$
June	23	$(13 + 16 + 19)/3 = 16$
July	26	$(16 + 19 + 23)/3 = 19\frac{1}{3}$
August	30	$(19 + 23 + 26)/3 = 22\frac{2}{3}$
September	28	$(23 + 26 + 30)/3 = 26\frac{1}{3}$
October	18	$(26 + 30 + 28)/3 = 28$
November	16	$(30 + 28 + 18)/3 = 25\frac{1}{3}$
December	14	$(28 + 18 + 16)/3 = 20\frac{2}{3}$

SOLUTION ▶ The forecast for December is $20\frac{2}{3}$. To project the demand for sheds in the coming January, we sum the October, November, and December sales and divide by 3: January forecast $= (18 + 16 + 14)/3 = 16$.

INSIGHT ▶ Management now has a forecast that averages sales for the last 3 months. It is easy to use and understand.

LEARNING EXERCISE ▶ If actual sales in December were 18 (rather than 14), what is the new January forecast? [Answer: $17\frac{1}{3}$.]

RELATED PROBLEMS ▶ 4.1a, 4.2b, 4.5a, 4.6, 4.8a, b, 4.10a, 4.13b, 4.15, 4.33 (4.35, 4.38 are available in MyOMLab)

EXCEL OM Data File Ch04Ex1.xls can be found in MyOMLab.

ACTIVE MODEL 4.1 This example is further illustrated in Active Model 4.1 in MyOMLab.

When a detectable trend or pattern is present, *weights* can be used to place more emphasis on recent values. This practice makes forecasting techniques more responsive to changes because more recent periods may be more heavily weighted. Choice of weights is somewhat arbitrary because there is no set formula to determine them. Therefore, deciding which weights to use requires some experience. For example, if the latest month or period is weighted too heavily, the forecast may reflect a large unusual change in the demand or sales pattern too quickly.

A weighted moving average may be expressed mathematically as:

$$\text{Weighted moving average} = \frac{\sum ((\text{Weight for period } n)(\text{Demand in period } n))}{\sum \text{Weights}} \quad (4\text{-}2)$$

Example 2 shows how to calculate a weighted moving average.

Example 2

DETERMINING THE WEIGHTED MOVING AVERAGE

Donna's Garden Supply (see Example 1) wants to forecast storage shed sales by weighting the past 3 months, with more weight given to recent data to make them more significant.

APPROACH ▶ Assign more weight to recent data, as follows:

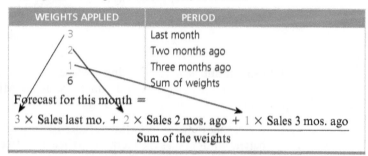

WEIGHTS APPLIED	PERIOD
3	Last month
2	Two months ago
1	Three months ago
6	Sum of weights

Forecast for this month =

$$\frac{3 \times \text{Sales last mo.} + 2 \times \text{Sales 2 mos. ago} + 1 \times \text{Sales 3 mos. ago}}{\text{Sum of the weights}}$$

SOLUTION ▶ The results of this weighted-average forecast are as follows:

MONTH	ACTUAL SHED SALES	3-MONTH WEIGHTED MOVING AVERAGE
January	10	
February	12	
March	13	
April	16	$[(3 \times 13) + (2 \times 12) + (10)]/6 = 12\frac{1}{6}$
May	19	$[(3 \times 16) + (2 \times 13) + (12)]/6 = 14\frac{1}{3}$
June	23	$[(3 \times 19) + (2 \times 16) + (13)]/6 = 17$
July	26	$[(3 \times 23) + (2 \times 19) + (16)]/6 = 20\frac{1}{2}$
August	30	$[(3 \times 26) + (2 \times 23) + (19)]/6 = 23\frac{5}{6}$
September	28	$[(3 \times 30) + (2 \times 26) + (23)]/6 = 27\frac{1}{2}$
October	18	$[(3 \times 28) + (2 \times 30) + (26)]/6 = 28\frac{1}{3}$
November	16	$[(3 \times 18) + (2 \times 28) + (30)]/6 = 23\frac{1}{3}$
December	14	$[(3 \times 16) + (2 \times 18) + (28)]/6 = 18\frac{2}{3}$

The forecast for January is $15\frac{1}{3}$. Do you see how this number is computed?

INSIGHT ▶ In this particular forecasting situation, you can see that more heavily weighting the latest month provides a more accurate projection.

LEARNING EXERCISE ▶ If the assigned weights were 0.50, 0.33, and 0.17 (instead of 3, 2, and 1), what is the forecast for January's weighted moving average? Why? [Answer: There is no change. These are the same *relative* weights. Note that $\sum$ weights = 1 now, so there is no need for a denominator. When the weights sum to 1, calculations tend to be simpler.]

RELATED PROBLEMS ▶ 4.1b, 4.2c, 4.5c, 4.6, 4.7, 4.10b (4.38 is available in MyOMLab)

EXCEL **OM** Data File **Ch04Ex2.xls** can be found in MyOMLab.

Figure **4.2**

Actual Demand vs. Moving-Average and Weighted-Moving-Average Methods for Donna's Garden Supply

Both simple and weighted moving averages are effective in smoothing out sudden fluctuations in the demand pattern to provide stable estimates. Moving averages do, however, present three problems:

1. Increasing the size of *n* (the number of periods averaged) does smooth out fluctuations better, but it makes the method less sensitive to changes in the data.
2. Moving averages cannot pick up trends very well. Because they are averages, they will always stay within past levels and will not predict changes to either higher or lower levels. That is, they *lag* the actual values.
3. Moving averages require extensive records of past data.

Figure 4.2, a plot of the data in Examples 1 and 2, illustrates the lag effect of the moving-average models. Note that both the moving-average and weighted-moving-average lines lag the actual demand. The weighted moving average, however, usually reacts more quickly to demand changes. Even in periods of downturn (see November and December), it more closely tracks the demand.

Exponential Smoothing

Exponential smoothing

A weighted-moving-average forecasting technique in which data points are weighted by an exponential function.

Exponential smoothing is another weighted-moving-average forecasting method. It involves very *little* record keeping of past data and is fairly easy to use. The basic exponential smoothing formula can be shown as follows:

New forecast = Last period's forecast

+ α (Last period's actual demand − Last period's forecast)　(4-3)

Smoothing constant

The weighting factor used in an exponential smoothing forecast, a number greater than or equal to 0 and less than or equal to 1.

where α is a weight, or **smoothing constant**, chosen by the forecaster, that has a value greater than or equal to 0 and less than or equal to 1. Equation (4-3) can also be written mathematically as:

$$F_t = F_{t-1} + \alpha(A_{t-1} - F_{t-1})\qquad(4\text{-}4)$$

where　F_t = new forecast

F_{t-1} = previous period's forecast

α = smoothing (or weighting) constant $(0 \le \alpha \le 1)$

A_{t-1} = previous period's actual demand

The concept is not complex. The latest estimate of demand is equal to the old forecast adjusted by a fraction of the difference between the last period's actual demand and last period's forecast. Example 3 shows how to use exponential smoothing to derive a forecast.

Example 3

DETERMINING A FORECAST VIA EXPONENTIAL SMOOTHING

In January, a car dealer predicted February demand for 142 Ford Mustangs. Actual February demand was 153 autos. Using a smoothing constant chosen by management of $\alpha = .20$, the dealer wants to forecast March demand using the exponential smoothing model.

APPROACH ▶ The exponential smoothing model in Equations (4-3) and (4-4) can be applied.

SOLUTION ▶ Substituting the sample data into the formula, we obtain:

$$\text{New forecast (for March demand)} = 142 + .2(153 - 142) = 142 + 2.2$$
$$= 144.2$$

Thus, the March demand forecast for Ford Mustangs is rounded to 144.

INSIGHT ▶ Using just two pieces of data, the forecast and the actual demand, plus a smoothing constant, we developed a forecast of 144 Ford Mustangs for March.

LEARNING EXERCISE ▶ If the smoothing constant is changed to .30, what is the new forecast? [Answer: 145.3]

RELATED PROBLEMS ▶ 4.1c, 4.3, 4.4, 4.5d, 4.6, 4.9d, 4.11, 4.12, 4.13a, 4.17, 4.18, 4.31, 4.33, 4.34 (4.36, 4.61a are available in MyOMLab)

The *smoothing constant*, α, is generally in the range from .05 to .50 for business applications. It can be changed to give more weight to recent data (when α is high) or more weight to past data (when α is low). When α reaches the extreme of 1.0, then in Equation (4-4), $F_t = 1.0A_{t-1}$. All the older values drop out, and the forecast becomes identical to the naive model mentioned earlier in this chapter. That is, the forecast for the next period is just the same as this period's demand.

The following table helps illustrate this concept. For example, when $\alpha = .5$, we can see that the new forecast is based almost entirely on demand in the last three or four periods. When $\alpha = .1$, the forecast places little weight on recent demand and takes many periods (about 19) of historical values into account.

			WEIGHT ASSIGNED TO		
SMOOTHING CONSTANT	MOST RECENT PERIOD (α)	2ND MOST RECENT PERIOD $\alpha(1-\alpha)$	3RD MOST RECENT PERIOD $\alpha(1-\alpha)^2$	4TH MOST RECENT PERIOD $\alpha(1-\alpha)^3$	5TH MOST RECENT PERIOD $\alpha(1-\alpha)^4$
$\alpha = .1$	.1	.09	.081	.073	.066
$\alpha = .5$	.5	.25	.125	.063	.031

Selecting the Smoothing Constant Exponential smoothing has been successfully applied in virtually every type of business. However, the appropriate value of the smoothing constant, α, can make the difference between an accurate forecast and an inaccurate forecast. High values of α are chosen when the underlying average is likely to change. Low values of α are used when the underlying average is fairly stable. In picking a value for the smoothing constant, the objective is to obtain the most accurate forecast.

Measuring Forecast Error

The overall accuracy of any forecasting model—moving average, exponential smoothing, or other—can be determined by comparing the forecasted values with the actual or observed

STUDENT TIP
Forecasts tend to be more accurate as they become shorter. Therefore, forecast error also tends to drop with shorter forecasts.

values. If F_t denotes the forecast in period t, and A_t denotes the actual demand in period t, the *forecast error* (or deviation) is defined as:

$$\text{Forecast error} = \text{Actual demand} - \text{Forecast value}$$
$$= A_t - F_t$$

LO 4.4 *Compute* three measures of forecast accuracy

Several measures are used in practice to calculate the overall forecast error. These measures can be used to compare different forecasting models, as well as to monitor forecasts to ensure they are performing well. Three of the most popular measures are mean absolute deviation (MAD), mean squared error (MSE), and mean absolute percent error (MAPE). We now describe and give an example of each.

Mean Absolute Deviation The first measure of the overall forecast error for a model is the mean absolute deviation (MAD). This value is computed by taking the sum of the absolute values of the individual forecast errors (deviations) and dividing by the number of periods of data (n):

Mean absolute
deviation (MAD)
A measure of the overall forecast
error for a model.

$$\text{MAD} = \frac{\sum |\text{Actual} - \text{Forecast}|}{n} \qquad (4\text{-}5)$$

Example 4 applies MAD, as a measure of overall forecast error, by testing two values of α.

Example 4

DETERMINING THE MEAN ABSOLUTE DEVIATION (MAD)

During the past 8 quarters, the Port of Baltimore has unloaded large quantities of grain from ships. The port's operations manager wants to test the use of exponential smoothing to see how well the technique works in predicting tonnage unloaded. He guesses that the forecast of grain unloaded in the first quarter was 175 tons. Two values of α are to be examined: $\alpha = .10$ and $\alpha = .50$.

APPROACH ▶ Compare the actual data with the data we forecast (using each of the two α values) and then find the absolute deviation and MADs.

SOLUTION ▶ The following table shows the *detailed* calculations for $\alpha = .10$ only:

QUARTER	ACTUAL TONNAGE UNLOADED	FORECAST WITH $\alpha = .10$	FORECAST WITH $\alpha = .50$
1	180	175	175
2	168	$175.50 = 175.00 + .10(180 - 175)$	177.50
3	159	$174.75 = 175.50 + .10(168 - 175.50)$	172.75
4	175	$173.18 = 174.75 + .10(159 - 174.75)$	165.88
5	190	$173.36 = 173.18 + .10(175 - 173.18)$	170.44
6	205	$175.02 = 173.36 + .10(190 - 173.36)$	180.22
7	180	$178.02 = 175.02 + .10(205 - 175.02)$	192.61
8	182	$178.22 = 178.02 + .10(180 - 178.02)$	186.30
9	?	$178.59 = 178.22 + .10(182 - 178.22)$	184.15

To evaluate the accuracy of each smoothing constant, we can compute forecast errors in terms of absolute deviations and MADs:

QUARTER	ACTUAL TONNAGE UNLOADED	FORECAST WITH $\alpha = .10$	ABSOLUTE DEVIATION FOR $\alpha = .10$	FORECAST WITH $\alpha = .50$	ABSOLUTE DEVIATION FOR $\alpha = .50$
1	180	175	5.00	175	5.00
2	168	175.50	7.50	177.50	9.50
3	159	174.75	15.75	172.75	13.75
4	175	173.18	1.82	165.88	9.12
5	190	173.36	16.64	170.44	19.56
6	205	175.02	29.98	180.22	24.78
7	180	178.02	1.98	192.61	12.61
8	182	178.22	3.78	186.30	4.30
	Sum of absolute deviations:		82.45		98.62
	$\text{MAD} = \dfrac{\sum |\text{Deviations}|}{n}$		10.31		12.33

INSIGHT ▶ On the basis of this comparison of the two MADs, a smoothing constant of $\alpha = .10$ is preferred to $\alpha = .50$ because its MAD is smaller.

LEARNING EXERCISE ▶ If the smoothing constant is changed from $\alpha = .10$ to $\alpha = .20$, what is the new MAD? [Answer: 10.21.]

RELATED PROBLEMS ▶ 4.5b, 4.8c, 4.9c, 4.14, 4.23, 4.59b (4.35d, 4.37a, 4.38c, 4.61b are available in MyOMLab)

EXCEL OM Data File **Ch04Ex4a.xls** and **Ch04Ex4b.xls** can be found in MyOMLab.

ACTIVE **MODEL** 4.2 This example is further illustrated in Active Model 4.2 in MyOMLab.

Most computerized forecasting software includes a feature that automatically finds the smoothing constant with the lowest forecast error. Some software modifies the α value if errors become larger than acceptable.

Mean Squared Error The mean squared error (MSE) is a second way of measuring overall forecast error. MSE is the average of the squared differences between the forecasted and observed values. Its formula is:

Mean squared error (MSE)
The average of the squared differences between the forecasted and observed values.

$$MSE = \frac{\Sigma(\text{Forecast errors})^2}{n} \qquad (4\text{-}6)$$

Example 5 finds the MSE for the Port of Baltimore problem introduced in Example 4.

Example 5

DETERMINING THE MEAN SQUARED ERROR (MSE)

The operations manager for the Port of Baltimore now wants to compute MSE for $\alpha = .10$.

APPROACH ▶ Using the same forecast data for $\alpha = .10$ from Example 4, compute the MSE with Equation (4-6).

SOLUTION ▶

QUARTER	ACTUAL TONNAGE UNLOADED	FORECAST FOR $\alpha = .10$	(ERROR)^2
1	180	175	$5^2 = 25$
2	168	175.50	$(-7.5)^2 = 56.25$
3	159	174.75	$(-15.75)^2 = 248.06$
4	175	173.18	$(1.82)^2 = 3.31$
5	190	173.36	$(16.64)^2 = 276.89$
6	205	175.02	$(29.98)^2 = 898.80$
7	180	178.02	$(1.98)^2 = 3.92$
8	182	178.22	$(3.78)^2 = 14.29$
			Sum of errors squared = 1,526.52

$$MSE = \frac{\Sigma(\text{Forecast errors})^2}{n} = 1,526.52/8 = 190.8$$

INSIGHT ▶ Is this MSE = 190.8 good or bad? It all depends on the MSEs for other forecasting approaches. A low MSE is better because we want to minimize MSE. MSE exaggerates errors because it squares them.

LEARNING EXERCISE ▶ Find the MSE for $\alpha = .50$. [Answer: MSE = 195.24. The result indicates that $\alpha = .10$ is a better choice because we seek a lower MSE. Coincidentally, this is the same conclusion we reached using MAD in Example 4.]

RELATED PROBLEMS ▶ 4.8d, 4.11c, 4.14, 4.15c, 4.16c, 4.20 (4.35d, 4.37b are available in MyOMLab)

The MSE tends to accentuate large deviations due to the squared term. For example, if the forecast error for period 1 is twice as large as the error for period 2, the squared error in period 1 is four times as large as that for period 2. Hence, using MSE as the measure of forecast error typically indicates that we prefer to have several smaller deviations rather than even one large deviation.

Mean Absolute Percent Error   A problem with both the MAD and MSE is that their values depend on the magnitude of the item being forecast. If the forecast item is measured in thousands, the MAD and MSE values can be very large. To avoid this problem, we can use the mean absolute percent error (MAPE). This is computed as the average of the absolute difference between the forecasted and actual values, expressed as a percentage of the actual values. That is, if we have forecasted and actual values for n periods, the MAPE is calculated as:

Mean absolute percent error (MAPE)

The average of the absolute differences between the forecast and actual values, expressed as a percent of actual values.

$$\text{MAPE} = \frac{\sum_{i=1}^{n} 100 \left| \text{Actual}_i - \text{Forecast}_i \right| / \text{Actual}_i}{n} \qquad (4\text{-}7)$$

Example 6 illustrates the calculations using the data from Examples 4 and 5.

Example 6

DETERMINING THE MEAN ABSOLUTE PERCENT ERROR (MAPE)

The Port of Baltimore wants to now calculate the MAPE when $\alpha = .10$.

APPROACH ▶   Equation (4-7) is applied to the forecast data computed in Example 4.

SOLUTION ▶

QUARTER	ACTUAL TONNAGE UNLOADED	FORECAST FOR $\alpha = .10$	ABSOLUTE PERCENT ERROR 100 (|ERROR|/ACTUAL)
1	180	175.00	100(5/180) = 2.78%
2	168	175.50	100(7.5/168) = 4.46%
3	159	174.75	100(15.75/159) = 9.90%
4	175	173.18	100(1.82/175) = 1.05%
5	190	173.36	100(16.64/190) = 8.76%
6	205	175.02	100(29.98/205) = 14.62%
7	180	178.02	100(1.98/180) = 1.10%
8	182	178.22	100(3.78/182) = 2.08%
			Sum of % errors = 44.75%

$$\text{MAPE} = \frac{\sum \text{absolute percent error}}{n} = \frac{44.75\%}{8} = 5.59\%$$

INSIGHT ▶   MAPE expresses the error as a percent of the actual values, undistorted by a single large value.

LEARNING EXERCISE ▶   What is MAPE when α is .50? [Answer: MAPE = 6.75%. As was the case with MAD and MSE, the $\alpha = .1$ was preferable for this series of data.]

RELATED PROBLEMS ▶   4.8e, 4.29c

The MAPE is perhaps the easiest measure to interpret. For example, a result that the MAPE is 6% is a clear statement that is not dependent on issues such as the magnitude of the input data. Table 4.1 summarizes how MAD, MSE, and MAPE differ.

Exponential Smoothing with Trend Adjustment

Simple exponential smoothing, the technique we just illustrated in Examples 3 to 6, is like any other moving-average technique: It fails to respond to trends. Other forecasting techniques that can deal with trends are certainly available. However, because exponential smoothing is such a popular modeling approach in business, let us look at it in more detail.

TABLE 4.1	Comparison of Measures of Forecast Error		
MEASURE	**MEANING**	**EQUATION**	**APPLICATION TO CHAPTER EXAMPLE**
Mean absolute deviation (MAD)	How much the forecast missed the target	$MAD = \dfrac{\Sigma\lvert Actual - Forecast\rvert}{n}$ (4-5)	For $\alpha = .10$ in Example 4, the forecast for grain unloaded was off by an average of 10.31 tons.
Mean squared error (MSE)	The square of how much the forecast missed the target	$MSE = \dfrac{\Sigma(Forecast\ errors)^2}{n}$ (4-6)	For $\alpha = .10$ in Example 5, the square of the forecast error was 190.8. This number does not have a physical meaning but is useful when compared to the MSE of another forecast.
Mean absolute percent error (MAPE)	The average percent error	$MAPE = \dfrac{\sum_{i=1}^{n} 100\lvert Actual_i - Forecast_i\rvert / Actual_i}{n}$ (4-7)	For $\alpha = .10$ in Example 6, the forecast is off by 5.59% on average. As in Examples 4 and 5, some forecasts were too high, and some were low.

Here is why exponential smoothing must be modified when a trend is present. Assume that demand for our product or service has been increasing by 100 units per month and that we have been forecasting with $\alpha = 0.4$ in our exponential smoothing model. The following table shows a severe lag in the second, third, fourth, and fifth months, even when our initial estimate for month 1 is perfect:

MONTH	ACTUAL DEMAND	FORECAST (F_t) FOR MONTHS 1–5
1	100	$F_1 = 100$ (given)
2	200	$F_2 = F_1 + \alpha(A_1 - F_1) = 100 + .4(100 - 100) = 100$
3	300	$F_3 = F_2 + \alpha(A_2 - F_2) = 100 + .4(200 - 100) = 140$
4	400	$F_4 = F_3 + \alpha(A_3 - F_3) = 140 + .4(300 - 140) = 204$
5	500	$F_5 = F_4 + \alpha(A_4 - F_4) = 204 + .4(400 - 204) = 282$

To improve our forecast, let us illustrate a more complex exponential smoothing model, one that adjusts for trend. The idea is to compute an exponentially smoothed average of the data and then adjust for positive or negative lag in trend. The new formula is:

Forecast including trend (FIT_t) = Exponentially smoothed forecast average (F_t)
+ Exponentially smoothed trend (T_t)   (4-8)

With trend-adjusted exponential smoothing, estimates for both the average and the trend are smoothed. This procedure requires two smoothing constants: α for the average and β for the trend. We then compute the average and trend each period:

$F_t = \alpha$(Actual demand last period) $+ (1 - \alpha)$(Forecast last period + Trend estimate last period)

or:

$$F_t = \alpha(A_{t-1}) + (1 - \alpha)(F_{t-1} + T_{t-1}) \quad (4\text{-}9)$$

$T_t = \beta$(Forecast this period − Forecast last period) $+ (1 - \beta)$(Trend estimate last period)

or:

$$T_t = \beta(F_t - F_{t-1}) + (1 - \beta)T_{t-1} \quad (4\text{-}10)$$

where F_t = exponentially smoothed forecast average of the data series in period t
T_t = exponentially smoothed trend in period t
A_t = actual demand in period t
α = smoothing constant for the average $(0 \le \alpha \le 1)$
β = smoothing constant for the trend $(0 \le \beta \le 1)$

So the three steps to compute a trend-adjusted forecast are:

STEP 1: Compute F_t, the exponentially smoothed forecast average for period t, using Equation (4-9).

STEP 2: Compute the smoothed trend, T_t, using Equation (4-10).

STEP 3: Calculate the forecast including trend, FIT_t, by the formula $FIT_t = F_t + T_t$ [from Equation (4-8)].

Example 7 shows how to use trend-adjusted exponential smoothing.

Example 7

COMPUTING A TREND-ADJUSTED EXPONENTIAL SMOOTHING FORECAST

A large Portland manufacturer wants to forecast demand for a piece of pollution-control equipment. A review of past sales, as shown below, indicates that an increasing trend is present:

MONTH (t)	ACTUAL DEMAND (A_t)	MONTH (t)	ACTUAL DEMAND (A_t)
1	12	6	21
2	17	7	31
3	20	8	28
4	19	9	36
5	24	10	?

Smoothing constants are assigned the values of $\alpha = .2$ and $\beta = .4$. The firm assumes the initial forecast average for month 1 (F_1) was 11 units and the trend over that period (T_1) was 2 units.

APPROACH ▶ A trend-adjusted exponential smoothing model, using Equations (4-9), (4-10), and (4-8) and the three steps above, is employed.

SOLUTION ▶

Step 1: Forecast average for month 2:

$$F_2 = \alpha A_1 + (1 - \alpha)(F_1 + T_1)$$
$$F_2 = (.2)(12) + (1 - .2)(11 + 2)$$
$$= 2.4 + (.8)(13) = 2.4 + 10.4 = 12.8 \text{ units}$$

Step 2: Compute the trend in period 2:

$$T_2 = \beta(F_2 - F_1) + (1 - \beta)T_1$$
$$= .4(12.8 - 11) + (1 - .4)(2)$$
$$= (.4)(1.8) + (.6)(2) = .72 + 1.2 = 1.92$$

Step 3: Compute the forecast including trend (FIT_t):

$$FIT_2 = F_2 + T_2$$
$$= 12.8 + 1.92$$
$$= 14.72 \text{ units}$$

We will also do the same calculations for the third month:

Step 1: $F_3 = \alpha A_2 + (1 - \alpha)(F_2 + T_2) = (.2)(17) + (1 - .2)(12.8 + 1.92)$
$$= 3.4 + (.8)(14.72) = 3.4 + 11.78 = 15.18$$

Step 2: $T_3 = \beta(F_3 - F_2) + (1 - \beta)T_2 = (.4)(15.18 - 12.8) + (1 - .4)(1.92)$
$$= (.4)(2.38) + (.6)(1.92) = .952 + 1.152 = 2.10$$

Step 3: $FIT_3 = F_3 + T_3$
$$= 15.18 + 2.10 = 17.28.$$

Table 4.2 completes the forecasts for the 10-month period.

MONTH	ACTUAL DEMAND	SMOOTHED FORECAST AVERAGE, F_t	SMOOTHED TREND, T_t	FORECAST INCLUDING TREND, FIT_t
1	12	11	2	13.00
2	17	12.80	1.92	14.72
3	20	15.18	2.10	17.28
4	19	17.82	2.32	20.14
5	24	19.91	2.23	22.14
6	21	22.51	2.38	24.89
7	31	24.11	2.07	26.18
8	28	27.14	2.45	29.59
9	36	29.28	2.32	31.60
10	—	32.48	2.68	35.16

TABLE 4.2 Forecast with $\alpha = .2$ and $\beta = .4$

INSIGHT ▶ Figure 4.3 compares actual demand (A_t) to an exponential smoothing forecast that includes trend (FIT_t). *FIT* picks up the trend in actual demand. A simple exponential smoothing model (as we saw in Examples 3 and 4) trails far behind.

LEARNING EXERCISE ▶ Using the data for actual demand for the 9 months, compute the exponentially smoothed forecast average *without* trend [using Equation (4-4) as we did earlier in Examples 3 and 4]. Apply $\alpha = .2$, and assume an initial forecast average for month 1 of 11 units. Then plot the months 2–10 forecast values on Figure 4.3. What do you notice? [Answer: Month 10 forecast = 24.65. All the points are below and lag the trend-adjusted forecast.]

RELATED PROBLEMS ▶ 4.19, 4.20, 4.21, 4.22, 4.32

ACTIVE **MODEL** 4.3 This example is further illustrated in Active Model 4.3 in MyOMLab.

EXCEL **OM** Data File **Ch04Ex7.xls** can be found in MyOMLab.

Figure **4.3**

Exponential Smoothing with Trend-Adjustment Forecasts Compared to Actual Demand Data

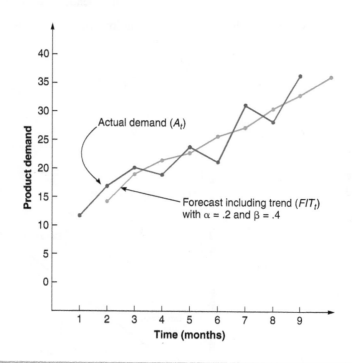

The value of the trend-smoothing constant, β, resembles the α constant because a high β is more responsive to recent changes in trend. A low β gives less weight to the most recent trends and tends to smooth out the present trend. Values of β can be found by the trial-and-error approach or by using sophisticated commercial forecasting software, with the MAD used as a measure of comparison.

Simple exponential smoothing is often referred to as *first-order smoothing*, and trend-adjusted smoothing is called *second-order smoothing* or *double smoothing*. Other advanced exponential-smoothing models are also used, including seasonal-adjusted and triple smoothing.

Trend Projections

Trend projection

A time-series forecasting method that fits a trend line to a series of historical data points and then projects the line into the future for forecasts.

The last time-series forecasting method we will discuss is trend projection. This technique fits a trend line to a series of historical data points and then projects the slope of the line into the future for medium- to long-range forecasts. Several mathematical trend equations can be developed (for example, exponential and quadratic), but in this section, we will look at *linear* (straight-line) trends only.

If we decide to develop a linear trend line by a precise statistical method, we can apply the *least-squares method*. This approach results in a straight line that minimizes the sum of the squares of the vertical differences or deviations from the line to each of the actual observations. Figure 4.4 illustrates the least-squares approach.

A least-squares line is described in terms of its *y*-intercept (the height at which it intercepts the *y*-axis) and its expected change (slope). If we can compute the *y*-intercept and slope, we can express the line with the following equation:

$$\hat{y} = a + bx \tag{4-11}$$

where $\hat{y}$ (called "y hat") = computed value of the variable to be predicted (called the *dependent variable*)

$\quad\quad\quad a =$ *y*-axis intercept

$\quad\quad\quad b =$ slope of the regression line (or the rate of change in *y* for given changes in *x*)

$\quad\quad\quad x =$ the independent variable (which in this case is *time*)

Statisticians have developed equations that we can use to find the values of *a* and *b* for any regression line. The slope *b* is found by:

$$b = \frac{\Sigma xy - n\bar{x}\,\bar{y}}{\Sigma x^2 - n\bar{x}^2} \tag{4-12}$$

Figure **4.4**

The Least-Squares Method for Finding the Best-Fitting Straight Line, Where the Asterisks Are the Locations of the Seven Actual Observations or Data Points

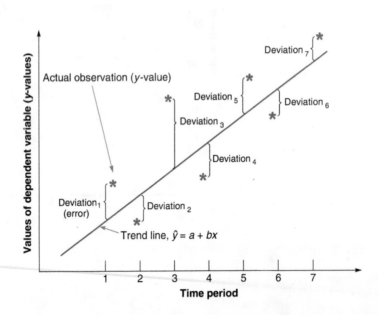

where b = slope of the regression line
Σ = summation sign
x = known values of the independent variable
y = known values of the dependent variable
$\bar{x}$ = average of the x-values
$\bar{y}$ = average of the y-values
n = number of data points or observations

We can compute the y-intercept a as follows:

$$a = \bar{y} - b\bar{x} \qquad (4\text{-}13)$$

Example 8 shows how to apply these concepts.

Example 8

FORECASTING WITH LEAST SQUARES

The demand for electric power at N.Y. Edison over the past 7 years is shown in the following table, in megawatts. The firm wants to forecast next year's demand by fitting a straight-line trend to these data.

YEAR	ELECTRICAL POWER DEMAND	YEAR	ELECTRICAL POWER DEMAND
1	74	5	105
2	79	6	142
3	80	7	122
4	90		

APPROACH ▶ Equations (4-12) and (4-13) can be used to create the trend projection model.

SOLUTION ▶

YEAR (x)	ELECTRIC POWER DEMAND (y)	x^2	xy
1	74	1	74
2	79	4	158
3	80	9	240
4	90	16	360
5	105	25	525
6	142	36	852
7	122	49	854
$\Sigma x = 28$	$\Sigma y = 692$	$\Sigma x^2 = 140$	$\Sigma xy = 3{,}063$

$$\bar{x} = \frac{\Sigma x}{n} = \frac{28}{7} = 4 \quad \bar{y} = \frac{\Sigma y}{n} = \frac{692}{7} = 98.86$$

$$b = \frac{\Sigma xy - n\bar{x}\bar{y}}{\Sigma x^2 - n\bar{x}^2} = \frac{3{,}063 - (7)(4)(98.86)}{140 - (7)(4^2)} = \frac{295}{28} = 10.54$$

$$a = \bar{y} - b\bar{x} = 98.86 - 10.54(4) = 56.70$$

Thus, the least-squares trend equation is $\hat{y} = 56.70 + 10.54x$. To project demand next year, $x = 8$:

$$\text{Demand in year 8} = 56.70 + 10.54(8)$$
$$= 141.02, \text{ or } 141 \text{ megawatts}$$

INSIGHT ▶ To evaluate the model, we plot both the historical demand and the trend line in Figure 4.5. In this case, we may wish to be cautious and try to understand the year 6 to year 7 swing in demand.

Figure 4.5

Electrical Power and the Computed Trend Line

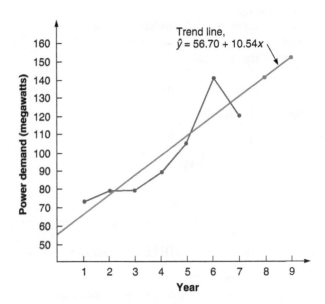

LEARNING EXERCISE ▶ Estimate demand for year 9. [Answer: 151.56, or 152 megawatts.]

RELATED PROBLEMS ▶ 4.6, 4.13c, 4.16, 4.24, 4.30, 4.34 (4.39, 4.42 are available in MyOMLab)

EXCEL **OM** Data File **Ch04Ex8.xls** can be found in MyOMLab.

ACTIVE **MODEL** 4.4 This example is further illustrated in Active Model 4.4 in MyOMLab.

Notes on the Use of the Least-Squares Method   Using the least-squares method implies that we have met three requirements:

1. We always plot the data because least-squares data assume a linear relationship. If a curve appears to be present, curvilinear analysis is probably needed.
2. We do not predict time periods far beyond our given database. For example, if we have 20 months' worth of average prices of Microsoft stock, we can forecast only 3 or 4 months into the future. Forecasts beyond that have little statistical validity. Thus, you cannot take 5 years' worth of sales data and project 10 years into the future. The world is too uncertain.
3. Deviations around the least-squares line (see Figure 4.4) are assumed to be random and normally distributed, with most observations close to the line and only a smaller number farther out.

Seasonal Variations in Data

Seasonal variations

Regular upward or downward movements in a time series that tie to recurring events.

Seasonal variations in data are regular movements in a time series that relate to recurring events such as weather or holidays. Demand for coal and fuel oil, for example, peaks during cold winter months. Demand for golf clubs or sunscreen may be highest in summer.

Seasonality may be applied to hourly, daily, weekly, monthly, or other recurring patterns. Fast-food restaurants experience *daily* surges at noon and again at 5 P.M. Movie theaters see higher demand on Friday and Saturday evenings. The post office, Toys "Я" Us, The Christmas Store, and Hallmark Card Shops also exhibit seasonal variation in customer traffic and sales.

Similarly, understanding seasonal variations is important for capacity planning in organizations that handle peak loads. These include electric power companies during extreme cold and warm periods, banks on Friday afternoons, and buses and subways during the morning and evening rush hours.

STUDENT TIP

John Deere understands seasonal variations: It has been able to obtain 70% of its orders in advance of seasonal use so it can smooth production.

Demand for many products is seasonal. Yamaha, the manufacturer of this jet ski and snowmobile, produces products with complementary demands to address seasonal fluctuations.

Time-series forecasts like those in Example 8 involve reviewing the trend of data over a series of time periods. The presence of seasonality makes adjustments in trend-line forecasts necessary. Seasonality is expressed in terms of the amount that actual values differ from average values in the time series. Analyzing data in monthly or quarterly terms usually makes it easy for a statistician to spot seasonal patterns. Seasonal indices can then be developed by several common methods.

In what is called a *multiplicative seasonal model*, seasonal factors are multiplied by an estimate of average demand to produce a seasonal forecast. Our assumption in this section is that trend has been removed from the data. Otherwise, the magnitude of the seasonal data will be distorted by the trend.

Here are the steps we will follow for a company that has "seasons" of 1 month:

1. Find the *average historical demand each season* (or month in this case) by summing the demand for that month in each year and dividing by the number of years of data available. For example, if, in January, we have seen sales of 8, 6, and 10 over the past 3 years, average January demand equals (8 + 6 + 10)/3 = 8 units.
2. Compute the *average demand over all months* by dividing the total average annual demand by the number of seasons. For example, if the total average demand for a year is 120 units and there are 12 seasons (each month), the average monthly demand is 120/12 = 10 units.

   LO 4.5 *Develop seasonal indices*

3. Compute a *seasonal index* for each season by dividing that *month's* historical average demand (from Step 1) by the average demand over all months (from Step 2). For example, if the average historical January demand over the past 3 years is 8 units and the average demand over all months is 10 units, the seasonal index for January is 8/10 = .80. Likewise, a seasonal index of 1.20 for February would mean that February's demand is 20% larger than the average demand over all months.
4. Estimate next year's total annual demand.
5. Divide this estimate of total annual demand by the number of seasons, then multiply it by the seasonal index for each month. This provides the *seasonal forecast*.

Example 9 illustrates this procedure as it computes seasonal indices from historical data.

Example 9 | DETERMINING SEASONAL INDICES

A Des Moines distributor of Sony laptop computers wants to develop monthly indices for sales. Data from the past 3 years, by month, are available.

APPROACH ▶ Follow the five steps listed above.

SOLUTION ▶

	DEMAND			AVERAGE PERIOD DEMAND	AVERAGE MONTHLY DEMAND[a]	SEASONAL INDEX[b]
MONTH	YEAR 1	YEAR 2	YEAR 3			
Jan.	80	85	105	90	94	.957 (= 90/94)
Feb.	70	85	85	80	94	.851 (= 80/94)
Mar.	80	93	82	85	94	.904 (= 85/94)
Apr.	90	95	115	100	94	1.064 (= 100/94)
May	113	125	131	123	94	1.309 (= 123/94)
June	110	115	120	115	94	1.223 (= 115/94)
July	100	102	113	105	94	1.117 (= 105/94)
Aug.	88	102	110	100	94	1.064 (= 100/94)
Sept.	85	90	95	90	94	.957 (= 90/94)
Oct.	77	78	85	80	94	.851 (= 80/94)
Nov.	75	82	83	80	94	.851 (= 80/94)
Dec.	82	78	80	80	94	.851 (= 80/94)

Total average annual demand = 1,128

[a]Average monthly demand $= \dfrac{1,128}{12 \text{ months}} = 94.$

[b]Seasonal index $= \dfrac{\text{Average monthly demand for past 3 years}}{\text{Average monthly demand}}.$

If we expect the annual demand for computers to be 1,200 units next year, we would use these seasonal indices to forecast the monthly demand as follows:

MONTH	DEMAND	MONTH	DEMAND
Jan.	$\dfrac{1,200}{12} \times .957 = 96$	July	$\dfrac{1,200}{12} \times 1.117 = 112$
Feb.	$\dfrac{1,200}{12} \times .851 = 85$	Aug.	$\dfrac{1,200}{12} \times 1.064 = 106$
Mar.	$\dfrac{1,200}{12} \times .904 = 90$	Sept.	$\dfrac{1,200}{12} \times .957 = 96$
Apr.	$\dfrac{1,200}{12} \times 1.064 = 106$	Oct.	$\dfrac{1,200}{12} \times .851 = 85$
May	$\dfrac{1,200}{12} \times 1.309 = 131$	Nov.	$\dfrac{1,200}{12} \times .851 = 85$
June	$\dfrac{1,200}{12} \times 1.223 = 122$	Dec.	$\dfrac{1,200}{12} \times .851 = 85$

INSIGHT ▶ Think of these indices as percentages of average sales. The average sales (without seasonality) would be 94, but with seasonality, sales fluctuate from 85% to 131% of average.

LEARNING EXERCISE ▶ If next year's annual demand is 1,150 laptops (instead of 1,200), what will the January, February, and March forecasts be? [Answer: 91.7, 81.5, and 86.6, which can be rounded to 92, 82, and 87.]

RELATED PROBLEMS ▶ 4.26, 4.27 (4.40, 4.41a are available in MyOMLab)

EXCEL **OM** Data File **Ch04Ex9.xls** can be found in MyOMLab.

For simplicity, only 3 periods (years) are used for each monthly index in the preceding example. Example 10 illustrates how indices that have already been prepared can be applied to adjust trend-line forecasts for seasonality.

Example 10

APPLYING BOTH TREND AND SEASONAL INDICES

San Diego Hospital wants to improve its forecasting by applying both trend and seasonal indices to 66 months of data it has collected. It will then forecast "patient-days" over the coming year.

APPROACH ▶ A trend line is created; then monthly seasonal indices are computed. Finally, a multiplicative seasonal model is used to forecast months 67 to 78.

SOLUTION ▶ Using 66 months of adult inpatient hospital days, the following equation was computed:

$$\hat{y} = 8,090 + 21.5x$$

where

$$\hat{y} = \text{patient days}$$
$$x = \text{time, in months}$$

Based on this model, which reflects only trend data, the hospital forecasts patient days for the next month (period 67) to be:

$$\text{Patient days} = 8,090 + (21.5)(67) = 9,530 \text{ (trend only)}$$

While this model, as plotted in Figure 4.6, recognized the upward trend line in the demand for inpatient services, it ignored the seasonality that the administration knew to be present.

Figure 4.6

Trend Data for San Diego Hospital

Source: From "Modern Methods Improve Hospital Forecasting" by W. E. Sterk and E. G. Shryock from *Healthcare Financial Management* 41, no. 3, p. 97. Reprinted by permission of Healthcare Financial Management Association.

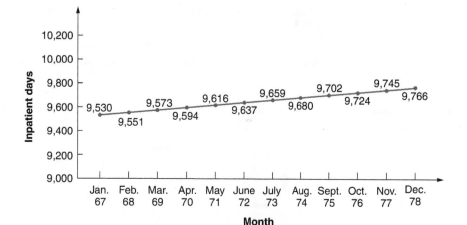

Month
(period = 67 for Jan. through 78 for Dec.)

The following table provides seasonal indices based on the same 66 months. Such seasonal data, by the way, were found to be typical of hospitals nationwide.

Seasonality Indices for Adult Inpatient Days at San Diego Hospital

MONTH	SEASONALITY INDEX	MONTH	SEASONALITY INDEX
January	1.04	July	1.03
February	0.97	August	1.04
March	1.02	September	0.97
April	1.01	October	1.00
May	0.99	November	0.96
June	0.99	December	0.98

These seasonal indices are graphed in Figure 4.7. Note that January, March, July, and August seem to exhibit significantly higher patient days on average, while February, September, November, and December experience lower patient days.

However, neither the trend data nor the seasonal data alone provide a reasonable forecast for the hospital. Only when the hospital multiplied the trend-adjusted data by the appropriate seasonal index did it obtain good forecasts. Thus, for period 67 (January):

$$\text{Patient days} = (\text{Trend-adjusted forecast})(\text{Monthly seasonal index}) = (9,530)(1.04) = 9,911$$

The patient-days for each month are:

Period	67	68	69	70	71	72	73	74	75	76	77	78
Month	Jan.	Feb.	March	April	May	June	July	Aug.	Sept.	Oct.	Nov.	Dec.
Forecast with Trend & Seasonality	9,911	9,265	9,764	9,691	9,520	9,542	9,949	10,068	9,411	9,724	9,355	9,572

A graph showing the forecast that combines both trend and seasonality appears in Figure 4.8.

Month
(period = 67 for Jan. through 78 for Dec.)

INSIGHT ▶ Notice that with trend only, the September forecast is 9,702, but with both trend and seasonal adjustments, the forecast is 9,411. By combining trend and seasonal data, the hospital was better able to forecast inpatient days and the related staffing and budgeting vital to effective operations.

LEARNING EXERCISE ▶ If the slope of the trend line for patient-days is 22.0 (rather than 21.5) and the index for December is .99 (instead of .98), what is the new forecast for December inpatient days? [Answer: 9,708.]

RELATED PROBLEMS ▶ 4.25, 4.28

Example 11 further illustrates seasonality for quarterly data at a wholesaler.

Example 11 | ADJUSTING TREND DATA WITH SEASONAL INDICES

Management at Jagoda Wholesalers, in Calgary, Canada, has used time-series regression based on point-of-sale data to forecast sales for the next 4 quarters. Sales estimates are $100,000, $120,000, $140,000, and $160,000 for the respective quarters. Seasonal indices for the four quarters have been found to be 1.30, .90, .70, and 1.10, respectively.

APPROACH ▶   To compute a seasonalized or adjusted sales forecast, we just multiply each seasonal index by the appropriate trend forecast:

$$\hat{y}_{seasonal} = Index \times \hat{y}_{trend\ forecast}$$

SOLUTION ▶
    Quarter I: $\hat{y}_I = (1.30)(\$100,000) = \$130,000$
    Quarter II: $\hat{y}_{II} = (.90)(\$120,000) = \$108,000$
    Quarter III: $\hat{y}_{III} = (.70)(\$140,000) = \$98,000$
    Quarter IV: $\hat{y}_{IV} = (1.10)(\$160,000) = \$176,000$

INSIGHT ▶   The straight-line trend forecast is now adjusted to reflect the seasonal changes.

LEARNING EXERCISE ▶   If the sales forecast for Quarter IV was $180,000 (rather than $160,000), what would be the seasonally adjusted forecast? [Answer: $198,000.]

RELATED PROBLEMS ▶   4.25, 4.28 (4.41b is available in MyOMLab)

Cyclical Variations in Data

Cycles are like seasonal variations in data but occur every several *years*, not weeks, months, or quarters. Forecasting cyclical variations in a time series is difficult. This is because cycles include a wide variety of factors that cause the economy to go from recession to expansion to recession over a period of years. These factors include national or industrywide overexpansion in times of euphoria and contraction in times of concern. Forecasting demand for individual products can also be driven by product life cycles—the stages products go through from introduction through decline. Life cycles exist for virtually all products; striking examples include floppy disks, video recorders, and the original Game Boy. We leave cyclical analysis to forecasting texts.

Developing associative techniques of variables that affect one another is our next topic.

Cycles
Patterns in the data that occur every several years.

Associative Forecasting Methods: Regression and Correlation Analysis

Unlike time-series forecasting, *associative forecasting* models usually consider *several* variables that are related to the quantity being predicted. Once these related variables have been found, a statistical model is built and used to forecast the item of interest. This approach is more powerful than the time-series methods that use only the historical values for the forecast variable.

Many factors can be considered in an associative analysis. For example, the sales of Dell PCs may be related to Dell's advertising budget, the company's prices, competitors' prices and promotional strategies, and even the nation's economy and unemployment rates. In this case, PC sales would be called the *dependent variable*, and the other variables would be called *independent variables*. The manager's job is to develop *the best statistical relationship between PC sales and the independent variables*. The most common quantitative associative forecasting model is linear-regression analysis.

◆ STUDENT TIP
We now deal with the same mathematical model that we saw earlier, the least-squares method. But we use any potential "cause-and-effect" variable as *x*.

Linear-regression analysis
A straight-line mathematical model to describe the functional relationships between independent and dependent variables.

Using Regression Analysis for Forecasting

We can use the same mathematical model that we employed in the least-squares method of trend projection to perform a linear-regression analysis. The dependent variables that we want to forecast will still be $\hat{y}$. But now the independent variable, x, need no longer be time. We use the equation:

$$\hat{y} = a + bx$$

where
    $\hat{y}$ = value of the dependent variable (in our example, sales)
    a = y-axis intercept
    b = slope of the regression line
    x = independent variable

Example 12 shows how to use linear regression.

LO 4.6 *Conduct* a regression and correlation analysis

Example 12

COMPUTING A LINEAR REGRESSION EQUATION

Nodel Construction Company renovates old homes in West Bloomfield, Michigan. Over time, the company has found that its dollar volume of renovation work is dependent on the West Bloomfield area payroll. Management wants to establish a mathematical relationship to help predict sales.

APPROACH ▶ Nodel's VP of operations has prepared the following table, which lists company revenues and the amount of money earned by wage earners in West Bloomfield during the past 6 years:

NODEL'S SALES (IN $ MILLIONS), y	AREA PAYROLL (IN $ BILLIONS), x	NODEL'S SALES (IN $ MILLIONS), y	AREA PAYROLL (IN $ BILLIONS), x
2.0	1	2.0	2
3.0	3	2.0	1
2.5	4	3.5	7

The VP needs to determine whether there is a straight-line (linear) relationship between area payroll and sales. He plots the known data on a scatter diagram:

STUDENT TIP ◆

A scatter diagram is a powerful data analysis tool. It helps quickly size up the relationship between two variables.

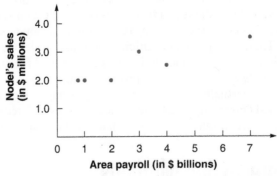

From the six data points, there appears to be a slight positive relationship between the independent variable (payroll) and the dependent variable (sales): As payroll increases, Nodel's sales tend to be higher.

SOLUTION ▶ We can find a mathematical equation by using the least-squares regression approach:

VIDEO 4.1
Forecasting Ticket Revenue for
Orlando Magic Basketball Games

SALES, y	PAYROLL, x	x^2	xy
2.0	1	1	2.0
3.0	3	9	9.0
2.5	4	16	10.0
2.0	2	4	4.0
2.0	1	1	2.0
3.5	7	49	24.5
$\Sigma y = 15.0$	$\Sigma x = 18$	$\Sigma x^2 = 80$	$\Sigma xy = 51.5$

$$\bar{x} = \frac{\Sigma x}{6} = \frac{18}{6} = 3$$

$$\bar{y} = \frac{\Sigma y}{6} = \frac{15}{6} = 2.5$$

$$b = \frac{\Sigma xy - n\bar{x}\bar{y}}{\Sigma x^2 - n\bar{x}^2} = \frac{51.5 - (6)(3)(2.5)}{80 - (6)(3^2)} = .25$$

$$a = \bar{y} - b\bar{x} = 2.5 - (.25)(3) = 1.75$$

The estimated regression equation, therefore, is:

$$\hat{y} = 1.75 + .25x$$

or:

$$\text{Sales} = 1.75 + .25 \text{ (payroll)}$$

If the local chamber of commerce predicts that the West Bloomfield area payroll will be $6 billion next year, we can estimate sales for Nodel with the regression equation:

$$\text{Sales (in \$ millions)} = 1.75 + .25(6)$$
$$= 1.75 + 1.50 = 3.25$$

or:

$$\text{Sales} = \$3{,}250{,}000$$

INSIGHT ▶ Given our assumptions of a straight-line relationship between payroll and sales, we now have an indication of the slope of that relationship: on average, sales increase at the rate of $\frac{1}{4}$ million dollars for every billion dollars in the local area payroll. This is because $b = .25$.

LEARNING EXERCISE ▶ What are Nodel's sales when the local payroll is $8 billion? [Answer: $3.75 million.]

RELATED PROBLEMS ▶ 4.34, 4.43–4.48, 4.50–4.54 (4.56a, 4.57, 4.58 are available in MyOMLab)

EXCEL OM Data File **Ch04Ex12.xls** can be found in MyOMLab.

The final part of Example 12 shows a central weakness of associative forecasting methods like regression. Even when we have computed a regression equation, we must provide a forecast of the independent variable x—in this case, payroll—before estimating the dependent variable y for the next time period. Although this is not a problem for all forecasts, you can imagine the difficulty of determining future values of *some* common independent variables (e.g., unemployment rates, gross national product, price indices, and so on).

Standard Error of the Estimate

The forecast of $3,250,000 for Nodel's sales in Example 12 is called a *point estimate* of y. The point estimate is really the *mean*, or *expected value*, of a distribution of possible values of sales. Figure 4.9 illustrates this concept.

To measure the accuracy of the regression estimates, we must compute the standard error of the estimate, $S_{y,x}$. This computation is called the *standard deviation of the regression:* It measures the error from the dependent variable, y, to the regression line, rather than to the mean. Equation (4-14) is a similar expression to that found in most statistics books for computing the standard deviation of an arithmetic mean:

Standard error of the estimate
A measure of variability around the regression line—its standard deviation.

$$S_{y,x} = \sqrt{\frac{\Sigma(y - y_c)^2}{n - 2}} \qquad (4\text{-}14)$$

where
$y = y$-value of each data point
$y_c =$ computed value of the dependent variable, from the regression equation
$n =$ number of data points

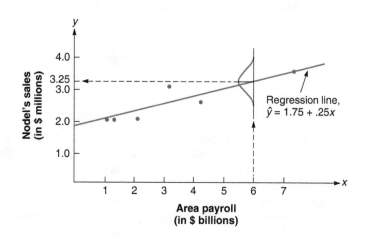

Figure 4.9

Distribution about the Point Estimate of $3.25 Million Sales

Glidden Paints' assembly lines require thousands of gallons every hour. To predict demand, the firm uses associative forecasting methods such as linear regression, with independent variables such as disposable personal income and GNP. Although housing starts would be a natural variable, Glidden found that it correlated poorly with past sales. It turns out that most Glidden paint is sold through retailers to customers who already own homes or businesses.

Michael Rosenfeld/Maximilian S/RGB Ventures/
SuperStock/Alamy

Equation (4-15) may look more complex, but it is actually an easier-to-use version of Equation (4-14). Both formulas provide the same answer and can be used in setting up prediction intervals around the point estimate:[2]

$$S_{y,x} = \sqrt{\frac{\sum y^2 - a\sum y - b\sum xy}{n - 2}} \tag{4-15}$$

Example 13 shows how we would calculate the standard error of the estimate in Example 12.

Example 13

COMPUTING THE STANDARD ERROR OF THE ESTIMATE

Nodel's VP of operations now wants to know the error associated with the regression line computed in Example 12.

APPROACH ▶ Compute the standard error of the estimate, $S_{y,x}$, using Equation (4-15).

SOLUTION ▶ The only number we need that is not available to solve for $S_{y,x}$ is $\sum y^2$. Some quick addition reveals $\sum y^2 = 39.5$. Therefore:

$$S_{y,x} = \sqrt{\frac{\sum y^2 - a\sum y - b\sum xy}{n - 2}}$$

$$= \sqrt{\frac{39.5 - 1.75(15.0) - .25(51.5)}{6 - 2}}$$

$$= \sqrt{.09375} = .306 \text{ (in \$ millions)}$$

The standard error of the estimate is then $306,000 in sales.

INSIGHT ▶ The interpretation of the standard error of the estimate is similar to the standard deviation; namely, ± 1 standard deviation $= .6827$. So there is a 68.27% chance of sales being $\pm \$306,000$ from the point estimate of $3,250,000.

LEARNING EXERCISE ▶ What is the probability sales will exceed $3,556,000? [Answer: About 16%.]

RELATED PROBLEMS ▶ 4.52e, 4.54b (4.56c, 4.57 are available in MyOMLab)

Correlation Coefficients for Regression Lines

The regression equation is one way of expressing the nature of the relationship between two variables. Regression lines are not "cause-and-effect" relationships. They merely describe the relationships among variables. The regression equation shows how one variable relates to the value and changes in another variable.

Another way to evaluate the relationship between two variables is to compute the coefficient of correlation. This measure expresses the degree or strength of the linear relationship (but note

Coefficient of correlation

A measure of the strength of the relationship between two variables.

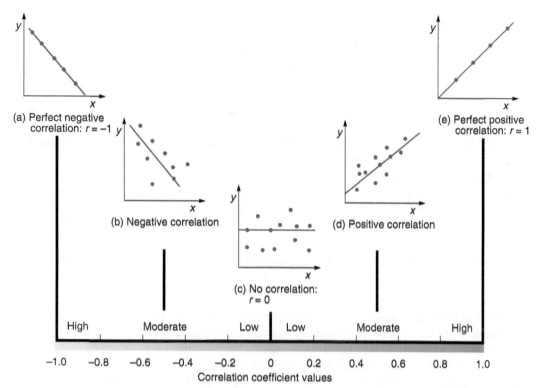

Figure **4.10**

Five Values of the Correlation Coefficient

that correlation does not necessarily imply causality). Usually identified as r, the coefficient of correlation can be any number between $+1$ and -1. Figure 4.10 illustrates what different values of r might look like.

To compute r, we use much of the same data needed earlier to calculate a and b for the regression line. The rather lengthy equation for r is:

$$r = \frac{n\Sigma xy - \Sigma x\Sigma y}{\sqrt{[n\Sigma x^2 - (\Sigma x)^2][n\Sigma y^2 - (\Sigma y)^2]}} \qquad (4\text{-}16)$$

Example 14 shows how to calculate the coefficient of correlation for the data given in Examples 12 and 13.

Example 14

DETERMINING THE COEFFICIENT OF CORRELATION

In Example 12, we looked at the relationship between Nodel Construction Company's renovation sales and payroll in its hometown of West Bloomfield. The VP now wants to know the strength of the association between area payroll and sales.

APPROACH ▶ We compute the r value using Equation (4-16). We need to first add one more column of calculations—for y^2.

SOLUTION ▶ The data, including the column for y^2 and the calculations, are shown here:

y	x	x^2	xy	y^2
2.0	1	1	2.0	4.0
3.0	3	9	9.0	9.0
2.5	4	16	10.0	6.25
2.0	2	4	4.0	4.0
2.0	1	1	2.0	4.0
3.5	7	49	24.5	12.25
$\Sigma y = 15.0$	$\Sigma x = 18$	$\Sigma x^2 = 80$	$\Sigma xy = 51.5$	$\Sigma y^2 = 39.5$

$$r = \frac{(6)(51.5) - (18)(15.0)}{\sqrt{[(6)(80) - (18)^2][(6)(39.5) - (15.0)^2]}}$$

$$= \frac{309 - 270}{\sqrt{(156)(12)}} = \frac{39}{\sqrt{1,872}}$$

$$= \frac{39}{43.3} = .901$$

INSIGHT ▶ This r of .901 appears to be a significant correlation and helps confirm the closeness of the relationship between the two variables.

LEARNING EXERCISE ▶ If the coefficient of correlation was $-.901$ rather than $+.901$, what would this tell you? [Answer: The negative correlation would tell you that as payroll went up, Nodel's sales went down—a rather unlikely occurrence that would suggest you recheck your math.]

RELATED PROBLEMS ▶ 4.43d, 4.48d, 4.50c, 4.52f, 4.54b (4.56b, 4.57 are available in MyOMLab)

Coefficient of determination

A measure of the amount of variation in the dependent variable about its mean that is explained by the regression equation.

Although the coefficient of correlation is the measure most commonly used to describe the relationship between two variables, another measure does exist. It is called the coefficient of determination and is simply the square of the coefficient of correlation—namely, r^2. The value of r^2 will always be a positive number in the range $0 \le r^2 \le 1$. The coefficient of determination is the percent of variation in the dependent variable (y) that is explained by the regression equation. In Nodel's case, the value of r^2 is .81, indicating that 81% of the total variation is explained by the regression equation.

Multiple-Regression Analysis

Multiple regression

An associative forecasting method with more than one independent variable.

Multiple regression is a practical extension of the simple regression model we just explored. It allows us to build a model with several independent variables instead of just one variable. For example, if Nodel Construction wanted to include average annual interest rates in its model for forecasting renovation sales, the proper equation would be:

$$\hat{y} = a + b_1 x_1 + b_2 x_2 \tag{4-17}$$

where
$y =$ dependent variable, sales
$a =$ a constant, the y intercept
x_1 and $x_2 =$ values of the two independent variables, area payroll and interest rates, respectively
b_1 and $b_2 =$ coefficients for the two independent variables

The mathematics of multiple regression becomes quite complex (and is usually tackled by computer), so we leave the formulas for a, b_1, and b_2 to statistics textbooks. However, Example 15 shows how to interpret Equation (4-17) in forecasting Nodel's sales.

Example 15 | **USING A MULTIPLE-REGRESSION EQUATION**

Nodel Construction wants to see the impact of a second independent variable, interest rates, on its sales.

APPROACH ▶ The new multiple-regression line for Nodel Construction, calculated by computer software, is:

$$\hat{y} = 1.80 + .30x_1 - 5.0x_2$$

We also find that the new coefficient of correlation is .96, implying the inclusion of the variable x_2, interest rates, adds even more strength to the linear relationship.

SOLUTION ▶ We can now estimate Nodel's sales if we substitute values for next year's payroll and interest rate. If West Bloomfield's payroll will be $6 billion and the interest rate will be .12 (12%), sales will be forecast as:

$$\text{Sales(\$ millions)} = 1.80 + .30(6) - 5.0(.12)$$
$$= 1.8 + 1.8 - .6$$
$$= 3.00$$

or:

$$\text{Sales} = \$3,000,000$$

INSIGHT ▶ By using both variables, payroll and interest rates, Nodel now has a sales forecast of $3 million and a higher coefficient of correlation. This suggests a stronger relationship between the two variables and a more accurate estimate of sales.

LEARNING EXERCISE ▶ If interest rates were only 6%, what would be the sales forecast? [Answer: $1.8 + 1.8 - 5.0(.06) = 3.3$, or $3,300,000.]

RELATED PROBLEMS ▶ 4.47, 4.49 (4.59 is available in MyOMLab)

The *OM in Action* box, "NYC's Potholes and Regression Analysis," provides an interesting example of one city's use of regression and multiple regression.

OM in Action | NYC's Potholes and Regression Analysis

New York is famous for many things, but one it does not like to be known for is its large and numerous potholes. David Letterman used to joke: "There is a pothole so big on 8th Avenue, it has its own Starbucks in it." When it comes to potholes, some years seem to be worse than others. The winter of 2014 was an exceptionally bad year. City workers filled a record 300,000 potholes during the first 4 months of the year. That's an astounding accomplishment.

But potholes are to some extent a measure of municipal competence—and they are costly. NYC's poor streets cost the average motorist an estimated $800 per year in repair work and new tires. There has been a steady and dramatic increase in potholes from around 70,000–80,000 in the 1990s to the devastatingly high 200,000–300,000 range in recent years. One theory is that bad weather causes the potholes. Using inches of snowfall as a measure of the severity of the winter, the graph below shows a plot of the number of potholes versus the inches of snow each winter.

Research showed that the city would need to resurface at least 1,000 miles of roads per year just to stay even with road deterioration.

Any amount below that would contribute to a "gap" or backlog of streets needing repair. The graph below shows the plot of potholes versus the gap. With an r^2 of .81, there is a very strong relationship between the increase in the "gap" and the number of potholes. It is obvious that the real reason for the steady and substantial increase in the number of potholes is due to the increasing gap in road resurfacing.

A third model performs a regression analysis using the resurfacing gap and inches of snow as two independent variables and number of potholes as the dependent variable. That regression model's r^2 is .91.

$$\text{Potholes} = 7,801.5 + 80.6 \times \text{Resurfacing gap} + 930.1 \times \text{Inches of snow}$$

Sources: OR/MS Today (June, 2014) and New York Daily News (March 5, 2014).

Monitoring and Controlling Forecasts

Once a forecast has been completed, it should not be forgotten. No manager wants to be reminded that his or her forecast is horribly inaccurate, but a firm needs to determine why actual demand (or whatever variable is being examined) differed significantly from that projected. If the forecaster is accurate, that individual usually makes sure that everyone is aware of his or her talents. Very seldom does one read articles in *Fortune, Forbes,* or *The Wall Street Journal,* however, about money managers who are consistently off by 25% in their stock market forecasts.

One way to monitor forecasts to ensure that they are performing well is to use a tracking signal. A tracking signal is a measurement of how well a forecast is predicting actual values. As forecasts are updated every week, month, or quarter, the newly available demand data are compared to the forecast values.

Tracking signal
A measurement of how well a forecast is predicting actual values.

The tracking signal is computed as the cumulative error divided by the *mean absolute deviation (MAD)*:

$$\text{Tracking signal} = \frac{\text{Cumulative error}}{\text{MAD}} \tag{4-18}$$

$$= \frac{\Sigma(\text{Actual demand in period } i - \text{Forecast demand in period } i)}{\text{MAD}}$$

where

$$\text{MAD} = \frac{\Sigma|\text{Actual} - \text{Forecast}|}{n}$$

STUDENT TIP ◆
Using a tracking signal is a good way to make sure the forecasting system is continuing to do a good job.

as seen earlier, in Equation (4-5).

Positive tracking signals indicate that demand is *greater* than forecast. *Negative* signals mean that demand is *less* than forecast. A good tracking signal—that is, one with a low cumulative error—has about as much positive error as it has negative error. In other words, small deviations are okay, but positive and negative errors should balance one another so that the tracking signal centers closely around zero. A consistent tendency for forecasts to be greater or less than the actual values (that is, for a high absolute cumulative error) is called a bias error. Bias can occur if, for example, the wrong variables or trend line are used or if a seasonal index is misapplied.

Bias
A forecast that is consistently higher or consistently lower than actual values of a time series.

Once tracking signals are calculated, they are compared with predetermined control limits. When a tracking signal exceeds an upper or lower limit, there is a problem with the forecasting method, and management may want to reevaluate the way it forecasts demand. Figure 4.11 shows the graph of a tracking signal that is exceeding the range of acceptable variation. If the model being used is exponential smoothing, perhaps the smoothing constant needs to be readjusted.

LO 4.7 *Use a tracking signal*

How do firms decide what the upper and lower tracking limits should be? There is no single answer, but they try to find reasonable values—in other words, limits not so low as to be triggered with every small forecast error and not so high as to allow bad forecasts to be regularly overlooked. One MAD is equivalent to approximately .8 standard deviations,

Figure 4.11

A Plot of Tracking Signals

± 2 MADs $= \pm 1.6$ standard deviations, ± 3 MADs $= \pm 2.4$ standard deviations, and ± 4 MADs $= \pm 3.2$ standard deviations. This fact suggests that for a forecast to be "in control," 89% of the errors are expected to fall within ± 2 MADs, 98% within ± 3 MADs, or 99.9% within ± 4 MADs.[3]

Example 16 shows how the tracking signal and cumulative error can be computed.

Example 16

COMPUTING THE TRACKING SIGNAL AT CARLSON'S BAKERY

Carlson's Bakery wants to evaluate performance of its croissant forecast.

APPROACH ▶ Develop a tracking signal for the forecast, and see if it stays within acceptable limits, which we define as ± 4 MADs.

SOLUTION ▶ Using the forecast and demand data for the past 6 quarters for croissant sales, we develop a tracking signal in the following table:

QUARTER	ACTUAL DEMAND	FORECAST DEMAND	ERROR	CUMULATIVE ERROR	ABSOLUTE FORECAST ERROR	CUMULATIVE ABSOLUTE FORECAST ERROR	MAD	TRACKING SIGNAL (CUMULATIVE ERROR/MAD)
1	90	100	−10	−10	10	10	10.0	−10/10 = −1
2	95	100	−5	−15	5	15	7.5	−15/7.5 = −2
3	115	100	+15	0	15	30	10.0	0/10 = 0
4	100	110	−10	−10	10	40	10.0	−10/10 = −1
5	125	110	+15	+5	15	55	11.0	+5/11 = +0.5
6	140	110	+30	+35	30	85	14.2	+35/14.2 = +2.5

$$\text{At the end of quarter 6, MAD} = \frac{\sum |\text{Forecast errors}|}{n} = \frac{85}{6} = 14.2$$

$$\text{and Tracking signal} = \frac{\text{Cumulative error}}{\text{MAD}} = \frac{35}{14.2} = 2.5 \text{ MADs}$$

INSIGHT ▶ Because the tracking signal drifted from −2 MAD to +2.5 MAD (between 1.6 and 2.0 standard deviations), we can conclude that it is within acceptable limits.

LEARNING EXERCISE ▶ If actual demand in quarter 6 was 130 (rather than 140), what would be the MAD and resulting tracking signal? [Answer: MAD for quarter 6 would be 12.5, and the tracking signal for period 6 would be 2 MADs.]

RELATED PROBLEMS ▶ 4.59, 4.60 (4.61c is available in MyOMLab)

Adaptive Smoothing

Adaptive forecasting refers to computer monitoring of tracking signals and self-adjustment if a signal passes a preset limit. For example, when applied to exponential smoothing, the α and β coefficients are first selected on the basis of values that minimize error forecasts and then adjusted accordingly whenever the computer notes an errant tracking signal. This process is called adaptive smoothing.

Adaptive smoothing
An approach to exponential smoothing forecasting in which the smoothing constant is automatically changed to keep errors to a minimum.

Focus Forecasting

Rather than adapt by choosing a smoothing constant, computers allow us to try a variety of forecasting models. Such an approach is called focus forecasting. Focus forecasting is based on two principles:

1. Sophisticated forecasting models are not always better than simple ones.
2. There is no single technique that should be used for all products or services.

Focus forecasting
Forecasting that tries a variety of computer models and selects the best one for a particular application.

Bernard Smith, inventory manager for American Hardware Supply, coined the term *focus forecasting*. Smith's job was to forecast quantities for 100,000 hardware products purchased by American's 21 buyers.[4] He found that buyers neither trusted nor understood the exponential smoothing model then in use. Instead, they used very simple approaches of their own. So Smith developed his new computerized system for selecting forecasting methods.

Smith chose to test seven forecasting methods. They ranged from the simple ones that buyers used (such as the naive approach) to statistical models. Every month, Smith applied the forecasts of all seven models to each item in stock. In these simulated trials, the forecast values were subtracted from the most recent actual demands, giving a simulated forecast error. The forecast method yielding the least error is selected by the computer, which then uses it to make next month's forecast. Although buyers still have an override capability, American Hardware finds that focus forecasting provides excellent results.

Forecasting in the Service Sector

Forecasting in the service sector presents some unusual challenges. A major technique in the retail sector is tracking demand by maintaining good short-term records. For instance, a barbershop catering to men expects peak flows on Fridays and Saturdays. Indeed, most barbershops are closed on Sunday and Monday, and many call in extra help on Friday and Saturday. A downtown restaurant, on the other hand, may need to track conventions and holidays for effective short-term forecasting.

Specialty Retail Shops Specialty retail facilities, such as flower shops, may have other unusual demand patterns, and those patterns will differ depending on the holiday. When Valentine's Day falls on a weekend, for example, flowers can't be delivered to offices, and those romantically inclined are likely to celebrate with outings rather than flowers. If a holiday falls on a Monday, some of the celebration may also take place on the weekend, reducing flower sales. However, when Valentine's Day falls in midweek, busy midweek schedules often make flowers the optimal way to celebrate. Because flowers for Mother's Day are to be delivered on Saturday or Sunday, this holiday forecast varies less. Due to special demand patterns, many service firms maintain records of sales, noting not only the day of the week but also unusual events, including the weather, so that patterns and correlations that influence demand can be developed.

Fast-Food Restaurants Fast-food restaurants are well aware not only of weekly, daily, and hourly but even 15-minute variations in demands that influence sales. Therefore, detailed forecasts of demand are needed. Figure 4.12(a) shows the hourly forecast for a typical fast-food restaurant. Note the lunchtime and dinnertime peaks. This contrasts to the mid-morning and mid-afternoon peaks at FedEx's call center in Figure 4.12(b).

Firms like Taco Bell now use point-of-sale computers that track sales every quarter hour. Taco Bell found that a 6-week moving average was the forecasting technique that minimized its mean squared error (MSE) of these quarter-hour forecasts. Building this forecasting methodology into each of Taco Bell's 6,500 U.S. stores' computers, the model makes weekly projections of customer transactions. These in turn are used by store managers to schedule staff, who begin in 15-minute increments, not 1-hour blocks as in other industries. The forecasting model has been so successful that Taco Bell has increased customer service while documenting more than $50 million in labor cost savings in 4 years of use.

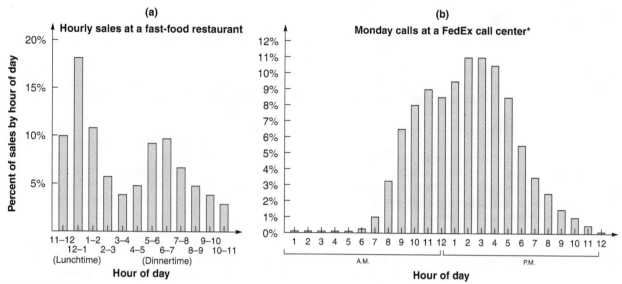

Figure **4.12**

Forecasts Are Unique: Note the Variations between (a) Hourly Sales at a Fast-Food Restaurant and (b) Hourly Call Volume at FedEx

*Based on historical data: see *Journal of Business Forecasting* (Winter 1999–2000): 6–11.

Summary

Forecasts are a critical part of the operations manager's function. Demand forecasts drive a firm's production, capacity, and scheduling systems and affect the financial, marketing, and personnel planning functions.

There are a variety of qualitative and quantitative forecasting techniques. Qualitative approaches employ judgment, experience, intuition, and a host of other factors that are difficult to quantify. Quantitative forecasting uses historical data and causal, or associative, relations to project future demands. The Rapid Review for this chapter summarizes the formulas we introduced in quantitative forecasting. Forecast calculations are seldom performed by hand. Most operations managers turn to software packages such as Forecast PRO, NCSS, Minitab, Systat, Statgraphics, SAS, or SPSS.

No forecasting method is perfect under all conditions. And even once management has found a satisfactory approach, it must still monitor and control forecasts to make sure errors do not get out of hand. Forecasting can often be a very challenging, but rewarding, part of managing.

Key Terms

Forecasting (p. 108)
Economic forecasts (p. 109)
Technological forecasts (p. 109)
Demand forecasts (p. 109)
Quantitative forecasts (p. 111)
Qualitative forecasts (p. 111)
Jury of executive opinion (p. 111)
Delphi method (p. 111)
Sales force composite (p. 111)
Market survey (p. 111)

Time series (p. 112)
Naive approach (p. 114)
Moving averages (p. 114)
Exponential smoothing (p. 116)
Smoothing constant (p. 116)
Mean absolute deviation (MAD) (p. 118)
Mean squared error (MSE) (p. 119)
Mean absolute percent error (MAPE) (p. 120)
Trend projection (p. 124)
Seasonal variations (p. 126)

Cycles (p. 131)
Linear-regression analysis (p. 131)
Standard error of the estimate (p. 133)
Coefficient of correlation (p. 134)
Coefficient of determination (p. 136)
Multiple regression (p. 136)
Tracking signal (p. 138)
Bias (p. 138)
Adaptive smoothing (p. 139)
Focus forecasting (p. 139)

Ethical Dilemma

We live in a society obsessed with test scores and maximum performance. Think of the SAT, ACT, GRE, GMAT, and LSAT. Though they take only a few hours, they are supposed to give schools and companies a snapshot of a student's abiding talents.

But these tests are often spectacularly bad at forecasting performance in the real world. The SAT does a decent job ($r^2 =$ .12) of predicting the grades of a college freshman. It is, however, less effective at predicting achievement *after* graduation.

LSAT scores bear virtually no correlation to career success as measured by income, life satisfaction, or public service.

What does the r^2 mean in this context? Is it ethical for colleges to base admissions and financial aid decisions on scores alone? What role do these tests take at your own school?

Robert Kneschke/Fotolia

Discussion Questions

1. What is a qualitative forecasting model, and when is its use appropriate?
2. Identify and briefly describe the two general forecasting approaches.
3. Identify the three forecasting time horizons. State an approximate duration for each.
4. Briefly describe the steps that are used to develop a forecasting system.
5. A skeptical manager asks what medium-range forecasts can be used for. Give the manager three possible uses/purposes.
6. Explain why such forecasting devices as moving averages, weighted moving averages, and exponential smoothing are not well suited for data series that have trends.
7. What is the basic difference between a weighted moving average and exponential smoothing?
8. What three methods are used to determine the accuracy of any given forecasting method? How would you determine whether time-series regression or exponential smoothing is better in a specific application?
9. Research and briefly describe the Delphi technique. How would it be used by an employer you have worked for?
10. What is the primary difference between a time-series model and an associative model?
11. Define *time series*.
12. What effect does the value of the smoothing constant have on the weight given to the recent values?
13. Explain the value of seasonal indices in forecasting. How are seasonal patterns different from cyclical patterns?
14. Which forecasting technique can place the most emphasis on recent values? How does it do this?
15. In your own words, explain adaptive forecasting.
16. What is the purpose of a tracking signal?
17. Explain, in your own words, the meaning of the correlation coefficient. Discuss the meaning of a negative value of the correlation coefficient.
18. What is the difference between a dependent and an independent variable?
19. Give examples of industries that are affected by seasonality. Why would these businesses want to filter out seasonality?
20. Give examples of industries in which demand forecasting is dependent on the demand for other products.

21. What happens to the ability to forecast for periods farther into the future?
22. CEO John Goodale, at Southern Illinois Power and Light, has been collecting data on demand for electric power in its western subregion for only the past 2 years. Those data are shown in the table below.

   To plan for expansion and to arrange to borrow power from neighboring utilities during peak periods, Goodale needs to be able to forecast demand for each month next year. However, the standard forecasting models discussed in this chapter will not fit the data observed for the 2 years.
   a) What are the weaknesses of the standard forecasting techniques as applied to this set of data?
   b) Because known models are not appropriate here, propose your own approach to forecasting. Although there is no perfect solution to tackling data such as these (in other words, there are no 100% right or wrong answers), justify your model.
   c) Forecast demand for each month next year using the model you propose.

DEMAND IN MEGAWATTS		
MONTH	LAST YEAR	THIS YEAR
January	5	17
February	6	14
March	10	20
April	13	23
May	18	30
June	15	38
July	23	44
August	26	41
September	21	33
October	15	23
November	12	26
December	14	17

Using Software in Forecasting

This section presents three ways to solve forecasting problems with computer software. First, you can create your own Excel spreadsheets to develop forecasts. Second, you can use the Excel OM software that comes with the text. Third, POM for Windows is another program that is located in MyOMLab.

CREATING YOUR OWN EXCEL SPREADSHEETS

Excel spreadsheets (and spreadsheets in general) are frequently used in forecasting. Exponential smoothing, trend analysis, and regression analysis (simple and multiple) are supported by built-in Excel functions.

Program 4.1 illustrates how to build an Excel forecast for the data in Example 8. The goal for N.Y. Edison is to create a trend analysis of the year 1 to year 7 data.

As an alternative, you may want to experiment with Excel's built-in regression analysis. To do so, under the Data menu bar selection choose Data Analysis, then Regression. Enter your Y and X data into two columns (say A and B). When the regression window appears, enter the Y and X ranges, then select OK. Excel offers several plots and tables to those interested in more rigorous analysis of regression problems.

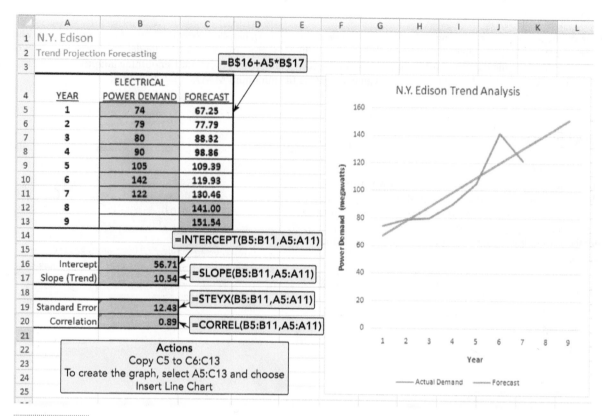

Program **4.1**

Using Excel to Develop Your Own Forecast, with Data from Example 8

✖ USING EXCEL OM

Excel OM's forecasting module has five components: (1) moving averages, (2) weighted moving averages, (3) exponential smoothing, (4) regression (with one variable only), and (5) decomposition. Excel OM's error analysis is much more complete than that available with the Excel add-in.

Program 4.2 illustrates Excel OM's input and output, using Example 2's weighted-moving-average data.

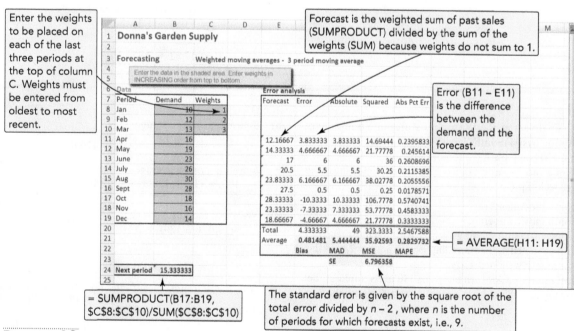

Program **4.2**

Analysis of Excel OM's Weighted-Moving-Average Program, Using Data from Example 2 as Input

P USING POM FOR WINDOWS
POM for Windows can project moving averages (both simple and weighted), handle exponential smoothing (both simple and trend adjusted), forecast with least squares trend projection, and solve linear regression (associative) models. A summary screen of error analysis and a graph of the data can also be generated. As a special example of exponential smoothing adaptive forecasting, when using an α of 0, POM for Windows will find the α value that yields the minimum MAD.
    Appendix IV provides further details.

Solved Problems   Virtual Office Hours help is available in MyOMLab.

SOLVED PROBLEM 4.1

Sales of Volkswagen's popular Beetle have grown steadily at auto dealerships in Nevada during the past 5 years (see table below). The sales manager had predicted before the new model was introduced that first year sales would be 410 VWs. Using exponential smoothing with a weight of $\alpha = .30$, develop forecasts for years 2 through 6.

YEAR	SALES	FORECAST
1	450	410
2	495	
3	518	
4	563	
5	584	
6	?	

SOLUTION

YEAR	FORECAST
1	410.0
2	$422.0 = 410 + .3 (450 - 410)$
3	$443.9 = 422 + .3 (495 - 422)$
4	$466.1 = 443.9 + .3 (518 - 443.9)$
5	$495.2 = 466.1 + .3 (563 - 466.1)$
6	$521.8 = 495.2 + .3 (584 - 495.2)$

SOLVED PROBLEM 4.2

In Example 7, we applied trend-adjusted exponential smoothing to forecast demand for a piece of pollution-control equipment for months 2 and 3 (out of 9 months of data provided). Let us now continue this process for month 4. We want to confirm the forecast for month 4 shown in Table 4.2 (p. 123) and Figure 4.3 (p. 123).
    For month 4, $A_4 = 19$, with $\alpha = .2$, and $\beta = .4$.

SOLUTION

$$F_4 = \alpha A_3 + (1 - \alpha)(F_3 + T_3)$$
$$= (.2)(20) + (1 - .2)(15.18 + 2.10)$$
$$= 4.0 + (.8)(17.28)$$
$$= 4.0 + 13.82$$
$$= 17.82$$
$$T_4 = \beta(F_4 - F_3) + (1 - \beta)T_3$$
$$= (.4)(17.82 - 15.18) + (1 - .4)(2.10)$$
$$= (.4)(2.64) + (.6)(2.10)$$
$$= 1.056 + 1.26$$
$$= 2.32$$
$$FIT_4 = 17.82 + 2.32$$
$$= 20.14$$

SOLVED PROBLEM 4.3

Sales of hair dryers at the Walgreens stores in Youngstown, Ohio, over the past 4 months have been 100, 110, 120, and 130 units (with 130 being the most recent sales).
    Develop a moving-average forecast for next month, using these three techniques:

a) 3-month moving average.
b) 4-month moving average.
c) Weighted 4-month moving average with the most recent month weighted 4, the preceding month 3, then 2, and the oldest month weighted 1.
d) If next month's sales turn out to be 140 units, forecast the following month's sales (months) using a 4-month moving average.

SOLUTION

a) 3-month moving average
$$= \frac{110 + 120 + 130}{3} = \frac{360}{3} = 120 \text{ dryers}$$

b) 4-month moving average
$$= \frac{100 + 110 + 120 + 130}{4} = \frac{460}{4} = 115 \text{ dryers}$$

c) Weighted moving average
$$= \frac{4(130) + 3(120) + 2(110) + 1(100)}{10}$$
$$= \frac{1,200}{10} = 120 \text{ dryers}$$

d) *Now* the four most recent sales are 110, 120, 130, and 140.
$$\text{4-month moving average} = \frac{110 + 120 + 130 + 140}{4}$$
$$= \frac{500}{4} = 125 \text{ dryers}$$

We note, of course, the lag in the forecasts, as the moving-average method does not immediately recognize trends.

SOLVED PROBLEM 4.4

The following data come from regression line projections:

PERIOD	FORECAST VALUES	ACTUAL VALUES
1	410	406
2	419	423
3	428	423
4	435	440

Compute the MAD and MSE.

SOLUTION

$$\text{MAD} = \frac{\Sigma \,|\text{Actual} - \text{Forecast}|}{n}$$

$$= \frac{|406 - 410| + |423 - 419| + |423 - 428| + |440 - 435|}{4}$$

$$= \frac{4 + 4 + 5 + 5}{4} = \frac{18}{4} = 4.5$$

$$\text{MSE} = \frac{\Sigma(\text{Forecast errors})^2}{n}$$

$$= \frac{(406-410)^2 + (423-419)^2 + (423-428)^2 + (440-435)^2}{4}$$

$$= \frac{4^2 + 4^2 + 5^2 + 5^2}{4} = \frac{16 + 16 + 25 + 25}{4} = 20.5$$

SOLVED PROBLEM 4.5

Room registrations in the Toronto Towers Plaza Hotel have been recorded for the past 9 years. To project future occupancy, management would like to determine the mathematical trend of guest registration. This estimate will help the hotel determine whether future expansion will be needed. Given the following time-series data, develop a regression equation relating registrations to time (e.g., a trend equation). Then forecast year 11 registrations. Room registrations are in the thousands:

Year 1: 17	Year 2: 16	Year 3: 16	Year 4: 21	Year 5: 20
Year 6: 20	Year 7: 23	Year 8: 25	Year 9: 24	

SOLUTION

YEAR	REGISTRANTS, y (IN THOUSANDS)	x^2	xy
1	17	1	17
2	16	4	32
3	16	9	48
4	21	16	84
5	20	25	100
6	20	36	120
7	23	49	161
8	25	64	200
9	24	81	216
$\Sigma x = 45$	$\Sigma y = 182$	$\Sigma x^2 = 285$	$\Sigma xy = 978$

$$b = \frac{\Sigma xy - n\overline{x}\,\overline{y}}{\Sigma x^2 - n\overline{x}^2} = \frac{978 - (9)(5)(20.22)}{285 - (9)(25)}$$

$$= \frac{978 - 909.9}{285 - 225} = \frac{68.1}{60} = 1.135$$

$$a = \overline{y} - b\overline{x} = 20.22 - (1.135)(5) = 20.22 - 5.675 = 14.545$$

$$\hat{y} = (\text{registrations}) = 14.545 + 1.135x$$

The projection of registrations in year 11 is:

$$\hat{y} = 14.545 + (1.135)(11) = 27.03 \text{ or } 27,030 \text{ guests in year 11.}$$

SOLVED PROBLEM 4.6

Quarterly demand for Ford F150 pickups at a New York auto dealer is forecast with the equation:

$$\hat{y} = 10 + 3x$$

where x = quarters, and:

Quarter I of year 1 = 0
Quarter II of year 1 = 1
Quarter III of year 1 = 2
Quarter IV of year 1 = 3
Quarter I of year 2 = 4
and so on

and:

$$\hat{y} = \text{quarterly demand}$$

The demand for trucks is seasonal, and the indices for Quarters I, II, III, and IV are 0.80, 1.00, 1.30, and 0.90, respectively. Forecast demand for each quarter of year 3. Then, seasonalize each forecast to adjust for quarterly variations.

SOLUTION

Quarter II of year 2 is coded $x = 5$; Quarter III of year 2, $x = 6$; and Quarter IV of year 2, $x = 7$. Hence, Quarter I of year 3 is coded $x = 8$; Quarter II, $x = 9$; and so on.

$$\hat{y}(\text{Year 3 Quarter I}) = 10 + 3(8) = 34$$
$$\hat{y}(\text{Year 3 Quarter II}) = 10 + 3(9) = 37$$
$$\hat{y}(\text{Year 3 Quarter III}) = 10 + 3(10) = 40$$
$$\hat{y}(\text{Year 3 Quarter IV}) = 10 + 3(11) = 43$$

Adjusted forecast = (.80)(34) = 27.2
Adjusted forecast = (1.00)(37) = 37
Adjusted forecast = (1.30)(40) = 52
Adjusted forecast = (.90)(43) = 38.7

SOLVED PROBLEM 4.7

Cengiz Haksever runs an Istanbul high-end jewelry shop. He advertises weekly in local Turkish newspapers and is thinking of increasing his ad budget. Before doing so, he decides to evaluate the past effectiveness of these ads. Five weeks are sampled, and the data are shown in the table below:

SALES ($1,000s)	AD BUDGET THAT WEEK ($100s)
11	5
6	3
10	7
6	2
12	8

Develop a regression model to help Cengiz evaluate his advertising.

SOLUTION

We apply the least-squares regression model as we did in Example 12.

SALES, y	ADVERTISING, x	x^2	xy
11	5	25	55
6	3	9	18
10	7	49	70
6	2	4	12
12	8	64	96
$\Sigma y = 45$	$\Sigma x = 25$	$\Sigma x^2 = 151$	$\Sigma xy = 251$

$$\bar{y} = \frac{45}{5} = 9 \qquad \bar{x} = \frac{25}{5} = 5$$

$$b = \frac{\Sigma xy - n\bar{x}\bar{y}}{\Sigma x^2 - n\bar{x}^2} = \frac{251 - (5)(5)(9)}{151 - (5)(5^2)}$$

$$= \frac{251 - 225}{151 - 125} = \frac{26}{26} = 1$$

$$a = \bar{y} - b\bar{x} = 9 - (1)(5) = 4$$

So the regression model is $\hat{y} = 4 + 1x$, or
Sales (in $1,000s) = 4 + 1 (Ad budget in $100s)
This means that for each 1-unit increase in x (or $100 in ads), sales increase by 1 unit (or $1,000).

SOLVED PROBLEM 4.8

Using the data in Solved Problem 4.7, find the coefficient of determination, r^2, for the model.

SOLUTION

To find r^2, we need to also compute Σy^2.

$$\Sigma y^2 = 11^2 + 6^2 + 10^2 + 6^2 + 12^2$$
$$= 121 + 36 + 100 + 36 + 144 = 437$$

The next step is to find the coefficient of correlation, r:

$$r = \frac{n\Sigma xy - \Sigma x \Sigma y}{\sqrt{[n\Sigma x^2 - (\Sigma x)^2][n\Sigma y^2 - (\Sigma y)^2]}}$$

$$= \frac{5(251) - (25)(45)}{\sqrt{[5(151) - (25)^2][5(437) - (45)^2]}}$$

$$= \frac{1,255 - 1,125}{\sqrt{(130)(160)}} = \frac{130}{\sqrt{20,800}} = \frac{130}{144.22}$$

$$= .9014$$

Thus, $r^2 = (.9014)^2 = .8125$, meaning that about 81% of the variability in sales can be explained by the regression model with advertising as the independent variable.

Problems

Note: **PX** means the problem may be solved with POM for Windows and/or Excel OM.

Problems 4.1–4.42 relate to Time-Series Forecasting

• **4.1** The following gives the number of pints of type B blood used at Woodlawn Hospital in the past 6 weeks:

WEEK OF	PINTS USED
August 31	360
September 7	389
September 14	410
September 21	381
September 28	368
October 5	374

a) Forecast the demand for the week of October 12 using a 3-week moving average.

b) Use a 3-week weighted moving average, with weights of .1, .3, and .6, using .6 for the most recent week. Forecast demand for the week of October 12.

c) Compute the forecast for the week of October 12 using exponential smoothing with a forecast for August 31 of 360 and α = .2. **PX**

•• **4.2**

YEAR	1	2	3	4	5	6	7	8	9	10	11
DEMAND	7	9	5	9	13	8	12	13	9	11	7

a) Plot the above data on a graph. Do you observe any trend, cycles, or random variations?

b) Starting in year 4 and going to year 12, forecast demand using a 3-year moving average. Plot your forecast on the same graph as the original data.

c) Starting in year 4 and going to year 12, forecast demand using a 3-year moving average with weights of .1, .3, and .6, using .6 for the most recent year. Plot this forecast on the same graph.

d) As you compare forecasts with the original data, which seems to give the better results? **Px**

•• **4.3**   Refer to Problem 4.2. Develop a forecast for years 2 through 12 using exponential smoothing with $\alpha = .4$ and a forecast for year 1 of 6. Plot your new forecast on a graph with the actual data and the naive forecast. Based on a visual inspection, which forecast is better? **Px**

• **4.4**   A check-processing center uses exponential smoothing to forecast the number of incoming checks each month. The number of checks received in June was 40 million, while the forecast was 42 million. A smoothing constant of .2 is used.

a) What is the forecast for July?

b) If the center received 45 million checks in July, what would be the forecast for August?

c) Why might this be an inappropriate forecasting method for this situation? **Px**

•• **4.5**   The Carbondale Hospital is considering the purchase of a new ambulance. The decision will rest partly on the anticipated mileage to be driven next year. The miles driven during the past 5 years are as follows:

YEAR	MILEAGE
1	3,000
2	4,000
3	3,400
4	3,800
5	3,700

a) Forecast the mileage for next year (6th year) using a 2-year moving average.

b) Find the MAD based on the 2-year moving average. (*Hint:* You will have only 3 years of matched data.)

c) Use a weighted 2-year moving average with weights of .4 and .6 to forecast next year's mileage. (The weight of .6 is for the most recent year.) What MAD results from using this approach to forecasting? (*Hint:* You will have only 3 years of matched data.)

d) Compute the forecast for year 6 using exponential smoothing, an initial forecast for year 1 of 3,000 miles, and $\alpha = .5$. **Px**

•• **4.6**   The monthly sales for Yazici Batteries, Inc., were as follows:

MONTH	SALES
January	20
February	21
March	15
April	14
May	13
June	16
July	17
August	18
September	20
October	20
November	21
December	23

a) Plot the monthly sales data.

b) Forecast January sales using each of the following:
   i)   Naive method.
   ii) A 3-month moving average.
   iii) A 6-month weighted average using .1, .1, .1, .2, .2, and .3, with the heaviest weights applied to the most recent months.
   iv) Exponential smoothing using an $\alpha = .3$ and a September forecast of 18.
   v)   A trend projection.

c) With the data given, which method would allow you to forecast next March's sales? **Px**

•• **4.7**   The actual demand for the patients at Omaha Emergency Medical Clinic for the first 6 weeks of this year follows:

WEEK	ACTUAL NO. OF PATIENTS
1	65
2	62
3	70
4	48
5	63
6	52

Clinic administrator Marc Schniederjans wants you to forecast patient demand at the clinic for week 7 by using this data. You decide to use a weighted moving average method to find this forecast. Your method uses four actual demand levels, with weights of 0.333 on the present period, 0.25 one period ago, 0.25 two periods ago, and 0.167 three periods ago.

a) What is the value of your forecast? **Px**

b) If instead the weights were 20, 15, 15, and 10, respectively, how would the forecast change? Explain why.

c) What if the weights were 0.40, 0.30, 0.20, and 0.10, respectively? Now what is the forecast for week 7?

• **4.8**   Daily high temperatures in St. Louis for the last week were as follows: 93, 94, 93, 95, 96, 88, 90 (yesterday).

a) Forecast the high temperature today, using a 3-day moving average.

b) Forecast the high temperature today, using a 2-day moving average.

c) Calculate the mean absolute deviation based on a 2-day moving average.

d) Compute the mean squared error for the 2-day moving average.

e) Calculate the mean absolute percent error for the 2-day moving average. **Px**

••• **4.9**   Lenovo uses the ZX-81 chip in some of its laptop computers. The prices for the chip during the past 12 months were as follows:

MONTH	PRICE PER CHIP	MONTH	PRICE PER CHIP
January	$1.80	July	1.80
February	1.67	August	1.83
March	1.70	September	1.70
April	1.85	October	1.65
May	1.90	November	1.70
June	1.87	December	1.75

a) Use a 2-month moving average on all the data and plot the averages and the prices.

b) Use a 3-month moving average and add the 3-month plot to the graph created in part (a).

c) Which is better (using the mean absolute deviation): the 2-month average or the 3-month average?

d) Compute the forecasts for each month using exponential smoothing, with an initial forecast for January of $1.80. Use α = .1, then α = .3, and finally α = .5. Using MAD, which α is the best? **P✗**

•• **4.10** Data collected on the yearly registrations for a Six Sigma seminar at the Quality College are shown in the following table:

YEAR	1	2	3	4	5	6	7	8	9	10	11
REGISTRATIONS (000)	4	6	4	5	10	8	7	9	12	14	15

a) Develop a 3-year moving average to forecast registrations from year 4 to year 12.

b) Estimate demand again for years 4 to 12 with a 3-year weighted moving average in which registrations in the most recent year are given a weight of 2, and registrations in the other 2 years are each given a weight of 1.

c) Graph the original data and the two forecasts. Which of the two forecasting methods seems better? **P✗**

• **4.11** Use exponential smoothing with a smoothing constant of 0.3 to forecast the registrations at the seminar given in Problem 4.10. To begin the procedure, assume that the forecast for year 1 was 5,000 people signing up.

a) What is the MAD? **P✗**

b) What is the MSE?

•• **4.12** Consider the following actual and forecast demand levels for Big Mac hamburgers at a local McDonald's restaurant:

DAY	ACTUAL DEMAND	FORECAST DEMAND
Monday	88	88
Tuesday	72	88
Wednesday	68	84
Thursday	48	80
Friday		

The forecast for Monday was derived by observing Monday's demand level and setting Monday's forecast level equal to this demand level. Subsequent forecasts were derived by using exponential smoothing with a smoothing constant of 0.25. Using this exponential smoothing method, what is the forecast for Big Mac demand for Friday? **P✗**

••• **4.13** As you can see in the following table, demand for heart transplant surgery at Washington General Hospital has increased steadily in the past few years:

YEAR	1	2	3	4	5	6
HEART TRANSPLANTS	45	50	52	56	58	?

The director of medical services predicted 6 years ago that demand in year 1 would be 41 surgeries.

Dmitry Kalinovsky/Shutterstock

a) Use exponential smoothing, first with a smoothing constant of .6 and then with one of .9, to develop forecasts for years 2 through 6.

b) Use a 3-year moving average to forecast demand in years 4, 5, and 6.

c) Use the trend-projection method to forecast demand in years 1 through 6.

d) With MAD as the criterion, which of the four forecasting methods is best? **P✗**

•• **4.14** Following are two weekly forecasts made by two different methods for the number of gallons of gasoline, in thousands, demanded at a local gasoline station. Also shown are actual demand levels, in thousands of gallons.

WEEK	FORECASTS		ACTUAL DEMAND
	METHOD 1	METHOD 2	
1	0.90	0.80	0.70
2	1.05	1.20	1.00
3	0.95	0.90	1.00
4	1.20	1.11	1.00

What are the MAD and MSE for each method?

• **4.15** Refer to Solved Problem 4.1 on page 144.

a) Use a 3-year moving average to forecast the sales of Volkswagen Beetles in Nevada through year 6.

b) What is the MAD? **P✗**

c) What is the MSE?

• **4.16** Refer to Solved Problem 4.1 on page 144.

a) Using the trend projection (regression) method, develop a forecast for the sales of Volkswagen Beetles in Nevada through year 6.

b) What is the MAD? **P✗**

c) What is the MSE?

• **4.17** Refer to Solved Problem 4.1 on page 144. Using smoothing constants of .6 and .9, develop forecasts for the sales of VW Beetles. What effect did the smoothing constant have on the forecast? Use MAD to determine which of the three smoothing constants (.3, .6, or .9) gives the most accurate forecast. **P✗**

•••• **4.18** Consider the following actual (A_t) and forecast (F_t) demand levels for a commercial multiline telephone at Office Max:

TIME PERIOD, t	ACTUAL DEMAND, A_t	FORECAST DEMAND, F_t
1	50	50
2	42	50
3	56	48
4	46	50
5		

The first forecast, F_1, was derived by observing A_1 and setting F_1 equal to A_1. Subsequent forecast averages were derived by exponential smoothing. Using the exponential smoothing method, find the forecast for time period 5. (*Hint:* You need to first find the smoothing constant, α.)

•••**4.19** Income at the architectural firm Spraggins and Yunes for the period February to July was as follows:

MONTH	FEBRUARY	MARCH	APRIL	MAY	JUNE	JULY
Income (in $ thousand)	70.0	68.5	64.8	71.7	71.3	72.8

Use trend-adjusted exponential smoothing to forecast the firm's August income. Assume that the initial forecast average for February is $65,000 and the initial trend adjustment is 0. The smoothing constants selected are $\alpha = .1$ and $\beta = .2$. **Px**

•••**4.20** Resolve Problem 4.19 with $\alpha = .1$ and $\beta = .8$. Using MSE, determine which smoothing constants provide a better forecast. **Px**

•**4.21** Refer to the trend-adjusted exponential smoothing illustration in Example 7 on pages 122–123. Using $\alpha = .2$ and $\beta = .4$, we forecast sales for 9 months, showing the detailed calculations for months 2 and 3. In Solved Problem 4.2, we continued the process for month 4.

In this problem, show your calculations for months 5 and 6 for F_t, T_t, and FIT_t. **Px**

•**4.22** Refer to Problem 4.21. Complete the trend-adjusted exponential-smoothing forecast computations for periods 7, 8, and 9. Confirm that your numbers for F_t, T_t, and FIT_t match those in Table 4.2 (p. 123). **Px**

••**4.23** Sales of quilt covers at Bud Banis's department store in Carbondale over the past year are shown below. Management prepared a forecast using a combination of exponential smoothing and its collective judgment for the 4 months (March, April, May, and June):

MONTH	UNIT SALES	MANAGEMENT'S FORECAST
July	100	
August	93	
September	96	
October	110	
November	124	
December	119	
January	92	
February	83	
March	101	120
April	96	114
May	89	110
June	108	108

a) Compute MAD and MAPE for management's technique.
b) Do management's results outperform (i.e., have smaller MAD and MAPE than) a naive forecast?
c) Which forecast do you recommend, based on lower forecast error? **Px**

•**4.24** The following gives the number of accidents that occurred on Florida State Highway 101 during the past 4 months:

MONTH	NUMBER OF ACCIDENTS
January	30
February	40
March	60
April	90

Forecast the number of accidents that will occur in May, using least-squares regression to derive a trend equation. **Px**

•**4.25** In the past, Peter Kelle's tire dealership in Baton Rouge sold an average of 1,000 radials each year. In the past 2 years, 200 and 250, respectively, were sold in fall, 350 and 300 in winter, 150 and 165 in spring, and 300 and 285 in summer. With a major expansion planned, Kelle projects sales next year to increase to 1,200 radials. What will be the demand during each season?

••**4.26** George Kyparisis owns a company that manufactures sailboats. Actual demand for George's sailboats during each of the past four seasons was as follows:

SEASON	YEAR 1	2	3	4
Winter	1,400	1,200	1,000	900
Spring	1,500	1,400	1,600	1,500
Summer	1,000	2,100	2,000	1,900
Fall	600	750	650	500

George has forecasted that annual demand for his sailboats in year 5 will equal 5,600 sailboats. Based on this data and the multiplicative seasonal model, what will the demand level be for George's sailboats in the spring of year 5?

••**4.27** Attendance at Orlando's newest Disneylike attraction, Lego World, has been as follows:

QUARTER	GUESTS (IN THOUSANDS)	QUARTER	GUESTS (IN THOUSANDS)
Winter Year 1	73	Summer Year 2	124
Spring Year 1	104	Fall Year 2	52
Summer Year 1	168	Winter Year 3	89
Fall Year 1	74	Spring Year 3	146
Winter Year 2	65	Summer Year 3	205
Spring Year 2	82	Fall Year 3	98

Compute seasonal indices using all of the data. **Px**

•**4.28** North Dakota Electric Company estimates its demand trend line (in millions of kilowatt hours) to be:

$$D = 77 + 0.43Q$$

where Q refers to the sequential quarter number and $Q = 1$ for winter of Year 1. In addition, the multiplicative seasonal factors are as follows:

QUARTER	FACTOR (INDEX)
Winter	.8
Spring	1.1
Summer	1.4
Fall	.7

Forecast energy use for the four quarters of year 26 (namely quarters 101 to 104), beginning with winter.

· 4.29 The number of disk drives (in millions) made at a plant in Taiwan during the past 5 years follows:

YEAR	DISK DRIVES
1	140
2	160
3	190
4	200
5	210

a) Forecast the number of disk drives to be made next year, using linear regression.
b) Compute the mean squared error (MSE) when using linear regression.
c) Compute the mean absolute percent error (MAPE). **Px**

·· 4.30 Dr. Lillian Fok, a New Orleans psychologist, specializes in treating patients who are agoraphobic (i.e., afraid to leave their homes). The following table indicates how many patients Dr. Fok has seen each year for the past 10 years. It also indicates what the robbery rate was in New Orleans during the same year:

YEAR	1	2	3	4	5	6	7	8	9	10
NUMBER OF PATIENTS	36	33	40	41	40	55	60	54	58	61
ROBBERY RATE PER 1,000 POPULATION	58.3	61.1	73.4	75.7	81.1	89.0	101.1	94.8	103.3	116.2

Using trend (linear regression) analysis, predict the number of patients Dr. Fok will see in years 11 and 12 as a function of time. How well does the model fit the data? **Px**

··· 4.31 Emergency calls to the 911 system of Durham, North Carolina, for the past 24 weeks are shown in the following table:

WEEK	1	2	3	4	5	6	7	8	9	10	11	12
CALLS	50	35	25	40	45	35	20	30	35	20	15	40
WEEK	13	14	15	16	17	18	19	20	21	22	23	24
CALLS	55	35	25	55	55	40	35	60	75	50	40	65

a) Compute the exponentially smoothed forecast of calls for each week. Assume an initial forecast of 50 calls in the first week, and use $\alpha = .2$. What is the forecast for week 25?
b) Reforecast each period using $\alpha = .6$.
c) Actual calls during week 25 were 85. Which smoothing constant provides a superior forecast? Explain and justify the measure of error you used. **Px**

··· 4.32 Using the 911 call data in Problem 4.31, forecast calls for weeks 2 through 25 with a trend-adjusted exponential smoothing model. Assume an initial forecast for 50 calls for week 1 and an initial trend of zero. Use smoothing constants of $\alpha = .3$ and $\beta = .2$. Is this model better than that of Problem 4.31? What adjustment might be useful for further improvement? (Again, assume that actual calls in week 25 were 85.) **Px**

··· 4.33 Storrs Cycles has just started selling the new Cyclone mountain bike, with monthly sales as shown in the table. First, co-owner Bob Day wants to forecast by exponential smoothing by initially setting February's forecast equal to January's sales with $\alpha = .1$. Co-owner Sherry Snyder wants to use a three-period moving average.

	SALES	BOB	SHERRY	BOB'S ERROR	SHERRY'S ERROR
JANUARY	400	—			
FEBRUARY	380	400			
MARCH	410				
APRIL	375				
MAY					

a) Is there a strong linear trend in sales over time?
b) Fill in the table with what Bob and Sherry each forecast for May and the earlier months, as relevant.
c) Assume that May's actual sales figure turns out to be 405. Complete the table's columns and then calculate the mean absolute deviation for both Bob's and Sherry's methods.
d) Based on these calculations, which method seems more accurate? **Px**

···· 4.34 Boulanger Savings and Loan is proud of its long tradition in Winter Park, Florida. Begun by Michelle Boulanger 22 years after World War II, the S&L has bucked the trend of financial and liquidity problems that has repeatedly plagued the industry. Deposits have increased slowly but surely over the years, despite recessions in 1983, 1988, 1991, 2001, and 2010. Ms. Boulanger believes it is necessary to have a long-range strategic plan for her firm, including a 1-year forecast and preferably even a 5-year forecast of deposits. She examines the past deposit data and also peruses Florida's gross state product (GSP) over the same 44 years. (GSP is analogous to gross national product [GNP] but on the state level.) The resulting data are in the following table.

YEAR	DEPOSITS[a]	GSP[b]	YEAR	DEPOSITS[a]	GSP[b]
1	.25	.4	13	.50	1.2
2	.24	.4	14	.95	1.2
3	.24	.5	15	1.70	1.2
4	.26	.7	16	2.3	1.6
5	.25	.9	17	2.8	1.5
6	.30	1.0	18	2.8	1.6
7	.31	1.4	19	2.7	1.7
8	.32	1.7	20	3.9	1.9
9	.24	1.3	21	4.9	1.9
10	.26	1.2	22	5.3	2.3
11	.25	1.1	23	6.2	2.5
12	.33	.9	24	4.1	2.8

(continued)

YEAR	DEPOSITS[a]	GSP[b]	YEAR	DEPOSITS[a]	GSP[b]
25	4.5	2.9	35	31.1	4.1
26	6.1	3.4	36	31.7	4.1
27	7.7	3.8	37	38.5	4.0
28	10.1	4.1	38	47.9	4.5
29	15.2	4.0	39	49.1	4.6
30	18.1	4.0	40	55.8	4.5
31	24.1	3.9	41	70.1	4.6
32	25.6	3.8	42	70.9	4.6
33	30.3	3.8	43	79.1	4.7
34	36.0	3.7	44	94.0	5.0

[a] In $ millions.
[b] In $ billions.

a) Using exponential smoothing, with $\alpha = .6$, then trend analysis, and finally linear regression, discuss which forecasting model fits best for Boulanger's strategic plan. Justify the selection of one model over another.

b) Carefully examine the data. Can you make a case for excluding a portion of the information? Why? Would that change your choice of model? **Px**

Additional problems 4.35–4.42 are available in MyOMLab.

Problems 4.43–4.58 relate to Associative Forecasting Methods

•• **4.43** Mark Gershon, owner of a musical instrument distributorship, thinks that demand for guitars may be related to the number of television appearances by the popular group Maroon 5 during the previous month. Mark has collected the data shown in the following table:

DEMAND FOR GUITARS	3	6	7	5	10	7
MAROON 5 TV APPEARANCES	3	4	7	6	8	5

a) Graph these data to see whether a linear equation might describe the relationship between the group's television shows and guitar sales.

b) Use the least-squares regression method to derive a forecasting equation.

c) What is your estimate for guitar sales if Maroon 5 performed on TV nine times last month?

d) What are the correlation coefficient (r) and the coefficient of determination (r^2) for this model, and what do they mean? **Px**

• **4.44** Lori Cook has developed the following forecasting model:

$$\hat{y} = 36 + 4.3x$$

where $\hat{y}$ = demand for Kool Air conditioners and
        x = the outside temperature (°F) **Px**

a) Forecast demand for the Kool Air when the temperature is 70°F.
b) What is demand when the temperature is 80°F?
c) What is demand when the temperature is 90°F? **Px**

•• **4.45** Café Michigan's manager, Gary Stark, suspects that demand for mocha latte coffees depends on the price being charged. Based on historical observations, Gary has gathered the following data, which show the numbers of these coffees sold over six different price values:

PRICE	NUMBER SOLD
$2.70	760
$3.50	510
$2.00	980
$4.20	250
$3.10	320
$4.05	480

Using these data, how many mocha latte coffees would be forecast to be sold according to simple linear regression if the price per cup were $2.80? **Px**

• **4.46** The following data relate the sales figures of the bar in Mark Kaltenbach's small bed-and-breakfast inn in Portland, to the number of guests registered that week:

WEEK	GUESTS	BAR SALES
1	16	$330
2	12	270
3	18	380
4	14	300

a) Perform a linear regression that relates bar sales to guests (not to time).

b) If the forecast is for 20 guests next week, what are the sales expected to be? **Px**

• **4.47** The number of auto accidents in Athens, Ohio, is related to the regional number of registered automobiles in thousands (X_1), alcoholic beverage sales in $10,000s ($X_2$), and rainfall in inches (X_3). Furthermore, the regression formula has been calculated as:

$$Y = a + b_1X_1 + b_2X_2 + b_3X_3$$

where

Y = number of automobile accidents
$a = 7.5$
$b_1 = 3.5$
$b_2 = 4.5$
$b_3 = 2.5$

Calculate the expected number of automobile accidents under conditions a, b, and c:

	X_1	X_2	X_3
(a)	2	3	0
(b)	3	5	1
(c)	4	7	2

•• **4.48** Rhonda Clark, a Slippery Rock, Pennsylvania, real estate developer, has devised a regression model to help determine residential housing prices in northwestern Pennsylvania. The model was developed using recent sales in a particular neighborhood. The price (Y) of the house is based on the size (square footage = X) of the house. The model is:

$$Y = 13,473 + 37.65X$$

The coefficient of correlation for the model is 0.63.

a) Use the model to predict the selling price of a house that is 1,860 square feet.

b) An 1,860-square-foot house recently sold for $95,000. Explain why this is not what the model predicted.

c) If you were going to use multiple regression to develop such a model, what other quantitative variables might you include?

d) What is the value of the coefficient of determination in this problem? **Px**

• **4.49** Accountants at the Tucson firm, Larry Youdelman, CPAs, believed that several traveling executives were submitting unusually high travel vouchers when they returned from business trips. First, they took a sample of 200 vouchers submitted from the past year. Then they developed the following multiple-regression equation relating expected travel cost to number of days on the road (x_1) and distance traveled (x_2) in miles:

$$\hat{y} = \$90.00 + \$48.50x_1 + \$.40x_2$$

The coefficient of correlation computed was .68.

a) If Donna Battista returns from a 300-mile trip that took her out of town for 5 days, what is the expected amount she should claim as expenses?

b) Battista submitted a reimbursement request for $685. What should the accountant do?

c) Should any other variables be included? Which ones? Why? **Px**

•• **4.50** City government has collected the following data on annual sales tax collections and new car registrations:

ANNUAL SALES TAX COLLECTIONS (IN MILLIONS)	1.0	1.4	1.9	2.0	1.8	2.1	2.3
NEW CAR REGISTRATIONS (IN THOUSANDS)	10	12	15	16	14	17	20

Determine the following:

a) The least-squares regression equation.

b) Using the results of part (a), find the estimated sales tax collections if new car registrations total 22,000.

c) The coefficients of correlation and determination. **Px**

•• **4.51** Using the data in Problem 4.30, apply linear regression to study the relationship between the robbery rate and Dr. Fok's patient load. If the robbery rate increases to 131.2 in year 11, how many phobic patients will Dr. Fok treat? If the robbery rate drops to 90.6, what is the patient projection? **Px**

••• **4.52** Bus and subway ridership for the summer months in London, England, is believed to be tied heavily to the number of tourists visiting the city. During the past 12 years, the data on the next page have been obtained:

YEAR (SUMMER MONTHS)	NUMBER OF TOURISTS (IN MILLIONS)	RIDERSHIP (IN MILLIONS)
1	7	1.5
2	2	1.0
3	6	1.3
4	4	1.5
5	14	2.5
6	15	2.7
7	16	2.4
8	12	2.0
9	14	2.7
10	20	4.4
11	15	3.4
12	7	1.7

a) Plot these data and decide if a linear model is reasonable.

b) Develop a regression relationship.

c) What is expected ridership if 10 million tourists visit London in a year?

d) Explain the predicted ridership if there are no tourists at all.

e) What is the standard error of the estimate?

f) What is the model's correlation coefficient and coefficient of determination? **Px**

•• **4.53** Thirteen students entered the business program at Sante Fe College 2 years ago. The following table indicates what each student scored on the high school SAT math exam and their grade-point averages (GPAs) after students were in the Sante Fe program for 2 years:

STUDENT	A	B	C	D	E	F	G
SAT SCORE	421	377	585	690	608	390	415
GPA	2.90	2.93	3.00	3.45	3.66	2.88	2.15
STUDENT	H	I	J	K	L	M	
SAT SCORE	481	729	501	613	709	366	
GPA	2.53	3.22	1.99	2.75	3.90	1.60	

a) Is there a meaningful relationship between SAT math scores and grades?

b) If a student scores a 350, what do you think his or her GPA will be?

c) What about a student who scores 800?

•• **4.54** Dave Fletcher, the general manager of North Carolina Engineering Corporation (NCEC), thinks that his firm's engineering services contracted to highway construction firms are directly related to the volume of highway construction business contracted with companies in his geographic area. He wonders if this is really so, and if it is, can this information help him plan his operations better by forecasting the quantity of his engineering services required by construction firms in each quarter of the year? The following table presents the sales of his services and total amounts of contracts for highway construction over the past eight quarters:

QUARTER	1	2	3	4	5	6	7	8
Sales of NCEC Services (in $ thousands)	8	10	15	9	12	13	12	16
Contracts Released (in $ thousands)	153	172	197	178	185	199	205	226

a) Using this data, develop a regression equation for predicting the level of demand of NCEC's services.

b) Determine the coefficient of correlation and the standard error of the estimate. Px

Additional problems **4.55-4.58** are available in MyOMLab.

Problems 4.59–4.61 relate to Monitoring and Controlling Forecasts

•• **4.59** Sales of tablet computers at Ted Glickman's electronics store in Washington, D.C., over the past 10 weeks are shown in the table below:

WEEK	DEMAND	WEEK	DEMAND
1	20	6	29
2	21	7	36
3	28	8	22
4	37	9	25
5	25	10	28

a) Forecast demand for each week, including week 10, using exponential smoothing with α = .5 (initial forecast = 20).

b) Compute the MAD.

c) Compute the tracking signal. Px

••• **4.60** The following are monthly actual and forecast demand levels for May through December for units of a product manufactured by the D. Bishop Company in Des Moines:

MONTH	ACTUAL DEMAND	FORECAST DEMAND
May	100	100
June	80	104
July	110	99
August	115	101
September	105	104
October	110	104
November	125	105
December	120	109

What is the value of the tracking signal as of the end of December?

Additional problem **4.61** is available in MyOMLab.

CASE STUDIES

Southwestern University: (B)*

Southwestern University (SWU), a large state college in Stephenville, Texas, enrolls close to 20,000 students. The school is a dominant force in the small city, with more students during fall and spring than permanent residents.

Always a football powerhouse, SWU is usually in the top 20 in college football rankings. Since the legendary Phil Flamm was hired as its head coach in 2009 (in hopes of reaching the elusive number 1 ranking), attendance at the five Saturday home games each year increased. Prior to Flamm's arrival, attendance generally averaged 25,000 to 29,000 per game. Season ticket sales bumped up by 10,000 just with the announcement of the new coach's arrival. Stephenville and SWU were ready to move to the big time!

Southwestern University Football Game Attendance, 2010–2015

GAME	2010 ATTENDEES	OPPONENT	2011 ATTENDEES	OPPONENT	2012 ATTENDEES	OPPONENT
1	34,200	Rice	36,100	Miami	35,900	USC
2[a]	39,800	Texas	40,200	Nebraska	46,500	Texas Tech
3	38,200	Duke	39,100	Ohio State	43,100	Alaska
4[b]	26,900	Arkansas	25,300	Nevada	27,900	Arizona
5	35,100	TCU	36,200	Boise State	39,200	Baylor

GAME	2013 ATTENDEES	OPPONENT	2014 ATTENDEES	OPPONENT	2015 ATTENDEES	OPPONENT
1	41,900	Arkansas	42,500	Indiana	46,900	LSU
2[a]	46,100	Missouri	48,200	North Texas	50,100	Texas
3	43,900	Florida	44,200	Texas A&M	45,900	South Florida
4[b]	30,100	Central Florida	33,900	Southern	36,300	Montana
5	40,500	LSU	47,800	Oklahoma	49,900	Arizona State

[a] Homecoming games.

[b] During the fourth week of each season, Stephenville hosted a hugely popular southwestern crafts festival. This event brought tens of thousands of tourists to the town, especially on weekends, and had an obvious negative impact on game attendance.

The immediate issue facing SWU, however, was not NCAA ranking. It was capacity. The existing SWU stadium, built in 1953, has seating for 54,000 fans. The following table indicates attendance at each game for the past 6 years.

One of Flamm's demands upon joining SWU had been a stadium expansion, or possibly even a new stadium. With attendance increasing, SWU administrators began to face the issue head-on. Flamm had wanted dormitories solely for his athletes in the stadium as an additional feature of any expansion.

SWU's president, Dr. Joel Wisner, decided it was time for his vice president of development to forecast when the existing stadium would "max out." The expansion was, in his mind, a given. But Wisner needed to know how long he could wait. He also sought a revenue projection, assuming an average ticket price of $50 in 2016 and a 5% increase each year in future prices.

Discussion Questions

1. Develop a forecasting model, justifying its selection over other techniques, and project attendance through 2017.

2. What revenues are to be expected in 2016 and 2017?

3. Discuss the school's options.

*This integrated case study runs throughout the text. Other issues facing Southwestern's football stadium include (A) managing the stadium project (Chapter 3); (C) quality of facilities (Chapter 6); (D) break-even analysis of food services (Supplement 7 Web site); (E) locating the new stadium (Chapter 8 Web site); (F) inventory planning of football programs (Chapter 12 Web site); and (G) scheduling of campus security officers/staff for game days (Chapter 13 Web site).

Forecasting Ticket Revenue for Orlando Magic Basketball Games

Video Case

For its first 2 decades of existence, the NBA's Orlando Magic basketball team set seat prices for its 41-game home schedule the same for each game. If a lower-deck seat sold for $150, that was the price charged, regardless of the opponent, day of the week, or time of the season. If an upper-deck seat sold for $10 in the first game of the year, it likewise sold for $10 for every game.

But when Anthony Perez, director of business strategy, finished his MBA at the University of Florida, he developed a valuable database of ticket sales. Analysis of the data led him to build a forecasting model he hoped would increase ticket revenue. Perez hypothesized that selling a ticket for similar seats should differ based on demand.

Studying individual sales of Magic tickets on the open Stub Hub marketplace during the prior season, Perez determined the additional potential sales revenue the Magic could have made had they charged prices the fans had proven they were willing to pay on Stub Hub. This became his dependent variable, y, in a multiple-regression model.

He also found that three variables would help him build the "true market" seat price for every game. With his model, it was possible that the same seat in the arena would have as many as seven different prices created at season onset—sometimes higher than expected on average and sometimes lower.

The major factors he found to be statistically significant in determining how high the demand for a game ticket, and hence, its price, would be were:

◆ The day of the week (x_1)
◆ A rating of how popular the opponent was (x_2)
◆ The time of the year (x_3)

For the day of the week, Perez found that Mondays were the least-favored game days (and he assigned them a value of 1). The rest of the weekdays increased in popularity, up to a Saturday game, which he rated a 6. Sundays and Fridays received 5 ratings, and holidays a 3 (refer to the footnote in Table 4.3).

His ratings of opponents, done just before the start of the season, were subjective and range from a low of 0 to a high of 8. A very high-rated team in that particular season may have had one or more superstars on its roster, or have won the NBA finals the prior season, making it a popular fan draw.

Fernando Medina

Finally, Perez believed that the NBA season could be divided into four periods in popularity:

◆ Early games (which he assigned 0 scores)
◆ Games during the Christmas season (assigned a 3)
◆ Games until the All-Star break (given a 2)
◆ Games leading into the play-offs (scored with a 3)

The first year Perez built his multiple-regression model, the dependent variable y, which was a "potential premium revenue score," yielded an $r^2 = .86$ with this equation:

$$y = 14,996 + 10,801x_1 + 23,397x_2 + 10,784x_3$$

Table 4.3 illustrates, for brevity in this case study, a sample of 12 games that year (out of the total 41 home game regular season), including the potential extra revenue per game (y) to be expected using the variable pricing model.

A leader in NBA variable pricing, the Orlando Magic have learned that regression analysis is indeed a profitable forecasting tool.

Discussion Questions*

1. Use the data in Table 4.3 to build a regression model with day of the week as the only independent variable.

TABLE 4.3	Data for Last Year's Magic Ticket Sales Pricing Model					
TEAM	DATE*	DAY OF WEEK*	TIME OF YEAR	RATING OF OPPONENT	ADDITIONAL SALES POTENTIAL	
Phoenix Suns	November 4	Wednesday	0	0	$12,331	
Detroit Pistons	November 6	Friday	0	1	$29,004	
Cleveland Cavaliers	November 11	Wednesday	0	6	$109,412	
Miami Heat	November 25	Wednesday	0	3	$75,783	
Houston Rockets	December 23	Wednesday	3	2	$42,557	
Boston Celtics	January 28	Thursday	1	4	$120,212	
New Orleans Pelicans	February 3	Monday	1	1	$20,459	
L. A. Lakers	March 7	Sunday	2	8	$231,020	
San Antonio Spurs	March 17	Wednesday	2	1	$28,455	
Denver Nuggets	March 23	Sunday	2	1	$110,561	
NY Knicks	April 9	Friday	3	0	$44,971	
Philadelphia 76ers	April 14	Wednesday	3	1	$30,257	

*Day of week rated as 1 = Monday, 2 = Tuesday, 3 = Wednesday, 4 = Thursday, 5 = Friday, 6 = Saturday, 5 = Sunday, 3 = holiday.

2. Use the data to build a model with rating of the opponent as the sole independent variable.

3. Using Perez's multiple-regression model, what would be the additional sales potential of a Thursday Miami Heat game played during the Christmas holiday?

4. What additional independent variables might you suggest to include in Perez's model?

*You may wish to view the video that accompanies this case before answering these questions.

Forecasting at Hard Rock Cafe

Video Case

With the growth of Hard Rock Cafe—from one pub in London in 1971 to more than 145 restaurants in 60 countries today—came a corporatewide demand for better forecasting. Hard Rock uses long-range forecasting in setting a capacity plan and intermediate-term forecasting for locking in contracts for leather goods (used in jackets) and for such food items as beef, chicken, and pork. Its short-term sales forecasts are conducted each month, by cafe, and then aggregated for a headquarters view.

The heart of the sales forecasting system is the point-of-sale (POS) system, which, in effect, captures transaction data on nearly every person who walks through a cafe's door. The sale of each entrée represents one customer; the entrée sales data are transmitted daily to the Orlando corporate headquarters' database. There, the financial team, headed by Todd Lindsey, begins the forecast process. Lindsey forecasts monthly guest counts, retail sales, banquet sales, and concert sales (if applicable) at each cafe. The general managers of individual cafes tap into the same database to prepare a daily forecast for their sites. A cafe manager pulls up prior years' sales for that day, adding information from the local Chamber of Commerce or Tourist Board on upcoming events such as a major convention, sporting event, or concert in the city where the cafe is located. The daily forecast is further broken into hourly sales, which drives employee scheduling. An hourly forecast of $5,500 in sales translates into 19 workstations, which are further broken down into a specific number of waitstaff, hosts, bartenders, and kitchen staff. Computerized scheduling software plugs in people based on their availability. Variances between forecast and actual sales are then examined to see why errors occurred.

Hard Rock doesn't limit its use of forecasting tools to sales. To evaluate managers and set bonuses, a 3-year weighted moving average is applied to cafe sales. If cafe general managers exceed their targets, a bonus is computed. Todd Lindsey, at corporate headquarters, applies weights of 40% to the most recent year's sales, 40% to the year before, and 20% to sales 2 years ago in reaching his moving average.

An even more sophisticated application of statistics is found in Hard Rock's menu planning. Using multiple regression, managers can compute the impact on demand of other menu items if the price of one item is changed. For example, if the price of a cheeseburger increases from $7.99 to $8.99, Hard Rock can predict the effect this will have on sales of chicken sandwiches, pork sandwiches, and salads. Managers do the same analysis on menu placement, with the center section driving higher sales volumes. When an item such as a hamburger is moved off the center to one of the side flaps, the corresponding effect on related items, say french fries, is determined.

HARD ROCK'S MOSCOW CAFE[a]										
MONTH	1	2	3	4	5	6	7	8	9	10
Guest count (in thousands)	21	24	27	32	29	37	43	43	54	66
Advertising (in $ thousand)	14	17	25	25	35	35	45	50	60	60

[a] These figures are used for purposes of this case study.

Discussion Questions*

1. Describe three different forecasting applications at Hard Rock. Name three other areas in which you think Hard Rock could use forecasting models.
2. What is the role of the POS system in forecasting at Hard Rock?
3. Justify the use of the weighting system used for evaluating managers for annual bonuses.
4. Name several variables besides those mentioned in the case that could be used as good predictors of daily sales in each cafe.

5. At Hard Rock's Moscow restaurant, the manager is trying to evaluate how a new advertising campaign affects guest counts. Using data for the past 10 months (see the table), develop a least-squares regression relationship and then forecast the expected guest count when advertising is $65,000.

*You may wish to view the video that accompanies this case before answering these questions.

- **Additional Case Studies:** Visit MyOMLab for these free case studies:
  North-South Airlines: Reflects the merger of two airlines and addresses their maintenance costs.
  Digital Cell Phone, Inc.: Uses regression analysis and seasonality to forecast demand at a cell phone manufacturer.

Endnotes

1. For a good review of statistical terms, refer to Tutorial 1, "Statistical Review for Managers," in MyOMLab.
2. When the sample size is large ($n > 30$), the prediction interval value of y can be computed using normal tables. When the number of observations is small, the t-distribution is appropriate. See D. Groebner et al., *Business Statistics*, 9th ed. (Upper Saddle River, NJ: Prentice Hall, 2014).

3. To prove these three percentages to yourself, just set up a normal curve for ± 1.6 standard deviations (z-values). Using the normal table in Appendix I, you find that the area under the curve is .89. This represents ± 2 MADs. Likewise, ± 3 MADs = ± 2.4 standard deviations encompass 98% of the area, and so on for ± 4 MADs.
4. Bernard T. Smith, *Focus Forecasting: Computer Techniques for Inventory Control* (Boston: CBI Publishing, 1978).

Main Heading	Review Material	MyOMLab
WHAT IS FORECASTING? (pp. 108–109)	■ **Forecasting**—The art and science of predicting future events. ■ **Economic forecasts**—Planning indicators that are valuable in helping organizations prepare medium- to long-range forecasts. ■ **Technological forecasts**—Long-term forecasts concerned with the rates of technological progress. ■ **Demand forecasts**—Projections of a company's sales for each time period in the planning horizon.	Concept Questions: 1.1–1.4
THE STRATEGIC IMPORTANCE OF FORECASTING (pp. 109–110)	*The forecast is the only estimate of demand until actual demand becomes known.* Forecasts of demand drive decisions in many areas, including: human resources, capacity, and supply chain management.	Concept Questions: 2.1–2.3
SEVEN STEPS IN THE FORECASTING SYSTEM (pp. 110–111)	■ Forecasting follows seven basic steps: (1) Determine the use of the forecast; (2) Select the items to be forecasted; (3) Determine the time horizon of the forecast; (4) Select the forecasting model(s); (5) Gather the data needed to make the forecast; (6) Make the forecast; (7) Validate and implement the results.	Concept Questions: 3.1–3.4
FORECASTING APPROACHES (pp. 111–112)	■ **Quantitative forecasts**—Forecasts that employ mathematical modeling to forecast demand. ■ **Qualitative forecast**—Forecasts that incorporate such factors as the decision maker's intuition, emotions, personal experiences, and value system. ■ **Jury of executive opinion**—Takes the opinion of a small group of high-level managers and results in a group estimate of demand. ■ **Delphi method**—Uses an interactive group process that allows experts to make forecasts. ■ **Sales force composite**—Based on salespersons' estimates of expected sales. ■ **Market survey**—Solicits input from customers or potential customers regarding future purchasing plans. ■ **Time series**—Uses a series of past data points to make a forecast.	Concept Questions: 4.1–4.4
TIME-SERIES FORECASTING (pp. 112–131)	■ **Naive approach**—Assumes that demand in the next period is equal to demand in the most recent period. ■ **Moving average**—Uses an average of the n most recent periods of data to forecast the next period. $$\text{Moving average} = \frac{\Sigma \text{demand in previous } n \text{ periods}}{n} \quad (4\text{-}1)$$ $$\text{Weighted moving average} = \frac{\Sigma((\text{Weight for period } n)(\text{Demand in period } n))}{\Sigma \text{Weights}} \quad (4\text{-}2)$$ ■ **Exponential smoothing**—A weighted-moving-average forecasting technique in which data points are weighted by an exponential function. ■ **Smoothing constant**—The weighting factor, α, used in an exponential smoothing forecast, a number between 0 and 1. Exponential smoothing formula: $$F_t = F_{t-1} + \alpha(A_{t-1} - F_{t-1}) \quad (4\text{-}4)$$ ■ **Mean absolute deviation (MAD)**—A measure of the overall forecast error for a model. $$\text{MAD} = \frac{\Sigma |\text{Actual} - \text{Forecast}|}{n} \quad (4\text{-}5)$$ ■ **Mean squared error (MSE)**—The average of the squared differences between the forecast and observed values. $$\text{MSE} = \frac{\Sigma(\text{Forecast errors})^2}{n} \quad (4\text{-}6)$$ ■ **Mean absolute percent error (MAPE)**—The average of the absolute differences between the forecast and actual values, expressed as a percentage of actual values. $$\text{MAPE} = \frac{\sum_{i=1}^{n} 100|\text{Actual}_i - \text{Forecast}_i|/\text{Actual}_i}{n} \quad (4\text{-}7)$$	Concept Questions: 5.1–5.4 Problems: 4.1–4.42 Virtual Office Hours for Solved Problems: 4.1–4.4 **ACTIVE MODELS 4.1–4.4**

Main Heading	Review Material	MyOMLab
	Exponential smoothing with trend adjustment Forecast including trend (FIT_t) = Exponentially smoothed forecast average (F_t) + Exponentially smoothed trend (T_t) (4-8) ■ **Trend projection**—A time-series forecasting method that fits a trend line to a series of historical data points and then projects the line into the future for forecasts. Trend projection and regression analysis $\hat{y} = a + bx$, where $b = \dfrac{\Sigma xy - n\bar{x}\bar{y}}{\Sigma x^2 - n\bar{x}^2}$ and $a = \bar{y} - b\bar{x}$ (4-11), (4-12), (4-13) ■ **Seasonal variations**—Regular upward or downward movements in a time series that tie to recurring events. ■ **Cycles**—Patterns in the data that occur every several years.	Virtual Office Hours for Solved Problems: 4.5–4.6
ASSOCIATIVE FORECASTING METHODS: REGRESSION AND CORRELATION ANALYSIS (pp. 131–137)	■ **Linear-regression analysis**—A straight-line mathematical model to describe the functional relationships between independent and dependent variables. ■ **Standard error of the estimate**—A measure of variability around the regression line. ■ **Coefficient of correlation**—A measure of the strength of the relationship between two variables. ■ **Coefficient of determination**—A measure of the amount of variation in the dependent variable about its mean that is explained by the regression equation. ■ **Multiple regression**—An associative forecasting method with > 1 independent variable. Multiple regression forecast: $\hat{y} = a + b_1x_1 + b_2x_2$ (4-17)	Concept Questions: 6.1–6.4 Problems: 4.43-4.58 **VIDEO** 4.1 Forecasting Ticket Revenue for Orlando Magic Basketball Games Virtual Office Hours for Solved Problems: 4.7–4.8
MONITORING AND CONTROLLING FORE-CASTS (pp. 138–140)	■ **Tracking signal**—A measurement of how well the forecast is predicting actual values. Tracking signal $= \dfrac{\Sigma(\text{Actual demand in period } i - \text{ Forecast demand in period } i)}{\text{MAD}}$ (4-18) ■ **Bias**—A forecast that is consistently higher or lower than actual values of a time series. ■ **Adaptive smoothing**—An approach to exponential smoothing forecasting in which the smoothing constant is automatically changed to keep errors to a minimum. ■ **Focus forecasting**—Forecasting that tries a variety of computer models and selects the best one for a particular application.	Concept Questions: 7.1–7.4 Problems: 4.59–4.61
FORECASTING IN THE SERVICE SECTOR (pp. 140–141)	Service-sector forecasting may require good short-term demand records, even per 15-minute intervals. Demand during holidays or specific weather events may also need to be tracked.	Concept Question: 8.1 **VIDEO** 4.2 Forecasting at Hard Rock Cafe

Self Test

■ **Before taking the self-test,** refer to the learning objectives listed at the beginning of the chapter and the key terms listed at the end of the chapter.

LO 4.1 Forecasting time horizons include:
    a) long range.   b) medium range.
    c) short range.   d) all of the above.

LO 4.2 Qualitative methods of forecasting include:
    a) sales force composite.   b) jury of executive opinion.
    c) consumer market survey.   d) exponential smoothing.
    e) all except (d).

LO 4.3 The difference between a *moving-average* model and an *exponential smoothing* model is that _____.

LO 4.4 Three popular measures of forecast accuracy are:
    a) total error, average error, and mean error.
    b) average error, median error, and maximum error.
    c) median error, minimum error, and maximum absolute error.
    d) mean absolute deviation, mean squared error, and mean absolute percent error.

LO 4.5 Average demand for iPods in the Rome, Italy, Apple store is 800 units per month. The May monthly index is 1.25. What is the seasonally adjusted sales forecast for May?
    a) 640 units   b) 798.75 units
    c) 800 units   d) 1,000 units
    e) cannot be calculated with the information given

LO 4.6 The main difference between simple and multiple regression is _____.

LO 4.7 The tracking signal is the:
    a) standard error of the estimate.
    b) cumulative error.
    c) mean absolute deviation (MAD).
    d) ratio of the cumulative error to MAD.
    e) mean absolute percent error (MAPE).

Answers: LO 4.1. d; LO 4.2. e; LO 4.3. exponential smoothing is a weighted moving-average model in which all prior values are weighted with a set of exponentially declining weights; LO 4.4. d; LO 4.5. d; LO 4.6. simple regression has only one independent variable; LO 4.7. d.

Managing Quality

CHAPTER OUTLINE

Alaska Air lines

Alaska Air lines

10 OM STRATEGY DECISIONS

- Design of Goods and Services
- *Managing Quality*
- Process Strategy
- Location Strategies
- Layout Strategies
- Human Resources
- Supply-Chain Management
- Inventory Management
- Scheduling
- Maintenance

CHAPTER 6

Managing Quality Provides a Competitive Advantage at Arnold Palmer Hospital

Since 1989, Arnold Palmer Hospital, named after its famous golfing benefactor, has touched the lives of over 7 million children and women and their families. Its patients come not only from its Orlando location but from all 50 states and around the world. More than 12,000 babies are delivered every year at Arnold Palmer, and its huge neonatal intensive care unit boasts one of the highest survival rates in the U.S.

Every hospital professes quality health care, but at Arnold Palmer quality is the mantra—practiced in a fashion like the Ritz-Carlton practices it in the hotel industry. The hospital typically scores in the top 10% of national benchmark studies in terms of patient satisfaction. And its managers follow patient questionnaire results daily. If anything is amiss, corrective action takes place immediately.

Virtually every quality management technique we present in this chapter is employed at Arnold Palmer Hospital:

♦ *Continuous improvement:* The hospital constantly seeks new ways to lower infection rates, readmission rates, deaths, costs, and hospital stay times.

The lobby of Arnold Palmer Hospital, with its 20-foot-high Genie, is clearly intended as a warm and friendly place for children.

Courtesy Arnold Palmer Medical Center

The Storkboard is a visible chart of the status of each baby about to be delivered, so all nurses and doctors are kept up to date at a glance.

Courtesy Arnold Palmer Medical Center

This PYXIS inventory station gives nurses quick access to medicines and supplies needed in their departments. When the nurse removes an item for patient use, the item is automatically billed to that account, and usage is noted at the main supply area.

The hospital has redesigned its neonatal rooms. In the old system, there were 16 neonatal beds in an often noisy and large room. The new rooms are semiprivate, with a quiet simulated-night atmosphere. These rooms have proven to help babies develop and improve more quickly.

* *Employee empowerment:* When employees see a problem, they are trained to take care of it; staff are empowered to give gifts to patients displeased with some aspect of service.
* *Benchmarking:* The hospital belongs to a 2,000-member organization that monitors standards in many areas and provides monthly feedback to the hospital.

When Arnold Palmer Hospital began planning for a new 11-story hospital across the street from its existing building, it decided on a circular pod design, creating a patient-centered environment. Rooms use warm colors, have pull-down Murphy beds for family members, 14-foot ceilings, and natural lighting with oversized windows. The pod concept also means there is a nursing station within a few feet of each 10-bed pod, saving much wasted walking time by nurses to reach the patient. The Video Case Study in Chapter 9 examines this layout in detail.

* *Just-in-time:* Supplies are delivered to Arnold Palmer on a JIT basis. This keeps inventory costs low and keeps quality problems from hiding.
* *Tools such as Pareto charts and flowcharts:* These tools monitor processes and help the staff graphically spot problem areas and suggest ways they can be improved.

From their first day of orientation, employees from janitors to nurses learn that the patient comes first. Staff standing in hallways will never be heard discussing their personal lives or commenting on confidential issues of health care. This culture of quality at Arnold Palmer Hospital makes a hospital visit, often traumatic to children and their parents, a warmer and more comforting experience.

Quality and Strategy

VIDEO 6.1
The Culture of Quality at Arnold Palmer Hospital

As Arnold Palmer Hospital and many other organizations have found, quality is a wonderful tonic for improving operations. Managing quality helps build successful strategies of *differentiation*, *low cost*, and *response*. For instance, defining customer quality expectations has helped Bose Corp. successfully *differentiate* its stereo speakers as among the best in the world. Nucor has learned to produce quality steel at *low cost* by developing efficient processes that produce consistent quality. And Dell Computers rapidly *responds* to customer orders because quality systems, with little rework, have allowed it to achieve rapid throughput in its plants. Indeed, quality may be the key success factor for these firms, just as it is at Arnold Palmer Hospital.

STUDENT TIP ◑

High-quality products and services are the most profitable.

As Figure 6.1 suggests, improvements in quality help firms increase sales and reduce costs, both of which can increase profitability. Increases in sales often occur as firms speed response, increase or lower selling prices, and improve their reputation for quality products. Similarly, improved quality allows costs to drop as firms increase productivity and lower rework, scrap, and warranty costs. One study found that companies with the highest quality were five times as productive (as measured by units produced per labor-hour) as companies with the poorest quality. Indeed, when the implications of an organization's long-term costs and the potential for increased sales are considered, total costs may well be at a minimum when 100% of the goods or services are perfect and defect free.

Quality, or the lack of quality, affects the entire organization from supplier to customer and from product design to maintenance. Perhaps more important, *building* an organization that can achieve quality is a demanding task. Figure 6.2 lays out the flow of activities for an organization to use to achieve total quality management (TQM). A successful quality strategy begins with an organizational culture that fosters quality, followed by an understanding of the principles of quality, and then engaging employees in the necessary activities to implement quality. When these things are done well, the organization typically satisfies its customers and obtains a competitive advantage. The ultimate goal is to win customers. Because quality causes so many other good things to happen, it is a great place to start.

Figure **6.1**

Ways Quality Improves Profitability

Two Ways Quality Improves Profitability

Sales Gains via
- Improved response
- Flexible pricing
- Improved reputation

Reduced Costs via
- Increased productivity
- Lower rework and scrap costs
- Lower warranty costs

Improved Quality → Increased Profits

Organizational practices
Leadership, Mission statement, Effective operating procedures,
Staff support, Training
Yields: What is important and what is to be accomplished.

Quality principles
Customer focus, Continuous improvement, Benchmarking,
Just-in-time, Tools of TQM
Yields: How to do what is important and to be accomplished.

Employee fulfillment
Empowerment, Organizational commitment
*Yields: Employee attitudes that can accomplish
what is important.*

Customer satisfaction
Winning orders, Repeat customers
*Yields: An effective organization with
a competitive advantage.*

Figure **6.2**

The Flow of Activities Necessary to Achieve Total Quality Management

Defining Quality

The operations manager's objective is to build a total quality management system that identifies and satisfies customer needs. Total quality management takes care of the customer. Consequently, we accept the definition of quality as adopted by the American Society for Quality (ASQ; **www.asq.org**): "The totality of features and characteristics of a product or service that bears on its ability to satisfy stated or implied needs."

Others, however, believe that definitions of quality fall into several categories. Some definitions are *user based*. They propose that quality "lies in the eyes of the beholder." Marketing people like this approach and so do customers. To them, higher quality means better performance, nicer features, and other (sometimes costly) improvements. To production managers, quality is *manufacturing based*. They believe that quality means conforming to standards and "making it right the first time." Yet a third approach is *product based*, which views quality as a precise and measurable variable. In this view, for example, really good ice cream has high butterfat levels.

This text develops approaches and techniques to address all three categories of quality. The characteristics that connote quality must first be identified through research (a user-based approach to quality). These characteristics are then translated into specific product attributes (a product-based approach to quality). Then, the manufacturing process is organized to ensure that products are made precisely to specifications (a manufacturing-based approach to quality). A process that ignores any one of these steps will not result in a quality product.

Implications of Quality

In addition to being a critical element in operations, quality has other implications. Here are three other reasons why quality is important:

1. *Company reputation:* An organization can expect its reputation for quality—be it good or bad—to follow it. Quality will show up in perceptions about the firm's new products, employment practices, and supplier relations. Self-promotion is not a substitute for quality products.

Quality
The ability of a product or service to meet customer needs.

LO 6.1 *Define* quality and TQM

◆ **STUDENT TIP**

To create a quality good or service, operations managers need to know what the customer expects.

2. *Product liability:* The courts increasingly hold organizations that design, produce, or distribute faulty products or services liable for damages or injuries resulting from their use. Legislation such as the Consumer Product Safety Act sets and enforces product standards by banning products that do not reach those standards. Impure foods that cause illness, nightgowns that burn, tires that fall apart, or auto fuel tanks that explode on impact can all lead to huge legal expenses, large settlements or losses, and terrible publicity.

3. *Global implications:* In this technological age, quality is an international, as well as OM, concern. For both a company and a country to compete effectively in the global economy, products must meet global quality, design, and price expectations. Inferior products harm a firm's profitability and a nation's balance of payments.

Malcolm Baldrige National Quality Award

The global implications of quality are so important that the U.S. has established the *Malcolm Baldrige National Quality Award* for quality achievement. The award is named for former Secretary of Commerce Malcolm Baldrige. Winners include such firms as Motorola, Milliken, Xerox, FedEx, Ritz-Carlton Hotels, AT&T, Cadillac, and Texas Instruments. (For details about the Baldrige Award and its 1,000-point scoring system, visit **www.nist.gov/baldrige/**.)

The Japanese have a similar award, the Deming Prize, named after an American, Dr. W. Edwards Deming.

ISO 9000 International Quality Standards

ISO 9000

A set of quality standards developed by the International Organization for Standardization (ISO).

The move toward global supply chains has placed so much emphasis on quality that the world has united around a single quality standard, ISO 9000. ISO 9000 is *the* quality standard with international recognition. Its focus is to enhance success through eight quality management principles: (1) top management leadership, (2) customer satisfaction, (3) continual improvement, (4) involvement of people, (5) process analysis, (6) use of data-driven decision making, (7) a systems approach to management, and (8) mutually beneficial supplier relationships.

LO 6.2 *Describe* the ISO international quality standards

The ISO standard encourages establishment of quality management procedures, detailed documentation, work instructions, and recordkeeping. Like the Baldrige Awards, the assessment includes self-appraisal and problem identification. Unlike the Baldrige, ISO certified organizations must be reaudited every three years.

The latest modification of the standard, ISO 9001: 2015, follows a structure that makes it more compatible with other management systems. This version gives greater emphasis to risk-based thinking, attempting to prevent undesirable outcomes.

STUDENT TIP ◆

International quality standards grow in prominence every year. See **www.iso.ch**.

Over one million certifications have been awarded to firms in 206 countries, including about 30,000 in the U.S. To do business globally, it is critical for a firm to be certified and listed in the ISO directory.

Cost of Quality (COQ)

Cost of quality (COQ)

The cost of doing things wrong—that is, the price of nonconformance.

Four major categories of costs are associated with quality. Called the cost of quality (COQ), they are:

- *Prevention costs:* costs associated with reducing the potential for defective parts or services (e.g., training, quality improvement programs).
- *Appraisal costs:* costs related to evaluating products, processes, parts, and services (e.g., testing, labs, inspectors).
- *Internal failure costs:* costs that result from production of defective parts or services before delivery to customers (e.g., rework, scrap, downtime).
- *External failure costs:* costs that occur after delivery of defective parts or services (e.g., rework, returned goods, liabilities, lost goodwill, costs to society).

TABLE 6.1	Leaders in the Field of Quality Management

LEADER	PHILOSOPHY/CONTRIBUTION
W. Edwards Deming	Deming insisted management accept responsibility for building good systems. The employee cannot produce products that on average exceed the quality of what the process is capable of producing. His 14 points for implementing quality improvement are presented in this chapter.
Joseph M. Juran	A pioneer in teaching the Japanese how to improve quality, Juran believed strongly in top-management commitment, support, and involvement in the quality effort. He was also a believer in teams that continually seek to raise quality standards. Juran varies from Deming somewhat in focusing on the customer and defining quality as fitness for use, not necessarily the written specifications.
Armand Feigenbaum	His 1961 book *Total Quality Control* laid out 40 steps to quality improvement processes. He viewed quality not as a set of tools but as a total field that integrated the processes of a company. His work in how people learn from each other's successes led to the field of cross-functional teamwork.
Philip B. Crosby	*Quality Is Free* was Crosby's attention-getting book published in 1979. Crosby believed that in the traditional trade-off between the cost of improving quality and the cost of poor quality, the cost of poor quality is understated. The cost of poor quality should include all of the things that are involved in not doing the job right the first time. Crosby coined the term *zero defects* and stated, "There is absolutely no reason for having errors or defects in any product or service."

Source: Based on *Quality Is Free* by Philip B. Crosby (New York, McGraw-Hill, 1979) p. 58.

The first three costs can be reasonably estimated, but external costs are very hard to quantify. When GE had to recall 3.1 million dishwashers (because of a defective switch alleged to have started seven fires), the cost of repairs exceeded the value of all the machines. This leads to the belief by many experts that the cost of poor quality is consistently underestimated.

Observers of quality management believe that, on balance, the cost of quality products is only a fraction of the benefits. They think the real losers are organizations that fail to work aggressively at quality. For instance, Philip Crosby stated that quality is free. "What costs money are the unquality things—all the actions that involve not doing it right the first time."[1]

Leaders in Quality   Besides Crosby there are several other giants in the field of quality management, including Deming, Feigenbaum, and Juran. Table 6.1 summarizes their philosophies and contributions.

Takumi is a Japanese character that symbolizes a broader dimension than quality, a deeper process than education, and a more perfect method than persistence.

Ethics and Quality Management

For operations managers, one of the most important jobs is to deliver healthy, safe, and quality products and services to customers. The development of poor-quality products, because of inadequate design and production processes, not only results in higher production costs but also leads to injuries, lawsuits, and increased government regulation.

If a firm believes that it has introduced a questionable product, ethical conduct must dictate the responsible action. This may be a worldwide recall, as conducted by both Johnson & Johnson (for Tylenol) and Perrier (for sparkling water), when each of these products was found to be contaminated. A manufacturer must accept responsibility for any poor-quality product released to the public.

There are many stakeholders involved in the production and marketing of poor-quality products, including stockholders, employees, customers, suppliers, distributors, and creditors. As a matter of ethics, management must ask if any of these stakeholders are being wronged. Every company needs to develop core values that become day-to-day guidelines for everyone from the CEO to production-line employees.

Total Quality Management

Total quality management (TQM) refers to a quality emphasis that encompasses the entire organization, from supplier to customer. TQM stresses a commitment by management to have a continuing companywide drive toward excellence in all aspects of products and services that are

Total quality management (TQM)

Management of an entire organization so that it excels in all aspects of products and services that are important to the customer.

TABLE 6.2	Deming's 14 Points for Implementing Quality Improvement

1. Create consistency of purpose.
2. Lead to promote change.
3. Build quality into the product; stop depending on inspections to catch problems.
4. Build long-term relationships based on performance instead of awarding business on the basis of price.
5. Continuously improve product, quality, and service.
6. Start training.
7. Emphasize leadership.
8. Drive out fear.
9. Break down barriers between departments.
10. Stop haranguing workers.
11. Support, help, and improve.
12. Remove barriers to pride in work.
13. Institute a vigorous program of education and self-improvement.
14. Put everybody in the company to work on the transformation.

Source: Deming, W. Edwards. *Out of the Crisis*, pp. 23–24, © 2000 W. Edwards Deming Institute, published by The MIT Press. Reprinted by permission.

important to the customer. Each of the 10 decisions made by operations managers deals with some aspect of identifying and meeting customer expectations. Meeting those expectations requires an emphasis on TQM if a firm is to compete as a leader in world markets.

Quality expert W. Edwards Deming used 14 points (see Table 6.2) to indicate how he implemented TQM. We develop these into seven concepts for an effective TQM program: (1) continuous improvement, (2) Six Sigma, (3) employee empowerment, (4) benchmarking, (5) just-in-time (JIT), (6) Taguchi concepts, and (7) knowledge of TQM tools.

Continuous Improvement

Total quality management requires a never-ending process of continuous improvement that covers people, equipment, suppliers, materials, and procedures. The basis of the philosophy is that every aspect of an operation can be improved. The end goal is perfection, which is never achieved but always sought.

Plan-Do-Check-Act Walter Shewhart, another pioneer in quality management, developed a circular model known as PDCA (plan, do, check, act) as his version of continuous improvement. Deming later took this concept to Japan during his work there after World War II. The PDCA cycle (also called a Deming circle or a Shewhart circle) is shown in Figure 6.3 as a circle to stress the continuous nature of the improvement process.

PDCA

A continuous improvement model of plan, do, check. act.

Figure **6.3**

PDCA Cycle

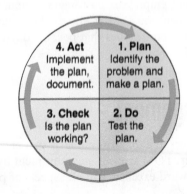

The Japanese use the word *kaizen* to describe this ongoing process of unending improvement—the setting and achieving of ever-higher goals. In the U.S., *TQM* and *zero defects* are also used to describe continuous improvement efforts. But whether it's PDCA, kaizen, TQM, or zero defects, the operations manager is a key player in building a work culture that endorses continuous improvement.

Six Sigma

The term Six Sigma, popularized by Motorola, Honeywell, and General Electric, has two meanings in TQM. In a *statistical* sense, it describes a process, product, or service with an extremely high capability (99.9997% accuracy). For example, if 1 million passengers pass through the St. Louis Airport with checked baggage each month, a Six Sigma program for baggage handling will result in only 3.4 passengers with misplaced luggage. The more common *three-sigma* program (which we address in the supplement to this chapter) would result in 2,700 passengers with misplaced bags every month. See Figure 6.4.

The second TQM definition of Six Sigma is a *program* designed to reduce defects to help lower costs, save time, and improve customer satisfaction. Six Sigma is a comprehensive system—a strategy, a discipline, and a set of tools—for achieving and sustaining business success:

- It is a *strategy* because it focuses on total customer satisfaction.
- It is a *discipline* because it follows the formal Six Sigma Improvement Model known as DMAIC. This five-step process improvement model (1) Defines the project's purpose, scope, and outputs and then identifies the required process information, keeping in mind the customer's definition of quality; (2) Measures the process and collects data; (3) Analyzes the data, ensuring repeatability (the results can be duplicated) and reproducibility (others get the same result); (4) Improves, by modifying or redesigning, existing processes and procedures; and (5) Controls the new process to make sure performance levels are maintained.
- It is a *set of seven tools* that we introduce shortly in this chapter: check sheets, scatter diagrams, cause-and-effect diagrams, Pareto charts, flowcharts, histograms, and statistical process control.

Motorola developed Six Sigma in the 1980s, in response to customer complaints about its products and in response to stiff competition. The company first set a goal of reducing defects by 90%. Within one year, it had achieved such impressive results—through benchmarking competitors, soliciting new ideas from employees, changing reward plans, adding training, and revamping critical processes—that it documented the procedures into what it called Six Sigma. Although the concept was rooted in manufacturing, GE later expanded Six Sigma into services, including human resources, sales, customer services, and financial/credit services. The concept of wiping out defects turns out to be the same in both manufacturing and services.

Six Sigma
A program to save time, improve quality, and lower costs.

LO 6.3 *Explain* Six Sigma

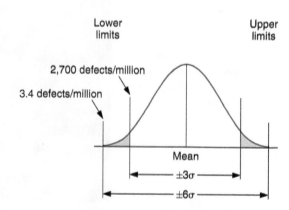

Lower limits   Upper limits

2,700 defects/million

3.4 defects/million

Mean

$\pm 3\sigma$

$\pm 6\sigma$

Figure **6.4**

Defects per Million for $\pm 3\sigma$ vs. $\pm 6\sigma$

⬥ **STUDENT TIP**

Recall that $\pm 3\sigma$ provides 99.73% accuracy, while $\pm 6\sigma$ is 99.9997%.

Implementing Six Sigma Implementing Six Sigma is a big commitment. Indeed, successful Six Sigma programs in every firm, from GE to Motorola to DuPont to Texas Instruments, require a major time commitment, especially from top management. These leaders have to formulate the plan, communicate their buy-in and the firm's objectives, and take a visible role in setting the example for others.

Successful Six Sigma projects are clearly related to the strategic direction of a company. It is a management-directed, team-based, and expert-led approach.[2]

Employee Empowerment

Employee empowerment

Enlarging employee jobs so that the added responsibility and authority is moved to the lowest level possible in the organization.

Employee empowerment means involving employees in every step of the production process. Consistently, research suggests that some 85% of quality problems have to do with materials and processes, not with employee performance. Therefore, the task is to design equipment and processes that produce the desired quality. This is best done with a high degree of involvement by those who understand the shortcomings of the system. Those dealing with the system on a daily basis understand it better than anyone else. One study indicated that TQM programs that delegate responsibility for quality to shop-floor employees tend to be twice as likely to succeed as those implemented with "top-down" directives.[3]

When nonconformance occurs, the worker is seldom at fault. Either the product was designed wrong, the process that makes the product was designed wrong, or the employee was improperly trained. Although the employee may be able to help solve the problem, the employee rarely causes it.

Techniques for building employee empowerment include (1) building communication networks that include employees; (2) developing open, supportive supervisors; (3) moving responsibility from both managers and staff to production employees; (4) building high-morale organizations; and (5) creating such formal organization structures as teams and quality circles.

Quality circle

A group of employees meeting regularly with a facilitator to solve work-related problems in their work area.

Teams can be built to address a variety of issues. One popular focus of teams is quality. Such teams are often known as quality circles. A **quality circle** is a group of employees who meet regularly to solve work-related problems. The members receive training in group planning, problem solving, and statistical quality control. They generally meet once a week (usually after work but sometimes on company time). Although the members are not rewarded financially, they do receive recognition from the firm. A specially trained team member, called the *facilitator*, usually helps train the members and keeps the meetings running smoothly. Teams with a quality focus have proven to be a cost-effective way to increase productivity as well as quality.

Benchmarking

Benchmarking

Selecting a demonstrated standard of performance that represents the very best performance for a process or an activity.

Benchmarking is another ingredient in an organization's TQM program. Benchmarking involves selecting a demonstrated standard of products, services, costs, or practices that represent

Workers at this TRW airbag manufacturing plant in Marshall, Illinois, are their own inspectors. Empowerment is an essential part of TQM. This man is checking the quality of a crash sensor he built.

TRW Automotive/General Manley Ford

TABLE 6.3	Best Practices for Resolving Customer Complaints
BEST PRACTICE	**JUSTIFICATION**
Make it easy for clients to complain.	It is free market research.
Respond quickly to complaints.	It adds customers and loyalty.
Resolve complaints on the first contact.	It reduces cost.
Use computers to manage complaints.	Discover trends, share them, and align your services.
Recruit the best for customer service jobs.	It should be part of formal training and career advancement.

Source: Based on Canadian Government Guide on Complaint Mechanism.

the very best performance for processes or activities very similar to your own. The idea is to develop a target at which to shoot and then to develop a standard or benchmark against which to compare your performance. The steps for developing benchmarks are:

1. Determine what to benchmark.
2. Form a benchmark team.
3. Identify benchmarking partners.
4. Collect and analyze benchmarking information.
5. Take action to match or exceed the benchmark.

Typical performance measures used in benchmarking include percentage of defects, cost per unit or per order, processing time per unit, service response time, return on investment, customer satisfaction rates, and customer retention rates.

In the ideal situation, you find one or more similar organizations that are leaders in the particular areas you want to study. Then you compare yourself (benchmark yourself) against them. The company need not be in your industry. Indeed, to establish world-class standards, it may be best to look outside your industry. If one industry has learned how to compete via rapid product development while yours has not, it does no good to study your industry.

This is exactly what Xerox and Mercedes-Benz did when they went to L.L. Bean for order-filling and warehousing benchmarks. Xerox noticed that L.L. Bean was able to "pick" orders three times faster. After benchmarking, Xerox was immediately able to pare warehouse costs by 10%. Mercedes-Benz observed that L.L. Bean warehouse employees used flowcharts to spot wasted motions. The auto giant followed suit and now relies more on problem solving at the worker level.

Benchmarks often take the form of "best practices" found in other firms or in other divisions. Table 6.3 illustrates best practices for resolving customer complaints.

Likewise, Britain's Great Ormond Street Hospital benchmarked the Ferrari Racing Team's pit stops to improve one aspect of medical care. (See the *OM in Action* box "A Hospital Benchmarks Against the Ferrari Racing Team?")

Internal Benchmarking When an organization is large enough to have many divisions or business units, a natural approach is the internal benchmark. Data are usually much more accessible than from outside firms. Typically, one internal unit has superior performance worth learning from.

Xerox's almost religious belief in benchmarking has paid off not only by looking outward to L.L. Bean but by examining the operations of its various country divisions. For example, Xerox Europe, a $6 billion subsidiary of Xerox Corp., formed teams to see how better sales could result through internal benchmarking. Somehow, France sold five times as many color copiers as did other divisions in Europe. By copying France's approach, namely, better sales training and use of dealer channels to supplement direct sales, Norway increased sales by 152%, Holland by 300%, and Switzerland by 328%!

Benchmarks can and should be established in a variety of areas. Total quality management requires no less.

LO 6.4 *Explain* how benchmarking is used in TQM

OM in Action   A Hospital Benchmarks Against the Ferrari Racing Team?

After surgeons successfully completed a 6-hour operation to fix a hole in a 3-year-old boy's heart, Dr. Angus McEwan supervised one of the most dangerous phases of the procedure: the boy's transfer from surgery to the intensive care unit.

Thousands of such "handoffs" occur in hospitals every day, and devastating mistakes can happen during them. In fact, at least 35% of preventable hospital mishaps take place because of handoff problems. Risks come from many sources: using temporary nursing staff, frequent shift changes for interns, surgeons working in larger teams, and an ever-growing tangle of wires and tubes connected to patients.

Using an unlikely benchmark, Britain's largest children's hospital turned to Italy's Formula One Ferrari racing team for help in revamping patient handoff techniques. Armed with videos and slides, the racing team described how they analyze pit crew performance. It also explained how its system for recording errors stressed the small ones that go unnoticed in pit-stop handoffs.

To move forward, Ferrari invited a team of doctors to attend practice sessions at the British Grand Prix in order to get closer looks at pit stops. Ferrari's technical director, Nigel Stepney, then watched a video of a hospital handoff. Stepney was not impressed. "In fact, he was amazed at how clumsy, chaotic, and informal the process appeared," said one hospital official. At that meeting, Stepney described how each Ferrari crew member is required to do a specific job, in a specific sequence, and in silence.

Oliver Multhaup/AP Images

The hospital handoff, in contrast, had several conversations going on at once, while different members of its team disconnected or reconnected patient equipment, but in no particular order.

Results of the benchmarking process: handoff errors fell over 40%, with a bonus of faster handoff time.

Sources: The Wall Street Journal (December 3, 2007) and (November 14, 2006).

Just-in-Time (JIT)

The philosophy behind just-in-time (JIT) is one of continuing improvement and enforced problem solving. JIT systems are designed to produce or deliver goods just as they are needed. JIT is related to quality in three ways:

- *JIT cuts the cost of quality:* This occurs because scrap, rework, inventory investment, and damage costs are directly related to inventory on hand. Because there is less inventory on hand with JIT, costs are lower. In addition, inventory hides bad quality, whereas JIT immediately *exposes* bad quality.

- *JIT improves quality:* As JIT shrinks lead time, it keeps evidence of errors fresh and limits the number of potential sources of error. JIT creates, in effect, an early warning system for quality problems, both within the firm and with vendors.

- *Better quality means less inventory and a better, easier-to-employ JIT system:* Often the purpose of keeping inventory is to protect against poor production performance resulting from unreliable quality. If consistent quality exists, JIT allows firms to reduce all the costs associated with inventory.

Taguchi Concepts

Most quality problems are the result of poor product and process design. Genichi Taguchi has provided us with three concepts aimed at improving both product and process quality: *quality robustness, target-oriented quality,* and the *quality loss function.*

Quality robust

Products that are consistently built to meet customer needs despite adverse conditions in the production process.

Quality robust products are products that can be produced uniformly and consistently in adverse manufacturing and environmental conditions. Taguchi's idea is to remove the *effects* of adverse conditions instead of removing the causes. Taguchi suggests that removing the effects

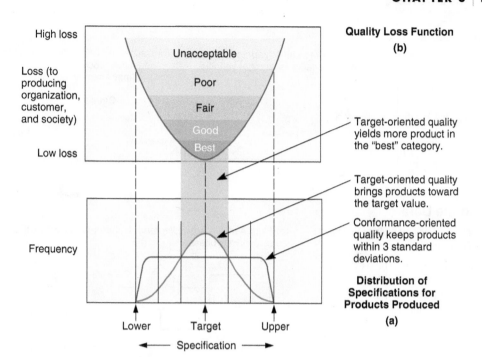

Quality Loss Function (b)

Target-oriented quality yields more product in the "best" category.

Target-oriented quality brings products toward the target value.

Conformance-oriented quality keeps products within 3 standard deviations.

Distribution of Specifications for Products Produced (a)

Figure **6.5**

(a) Distribution of Products Produced and (b) Quality Loss Function

Taguchi aims for the target because products produced near the upper and lower acceptable specifications result in a higher quality loss.

is often cheaper than removing the causes and more effective in producing a robust product. In this way, small variations in materials and process do not destroy product quality.

A study found that U.S. consumers preferred Sony TVs made in Japan to Sony TVs made in the U.S., even though both factories used the exact same designs and specifications. The difference in approaches to quality generated the difference in consumer preferences. In particular, the U.S. factory was *conformance-oriented*, accepting all components that were produced within specification limits. On the other hand, the Japanese factory strove to produce as many components as close to the actual target as possible (see Figure 6.5(a)).

This suggests that even though components made close to the boundaries of the specification limits may technically be acceptable, they may still create problems. For example, TV screens produced near their diameter's lower spec limit may provide a loose fit with screen frames produced near their upper spec limit, and vice versa. This implies that a final product containing many parts produced near their specification boundaries may contain numerous loose and tight fits, which could cause assembly, performance, or aesthetic concerns. Customers may be dissatisfied, resulting in possible returns, service work, or decreased future demand.

Taguchi introduced the concept of target-oriented quality as a philosophy of continuous improvement to bring the product exactly on target. As a measure, Taguchi's quality loss function (QLF) attempts to estimate the cost of deviating from the target value. Even though the item is produced within specification limits, the variation in quality can be expected to increase costs as the item output moves away from its target value. (These quality-related costs are estimates of the average cost over many such units produced.)

The QLF is an excellent way to estimate quality costs of different processes. A process that produces closer to the actual target value may be more expensive, but it may yield a more valuable product. The QLF is the tool that helps the manager determine if this added cost is worthwhile. The QLF takes the general form of a simple quadratic equation (see Figure 6.5(b)).

Knowledge of TQM Tools

To empower employees and implement TQM as a continuing effort, everyone in the organization must be trained in the techniques of TQM. In the following section, we focus on some of the diverse and expanding tools that are used in the TQM crusade.

LO 6.5 *Explain* quality robust products and Taguchi concepts

Target-oriented quality
A philosophy of continuous improvement to bring a product exactly on target.

Quality loss function (QLF)
A mathematical function that identifies all costs connected with poor quality and shows how these costs increase as output moves away from the target value.

Tools for Generating Ideas

(a) *Check Sheet:* An organized method of recording data

Defect	\multicolumn{8}{c}{Hour}
	1	2	3	4	5	6	7	8
A	///	/		/	/	/	///	/
B	//	/	/	/			//	///
C	/	//					//	////

(b) *Scatter Diagram:* A graph of the value of one variable vs. another variable

(c) *Cause-and-Effect Diagram:* A tool that identifies process elements (causes) that may affect an outcome

Tools for Organizing the Data

(d) *Pareto Chart:* A graph that identifies and plots problems or defects in descending order of frequency

(e) *Flowchart (Process Diagram):* A chart that describes the steps in a process

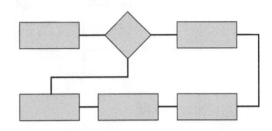

Tools for Identifying Problems

(f) *Histogram:* A distribution that shows the frequency of occurrences of a variable

(g) *Statistical Process Control Chart:* A chart with time on the horizontal axis for plotting values of a statistic

Figure **6.6**

Seven Tools of TQM

Tools of TQM

Seven tools that are particularly helpful in the TQM effort are shown in Figure 6.6. We will now introduce these tools.

Check Sheets

A check sheet is any kind of a form that is designed for recording data. In many cases, the recording is done so the patterns are easily seen while the data are being taken [see Figure 6.6(a)]. Check sheets help analysts find the facts or patterns that may aid subsequent analysis. An example might be a drawing that shows a tally of the areas where defects are occurring or a check sheet showing the type of customer complaints.

LO 6.6 *Use* the seven tools of TQM

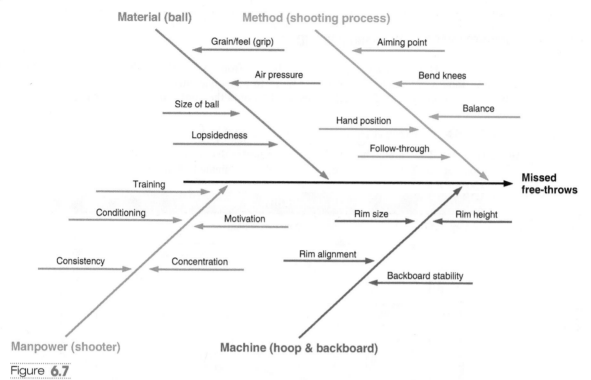

Figure **6.7**

Fish-Bone Chart (or Cause-and-Effect Diagram) for Problems with Missed Free-Throws
Source: Adapted from MoreSteam.com, 2007.

Scatter Diagrams

Scatter diagrams show the relationship between two measurements. An example is the positive relationship between length of a service call and the number of trips a repair person makes back to the truck for parts. Another example might be a plot of productivity and absenteeism, as shown in Figure 6.6(b). If the two items are closely related, the data points will form a tight band. If a random pattern results, the items are unrelated.

Cause-and-Effect Diagrams

Another tool for identifying quality issues and inspection points is the cause-and-effect diagram, also known as an Ishikawa diagram or a fish-bone chart. Figure 6.7 illustrates a chart (note the shape resembling the bones of a fish) for a basketball quality control problem—missed free-throws. Each "bone" represents a possible source of error.

The operations manager starts with four categories: material, machinery/equipment, manpower, and methods. These four *M*s are the "causes." They provide a good checklist for initial analysis. Individual causes associated with each category are tied in as separate bones along that branch, often through a brainstorming process. For example, the method branch in Figure 6.7 has problems caused by hand position, follow-through, aiming point, bent knees, and balance. When a fish-bone chart is systematically developed, possible quality problems and inspection points are highlighted.

Cause-and-effect diagram
A schematic technique used to discover possible locations of quality problems.

Pareto Charts

Pareto charts are a method of organizing errors, problems, or defects to help focus on problem-solving efforts. They are based on the work of Vilfredo Pareto, a 19th-century economist. Joseph M. Juran popularized Pareto's work when he suggested that 80% of a firm's problems are a result of only 20% of the causes.

Example 1 indicates that of the five types of complaints identified, the vast majority were of one type—poor room service.

Pareto charts
A graphic way of classifying problems by their level of importance, often referred to as the 80–20 rule.

Example 1

A PARETO CHART AT THE HARD ROCK HOTEL

The Hard Rock Hotel in Bali has just collected the data from 75 complaint calls to the general manager during the month of October. The manager wants to prepare an analysis of the complaints. The data provided are room service, 54; check-in delays, 12; hours the pool is open, 4; minibar prices, 3; and miscellaneous, 2.

APPROACH ▶   A Pareto chart is an excellent choice for this analysis.

SOLUTION ▶   The Pareto chart shown below indicates that 72% of the calls were the result of one cause: room service. The majority of complaints will be eliminated when this one cause is corrected.

INSIGHT ▶   This visual means of summarizing data is very helpful—particularly with large amounts of data, as in the Southwestern University case study at the end of this chapter. We can immediately spot the top problems and prepare a plan to address them.

LEARNING EXERCISE ▶   Hard Rock's bar manager decides to do a similar analysis on complaints she has collected over the past year: too expensive, 22; weak drinks, 15; slow service, 65; short hours, 8; unfriendly bartender, 12. Prepare a Pareto chart. [Answer: slow service, 53%; expensive, 18%; drinks, 12%; bartender, 10%; hours, 7%.]

RELATED PROBLEMS ▶   6.1, 6.3, 6.7b, 6.12, 6.13, 6.16c, 6.17b

ACTIVE **MODEL** 6.1 This example is further illustrated in Active Model 6.1 in MyOMLab.

Pareto analysis indicates which problems may yield the greatest payoff. Pacific Bell discovered this when it tried to find a way to reduce damage to buried phone cable, the number-one cause of phone outages. Pareto analysis showed that 41% of cable damage was caused by construction work. Armed with this information, Pacific Bell was able to devise a plan to reduce cable cuts by 24% in one year, saving $6 million.

Likewise, Japan's Ricoh Corp., a copier maker, used the Pareto principle to tackle the "callback" problem. Callbacks meant the job was not done right the first time and that a second visit, at Ricoh's expense, was needed. Identifying and retraining only the 11% of the customer engineers with the most callbacks resulted in a 19% drop in return visits.

Flowcharts

Flowcharts

Block diagrams that graphically describe a process or system.

Flowcharts graphically present a process or system using annotated boxes and interconnected lines [see Figure 6.6(e)]. They are a simple but great tool for trying to make sense of a process or explain a process. Example 2 uses a flowchart to show the process of completing an MRI at a hospital.

Example 2

A FLOWCHART FOR HOSPITAL MRI SERVICE

Arnold Palmer Hospital has undertaken a series of process improvement initiatives. One of these is to make the MRI service efficient for patient, doctor, and hospital. The first step, the administrator believes, is to develop a flowchart for this process.

APPROACH ▶ A process improvement staffer observed a number of patients and followed them (and information flow) from start to end. Here are the 11 steps:

1. Physician schedules MRI after examining patient (START).
2. Patient taken from the examination room to the MRI lab with test order and copy of medical records.
3. Patient signs in, completes required paperwork.
4. Patient is prepped by technician for scan.
5. Technician carries out the MRI scan.
6. Technician inspects film for clarity.
7. If MRI not satisfactory (20% of time), Steps 5 and 6 are repeated.
8. Patient taken back to hospital room.
9. MRI is read by radiologist and report is prepared.
10. MRI and report are transferred electronically to physician.
11. Patient and physician discuss report (END).

SOLUTION ▶ Here is the flowchart:

STUDENT TIP ◖

Flowcharting any
process is an
excellent way to
understand and then
try to improve that
process.

INSIGHT ▶ With the flowchart in hand, the hospital can analyze each step and identify value-added activities and activities that can be improved or eliminated.

LEARNING EXERCISE ▶ A new procedure requires that if the patient's blood pressure is over 200/120 when being prepped for the MRI, she is taken back to her room for 2 hours and the process returns to Step 2. How does the flowchart change? Answer:

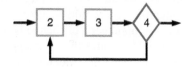

RELATED PROBLEMS ▶ 6.6, 6.15

Histograms

Histograms show the range of values of a measurement and the frequency with which each value occurs [see Figure 6.6(f)]. They show the most frequently occurring readings as well as the variations in the measurements. Descriptive statistics, such as the average and standard deviation, may be calculated to describe the distribution. However, the data should always be plotted so the shape of the distribution can be "seen." A visual presentation of the distribution may also provide insight into the cause of the variation.

Statistical Process Control (SPC)

Statistical process control (SPC) monitors standards, makes measurements, and takes corrective action as a product or service is being produced. Samples of process outputs are examined; if they are within acceptable limits, the process is permitted to continue. If they fall outside certain specific ranges, the process is stopped and, typically, the assignable cause located and removed.

Statistical process control (SPC)
A process used to monitor standards, make measurements, and take corrective action as a product or service is being produced.

Figure **6.8**

Control Chart for Percentage of Free-throws Missed by the Orlando Magic in Their First Nine Games of the New Season

Control charts

Graphic presentations of process data over time, with predetermined control limits.

Control charts are graphic presentations of data over time that show upper and lower limits for the process we want to control [see Figure 6.6(g)]. Control charts are constructed in such a way that new data can be quickly compared with past performance data. We take samples of the process output and plot the average of each of these samples on a chart that has the limits on it. The upper and lower limits in a control chart can be in units of temperature, pressure, weight, length, and so on.

Figure 6.8 shows the plot of sample averages in a control chart. When the samples fall within the upper and lower control limits and no discernible pattern is present, the process is said to be in control with only natural variation present. Otherwise, the process is out of control or out of adjustment.

The supplement to this chapter details how control charts of different types are developed. It also deals with the statistical foundation underlying the use of this important tool.

The Role of Inspection

Inspection

A means of ensuring that an operation is producing at the quality level expected.

To make sure a system is producing as expected, control of the process is needed. The best processes have little variation from the standard expected. In fact, if variation were completely eliminated, there would be no need for inspection because there would be no defects. The operations manager's challenge is to build such systems. However, inspection must often be performed to ensure that processes are performing to standard. This inspection can involve measurement, tasting, touching, weighing, or testing of the product (sometimes even destroying it when doing so). Its goal is to detect a bad process immediately. Inspection does not correct deficiencies in the system or defects in the products, nor does it change a product or increase its value. Inspection only finds deficiencies and defects. Moreover, inspections are expensive and do not add value to the product.

Inspection should be thought of as a vehicle for improving the system. Operations managers need to know critical points in the system: (1) *when to inspect* and (2) *where to inspect*.

When and Where to Inspect

Deciding when and where to inspect depends on the type of process and the value added at each stage. Inspections can take place at any of the following points:

1. At your supplier's plant while the supplier is producing.
2. At your facility upon receipt of goods from your supplier.
3. Before costly or irreversible processes.
4. During the step-by-step production process.
5. When production or service is complete.
6. Before delivery to your customer.
7. At the point of customer contact.

Good methods analysis and the proper tools can result in poka-yokes that improve both quality and speed. Here, two poka-yokes are demonstrated. First, the aluminum scoop automatically positions the french fries vertically, and second, the properly sized container ensures that the portion served is correct. McDonald's thrives by bringing rigor and consistency to the restaurant business.

The seven tools of TQM discussed in the previous section aid in this "when and where to inspect" decision. However, inspection is not a substitute for a robust product produced by well-trained employees in a good process. In one well-known experiment conducted by an independent research firm, 100 defective pieces were added to a "perfect" lot of items and then subjected to 100% inspection. The inspectors found only 68 of the defective pieces in their first inspection. It took another three passes by the inspectors to find the next 30 defects. The last two defects were never found. So the bottom line is that there is variability in the inspection process. In addition, inspectors are only human: They become bored, they become tired, and the inspection equipment itself has variability. Even with 100% inspection, inspectors cannot guarantee perfection. Therefore, good processes, employee empowerment, and source control are a better solution than trying to find defects by inspection. You cannot inspect quality into the product.

For example, at Velcro Industries, as in many other organizations, quality was viewed by machine operators as the job of "those quality people." Inspections were based on random sampling, and if a part showed up bad, it was thrown out. The company decided to pay more attention to the system (operators, machine repair and design, measurement methods, communications, and responsibilities) and to invest more money in training. Over time as defects declined, Velcro was able to pull half its quality control people out of the process.

Source Inspection

The best inspection can be thought of as no inspection at all; this "inspection" is always done at the source—it is just doing the job properly with the operator ensuring that this is so. This may be called source inspection (or source control) and is consistent with the concept of employee empowerment, where individual employees self-check their own work. The idea is that each supplier, process, and employee *treats the next step in the process as the customer*, ensuring perfect product to the next "customer." This inspection may be assisted by the use of checklists and controls such as a fail-safe device called a *poka-yoke*, a name borrowed from the Japanese.

A poka-yoke is a foolproof device or technique that ensures production of good units every time. These special devices avoid errors and provide quick feedback of problems. A simple example of a poka-yoke device is the diesel gas pump nozzle that will not fit into the "unleaded" gas tank opening on your car. In McDonald's, the french fry scoop and standard-size container used to measure the correct quantity are poka-yokes. Similarly, in a hospital, the prepackaged surgical coverings that contain exactly the items needed for a medical procedure are poka-yokes.

Checklists are a type of poka-yoke to help ensure consistency and completeness in carrying out a task. A basic example is a to-do list. This tool may take the form of preflight checklists used by airplane pilots, surgical safety checklists used by doctors, or software quality assurance lists used by programmers. The *OM in Action* box "Safe Patients, Smart Hospitals" illustrates the important role checklists have in hospital quality.

The idea of source inspection, poka-yokes, and checklists is to guarantee 100% good product or service at each step of a process.

STUDENT TIP

One of our themes of quality is that "quality cannot be inspected into a product."

Source inspection

Controlling or monitoring at the point of production or purchase—at the source.

Poka-yoke

Literally translated, "mistake proofing"; it has come to mean a device or technique that ensures the production of a good unit every time.

Checklist

A type of poka-yoke that lists the steps needed to ensure consistency and completeness in a task.

OM in Action | Safe Patients, Smart Hospitals

Simple and avoidable errors are made in hospitals each day, causing patients to die. Inspired by two tragic medical mistakes—his father's misdiagnosed cancer and sloppiness that killed an 18-month-old child at Johns Hopkins—Dr. Peter Pronovost has made it his mission, often swimming upstream against the medical culture, to improve patient safety and prevent deaths.

He began by developing a basic 5-step checklist to reduce catheter infections. Inserted into veins in the groin, neck, or chest to administer fluids and medicines, catheters can save lives. But every year, 80,000 Americans get infections from *central venous catheters* (or lines), and over 30,000 of these patients die. Pronovost's checklist has dropped infection rates at hospitals that use it down to zero, saving thousands of lives and tens of millions of dollars.

His steps for doctors and nurses are simple: (1) wash your hands; (2) use sterile gloves, masks, and drapes; (3) use antiseptic on the area being opened for the catheter; (4) avoid veins in the arms and legs; and (5) take the catheter out as soon as possible. He also created a special cart, where all supplies needed are stored.

Dr. Provonost believes that many hospital errors are due to lack of standardization, poor communications, and a noncollaborative culture that is "antiquated

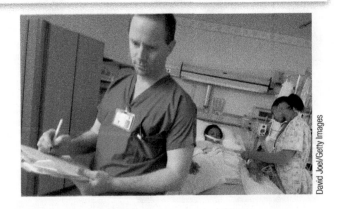

David Joel/Getty Images

and toxic." He points out that checklists in the airline industry are a science, and *every* crew member works as part of the safety team. Provonost's book has shown that one person, with small changes, can make a huge difference.

Sources: Safe Patients, Smart Hospitals (Penguin Publishers, 2011); and *The Wall Street Journal* (December 13, 2014).

Service Industry Inspection

VIDEO 6.2
Quality Counts at Alaska Airlines

In *service*-oriented organizations, inspection points can be assigned at a wide range of locations, as illustrated in Table 6.4. Again, the operations manager must decide where inspections are justified and may find the seven tools of TQM useful when making these judgments.

TABLE 6.4	Examples of Inspection in Services	
ORGANIZATION	**WHAT IS INSPECTED**	**STANDARD**
Alaska Airlines	Last bag on carousel	Less than 20 minutes after arrival at the gate
	Airplane door opened	Less than 2 minutes after arrival at the gate
Jones Law Offices	Receptionist performance	Phone answered by the second ring
	Billing	Accurate, timely, and correct format
	Attorney	Promptness in returning calls
Hard Rock Hotel	Reception desk	Use customer's name
	Doorman	Greet guest in less than 30 seconds
	Room	All lights working, spotless bathroom
	Minibar	Restocked and charges accurately posted to bill
Arnold Palmer Hospital	Billing	Accurate, timely, and correct format
	Pharmacy	Prescription accuracy, inventory accuracy
	Lab	Audit for lab-test accuracy
	Nurses	Charts immediately updated
	Admissions	Data entered correctly and completely
Olive Garden Restaurant	Busboy	Serves water and bread within one minute
	Busboy	Clears all entrée items and crumbs prior to dessert
	Waiter	Knows and suggests specials, desserts
Nordstrom Department Store	Display areas	Attractive, well organized, stocked, good lighting
	Stockrooms	Rotation of goods, organized, clean
	Salesclerks	Neat, courteous, very knowledgeable

Inspection of Attributes versus Variables

When inspections take place, quality characteristics may be measured as either *attributes* or *variables*. Attribute inspection classifies items as being either good or defective. It does not address the *degree* of failure. For example, the lightbulb burns or it does not. Variable inspection measures such dimensions as weight, speed, size, or strength to see if an item falls within an acceptable range. If a piece of electrical wire is supposed to be 0.01 inch in diameter, a micrometer can be used to see if the product is close enough to pass inspection.

Knowing whether attributes or variables are being inspected helps us decide which statistical quality control approach to take, as we will see in the supplement to this chapter.

Attribute inspection
An inspection that classifies items as being either good or defective.

Variable inspection
Classifications of inspected items as falling on a continuum scale, such as dimension or strength.

TQM in Services

The personal component of services is more difficult to measure than the quality of the tangible component. Generally, the user of a service, like the user of a good, has features in mind that form a basis for comparison among alternatives. Lack of any one feature may eliminate the service from further consideration. Quality also may be perceived as a bundle of attributes in which many lesser characteristics are superior to those of competitors. This approach to product comparison differs little between goods and services. However, what is very different about the selection of services is the poor definition of the (1) *intangible differences between products* and (2) *the intangible expectations customers have of those products*. Indeed, the intangible attributes may not be defined at all. They are often unspoken images in the purchaser's mind. This is why all of those marketing issues such as advertising, image, and promotion can make a difference.

The operations manager plays a significant role in addressing several major aspects of service quality. First, the *tangible component of many services is important*. How well the service is designed and produced does make a difference. This might be how accurate, clear, and complete your checkout bill at the hotel is, how warm the food is at Taco Bell, or how well your car runs after you pick it up at the repair shop.

Second, another aspect of service and service quality is the process. Notice in Table 6.5 that 9 out of 10 of the determinants of service quality are related to *the service process*. Such things as reliability and courtesy are part of the process. An operations manager can

TABLE 6.5	Determinants of Service Quality
Reliability involves consistency of performance and dependability. It means that the firm performs the service right the first time and that the firm honors its promises.	
Responsiveness concerns the willingness or readiness of employees to provide service. It involves timeliness of service.	
Competence means possession of the required skills and knowledge to perform the service.	
Access involves approachability and ease of contact.	
Courtesy involves politeness, respect, consideration, and friendliness of contact personnel (including receptionists, telephone operators, etc.).	
Communication means keeping customers informed in language they can understand and listening to them. It may mean that the company has to adjust its language for different consumers—increasing the level of sophistication with a well-educated customer and speaking simply and plainly with a novice.	
Credibility involves trustworthiness, believability, and honesty. It involves having the customer's best interests at heart.	
Security is the freedom from danger, risk, or doubt.	
Understanding/knowing the customer involves making the effort to understand the customer's needs.	
Tangibles include the physical evidence of the service.	

Sources: Adapted from A. Parasuranam, Valarie A. Zeithaml, and Leonard L. Berry, "A Conceptual Model of Service Quality and Its Implications for Future Research," *Journal of Marketing* (1985): 49. Copyright © 1985 by the American Marketing Association. Reprinted with permission.

First passenger boarded
40 min. before departure

Flight attendants on-board
45 min. before departure

Final load
closeout
2 min. before
departure

Aircraft 97%
boarded 10 min.
before departure
time

First bag to
conveyor belt
15 min. after
arrival

Cargo door opened
1 min. after arrival

On board
check-in count
5 min. before
departure

All doors closed
2 min. before
departure

Alaska Airlines

Like many service organizations, Alaska Airlines sets quality standards in areas such as courtesy, appearance, and time. Shown here are some of Alaska Airlines 50 quality checkpoints, based on a timeline for each departure.

design processes that have these attributes and can ensure their quality through the TQM techniques discussed in this chapter. (See the Alaska Airlines photo.)

Third, the operations manager should realize that the customer's expectations are the standard against which the service is judged. Customers' perceptions of service quality result from a comparison of their "before-service expectations" with their "actual-service experience." In other words, service quality is judged on the basis of whether it meets expectations. *The manager may be able to influence both the quality of the service and the expectation.* Don't promise more than you can deliver.

Fourth, the manager must expect exceptions. There is a standard quality level at which the regular service is delivered, such as the bank teller's handling of a transaction. However, there are "exceptions" or "problems" initiated by the customer or by less-than-optimal operating conditions (e.g., the computer "crashed"). This implies that the quality control system must recognize and *have a set of alternative plans for less-than-optimal operating conditions.*

Service recovery

Training and empowering frontline workers to solve a problem immediately.

Well-run companies have service recovery strategies. This means they train and empower frontline employees to immediately solve a problem. For instance, staff at Marriott Hotels are drilled in the LEARN routine—Listen, Empathize, Apologize, React, Notify—with the final step ensuring that the complaint is fed back into the system. And at the Ritz-Carlton, staff members are trained not to say merely "sorry" but "please accept my apology." The Ritz gives them a budget for reimbursing upset guests. Similarly, employees at Alaska Airlines are empowered to soothe irritated travelers by drawing from a "toolkit" of options at their disposal.

SERVQUAL

A popular measurement scale for service quality that compares service expectations with service performance.

Managers of service firms may find SERVQUAL useful when evaluating performance. SERVQUAL is a widely used instrument that provides direct comparisons between customer service expectations and the actual service provided. SERVQUAL focuses on the *gaps* between the customer service expectations and the service provided on 10 service quality determinants. The most common version of the scale collapses the 10 service quality determinants shown in Table 6.5 into five factors for measurement: reliability, assurance, tangibles, empathy, and responsiveness.

Designing the product, managing the service process, matching customer expectations to the product, and preparing for the exceptions are keys to quality services. The *OM in Action* box "Richey International's Spies" provides another glimpse of how OM managers improve quality in services.

VIDEO 6.3
TQM at Ritz-Carlton Hotels

OM in Action   Richey International's Spies

How do luxury hotels maintain quality? They inspect. But when the product is one-on-one service, largely dependent on personal behavior, how do you inspect? You hire spies!

Richey International is the spy. Preferred Hotels and Resorts Worldwide and Intercontinental Hotels have both hired Richey to do quality evaluations via spying. Richey employees posing as customers perform the inspections. However, even then management must have established what the customer expects and specific services that yield customer satisfaction. Only then do managers know where and how to inspect. Aggressive training and objective inspections reinforce behavior that will meet those customer expectations.

The hotels use Richey's undercover inspectors to ensure performance to exacting standards. The hotels do not know when the evaluators will arrive. Nor what aliases they will use. Over 50 different standards are evaluated before the inspectors even check in at a luxury hotel. Over the next 24 hours, using checklists, tape recordings, and photos, written reports are prepared. The reports include evaluation of standards such as:

- Does the doorman greet each guest in less than 30 seconds?
- Does the front-desk clerk use the guest's name during check-in?
- Are the bathroom tub and shower spotlessly clean?
- How many minutes does it take to get coffee after the guest sits down for breakfast?
- Did the waiter make eye contact?
- Were minibar charges posted correctly on the bill?

Established standards, aggressive training, and inspections are part of the TQM effort at these hotels. Quality does not happen by accident.

Sources: Hotelier (Feb. 6, 2010); *Hotel and Motel Management* (August 2002); and *The Wall Street Journal* (May 12, 1999).

Summary

Quality is a term that means different things to different people. We define quality as "the totality of features and characteristics of a product or service that bears on its ability to satisfy stated or implied needs." Defining quality expectations is critical to effective and efficient operations.

Quality requires building a total quality management (TQM) environment because quality cannot be inspected into a product. The chapter also addresses seven TQM *concepts*: continuous improvement, Six Sigma, employee empowerment, benchmarking, just-in-time, Taguchi concepts, and knowledge of TQM tools. The seven TQM *tools* introduced in this chapter are check sheets, scatter diagrams, cause-and-effect diagrams, Pareto charts, flowcharts, histograms, and statistical process control (SPC).

Key Terms

Quality (p. 217)
ISO 9000 (p. 218)
Cost of quality (COQ) (p. 218)
Total quality management (TQM) (p. 219)
PDCA (p. 220)
Six Sigma (p. 221)
Employee empowerment (p. 222)
Quality circle (p. 222)
Benchmarking (p. 222)

Quality robust (p. 224)
Target-oriented quality (p. 225)
Quality loss function (QLF) (p. 225)
Cause-and-effect diagram, Ishikawa diagram, or fish-bone chart (p. 227)
Pareto charts (p. 227)
Flowcharts (p. 228)
Statistical process control (SPC) (p. 229)
Control charts (p. 230)

Inspection (p. 230)
Source inspection (p. 231)
Poka-yoke (p. 231)
Checklist (p. 231)
Attribute inspection (p. 233)
Variable inspection (p. 233)
Service recovery (p. 234)
SERVQUAL (p. 234)

Ethical Dilemma

A lawsuit a few years ago made headlines worldwide when a McDonald's drive-through customer spilled a cup of scalding hot coffee on herself. Claiming the coffee was too hot to be safely consumed in a car, the badly burned 80-year-old woman won $2.9 million in court. (The judge later reduced the award to $640,000.) McDonald's claimed the product was served to the correct specifications and was of proper quality. Further, the cup read "Caution—Contents May Be Hot." McDonald's coffee, at 180°, is substantially hotter (by corporate rule) than typical restaurant coffee, despite hundreds of coffee-scalding complaints in the past 10 years. Similar court cases, incidentally, resulted in smaller verdicts, but again in favor of the plaintiffs. For example, Motor City Bagel Shop was sued for a spilled cup of coffee by a drive-through patron, and Starbucks by a customer who spilled coffee on her own ankle.

Are McDonald's, Motor City, and Starbucks at fault in situations such as these? How do quality and ethics enter into these cases?

Discussion Questions

1. Explain how improving quality can lead to reduced costs.
2. As an Internet exercise, determine the Baldrige Award criteria. See the Web site **www.nist.gov/baldrige/**.
3. Which 3 of Deming's 14 points do you think are most critical to the success of a TQM program? Why?
4. List the seven concepts that are necessary for an effective TQM program. How are these related to Deming's 14 points?
5. Name three of the important people associated with the quality concepts of this chapter. In each case, write a sentence about each one summarizing his primary contribution to the field of quality management.
6. What are seven tools of TQM?
7. How does fear in the workplace (and in the classroom) inhibit learning?
8. How can a university control the quality of its output (that is, its graduates)?
9. Philip Crosby said that quality is free. Why?
10. List the three concepts central to Taguchi's approach.
11. What is the purpose of using a Pareto chart for a given problem?

12. What are the four broad categories of "causes" to help initially structure an Ishikawa diagram or cause-and-effect diagram?
13. Of the several points where inspection may be necessary, which apply especially well to manufacturing?
14. What roles do operations managers play in addressing the major aspects of service quality?
15. Explain, in your own words, what is meant by *source inspection*.
16. What are 10 determinants of service quality?
17. Name several products that do not require high quality.
18. In this chapter, we have suggested that building quality into a process and its people is difficult. Inspections are also difficult. To indicate just how difficult inspections are, count the number of *E*s (both capital *E* and lowercase *e*) in the *OM in Action* box "Richey International's Spies" on page 235 (include the title but not the source note). How many did you find? If each student does this individually, you are very likely to find a distribution rather than a single number!

Solved Problems   Virtual Office Hours help is available in MyOMLab.

SOLVED PROBLEM 6.1

Northern Airlines's frequent flyer complaints about redeeming miles for free, discounted, and upgraded travel are summarized below, in five categories, from 600 letters received this year.

COMPLAINT	FREQUENCY
Could not get through to customer service to make requests	125
Seats not available on date requested	270
Had to pay fees to get "free" seats	62
Seats were available but only on flights at odd hours	110
Rules kept changing whenever customer called	33

Develop a Pareto chart for the data.

SOLUTION

Problems

Problems 6.1–6.20 relate to Tools of TQM

· 6.1 An avant-garde clothing manufacturer runs a series of high-profile, risqué ads on a billboard on Highway 101 and regularly collects protest calls from people who are offended by them. The company has no idea how many people in total see the ads, but it has been collecting statistics on the number of phone calls from irate viewers:

TYPE	DESCRIPTION	NUMBER OF COMPLAINTS
R	Offensive racially/ethnically	10
M	Demeaning to men	4
W	Demeaning to women	14
I	Ad is incomprehensible	6
O	Other	2

a) Depict this data with a Pareto chart. Also depict the cumulative complaint line.
b) What percent of the total complaints can be attributed to the most prevalent complaint?

· 6.2 Develop a scatter diagram for two variables of interest [say pages in the newspaper by day of the week; see the example in Figure 6.6(b)].

· 6.3 Develop a Pareto chart of the following causes of poor grades on an exam:

REASON FOR POOR GRADE	FREQUENCY
Insufficient time to complete	15
Late arrival to exam	7
Difficulty understanding material	25
Insufficient preparation time	2
Studied wrong material	2
Distractions in exam room	9
Calculator batteries died during exam	1
Forgot exam was scheduled	3
Felt ill during exam	4

· 6.4 Develop a histogram of the time it took for you or your friends to receive six recent orders at a fast-food restaurant.

·· 6.5 Kathleen McFadden's restaurant in Boston has recorded the following data for eight recent customers:

CUSTOMER NUMBER, i	MINUTES FROM TIME FOOD ORDERED UNTIL FOOD ARRIVED (y_i)	NO. OF TRIPS TO KITCHEN BY WAITRESS (x_i)
1	10.50	4
2	12.75	5
3	9.25	3
4	8.00	2
5	9.75	3
6	11.00	4
7	14.00	6
8	10.75	5

a) McFadden wants you to graph the eight points (x_i, y_i), $i = 1$, 2, ... 8. She has been concerned because customers have been waiting too long for their food, and this graph is intended to help her find possible causes of the problem.
b) This is an example of what type of graph?

·· 6.6 Develop a flowchart [as in Figure 6.6(e) and Example 2] showing all the steps involved in planning a party.

·· 6.7 Consider the types of poor driving habits that might occur at a traffic light. Make a list of the 10 you consider most likely to happen. Add the category of "other" to that list.
a) Compose a check sheet [like that in Figure 6.6(a)] to collect the frequency of occurrence of these habits. Using your check sheet, visit a busy traffic light intersection at four different times of the day, with two of these times being during high-traffic periods (rush hour, lunch hour). For 15 to 20 minutes each visit, observe the frequency with which the habits you listed occurred.
b) Construct a Pareto chart showing the relative frequency of occurrence of each habit.

·· 6.8 Draw a fish-bone chart detailing reasons why an airline customer might be dissatisfied.

·· 6.9 Consider the everyday task of getting to work on time or arriving at your first class on time in the morning. Draw a fish-bone chart showing reasons why you might arrive late in the morning.

··6.10 Construct a cause-and-effect diagram to reflect "student dissatisfied with university registration process." Use the "four Ms" or create your own organizing scheme. Include at least 12 causes.

··6.11 Draw a fish-bone chart depicting the reasons that might give rise to an incorrect fee statement at the time you go to pay for your registration at school.

···6.12 Mary Beth Marrs, the manager of an apartment complex, feels overwhelmed by the number of complaints she is receiving. Below is the check sheet she has kept for the past 12 weeks. Develop a Pareto chart using this information. What recommendations would you make?

WEEK	GROUNDS	PARKING/DRIVES	POOL	TENANT ISSUES	ELECTRICAL/PLUMBING
1	✓✓✓	✓✓	✓	✓✓✓	
2	✓	✓✓✓	✓✓	✓✓	✓
3	✓✓✓	✓✓✓	✓✓	✓	
4	✓	✓✓✓✓	✓	✓	✓✓
5	✓✓	✓✓✓	✓✓✓✓	✓✓	
6	✓	✓✓✓✓	✓✓		
7		✓✓✓	✓✓	✓✓	
8	✓	✓✓✓✓	✓✓	✓✓✓	✓
9	✓	✓✓	✓		
10	✓	✓✓✓✓	✓✓	✓✓	
11		✓✓✓	✓✓	✓	
12	✓✓	✓✓✓	✓✓✓	✓	

• **6.13** Use Pareto analysis to investigate the following data collected on a printed-circuit-board assembly line:

DEFECT	NUMBER OF DEFECT OCCURRENCES
Components not adhering	143
Excess adhesive	71
Misplaced transistors	601
Defective board dimension	146
Mounting holes improperly positioned	12
Circuitry problems on final test	90
Wrong component	212

a) Prepare a graph of the data.
b) What conclusions do you reach?

•• **6.14** A list of 16 issues that led to incorrect formulations in Tuncey Bayrak's jam manufacturing unit in New England is provided below:

List of Issues

1. Incorrect measurement	9. Variability in scale accuracy
2. Antiquated scales	10. Equipment in disrepair
3. Lack of clear instructions	11. Technician calculation off
4. Damaged raw material	12. Jars mislabeled
5. Operator misreads display	13. Temperature controls off
6. Inadequate cleanup	14. Incorrect weights
7. Incorrect maintenance	15. Priority miscommunication
8. Inadequate flow controls	16. Inadequate instructions

Create a fish-bone diagram and categorize each of these issues correctly, using the "four *M*s" method.

•• **6.15** Develop a flowchart for one of the following:
a) Filling up with gasoline at a self-serve station.
b) Determining your account balance and making a withdrawal at an ATM.
c) Getting a cone of yogurt or ice cream from an ice cream store.

•••• **6.16** Boston Electric Generators has been getting many complaints from its major customer, Home Station, about the quality of its shipments of home generators. Daniel Shimshak, the plant manager, is alarmed that a customer is providing him with the only information the company has on shipment quality. He decides to collect information on defective shipments through a form he has asked his drivers to complete on arrival at customers' stores. The forms for the first 279 shipments have been turned in. They show the following over the past 8 weeks:

WEEK	NO. OF SHIP- MENTS	NO. OF SHIP- MENTS WITH DEFECTS	INCORRECT BILL OF LADING	INCORRECT TRUCK- LOAD	DAMAGED PRODUCT	TRUCKS LATE
			REASON FOR DEFECTIVE SHIPMENT			
1	23	5	2	2	1	
2	31	8	1	4	1	2
3	28	6	2	3	1	
4	37	11	4	4	1	2
5	35	10	3	4	2	1
6	40	14	5	6	3	
7	41	12	3	5	3	1
8	44	15	4	7	2	2

Even though Daniel increased his capacity by adding more workers to his normal contingent of 30, he knew that for many weeks he exceeded his regular output of 30 shipments per week. A review of his turnover over the past 8 weeks shows the following:

WEEK	NO. OF NEW HIRES	NO. OF TERMINATIONS	TOTAL NO. OF WORKERS
1	1	0	30
2	2	1	31
3	3	2	32
4	2	0	34
5	2	2	34
6	2	4	32
7	4	1	35
8	3	2	36

a) Develop a scatter diagram using total number of shipments and number of defective shipments. Does there appear to be any relationship?
b) Develop a scatter diagram using the variable "turnover" (number of new hires plus number of terminations) and the number of defective shipments. Does the diagram depict a relationship between the two variables?
c) Develop a Pareto chart for the type of defects that have occurred.
d) Draw a fish-bone chart showing the possible causes of the defective shipments.

••• **6.17** A recent Gallup poll of 519 adults who flew in the past year found the following number of complaints about flying: cramped seats (45), cost (16), dislike or fear of flying (57), security measures (119), poor service (12), connecting flight problems (8), overcrowded planes (42), late planes/waits (57), food (7), lost luggage (7), and other (51).
a) What percentage of those surveyed found nothing they disliked?
b) Draw a Pareto chart summarizing these responses. Include the "no complaints" group.
c) Use the "four *M*s" method to create a fish-bone diagram for the 10 specific categories of dislikes (exclude "other" and "no complaints").
d) If you were managing an airline, what two or three specific issues would you tackle to improve customer service? Why?

Christophe Testi/Shutterstock

Problems **6.18–6.20** *are available in* MyOMLab.

Problem 6.21 (available in MyOMLab**) relates to TQM in Services**

CASE STUDIES

Southwestern University: (C)*

The popularity of Southwestern University's football program under its new coach Phil Flamm surged in each of the 5 years since his arrival at the Stephenville, Texas, college. (See Southwestern University: (A) in Chapter 3 and (B) in Chapter 4.) With a football stadium close to maxing out at 54,000 seats and a vocal coach pushing for a new stadium, SWU president Joel Wisner faced some difficult decisions. After a phenomenal upset victory over its archrival, the University of Texas, at the homecoming game in the fall, Dr. Wisner was not as happy as one would think. Instead of ecstatic alumni, students, and faculty, all Wisner heard were complaints. "The lines at the concession stands were too long"; "Parking was harder to find and farther away than in the old days" (that is, before the team won regularly); "Seats weren't comfortable"; "Traffic was backed up halfway to Dallas"; and

on and on. "A college president just can't win," muttered Wisner to himself.

At his staff meeting the following Monday, Wisner turned to his VP of administration, Leslie Gardner. "I wish you would take care of these football complaints, Leslie," he said. "See what the *real* problems are and let me know how you've resolved them." Gardner wasn't surprised at the request. "I've already got a handle on it, Joel," she replied. "We've been randomly surveying 50 fans per game for the past year to see what's on their minds. It's all part of my campuswide TQM effort. Let me tally things up and I'll get back to you in a week."

When she returned to her office, Gardner pulled out the file her assistant had compiled (see Table 6.6). "There's a lot of information here," she thought.

TABLE 6.6	Fan Satisfaction Survey Results (N = 250)					
		OVERALL GRADE				
		A	B	C	D	F
Game Day	A. Parking	90	105	45	5	5
	B. Traffic	50	85	48	52	15
	C. Seating	45	30	115	35	25
	D. Entertainment	160	35	26	10	19
	E. Printed Program	66	34	98	22	30
Tickets	A. Pricing	105	104	16	15	10
	B. Season Ticket Plans	75	80	54	41	0
Concessions	A. Prices	16	116	58	58	2
	B. Selection of Foods	155	60	24	11	0
	C. Speed of Service	35	45	46	48	76
Respondents						
Alumnus	113					
Student	83					
Faculty/Staff	16					
None of the above	38					

Open-Ended Comments on Survey Cards:

Parking a mess	More hot dog stands	Put in bigger seats	My company will buy a skybox—
Add a skybox	Seats are all metal	Friendly ushers	build it!
Get better cheerleaders	Need skyboxes	Need better seats	Programs overpriced
Double the parking attendants	Seats stink	Expand parking lots	Want softer seats
Everything is okay	Go SWU!	Hate the bleacher seats	Beat those Longhorns!
Too crowded	Lines are awful	Hot dogs cold	I'll pay for a skybox
Seats too narrow	Seats are uncomfortable	$3 for a coffee? No way!	Seats too small
Great food	I will pay more for better view	Get some skyboxes	Band was terrific
Phil F. for President!	Get a new stadium	Love the new uniforms	Love Phil Flamm
I smelled drugs being smoked	Student dress code needed	Took an hour to park	Everything is great
Stadium is ancient	I want cushioned seats	Coach is terrific	Build new stadium
Seats are like rocks	Not enough police	More water fountains	Move games to Dallas
Not enough cops for traffic	Students too rowdy	Better seats	No complaints
Game starts too late	Parking terrible	Seats not comfy	Dirty bathroom
Hire more traffic cops	Toilets weren't clean	Bigger parking lot	
Need new band	Not enough handicap spots in lot	I'm too old for bench seats	
Great!	Well done, SWU	Cold coffee served at game	

Discussion Questions

1. Using at least two different quality tools, analyze the data and present your conclusions.
2. How could the survey have been more useful?
3. What is the next step?

*This integrated case study runs throughout the text. Other issues facing Southwestern's football stadium include: (A) Managing the renovation project (Chapter 3); (B) Forecasting game attendance (Chapter 4); (D) Break-even analysis of food services (Supplement 7 Web site); (E) Locating the new stadium (Chapter 8 Web site); (F) Inventory planning of football programs (Chapter 12 Web site); and (G) Scheduling of campus security officers/staff for game days (Chapter 13 Web site).

The Culture of Quality at Arnold Palmer Hospital

Video Case

Founded in 1989, Arnold Palmer Hospital is one of the largest hospitals for women and children in the U.S., with 431 beds in two facilities totaling 676,000 square feet. Located in downtown Orlando, Florida, and named after its famed golf benefactor, the hospital, with more than 2,000 employees, serves an 18-county area in central Florida and is the only Level 1 trauma center for children in that region. Arnold Palmer Hospital provides a broad range of medical services including neonatal and pediatric intensive care, pediatric oncology and cardiology, care for high-risk pregnancies, and maternal intensive care.

The Issue of Assessing Quality Health Care

Quality health care is a goal all hospitals profess, but Arnold Palmer Hospital has actually developed comprehensive and scientific means of asking customers to judge the quality of care they receive. Participating in a national benchmark comparison against other hospitals, Arnold Palmer Hospital consistently scores in the top 10% in overall patient satisfaction. Executive Director Kathy Swanson states, "Hospitals in this area will be distinguished largely on the basis of their customer satisfaction. We must have accurate information about how our patients and their families judge the quality of our care, so I follow the questionnaire results daily. The in-depth survey helps me and others on my team to gain quick knowledge from patient feedback." Arnold Palmer Hospital employees are empowered to provide gifts in value up to $200 to patients who find reason to complain about any hospital service such as food, courtesy, responsiveness, or cleanliness.

Swanson doesn't focus just on the customer surveys, which are mailed to patients one week after discharge, but also on a variety of internal measures. These measures usually start at the grass-roots level, where the staff sees a problem and develops ways to track performance. The hospital's longstanding philosophy supports the concept that each patient is important and respected as a person. That patient has the right to comprehensive, compassionate family-centered health care provided by a knowledgeable physician-directed team.

Some of the measures Swanson carefully monitors for continuous improvement are morbidity, infection rates, readmission rates, costs per case, and length of stays. The tools she uses daily include Pareto charts, flowcharts, and process charts, in addition to benchmarking against hospitals both nationally and in the southeast region.

The result of all of these efforts has been a quality culture as manifested in Arnold Palmer's high ranking in patient satisfaction and one of the highest survival rates of critically ill babies.

Discussion Questions*

1. Why is it important for Arnold Palmer Hospital to get a patient's assessment of health care quality? Does the patient have the expertise to judge the health care she receives?
2. How would you build a culture of quality in an organization such as Arnold Palmer Hospital?
3. What techniques does Arnold Palmer Hospital practice in its drive for quality and continuous improvement?
4. Develop a fish-bone diagram illustrating the quality variables for a patient who just gave birth at Arnold Palmer Hospital (or any other hospital).

*You may wish to view the video that accompanies this case before answering these questions.

Quality Counts at Alaska Airlines

Video Case

Alaska Airlines, with nearly 100 destinations, including regular service to Alaska, Hawaii, Canada, and Mexico, is the seventh-largest U.S. carrier. Alaska Airlines has won the J.D. Power and Associates Award for highest customer satisfaction in the industry for eight years in a row while being the number one on-time airline for five years in a row.

Management's unwavering commitment to quality has driven much of the firm's success and generated an extremely loyal customer base. Executive V.P. Ben Minicucci exclaims, "We have rewritten our DNA." Building an organization that can achieve quality is a demanding task, and the management at Alaska Airlines accepted the challenge. This is a highly participative quality culture, reinforced by leadership training, constant process improvement, comprehensive metrics, and frequent review of those metrics. The usual training of flight crews and pilots is supplemented with

Alaska Air lines

ELEMENTS	WEIGHTING	PERFORMANCE	SCORE	BONUS POINTS	TOTAL	GRADE
Process Compliance	20		15		15	B
Staffing	15		15	5	20	A+
MAP Rate (for bags)	20		15		15	B
Delays	10		9		9	A
Time to Carousel (total weight = 10)			10		10	A
Percentage of flights scanned	2	98.7%				
Percentage of bags scanned	2	70.9%				
20 Minutes all bags dropped (% compliance)	4	92.5%				
Outliers (>25mins)	2	2				
Safety Compliance	15		15	5	20	A+
Quality Compliance	10		10		10	A
Total - 100%	**100**		**89**	**10**	**99**	**A+**

Time to Carousel

Points	2	1.5	1	0
Percentage of flights scanned	95%–100%	90%–94.9%	89.9%–85%	< 84.9%

Points	2	0
Percentage of bags scanned	60% or above	≤ 59.9%

Points	0	4
Last bag percent compliance	Below 89.9%	90%–100%

Points	0	1	1.5	2
Last Bag >25 min. (Outliers)	20	15	10	5

classroom training in areas such as Six Sigma. Over 200 managers have obtained Six Sigma Green Belt certification.

Alaska collects more than 100 quality and performance metrics every day. For example, the accompanying picture tells the crew that it has 6 minutes to close the door and back away from the gate to meet the "time to pushback" target. Operations personnel review each airport hub's performance scorecard daily and the overall operations scorecard weekly. As Director of System Operations Control, Wayne Newton proclaims, "If it is not measured, it is not managed." The focus is on identifying problem areas or trends, determining causes, and working on preventive measures.

Within the operations function there are numerous detailed input metrics for station operations (such as the percentage of time that hoses are free of twists, the ground power cord is stowed, and no vehicles are parked in prohibited zones). Management operates under the assumption that if all the detailed input metrics are acceptable, the major key performance indicators, such as Alaska's on-time performance and 20-minute luggage guarantee, will automatically score well.

The accompanying table displays a sample monthly scorecard for Alaska's ground crew provider in Seattle. The major evaluation categories include process compliance, staffing (degree that crew members are available when needed), MAP rate (minimum acceptable performance for mishandled bags), delays, time to carousel, safety compliance, and quality compliance. The quality compliance category alone tracks 64 detailed input metrics using approximately 30,000 monthly observations. Each of the major categories on the scorecard has an importance weight, and the provider is assigned a weighted average score at the end of each month. The contract with the supplier provides for up to a 3.7% bonus for outstanding performance and as much as a 5.0%

penalty for poor performance. The provider's line workers receive a portion of the bonus when top scores are achieved.

As a company known for outstanding customer service, service recovery efforts represent a necessary area of emphasis. When things go wrong, employees mobilize to first communicate with, and in many cases compensate, affected customers. "It doesn't matter if it's not our fault," says Minicucci. Front-line workers are empowered with a "toolkit" of options to offer to inconvenienced customers, including the ability to provide up to 5,000 frequent flyer miles and/or vouchers for meals, hotels, luggage, and tickets. When an Alaska flight had to make an emergency landing in Eugene, Oregon, due to a malfunctioning oven, passengers were immediately texted with information about what happened and why, and they were told that a replacement plane would be arriving within one hour. Within that hour, an apology letter along with a $450 ticket voucher were already in the mail to each passenger's home. No customer complaints subsequently appeared on Twitter or Facebook. It's no wonder why Alaska's customers return again and again.

Discussion Questions*

1. What are some ways that Alaska can ensure that quality and performance metric standards are met when the company outsources its ground operations to a contract provider?
2. Identify several quality metrics, in addition to those identified earlier, that you think Alaska tracks or should be tracking.
3. Think about a previous problem that you had when flying, for example, a late flight, a missed connection, or lost luggage. How, if at all, did the airline respond? Did the airline adequately address your situation? If not, what else should they

have done? Did your experience affect your desire (positively or negative) to fly with that airline in the future?

4. See the accompanying table. The contractor received a perfect Time to Carousel score of 10 total points, even though its performance was not "perfect." How many total points would the contractor have received with the following performance

scores: 93.2% of flights scanned, 63.5% of bags scanned, 89.6% of all bags dropped within 20 minutes, and 15 bags arriving longer than 25 minutes?

*You may wish to view the video that accompanies this case before addressing these questions.

Quality at the Ritz-Carlton Hotel Company

Video Case

Ritz-Carlton. The name alone evokes images of luxury and quality. As the first hotel company to win the Malcolm Baldrige National Quality Award, the Ritz treats quality as if it is the heartbeat of the company. This means a daily commitment to meeting customer expectations and making sure that each hotel is free of any deficiency.

In the hotel industry, quality can be hard to quantify. Guests do not purchase a product when they stay at the Ritz: They buy an experience. Thus, creating the right combination of elements to make the experience stand out is the challenge and goal of every employee, from maintenance to management.

Before applying for the Baldrige Award, company management undertook a rigorous self-examination of its operations in an attempt to measure and quantify quality. Nineteen processes were studied, including room service delivery, guest reservation and registration, message delivery, and breakfast service. This period of self-study included statistical measurement of process work flows and cycle times for areas ranging from room service delivery times and reservations to valet parking and housekeeping efficiency. The results were used to develop performance benchmarks against which future activity could be measured.

With specific, quantifiable targets in place, Ritz-Carlton managers and employees now focus on continuous improvement. The goal is 100% customer satisfaction: If a guest's experience does not meet expectations, the Ritz-Carlton risks losing that guest to competition.

One way the company has put more meaning behind its quality efforts is to organize its employees into "self-directed" work teams. Employee teams determine work scheduling, what work needs to be done, and what to do about quality problems in their own areas. In order to see the relationship of their specific area to the overall goals, employees are also given the opportunity to take additional training in hotel operations. Ritz-Carlton believes that a more educated and informed employee is in a better position to make decisions in the best interest of the organization.

Discussion Questions*

1. In what ways could the Ritz-Carlton monitor its success in achieving quality?
2. Many companies say that their goal is to provide quality products or services. What actions might you expect from a company that intends quality to be more than a slogan or buzzword?
3. Why might it cost the Ritz-Carlton less to "do things right" the first time?
4. How could control charts, Pareto diagrams, and cause-and-effect diagrams be used to identify quality problems at a hotel?
5. What are some nonfinancial measures of customer satisfaction that might be used by the Ritz-Carlton?

*You may wish to view the video that accompanies this case before addressing these questions.

Source: Adapted from C. T. Horngren, S. M. Datar, and G. Foster, *Cost Accounting*, 15th ed. (Upper Saddle River, NJ: Prentice Hall, 2014).

- **Additional Case Study:** Visit MyOMLab for this free case study:
  Westover Electrical, Inc.: This electric motor manufacturer has a large log of defects in its wiring process.

Endnotes

1. Philip B. Crosby, *Quality Is Free* (New York: McGraw-Hill, 1979). Further, J. M. Juran states, in his book *Juran on Quality by Design* (The Free Press 1992, p. 119), that costs of poor quality "are huge, but the amounts are not known with precision. In most companies the accounting system provides only a minority of the information needed to quantify this cost of poor quality. It takes a great deal of time and effort to extend the accounting system so as to provide full coverage."

2. To train employees in how to improve quality and its relationship to customers, there are three other key players in the Six Sigma program: Master Black Belts, Black Belts, and Green Belts.

3. "The Straining of Quality," *The Economist* (January 14, 1995): 55. We also see that this is one of the strengths of Southwest Airlines, which offers bare-bones domestic service but whose friendly and humorous employees help it obtain number-one ranking for quality. (See *Fortune* [March 6, 2006]: 65–69.)

Main Heading	Review Material	MyOMLab
QUALITY AND STRATEGY (pp. 216–217)	Managing quality helps build successful strategies of differentiation, low cost, and *response.* Two ways that quality improves profitability are: ■ *Sales gains* via improved response, price flexibility, increased market share, and/or improved reputation ■ *Reduced costs* via increased productivity, lower rework and scrap costs, and/or lower warranty costs	Concept Questions: 1.1–1.4 **VIDEO 6.1** The Culture and Quality at Arnold Palmer Hospital
DEFINING QUALITY (pp. 217–219)	An operations manager's objective is to build a total quality management system that identifies and satisfies customer needs. ■ **Quality**—The ability of a product or service to meet customer needs. The American Society for Quality (ASQ) defines quality as "the totality of features and characteristics of a product or service that bears on its ability to satisfy stated or implied needs." The two most well-known quality awards are: ■ *U.S.*: Malcolm Baldrige National Quality Award, named after a former secretary of commerce ■ *Japan*: Deming Prize, named after an American, Dr. W. Edwards Deming ■ **ISO 9000**—A set of quality standards developed by the International Organization for Standardization (ISO). ISO 9000 is the only quality standard with international recognition. To do business globally, being listed in the ISO directory is critical. ■ **Cost of quality (COQ)**—The cost of doing things wrong; that is, the price of nonconformance. The four major categories of costs associated with quality are *prevention costs, appraisal costs, internal failure costs,* and *external failure costs.* Four leaders in the field of quality management are W. Edwards Deming, Joseph M. Juran, Armand Feigenbaum, and Philip B. Crosby.	Concept Questions: 2.1–2.4
TOTAL QUALITY MANAGEMENT (pp. 219–226)	■ **Total quality management (TQM)**—Management of an entire organization so that it excels in all aspects of products and services that are important to the customer. Seven concepts for an effective TQM program are (1) continuous improvement, (2) Six Sigma, (3) employee empowerment, (4) benchmarking, (5) just-in-time (JIT), (6) Taguchi concepts, and (7) knowledge of TQM tools. ■ **PDCA**—A continuous improvement model that involves four stages: plan, do, check, and act. The Japanese use the word *kaizen* to describe the ongoing process of unending improvement—the setting and achieving of ever-higher goals. ■ **Six Sigma**—A program to save time, improve quality, and lower costs. In a statistical sense, Six Sigma describes a process, product, or service with an extremely high capability—99.9997% accuracy, or 3.4 defects per million. ■ **Employee empowerment**—Enlarging employee jobs so that the added responsibility and authority are moved to the lowest level possible in the organization. Business literature suggests that some 85% of quality problems have to do with materials and processes, not with employee performance. ■ **Quality circle**—A group of employees meeting regularly with a facilitator to solve work-related problems in their work area. ■ **Benchmarking**—Selecting a demonstrated standard of performance that represents the very best performance for a process or an activity. The philosophy behind just-in-time (JIT) involves continuing improvement and enforced problem solving. JIT systems are designed to produce or deliver goods just as they are needed. ■ **Quality robust**—Products that are consistently built to meet customer needs, despite adverse conditions in the production process. ■ **Target-oriented quality**—A philosophy of continuous improvement to bring the product exactly on target. ■ **Quality loss function (QLF)**—A mathematical function that identifies all costs connected with poor quality and shows how these costs increase as output moves away from the target value.	Concept Questions: 3.1–3.4

Main Heading	Review Material	MyOMLab
TOOLS OF TQM (pp. 226–230)	TQM tools that generate ideas include the *check sheet* (organized method of recording data), *scatter diagram* (graph of the value of one variable vs. another variable), and *cause-and-effect diagram*. Tools for organizing the data are the *Pareto chart* and *flowchart*. Tools for identifying problems are the *histogram* (distribution showing the frequency of occurrences of a variable) and *statistical process control chart*. ■ **Cause-and-effect diagram**—A schematic technique used to discover possible locations of quality problems. (Also called an Ishikawa diagram or a fish-bone chart.) The 4 *Ms* (material, machinery/equipment, manpower, and methods) may be broad "causes." ■ **Pareto chart**—A graphic that identifies the few critical items as opposed to many less important ones. ■ **Flowchart**—A block diagram that graphically describes a process or system. ■ **Statistical process control (SPC)**—A process used to monitor standards, make measurements, and take corrective action as a product or service is being produced. ■ **Control chart**—A graphic presentation of process data over time, with predetermined control limits.	Concept Questions: 4.1–4.4 Problems: 6.1, 6.3, 6.5, 6.8–6.14, 6.16–6.20 ACTIVE MODEL 6.1 Virtual Office Hours for Solved Problem: 6.1
THE ROLE OF INSPECTION (pp. 230–233)	■ **Inspection**—A means of ensuring that an operation is producing at the quality level expected. ■ **Source inspection**—Controlling or monitoring at the point of production or purchase: at the source. ■ **Poka-yoke**—Literally translated, "mistake proofing"; it has come to mean a device or technique that ensures the production of a good unit every time. ■ **Checklist**—A type of poka-yoke that lists the steps needed to ensure consistency and completeness in a task. ■ **Attribute inspection**—An inspection that classifies items as being either good or defective. ■ **Variable inspection**—Classifications of inspected items as falling on a continuum scale, such as dimension, size, or strength.	Concept Questions: 5.1–5.4 **VIDEO 6.2** Quality Counts at Alaska Airlines
TQM IN SERVICES (pp. 233–235)	Determinants of service quality: reliability, responsiveness, competence, access, courtesy, communication, credibility, security, understanding/knowing the customer, and tangibles. ■ **Service recovery**—Training and empowering frontline workers to solve a problem immediately. ■ **SERVQUAL**—A popular measurement scale for service quality that compares service expectations with service performance.	Concept Questions: 6.1–6.4 Problem: 6.21 **VIDEO 6.3** TQM at Ritz-Carlton Hotels

Self Test

■ **Before taking the self-test,** refer to the learning objectives listed at the beginning of the chapter and the key terms listed at the end of the chapter.

LO 6.1 In this chapter, *quality* is defined as:
 a) the degree of excellence at an acceptable price and the control of variability at an acceptable cost.
 b) how well a product fits patterns of consumer preferences.
 c) the totality of features and characteristics of a product or service that bears on its ability to satisfy stated or implied needs.
 d) being impossible to define, but you know what it is.

LO 6.2 ISO 9000 is an international standard that addresses _____.

LO 6.3 If 1 million passengers pass through the Jacksonville Airport with checked baggage each year, a successful Six Sigma program for baggage handling would result in how many passengers with misplaced luggage?
 a) 3.4
 b) 6.0
 c) 34
 d) 2,700
 e) 6 times the monthly standard deviation of passengers

LO 6.4 The process of identifying other organizations that are best at some facet of your operations and then modeling your organization after them is known as:
 a) continuous improvement. b) employee empowerment.
 c) benchmarking. d) copycatting.
 e) patent infringement.

LO 6.5 The Taguchi method includes all except which of the following major concepts?
 a) Employee involvement
 b) Remove the effects of adverse conditions
 c) Quality loss function
 d) Target specifications

LO 6.6 The seven tools of total quality management are _____, _____, _____, _____, _____, _____, and _____.

Answers: LO 6.1. c; LO 6.2. quality management systems; LO 6.3. a; LO 6.4. c; LO 6.5. a; LO 6.6. check sheets, scatter diagrams, cause-and-effect diagrams, Pareto charts, flowcharts, histograms, SPC charts.

Statistical Process Control

6

Alaska Airlines

Alaska Airlines

As part of its statistical process control system, Flowers Bakery, in Georgia, uses a digital camera to inspect just-baked sandwich buns as they move along the production line. Items that don't measure up in terms of color, shape, seed distribution, or size are identified and removed automatically from the conveyor.

Georgia Tech

Statistical Process Control (SPC)

In this supplement, we address statistical process control—the same techniques used at BetzDearborn, at Arnold Palmer Hospital, at GE, and at Southwest Airlines to achieve quality standards. Statistical process control (SPC) is the application of statistical techniques to ensure that processes meet standards. All processes are subject to a certain degree of variability. While studying process data in the 1920s, Walter Shewhart of Bell Laboratories made the distinction between the common (natural) and special (assignable) causes of variation. He developed a simple but powerful tool to separate the two—the control chart.

A process is said to be operating *in statistical control* when the only source of variation is common (natural) causes. The process must first be brought into statistical control by detecting and eliminating special (assignable) causes of variation.[1] Then its performance is predictable, and its ability to meet customer expectations can be assessed. The *objective* of a process control system is to *provide a statistical signal when assignable causes of variation are present*. Such a signal can quicken appropriate action to eliminate assignable causes.

Natural Variations   Natural variations affect almost every process and are to be expected. Natural variations are the many sources of variation that occur within a process, even one that is in statistical control. Natural variations form a pattern that can be described as a *distribution*.

As long as the distribution (output measurements) remains within specified limits, the process is said to be "in control," and natural variations are tolerated.

Statistical process control (SPC)

A process used to monitor standards by taking measurements and corrective action as a product or service is being produced.

Control chart

A graphical presentation of process data over time.

Natural variations

Variability that affects every production process to some degree and is to be expected; also known as common cause.

(a) Samples of the product, say five boxes of cereal taken off the filling machine line, vary from one another in weight.

Each of these represents one sample of five boxes of cereal.

Figure **S6.1**

Natural and Assignable Variation

(b) After enough sample means are taken from a stable process, they form a pattern called a *distribution*.

The solid line represents the distribution.

(c) There are many types of distributions, including the normal (bell-shaped) distribution, but distributions do differ in terms of central tendency (mean), standard deviation or variance, and shape.

Measure of central tendency (mean)   Variation (std. deviation)   Shape

(d) If only natural causes of variation are present, the output of a process forms a distribution that is stable over time and is predictable.

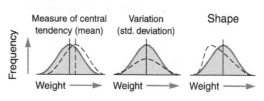

Prediction

(e) If assignable causes of variation are present, the process output is not stable over time and is not predictable. That is, when causes that are not an expected part of the process occur, the samples will yield unexpected distributions that vary by central tendency, standard deviation, and shape.

Prediction

Assignable Variations   Assignable variation in a process can be traced to a specific reason. Factors such as machine wear, misadjusted equipment, fatigued or untrained workers, or new batches of raw material are all potential sources of assignable variations.

Natural and assignable variations distinguish two tasks for the operations manager. The first is to *ensure that the process is capable* of operating under control with only natural variation. The second is, of course, to *identify and eliminate assignable variations* so that the processes will remain under control.

Samples   Because of natural and assignable variation, statistical process control uses averages of small samples (often of four to eight items) as opposed to data on individual parts. Individual pieces tend to be too erratic to make trends quickly visible.

Figure S6.1 provides a detailed look at the important steps in determining process variation. The horizontal scale can be weight (as in the number of ounces in boxes of cereal) or length (as in fence posts) or any physical measure. The vertical scale is frequency. The samples of five boxes of cereal in Figure S6.1 **(a)** are weighed, **(b)** form a distribution, and **(c)** can vary. The distributions formed in **(b)** and **(c)** will fall in a predictable pattern **(d)** if only natural variation is present. If assignable causes of variation are present, then we can expect either the mean to vary or the dispersion to vary, as is the case in **(e)**.

Control Charts   The process of building control charts is based on the concepts presented in Figure S6.2. This figure shows three distributions that are the result of outputs from three types of processes. We plot small samples and then examine characteristics of the resulting data to see if the process is within "control limits." The purpose of control charts is to help distinguish between natural variations and variations due to assignable causes. As seen in Figure S6.2, a process is **(a)** in control *and the process is capable of producing within established control limits*, **(b)** in control *but the process is not capable of producing within established*

Assignable variation
Variation in a production process that can be traced to specific causes.

LO S6.1 *Explain* the purpose of a control chart

Figure **S6.2**

**Process Control: Three Types
of Process Outputs**

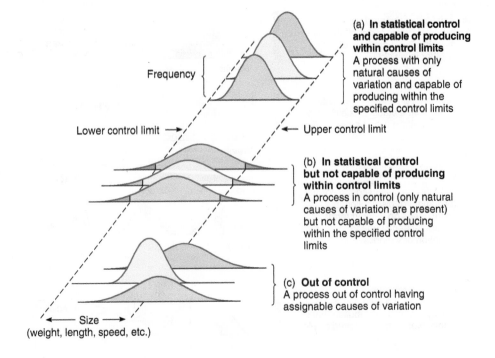

Figure **S6.2**

Process Control: Three Types of Process Outputs

limits, or **(c)** out of control. We now look at ways to build control charts that help the operations manager keep a process under control.

Control Charts for Variables

The variables of interest here are those that have continuous dimensions. They have an infinite number of possibilities. Examples are weight, speed, length, or strength. Control charts for the mean, $\bar{x}$ or x-bar, and the range, R, are used to monitor processes that have continuous dimensions. The $\bar{x}$-chart tells us whether changes have occurred in the central tendency (the mean, in this case) of a process. These changes might be due to such factors as tool wear, a gradual increase in temperature, a different method used on the second shift, or new and stronger materials. The R-chart values indicate that a gain or loss in dispersion has occurred. Such a change may be due to worn bearings, a loose tool, an erratic flow of lubricants to a machine, or to sloppiness on the part of a machine operator. The two types of charts go hand in hand when monitoring variables because they measure the two critical parameters: central tendency and dispersion.

The Central Limit Theorem

The theoretical foundation for $\bar{x}$-charts is the central limit theorem. This theorem states that regardless of the distribution of the population, the distribution of $\bar{x}$s (each of which is a mean of a sample drawn from the population) will tend to follow a normal curve as the number of samples increases. Fortunately, even if each sample (n) is fairly small (say, 4 or 5), the distributions of the averages will still roughly follow a normal curve. The theorem also states that: (1) the mean of the distribution of the $\bar{x}$s (called $\bar{\bar{x}}$) will equal the mean of the overall population (called μ); and (2) the standard deviation of the *sampling distribution*, $\sigma_{\bar{x}}$, will be the *population (process) standard deviation*, divided by the square root of the sample size, n. In other words:[2]

$$\bar{\bar{x}} = \mu \tag{S6-1}$$

and

$$\sigma_{\bar{x}} = \frac{\sigma}{\sqrt{n}} \tag{S6-2}$$

$\bar{x}$-chart

A quality control chart for variables that indicates when changes occur in the central tendency of a production process.

R-chart

A control chart that tracks the "range" within a sample; it indicates that a gain or loss in uniformity has occurred in dispersion of a production process.

Central limit theorem

The theoretical foundation for $\bar{x}$-charts, which states that regardless of the distribution of the population of all parts or services, the distribution of $\bar{x}$s tends to follow a normal curve as the number of samples increases.

LO S6.2 *Explain* the role of the central limit theorem in SPC

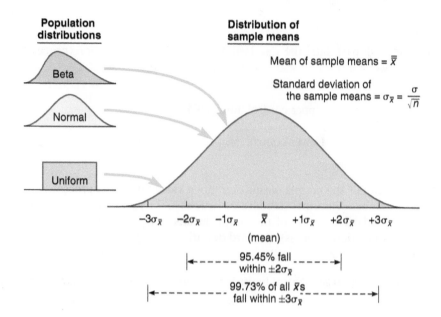

Figure **S6.3**

The Relationship Between Population and Sampling Distributions

Even though the population distributions will differ (e.g., normal, beta, uniform), each with its own mean (μ) and standard deviation (σ), the distribution of sample means always approaches a normal distribution.

Figure S6.3 shows three possible population distributions, each with its own mean, μ, and standard deviation, σ. If a series of random samples ($\bar{x}_1$, $\bar{x}_2$, $\bar{x}_3$, $\bar{x}_4$, and so on), each of size n, is drawn from any population distribution (which could be normal, beta, uniform, and so on), the resulting distribution of $\bar{x}_i$s will approximate a normal distribution (see Figure S6.3).

Moreover, the sampling distribution, as is shown in Figure S6.4(a), will have less variability than the process distribution. Because the sampling distribution is normal, we can state that:

- 95.45% of the time, the sample averages will fall within $\pm 2\sigma_{\bar{x}}$ if the process has only natural variations.
- 99.73% of the time, the sample averages will fall within $\pm 3\sigma_{\bar{x}}$ if the process has only natural variations.

If a point on the control chart falls outside of the $\pm 3\sigma_{\bar{x}}$ control limits, then we are 99.73% sure the process has changed. Figure S6.4(b) shows that as the sample size increases, the sampling distribution becomes narrower. So the sample statistic is closer to the true value of the population for larger sample sizes. This is the theory behind control charts.

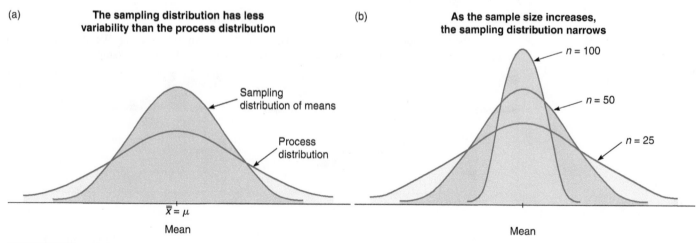

Figure **S6.4**

The Sampling Distribution of Means Is Normal

The process distribution from which the sample was drawn was also normal, but it could have been any distribution.

Setting Mean Chart Limits ($\bar{x}$-Charts)

If we know, through past data, the standard deviation of the population (process), σ, we can set upper and lower control limits[3] by using these formulas:

$$\text{Upper control limit (UCL)} = \bar{\bar{x}} + z\sigma_{\bar{x}} \qquad \text{(S6-3)}$$

$$\text{Lower control limit (LCL)} = \bar{\bar{x}} - z\sigma_{\bar{x}} \qquad \text{(S6-4)}$$

LO S6.3 *Build $\bar{x}$-charts and R-charts*

where

$\bar{\bar{x}}$ = mean of the sample means or a target value set for the process
z = number of normal standard deviations (2 for 95.45% confidence, 3 for 99.73%)
$\sigma_{\bar{x}}$ = standard deviation of the sample means = $\sigma/\sqrt{n}$
σ = population (process) standard deviation
n = sample size

Example S1 shows how to set control limits for sample means using standard deviations.

Example S1

SETTING CONTROL LIMITS USING SAMPLES

The weights of boxes of Oat Flakes within a large production lot are sampled each hour. Managers want to set control limits that include 99.73% of the sample means.

APPROACH ▶ Randomly select and weigh nine ($n = 9$) boxes each hour. Then find the overall mean and use Equations (S6-3) and (S6-4) to compute the control limits. Here are the nine boxes chosen for Hour 1:

| Oat Flakes 17 oz. | Oat Flakes 13 oz. | Oat Flakes 16 oz. | Oat Flakes 18 oz. | Oat Flakes 17 oz. | Oat Flakes 16 oz. | Oat Flakes 15 oz. | Oat Flakes 17 oz. | Oat Flakes 16 oz. |

SOLUTION ▶

$$\text{The average weight in the first hourly sample} = \frac{17 + 13 + 16 + 18 + 17 + 16 + 15 + 17 + 16}{9}$$

$$= 16.1 \text{ ounces.}$$

Also, the *population (process)* standard deviation (σ) is known to be 1 ounce. We do not show each of the boxes randomly selected in hours 2 through 12, but here are all 12 hourly samples:

WEIGHT OF SAMPLE		WEIGHT OF SAMPLE		WEIGHT OF SAMPLE	
HOUR	(AVG. OF 9 BOXES)	HOUR	(AVG. OF 9 BOXES)	HOUR	(AVG. OF 9 BOXES)
1	16.1	5	16.5	9	16.3
2	16.8	6	16.4	10	14.8
3	15.5	7	15.2	11	14.2
4	16.5	8	16.4	12	17.3

The average mean $\bar{\bar{x}}$ of the 12 samples is calculated to be exactly 16 ounces $\left[\bar{\bar{x}} = \dfrac{\sum\limits_{i=1}^{12} (\text{Avg. of 9 Boxes})}{12} \right]$.

We therefore have $\bar{\bar{x}} = 16$ ounces, $\sigma = 1$ ounce, $n = 9$, and $z = 3$. The control limits are:

$$\text{UCL}_{\bar{x}} = \bar{\bar{x}} + z\sigma_{\bar{x}} = 16 + 3\left(\frac{1}{\sqrt{9}}\right) = 16 + 3\left(\frac{1}{3}\right) = 17 \text{ ounces}$$

$$\text{LCL}_{\bar{x}} = \bar{\bar{x}} - z\sigma_{\bar{x}} = 16 - 3\left(\frac{1}{\sqrt{9}}\right) = 16 - 3\left(\frac{1}{3}\right) = 15 \text{ ounces}$$

The 12 samples are then plotted on the following control chart:

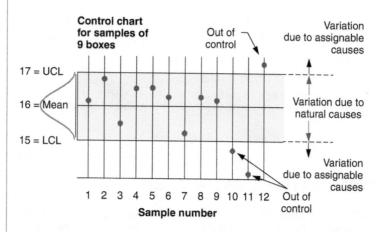

INSIGHT ▶ Because the means of recent sample averages fall outside the upper and lower control limits of 17 and 15, we can conclude that the process is becoming erratic and is *not* in control.

LEARNING EXERCISE ▶ If Oat Flakes's population standard deviation (σ) is 2 (instead of 1), what is your conclusion? [Answer: LCL = 14, UCL = 18; the process would be in control.]

RELATED PROBLEMS ▶ S6.1, S6.2, S6.4, S6.8, S6.10a,b (S6.28 is available in MyOMLab)

ACTIVE MODEL S6.1 This example is further illustrated in Active Model S6.1 in MyOMLab.

EXCEL OM Data File CH06ExS1.XLS can be found in MyOMLab.

Because process standard deviations are often not available, we usually calculate control limits based on the average *range* values rather than on standard deviations. Table S6.1 provides the necessary conversion for us to do so. The *range* (R_i) is defined as the difference between the largest and smallest items in one sample. For example, the heaviest box of Oat Flakes in Hour 1 of Example S1 was 18 ounces and the lightest was 13 ounces, so the range for that hour is 5 ounces. We use Table S6.1 and the equations:

$$\text{UCL}_{\bar{x}} = \bar{\bar{x}} + A_2\bar{R} \qquad (S6\text{-}5)$$

and:

$$\text{LCL}_{\bar{x}} = \bar{\bar{x}} - A_2\bar{R} \qquad (S6\text{-}6)$$

where $\bar{R} = \dfrac{\sum\limits_{i=1}^{k} R_i}{k}$ = average range of all the samples; R_i = range for sample i

A_2 = value found in Table S6.1 $\qquad\qquad k$ = total number of samples

$\bar{\bar{x}}$ = mean of the sample means

Example S2 shows how to set control limits for sample means by using Table S6.1 and the average range.

TABLE S6.1	Factors for Computing Control Chart Limits (3 sigma)		
SAMPLE SIZE, n	MEAN FACTOR, A_2	UPPER RANGE, D_4	LOWER RANGE, D_3
2	1.880	3.268	0
3	1.023	2.574	0
4	.729	2.282	0
5	.577	2.115	0
6	.483	2.004	0
7	.419	1.924	0.076
8	.373	1.864	0.136
9	.337	1.816	0.184
10	.308	1.777	0.223
12	.266	1.716	0.284

Source: Reprinted by permission of American Society for Testing Materials. Copyright 1951. Taken from Special Technical Publication 15–C, "Quality Control of Materials," pp. 63 and 72. Copyright ASTM INTERNATIONAL. Reprinted with permission.

Example S2

SETTING MEAN LIMITS USING TABLE VALUES

Super Cola bottles soft drinks labeled "net weight 12 ounces." Indeed, an overall process average of 12 ounces has been found by taking 10 samples, in which each sample contained 5 bottles. The OM team wants to determine the upper and lower control limits for averages in this process.

APPROACH ▶ Super Cola first examines the 10 samples to compute the average range of the process. Here are the data and calculations:

SAMPLE	WEIGHT OF LIGHTEST BOTTLE IN SAMPLE OF $n = 5$	WEIGHT OF HEAVIEST BOTTLE IN SAMPLE OF $n = 5$	RANGE (R_i) = DIFFERENCE BETWEEN THESE TWO
1	11.50	11.72	.22
2	11.97	12.00	.03
3	11.55	12.05	.50
4	12.00	12.20	.20
5	11.95	12.00	.05
6	10.55	10.75	.20
7	12.50	12.75	.25
8	11.00	11.25	.25
9	10.60	11.00	.40
10	11.70	12.10	.40
			$\sum R_i = 2.50$

$$\text{Average Range} = \frac{2.50}{10 \text{ samples}} = .25 \text{ ounces}$$

Now Super Cola applies Equations (S6-5) and (S6-6) and uses the A_2 column of Table S6.1.

SOLUTION ▶ Looking in Table S6.1 for a sample size of 5 in the mean factor A_2 column, we find the value .577. Thus, the upper and lower control chart limits are:

$$\text{UCL}_{\bar{x}} = \bar{\bar{x}} + A_2\bar{R}$$

$$= 12 + (.577)(.25)$$

$$= 12 + .144$$

$$= 12.144 \text{ ounces}$$

$$LCL_{\bar{x}} = \bar{\bar{x}} - A_2\bar{R}$$

$$= 12 - .144$$

$$= 11.856 \text{ ounces}$$

INSIGHT ▶ The advantage of using this range approach, instead of the standard deviation, is that it is easy to apply and may be less confusing.

LEARNING EXERCISE ▶ If the sample size was $n = 4$ and the average range $= .20$ ounces, what are the revised $UCL_{\bar{x}}$ and $LCL_{\bar{x}}$? [Answer: 12.146, 11.854.]

RELATED PROBLEMS ▶ S6.3a, S6.5, S6.6, S6.7, S6.9, S6.10b,c,d, S6.11, S6.26 (S6.29a, S6.30a, S6.31a, S6.32a, S6.33a are available in MyOMLab)

EXCEL **OM** Data File **CH06ExS2.xls** can be found in MyOMLab.

Setting Range Chart Limits (R-Charts)

In Examples S1 and S2, we determined the upper and lower control limits for the process *average*. In addition to being concerned with the process average, operations managers are interested in the process *dispersion*, or *range*. Even though the process average is under control, the dispersion of the process may not be. For example, something may have worked itself loose in a piece of equipment that fills boxes of Oat Flakes. As a result, the average of the samples may remain the same, but the variation within the samples could be entirely too large. For this reason, operations managers use control charts for ranges to monitor the process variability, as well as control charts for averages, which monitor the process central tendency. The theory behind the control charts for ranges is the same as that for process average control charts. Limits are established that contain ± 3 standard deviations of the distribution for the average range $\bar{R}$. We can use the following equations to set the upper and lower control limits for ranges:

$$UCL_R = D_4\bar{R} \tag{S6-7}$$

$$LCL_R = D_3\bar{R} \tag{S6-8}$$

where

$$UCL_R = \text{upper control chart limit for the range}$$
$$LCL_R = \text{lower control chart limit for the range}$$
$$D_4 \text{ and } D_3 = \text{values from Table S6.1}$$

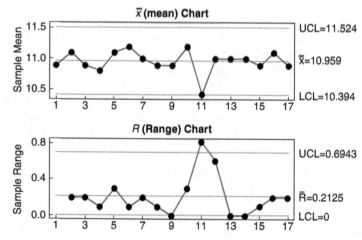

Salmon filets are monitored by Darden Restaurant's SPC software, which includes $\bar{x}$-(mean) charts and R-(range) charts. Darden uses average weight as a measure of central tendency for salmon filets. The range is the difference between the heaviest and the lightest filets in each sample. The video case study "Farm to Fork," at the end of this supplement, asks you to interpret these figures.

VIDEO S6.1
Farm to Fork: Quality of Darden Restaurants

Example S3 shows how to set control limits for sample ranges using Table S6.1 and the average range.

Example S3	**SETTING RANGE LIMITS USING TABLE VALUES**

Roy Clinton's mail-ordering business wants to measure the response time of its operators in taking customer orders over the phone. Clinton lists below the time recorded (in minutes) from five different samples of the ordering process with four customer orders per sample. He wants to determine the upper and lower range control chart limits.

APPROACH ▶ Looking in Table S6.1 for a sample size of 4, he finds that $D_4 = 2.282$ and $D_3 = 0$.

SOLUTION ▶

SAMPLE	OBSERVATIONS (MINUTES)	SAMPLE RANGE (R_i)
1	5, 3, 6, 10	$10 - 3 = 7$
2	7, 5, 3, 5	$7 - 3 = 4$
3	1, 8, 3, 12	$12 - 1 = 11$
4	7, 6, 2, 1	$7 - 1 = 6$
5	3, 15, 6, 12	$15 - 3 = 12$
		$\Sigma R_i = 40$

$$\bar{R} = \frac{40}{5} = 8$$

$$\text{UCL}_R = 2.282(8) = 18.256 \text{ minutes}$$

$$\text{LCL}_R = 0(8) = 0 \text{ minutes}$$

INSIGHT ▶ Computing ranges with Table S6.1 is straightforward and an easy way to evaluate dispersion. No sample ranges are out of control.

LEARNING EXERCISE ▶ Clinton decides to increase the sample size to $n = 6$ (with no change in average range, $\bar{R}$). What are the new UCL_R and LCL_R values? [Answer: 16.032, 0.]

RELATED PROBLEMS ▶ S6.3b, S6.5, S6.6, S6.7, S6.9, S6.10c, S6.11, S6.12, S6.26 (S6.29b, S6.30b, S6.31b, S6.32b, S6.33b are available in MyOMLab)

Using Mean and Range Charts

The normal distribution is defined by two parameters, the *mean* and *standard deviation*. The $\bar{x}$ (mean)-chart and the R-chart mimic these two parameters. The $\bar{x}$-chart is sensitive to shifts in the process mean, whereas the R-chart is sensitive to shifts in the process standard deviation. Consequently, by using both charts we can track changes in the process distribution.

For instance, the samples and the resulting $\bar{x}$-chart in Figure S6.5(a) show the shift in the process mean, but because the dispersion is constant, no change is detected by the R-chart. Conversely, the samples and the $\bar{x}$-chart in Figure S6.5(b) detect no shift (because none is present), but the R-chart does detect the shift in the dispersion. Both charts are required to track the process accurately.

LO S6.4 *List* the five steps involved in building control charts

Steps to Follow When Building Control Charts There are five steps that are generally followed in building $\bar{x}$- and R-charts:

1. Collect 20 to 25 samples, often of $n = 4$ or $n = 5$ observations each, from a stable process, and compute the mean and range of each.
2. Compute the overall means ($\bar{\bar{x}}$ and $\bar{R}$), set appropriate control limits, usually at the 99.73% level, and calculate the preliminary upper and lower control limits. Refer to Table S6.2 for other control limits. *If the process is not currently stable and in control*, use the desired mean, μ, instead of $\bar{\bar{x}}$ to calculate limits.

(a)

These sampling distributions result in the charts below.

(Sampling mean is shifting upward, but range is consistent.)

$\bar{x}$-chart

UCL

($\bar{x}$-chart detects shift in central tendency.)

LCL

R-chart

UCL

(R-chart indicates no change in dispersion [mean].)

LCL

(b)

These sampling distributions result in the charts below.

(Sampling mean is constant, but dispersion is increasing.)

$\bar{x}$-chart

UCL

($\bar{x}$-chart indicates no change in central tendency.)

LCL

R-chart

UCL

(R-chart detects increase in dispersion [range].)

LCL

Figure S6.5

Mean and Range Charts Complement Each Other by Showing the Mean and Dispersion of the Normal Distribution

◈ **STUDENT TIP**

Mean ($\bar{x}$) charts are a measure of *central tendency*, while range (R) charts are a measure of *dispersion*. SPC requires both charts for a complete assessment because a sample mean could be out of control while the range is in control and vice versa.

3. Graph the sample means and ranges on their respective control charts, and determine whether they fall outside the acceptable limits.
4. Investigate points or patterns that indicate the process is out of control. Try to assign causes for the variation, address the causes, and then resume the process.
5. Collect additional samples and, if necessary, revalidate the control limits using the new data.

TABLE S6.2

Common z Values

DESIRED CONTROL LIMIT (%)	Z-VALUE (STANDARD DEVIATION REQUIRED FOR DESIRED LEVEL OF CONFIDENCE)
90.0	1.65
95.0	1.96
95.45	2.00
99.0	2.58
99.73	3.00

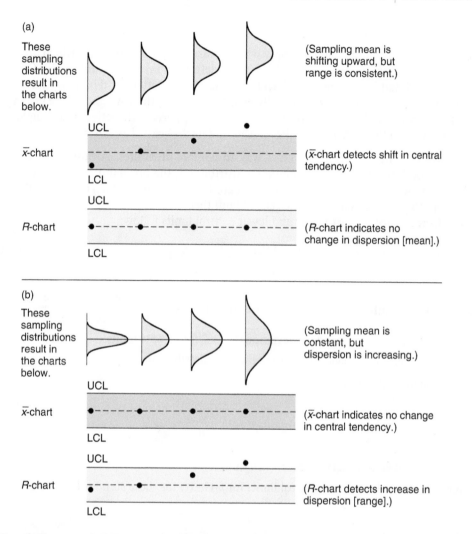

WEIGHTED SINGLE SAMPLE CENTERLINING CHART

FritoLay

FL-5885 (Rev. 11/03)

SHIFT	NUMBER OF CHECKS	MAX. TIME GAP BETWEEN CHECKS
1st SHIFT	10 Checks	40 min
2nd SHIFT		
3rd SHIFT		

INSTRUCTIONS

1. CURRENT VALUE MUST BE WITHIN SPECIFICATION LIMITS. IF NOT, FOLLOW PRESCRIBED PROCEDURES (ABORT, HOLD, ETC.). RECORD CORRECTIVE ACTION AT BOTTOM OF CHART.
2. PREDICTED VALUE = AVERAGE OF CURRENT VALUE AND PREVIOUS PREDICTED VALUE. THE PREDICTED VALUE IS ALWAYS PLOTTED ON THE CHART.
3. DECISION RULE: ANY PREDICTED VALUE IN THE YELLOW (RED TAKE ACTION) INDICATES IMMEDIATE CORRECTIVE ACTION IS REQUIRED. RECORD CORRECTIVE ACTION AT BOTTOM OF CHART.
4. AT STARTUP OR AFTER MAJOR PROCESS ADJUSTMENTS THE CURRENT VALUE WILL ALSO BE USED AS THE PREDICTED VALUE.

RED ABORT SPECIFICATION LIMITS
1.70–2.50

TIME:	710	750	830	910	950	1000	1055	1115	1155	1235	115
CURRENT VALUE	218	182	210	215	194	Break	199	193	193	205	191
PREDICTED VALUE (PLOT ON CHART)	218	200	205	210	202	↓	201	197	193	199	195

ADJUST

UCL = 2.22

216

AIM = 2.10

204

LCL = 1.98

ADJUST

Frito-Lay uses $\bar{x}$ charts to control production quality at critical points in the process. About every 40 minutes, three batches of chips are taken from the conveyor (on the left) and analyzed electronically to get an average salt content, which is plotted on an $\bar{x}$-chart (on the right). Points plotted in the green zone are "in control," while those in the yellow zone are "out of control." The SPC chart is displayed where all production employees can monitor process stability.

Control Charts for Attributes

Control charts for $\bar{x}$ and R do not apply when we are sampling *attributes*, which are typically classified as *defective* or *nondefective*. Measuring defectives involves counting them (for example, number of bad lightbulbs in a given lot, or number of letters or data entry records typed with errors), whereas *variables* are usually measured for length or weight. There are two kinds of attribute control charts: (1) those that measure the *percent* defective in a sample—called *p*-charts—and (2) those that count the *number* of defects—called *c*-charts.

p-chart

A quality control chart that is used to control attributes.

p-Charts Using *p*-charts is the chief way to control attributes. Although attributes that are either good or bad follow the binomial distribution, the normal distribution can be used to calculate *p*-chart limits when sample sizes are large. The procedure resembles the $\bar{x}$-chart approach, which is also based on the central limit theorem.

The formulas for *p*-chart upper and lower control limits follow:

$$UCL_p = \bar{p} + z\sigma_p \tag{S6-9}$$

$$LCL_p = \bar{p} - z\sigma_p \tag{S6-10}$$

where $\bar{p} = $ mean fraction (percent) defective in the samples $= \dfrac{\text{total number of defects}}{\text{sample size} \times \text{number of samples}}$

$z = $ number of standard deviations ($z = 2$ for 95.45% limits; $z = 3$ for 99.73% limits)

$\sigma_p = $ standard deviation of the sampling distribution

σ_p is estimated by the formula:

$$\hat{\sigma}_p = \sqrt{\frac{\bar{p}(1 - \bar{p})}{n}} \tag{S6-11}$$

where $n = $ number of observations in *each* sample[4]

Example S4 shows how to set control limits for *p*-charts for these standard deviations.

Example S4

SETTING CONTROL LIMITS FOR PERCENT DEFECTIVE

Clerks at Mosier Data Systems key in thousands of insurance records each day for a variety of client firms. CEO Donna Mosier wants to set control limits to include 99.73% of the random variation in the data entry process when it is in control.

APPROACH ▶ Samples of the work of 20 clerks are gathered (and shown in the table). Mosier carefully examines 100 records entered by each clerk and counts the number of errors. She also computes the fraction defective in each sample. Equations (S6-9), (S6-10), and (S6-11) are then used to set the control limits.

SAMPLE NUMBER	NUMBER OF ERRORS	FRACTION DEFECTIVE	SAMPLE NUMBER	NUMBER OF ERRORS	FRACTION DEFECTIVE
1	6	.06	11	6	.06
2	5	.05	12	1	.01
3	0	.00	13	8	.08
4	1	.01	14	7	.07
5	4	.04	15	5	.05
6	2	.02	16	4	.04
7	5	.05	17	11	.11
8	3	.03	18	3	.03
9	3	.03	19	0	.00
10	2	.02	20	4	.04
				80	

SOLUTION ▶

$$\bar{p} = \frac{\text{Total number of errors}}{\text{Total number of records examined}} = \frac{80}{(100)(20)} = .04$$

$$\hat{\sigma}_p = \sqrt{\frac{(.04)(1 - .04)}{100}} = .02 \text{ (rounded up from .0196)}$$

(*Note:* 100 is the size of *each* sample = *n*.)

$$\text{UCL}_p = \bar{p} + z\hat{\sigma}_p = .04 + 3(.02) = .10$$

$$\text{LCL}_p = \bar{p} - z\hat{\sigma}_p = .04 - 3(.02) = 0$$

(because we cannot have a negative percentage defective)

INSIGHT ▶ When we plot the control limits and the sample fraction defectives, we find that only one data-entry clerk (number 17) is out of control. The firm may wish to examine that individual's work a bit more closely to see if a serious problem exists (see Figure S6.6).

Figure **S6.6**

p-Chart for Data Entry for Example S4

STUDENT TIP ◀

We are always pleased to be at zero or below the center line in a *p*-chart.

LEARNING EXERCISE ▶ Mosier decides to set control limits at 95.45% instead. What are the new UCL_p and LCL_p? [Answer: 0.08, 0]

RELATED PROBLEMS ▶ S6.13–S6.20, S6.25, S6.27 (S6.35–S6.39 are available in MyOMLab)

ACTIVE **MODEL** S6.2 This example is further illustrated in Active Model S6.2 in MyOMLab.

EXCEL **OM** Data File **Ch06ExS4.xls** can be found in MyOMLab.

The *OM in Action* box "Trying to Land a Seat with Frequent Flyer Miles" provides a real-world follow-up to Example S4.

c-Charts   In Example S4, we counted the number of defective records entered. A defective record was one that was not exactly correct because it contained at least one defect. However, a bad record may contain more than one defect. We use *c*-charts to control the *number* of defects per unit of output (or per insurance record, in the preceding case).

c-chart

A quality control chart used to control the number of defects per unit of output.

OM in Action | Trying to Land a Seat with Frequent Flyer Miles

How hard is it to redeem your 25,000 frequent flyer points for airline tickets? That depends on the airline. (It also depends on the city. Don't try to get into or out of San Francisco!) When the consulting firm Idea Works made 280 requests for a standard mileage award to each of 24 airlines' Web sites (a total of 6,720 requests), the success rates ranged from a low of 25.7% and 27.1% (at US Airways and Delta, respectively) to a high of 100% at GOL-Brazil and 99.3% at Southwest.

The overall average of 68.6% for the two dozen carriers provides the center line in a *p*-chart. With 3-sigma upper and lower control limits of 82.5% and 54.7%, the other top and bottom performers are easily spotted. "Out of control" (but in a positive *outperforming* way) are GOL and Southwest,

Lufthansa (85.0%), Singapore (90.7%), Virgin Australia (91.4%), and Air Berlin (96.4%).

Out of control *on the negative side* are US Airways and Delta, plus Emirates (35.7%), AirTran (47.1%), Turkish (49.3%), and SAS (52.9%).

Control charts can help airlines see where they stand relative to competitors in such customer service activities as lost bags, on-time rates, and ease of redeeming mileage points. "I think airlines are getting the message that availability is important. Are airlines where they need to be? I don't think so," says the president of Idea Works.

Sources: Wall Street Journal (May 26, 2011); and *Consumer Reports* (November 2014).

Sampling wine from these wooden barrels, to make sure it is aging properly, uses both SPC (for alcohol content and acidity) and subjective measures (for taste).

Charles O'Rear/Corbis

Control charts for defects are helpful for monitoring processes in which a large number of potential errors can occur, but the actual number that do occur is relatively small. Defects may be errors in newspaper words, bad circuits in a microchip, blemishes on a table, or missing pickles on a fast-food hamburger.

The Poisson probability distribution,[5] which has a variance equal to its mean, is the basis for c-charts. Because $\bar{c}$ is the mean number of defects per unit, the standard deviation is equal to $\sqrt{\bar{c}}$. To compute 99.73% control limits for $\bar{c}$, we use the formula:

$$\text{Control limits} = \bar{c} \pm 3\sqrt{\bar{c}} \qquad (S6\text{-}12)$$

Example S5 shows how to set control limits for a $\bar{c}$-chart.

Example S5

SETTING CONTROL LIMITS FOR NUMBER OF DEFECTS

Red Top Cab Company receives several complaints per day about the behavior of its drivers. Over a 9-day period (where days are the units of measure), the owner, Gordon Hoft, received the following numbers of calls from irate passengers: 3, 0, 8, 9, 6, 7, 4, 9, 8, for a total of 54 complaints. Hoft wants to compute 99.73% control limits.

APPROACH ▶ He applies Equation (S6–12).

SOLUTION ▶ $\bar{c} = \dfrac{54}{9} = 6$ complaints per day

Thus:

$$\text{UCL}_c = \bar{c} + 3\sqrt{\bar{c}} = 6 + 3\sqrt{6} = 6 + 3(2.45) = 13.35, \text{ or } 13$$

$$\text{LCL}_c = \bar{c} - 3\sqrt{\bar{c}} = 6 - 3\sqrt{6} = 6 - 3(2.45) = 0 \leftarrow \text{(since it cannot be negative)}$$

INSIGHT ▶ After Hoft plotted a control chart summarizing these data and posted it prominently in the drivers' locker room, the number of calls received dropped to an average of three per day. Can you explain why this occurred?

LEARNING EXERCISE ▶ Hoft collects 3 more days' worth of complaints (10, 12, and 8 complaints) and wants to combine them with the original 9 days to compute updated control limits. What are the revised UCL_c and LCL_c? [Answer: 14.94, 0.]

RELATED PROBLEMS ▶ S6.21, S6.22, S6.23, S6.24

EXCEL OM Data File **Ch06SExS5.xls** can be found in MyOMLab.

TABLE S6.3	Helping You Decide Which Control Chart to Use

VARIABLE DATA
USING AN x̄-CHART AND AN R-CHART

1. Observations are *variables*, which are usually products measured for size or weight. Examples are the width or length of a wire and the weight of a can of Campbell's soup.
2. Collect 20 to 25 samples, usually of $n = 4$, $n = 5$, or more, each from a stable process, and compute the means for an x̄-chart and the ranges for an R-chart.
3. We track samples of n observations each, as in Example S1.

ATTRIBUTE DATA
USING A p-CHART

1. Observations are *attributes* that can be categorized as good or bad (or pass–fail, or functional–broken); that is, in two states.
2. We deal with fraction, proportion, or percent defectives.
3. There are several samples, with many observations in each. For example, 20 samples of $n = 100$ observations in each, as in Example S4.

ATTRIBUTE DATA
USING A c-CHART

1. Observations are *attributes* whose defects per unit of output can be counted.
2. We deal with the number counted, which is a small part of the possible occurrences.
3. Defects may be: number of blemishes on a desk; flaws in a bolt of cloth; crimes in a year; broken seats in a stadium; typos in a chapter of this text; or complaints in a day, as is shown in Example S5.

Managerial Issues and Control Charts

In an ideal world, there is no need for control charts. Quality is uniform and so high that employees need not waste time and money sampling and monitoring variables and attributes. But because most processes have not reached perfection, managers must make three major decisions regarding control charts.

First, managers must select the points in their process that need SPC. They may ask "Which parts of the job are critical to success?" or "Which parts of the job have a tendency to become out of control?"

Second, managers need to decide if variable charts (i.e., x̄ and R) or attribute charts (i.e., p and c) are appropriate. Variable charts monitor weights or dimensions. Attribute charts are more of a "yes–no" or "go–no go" gauge and tend to be less costly to implement. Table S6.3 can help you understand when to use each of these types of control charts.

Third, the company must set clear and specific SPC policies for employees to follow. For example, should the data-entry process be halted if a trend is appearing in percent defective records being keyed? Should an assembly line be stopped if the average length of five successive samples is above the centerline? Figure S6.7 illustrates some of the patterns to look for over time in a process.

Figure S6.7

Patterns to Look for on Control Charts

Source: Adapted from Bertrand L. Hansen, *Quality Control: Theory and Applications* (1991): 65. Reprinted by permission of Prentice Hall, Upper Saddle River, NJ.

Upper control limit / Target / Lower control limit

Normal behavior. Process is "in control."

One point out above (or below). Investigate for cause. Process is "out of control."

Trends in either direction, 5 points. Investigate for cause of progressive change. This could be the result of gradual tool wear.

Two points very near lower (or upper) control. Investigate for cause.

Run of 5 points above (or below) central line. Investigate for cause.

Erratic behavior. Investigate.

Run test

A test used to examine the points in a control chart to see if nonrandom variation is present.

A tool called a run test is available to help identify the kind of abnormalities in a process that we see in Figure S6.7. In general, a run of 5 points above or below the target or centerline may suggest that an assignable, or nonrandom, variation is present. When this occurs, even though all the points may fall inside the control limits, a flag has been raised. This means the process may not be statistically in control. A variety of run tests are described in books on the subject of quality methods.

STUDENT TIP ◆ # Process Capability

Here we deal with whether a process meets the specification it was *designed* to yield.

Statistical process control means keeping a process in control. This means that the natural variation of the process must be stable. However, a process that is in statistical control may not yield goods or services that meet their *design specifications* (tolerances). In other words, the variation should be small enough to produce consistent output within specifications. The ability of a process to meet design specifications, which are set by engineering design or customer requirements, is called process capability. Even though that process may be statistically in control (stable), the output of that process may not conform to specifications.

Process capability

The ability to meet design specifications.

For example, let's say the time a customer expects to wait for the completion of a lube job at Quik Lube is 12 minutes, with an acceptable tolerance of ± 2 minutes. This tolerance gives an upper specification of 14 minutes and a lower specification of 10 minutes. The lube process has to be capable of operating within these design specifications—if not, some customers will not have their requirements met. As a manufacturing example, the tolerances for Harley-Davidson cam gears are extremely low, only 0.0005 inch—and a process must be designed that is capable of achieving this tolerance.

LO S6.6 *Explain* process capability and compute C_p and C_{pk}

There are two popular measures for quantitatively determining if a process is capable: process capability ratio (C_p) and process capability index (C_{pk}).

Process Capability Ratio (C_p)

For a process to be capable, its values must fall within upper and lower specifications. This typically means the process capability is within ± 3 standard deviations from the process mean. Because this range of values is 6 standard deviations, a capable process tolerance, which is the difference between the upper and lower specifications, must be greater than or equal to 6.

C_p

A ratio for determining whether a process meets design specifications; a ratio of the specification to the process variation.

The process capability ratio, C_p, is computed as:

$$C_p = \frac{\text{Upper specification} - \text{Lower specification}}{6\sigma} \qquad \text{(S6-13)}$$

Example S6 shows the computation of C_p.

Example S6

PROCESS CAPABILITY RATIO (C_p)

In a GE insurance claims process, $\bar{x} = 210.0$ minutes, and $\sigma = .516$ minutes.

The design specification to meet customer expectations is 210 ± 3 minutes. So the Upper Specification is 213 minutes and the lower specification is 207 minutes. The OM manager wants to compute the process capability ratio.

APPROACH ▶ GE applies Equation (S6-13).

SOLUTION ▶ $C_p = \dfrac{\text{Upper specification} - \text{Lower specification}}{6\sigma} = \dfrac{213 - 207}{6(.516)} = 1.938$

INSIGHT ▶ Because a ratio of 1.00 means that 99.73% of a process's outputs are within specifications, this ratio suggests a very capable process, with nonconformance of less than 4 claims per million.

LEARNING EXERCISE ▶ If $\sigma = .60$ (instead of .516), what is the new C_p? [Answer: 1.667, a very capable process still.]

RELATED PROBLEMS ▶ S6.40, S6.41 (S6.50 is available in MyOMLab)

ACTIVE **MODEL** S6.3 This example is further illustrated in Active Model S6.3 in MyOMLab.

EXCEL **OM** Data File Ch06SExS6.xls can be found in MyOMLab.

A capable process has a C_p of at least 1.0. If the C_p is less than 1.0, the process yields products or services that are outside their allowable tolerance. With a C_p of 1.0, 2.7 parts in 1,000 can be expected to be "out of spec."[6] The higher the process capability ratio, the greater the likelihood the process will be within design specifications. Many firms have chosen a C_p of 1.33 (a 4-sigma standard) as a target for reducing process variability. This means that only 64 parts per million can be expected to be out of specification.

Recall that in Chapter 6 we mentioned the concept of *Six Sigma* quality, championed by GE and Motorola. This standard equates to a C_p of 2.0, with only 3.4 defective parts per million (very close to zero defects) instead of the 2.7 parts per 1,000 with 3-sigma limits.

Although C_p relates to the spread (dispersion) of the process output relative to its tolerance, it does not look at how well the process average is centered on the target value.

Process Capability Index (C$_{pk}$)

The process capability index, C_{pk}, measures the difference between the desired and actual dimensions of goods or services produced.

The formula for C_{pk} is:

> C_{pk}
> A proportion of variation (3σ) between the center of the process and the nearest specification limit.

$$C_{pk} = \text{Minimum of} \left[\frac{\text{Upper specification limit} - \overline{X}}{3\sigma}, \frac{\overline{X} - \text{Lower specification limit}}{3\sigma} \right]$$

(S6-14)

where $\overline{X}$ = process mean

σ = standard deviation of the process population

When the C_{pk} index for both the upper and lower specification limits equals 1.0, the process variation is centered and the process is capable of producing within ±3 standard deviations (fewer than 2,700 defects per million). A C_{pk} of 2.0 means the process is capable of producing fewer than 3.4 defects per million. For C_{pk} to exceed 1, σ must be less than $\frac{1}{3}$ of the difference between the specification and the process mean ($\overline{X}$). Figure S6.8 shows the meaning of various measures of C_{pk}, and Example S7 shows an application of C_{pk}.

Example S7

PROCESS CAPABILITY INDEX (C$_{pk}$)

You are the process improvement manager and have developed a new machine to cut insoles for the company's top-of-the-line running shoes. You are excited because the company's goal is no more than 3.4 defects per million, and this machine may be the innovation you need. The insoles cannot be more than $\pm.001$ of an inch from the required thickness of .250". You want to know if you should replace the existing machine, which has a C_{pk} of 1.0.

Mean of the new process $\overline{X} = .250$ inches.
Standard deviation of the new process = σ = .0005 inches.

APPROACH ▶ You decide to determine the C_{pk}, using Equation (S6-14), for the new machine and make a decision on that basis.

SOLUTION ▶
Upper specification limit = .251 inches

Lower specification limit = .249 inches

$$C_{pk} = \text{Minimum of} \left[\frac{\text{Upper specification limit} - \overline{X}}{3\sigma}, \frac{\overline{X} - \text{Lower specification limit}}{3\sigma} \right]$$

$$C_{pk} = \text{Minimum of} \left[\frac{.251 - .250}{(3).0005}, \frac{.250 - .249}{(3).0005} \right]$$

Both calculations result in: $\dfrac{.001}{.0015} = .67$.

INSIGHT ▶ Because the new machine has a C_{pk} of only 0.67, the new machine should *not* replace the existing machine.

LEARNING EXERCISE ▶ If the insoles can be $\pm .002''$ (instead of .001″) from the required .250″, what is the new C_{pk}? [Answer: 1.33 and the new machine *should* replace the existing one.]

RELATED PROBLEMS ▶ S6.41–S6.45 (S6.46–S6.49 are available in MyOMLab)

ACTIVE **MODEL** S6.2 This example is further illustrated in Active Model S6.2 in MyOMLab.

EXCEL **OM** Data File **Ch06SExS7.xls** can be found in MyOMLab.

Note that C_p and C_{pk} will be the same when the process is centered. However, if the mean of the process is not centered on the desired (specified) mean, then the smaller numerator in Equation (S6-14) is used (the minimum of the difference between the upper specification limit and the mean or the lower specification limit and the mean). This application of C_{pk} is shown in Solved Problem S6.4. C_{pk} is the standard criterion used to express process performance.

Acceptance Sampling[7]

Acceptance sampling

A method of measuring random samples of lots or batches of products against predetermined standards.

LO S6.7 *Explain acceptance sampling*

Acceptance sampling is a form of testing that involves taking random samples of "lots," or batches, of finished products and measuring them against predetermined standards. Sampling is more economical than 100% inspection. The quality of the sample is used to judge the quality of all items in the lot. Although both attributes and variables can be inspected by acceptance sampling, attribute inspection is more commonly used, as illustrated in this section.

Acceptance sampling can be applied either when materials arrive at a plant or at final inspection, but it is usually used to control incoming lots of purchased products. A lot of items rejected, based on an unacceptable level of defects found in the sample, can (1) be returned to the supplier or (2) be 100% inspected to cull out all defects, with the cost of this screening usually billed to the supplier. However, acceptance sampling is not a substitute for adequate process controls. In fact, the current approach is to build statistical quality controls at suppliers so that acceptance sampling can be eliminated.

Figure **S6.8**

Meanings of C_{pk} Measures

A C_{pk} index of 1.0 for both the upper and lower specification limits indicates that the process variation is within the upper and lower specification limits. As the C_{pk} index goes above 1.0, the process becomes increasingly target oriented, with fewer defects. If the C_{pk} is less than 1.0, the process will not produce within the specified tolerance. Because a process may not be centered, or may "drift," a C_{pk} above 1 is desired.

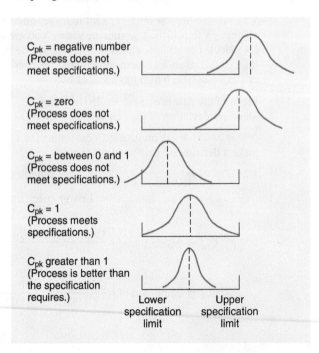

C_{pk} = negative number (Process does not meet specifications.)

C_{pk} = zero (Process does not meet specifications.)

C_{pk} = between 0 and 1 (Process does not meet specifications.)

C_{pk} = 1 (Process meets specifications.)

C_{pk} greater than 1 (Process is better than the specification requires.)

Lower specification limit   Upper specification limit

Raw data for Statistical Process Control is collected in a wide variety of ways. Here physical measures using a micrometer (on the left) and a microscope (on the right) are being made.

Operating Characteristic Curve

The operating characteristic (OC) curve describes how well an acceptance plan discriminates between good and bad lots. A curve pertains to a specific plan—that is, to a combination of n (sample size) and c (acceptance level). It is intended to show the probability that the plan will accept lots of various quality levels.

With acceptance sampling, two parties are usually involved: the producer of the product and the consumer of the product. In specifying a sampling plan, each party wants to avoid costly mistakes in accepting or rejecting a lot. The producer usually has the responsibility of replacing all defects in the rejected lot or of paying for a new lot to be shipped to the customer. The producer, therefore, wants to avoid the mistake of having a good lot rejected (producer's risk). On the other hand, the customer or consumer wants to avoid the mistake of accepting a bad lot because defects found in a lot that has already been accepted are usually the responsibility of the customer (consumer's risk). The OC curve shows the features of a particular sampling plan, including the risks of making a wrong decision. The steeper the curve, the better the plan distinguishes between good and bad lots.[8]

Figure S6.9 can be used to illustrate one sampling plan in more detail. Four concepts are illustrated in this figure.

The acceptable quality level (AQL) is the poorest level of quality that we are willing to accept. In other words, we wish to accept lots that have this or a better level of quality, but no worse. If an acceptable quality level is 20 defects in a lot of 1,000 items or parts, then AQL is 20/1,000 = 2% defectives.

The lot tolerance percentage defective (LTPD) is the quality level of a lot that we consider bad. We wish to reject lots that have this or a poorer level of quality. If it is agreed that an unacceptable quality level is 70 defects in a lot of 1,000, then the LTPD is 70/1,000 = 7% defective.

To derive a sampling plan, producer and consumer must define not only "good lots" and "bad lots" through the AQL and LTPD, but they must also specify risk levels.

Producer's risk (α) is the probability that a "good" lot will be rejected. This is the risk that a random sample might result in a much higher proportion of defects than the population of all items. A lot with an acceptable quality level of AQL still has an α chance of being rejected. Sampling plans are often designed to have the producer's risk set at $\alpha = .05$, or 5%.

Consumer's risk (β) is the probability that a "bad" lot will be accepted. This is the risk that a random sample may result in a lower proportion of defects than the overall population of items. A common value for consumer's risk in sampling plans is $\beta = .10$, or 10%.

The probability of rejecting a good lot is called a type I error. The probability of accepting a bad lot is a type II error.

Sampling plans and OC curves may be developed by computer (as seen in the software available with this text), by published tables, or by calculation, using binomial or Poisson distributions.

Operating characteristic (OC) curve

A graph that describes how well an acceptance plan discriminates between good and bad lots.

Producer's risk

The mistake of having a producer's good lot rejected through sampling.

Consumer's risk

The mistake of a customer's acceptance of a bad lot overlooked through sampling.

Acceptable quality level (AQL)

The quality level of a lot considered good.

Lot tolerance percentage defective (LTPD)

The quality level of a lot considered bad.

Type I error

Statistically, the probability of rejecting a good lot.

Type II error

Statistically, the probability of accepting a bad lot.

Figure **S6.9**

An Operating Characteristic (OC) Curve Showing Producer's and Consumer's Risks

A good lot for this particular acceptance plan has less than or equal to 2% defectives. A bad lot has 7% or more defectives.

Average Outgoing Quality

In most sampling plans, when a lot is rejected, the entire lot is inspected and all defective items replaced. Use of this replacement technique improves the average outgoing quality in terms of percent defective. In fact, given (1) any sampling plan that replaces all defective items encountered and (2) the true incoming percent defective for the lot, it is possible to determine the average outgoing quality (AOQ) in percentage defective. The equation for AOQ is:

Average outgoing quality (AOQ)

The percentage defective in an average lot of goods inspected through acceptance sampling.

$$AOQ = \frac{(P_d)(P_a)(N - n)}{N} \tag{S6-15}$$

where

P_d = true percentage defective of the lot
P_a = probability of accepting the lot for a given sample size and quantity defective
N = number of items in the lot
n = number of items in the sample

The maximum value of AOQ corresponds to the highest average percentage defective or the lowest average quality for the sampling plan. It is called the *average outgoing quality limit (AOQL)*.

This laser tracking device, by Faro Technologies, enables quality control personnel to measure and inspect parts and tools during production. The portable tracker can measure objects from 262 feet away and takes to up 1,000 accurate readings per second.

Faro Technologies

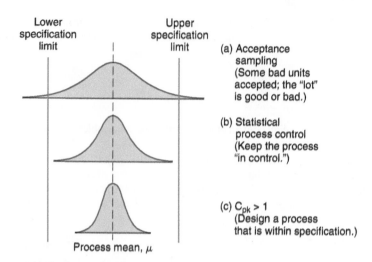

Figure **S6.10**

The Application of Statistical Process Control Techniques Contributes to the Identification and Systematic Reduction of Process Variability

Acceptance sampling is useful for screening incoming lots. When the defective parts are replaced with good parts, acceptance sampling helps to increase the quality of the lots by reducing the outgoing percent defective.

Figure S6.10 compares acceptance sampling, SPC, and C_{pk}. As the figure shows, (a) acceptance sampling by definition accepts some bad units, (b) control charts try to keep the process in control, but (c) the C_{pk} index places the focus on improving the process. As operations managers, that is what we want to do—improve the process.

Summary

Statistical process control is a major statistical tool of quality control. Control charts for SPC help operations managers distinguish between natural and assignable variations. The $\bar{x}$-chart and the R-chart are used for variable sampling, and the p-chart and the c-chart for attribute sampling.

The C_{pk} index is a way to express process capability. Operating characteristic (OC) curves facilitate acceptance sampling and provide the manager with tools to evaluate the quality of a production run or shipment.

Key Terms

Statistical process control (SPC) (p. 246)
Control chart (p. 246)
Natural variations (p. 246)
Assignable variation (p. 247)
$\bar{x}$-chart (p. 248)
R-chart (p. 248)
Central limit theorem (p. 248)
p-chart (p. 255)

c-chart (p. 257)
Run test (p. 260)
Process capability (p. 260)
C_p (p. 260)
C_{pk} (p. 261)
Acceptance sampling (p. 262)
Operating characteristic (OC) curve (p. 263)
Producer's risk (p. 263)
Consumer's risk (p. 263)

Acceptable quality level (AQL) (p. 263)
Lot tolerance percentage defective (LTPD) (p. 263)
Type I error (p. 263)
Type II error (p. 263)
Average outgoing quality (AOQ) (p. 264)

Discussion Questions

1. List Shewhart's two types of variation. What are they also called?
2. Define "in statistical control."
3. Explain briefly what an $\bar{x}$-chart and an R-chart do.
4. What might cause a process to be out of control?
5. List five steps in developing and using $\bar{x}$-charts and R-charts.
6. List some possible causes of assignable variation.
7. Explain how a person using 2-sigma control charts will more easily find samples "out of bounds" than 3-sigma control charts. What are some possible consequences of this fact?
8. When is the desired mean, μ, used in establishing the centerline of a control chart instead of $\bar{\bar{x}}$?

9. Can a production process be labeled as "out of control" because it is too good? Explain.
10. In a control chart, what would be the effect on the control limits if the sample size varied from one sample to the next?
11. Define C_{pk} and explain what a C_{pk} of 1.0 means. What is C_p?
12. What does a run of 5 points above or below the centerline in a control chart imply?
13. What are the acceptable quality level (AQL) and the lot tolerance percentage defective (LTPD)? How are they used?
14. What is a run test, and when is it used?
15. Discuss the managerial issues regarding the use of control charts.
16. What is an OC curve?

17. What is the purpose of acceptance sampling?
18. What two risks are present when acceptance sampling is used?

19. Is a *capable* process a *perfect* process? That is, does a capable process generate only output that meets specifications? Explain.

Using Software for SPC

Excel, Excel OM, and POM for Windows may be used to develop control charts for most of the problems in this chapter.

✗ CREATING YOUR OWN EXCEL SPREADSHEETS TO DETERMINE CONTROL LIMITS FOR A C-CHART

Excel and other spreadsheets are extensively used in industry to maintain control charts. Program S6.1 is an example of how to use Excel to determine the control limits for a *c*-chart. A *c*-chart is used when the number of defects per unit of output is known. The data from Example S5 are used here. In this example, 54 complaints occurred over 9 days. Excel also contains a built-in graphing ability with Chart Wizard.

Program S6.1

An Excel Spreadsheet for Creating a *c*-Chart for Example S5

✗ USING EXCEL OM

Excel OM's Quality Control module has the ability to develop $\bar{x}$-charts, *p*-charts, and *c*-charts. It also handles OC curves, acceptance sampling, and process capability. Program S6.2 illustrates Excel OM's spreadsheet approach to computing the $\bar{x}$ control limits for the Oat Flakes company in Example S1.

Program S6.2

Excel OM Input and Selected Formulas for the Oat Flakes Company in Example S1

P USING POM FOR WINDOWS
The POM for Windows Quality Control module has the ability to compute all the SPC control charts we introduced in this supplement, as well as OC curves, acceptance sampling, and process capability. See Appendix IV for further details.

Solved Problems   Virtual Office Hours help is available in MyOMLab.

SOLVED PROBLEM S6.1

A manufacturer of precision machine parts produces round shafts for use in the construction of drill presses. The average diameter of a shaft is .56 inch. Inspection samples contain 6 shafts each. The average range of these samples is .006 inch. Determine the upper and lower $\bar{x}$ control chart limits.

SOLUTION

The mean factor A_2 from Table S6.1, where the sample size is 6, is seen to be .483. With this factor, you can obtain the upper and lower control limits:

$$\text{UCL}_{\bar{x}} = .56 + (.483)(.006)$$
$$= .56 + .0029$$
$$= .5629 \text{ inch}$$
$$\text{LCL}_{\bar{x}} = .56 - .0029$$
$$= .5571 \text{ inch}$$

SOLVED PROBLEM S6.2

Nocaf Drinks, Inc., a producer of decaffeinated coffee, bottles Nocaf. Each bottle should have a net weight of 4 ounces. The machine that fills the bottles with coffee is new, and the operations manager wants to make sure that it is properly adjusted. Bonnie Crutcher, the operations manager, randomly selects and weighs $n = 8$ bottles and records the average and range in ounces for each sample. The data for several samples is given in the following table. Note that every sample consists of 8 bottles.

SAMPLE	SAMPLE RANGE	SAMPLE AVERAGE	SAMPLE	SAMPLE RANGE	SAMPLE AVERAGE
A	.41	4.00	E	.56	4.17
B	.55	4.16	F	.62	3.93
C	.44	3.99	G	.54	3.98
D	.48	4.00	H	.44	4.01

Is the machine properly adjusted and in control?

SOLUTION

We first find that $\bar{\bar{x}} = 4.03$ and $\bar{R} = .505$. Then, using Table S6.1, we find:

$$\text{UCL}_{\bar{x}} = \bar{\bar{x}} + A_2\bar{R} = 4.03 + (.373)(.505) = 4.22$$
$$\text{LCL}_{\bar{x}} = \bar{\bar{x}} - A_2\bar{R} = 4.03 - (.373)(.505) = 3.84$$
$$\text{UCL}_R = D_4\bar{R} = (1.864)(.505) = .94$$
$$\text{LCL}_R = D_3\bar{R} = (.136)(.505) = .07$$

It appears that the process average and range are both in statistical control.

The operations manager needs to determine if a process with a mean (4.03) slightly above the desired mean of 4.00 is satisfactory; if it is not, the process will need to be changed.

SOLVED PROBLEM S6.3

Altman Distributors, Inc., fills catalog orders. Samples of size $n = 100$ orders have been taken each day over the past 6 weeks. The average defect rate was .05. Determine the upper and lower limits for this process for 99.73% confidence.

SOLUTION

$z = 3, \bar{p} = .05$. Using Equations (S6-9), (S6-10), and (S6-11):

$$\text{UCL}_p = \bar{p} + 3\sqrt{\frac{\bar{p}(1 - \bar{p})}{n}} = .05 + 3\sqrt{\frac{(.05)(1 - .05)}{100}}$$
$$= .05 + 3(0.0218) = .1154$$

$$\text{LCL}_p = \bar{p} - 3\sqrt{\frac{\bar{p}(1 - \bar{p})}{n}} = .05 - 3(0.0218)$$
$$= .05 - .0654 = 0 \quad \text{(because percentage defective cannot be negative)}$$

SOLVED PROBLEM S6.4

Ettlie Engineering has a new catalyst injection system for your countertop production line. Your process engineering department has conducted experiments and determined that the mean is 8.01 grams with a standard deviation of .03. Your specifications are: $\mu = 8.0$ and $\sigma = .04$, which means an upper specification limit of 8.12 [$= 8.0 + 3(.04)$] and a lower specification limit of 7.88 [$= 8.0 - 3(.04)$].

What is the C_{pk} performance of the injection system?

SOLUTION

Using Equation (S6-14):

$$C_{pk} = \text{Minimum of} \left[\frac{\text{Upper specification limit} - \overline{X}}{3\sigma}, \frac{\overline{X} - \text{Lower specification limit}}{3\sigma} \right]$$

where

$\overline{X} = $ process mean
$\sigma = $ standard deviation of the process population

$$C_{pk} = \text{Minimum of} \left[\frac{8.12 - 8.01}{(3)(.03)}, \frac{8.01 - 7.88}{(3)(.03)} \right]$$

$$\left[\frac{.11}{.09} = 1.22, \frac{.13}{.09} = 1.44 \right]$$

The minimum is 1.22, so the C_{pk} is within specifications and has an implied error rate of less than 2,700 defects per million.

SOLVED PROBLEM S6.5

Airlines lose thousands of checked bags every day, and America South Airlines is no exception to the industry rule. Over the past 6 weeks, the number of bags "misplaced" on America South flights has been 18, 10, 4, 6, 12, and 10. The head of customer service wants to develop a c-chart at 99.73% levels.

SOLUTION

She first computes $\bar{c} = \dfrac{18 + 10 + 4 + 6 + 12 + 10}{6} = \dfrac{60}{6} = 10$ bags/week

Then, using Equation (S6-12):

$$UCL_c = \bar{c} + 3\sqrt{\bar{c}} = 10 + 3\sqrt{10} = 10 + 3(3.16) = 19.48 \text{ bags}$$

$$LCL_c = \bar{c} - 3\sqrt{\bar{c}} = 10 - 3\sqrt{10} = 10 - 3(3.16) = .52 \text{ bag}$$

Problems   Note: Px means the problem may be solved with POM for Windows and/or Excel OM/Excel.

Problems S6.1–S6.39 relate to Statistical Process Control (SPC)

• **S6.1**   Boxes of Honey-Nut Oatmeal are produced to contain 14 ounces, with a standard deviation of .1 ounce. Set up the 3-sigma $\bar{x}$-chart for a sample size of 36 boxes. Px

• **S6.2**   The overall average on a process you are attempting to monitor is 50 units. The process population standard deviation is 1.72. Determine the upper and lower control limits for a mean chart, if you choose to use a sample size of 5. Px
a) Set $z = 3$.
b) Now set $z = 2$. How do the control limits change?

• **S6.3**   Thirty-five samples of size 7 each were taken from a fertilizer-bag-filling machine. The results were overall mean = 57.75 lb; average range = 1.78 lb.
a) Determine the upper and lower control limits of the $\bar{x}$-chart, where $\sigma = 3$.
b) Determine the upper and lower control limits of the R-chart, where $\sigma = 3$. Px

• **S6.4**   Rosters Chicken advertises "lite" chicken with 30% fewer calories than standard chicken. When the process for "lite" chicken breast production is in control, the average chicken breast contains 420 calories, and the standard deviation in caloric content of the chicken breast population is 25 calories.
   Rosters wants to design an $\bar{x}$-chart to monitor the caloric content of chicken breasts, where 25 chicken breasts would be chosen at random to form each sample.
a) What are the lower and upper control limits for this chart if these limits are chosen to be *four* standard deviations from the target?
b) What are the limits with three standard deviations from the target? Px

• **S6.5**   Ross Hopkins is attempting to monitor a filling process that has an overall average of 705 cc. The average range is 6 cc. If you use a sample size of 10, what are the upper and lower control limits for the mean and range?

•• **S6.6**   Sampling four pieces of precision-cut wire (to be used in computer assembly) every hour for the past 24 hours has produced the following results:

HOUR	$\bar{X}$	R	HOUR	$\bar{X}$	R
1	3.25"	.71"	13	3.11"	.85"
2	3.10	1.18	14	2.83	1.31
3	3.22	1.43	15	3.12	1.06
4	3.39	1.26	16	2.84	.50
5	3.07	1.17	17	2.86	1.43
6	2.86	.32	18	2.74	1.29
7	3.05	.53	19	3.41	1.61
8	2.65	1.13	20	2.89	1.09
9	3.02	.71	21	2.65	1.08
10	2.85	1.33	22	3.28	.46
11	2.83	1.17	23	2.94	1.58
12	2.97	.40	24	2.64	.97

Develop appropriate control charts and determine whether there is any cause for concern in the cutting process. Plot the information and look for patterns. Px

•• **S6.7**   Auto pistons at Wemming Chung's plant in Shanghai are produced in a forging process, and the diameter is a critical factor that must be controlled. From sample sizes of 10 pistons produced each day, the mean and the range of this diameter have been as follows:

DAY	MEAN (MM)	RANGE (MM)
1	156.9	4.2
2	153.2	4.6
3	153.6	4.1
4	155.5	5.0
5	156.6	4.5

a) What is the value of $\bar{\bar{x}}$?
b) What is the value of $\bar{R}$?
c) What are the $UCL_{\bar{x}}$ and $LCL_{\bar{x}}$, using 3σ? Plot the data.
d) What are the UCL_R and LCL_R, using 3σ? Plot the data.
e) If the true diameter mean should be 155 mm and you want this as your center (nominal) line, what are the new $UCL_{\bar{x}}$ and $LCL_{\bar{x}}$? Px

•• **S6.8**   A. Choudhury's bowling ball factory in Illinois makes bowling balls of adult size and weight only. The standard deviation in the weight of a bowling ball produced at the factory is known to be 0.12 pounds. Each day for 24 days, the average weight, in pounds, of nine of the bowling balls produced that day has been assessed as follows:

DAY	AVERAGE (lb)	DAY	AVERAGE (lb)
1	16.3	13	16.3
2	15.9	14	15.9
3	15.8	15	16.3
4	15.5	16	16.2
5	16.3	17	16.1
6	16.2	18	15.9
7	16.0	19	16.2
8	16.1	20	15.9
9	15.9	21	15.9
10	16.2	22	16.0
11	15.9	23	15.5
12	15.9	24	15.8

a) Establish a control chart for monitoring the average weights of the bowling balls in which the upper and lower control limits are each two standard deviations from the mean. What are the values of the control limits?
b) If three standard deviations are used in the chart, how do these values change? Why? Px

··S6.9 Organic Grains LLC uses statistical process control to ensure that its health-conscious, low-fat, multigrain sandwich loaves have the proper weight. Based on a previously stable and in-control process, the control limits of the $\bar{x}$- and R-charts are $UCL_{\bar{x}} = 6.56$. $LCL_{\bar{x}} = 5.84$, $UCL_R = 1.141$, $LCL_R = 0$. Over the past few days, they have taken five random samples of four loaves each and have found the following:

SAMPLE	NET WEIGHT			
	LOAF #1	LOAF #2	LOAF #3	LOAF #4
1	6.3	6.0	5.9	5.9
2	6.0	6.0	6.3	5.9
3	6.3	4.8	5.6	5.2
4	6.2	6.0	6.2	5.9
5	6.5	6.6	6.5	6.9

Is the process still in control? Explain why or why not. **PX**

···S6.10 A process that is considered to be in control measures an ingredient in ounces. Below are the last 10 samples (each of size $n = 5$) taken. The population process standard deviation, σ, is 1.36.

SAMPLES									
1	2	3	4	5	6	7	8	9	10
10	9	13	10	12	10	10	13	8	10
9	9	9	10	10	10	11	10	8	12
10	11	10	11	9	8	10	8	12	9
9	11	10	10	11	12	8	10	12	8
12	10	9	10	10	9	9	8	9	12

a) What is $\sigma_{\bar{x}}$?
b) If $z = 3$, what are the control limits for the mean chart?
c) What are the control limits for the range chart?
d) Is the process in control? **PX**

···S6.11 Twelve samples, each containing five parts, were taken from a process that produces steel rods at Emmanuel Kodzi's factory. The length of each rod in the samples was determined. The results were tabulated and sample means and ranges were computed. The results were:

SAMPLE	SAMPLE MEAN (in.)	RANGE (in.)
1	10.002	0.011
2	10.002	0.014
3	9.991	0.007
4	10.006	0.022
5	9.997	0.013
6	9.999	0.012
7	10.001	0.008
8	10.005	0.013
9	9.995	0.004
10	10.001	0.011
11	10.001	0.014
12	10.006	0.009

a) Determine the upper and lower control limits and the overall means for $\bar{x}$-charts and R-charts.
b) Draw the charts and plot the values of the sample means and ranges.
c) Do the data indicate a process that is in control?
d) Why or why not? **PX**

··S6.12 Eagletrons are all-electric automobiles produced by Mogul Motors, Inc. One of the concerns of Mogul Motors is that the Eagletrons be capable of achieving appropriate maximum speeds. To monitor this, Mogul executives take samples of eight Eagletrons at a time. For each sample, they determine the average maximum speed and the range of the maximum speeds within the sample. They repeat this with 35 samples to obtain 35 sample means and 35 ranges. They find that the average sample mean is 88.50 miles per hour, and the average range is 3.25 miles per hour. Using these results, the executives decide to establish an R chart. They would like this chart to be established so that when it shows that the range of a sample is not within the control limits, there is only approximately a 0.0027 probability that this is due to natural variation. What will be the upper control limit (UCL) and the lower control limit (LCL) in this chart? **PX**

··S6.13 The defect rate for data entry of insurance claims has historically been about 1.5%.
a) What are the upper and lower control chart limits if you wish to use a sample size of 100 and 3-sigma limits?
b) What if the sample size used were 50, with 3σ?
c) What if the sample size used were 100, with 2σ?
d) What if the sample size used were 50, with 2σ?
e) What happens to $\hat{\sigma}_p$ when the sample size is larger?
f) Explain why the lower control limit cannot be less than 0. **PX**

··S6.14 You are attempting to develop a quality monitoring system for some parts purchased from Charles Sox Manufacturing Co. These parts are either good or defective. You have decided to take a sample of 100 units. Develop a table of the appropriate upper and lower control chart limits for various values of the average fraction defective in the samples taken. The values for $\bar{p}$ in this table should range from 0.02 to 0.10 in increments of 0.02. Develop the upper and lower control limits for a 99.73% confidence level.

N = 100		
$\bar{P}$	UCL	LCL
0.02		
0.04		
0.06		
0.08		
0.10		

PX

··S6.15 The results of an inspection of DNA samples taken over the past 10 days are given below. Sample size is 100.

DAY	1	2	3	4	5	6	7	8	9	10
DEFECTIVES	7	6	6	9	5	6	0	8	9	1

a) Construct a 3-sigma p-chart using this information.
b) Using the control chart in part (a), and finding that the number of defectives on the next three days are 12, 5, and 13, is the process in control? **PX**

·S6.16 In the past, the defective rate for your product has been 1.5%. What are the upper and lower control chart limits if you wish to use a sample size of 500 and $z = 3$? **PX**

·S6.17 Refer to Problem S6.16. If the defective rate was 3.5% instead of 1.5%, what would be the control limits ($z = 3$)? **PX**

··S6.18 Five data entry operators work at the data processing department of the Birmingham Bank. Each day for 30 days, the number of defective records in a sample of 250 records typed by these operators has been noted, as follows:

SAMPLE NO.	NO. DEFECTIVE	SAMPLE NO.	NO. DEFECTIVE	SAMPLE NO.	NO. DEFECTIVE
1	7	11	18	21	17
2	5	12	5	22	12
3	19	13	16	23	6
4	10	14	4	24	7
5	11	15	11	25	13
6	8	16	8	26	10
7	12	17	12	27	14
8	9	18	4	28	6
9	6	19	6	29	12
10	13	20	16	30	3

a) Establish 3σ upper and lower control limits.
b) Why can the lower control limit not be a negative number?
c) The industry standards for the upper and lower control limits are 0.10 and 0.01, respectively. What does this imply about Birmingham Bank's own standards? **Px**

··S6.19 Houston North Hospital is trying to improve its image by providing a positive experience for its patients and their relatives. Part of the "image" program involves providing tasty, inviting patient meals that are also healthful. A questionnaire accompanies each meal served, asking the patient, among other things, whether he or she is satisfied or unsatisfied with the meal. A 100-patient sample of the survey results over the past 7 days yielded the following data:

DAY	NO. OF UNSATISFIED PATIENTS	SAMPLE SIZE
1	24	100
2	22	100
3	8	100
4	15	100
5	10	100
6	26	100
7	17	100

Construct a *p*-chart that plots the percentage of patients unsatisfied with their meals. Set the control limits to include 99.73% of the random variation in meal satisfaction. Comment on your results. **Px**

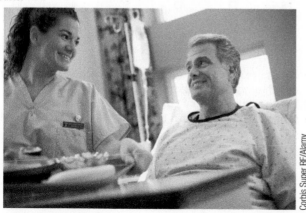

Corbis Super RF/Alamy

··S6.20 Jamison Kovach Supply Company manufactures paper clips and other office products. Although inexpensive, paper clips have provided the firm with a high margin of profitability. Sample size is 200. Results are given for the last 10 samples:

SAMPLE	1	2	3	4	5	6	7	8	9	10
DEFECTIVES	5	7	4	4	6	3	5	6	2	8

a) Establish upper and lower control limits for the control chart and graph the data.
b) Has the process been in control?
c) If the sample size were 100 instead, how would your limits and conclusions change? **Px**

·S6.21 Peter Ittig's department store, Ittig Brothers, is Amherst's largest independent clothier. The store receives an average of six returns per day. Using $z = 3$, would nine returns in a day warrant action? **Px**

··S6.22 An ad agency tracks the complaints, by week received, about the billboards in its city:

WEEK	NO. OF COMPLAINTS
1	4
2	5
3	4
4	11
5	3
6	9

a) What type of control chart would you use to monitor this process? Why?
b) What are the 3-sigma control limits for this process? Assume that the historical complaint rate is unknown.
c) Is the process in control, according to the control limits? Why or why not?
d) Assume now that the historical complaint rate has been four calls a week. What would the 3-sigma control limits for this process be now? Has the process been in control according to the control limits? **Px**

··S6.23 The school board is trying to evaluate a new math program introduced to second-graders in five elementary schools across the county this year. A sample of the student scores on standardized math tests in each elementary school yielded the following data:

SCHOOL	NO. OF TEST ERRORS
A	52
B	27
C	35
D	44
E	55

Construct a *c*-chart for test errors, and set the control limits to contain 99.73% of the random variation in test scores. What does the chart tell you? Has the new math program been effective? **Px**

•• **S6.24** Telephone inquiries of 100 IRS "customers" are monitored daily at random. Incidents of incorrect information or other nonconformities (such as impoliteness to customers) are recorded. The data for last week follow:

DAY	NO. OF NONCONFORMITIES
1	5
2	10
3	23
4	20
5	15

a) Construct a 3-standard deviation c-chart of nonconformities.
b) What does the control chart tell you about the IRS telephone operators? **Px**

••• **S6.25** The accounts receivable department at Rick Wing Manufacturing has been having difficulty getting customers to pay the full amount of their bills. Many customers complain that the bills are not correct and do not reflect the materials that arrived at their receiving docks. The department has decided to implement SPC in its billing process. To set up control charts, 10 samples of 50 bills each were taken over a month's time and the items on the bills checked against the bill of lading sent by the company's shipping department to determine the number of bills that were not correct. The results were:

SAMPLE NO.	NO. OF INCORRECT BILLS	SAMPLE NO.	NO. OF INCORRECT BILLS
1	6	6	5
2	5	7	3
3	11	8	4
4	4	9	7
5	0	10	2

a) Determine the value of p-bar, the mean fraction defective. Then determine the control limits for the p-chart using a 99.73% confidence level (3 standard deviations). Has this process been in control? If not, which samples were out of control?
b) How might you use the quality tools discussed in Chapter 6 to determine the source of the billing defects and where you might start your improvement efforts to eliminate the causes? **Px**

••• **S6.26** West Battery Corp. has recently been receiving complaints from retailers that its 9-volt batteries are not lasting as long as other name brands. James West, head of the TQM program at West's Austin plant, believes there is no problem because his batteries have had an average life of 50 hours, about 10% longer than competitors' models. To raise the lifetime above this level would require a new level of technology not available to West. Nevertheless, he is concerned enough to set up hourly assembly line checks. Previously, after ensuring that the process was running properly, West took size $n = 5$ samples of 9-volt batteries for each of 25 hours to establish the standards for control chart limits. Those samples are shown in the following table:

West Battery Data—Battery Lifetimes (in hours)

HOUR SAMPLE TAKEN	SAMPLE 1	2	3	4	5	$\bar{X}$	R
1	51	50	49	50	50	50.0	2
2	45	47	70	46	36	48.8	34
3	50	35	48	39	47	43.8	15
4	55	70	50	30	51	51.2	40
5	49	38	64	36	47	46.8	28
6	59	62	40	54	64	55.8	24
7	36	33	49	48	56	44.4	23
8	50	67	53	43	40	50.6	27
9	44	52	46	47	44	46.6	8
10	70	45	50	47	41	50.6	29
11	57	54	62	45	36	50.8	26
12	56	54	47	42	62	52.2	20
13	40	70	58	45	44	51.4	30
14	52	58	40	52	46	49.6	18
15	57	42	52	58	59	53.6	17
16	62	49	42	33	55	48.2	29
17	40	39	49	59	48	47.0	20
18	64	50	42	57	50	52.6	22
19	58	53	52	48	50	52.2	10
20	60	50	41	41	50	48.4	19
21	52	47	48	58	40	49.0	18
22	55	40	56	49	45	49.0	16
23	47	48	50	50	48	48.6	3
24	50	50	49	51	51	50.2	2
25	51	50	51	51	62	53.0	12

With these limits established, West now takes 5 more hours of data, which are shown in the following table:

HOUR	SAMPLE 1	2	3	4	5
26	48	52	39	57	61
27	45	53	48	46	66
28	63	49	50	45	53
29	57	70	45	52	61
30	45	38	46	54	52

a) Determine means and the upper and lower control limits for $\bar{x}$ and R (using the first 25 hours only).
b) Has the manufacturing process been in control?
c) Comment on the lifetimes observed. **Px**

•••• **S6.27** One of New England Air's top competitive priorities is on-time arrivals. Quality VP Clair Bond decided to personally monitor New England Air's performance. Each week for the past 30 weeks, Bond checked a random sample of 100 flight arrivals for on-time performance. The table that follows contains the number of flights that did not meet New England Air's definition of "on time":

SAMPLE (WEEK)	LATE FLIGHTS	SAMPLE (WEEK)	LATE FLIGHTS
1	2	16	2
2	4	17	3
3	10	18	7
4	4	19	3
5	1	20	2
6	1	21	3
7	13	22	7
8	9	23	4
9	11	24	3
10	0	25	2
11	3	26	2
12	4	27	0
13	2	28	1
14	2	29	3
15	8	30	4

a) Using a 95% confidence level, plot the overall percentage of late flights ($\bar{p}$) and the upper and lower control limits on a control chart.

b) Assume that the airline industry's upper and lower control limits for flights that are not on time are .1000 and .0400, respectively. Draw them on your control chart.

c) Plot the percentage of late flights in each sample. Do all samples fall within New England Air's control limits? When one falls outside the control limits, what should be done?

d) What can Clair Bond report about the quality of service? **Px**

Additional problems **S6.28–S6.39** are available in MyOMLab.

Problems S6.40–S6.50 relate to Process Capability

• **S6.40** The difference between the upper specification and the lower specification for a process is 0.6". The standard deviation is 0.1". What is the process capability ratio, C_p? Interpret this number. **Px**

•• **S6.41** Meena Chavan Corp.'s computer chip production process yields DRAM chips with an average life of 1,800 hours and $\sigma = 100$ hours. The tolerance upper and lower specification limits are 2,400 hours and 1,600 hours, respectively. Is this process capable of producing DRAM chips to specification? **Px**

•• **S6.42** Linda Boardman, Inc., an equipment manufacturer in Boston, has submitted a sample cutoff valve to improve your manufacturing process. Your process engineering department has conducted experiments and found that the valve has a mean (μ) of 8.00 and a standard deviation (σ) of .04. Your desired performance is $\mu = 8.0 \pm 3\sigma$, where $\sigma = .045$. What is the C_{pk} of the Boardman valve? **Px**

•• **S6.43** The specifications for a plastic liner for concrete highway projects calls for a thickness of 3.0 mm $\pm .1$ mm. The standard deviation of the process is estimated to be .02 mm. What are the upper and lower specification limits for this product? The process is known to operate at a mean thickness of 3.0 mm. What is the C_{pk} for this process? About what percentage of all units of this liner will meet specifications? **Px**

•• **S6.44** Frank Pianki, the manager of an organic yogurt processing plant, desires a quality specification with a mean of 16 ounces, an upper specification limit of 16.5, and a lower specification limit of 15.5. The process has a mean of 16 ounces and a standard deviation of 1 ounce. Determine the C_{pk} of the process. **Px**

•• **S6.45** A process filling small bottles with baby formula has a target of 3 ounces ± 0.150 ounce. Two hundred bottles from the process were sampled. The results showed the average amount of formula placed in the bottles to be 3.042 ounces. The standard deviation of the amounts was 0.034 ounce. Determine the value of C_{pk}. Roughly what proportion of bottles meet the specifications? **Px**

Additional problems **S6.46–S6.50** are available in MyOMLab.

Problems S6.51–S6.55 relate to Acceptance Sampling

•• **S6.51** As the supervisor in charge of shipping and receiving, you need to determine *the average outgoing quality* in a plant where the known incoming lots from your assembly line have an average defective rate of 3%. Your plan is to sample 80 units of every 1,000 in a lot. The number of defects in the sample is not to exceed 3. Such a plan provides you with a probability of acceptance of each lot of .79 (79%). What is your average outgoing quality? **Px**

•• **S6.52** An acceptance sampling plan has lots of 500 pieces and a sample size of 60. The number of defects in the sample may not exceed 2. This plan, based on an OC curve, has a probability of .57 of accepting lots when the incoming lots have a defective rate of 4%, which is the historical average for this process. What do you tell your customer the average outgoing quality is? **Px**

••• **S6.53** The percent defective from an incoming lot is 3%. An OC curve showed the probability of acceptance to be 0.55. Given a lot size of 2,000 and a sample of 100, determine the average outgoing quality in percent defective.

•• **S6.54** In an acceptance sampling plan developed for lots containing 1,000 units, the sample size n is 85. The percent defective of the incoming lots is 2%, and the probability of acceptance is 0.64. What is the average outgoing quality?

•• **S6.55** We want to determine the AOQ for an acceptance sampling plan when the quality of the incoming lots in percent defective is 1.5%, and then again when the incoming percent defective is 5%. The sample size is 80 units for a lot size of 550 units. Furthermore, P_a at 1.5% defective levels is 0.95. At 5% incoming defective levels, the P_a is found to be 0.5. Determine the average outgoing quality for both incoming percent defective levels.

CASE STUDIES

Bayfield Mud Company

In November 2015, John Wells, a customer service representative of Bayfield Mud Company, was summoned to the Houston warehouse of Wet-Land Drilling, Inc., to inspect three boxcars of mudtreating agents that Bayfield had shipped to the Houston firm. (Bayfield's corporate offices and its largest plant are located in Orange, Texas, which is just west of the Louisiana–Texas border.) Wet-Land had filed a complaint that the 50-pound bags of treating agents just received from Bayfield were short-weight by approximately 5%.

The short-weight bags were initially detected by one of Wet-Land's receiving clerks, who noticed that the railroad scale tickets indicated that net weights were significantly less on all three boxcars than those of identical shipments received on October 25, 2015. Bayfield's traffic department was called to determine if lighter-weight pallets were used on the shipments. (This might explain the lighter net weights.) Bayfield indicated, however, that no changes had been made in loading or palletizing procedures. Thus, Wet-Land engineers randomly checked 50 bags and discovered that the average net weight was 47.51 pounds. They noted from past shipments that the process yielded bag net weights averaging exactly 50.0 pounds, with an acceptable standard deviation σ of 1.2 pounds. Consequently, they concluded that the sample indicated a significant short-weight. (The reader may wish to verify this conclusion.) Bayfield was then contacted, and Wells was sent to investigate the complaint. Upon arrival, Wells verified the complaint and issued a 5% credit to Wet-Land.

Wet-Land management, however, was not completely satisfied with the issuance of credit. The charts followed by their mud engineers on the drilling platforms were based on 50-pound bags of treating agents. Lighter-weight bags might result in poor chemical control during the drilling operation and thus adversely affect drilling efficiency. (Mud-treating agents are used to control the pH and other chemical properties of the core during drilling operation.) This defect could cause severe economic consequences because of the extremely high cost of oil and natural gas well-drilling operations. Consequently, special-use instructions had to accompany the delivery of these shipments to the drilling platforms. Moreover, the short-weight shipments had to be isolated in Wet-Land's warehouse, causing extra handling and poor space utilization. Thus, Wells was informed that Wet-Land might seek a new supplier of mud-treating agents if, in the future, it received bags that deviated significantly from 50 pounds.

The quality control department at Bayfield suspected that the lightweight bags might have resulted from "growing pains" at the Orange plant. Because of the earlier energy crisis, oil and natural gas exploration activity had greatly increased. In turn, this increased activity created increased demand for products produced by related industries, including drilling muds. Consequently, Bayfield had to expand from a one-shift (6:00 A.M. to 2:00 P.M.) to a two-shift (2:00 P.M. to 10:00 P.M.) operation in mid-2010, and finally to a three-shift operation (24 hours per day) in the fall of 2015.

| TIME | AVERAGE WEIGHT (POUNDS) | RANGE | | TIME | AVERAGE WEIGHT (POUNDS) | RANGE | |
		SMALLEST	LARGEST			SMALLEST	LARGEST
6:00 A.M.	49.6	48.7	50.7	6:00 P.M.	46.8	41.0	51.2
7:00	50.2	49.1	51.2	7:00	50.0	46.2	51.7
8:00	50.6	49.6	51.4	8:00	47.4	44.0	48.7
9:00	50.8	50.2	51.8	9:00	47.0	44.2	48.9
10:00	49.9	49.2	52.3	10:00	47.2	46.6	50.2
11:00	50.3	48.6	51.7	11:00	48.6	47.0	50.0
12 noon	48.6	46.2	50.4	12 midnight	49.8	48.2	50.4
1:00 P.M.	49.0	46.4	50.0	1:00 A.M.	49.6	48.4	51.7
2:00	49.0	46.0	50.6	2:00	50.0	49.0	52.2
3:00	49.8	48.2	50.8	3:00	50.0	49.2	50.0
4:00	50.3	49.2	52.7	4:00	47.2	46.3	50.5
5:00	51.4	50.0	55.3	5:00	47.0	44.1	49.7
6:00	51.6	49.2	54.7	6:00	48.4	45.0	49.0
7:00	51.8	50.0	55.6	7:00	48.8	44.8	49.7
8:00	51.0	48.6	53.2	8:00	49.6	48.0	51.8
9:00	50.5	49.4	52.4	9:00	50.0	48.1	52.7
10:00	49.2	46.1	50.7	10:00	51.0	48.1	55.2
11:00	49.0	46.3	50.8	11:00	50.4	49.5	54.1
12 midnight	48.4	45.4	50.2	12 noon	50.0	48.7	50.9
1:00 A.M.	47.6	44.3	49.7	1:00 P.M.	48.9	47.6	51.2
2:00	47.4	44.1	49.6	2:00	49.8	48.4	51.0
3:00	48.2	45.2	49.0	3:00	49.8	48.8	50.8
4:00	48.0	45.5	49.1	4:00	50.0	49.1	50.6
5:00	48.4	47.1	49.6	5:00	47.8	45.2	51.2

(cont'd)

| TIME | AVERAGE WEIGHT (POUNDS) | RANGE | | TIME | AVERAGE WEIGHT (POUNDS) | RANGE | |
		SMALLEST	LARGEST			SMALLEST	LARGEST
6:00 A.M.	48.6	47.4	52.0	6:00 P.M.	46.4	44.0	49.7
7:00	50.0	49.2	52.2	7:00	46.4	44.4	50.0
8:00	49.8	49.0	52.4	8:00	47.2	46.6	48.9
9:00	50.3	49.4	51.7	9:00	48.4	47.2	49.5
10:00	50.2	49.6	51.8	10:00	49.2	48.1	50.7
11:00	50.0	49.0	52.3	11:00	48.4	47.0	50.8
12 noon	50.0	48.8	52.4	12 midnight	47.2	46.4	49.2
1:00 P.M.	50.1	49.4	53.6	1:00 A.M.	47.4	46.8	49.0
2:00	49.7	48.6	51.0	2:00	48.8	47.2	51.4
3:00	48.4	47.2	51.7	3:00	49.6	49.0	50.6
4:00	47.2	45.3	50.9	4:00	51.0	50.5	51.5
5:00	46.8	44.1	49.0	5:00	50.5	50.0	51.9

The additional night-shift bagging crew was staffed entirely by new employees. The most experienced foremen were temporarily assigned to supervise the night-shift employees. Most emphasis was placed on increasing the output of bags to meet ever-increasing demand. It was suspected that only occasional reminders were made to double-check the bag weight-feeder. (A double-check is performed by systematically weighing a bag on a scale to determine if the proper weight is being loaded by the weight-feeder. If there is significant deviation from 50 pounds, corrective adjustments are made to the weight-release mechanism.)

To verify this expectation, the quality control staff randomly sampled the bag output and prepared the chart on the previous page. Six bags were sampled and weighed each hour.

Discussion Questions

1. What is your analysis of the bag-weight problem?

2. What procedures would you recommend to maintain proper quality control?

Source: Professor Jerry Kinard, Western Carolina University. Reprinted with permission.

Frito-Lay's Quality-Controlled Potato Chips

Video Case

Frito-Lay, the multi-billion-dollar snack food giant, produces billions of pounds of product every year at its dozens of U.S. and Canadian plants. From the farming of potatoes—in Florida, North Carolina, and Michigan—to factory and to retail stores, the ingredients and final product of Lay's chips, for example, are inspected at least 11 times: in the field, before unloading at the plant, after washing and peeling, at the sizing station, at the fryer, after seasoning, when bagged (for weight), at carton filling, in the warehouse, and as they are placed on the store shelf by Frito-Lay personnel. Similar inspections take place for its other famous products, including Cheetos, Fritos, Ruffles, and Tostitos.

In addition to these employee inspections, the firm uses proprietary vision systems to look for defective potato chips. Chips are pulled off the high-speed line and checked twice if the vision system senses them to be too brown.

The company follows the very strict standards of the American Institute of Baking (AIB), standards that are much tougher than those of the U.S. Food and Drug Administration. Two unannounced AIB site visits per year keep Frito-Lay's plants on their toes. Scores, consistently in the "excellent" range, are posted, and every employee knows exactly how the plant is doing.

There are two key metrics in Frito-Lay's continuous improvement quality program: (1) total customer complaints (measured on a complaints per million bag basis) and (2) hourly or daily statistical process control scores (for oil, moisture, seasoning, and salt content, for chip thickness, for fryer temperature, and for weight).

In the Florida plant, Angela McCormack, who holds engineering and MBA degrees, oversees a 15-member quality

assurance staff. They watch all aspects of quality, including training employees on the factory floor, monitoring automated processing equipment, and developing and updating statistical process control (SPC) charts. The upper and lower control limits for one checkpoint, salt content in Lay's chips, are 2.22% and 1.98%, respectively. To see exactly how these limits are created using SPC, watch the video that accompanies this case.

Discussion Questions*

1. Angela is now going to evaluate a new salt process delivery system and wants to know if the upper and lower control limits at 3 standard deviations for the new system will meet the upper and lower control specifications noted earlier.

   The data (in percents) from the initial trial samples are:

   Sample 1: 1.98, 2.11, 2.15, 2.06
   Sample 2: 1.99, 2.0, 2.08, 1.99
   Sample 3: 2.20, 2.10. 2.20, 2.05
   Sample 4: 2.18, 2.01, 2.23, 1.98
   Sample 5: 2.01, 2.08, 2.14, 2.16

   Provide the report to Angela.

2. What are the advantages and disadvantages of Frito-Lay drivers stocking their customers' shelves?

3. Why is quality a critical function at Frito-Lay?

*You may wish to view the video that accompanies this case before answering these questions.

Farm to Fork: Quality at Darden Restaurants

Darden Restaurants, the $6.3 billion owner of such popular brands as Olive Garden, Seasons 52, and Bahama Breeze, serves more than 320 million meals annually in its 1,500 restaurants across the U.S. and Canada. Before any one of these meals is placed before a guest, the ingredients for each recipe must pass quality control inspections at the source, ranging from measurement and weighing to tasting, touching, or lab testing. Darden has differentiated itself from its restaurant peers by developing the gold standard in continuous improvement.

To assure both customers and the company that quality expectations are met, Darden uses a rigorous inspection process, employing statistical process control (SPC) as part of its "Farm to Fork" program. More than 50 food scientists, microbiologists, and public health professionals report to Ana Hooper, vice president of quality assurance.

As part of Darden's Point Source program, Hooper's team, based in Southeast Asia (in China, Thailand, and Singapore) and Latin America (in Equador, Honduras, and Chile), approves and inspects—and works with Darden buyers to purchase—more than 50 million pounds of seafood each year for restaurant use. Darden used to build quality in at the end by inspecting shipments as they reached U.S. distribution centers. Now, thanks to coaching and partnering with vendors abroad, Darden needs but a few domestic inspection labs to verify compliance to its exacting standards. Food vendors in source countries know that when supplying Darden, they are subject to regular audits that are stricter than U.S. Food and Drug Administration (FDA) standards.

Two Quality Success Stories

Quality specialists' jobs include raising the bar and improving quality and safety at all plants in their geographic area. The Thai quality representative, for example, worked closely with several of Darden's largest shrimp vendors to convert them to a production-line-integrated quality assurance program. The vendors were able to improve the quality of shrimp supplied and reduce the percentage of defects by 19%.

Likewise, when the Darden quality teams visited fields of growers/shippers in Mexico recently, it identified challenges such as low employee hygiene standards, field food safety problems, lack of portable toilets, child labor, and poor working conditions. Darden addressed these concerns and hired third-party independent food safety verification firms to ensure continued compliance to standards.

SPC Charts

SPC charts, such as the one shown on page 253 in this supplement, are particularly important. These charts document precooked food weights; meat, seafood and poultry temperatures; blemishes on produce; and bacteria counts on shrimp—just to name a few. Quality assurance is part of a much bigger process that is key to Darden's success—its supply chain (see Chapters 2 and 11 for discussion and case studies on this topic). That's because quality comes from the source and flows through distribution to the restaurant and guests.

Discussion Questions*

1. How does Darden build quality into the supply chain?
2. Select two potential problems—one in the Darden supply chain and one in a restaurant—that can be analyzed with a fish-bone chart. Draw a complete chart to deal with each problem.
3. Darden applies SPC in many product attributes. Identify where these are probably used.
4. The SPC chart on page 253 illustrates Darden's use of control charts to monitor the weight of salmon filets. Given these data, what conclusion do you, as a Darden quality control inspector, draw? What report do you issue to your supervisor? How do you respond to the salmon vendor?

*You might want to view the video that accompanies this case before answering these questions.

- **Additional Case Study:** Visit MyOMLab for this free case study:
  Green River Chemical Company: Involves a company that needs to set up a control chart to monitor sulfate content because of customer complaints.

Endnotes

1. Removing assignable causes is work. Quality expert W. Edwards Deming observed that a state of statistical control is not a natural state for a manufacturing process. Deming instead viewed it as an achievement, arrived at by elimination, one by one, by determined effort, of special causes of excessive variation.
2. The standard deviation is easily calculated as
$$\sigma = \sqrt{\frac{\sum_{i=1}^{n}(x_i - \overline{x})^2}{n - 1}}.$$ For a good review of this and other statistical terms, refer to Tutorial 1, "Statistical Review for Managers," in MyOMLab.
3. Lower control limits cannot take negative values in control charts. So the LCL $= max\ (0, \overline{\overline{x}} - z\sigma_{\overline{x}})$.
4. If the sample sizes are not the same, other techniques must be used.
5. A Poisson probability distribution is a discrete distribution commonly used when the items of interest (in this case, defects) are infrequent or occur in time or space.

6. This is because a C_p of 1.0 has 99.73% of outputs within specifications. So $1.00 - .9973 = .0027$; with 1,000 parts, there are $.0027 = 1,000 = 2.7$ defects.

   For a C_p of 2.0, 99.99966% of outputs are "within spec." So $1.00 - .9999966 = .0000034$; with 1 million parts, there are 3.4 defects.
7. Refer to Tutorial 2 in MyOMLab for an extended discussion of acceptance sampling.
8. Note that sampling always runs the danger of leading to an erroneous conclusion. Let us say that in one company the total population under scrutiny is a load of 1,000 computer chips, of which in reality only 30 (or 3%) are defective. This means that we would want to accept the shipment of chips, because for this particular firm 4% is the allowable defect rate. However, if a random sample of $n = 50$ chips was drawn, we could conceivably end up with 0 defects and accept that shipment (that is, it is okay), or we could find all 30 defects in the sample. If the latter happened, we could wrongly conclude that the whole population was 60% defective and reject them all.

Main Heading	Review Material	MyOMLab
STATISTICAL PROCESS CONTROL (SPC) (pp. 246–260)	■ **Statistical process control (SPC)**—A process used to monitor standards by taking measurements and corrective action as a product or service is being produced. ■ **Control chart**—A graphical presentation of process data over time. A process is said to be operating *in statistical control* when the only source of variation is common (natural) causes. The process must first be brought into statistical control by detecting and eliminating special (assignable) causes of variation. *The objective of a process control system is to provide a statistical signal when assignable causes of variation are present.* ■ **Natural variations**—The variability that affects every production process to some degree and is to be expected; also known as common cause. When natural variations form a *normal distribution,* they are characterized by two parameters: ■ Mean, μ (the measure of central tendency—in this case, the average value) ■ Standard deviation, σ (the measure of dispersion) As long as the distribution (output measurements) remains within specified limits, the process is said to be "in control," and natural variations are tolerated. ■ **Assignable variation**—Variation in a production process that can be traced to specific causes. Control charts for the mean, $\bar{x}$, and the range, R, are used to monitor *variables* (outputs with continuous dimensions), such as weight, speed, length, or strength. ■ **$\bar{x}$-chart**—A quality control chart for variables that indicates when changes occur in the central tendency of a production process. ■ **R-chart**—A control chart that tracks the range within a sample; it indicates that a gain or loss in uniformity has occurred in dispersion of a production process. ■ **Central limit theorem**—The theoretical foundation for $\bar{x}$-charts, which states that regardless of the distribution of the population of all parts or services, the $\bar{x}$ distribution will tend to follow a normal curve as the number of samples increases: $$\bar{\bar{x}} = \mu \qquad \text{(S6-1)}$$ $$\sigma_{\bar{x}} = \frac{\sigma}{\sqrt{n}} \qquad \text{(S6-2)}$$ The $\bar{x}$-chart limits, if we know the true standard deviation σ of the process population, are: $$\text{Upper control limit (UCL)} = \bar{\bar{x}} + z\sigma_{\bar{x}} \qquad \text{(S6-3)}$$ $$\text{Lower control limit (LCL)} = \bar{\bar{x}} - z\sigma_{\bar{x}} \qquad \text{(S6-4)}$$ where z = confidence level selected (e.g., $z = 3$ is 99.73% confidence). The *range, R,* of a sample is defined as the difference between the largest and smallest items. If we do not know the true standard deviation, σ, of the population, the $\bar{x}$-chart limits are: $$\text{UCL}_{\bar{x}} = \bar{\bar{x}} + A_2\bar{R} \qquad \text{(S6-5)}$$ $$\text{LCL}_{\bar{x}} = \bar{\bar{x}} - A_2\bar{R} \qquad \text{(S6-6)}$$ In addition to being concerned with the process average, operations managers are interested in the process dispersion, or range. The R-chart control limits for the range of a process are: $$\text{UCL}_R = D_4\bar{R} \qquad \text{(S6-7)}$$ $$\text{LCL}_R = D_3\bar{R} \qquad \text{(S6-8)}$$ Attributes are typically classified as *defective* or *nondefective.* The two attribute charts are (1) p-charts (which measure the *percent* defective in a sample), and (2) c-charts (which *count* the number of defects in a sample). ■ **p-chart**—A quality control chart that is used to control attributes: $$\text{UCL}_p = \bar{p} + z\sigma_p \qquad \text{(S6-9)}$$ $$\text{LCL}_p = \bar{p} - z\sigma_p \qquad \text{(S6-10)}$$ $$\hat{\sigma}_p = \sqrt{\frac{\bar{p}(1 - \bar{p})}{n}} \qquad \text{(S6-11)}$$ ■ **c-chart**—A quality control chart used to control the number of defects per unit of output. The Poisson distribution is the basis for c-charts, whose 99.73% limits are computed as: $$\text{Control limits} = \bar{c} \pm 3\sqrt{\bar{c}} \qquad \text{(S6-12)}$$ ■ **Run test**—A test used to examine the points in a control chart to determine whether nonrandom variation is present.	Concept Questions: 1.1–1.4 Problems: S6.1–S6.39 **VIDEO S6.1** Farm to Fork: Quality at Darden Restaurants Virtual Office Hours for Solved Problems: S6.1–S6.3 ACTIVE MODELS S6.1 and S6.2 **VIDEO S6.2** Frito-Lay's Quality-Controlled Potato Chips Virtual Office Hours for Solved Problem: S6.5

Main Heading	Review Material	MyOMLab
PROCESS CAPABILITY (pp. 260–262)	▪ **Process capability**—The ability to meet design specifications. ▪ C_p—A ratio for determining whether a process meets design specifications. $$C_p = \frac{(\text{Upper specification} - \text{Lower specification})}{6\sigma} \quad \text{(S6-13)}$$ ▪ C_{pk}—A proportion of variation (3σ) between the center of the process and the nearest specification limit: $$C_{pk} = \text{Minimum of}\left[\frac{\text{Upper spec limit} - \overline{X}}{3\sigma}, \frac{\overline{X} - \text{Lower spec limit}}{3\sigma}\right] \quad \text{(S6-14)}$$	Concept Questions: 2.1–2.4 Problems: S6.40–S6.50 Virtual Office Hours for Solved Problems: S6.4 **ACTIVE MODEL S6.3**
ACCEPTANCE SAMPLING (pp. 262–265)	▪ **Acceptance sampling**—A method of measuring random samples of lots or batches of products against predetermined standards. ▪ **Operating characteristic (OC) curve**—A graph that describes how well an acceptance plan discriminates between good and bad lots. ▪ **Producer's risk**—The mistake of having a producer's good lot rejected through sampling. ▪ **Consumer's risk**—The mistake of a customer's acceptance of a bad lot overlooked through sampling. ▪ **Acceptable quality level (AQL)**—The quality level of a lot considered good. ▪ **Lot tolerance percent defective (LTPD)**—The quality level of a lot considered bad. ▪ **Type I error**—Statistically, the probability of rejecting a good lot. ▪ **Type II error**—Statistically, the probability of accepting a bad lot. ▪ **Average outgoing quality (AOQ)**—The percent defective in an average lot of goods inspected through acceptance sampling: $$\text{AOQ} = \frac{(P_d)(P_a)(N-n)}{N} \quad \text{(S6-15)}$$	Concept Questions: 3.1–3.4 Problems: S6.51–S6.55

Self Test

▪ **Before taking the self-test,** refer to the learning objectives listed at the beginning of the supplement and the key terms listed at the end of the supplement.

LO S6.1 If the mean of a particular sample is within control limits and the range of that sample is not within control limits:
  a) the process is in control, with only assignable causes of variation.
  b) the process is not producing within the established control limits.
  c) the process is producing within the established control limits, with only natural causes of variation.
  d) the process has both natural and assignable causes of variation.

LO S6.2 The central limit theorem:
  a) is the theoretical foundation of the *c*-chart.
  b) states that the average of assignable variations is zero.
  c) allows managers to use the normal distribution as the basis for building some control charts.
  d) states that the average range can be used as a proxy for the standard deviation.
  e) controls the steepness of an operating characteristic curve.

LO S6.3 The type of chart used to control the central tendency of variables with continuous dimensions is:
  a) $\overline{x}$-chart.
  b) *R*-chart.
  c) *p*-chart.
  d) *c*-chart.
  e) none of the above.

LO S6.4 If parts in a sample are measured and the mean of the sample measurement is outside the control limits:
  a) the process is out of control, and the cause should be established.
  b) the process is in control but not capable of producing within the established control limits.
  c) the process is within the established control limits, with only natural causes of variation.
  d) all of the above are true.

LO S6.5 Control charts for attributes are:
  a) *p*-charts.
  b) *c*-charts.
  c) *R*-charts.
  d) $\overline{x}$-charts.
  e) both a and b.

LO S6.6 The ability of a process to meet design specifications is called:
  a) Taguchi.
  b) process capability.
  c) capability index.
  d) acceptance sampling.
  e) average outgoing quality.

LO S6.7 The _____ risk is the probability that a lot will be rejected despite the quality level exceeding or meeting the _____.

Answers: LO S6.1. b; LO S6.2. c; LO S6.3. a; LO S6.4. a; LO S6.5. e; LO S6.6. b; LO S6.7. producer's, AQL

Capacity and Constraint Management

SUPPLEMENT OUTLINE

Alaska Airlines

Alaska Airlines

When designing a concert hall, management hopes that the forecasted capacity (the product mix—opera, symphony, and special events—and the technology needed for these events) is accurate and adequate for operation above the break-even point. However, in many concert halls, even when operating at full capacity, break-even is not achieved, and supplemental funding must be obtained.

Klaus Lang/All Canada Photos/Alamy

Capacity

LO S7.1 *Define capacity*

What should be the seating capacity of a concert hall? How many customers per day should an Olive Garden or a Hard Rock Cafe be able to serve? How large should a Frito-Lay plant be to produce 75,000 bags of Ruffles in an 8-hour shift? In this supplement we look at tools that help a manager make these decisions.

After selection of a production process (Chapter 7), managers need to determine capacity. Capacity is the "throughput," or the number of units a facility can hold, receive, store, or produce in a given time. Capacity decisions often determine capital requirements and therefore a large portion of fixed cost. Capacity also determines whether demand will be satisfied or whether facilities will be idle. If a facility is too large, portions of it will sit unused and add cost to existing production. If a facility is too small, customers—and perhaps entire markets—will be lost. Determining facility size, with an objective of achieving high levels of utilization and a high return on investment, is critical.

Capacity
The "throughput," or number of units a facility can hold, receive, store, or produce in a period of time.

Capacity planning can be viewed in three time horizons. In Figure S7.1 we note that long-range capacity (generally greater than 3 years) is a function of adding facilities and equipment that have a long lead time. In the intermediate range (usually 3 to 36 months), we can add equipment, personnel, and shifts; we can subcontract; and we can build or use inventory. This is the "aggregate planning" task. In the short run (usually up to 3 months), we are primarily concerned with scheduling jobs and people, as well as allocating machinery. Modifying capacity in the short run is difficult, as we are usually constrained by existing capacity.

STUDENT TIP ◆
Too little capacity loses customers and too much capacity is expensive. Like Goldilocks's porridge, capacity needs to be *just* right.

Options for Adjusting Capacity

Time Horizon	Modify capacity	Use capacity
Long-range planning	Design new production processes. Add (or sell existing) long-lead-time equipment. Acquire or sell facilities. Acquire competitors.	*
Intermediate-range planning (aggregate planning)	Subcontract. Add or sell equipment. Add or reduce shifts.	Build or use inventory. More or improved training. Add or reduce personnel.
Short-range planning (scheduling)	*	Schedule jobs. Schedule personnel. Allocate machinery.

* Difficult to adjust capacity, as limited options exist

Design and Effective Capacity

Design capacity is the maximum theoretical output of a system in a given period under ideal conditions. It is normally expressed as a rate, such as the number of tons of steel that can be produced per week, per month, or per year. For many companies, measuring capacity can be straightforward: it is the maximum number of units the company is capable of producing in a specific time. However, for some organizations, determining capacity can be more difficult. Capacity can be measured in terms of beds (a hospital), active members (a church), or billable hours (a CPA firm). Other organizations use total work time available as a measure of overall capacity.

Most organizations operate their facilities at a rate less than the design capacity. They do so because they have found that they can operate more efficiently when their resources are not stretched to the limit. For example, Ian's Bistro has tables set with 2 or 4 chairs seating a total of 270 guests. But the tables are never filled that way. Some tables will have 1 or 3 guests; tables can be pulled together for parties of 6 or 8. There are always unused chairs. *Design capacity* is 270, but *effective capacity* is often closer to 220, which is 81% of design capacity.

Effective capacity is the capacity a firm *expects* to achieve given the current operating constraints. Effective capacity is often lower than design capacity because the facility may have been designed for an earlier version of the product or a different product mix than is currently being produced. Table S7.1 further illustrates the relationship between design capacity, effective capacity, and *actual output*.

Design capacity
The theoretical maximum output of a system in a given period under ideal conditions.

Effective capacity
The capacity a firm can expect to achieve, given its product mix, methods of scheduling, maintenance, and standards of quality.

TABLE S7.1 | **Capacity Measurements**

MEASURE	DEFINITION	EXAMPLE
Design capacity	Ideal conditions exist during the time that the system is available.	If machines at Frito-Lay are designed to produce 1,000 bags of chips/hr., and the plant operates 16 hrs./day. **Design Capacity = 1,000 bags/hr. × 16 hrs.** **= 16,000 bags/day**
Effective capacity	Design capacity minus lost output because of *planned* resource unavailability (e.g., preventive maintenance, machine setups/changeovers, changes in product mix, scheduled breaks)	If Frito-Lay loses 3 hours of output per day (namely 0.5 hrs./day on preventive maintenance + 1 hr./day on employee breaks + 1.5 hrs./day setting up machines for different products). **Effective Capacity = 16,000 bags/day − (1,000 bags/hr.)(3 hrs./day)** **= 16,000 bags/day − 3,000 bags/day** **= 13,000 bags/day**
Actual output	Effective capacity minus lost output during *unplanned* resource idleness (e.g., absenteeism, machine breakdowns, unavailable parts, quality problems)	On average, if machines at Frito-Lay are not running 1 hr./day due to late parts and machine breakdowns. **Actual Output = 13,000 bags/day − (1,000 bags/hr.)(1 hr./day)** **= 13,000 bags/day − 1,000 bags/day** **= 12,000 bags/day**

Utilization
Actual output as a percent of design capacity.

Efficiency
Actual output as a percent of effective capacity.

LO S7.2 *Determine* design capacity, effective capacity, and utilization

Two measures of system performance are particularly useful: utilization and efficiency. Utilization is simply the percent of *design capacity* actually achieved. Efficiency is the percent of *effective capacity* actually achieved. Depending on how facilities are used and managed, it may be difficult or impossible to reach 100% efficiency. Operations managers tend to be evaluated on efficiency. The key to improving efficiency is often found in correcting quality problems and in effective scheduling, training, and maintenance. Utilization and efficiency are computed below:

$$\text{Utilization} = \text{Actual output}/\text{Design capacity} \tag{S7-1}$$

$$\text{Efficiency} = \text{Actual output}/\text{Effective capacity} \tag{S7-2}$$

In Example S1 we determine these values.

Example S1 | DETERMINING CAPACITY UTILIZATION AND EFFICIENCY

Sara James Bakery has a plant for processing *Deluxe* breakfast rolls and wants to better understand its capability. Last week the facility produced 148,000 rolls. The effective capacity is 175,000 rolls. The production line operates 7 days per week, with three 8-hour shifts per day. The line was designed to process the nut-filled, cinnamon-flavored *Deluxe* roll at a rate of 1,200 per hour. Determine the design capacity, utilization, and efficiency for this plant when producing this *Deluxe* roll.

APPROACH ▶ First compute the design capacity and then use Equation (S7-1) to determine utilization and Equation (S7-2) to determine efficiency.

SOLUTION ▶

$$\text{Design capacity} = (7\text{ days} \times 3\text{ shifts} \times 8\text{ hours}) \times (1{,}200\text{ rolls per hour}) = 201{,}600\text{ rolls}$$

$$\text{Utilization} = \text{Actual output}/\text{Design capacity} = 148{,}000/201{,}600 = 73.4\%$$

$$\text{Efficiency} = \text{Actual output}/\text{Effective capacity} = 148{,}000/175{,}000 = 84.6\%$$

INSIGHT ▶ The bakery now has the information necessary to evaluate efficiency.

LEARNING EXERCISE ▶ If the actual output is 150,000, what is the efficiency? [Answer: 85.7%.]

RELATED PROBLEMS ▶ S7.1, S7.2, S7.3, S7.4, S7.5, S7.6, S7.7, S7.8

ACTIVE **MODEL** S7.1 This example is further illustrated in Active Model S7.1 in MyOMLab.

In Example S2 we see how the effectiveness of new capacity additions depends on how well management can perform on the utilization and efficiency of those additions.

Example S2 | EXPANDING CAPACITY

The manager of Sara James Bakery (see Example S1) now needs to increase production of the increasingly popular *Deluxe* roll. To meet this demand, she will be adding a second production line. The second line has the same design capacity (201,600) and effective capacity (175,000) as the first line; however, new workers will be operating the second line. Quality problems and other inefficiencies stemming from the inexperienced workers are expected to reduce output on the second line to 130,000 (compared to 148,000 on the first). The utilization and efficiency were 73.4% and 84.6%, respectively, on the first line. Determine the new utilization and efficiency for the *Deluxe* roll operation after adding the second line.

APPROACH ▶ First, determine the new design capacity, effective capacity, and actual output after adding the second line. Then, use Equation (S7-1) to determine utilization and Equation (S7-2) to determine efficiency.

SOLUTION ▶ Design capacity = 201,600 × 2 = 403,200 rolls

Effective capacity = 175,000 × 2 = 350,000 rolls

Actual output = 148,000 + 130,000 = 278,000 rolls

Utilization = Actual output/Design capacity = 278,000 / 403,200 = 68.95%

Efficiency = Actual output/Effective capacity = 278,000 / 350,000 = 79.43%

INSIGHT ▶ Although adding equipment increases capacity, that equipment may not be operated as efficiently with new employees as might be the case with experienced employees. For Sara James Bakery, a doubling of equipment investment did not result in a doubling of output; other variables drove both utilization and efficiency lower.

LEARNING EXERCISE ▶ Suppose that Sara James reduces changeover time (setup time) by three fewer hours per week. What will be the new values of utilization and efficiency? [Answer: utilization is still 68.95%, efficiency now increases to 81.10%]

RELATED PROBLEMS ▶ S7.1, S7.2, S7.3, S7.4, S7.5, S7.6, S7.7, S7.8

Actual output, as used in Equation (S7-2), represents current conditions. Alternatively, with a knowledge of effective capacity and a current or target value for efficiency, the future *expected output* can be computed by reversing Equation (S7-2):

$$\text{Expected output} = \text{Effective capacity} \times \text{Efficiency}$$

If the expected output is inadequate, additional capacity may be needed. Much of the remainder of this supplement addresses how to effectively and efficiently add that capacity.

Capacity and Strategy

Sustained profits come from building competitive advantage, not just from a good financial return on a specific process. Capacity decisions must be integrated into the organization's mission and strategy. Investments are not to be made as isolated expenditures, but as part of a coordinated plan that will place the firm in an advantageous position. The questions to be asked are, "Will these investments eventually win profitable customers?" and "What competitive advantage (such as process flexibility, speed of delivery, improved quality, and so on) do we obtain?"

All 10 OM decisions we discuss in this text, as well as other organizational elements such as marketing and finance, are affected by changes in capacity. Change in capacity will have sales and cash flow implications, just as capacity changes have quality, supply chain, human resource, and maintenance implications. All must be considered.

Capacity Considerations

In addition to tight integration of strategy and investments, there are four special considerations for a good capacity decision:

1. *Forecast demand accurately:* Product additions and deletions, competition actions, product life cycle, and unknown sales volumes all add challenge to accurate forecasting.
2. *Match technology increments and sales volume:* Capacity options are often constrained by technology. Some capacity increments may be large (e.g., steel mills or power plants), while others may be small (hand-crafted Louis Vuitton handbags). Large capacity increments complicate the difficult but necessary job of matching capacity to sales.
3. *Find the optimum operating size (volume):* Economies and diseconomies of scale often dictate an optimal size for a facility. *Economies of scale* exist when average cost declines as size increases, whereas *diseconomies of scale* occur when a larger size raises the average cost. As Figure S7.2 suggests, most businesses have an optimal size—at least until someone comes along with a new business model. For decades, very large integrated steel mills were considered optimal. Then along came Nucor, CMC, and other minimills, with a new process and a new business model that radically reduced the optimum size of a steel mill.
4. *Build for change:* Managers build flexibility into facilities and equipment; changes will occur in processes, as well as products, product volume, and product mix.

◆ **STUDENT TIP**

Each industry and technology has an optimum size.

Next, we note that rather than strategically manage capacity, managers may tactically manage demand.

Figure **S7.2**

Economies and Diseconomies of Scale

Krispy Kreme originally had 8,000-square-foot stores but found them too large and too expensive for many markets. Then they tried tiny 1,300-square-foot stores, which required less investment, but such stores were too small to provide the mystique of seeing and smelling Krispy Kreme doughnuts being made. Krispy Kreme finally got it right with a 2,600-foot-store.

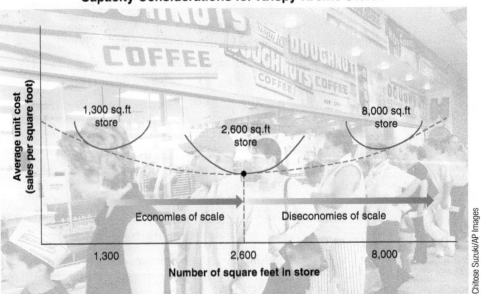

Capacity Considerations for Krispy Kreme Stores

Managing Demand

Even with good forecasting and facilities built to accomodate that forecast, there may be a poor match between the actual demand that occurs and available capacity. A poor match may mean demand exceeds capacity or capacity exceeds demand. However, in both cases, firms have options.

Demand Exceeds Capacity   When *demand exceeds capacity*, the firm may be able to curtail demand simply by raising prices, scheduling long lead times (which may be inevitable), and discouraging marginally profitable business. However, because inadequate facilities reduce revenue below what is possible, the long-term solution is usually to increase capacity.

Capacity Exceeds Demand   When *capacity exceeds demand*, the firm may want to stimulate demand through price reductions or aggressive marketing, or it may accommodate the market through product changes. When decreasing customer demand is combined with old and inflexible processes, layoffs and plant closings may be necessary to bring capacity in line with demand.

Adjusting to Seasonal Demands   A seasonal or cyclical pattern of demand is another capacity challenge. In such cases, management may find it helpful to offer products with complementary demand patterns—that is, products for which the demand is high for one when low for the other. For example, in Figure S7.3 the firm is adding a line of snowmobile motors to its line of jet skis to smooth demand. With appropriate complementing of products, perhaps the utilization of facility, equipment, and personnel can be smoothed (as we see in the *OM in Action* box "Matching Airline Capacity to Demand").

Figure **S7.3**

By Combining Products That Have Complementary Seasonal Patterns, Capacity Can Be Better Utilized

OM in Action | Matching Airline Capacity to Demand

Airlines constantly struggle to control their capital expenditures and to adapt to unstable demand patterns.

Southwest and Lufthansa have each taken their own approach to increasing capacity while holding down capital investment. To manage capacity constraints on the cheap, Southwest squeezes seven flight segments out of its typical plane schedule per day—one more than most competitors. Its operations personnel find that quick ground turnaround, long a Southwest strength, is a key to this capital-saving technique.

Lufthansa has cut hundreds of millions of dollars in new jet purchases by squashing rows of seats 2 inches closer together. On the A320, for example, Lufthansa added two rows of seats, giving the plane 174 seats instead of 162. For its European fleet, this is the equivalent of having 12 more Airbus A320 jets. But Lufthansa will tell you that squeezing in more seats is not quite as bad as it sounds, as the new generation of ultra-thin seats provides passengers with more leg room. Using a strong mesh, similar to that in fancy office chairs

(instead of inches of foam padding), and moving magazine pockets to the top of seat backs, there is actually more knee room than with the old chairs.

Unstable demands in the airline industry provide another capacity challenge. Seasonal patterns (e.g., fewer people fly in the winter), compounded by spikes in demand during major holidays and summer vacations, play havoc with efficient use of capacity. Airlines attack costly seasonality in several ways. First, they schedule more planes for maintenance and renovations during slow winter months, curtailing winter capacity; second, they seek out contra-seasonal routes. And when capacity is substantially above demand, placing planes in storage (as shown in the photo) may be the most economical answer.

Airlines also use revenue management (see Chapter 13) to maximize per-seat pricing of available capacity, regardless of current demand patterns.

Sources: The Wall Street Journal (February 29, 2012) and (October 6, 2011).

Tactics for Matching Capacity to Demand   Various tactics for adjusting capacity to demand include:

1. Making staffing changes (increasing or decreasing the number of employees or shifts)
2. Adjusting equipment (purchasing additional machinery or selling or leasing out existing equipment)
3. Improving processes to increase throughput (e.g., reducing setup times at M2 Global Technology added the equivalent of 17 shifts of capacity)
4. Redesigning products to facilitate more throughput
5. Adding process flexibility to better meet changing product preferences
6. Closing facilities

The foregoing tactics can be used to adjust demand to existing facilities. The strategic issue is, of course, how to have a facility of the correct size.

Service-Sector Demand and Capacity Management

In the service sector, scheduling customers is *demand management*, and scheduling the workforce is *capacity management*.

Recessions (e.g., 2008–2010) and terrorist attacks (e.g., September 11, 2001) can make even the best capacity decision for an airline look bad. And excess capacity for an airline can be very expensive, with storage costs running as high as $60,000 per month per aircraft. Here, as a testimonial to excess capacity, aircraft sit idle in the Mojave Desert.

Joe McNally/Getty Images

Many U.S. hospitals use services abroad to manage capacity for radiologists during night shifts. Night Hawk, an Idaho-based service with 50 radiologists in Zurich and Sydney, contracts with 900 facilities (20% of all U.S. hospitals). These trained experts, wide awake and alert in their daylight hours, usually return a diagnosis in 10 to 20 minutes, with a guarantee of 30 minutes.

Demand Management   When demand and capacity are fairly well matched, demand management can often be handled with appointments, reservations, or a first-come, first-served rule. In some businesses, such as doctors' and lawyers' offices, an *appointment system* is the schedule and is adequate. *Reservations systems* work well in rental car agencies, hotels, and some restaurants as a means of minimizing customer waiting time and avoiding disappointment over unfilled service. In retail shops, a post office, or a fast-food restaurant, a *first-come, first-served* rule for serving customers may suffice. Each industry develops its own approaches to matching demand and capacity. Other more aggressive approaches to demand management include many variations of discounts: "early bird" specials in restaurants, discounts for matinee performances or for seats at odd hours on an airline, and cheap weekend hotel rooms.

Capacity Management   When managing demand is not feasible, then managing capacity through changes in full-time, temporary, or part-time staff may be an option. This is the approach in many services. For instance, hospitals may find capacity limited by a shortage of board-certified radiologists willing to cover the graveyard shifts. Getting fast and reliable radiology readings can be the difference between life and death for an emergency room patient. As the photo above illustrates, when an overnight reading is required (and 40% of CT scans are done between 8 P.M. and 8 A.M.), the image can be sent by e-mail to a doctor in Europe or Australia for immediate analysis.

Bottleneck Analysis and the Theory of Constraints

As managers seek to match capacity to demand, decisions must be made about the size of specific operations or work areas in the larger system. Each of the interdependent work areas can be expected to have its own unique capacity. Capacity analysis involves determining the throughput capacity of workstations in a system and ultimately the capacity of the entire system.

A key concept in capacity analysis is the role of a constraint or bottleneck. A bottleneck is an operation that is the limiting factor or constraint. The term *bottleneck* refers to the literal neck of a bottle that constrains flow or, in the case of a production system, constrains throughput. A bottleneck has the lowest effective capacity of any operation in the system and thus limits the system's output. Bottlenecks occur in all facets of life—from job shops where a machine is constraining the work flow to highway traffic where two lanes converge into one inadequate lane, resulting in traffic congestion.

We define the process time of a station as the time to produce a unit (or a specified batch size of units) at that workstation. For example, if 16 customers can be checked out in a supermarket line every 60 minutes, then the process time at that station is 3.75 minutes per customer (= 60/16). (Process time is simply the inverse of capacity, which in this case is 60 minutes per hour/3.75 minutes per customer = 16 customers per hour.)

Capacity analysis

A means of determining throughput capacity of workstations or an entire production system.

Bottleneck

The limiting factor or constraint in a system.

Process time

The time to produce a unit (or specified batch of units) at a workstation.

To determine the bottleneck in a production system, simply identify the station with the slowest process time. The bottleneck time is the process time of the slowest workstation (the one that takes the longest) in a production system. For example, the flowchart in Figure S7.4 shows a simple assembly line. Individual station process times are 2, 4, and 3 minutes, respectively. The bottleneck time is 4 minutes. This is because station B is the slowest station. Even if we were to speed up station A, the entire production process would not be faster. Inventory would simply pile up in front of station B even more than now. Likewise, if station C could work faster, we could not tap its excess capacity because station B will not be able to feed products to it any faster than 1 every 4 minutes.

Bottleneck time

The process time of the longest (slowest) process, i.e., the bottleneck.

Station A		Station B		Station C
2 min/unit		4 min/unit		3 min/unit

The throughput time, on the other hand, is the time it takes a unit to go through production from start to end, *with no waiting*. (Throughput time describes the behavior in an empty system. In contrast, flow time describes the time to go through a production process from beginning to end, including idle time waiting for stations to finish working on other units.) The throughput time to produce a new completed unit in Figure S7.4 is 9 minutes (= 2 minutes + 4 minutes + 3 minutes).

Bottleneck time and *throughput time* may be quite different. For example, a Ford assembly line may roll out a new car every minute (bottleneck time), but it may take 25 hours to actually make a car from start to finish (throughput time). This is because the assembly line has many workstations, with each station contributing to the completed car. Thus, bottleneck time determines the system's capacity (one car per minute), while its throughput time determines potential ability to produce a newly ordered product from scratch in 25 hours.

The following two examples illustrate capacity analysis for slightly more complex systems. Example S3 introduces the concept of parallel processes, and Example S4 introduces the concept of simultaneous processing.

Figure S7.4

Three-Station Assembly Line

A box represents an operation, a triangle represents inventory, and arrows represent precedence relationships

Throughput time

The time it takes for a product to go through the production process *with no waiting*. It is the time of the longest path through the system.

Example S3

CAPACITY ANALYSIS WITH PARALLEL PROCESSES

Howard Kraye's sandwich shop provides healthy sandwiches for customers. Howard has two identical sandwich assembly lines. A customer first places an order, which takes 30 seconds. The order is then sent to one of the two assembly lines. Each assembly line has two workers and three operations: (1) assembly worker 1 retrieves and cuts the bread (15 seconds/sandwich), (2) assembly worker 2 adds ingredients and places the sandwich onto the toaster conveyor belt (20 seconds/sandwich), and (3) the toaster heats the sandwich (40 seconds/sandwich). Finally, another employee wraps the heated sandwich coming out of the toaster and delivers it to the customer (37.5 seconds/sandwich). A flowchart of the process is shown below. Howard wants to determine the bottleneck time and throughput time of this process.

LO S7.3 *Perform* bottleneck analysis

APPROACH ▶ Clearly the toaster is the single-slowest resource in the five-step process, but is it the bottleneck? Howard should first determine the bottleneck time of each of the two assembly lines separately, then the bottleneck time of the combined assembly lines, and finally the bottleneck time of the entire operation. For throughput time, each assembly line is identical, so Howard should just sum the process times for all five operations.

SOLUTION ▶ Because each of the three assembly-line operations uses a separate resource (worker or machine), different partially completed sandwiches can be worked on simultaneously at each station. Thus, the bottleneck time of each assembly line is the longest process time of each of the three operations. In this case, the 40-second toasting time represents the bottleneck time of each assembly line. Next, the bottleneck time of the *combined* assembly line operations is 40 seconds per *two* sandwiches, or 20 seconds per sandwich. Therefore, the wrapping and delivering operation, with a process time of 37.5 seconds, appears to be the bottleneck for the entire operation. The capacity per hour equals 3,600 seconds per hour/37.5 seconds per sandwich = 96 sandwiches per hour. The throughput time equals 30 + 15 + 20 + 40 + 37.5 = 142.5 seconds (or 2 minutes and 22.5 seconds), assuming no wait time in line to begin with.

INSIGHT ▶ Doubling the resources at a workstation effectively cuts the time at that station in half. (If *n* parallel [redundant] operations are added, the process time of the combined workstation operation will equal $1/n$ times the original process time.)

LEARNING EXERCISE ▶ If Howard hires an additional wrapper, what will be the new hourly capacity? [Answer: The new bottleneck is now the order-taking station: Capacity = 3,600 seconds per hour/30 seconds per sandwich = 120 sandwiches per hour]

RELATED PROBLEMS ▶ S7.9, S7.10, S7.11, S7.12, S7.13

In Example S3, how could we claim that the process time of the toaster was 20 seconds per sandwich when it takes 40 seconds to toast a sandwich? The reason is that we had two toasters; thus, two sandwiches could be toasted every 40 seconds, for an average of one sandwich every 20 seconds. And that time for a toaster can actually be achieved if the start times for the two are *staggered* (i.e., a new sandwich is placed in a toaster every 20 seconds). In that case, even though each sandwich will sit in the toaster for 40 seconds, a sandwich could emerge from one of the two toasters every 20 seconds. As we see, doubling the number of resources effectively cuts the process time at that station in half, resulting in a doubling of the capacity of those resources.

Example S4 | CAPACITY ANALYSIS WITH SIMULTANEOUS PROCESSES

Dr. Cynthia Knott's dentistry practice has been cleaning customers' teeth for decades. The process for a basic dental cleaning is relatively straightforward: (1) the customer checks in (2 minutes); (2) a lab technician takes and develops X-rays (2 and 4 minutes, respectively); (3) the dentist processes and examines the X-rays (5 minutes) *while* the hygienist cleans the teeth (24 minutes); (4) the dentist meets with the patient to poke at a few teeth, explain the X-ray results, and tell the patient to floss more often (8 minutes); and (5) the customer pays and books her next appointment (6 minutes). A flowchart of the customer visit is shown below. Dr. Knott wants to determine the bottleneck time and throughput time of this process.

APPROACH ▶ With simultaneous processes, an order or a product is essentially *split* into different paths to be rejoined later on. To find the bottleneck time, each operation is treated separately, just as though all operations were on a sequential path. To find the throughput time, the time over *all* paths must be computed, and the throughput time is the time of the *longest* path.

SOLUTION ▶ The bottleneck in this system is the hygienist cleaning operation at 24 minutes per patient, resulting in an hourly system capacity of 60 minutes/24 minutes per patient = 2.5 patients. The throughput time is the maximum of the two paths through the system. The path through the X-ray exam is $2 + 2 + 4 + 5 + 8 + 6 = 27$ minutes, while the path through the hygienist cleaning operation is $2 + 2 + 4 + 24 + 8 + 6 = 46$ minutes. Thus a patient should be out the door after 46 minutes (i.e., the maximum of 27 and 46).

INSIGHT ▶ With simultaneous processing, all operation times in the entire system are not simply added together to compute throughput time because some operations are occurring simultaneously. Instead, the time of the longest path through the system is deemed the throughput time.

LEARNING EXERCISE ▶ Suppose that the same technician now has the hygienist start immediately after the X-rays are taken (allowing the hygienist to start 4 minutes sooner). The technician then develops the X-rays while the hygienist is cleaning teeth. The dentist still examines the X-rays while the teeth cleaning is occurring. What would be the new system capacity and throughput time? [Answer: The X-ray development operation is now on the parallel path with cleaning and X-ray exam, reducing the total patient visit duration by 4 minutes, for a throughput time of 42 minutes (the maximum of 27 and 42). However, the hygienist cleaning operation is still the bottleneck, so the capacity remains 2.5 patients per hour.]

RELATED PROBLEMS ▶ S7.14, S7.15

To summarize: (1) the *bottleneck* is the operation with the longest (slowest) process time, after dividing by the number of parallel (redundant) operations, (2) the *system capacity* is the inverse of the *bottleneck time*, and (3) the *throughput time* is the total time through the longest path in the system, assuming no waiting.

Theory of Constraints

The theory of constraints (TOC) has been popularized by the book *The Goal: A Process of Ongoing Improvement,* by Goldratt and Cox.[1] TOC is a body of knowledge that deals with anything that limits or constrains an organization's ability to achieve its goals. Constraints can be physical (e.g., process or personnel availability, raw materials, or supplies) or nonphysical (e.g., procedures, morale, and training). Recognizing and managing these limitations through a five-step process is the basis of TOC.

Theory of constraints (TOC)
A body of knowledge that deals with anything that limits an organization's ability to achieve its goals.

STEP 1: Identify the constraints.

STEP 2: Develop a plan for overcoming the identified constraints.

STEP 3: Focus resources on accomplishing Step 2.

STEP 4: Reduce the effects of the constraints by offloading work or by expanding capability. Make sure that the constraints are recognized by all those who can have an impact on them.

STEP 5: When one set of constraints is overcome, go back to Step 1 and identify new constraints.

Bottleneck Management

A crucial constraint in any system is the bottleneck, and managers must focus significant attention on it. We present four principles of bottleneck management:

◆ STUDENT TIP
There are always bottlenecks; a manager must identify and manage them.

1. *Release work orders to the system at the pace set by the bottleneck's capacity:* The theory of constraints utilizes the concept of *drum, buffer, rope* to aid in the implementation of bottleneck and nonbottleneck scheduling. In brief, the *drum* is the beat of the system. It provides the schedule—the pace of production. The *buffer* is the resource, usually inventory, which may be helpful to keep the bottleneck operating at the pace of the drum. Finally, the *rope* provides the synchronization or communication necessary to pull units through the system. The rope can be thought of as signals between workstations.

2. *Lost time at the bottleneck represents lost capacity for the whole system:* This principle implies that the bottleneck should always be kept busy with work. Well-trained and cross-trained employees and inspections prior to the bottleneck can reduce lost capacity at a bottleneck.

3. *Increasing the capacity of a nonbottleneck station is a mirage:* Increasing the capacity of *nonbottleneck* stations has no impact on the system's overall capacity. Working faster on

a nonbottleneck station may just create extra inventory, with all of its adverse effects. This implies that nonbottlenecks should have planned idle time. Extra work or setups at nonbottleneck stations will not cause delay, which allows for smaller batch sizes and more frequent product changeovers at nonbottleneck stations.

4. *Increasing the capacity of the bottleneck increases capacity for the whole system:* Managers should focus improvement efforts on the bottleneck. Bottleneck capacity may be improved by various means, including offloading some of the bottleneck operations to another workstation (e.g., let the beer foam settle next to the tap at the bar, not under it, so the next beer can be poured), increasing capacity of the bottleneck (adding resources, working longer or working faster), subcontracting, developing alternative routings, and reducing setup times.

Even when managers have process and quality variability under control, changing technology, personnel, products, product mixes, and volumes can create multiple and shifting bottlenecks. Identifying and managing bottlenecks is a required operations task, but by definition, bottlenecks cannot be "eliminated." A system will always have at least one.

Break-Even Analysis

Break-even analysis

A means of finding the point, in dollars and units, at which costs equal revenues.

Break-even analysis is the critical tool for determining the capacity a facility must have to achieve profitability. The objective of break-even analysis is to find the point, in dollars and units, at which costs equal revenue. This point is the break-even point. Firms must operate above this level to achieve profitability. As shown in Figure S7.5, break-even analysis requires an estimation of fixed costs, variable costs, and revenue.

Fixed costs are costs that continue even if no units are produced. Examples include depreciation, taxes, debt, and mortgage payments. *Variable costs* are those that vary with the volume of units produced. The major components of variable costs are labor and materials. However, other costs, such as the portion of the utilities that varies with volume, are also variable costs. The difference between selling price and variable cost is *contribution*. Only when total contribution exceeds total fixed cost will there be profit.

Another element in break-even analysis is the *revenue function*. In Figure S7.5, revenue begins at the origin and proceeds upward to the right, increasing by the selling price of each unit. Where the revenue function crosses the total cost line (the sum of fixed and variable costs) is the break-even point, with a profit corridor to the right and a loss corridor to the left.

Assumptions A number of assumptions underlie the basic break-even model. Notably, costs and revenue are shown as straight lines. They are shown to increase linearly—that is,

Figure S7.5

Basic Break-Even Point

in direct proportion to the volume of units being produced. However, neither fixed costs nor variable costs (nor, for that matter, the revenue function) need be a straight line. For example, fixed costs change as more capital equipment or warehouse space is used; labor costs change with overtime or as marginally skilled workers are employed; the revenue function may change with such factors as volume discounts.

Single-Product Case

The formulas for the break-even point in units and dollars for a single product are shown below. Let:

LO S7.4 *Compute break-even*

BEP_x = break-even point in units
$BEP_\$$ = break-even point in dollars
P = price per unit (after all discounts)
x = number of units produced

TR = total revenue = Px
F = fixed costs
V = variable costs per unit
TC = total costs = $F + Vx$

The break-even point occurs where total revenue equals total costs. Therefore:

$$TR = TC \quad \text{or} \quad Px = F + Vx$$

Solving for x, we get:

$$\text{Break-even point in units } (BEP_x) = \frac{F}{P - V}$$

and:

$$\text{Break-even point in dollars } (BEP_\$) = BEP_x P = \frac{F}{P - V}P = \frac{F}{(P - V)/P} = \frac{F}{1 - V/P}$$

$$\text{Profit} = TR - TC = Px - (F + Vx) = Px - F - Vx = (P - V)x - F$$

Using these equations, we can solve directly for break-even point and profitability. The two break-even formulas of particular interest are:

$$\text{Break-even in units } (BEP_x) = \frac{\text{Total fixed cost}}{\text{Price} - \text{Variable cost}} = \frac{F}{P - V} \qquad \text{(S7-3)}$$

$$\text{Break-even in dollars } (BEP_\$) = \frac{\text{Total fixed cost}}{1 - \dfrac{\text{Variable cost}}{\text{Price}}} = \frac{F}{1 - \dfrac{V}{P}} \qquad \text{(S7-4)}$$

In Example S5, we determine the break-even point in dollars and units for one product.

Example S5 | SINGLE-PRODUCT BREAK-EVEN ANALYSIS

Stephens, Inc., wants to determine the minimum dollar volume and unit volume needed at its new facility to break even.

APPROACH ▶ The firm first determines that it has fixed costs of $10,000 this period. Direct labor is $1.50 per unit, and material is $.75 per unit. The selling price is $4.00 per unit.

SOLUTION ▶ The break-even point in dollars is computed as follows:

$$BEP_\$ = \frac{F}{1 - (V/P)} = \frac{\$10,000}{1 - [(1.50 + .75)/(4.00)]} = \frac{\$10,000}{.4375} = \$22,857.14$$

The break-even point in units is:

$$BEP_x = \frac{F}{P - V} = \frac{\$10,000}{4.00 - (1.50 + .75)} = 5,714$$

Note that we use total variable costs (that is, both labor and material).

INSIGHT ▶ The management of Stevens, Inc., now has an estimate in both units and dollars of the volume necessary for the new facility.

LEARNING EXERCISE ▶ If Stevens finds that fixed cost will increase to $12,000, what happens to the break-even in units and dollars? [Answer: The break-even in units increases to 6,857, and break-even in dollars increases to $27,428.57.]

RELATED PROBLEMS ▶ S7.16–S7.25 (S7.28–S7.31 are available in MyOMLab)

EXCEL **OM** Data File **Ch07SExS3**.xls can be found in MyOMLab.

ACTIVE **MODEL** S7.2 This example is further illustrated in Active Model S7.2 in MyOMLab.

Multiproduct Case

Most firms, from manufacturers to restaurants, have a variety of offerings. Each offering may have a different selling price and variable cost. Utilizing break-even analysis, we modify Equation (S7-4) to reflect the proportion of sales for each product. We do this by "weighting" each product's contribution by its proportion of sales. The formula is then:

$$\text{Break-even point in dollars } (BEP_\$) = \frac{F}{\sum\left[1 - \left(\frac{V_i}{P_i}\right) \times (W_i)\right]} \tag{S7-5}$$

where V = variable cost per unit W = percent each product is of total dollar sales
P = price per unit i = each product
F = fixed cost

Paper machines such as the one shown here require a high capital investment. This investment results in a high fixed cost but allows production of paper at a very low variable cost. The production manager's job is to maintain utilization above the break-even point to achieve profitability.

Image Ideas/Stockbyte/Getty Images

Example S6 shows how to determine the break-even point for the multiproduct case at the Le Bistro restaurant.

Example S6 | MULTIPRODUCT BREAK-EVEN ANALYSIS

Le Bistro, like most other resturants, makes more than one product and would like to know its break-even point in dollars. Information for Le Bistro follows. Fixed costs are $3,000 per month.

ITEM	ANNUAL FORECASTED SALES UNITS	PRICE	COST
Sandwich	9,000	$5.00	$3.00
Drinks	9,000	1.50	0.50
Baked potato	7,000	2.00	1.00

APPROACH ▶ With a variety of offerings, we proceed with break-even analysis just as in a single-product case, except that we weight each of the products by its proportion of total sales using Equation (S7-5).

SOLUTION ▶ Multiproduct Break-Even: Determining Contribution

1	2	3	4	5	6	7	8	9
ITEM (*i*)	ANNUAL FORECASTED SALES UNITS	SELLING PRICE (P_i)	VARIABLE COST (V_i)	(V_i/P_i)	CONTRI-BUTION $1-(V_i/P_i)$	ANNUAL FORECASTED SALES $	% OF SALES (W_i)	WEIGHTED CONTRIBUTION (COL. 6 × COL. 8)
Sandwich	9,000	$5.00	$3.00	.60	.40	$45,000	.621	.248
Drinks	9,000	1.50	0.50	.33	.67	13,500	.186	.125
Baked potato	7,000	2.00	1.00	.50	.50	14,000	.193	.097
						$72,500	1.000	.470

Note: Revenue for sandwiches is $45,000 (= 5.00 × 9,000), which is 62.1% of the total revenue of $72,500. Therefore, the contribution for sandwiches is "weighted" by .621. The weighted contribution is .621 × .40 = .248. In this manner, its *relative* contribution is properly reflected.

Using this approach for each product, we find that the total weighted contribution is .47 for each dollar of sales, and the break-even point in dollars is $76,596:

$$BEP_\$ = \frac{F}{\sum\left[1 - \left(\frac{V_i}{P_i}\right) \times (W_i)\right]} = \frac{\$3,000 \times 12}{.47} = \frac{\$36,000}{.47} = \$76,596$$

The information given in this example implies total daily sales (52 weeks at 6 days each) of:

$$\frac{\$76,596}{312 \text{ days}} = \$245.50$$

INSIGHT ▶ The management of Le Bistro now knows that it must generate average sales of $245.50 each day to break even. Management also knows that if the forecasted sales of $72,500 are correct, Le Bistro will lose money, as break-even is $76,596.

LEARNING EXERCISE ▶ If the manager of Le Bistro wants to make an additional $1,000 per month in salary, and considers this a fixed cost, what is the new break-even point in average sales per day? [Answer: $327.33.]

RELATED PROBLEMS ▶ S7.26, S7.27

Break-even figures by product provide the manager with added insight as to the realism of his or her sales forecast. They indicate exactly what must be sold each day, as we illustrate in Example S7.

Example S7

UNIT SALES AT BREAK-EVEN

Le Bistro also wants to know the break-even for the number of sandwiches that must be sold every day.

APPROACH ▶ Using the data in Example S6, we take the forecast sandwich sales of 62.1% times the daily break-even of $245.50 divided by the selling price of each sandwich ($5.00).

SOLUTION ▶ At break-even, sandwich sales must then be:

$$\frac{.621 \times \$245.50}{5.00} = \text{Number of sandwiches} = 30.5 \approx 31 \text{ sandwiches each day}$$

INSIGHT ▶   With knowledge of individual product sales, the manager has a basis for determining material and labor requirements.

LEARNING EXERCISE ▶   At a dollar break-even of $327.33 per day, how many sandwiches must Le Bistro sell each day? [Answer: ≈ 41.]

RELATED PROBLEMS ▶   S7.26b, S7.27b

Once break-even analysis has been prepared, analyzed, and judged to be reasonable, decisions can be made about the type and capacity of equipment needed. Indeed, a better judgment of the likelihood of success of the enterprise can now be made.

Reducing Risk with Incremental Changes

When demand for goods and services can be forecast with a reasonable degree of precision, determining a break-even point and capacity requirements can be rather straightforward. But, more likely, determining the capacity and how to achieve it will be complicated, as many factors are difficult to measure and quantify. Factors such as technology, competitors, building restrictions, cost of capital, human resource options, and regulations make the decision interesting. To complicate matters further, demand growth is usually in small units, while capacity additions are likely to be both instantaneous and in large units. This contradiction adds to the capacity decision risk. To reduce risk, incremental changes that hedge demand forecasts may be a good option. Figure S7.6 illustrates four approaches to new capacity.

Alternative Figure S7.6(a) *leads* capacity—that is, acquires capacity to stay ahead of demand, with new capacity being acquired at the beginning of period 1. This capacity handles increased demand until the beginning of period 2. At the beginning of period 2, new capacity is again acquired, allowing the organization to stay ahead of demand until the beginning of period 3. This process can be continued indefinitely into the future. Here capacity is acquired *incrementally*—at the beginning of period 1 *and* at the beginning of period 2.

But managers can also elect to make a larger increase at the beginning of period 1 [Figure S7.6(b)]—an increase that may satisfy expected demand until the beginning of period 3. Excess capacity gives operations managers flexibility. For instance, in the hotel industry, added (extra) capacity in the form of rooms can allow a wider variety of room options and perhaps flexibility in room cleanup schedules. In manufacturing, excess capacity can be used to do more setups, shorten production runs, and drive down inventory costs.

STUDENT TIP◔
Capacity decisions require matching capacity to forecasts, which is always difficult.

VIDEO S7.1
Capacity Planning at Arnold Palmer Hospital

Figure **S7.6**

Four Approaches to Capacity Expansion

Figure S7.6(c) shows an option that *lags* capacity, perhaps using overtime or subcontracting to accommodate excess demand. Finally, Figure S7.6(d) *straddles* demand by building capacity that is "average," sometimes lagging demand and sometimes leading it. Both the lag and straddle option have the advantage of delaying capital expenditure.

In cases where the business climate is stable, deciding between alternatives can be relatively easy. The total cost of each alternative can be computed, and the alternative with the least total cost can be selected. However, when capacity requirements are subject to significant unknowns, "probabilistic" models may be appropriate. One technique for making successful capacity planning decisions with an uncertain demand is decision theory, including the use of expected monetary value.

> **◆ STUDENT TIP**
> Uncertainty in capacity decisions makes EMV a helpful tool.

Applying Expected Monetary Value (EMV) to Capacity Decisions

Determining expected monetary value (EMV) requires specifying alternatives and various states of nature. For capacity-planning situations, the state of nature usually is future demand or market favorability. By assigning probability values to the various states of nature, we can make decisions that maximize the expected value of the alternatives. Example S8 shows how to apply EMV to a capacity decision.

> **LO S7.5** *Determine expected monetary value of a capacity decision*

Example S8

EMV APPLIED TO CAPACITY DECISION

Southern Hospital Supplies, a company that makes hospital gowns, is considering capacity expansion.

APPROACH: ▶ Southern's major alternatives are to do nothing, build a small plant, build a medium plant, or build a large plant. The new facility would produce a new type of gown, and currently the potential or marketability for this product is unknown. If a large plant is built and a favorable market exists, a profit of $100,000 could be realized. An unfavorable market would yield a $90,000 loss. However, a medium plant would earn a $60,000 profit with a favorable market. A $10,000 loss would result from an unfavorable market. A small plant, on the other hand, would return $40,000 with favorable market conditions and lose only $5,000 in an unfavorable market. Of course, there is always the option of doing nothing.

Recent market research indicates that there is a .4 probability of a favorable market, which means that there is also a .6 probability of an unfavorable market. With this information, the alternative that will result in the highest expected monetary value (EMV) can be selected.

SOLUTION ▶ Compute the EMV for each alternative:

$$\text{EMV (large plant)} = (.4)(\$100{,}000) + (.6)(-\$90{,}000) = -\$14{,}000$$
$$\text{EMV (medium plant)} = (.4)(\$60{,}000) + (.6)(-\$10{,}000) = +\$18{,}000$$
$$\text{EMV (small plant)} = (.4)(\$40{,}000) + (.6)(-\$5{,}000) = +\$13{,}000$$
$$\text{EMV (do nothing)} = \$0$$

Based on EMV criteria, Southern should build a medium plant.

INSIGHT ▶ If Southern makes many decisions like this, then determining the EMV for each alternative and selecting the highest EMV is a good decision criterion.

LEARNING EXERCISE ▶ If a new estimate of the loss from a medium plant in an unfavorable market increases to –$20,000, what is the new EMV for this alternative? [Answer: $12,000, which changes the decision because the small plant EMV is now higher.]

RELATED PROBLEMS ▶ S7.32, S7.33

Applying Investment Analysis to Strategy-Driven Investments

Once the strategy implications of potential investments have been considered, traditional investment analysis is appropriate. We introduce the investment aspects of capacity next.

Investment, Variable Cost, and Cash Flow

Because capacity and process alternatives exist, so do options regarding capital investment and variable cost. Managers must choose from among different financial options as well as capacity and process alternatives. Analysis should show the capital investment, variable cost, and cash flows as well as net present value for each alternative.

Net Present Value

Net present value
A means of determining the discounted value of a series of future cash receipts.

Determining the discount value of a series of future cash receipts is known as the net present value technique. By way of introduction, let us consider the time value of money. Say you invest $100.00 in a bank at 5% for 1 year. Your investment will be worth $100.00 + ($100.00)(.05) = $105.00. If you invest the $105.00 for a second year, it will be worth $105.00 + ($105.00)(.05) = $110.25 at the end of the second year. Of course, we could calculate the future value of $100.00 at 5% for as many years as we wanted by simply extending this analysis. However, there is an easier way to express this relationship mathematically. For the first year:

$$\$105 = \$100(1 + .05)$$

For the second year:

$$\$110.25 = \$105(1 + .05) = \$100(1 + .05)^2$$

In general:

$$F = P(1 + i)^N \tag{S7-6}$$

where F = future value (such as $110.25 or $105)
  P = present value (such as $100.00)
  i = interest rate (such as .05)
  N = number of years (such as 1 year or 2 years)

LO S7.6 *Compute* net present value

In most investment decisions, however, we are interested in calculating the present value of a series of future cash receipts. Solving for P, we get:

$$P = \frac{F}{(1 + i)^N} \tag{S7-7}$$

When the number of years is not too large, the preceding equation is effective. However, when the number of years, N, is large, the formula is cumbersome. For 20 years, you would have to compute $(1 + i)^{20}$. Interest-rate tables, such as Table S7.2, can help. We restate the present value equation:

$$P = \frac{F}{(1 + i)^N} = FX \tag{S7-8}$$

where X = a factor from Table S7.2 defined as = $1/(1 + i)^N$ and F = future value

Thus, all we have to do is find the factor X and multiply it by F to calculate the present value, P. The factors, of course, are a function of the interest rate, i, and the number of years, N. Table S7.2 lists some of these factors.

Equations (S7-7) and (S7-8) are used to determine the present value of one future cash amount, but there are situations in which an investment generates a series of uniform and equal

TABLE S7.2	Present Value of $1							
YEAR	5%	6%	7%	8%	9%	10%	12%	14%
1	.952	.943	.935	.926	.917	.909	.893	.877
2	.907	.890	.873	.857	.842	.826	.797	.769
3	.864	.840	.816	.794	.772	.751	.712	.675
4	.823	.792	.763	.735	.708	.683	.636	.592
5	.784	.747	.713	.681	.650	.621	.567	.519
6	.746	.705	.666	.630	.596	.564	.507	.456
7	.711	.665	.623	.583	.547	.513	.452	.400
8	.677	.627	.582	.540	.502	.467	.404	.351
9	.645	.592	.544	.500	.460	.424	.361	.308
10	.614	.558	.508	.463	.422	.386	.322	.270
15	.481	.417	.362	.315	.275	.239	.183	.140
20	.377	.312	.258	.215	.178	.149	.104	.073

cash amounts. This type of investment is called an *annuity*. For example, an investment might yield $300 per year for 3 years. Easy-to-use factors have been developed for the present value of annuities. These factors are shown in Table S7.3. The basic relationship is:

$$S = RX$$

where X = factor from Table S7.3
   S = present value of a series of uniform annual receipts
   R = receipts that are received every year for the life of the investment (the annuity)

The present value of a uniform annual series of amounts is an extension of the present value of a single amount, and thus Table S7.3 can be directly developed from Table S7.2. The factors for any given interest rate in Table S7.3 are the cumulative sum of the values in Table S7.2. In Table S7.2, for example, .943, .890, and .840 are the factors for years 1, 2, and 3 when the interest rate is 6%. The cumulative sum of these factors is 2.673. Now look at the point in Table S7.3 where the interest rate is 6% and the number of years is 3. The factor for the present value of an annuity is 2.673, as you would expect. Alternatively, the PV formula in Microsoft Excel can be used: $=-\text{PV}(\text{interest rate},\text{year},1)$, e.g., $=-\text{PV}(.06,3,1) = 2.673$.

TABLE S7.3	Present Value of an Annuity of $1							
YEAR	5%	6%	7%	8%	9%	10%	12%	14%
1	.952	.943	.935	.926	.917	.909	.893	.877
2	1.859	1.833	1.808	1.783	1.759	1.736	1.690	1.647
3	2.723	2.673	2.624	2.577	2.531	2.487	2.402	2.322
4	3.546	3.465	3.387	3.312	3.240	3.170	3.037	2.914
5	4.329	4.212	4.100	3.993	3.890	3.791	3.605	3.433
6	5.076	4.917	4.766	4.623	4.486	4.355	4.111	3.889
7	5.786	5.582	5.389	5.206	5.033	4.868	4.564	4.288
8	6.463	6.210	5.971	5.747	5.535	5.335	4.968	4.639
9	7.108	6.802	6.515	6.247	5.985	5.759	5.328	4.946
10	7.722	7.360	7.024	6.710	6.418	6.145	5.650	5.216
15	10.380	9.712	9.108	8.559	8.060	7.606	6.811	6.142
20	12.462	11.470	10.594	9.818	9.128	8.514	7.469	6.623

Example S9 shows how to determine the present value of an annuity.

Example S9 | DETERMINING NET PRESENT VALUE OF FUTURE RECEIPTS OF EQUAL VALUE

River Road Medical Clinic is thinking of investing in a sophisticated new piece of medical equipment. It will generate $7,000 per year in receipts for 5 years.

APPROACH ▶ Determine the present value of this cash flow; assume an interest rate of 6%.

SOLUTION ▶ The factor from Table S7.3 (4.212) is obtained by finding that value when the interest rate is 6% and the number of years is 5 (alternatively using the Excel formula $= -PV\,(.06,5,1)$):

$$S = RX = \$7,000(4.212) = \$29,484$$

INSIGHT ▶ There is another way of looking at this example. If you went to a bank and took a loan for $29,484 today, your payments would be $7,000 per year for 5 years if the bank used an interest rate of 6% compounded yearly. Thus, $29,484 is the present value.

LEARNING EXERCISE ▶ If the interest rate is 8%, what is the present value? [Answer: $27,951.]

RELATED PROBLEMS ▶ S7.34–S7.39 (S7.40–S7.45 are available in MyOMLab)

EXCEL OM Data File Ch07SExS9.xls can be found in MyOMLab.

The net present value method is straightforward: You simply compute the present value of all cash flows for each investment alternative. When deciding among investment alternatives, you pick the investment with the highest net present value. Similarly, when making several investments, those with higher net present values are preferable to investments with lower net present values.

Solved Problem S7.4 shows how to use the net present value to choose between investment alternatives.

Although net present value is one of the best approaches to evaluating investment alternatives, it does have its faults. Limitations of the net present value approach include the following:

1. Investments with the same net present value may have significantly different projected lives and different salvage values.
2. Investments with the same net present value may have different cash flows. Different cash flows may make substantial differences in the company's ability to pay its bills.
3. The assumption is that we know future interest rates, which we do not.
4. Payments are always made at the end of the period (week, month, or year), which is not always the case.

Summary

Managers tie equipment selection and capacity decisions to the organization's missions and strategy. Four additional considerations are critical: (1) accurately forecasting demand; (2) understanding the equipment, processes, and capacity increments; (3) finding the optimum operating size; and (4) ensuring the flexibility needed for adjustments in technology, product features and mix, and volumes.

Techniques that are particularly useful to operations managers when making capacity decisions include good forecasting, bottleneck analysis, break-even analysis, expected monetary value, cash flow, and net present value.

The single most important criterion for investment decisions is the contribution to the overall strategic plan and the winning of profitable orders. Successful firms select the correct process and capacity.

Key Terms

Capacity (p. 308)
Design capacity (p. 309)
Effective capacity (p. 309)
Utilization (p. 310)
Efficiency (p. 310)

Capacity analysis (p. 314)
Bottleneck (p. 314)
Process time (p. 314)
Bottleneck time (p. 315)
Throughput time (p. 315)

Theory of constraints (TOC) (p. 317)
Break-even analysis (p. 318)
Net present value (p. 324)

Discussion Questions

1. Distinguish between design capacity and effective capacity.
2. What is effective capacity?
3. What is efficiency?
4. Distinguish between effective capacity and actual output.
5. Explain why doubling the capacity of a bottleneck may not double the system capacity.
6. Distinguish between bottleneck time and throughput time.
7. What is the theory of constraints?
8. What are the assumptions of break-even analysis?
9. What keeps plotted revenue data from falling on a straight line in a break-even analysis?

10. Under what conditions would a firm want its capacity to lag demand? to lead demand?
11. Explain how net present value is an appropriate tool for comparing investments.
12. Describe the five-step process that serves as the basis of the theory of constraints.
13. What are the techniques available to operations managers to deal with a bottleneck operation? Which of these does not decrease throughput time?

Using Software for Break-Even Analysis

Excel, Excel OM, and POM for Windows all handle break-even and cost–volume analysis problems.

CREATING YOUR OWN EXCEL SPREADSHEETS

It is a straightforward task to develop the formulas to conduct a single-product break-even analysis in Excel. Although we do not demonstrate the basics here, Active Model S7.2 provides a working example. Program S7.1 illustrates how you can make an Excel model to solve Example S6, which is a multiproduct break-even analysis.

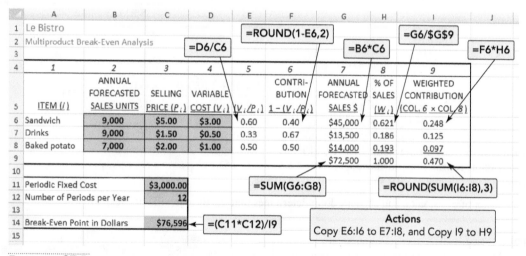

Program **S7.1**

An Excel Spreadsheet for Performing Break-Even Analysis for Example S6

✗ USING EXCEL OM

Excel OM's Break-Even Analysis module provides the Excel formulas needed to compute the break-even points, and the solution and graphical output.

P USING POM FOR WINDOWS

Similar to Excel OM, POM for Windows also contains a break-even/cost–volume analysis module.

Solved Problems   Virtual Office Hours help is available in MyOMLab.

SOLVED PROBLEM S7.1

Sara James Bakery, described in Examples S1 and S2, has decided to increase its facilities by adding one additional process line. The firm will have two process lines, each working 7 days a week, 3 shifts per day, 8 hours per shift, with effective capacity of 300,000 rolls. This addition, however, will reduce overall system efficiency to 85%. Compute the expected production with this new effective capacity.

SOLUTION

Expected production = (Effective capacity)(Efficiency)
= 300,000(.85)
= 255,000 rolls per week

SOLVED PROBLEM S7.2

Marty McDonald has a business packaging software in Wisconsin. His annual fixed cost is $10,000, direct labor is $3.50 per package, and material is $4.50 per package. The selling price will be $12.50 per package. What is the break-even point in dollars? What is break-even in units?

SOLUTION

$$BEP_\$ = \frac{F}{1-(V/P)} = \frac{\$10,000}{1-(\$8.00/\$12.50)} = \frac{\$10,000}{.36} = \$27,777$$

$$BEP_x = \frac{F}{P-V} = \frac{\$10,000}{\$12.50-\$8.00} = \frac{\$10,000}{\$4.50} = 2,222 \text{ units}$$

SOLVED PROBLEM S7.3

John has been asked to determine whether the $22.50 cost of tickets for the community dinner theater will allow the group to achieve break-even and whether the 175 seating capacity is adequate. The cost for each performance of a 10-performance run is $2,500. The facility rental cost for the entire 10 performances is $10,000. Drinks and parking are extra charges and have their own price and variable costs, as shown below:

1	2	3	4	5	6	7	8	9
	SELLING PRICE (P)	VARIABLE COST (V)	PERCENT VARIABLE COST (V/P)	CONTRIBUTION 1 − (V/P)	ESTIMATED QUANTITY OF SALES UNITS (SALES)	DOLLAR SALES (SALES × P)	PERCENT OF SALES	CONTRIBUTION WEIGHTED BY PERCENT SALES (COL.5 × COL. 8)
Tickets with dinner	$22.50	$10.50	0.467	0.533	175	$3,938	0.741	0.395
Drinks	$5.00	$1.75	0.350	0.650	175	$875	0.165	0.107
Parking	$5.00	$2.00	0.400	0.600	100	$500	0.094	0.056
					450	$5,313	1.000	0.558

SOLUTION

$$BEP_\$ = \frac{F}{\sum\left[\left(1-\frac{V_i}{P_i}\right)\times(W_i)\right]} = \frac{\$(10\times2,500)+\$10,000}{0.558} = \frac{\$35,000}{0.558} = \$62,724$$

Revenue for each performance (from column 7) = $5,313
Total forecasted revenue for the 10 performances = (10 × $5,313) = $53,130
Forecasted revenue with this mix of sales shows a break-even of $62,724

Thus, given this mix of costs, sales, and capacity John determines that the theater will not break even.

SOLVED PROBLEM S7.4

Your boss has told you to evaluate the cost of two machines. After some questioning, you are assured that they have the costs shown at the right. Assume:

a) The life of each machine is 3 years.
b) The company thinks it knows how to make 14% on investments no riskier than this one.

Determine via the present value method which machine to purchase.

	MACHINE A	MACHINE B
Original cost	$13,000	$20,000
Labor cost per year	2,000	3,000
Floor space per year	500	600
Energy (electricity) per year	1,000	900
Maintenance per year	2,500	500
Total annual cost	$6,000	$5,000
Salvage value	$2,000	$7,000

SOLUTION

		MACHINE A			MACHINE B		
		COLUMN 1	COLUMN 2	COLUMN 3	COLUMN 4	COLUMN 5	COLUMN 6
Now	Expense	1.000	$13,000	$13,000	1.000	$20,000	$20,000
1 yr.	Expense	.877	6,000	5,262	.877	5,000	4,385
2 yr.	Expense	.769	6,000	4,614	.769	5,000	3,845
3 yr.	Expense	.675	6,000	4,050	.675	5,000	3,375
				$26,926			$31,605
3 yr.	Salvage revenue	.675	$ 2,000	−1,350	.675	$ 7,000	−4,725
				$25,576			$26,880

We use 1.0 for payments with no discount applied against them (that is, when payments are made now, there is no need for a discount). The other values in columns 1 and 4 are from the 14% column and the respective year in Table S7.2 (for example, the intersection of 14% and 1 year is .877, etc.). Columns 3 and 6 are the products of the present value figures times the combined costs. This computation is made for each year and for the salvage value.

The calculation for machine A for the first year is:

$$.877 \times (\$2,000 + \$500 + \$1,000 + \$2,500) = \$5,262$$

The salvage value of the product is subtracted from the summed costs, because it is a receipt of cash. Because the sum of the net costs for machine B is larger than the sum of the net costs for machine A, machine A is the low-cost purchase, and your boss should be so informed.

SOLVED PROBLEM S7.5

T. Smunt Manufacturing Corp. has the process displayed below. The drilling operation occurs separately from and simultaneously with the sawing and sanding operations. The product only needs to go through one of the three assembly operations (the assembly operations are "parallel").

a) Which operation is the bottleneck?
b) What is the throughput time for the overall system?

c) If the firm operates 8 hours per day, 22 days per month, what is the monthly capacity of the manufacturing process?
d) Suppose that a second drilling machine is added, and it takes the same time as the original drilling machine. What is the new bottleneck time of the system?
e) Suppose that a second drilling machine is added, and it takes the same time as the original drilling machine. What is the new throughput time?

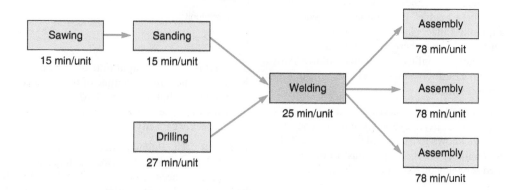

SOLUTION

a) The time for *assembly* is 78 minutes/3 operators = 26 minutes per unit, so the station that takes the longest time, hence the bottleneck, is *drilling*, at 27 minutes.
b) System throughput time is the maximum of (15 + 15 + 25 + 78), (27 + 25 + 78) = maximum of (133, 130) = 133 minutes
c) Monthly capacity = (60 minutes)(8 hours)(22 days)/27 minutes per unit = 10,560 minutes per month/27 minutes per unit = 391.11 units/month.
d) The bottleneck shifts to *Assembly*, with a time of 26 minutes per unit.
e) Redundancy does not affect throughput time. It is still 133 minutes.

Problems   *Note:* **Px** means the problem may be solved with POM for Windows and/or Excel OM.

Problems S7.1–S7.8 relate to Capacity

• **S7.1**   Amy Xia's plant was designed to produce 7,000 hammers per day but is limited to making 6,000 hammers per day because of the time needed to change equipment between styles of hammers. What is the utilization?

• **S7.2**   For the past month, the plant in Problem S7.1, which has an effective capacity of 6,500, has made only 4,500 hammers per day because of material delay, employee absences, and other problems. What is its efficiency?

•• **S7.3**   If a plant has an effective capacity of 6,500 and an efficiency of 88%, what is the actual (planned) output?

• **S7.4**   A plant has an effective capacity of 900 units per day and produces 800 units per day with its product mix; what is its efficiency?

• **S7.5**   Material delays have routinely limited production of household sinks to 400 units per day. If the plant efficiency is 80%, what is the effective capacity?

•• **S7.6**   The effective capacity and efficiency for the next quarter at MMU Mfg. in Waco, Texas, for each of three departments are shown:

DEPARTMENT	EFFECTIVE CAPACITY	RECENT EFFICIENCY
Design	93,600	.95
Fabrication	156,000	1.03
Finishing	62,400	1.05

Compute the expected production for next quarter for each department.

•• **S7.7**   Southeastern Oklahoma State University's business program has the facilities and faculty to handle an enrollment of 2,000 new students per semester. However, in an effort to limit class sizes to a "reasonable" level (under 200, generally), Southeastern's dean, Holly Lutze, placed a ceiling on enrollment of 1,500 new students. Although there was ample demand for business courses last semester, conflicting schedules allowed only 1,450 new students to take business courses. What are the utilization and efficiency of this system?

•• **S7.8**   Under ideal conditions, a service bay at a Fast Lube can serve 6 cars per hour. The effective capacity and efficiency of a Fast Lube service bay are known to be 5.5 and 0.880, respectively. What is the minimum number of service bays Fast Lube needs to achieve an anticipated servicing of 200 cars per 8-hour day?

Problems S7.9–S7.15 relate to Bottleneck Analysis and the Theory of Constraints

• **S7.9**   A production line at V. J. Sugumaran's machine shop has three stations. The first station can process a unit in 10 minutes. The second station has two identical machines, each of which can process a unit in 12 minutes. (Each unit only needs to be processed on one of the two machines.) The third station can process a unit in 8 minutes. Which station is the bottleneck station?

•• **S7.10**   A work cell at Chris Ellis Commercial Laundry has a workstation with two machines, and each unit produced at the station needs to be processed by both of the machines. (The same unit cannot be worked on by both machines simultaneously.) Each machine has a production capacity of 4 units per hour. What is the throughput time of the work cell?

•• **S7.11**   The three-station work cell illustrated in Figure S7.7 has a product that must go through one of the two machines at station 1 (they are parallel) before proceeding to station 2.

Figure **S7.7**

a) What is the bottleneck time of the system?
b) What is the bottleneck station of this work cell?
c) What is the throughput time?
d) If the firm operates 10 hours per day, 5 days per week, what is the weekly capacity of this work cell?

•• **S7.12**   The three-station work cell at Pullman Mfg., Inc. is illustrated in Figure S7.8. It has two machines at station 1 in parallel (i.e., the product needs to go through only one of the two machines before proceeding to station 2).

Figure **S7.8**

a) What is the throughput time of this work cell?
b) What is the bottleneck time of this work cell?
c) What is the bottleneck station?
d) If the firm operates 8 hours per day, 6 days per week, what is the weekly capacity of this work cell?

•• **S7.13**   The Pullman Mfg., Inc., three-station work cell illustrated in Figure S7.8 has two machines at station 1 in parallel. (The product needs to go through only one of the two machines before proceeding to station 2.) The manager, Ms. Hartley, has asked you to evaluate the system if she adds a parallel machine at station 2.
a) What is the throughput time of the new work cell?
b) What is the bottleneck time of the new work cell?
c) If the firm operates 8 hours per day, 6 days per week, what is the weekly capacity of this work cell?
d) How did the addition of the second machine at workstation 2 affect the performance of the work cell from Problem S7.12?

• **S7.14**   Klassen Toy Company, Inc., assembles two parts (parts 1 and 2): Part 1 is first processed at workstation A for 15 minutes per unit and then processed at workstation B for

10 minutes per unit. Part 2 is simultaneously processed at work-station C for 20 minutes per unit. Work stations B and C feed the parts to an assembler at workstation D, where the two parts are assembled. The time at workstation D is 15 minutes.
a) What is the bottleneck of this process?
b) What is the hourly capacity of the process?

•• **S7.15**   A production process at Kenneth Day Manufacturing is shown in Figure S7.9. The drilling operation occurs separately from, and simultaneously with, sawing and sanding, which are

independent and sequential operations. A product needs to go through only one of the three assembly operations (the operations are in parallel).
a) Which operation is the bottleneck?
b) What is the bottleneck time?
c) What is the throughput time of the overall system?
d) If the firm operates 8 hours per day, 20 days per month, what is the monthly capacity of the manufacturing process?

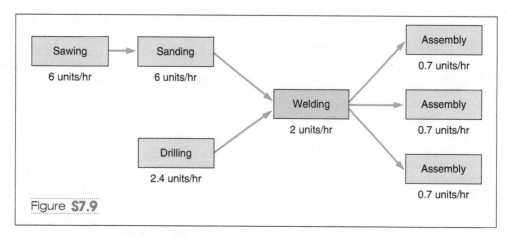

Figure **S7.9**

Problems S7.16–S7.31 relate to Break-Even Analysis

• **S7.16**   Smithson Cutting is opening a new line of scissors for supermarket distribution. It estimates its fixed cost to be $500.00 and its variable cost to be $0.50 per unit. Selling price is expected to average $0.75 per unit.
a) What is Smithson's break-even point in units?
b) What is the break-even point in dollars? **Px**

• **S7.17**   Markland Manufacturing intends to increase capacity by overcoming a bottleneck operation by adding new equipment. Two vendors have presented proposals. The fixed costs for proposal A are $50,000, and for proposal B, $70,000. The variable cost for A is $12.00, and for B, $10.00. The revenue generated by each unit is $20.00.
a) What is the break-even point in units for proposal A?
b) What is the break-even point in units for proposal B? **Px**

• **S7.18**   Using the data in Problem S7.17:
a) What is the break-even point in dollars for proposal A if you add $10,000 installation to the fixed cost?
b) What is the break-even point in dollars for proposal B if you add $10,000 installation to the fixed cost? **Px**

• **S7.19**   Given the data in Problem S7.17, at what volume (units) of output would the two alternatives yield the same profit? **Px**

•• **S7.20**   Janelle Heinke, the owner of Ha'Peppas!, is consider-ing a new oven in which to bake the firm's signature dish, vegetar-ian pizza. Oven type A can handle 20 pizzas an hour. The fixed costs associated with oven A are $20,000 and the variable costs are $2.00 per pizza. Oven B is larger and can handle 40 pizzas an hour. The fixed costs associated with oven B are $30,000 and the variable costs are $1.25 per pizza. The pizzas sell for $14 each.
a) What is the break-even point for each oven?
b) If the owner expects to sell 9,000 pizzas, which oven should she purchase?

c) If the owner expects to sell 12,000 pizzas, which oven should she purchase?
d) At what volume should Janelle switch ovens? **Px**

•• **S7.21**   Given the following data, calculate a) BEP_x; b) $BEP_\$$; and c) the profit at 100,000 units:

$$P = \$8/\text{unit} \quad V = \$4/\text{unit} \quad F = \$50,000 \ \text{Px}$$

•• **S7.22**   You are considering opening a copy service in the student union. You estimate your fixed cost at $15,000 and the variable cost of each copy sold at $.01. You expect the selling price to average $.05.
a) What is the break-even point in dollars?
b) What is the break-even point in units? **Px**

•• **S7.23**   An electronics firm is currently manufacturing an item that has a variable cost of $.50 per unit and a selling price of $1.00 per unit. Fixed costs are $14,000. Current volume is

30,000 units. The firm can substantially improve the product quality by adding a new piece of equipment at an additional fixed cost of $6,000. Variable cost would increase to $.60, but volume should jump to 50,000 units due to a higher-quality product. Should the company buy the new equipment? **Px**

•• **S7.24** The electronics firm in Problem S7.23 is now considering the new equipment and increasing the selling price to $1.10 per unit. With the higher-quality product, the new volume is expected to be 45,000 units. Under these circumstances, should the company purchase the new equipment and increase the selling price? **Px**

•••• **S7.25** Zan Azlett and Angela Zesiger have joined forces to start A&Z Lettuce Products, a processor of packaged shredded lettuce for institutional use. Zan has years of food processing experience, and Angela has extensive commercial food preparation experience. The process will consist of opening crates of lettuce and then sorting, washing, slicing, preserving, and finally packaging the prepared lettuce. Together, with help from vendors, they think they can adequately estimate demand, fixed costs, revenues, and variable cost per 5-pound bag of lettuce. They think a largely manual process will have monthly fixed costs of $37,500 and variable costs of $1.75 per bag. A more mechanized process will have fixed costs of $75,000 per month with variable costs of $1.25 per 5-pound bag. They expect to sell the shredded lettuce for $2.50 per 5-pound bag.
a) What is the break-even quantity for the manual process?
b) What is the revenue at the break-even quantity for the manual process?
c) What is the break-even quantity for the mechanized process?
d) What is the revenue at the break-even quantity for the mechanized process?
e) What is the monthly profit or loss of the *manual* process if they expect to sell 60,000 bags of lettuce per month?
f) What is the monthly profit or loss of the *mechanized* process if they expect to sell 60,000 bags of lettuce per month?
g) At what quantity would Zan and Angela be indifferent to the process selected?
h) Over what range of demand would the *manual* process be preferred over the mechanized process? Over what range of demand would the *mechanized* process be preferred over the manual process? **Px**

•••• **S7.26** As a prospective owner of a club known as the Red Rose, you are interested in determining the volume of sales dollars necessary for the coming year to reach the break-even point. You have decided to break down the sales for the club into four categories, the first category being beer. Your estimate of the beer sales is that 30,000 drinks will be served. The selling price for each unit will average $1.50; the cost is $.75. The second major category is meals, which you expect to be 10,000 units with an average price of $10.00 and a cost of $5.00. The third major category is desserts and wine, of which you also expect to sell 10,000 units, but with an average price of $2.50 per unit sold and a cost of $1.00 per unit. The final category is lunches and inexpensive sandwiches, which you expect to total 20,000 units at an average price of $6.25 with a food cost of $3.25. Your fixed cost (i.e., rent, utilities, and so on) is $1,800 per month plus $2,000 per month for entertainment.
a) What is your break-even point in dollars per month?
b) What is the expected number of meals each day if you are open 30 days a month?

••• **S7.27** As manager of the St. Cloud Theatre Company, you have decided that concession sales will support themselves. The following table provides the information you have been able to put together thus far:

ITEM	SELLING PRICE	VARIABLE COST	% OF REVENUE
Soft drink	$1.00	$.65	25
Wine	1.75	.95	25
Coffee	1.00	.30	30
Candy	1.00	.30	20

Last year's manager, Jim Freeland, has advised you to be sure to add 10% of variable cost as a waste allowance for all categories.

You estimate labor cost to be $250.00 (5 booths with 2 people each). Even if nothing is sold, your labor cost will be $250.00, so you decide to consider this a fixed cost. Booth rental, which is a contractual cost at $50.00 for *each* booth per night, is also a fixed cost.
a) What is the break-even volume per evening performance?
b) How much wine would you expect to sell each evening at the break-even point?

Additional problems **S7.28–S7.31** *are available in* MyOMLab.

Problems S7.32–S7.33 relate to Applying Expected Monetary Value (EMV) to Capacity Decisions

•• **S7.32** James Lawson's Bed and Breakfast, in a small historic Mississippi town, must decide how to subdivide (remodel) the large old home that will become its inn. There are three alternatives: Option A would modernize all baths and combine rooms, leaving the inn with four suites, each suitable for two to four adults. Option B would modernize only the second floor; the results would be six suites, four for two to four adults, two for two adults only. Option C (the status quo option) leaves all walls intact. In this case, there are eight rooms available, but only two are suitable for four adults, and four rooms will not have private baths. Below are the details of profit and demand patterns that will accompany each option:

ALTERNATIVES	ANNUAL PROFIT UNDER VARIOUS DEMAND PATTERNS			
	HIGH	P	AVERAGE	P
A (modernize all)	$90,000	.5	$25,000	.5
B (modernize 2nd)	$80,000	.4	$70,000	.6
C (status quo)	$60,000	.3	$55,000	.7

Which option has the highest expected monetary value? **Px**

•••• **S7.33** As operations manager of Holz Furniture, you must make a decision about adding a line of rustic furniture. In discussing the possibilities with your sales manager, Steve Gilbert, you decide that there will definitely be a market and that your firm should enter that market. However, because rustic furniture has a different finish than your standard offering, you decide you need another process line. There is no doubt in your mind about the decision, and you are sure that you should have a second process. But you do question how large to make it. A large process line is going to cost $400,000; a small process line will cost $300,000. The question, therefore, is the demand for rustic furniture. After extensive discussion with Mr. Gilbert and Tim Ireland of Ireland Market Research, Inc., you determine that the best estimate you can make is that there is a two-out-of-three chance of profit from sales as large as $600,000 and a one-out-of-three chance as low as $300,000.

With a large process line, you could handle the high figure of $600,000. However, with a small process line you could not and would be forced to expand (at a cost of $150,000), after which time your profit from sales would be $500,000 rather than the $600,000 because of the lost time in expanding the process. If you do not expand the small process, your profit from sales would be held to $400,000. If you build a small process and the demand is low, you can handle all of the demand.

Should you open a large or small process line?

Problems S7.34–S7.45 relate to Applying Investment Analysis to Strategy-Driven Investments

·· S7.34 What is the net present value of an investment that costs $75,000 and has a salvage value of $45,000? The annual profit from the investment is $15,000 each year for 5 years. The cost of capital at this risk level is 12%. $\mathbf{P_X}$

· S7.35 The initial cost of an investment is $65,000 and the cost of capital is 10%. The return is $16,000 per year for 8 years. What is the net present value? $\mathbf{P_X}$

· S7.36 What is the present value of $5,600 when the interest rate is 8% and the return of $5,600 will not be received for 15 years? $\mathbf{P_X}$

·· S7.37 Tim Smunt has been asked to evaluate two machines. After some investigation, he determines that they have the costs shown in the following table. He is told to assume that:
1. The life of each machine is 3 years.
2. The company thinks it knows how to make 12% on investments no more risky than this one.
3. Labor and maintenance are paid at the end of the year.

	MACHINE A	MACHINE B
Original cost	$10,000	$20,000
Labor per year	2,000	4,000
Maintenance per year	4,000	1,000
Salvage value	2,000	7,000

Determine, via the present value method, which machine Tim should recommend.

···· S7.38 Your boss has told you to evaluate two ovens for Tink-the-Tinkers, a gourmet sandwich shop. After some questioning of vendors and receipt of specifications, you are assured that the ovens have the attributes and costs shown in the following table. The following two assumptions are appropriate:
1. The life of each machine is 5 years.
2. The company thinks it knows how to make 14% on investments no more risky than this one.
a) Determine via the present value method which machine to tell your boss to purchase.
b) What assumption are you making about the ovens?
c) What assumptions are you making in your methodology?

	THREE SMALL OVENS AT $1,250 EACH	TWO LARGE OVENS AT $2,500 EACH
Original cost	$3,750	$5,000
Labor per year in excess of larger models	$ 750 (total)	
Cleaning/ maintenance	$ 750 ($250 each)	$ 400 ($200 each)
Salvage value	$ 750 ($250 each)	$1,000 ($500 each)

···· S7.39 Bold's Gym, a health club chain, is considering expanding into a new location: the initial investment would be $1 million in equipment, renovation, and a 6-year lease, and its annual upkeep and expenses would be $75,000 (paid at the beginning of the year). Its planning horizon is 6 years out, and at the end, it can sell the equipment for $50,000. Club capacity is 500 members who would pay an annual fee of $600. Bold's expects to have no problems filling membership slots. Assume that the interest rate is 10%. (See Table S7.2.)
a) What is the present value profit/loss of the deal?
b) The club is considering offering a special deal to the members in the first year. For $3,000 upfront they get a full 6-year membership (i.e., 1 year free). Would it make financial sense to offer this deal?

Additional problems S7.40–S7.45 are available in MyOMLab.

CASE STUDY

Capacity Planning at Arnold Palmer Hospital

Video Case

Since opening day, Arnold Palmer Hospital has experienced an explosive growth in demand for its services. One of only six hospitals in the U.S. to specialize in health care for women and children, Arnold Palmer Hospital has cared for over 1,500,000 patients who came to the Orlando facility from all 50 states and more than 100 other countries. With patient satisfaction scores in the top 10% of U.S. hospitals surveyed (over 95% of patients would recommend the hospital to others), one of Arnold Palmer Hospital's main focuses is delivery of babies. Originally built with

281 beds and a capacity for 6,500 births per year, the hospital steadily approached and then passed 10,000 births. Looking at Table S7.4, Executive Director Kathy Swanson knew an expansion was necessary.

With continuing population growth in its market area serving 18 central Florida counties, Arnold Palmer Hospital was delivering the equivalent of a kindergarten class of babies every day and still not meeting demand. Supported with substantial additional demographic analysis, the hospital was ready to move ahead with a capacity expansion plan and a new 11-story hospital building across the street from the existing facility.

Thirty-five planning teams were established to study such issues as (1) specific forecasts, (2) services that would transfer to the new facility, (3) services that would remain in the existing facility, (4) staffing needs, (5) capital equipment, (6) pro forma accounting data, and (7) regulatory requirements. Ultimately, Arnold Palmer Hospital was ready to move ahead with a budget of $100 million and a commitment to an additional 150 beds. But given the growth of the central Florida region, Swanson decided to expand the hospital in stages: the top two floors would be empty interiors ("shell") to be completed at a later date, and the fourth-floor operating room could be doubled in size when needed. "With the new facility in place, we are now able to handle up to 16,000 births per year," says Swanson.

Discussion Questions*

1. Given the capacity planning discussion in the text (see Figure S7.6), what approach is being taken by Arnold Palmer Hospital toward matching capacity to demand?
2. What kind of major changes could take place in Arnold Palmer Hospital's demand forecast that would leave the hospital with an underutilized facility (namely, what are the risks connected with this capacity decision)?
3. Use regression analysis to forecast the point at which Swanson needs to "build out" the top two floors of the new building, namely, when demand will exceed 16,000 births.

*You may wish to view the video that accompanies the case before addressing these questions.

TABLE S7.4	Births at Arnold Palmer Hospital
YEAR	**BIRTHS**
1995	6,144
1996	6,230
1997	6,432
1998	6,950
1999	7,377
2000	8,655
2001	9,536
2002	9,825
2003	10,253
2004	10,555
2005	12,316
2006	13,070
2007	14,028
2008	14,241
2009	13,050
2010	12,571
2011	12,978
2012	13,529
2013	13,576
2014	13,994

- **Additional Case Study:** Visit MyOMLab for this free case study:
  Southwestern University (D): Requires the development of a multiproduct break-even solution.

Endnote

1. See E. M. Goldratt and J. Cox, *The Goal: A Process of Ongoing Improvement*, 3rd rev. ed., Great Barrington, MA: North River Press, 2004.

Supplement 7 *Rapid* Review

Main Heading	Review Material	MyOMLab
CAPACITY (pp. 308–314)	■ **Capacity**—The "throughput," or number of units a facility can hold, receive, store, or produce in a period of time. Capacity decisions often determine capital requirements and therefore a large portion of fixed cost. Capacity also determines whether demand will be satisfied or whether facilities will be idle. *Determining facility size, with an objective of achieving high levels of utilization and a high return on investment, is critical.* Capacity planning can be viewed in three time horizons: 1. *Long-range* (> 1 year)—Adding facilities and long lead-time equipment 2. *Intermediate-range* (3–18 months)—"Aggregate planning" tasks, including adding equipment, personnel, and shifts; subcontracting; and building or using inventory 3. *Short-range* (< 3 months)—Scheduling jobs and people, and allocating machinery ■ **Design capacity**—The theoretical maximum output of a system in a given period, under ideal conditions. Most organizations operate their facilities at a rate less than the design capacity. ■ **Effective capacity**—The capacity a firm can expect to achieve, given its product mix, methods of scheduling, maintenance, and standards of quality. ■ **Utilization**—Actual output as a percent of design capacity. ■ **Efficiency**—Actual output as a percent of effective capacity. $$\text{Utilization} = \text{Actual output/Design capacity} \quad (S7\text{-}1)$$ $$\text{Efficiency} = \text{Actual output/Effective capacity} \quad (S7\text{-}2)$$ When demand exceeds capacity, a firm may be able to curtail demand simply by raising prices, increasing lead times (which may be inevitable), and discouraging marginally profitable business. When capacity exceeds demand, a firm may want to stimulate demand through price reductions or aggressive marketing, or it may accommodate the market via product changes. In the service sector, scheduling customers is *demand management,* and scheduling the workforce is *capacity management.* When demand and capacity are fairly well matched, demand management in services can often be handled with appointments, reservations, or a first-come, first-served rule. Otherwise, discounts based on time of day may be used (e.g., "early bird" specials, matinee pricing). When managing demand in services is not feasible, managing capacity through changes in full-time, temporary, or part-time staff may be an option.	Concept Questions: 1.1–1.4 Problems: S7.1–S7.8 Virtual Office Hours for Solved Problem: S7.1 ACTIVE MODEL S7.1
BOTTLENECK ANALYSIS AND THE THEORY OF CONSTRAINTS (pp. 314–318)	■ **Capacity analysis**—Determining throughput capacity of workstations or an entire production system. ■ **Bottleneck**—The limiting factor or constraint in a system. ■ **Process time**—The time to produce a unit (or batch) at a workstation. ■ **Bottleneck time**—The process time of the longest (slowest) process. ■ **Throughput time**—The time it takes for a product to go through the production process *with no waiting,* i.e., the time of the longest path through the system. If *n* parallel (redundant) operations are added, the process time of the combined operations will equal $1/n$ times the process time of the original. With simultaneous processing, an order or product is essentially *split* into different paths to be rejoined later on. The longest path through the system is deemed the throughput time. ■ **Theory of constraints (TOC)**—A body of knowledge that deals with anything limiting an organization's ability to achieve its goals.	Concept Questions: 2.1–2.4 Problems: S7.9–S7.15 Virtual Office Hours for Solved Problem: S7.5

MyOMLab

Main Heading	Review Material	
BREAK-EVEN ANALYSIS (pp. 318–322)	■ **Break-even analysis**—A means of finding the point, in dollars and units, at which costs equal revenues. *Fixed costs* are costs that exist even if no units are produced. Variable costs are those that vary with the volume of units produced. In the break-even model, costs and revenue are assumed to increase linearly. $$\text{Break-even in units} = \frac{\text{Total Fixed cost}}{\text{Price} - \text{Variable cost}} = \frac{F}{P - V} \quad (S7\text{-}3)$$ $$\text{Break-even in dollars} = \frac{\text{Total Fixed cost}}{1 - \frac{\text{Variable cost}}{\text{Price}}} = \frac{F}{1 - \left(\frac{V}{P}\right)} \quad (S7\text{-}4)$$ $$\text{Multiproduct break-even point in dollars} = BEP_\$ = \frac{F}{\sum\left[\left(1 - \frac{V_i}{P_i}\right) \times (W_i)\right]} \quad (S7\text{-}5)$$	Concept Questions: 3.1–3.4 Problems: S7.16–S7.31 Virtual Office Hours for Solved Problem: S7.3 ACTIVE MODEL S7.2
REDUCING RISK WITH INCREMENTAL CHANGES (pp. 322–323)	Demand growth is usually in small units, while capacity additions are likely to be both instantaneous and in large units. To reduce risk, incremental changes that hedge demand forecasts may be a good option. Four approaches to capacity expansion are (1) *leading* strategy, with incremental expansion, (2) *leading* strategy with one step expansion, (3) *lag* strategy, and (4) *straddle* strategy. Both lag strategy and straddle strategy delay capital expenditure.	Concept Questions: 4.1–4.4 **VIDEO S7.1** Capacity Planning at Arnold Palmer Hospital
APPLYING EXPECTED MONETARY VALUE (p. 323)	Determining expected monetary value requires specifying alternatives and various states of nature (e.g., demand or market favorability). By assigning probability values to the various states of nature, we can make decisions that maximize the expected value of the alternatives.	Concept Questions: 5.1–5.4 Problems: S7.32–S7.33
APPLYING INVESTMENT ANALYSIS TO STRATEGY-DRIVEN INVESTMENTS (pp. 324–326)	■ **Net present value**—A means of determining the discounted value of a series of future cash receipts. $$F = P(1 + i)^N \quad (S7\text{-}6)$$ $$P = \frac{F}{(1 + i)^N} \quad (S7\text{-}7)$$ $$P = \frac{F}{(1 + i)^N} = FX \quad (S7\text{-}8)$$ When making several investments, those with higher net present values are preferable to investments with lower net present values.	Concept Questions: 6.1–6.4 Problems: S7.34–S7.45 Virtual Office Hours for Solved Problem: S7.4

Self Test

■ **Before taking the self-test,** refer to the learning objectives listed at the beginning of the supplement and the key terms listed at the end of the supplement.

LO S7.1 Capacity decisions should be made on the basis of:
a) building sustained competitive advantage.
b) good financial returns.
c) a coordinated plan.
d) integration into the company's strategy.
e) all of the above.

LO S7.2 Effective capacity is:
a) the capacity a firm expects to achieve, given the current operating constraints.
b) the percentage of design capacity actually achieved.
c) the percentage of capacity actually achieved.
d) actual output.
e) efficiency.

LO S7.3 System capacity is based on:
a) the bottleneck.
b) throughput time.
c) time of the fastest station.
d) throughput time plus waiting time.
e) none of the above.

LO S7.4 The break-even point is:
a) adding processes to meet the point of changing product demands.
b) improving processes to increase throughput.
c) the point in dollars or units at which cost equals revenue.
d) adding or removing capacity to meet demand.
e) the total cost of a process alternative.

LO S7.5 Expected monetary value is most appropriate:
a) when the payoffs are equal.
b) when the probability of each decision alternative is known.
c) when probabilities are the same.
d) when both revenue and cost are known.
e) when probabilities of each state of nature are known.

LO S7.6 Net present value:
a) is greater if cash receipts occur later rather than earlier.
b) is greater if cash receipts occur earlier rather than later.
c) is revenue minus fixed cost.
d) is preferred over break-even analysis.
e) is greater if $100 monthly payments are received in a lump sum ($1,200) at the end of the year.

Answers: LO S7.1. e; LO S7.2. a; LO S7.3. a; LO S7.4. c; LO S7.5. b; LO S7.6. b.

Inventory Management

12 CHAPTER

Alaska Airlines

10 OM STRATEGY DECISIONS

- Design of Goods and Services
- Managing Quality
- Process Strategy
- Location Strategies
- Layout Strategies
- Human Resources
- Supply-Chain Management
- *Inventory Management*
  - ■ *Independent Demand (Ch. 12)*
  - ■ Dependent Demand (Ch. 14)
  - ■ Lean Operations (Ch. 16)
- Scheduling
- Maintenance

Inventory Management Provides Competitive Advantage at Amazon.com

W hen Jeff Bezos opened his revolutionary business in 1995, Amazon.com was intended to be a "virtual" retailer—no inventory, no warehouses, no overhead—just a bunch of computers taking orders for books and authorizing others to fill them. Things clearly didn't work out that way. Now, Amazon stocks millions of items of inventory, amid hundreds of thousands of bins on shelves in over 150 warehouses around the world. Additionally, Amazon's

Marilyn Newton/Reno Gazette–Journal

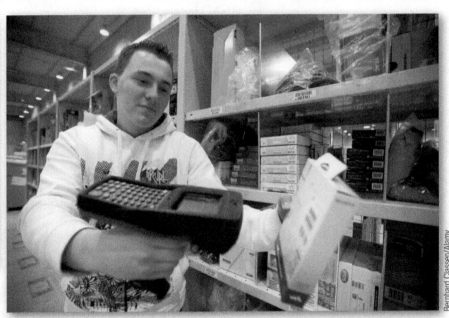

Bernhard Classen/Alamy

1. You order three items, and a computer in Seattle takes charge. A computer assigns your order—a book, a game, and a digital camera—to one of Amazon's massive U.S. distribution centers.

2. The "flow meister" at the distribution center receives your order. She determines which workers go where to fill your order.

3. Amazon's current system doubles the picking speed of manual operators and drops the error rate to nearly zero.

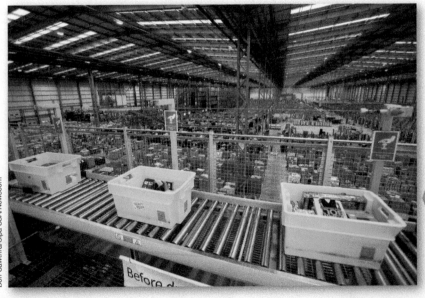

Ben Cawthra/Sipa USA/Newscom

4. Your items are put into crates on moving belts. Each item goes into a large yellow crate that contains many customers' orders. When full, the crates ride a series of conveyor belts that wind more than 10 miles through the plant at a constant speed of 2.9 feet per second. The bar code on each item is scanned 15 times, by machines and by many of the 600 workers. The goal is to reduce errors to zero—returns are very expensive.

5. All three items converge in a chute and then inside a box. All the crates arrive at a central point where bar codes are matched with order numbers to determine who gets what. Your three items end up in a 3-foot-wide chute—one of several thousand—and are placed into a corrugated box with a new bar code that identifies your order. Picking is sequenced to reduce operator travel.

6. Any gifts you've chosen are wrapped by hand. Amazon trains an elite group of gift wrappers, each of whom processes 30 packages an hour.

software is so good that Amazon sells its order taking, processing, and billing expertise to others. It is estimated that 200 million items are now available via the Amazon Web site.

Bezos expects the customer experience at Amazon to be one that yields the lowest price, the fastest delivery, and an error-free order fulfillment process so no other contact with Amazon is necessary. Exchanges and returns are very expensive.

Managing this massive inventory precisely is the key for Amazon to be the world-class leader in warehouse automation and management. The time to receive, process, and position the stock in storage and to then accurately "pull" and package an order requires a labor investment of less than 3 minutes. And 70% of these orders are multiproduct orders. This underlines the high benchmark that Amazon has achieved. This is world-class performance.

When you place an order with Amazon .com, you are doing business with a company that obtains competitive advantage through inventory management. This *Global Company Profile* shows how Amazon does it.

Adrian Sherratt/Alamy

7. The box is packed, taped, weighed, and labeled before leaving the warehouse in a truck. A typical plant is designed to ship as many as 200,000 pieces a day. About 60% of orders are shipped via the U.S. Postal Service; nearly everything else goes through United Parcel Service.

8. Your order arrives at your doorstep. In 1 or 2 days, your order is delivered.

The Importance of Inventory

As Amazon.com well knows, inventory is one of the most expensive assets of many companies, representing as much as 50% of total invested capital. Operations managers around the globe have long recognized that good inventory management is crucial. On the one hand, a firm can reduce costs by reducing inventory. On the other hand, production may stop and customers become dissatisfied when an item is out of stock. *The objective of inventory management is to strike a balance between inventory investment and customer service.* You can never achieve a low-cost strategy without good inventory management.

All organizations have some type of inventory planning and control system. A bank has methods to control its inventory of cash. A hospital has methods to control blood supplies and pharmaceuticals. Government agencies, schools, and, of course, virtually every manufacturing and production organization are concerned with inventory planning and control.

In cases involving physical products, the organization must determine whether to produce goods or to purchase them. Once this decision has been made, the next step is to forecast demand, as discussed in Chapter 4. Then operations managers determine the inventory necessary to service that demand. In this chapter, we discuss the functions, types, and management of inventory. We then address two basic inventory issues: how much to order and when to order.

Functions of Inventory

VIDEO 12.1
Managing Inventory at Frito-Lay

Inventory can serve several functions that add flexibility to a firm's operations. The four functions of inventory are:

1. *To provide a selection of goods for anticipated customer demand and to separate the firm from fluctuations in that demand.* Such inventories are typical in retail establishments.
2. To *decouple various parts of the production process.* For example, if a firm's supplies fluctuate, extra inventory may be necessary to decouple the production process from suppliers.
3. To *take advantage of quantity discounts*, because purchases in larger quantities may reduce the cost of goods or their delivery.
4. To *hedge against inflation* and upward price changes.

Types of Inventory

Raw material inventory
Materials that are usually purchased but have yet to enter the manufacturing process.

Work-in-process (WIP) inventory
Products or components that are no longer raw materials but have yet to become finished products.

Maintenance/repair/operating (MRO) inventory
Maintenance, repair, and operating materials.

To accommodate the functions of inventory, firms maintain four types of inventories: (1) raw material inventory, (2) work-in-process inventory, (3) maintenance/repair/operating supply (MRO) inventory, and (4) finished-goods inventory.

Raw material inventory has been purchased but not processed. This inventory can be used to decouple (i.e., separate) suppliers from the production process. However, the preferred approach is to eliminate supplier variability in quality, quantity, or delivery time so that separation is not needed. Work-in-process (WIP) inventory is components or raw material that have undergone some change but are not completed. WIP exists because of the time it takes for a product to be made (called *cycle time*). Reducing cycle time reduces inventory. Often this task is not difficult: during most of the time a product is "being made," it is in fact sitting idle. As Figure 12.1 shows, actual work time, or "run" time, is a small portion of the material flow time, perhaps as low as 5%.

MROs are inventories devoted to maintenance/repair/operating supplies necessary to keep machinery and processes productive. They exist because the need and timing for maintenance and

Figure **12.1**

The Material Flow Cycle

Most of the time that work is in-process (95% of the cycle time) is not productive time.

repair of some equipment are unknown. Although the demand for MRO inventory is often a function of maintenance schedules, other unscheduled MRO demands must be anticipated. Finished-goods inventory is completed product awaiting shipment. Finished goods may be inventoried because future customer demands are unknown.

Finished-goods inventory
An end item ready to be sold, but still an asset on the company's books.

Managing Inventory

Operations managers establish systems for managing inventory. In this section, we briefly examine two ingredients of such systems: (1) how inventory items can be classified (called *ABC analysis*) and (2) how accurate inventory records can be maintained. We will then look at inventory control in the service sector.

ABC Analysis

ABC analysis divides on-hand inventory into three classifications on the basis of annual dollar volume. ABC analysis is an inventory application of what is known as the *Pareto principle* (named after Vilfredo Pareto, a 19th-century Italian economist). The Pareto principle states that there are a "critical few and trivial many." The idea is to establish inventory policies that focus resources on the *few critical* inventory parts and not the many trivial ones. It is not realistic to monitor inexpensive items with the same intensity as very expensive items.

To determine annual dollar volume for ABC analysis, we measure the *annual demand* of each inventory item times the *cost per unit*. Class A items are those on which the annual dollar volume is high. Although such items may represent only about 15% of the total inventory items, they represent 70% to 80% of the total dollar usage. Class B items are those inventory items of medium annual dollar volume. These items may represent about 30% of inventory items and 15% to 25% of the total value. Those with low annual dollar volume are Class C, which may represent only 5% of the annual dollar volume but about 55% of the total inventory items.

Graphically, the inventory of many organizations would appear as presented in Figure 12.2.

ABC analysis
A method for dividing on-hand inventory into three classifications based on annual dollar volume.

STUDENT TIP

A, B, and C categories need not be exact. The idea is to recognize that levels of control should match the risk.

Figure **12.2**

Graphic Representation of ABC Analysis

An example of the use of ABC analysis is shown in Example 1.

Example 1

LO 12.1 *Conduct an*
ABC analysis

ABC ANALYSIS FOR A CHIP MANUFACTURER

Silicon Chips, Inc., maker of superfast DRAM chips, wants to categorize its 10 major inventory items using ABC analysis.

APPROACH ▶ ABC analysis organizes the items on an annual dollar-volume basis. Shown below (in columns 1–4) are the 10 items (identified by stock numbers), their annual demands, and unit costs.

SOLUTION ▶ Annual dollar volume is computed in column 5, along with the percentage of the total represented by each item in column 6. Column 7 groups the 10 items into A, B, and C categories.

ABC Calculation

(1) ITEM STOCK NUMBER	(2) PERCENTAGE OF NUMBER OF ITEMS STOCKED	(3) ANNUAL VOLUME (UNITS)	×	(4) UNIT COST	=	(5) ANNUAL DOLLAR VOLUME	(6) PERCENTAGE OF ANNUAL DOLLAR VOLUME		(7) CLASS
#10286	20%	1,000		$ 90.00		$ 90,000	38.8%	72%	A
#11526		500		154.00		77,000	33.2%		A
#12760	30%	1,550		17.00		26,350	11.3%	23%	B
#10867		350		42.86		15,001	6.4%		B
#10500		1,000		12.50		12,500	5.4%		B
#12572	50%	600		14.17		8,502	3.7%	5%	C
#14075		2,000		.60		1,200	.5%		C
#01036		100		8.50		850	.4%		C
#01307		1,200		.42		504	.2%		C
#10572		250		.60		150	.1%		C
		8,550				$232,057	100.0%		

INSIGHT ▶ The breakdown into A, B, and C categories is not hard and fast. The objective is to try to separate the "important" from the "unimportant."

LEARNING EXERCISE ▶ The unit cost for Item #10286 has increased from $90.00 to $120.00. How does this impact the ABC analysis? [Answer: The total annual dollar volume increases by $30,000, to $262,057, and the two A items now comprise 75% of that amount.]

RELATED PROBLEMS ▶ 12.1, 12.2, 12.3 (12.5–12.6 are available in MyOMLab)

EXCEL **OM** Data File **Ch12Ex1.xls** can be found in MyOMLab.

Criteria other than annual dollar volume can determine item classification. For instance, high shortage or holding cost, anticipated engineering changes, delivery problems, or quality problems may dictate upgrading items to a higher classification. The advantage of dividing inventory items into classes allows policies and controls to be established for each class.

Policies that may be based on ABC analysis include the following:

1. Purchasing resources expended on supplier development should be much higher for individual A items than for C items.
2. A items, as opposed to B and C items, should have tighter physical inventory control; perhaps they belong in a more secure area, and perhaps the accuracy of inventory records for A items should be verified more frequently.
3. Forecasting A items may warrant more care than forecasting other items.

Better forecasting, physical control, supplier reliability, and an ultimate reduction in inventory can all result from classification systems such as ABC analysis.

OM in Action   Inventory Accuracy at Milton Bradley

Milton Bradley, a division of Hasbro, Inc., has been manufacturing toys for 150 years. Founded by Milton Bradley in 1860, the company started by making a lithograph of Abraham Lincoln. Using his printing skills, Bradley developed games, including The Game of Life, Chutes and Ladders, Candy Land, Scrabble, and Lite Brite. Today, the company produces hundreds of games, requiring billions of plastic parts.

Once Milton Bradley has determined the optimal quantities for each production run, it must make them and assemble them as a part of the proper game. Some games require literally hundreds of plastic parts, including spinners, hotels, people, animals, cars, and so on. According to Gary Brennan, director of manufacturing, getting the right number of pieces to the right toys and production lines is the most important issue for the credibility of the company. Some orders can require 20,000 or more perfectly assembled games delivered to their warehouses in a matter of days.

Games with the incorrect number of parts and pieces can result in some very unhappy customers. It is also time-consuming and expensive for Milton Bradley to

supply the extra parts or to have toys or games returned. When shortages are found during the assembly stage, the entire production run is stopped until the problem is corrected.

Counting parts by hand or machine is not always accurate. As a result, Milton Bradley now weighs pieces and completed games to determine if the correct number of parts have been included. If the weight is not exact, there is a problem that is resolved before shipment. Using highly accurate digital scales, Milton Bradley is now able to get the right parts in the right game at the right time. Without this simple innovation, the company's most sophisticated production schedule would be meaningless.

Sources: Forbes (February 7, 2011); and *The Wall Street Journal* (April 15, 1999).

Record Accuracy

Record accuracy is a prerequisite to inventory management, production scheduling, and, ultimately, sales. Accuracy can be maintained by either periodic or perpetual systems. *Periodic systems* require regular (periodic) checks of inventory to determine quantity on hand. Some small retailers and facilities with vendor-managed inventory (the vendor checks quantity on hand and resupplies as necessary) use these systems. However, the downside is lack of control between reviews and the necessity of carrying extra inventory to protect against shortages.

A variation of the periodic system is a *two-bin system*. In practice, a store manager sets up two containers (each with adequate inventory to cover demand during the time required to receive another order) and places an order when the first container is empty.

Alternatively, *perpetual inventory* tracks both receipts and subtractions from inventory on a continuing basis. Receipts are usually noted in the receiving department in some semiautomated way, such as via a bar-code reader, and disbursements are noted as items leave the stockroom or, in retailing establishments, at the point-of-sale (POS) cash register.

Regardless of the inventory system, record accuracy requires good incoming and outgoing record keeping as well as good security. Stockrooms will have limited access, good housekeeping, and storage areas that hold fixed amounts of inventory. In both manufacturing and retail facilities, bins, shelf space, and individual items must be stored and labeled accurately. Meaningful decisions about ordering, scheduling, and shipping, are made only when the firm knows what it has on hand. (See the *OM in Action* box, "Inventory Accuracy at Milton Bradley.")

In this hospital, these vertically rotating storage carousels provide rapid access to hundreds of critical items and at the same time save floor space. This Omnicell inventory management carousel is also secure and has the added advantage of printing bar code labels.

Cycle Counting

Even though an organization may have made substantial efforts to record inventory accurately, these records must be verified through a continuing audit. Such audits are known as cycle counting. Historically, many firms performed annual physical inventories. This practice often meant shutting down the facility and having inexperienced people count parts and material. Inventory records should instead be verified via cycle counting. Cycle counting uses inventory classifications developed through ABC analysis. With cycle counting procedures, items are counted, records are verified, and inaccuracies are periodically documented. The cause of inaccuracies is then traced and appropriate remedial action taken to ensure integrity of the inventory system. **A** items will be counted frequently, perhaps once a month; **B** items will be counted less frequently, perhaps once a quarter; and **C** items will be counted perhaps once every 6 months. Example 2 illustrates how to compute the number of items of each classification to be counted each day.

Cycle counting
A continuing reconciliation of inventory with inventory records.

LO 12.2 *Explain* and use cycle counting

Example 2

CYCLE COUNTING AT COLE'S TRUCKS, INC.

Cole's Trucks, Inc., a builder of high-quality refuse trucks, has about 5,000 items in its inventory. It wants to determine how many items to cycle count each day.

APPROACH ▶ After hiring Matt Clark, a bright young OM student, for the summer, the firm determined that it has 500 A items, 1,750 B items, and 2,750 C items. Company policy is to count all A items every month (every 20 working days), all B items every quarter (every 60 working days), and all C items every 6 months (every 120 working days). The firm then allocates some items to be counted each day.

SOLUTION ▶

ITEM CLASS	QUANTITY	CYCLE-COUNTING POLICY	NUMBER OF ITEMS COUNTED PER DAY
A	500	Each month (20 working days)	500/20 = 25/day
B	1,750	Each quarter (60 working days)	1,750/60 = 29/day
C	2,750	Every 6 months (120 working days)	2,750/120 = 23/day
			77/day

Each day, 77 items are counted.

INSIGHT ▶ This daily audit of 77 items is much more efficient and accurate than conducting a massive inventory count once a year.

LEARNING EXERCISE ▶ Cole's reclassifies some B and C items so there are now 1,500 B items and 3,000 C items. How does this change the cycle count? [Answer: B and C both change to 25 items each per day, for a total of 75 items per day.]

RELATED PROBLEM ▶ 12.4

In Example 2, the particular items to be cycle counted can be sequentially or randomly selected each day. Another option is to cycle count items when they are reordered.

Cycle counting also has the following advantages:

Shrinkage

Retail inventory that is unaccounted for between receipt and sale.

Pilferage

A small amount of theft.

1. Eliminates the shutdown and interruption of production necessary for annual physical inventories.
2. Eliminates annual inventory adjustments.
3. Trained personnel audit the accuracy of inventory.
4. Allows the cause of the errors to be identified and remedial action to be taken.
5. Maintains accurate inventory records.

Robin Nelson/ZUMA Press, Inc./Alamy

Pharmaceutical distributor McKesson Corp., which is one of Arnold Palmer Hospital's main suppliers of surgical materials, makes heavy use of bar-code readers to automate inventory control. The device on the warehouse worker's arm combines a scanner, a computer, and a two-way radio to check orders. With rapid and accurate data, items are easily verified, improving inventory and shipment accuracy.

Control of Service Inventories

Although we may think of the service sector of our economy as not having inventory, that is seldom the case. Extensive inventory is held in wholesale and retail businesses, making inventory management crucial. In the food-service business, control of inventory is often the difference between success and failure. Moreover, inventory that is in transit or idle in a warehouse is lost value. Similarly, inventory damaged or stolen prior to sale is a loss. In retailing, inventory that is unaccounted for between receipt and time of sale is known as shrinkage. Shrinkage occurs from damage and theft as well as from sloppy paperwork. Inventory theft is also known as pilferage. Retail inventory loss of 1% of sales is considered good, with losses in many stores exceeding 3%. Because the impact on profitability is substantial, inventory accuracy and control are critical. Applicable techniques include the following:

1. *Good personnel selection, training, and discipline:* These are never easy but very necessary in food-service, wholesale, and retail operations, where employees have access to directly consumable merchandise.

OM in Action   Retail's Last 10 Yards

Retail managers commit huge resources to inventory and its management. Even with retail inventory representing 36% of total assets, nearly 1 of 6 items a retail store thinks it has available to its customers is not! Amazingly, close to two-thirds of inventory records are wrong. Failure to have product available is due to poor ordering, poor stocking, mislabeling, merchandise exchange errors, and merchandise being in the wrong location. Despite major investments in bar coding, RFID, and IT, *the last 10 yards* of retail inventory management is a disaster.

The huge number and variety of stock keeping units (SKUs) at the retail level adds complexity to inventory management. Does the customer really need 32 different offerings of Crest toothpaste or 26 offerings of Colgate? The proliferation of SKUs increases confusion, store size, purchasing, inventory, and stocking costs, as well as subsequent markdown costs. With

so many SKUs, stores have little space to stock and display a full case of many products, leading to labeling and "broken case" issues in the back room. Supervalu, the nation's 4th largest food retailer, is reducing the number of SKUs by 25% as one way to cut costs and add focus to its own store-branded items.

Reducing the variation in delivery lead time, improving forecasting accuracy, and cutting the huge variety of SKUs may all help. But reducing the number of SKUs may not improve customer service. Training and educating employees about the importance of inventory management may be a better way to improve the *last 10 yards*.

Sources: The Wall Street Journal (January 13, 2010); *Management Science* (February 2005); and *California Management Review* (Spring 2001).

---

2. *Tight control of incoming shipments:* This task is being addressed by many firms through the use of Universal Product Code (or bar code) and radio frequency ID (RFID) systems that read every incoming shipment and automatically check tallies against purchase orders. When properly designed, these systems—where each stock keeping unit (SKU; pronounced "skew") has its own identifier—can be very hard to defeat.
3. *Effective control of all goods leaving the facility:* This job is accomplished with bar codes, RFID tags, or magnetic strips on merchandise, and via direct observation. Direct observation can be personnel stationed at exits (as at Costco and Sam's Club wholesale stores) and in potentially high-loss areas or can take the form of one-way mirrors and video surveillance.

A handheld reader can scan RFID tags, aiding control of both incoming and outgoing shipments.

Successful retail operations require very good store-level control with accurate inventory in its proper location. Major retailers lose 10% to 25% of overall profits due to poor or inaccurate inventory records.[1] (See the *OM in Action* box, "Retail's Last 10 Yards.")

Inventory Models

We now examine a variety of inventory models and the costs associated with them.

VIDEO 12.2
Inventory Control at Wheeled Coach
Ambulance

Independent vs. Dependent Demand

Inventory control models assume that demand for an item is either independent of or dependent on the demand for other items. For example, the demand for refrigerators is *independent* of the demand for toaster ovens. However, the demand for toaster oven components is *dependent* on the requirements of toaster ovens.

This chapter focuses on managing inventory where demand is *independent*. Chapter 14 presents *dependent* demand management.

Holding, Ordering, and Setup Costs

Holding costs are the costs associated with holding or "carrying" inventory over time. Therefore, holding costs also include obsolescence and costs related to storage, such as insurance, extra staffing, and interest payments. Table 12.1 shows the kinds of costs that need to be evaluated to determine holding costs. Many firms fail to include all the inventory holding costs. Consequently, inventory holding costs are often understated.

Ordering cost includes costs of supplies, forms, order processing, purchasing, clerical support, and so forth. When orders are being manufactured, ordering costs also exist, but they are a part

Holding cost

The cost to keep or carry inventory in stock.

Ordering cost

The cost of the ordering process.

TABLE 12.1	Determining Inventory Holding Costs	
CATEGORY		COST (AND RANGE) AS A PERCENTAGE OF INVENTORY VALUE
Housing costs (building rent or depreciation, operating cost, taxes, insurance)		6% (3–10%)
Material-handling costs (equipment lease or depreciation, power, operating cost)		3% (1–3.5%)
Labor cost (receiving, warehousing, security)		3% (3–5%)
Investment costs (borrowing costs, taxes, and insurance on inventory)		11% (6–24%)
Pilferage, scrap, and obsolescence (much higher in industries undergoing rapid change like tablets and smart phones)		3% (2–5%)
Overall carrying cost		26%

Note: All numbers are approximate, as they vary substantially depending on the nature of the business, location, and current interest rates.

Setup cost

The cost to prepare a machine or process for production.

Setup time

The time required to prepare a machine or process for production.

of what is called setup costs. Setup cost is the cost to prepare a machine or process for manufacturing an order. This includes time and labor to clean and change tools or holders. Operations managers can lower ordering costs by reducing setup costs and by using such efficient procedures as electronic ordering and payment.

In manufacturing environments, setup cost is highly correlated with setup time. Setups usually require a substantial amount of work even before a setup is actually performed at the work center. With proper planning, much of the preparation required by a setup can be done prior to shutting down the machine or process. Setup times can thus be reduced substantially. Machines and processes that traditionally have taken hours to set up are now being set up in less than a minute by the more imaginative world-class manufacturers. Reducing setup times is an excellent way to reduce inventory investment and to improve productivity.

Inventory Models for Independent Demand

In this section, we introduce three inventory models that address two important questions: *when to order* and *how much to order*. These *independent* demand models are:

1. Basic economic order quantity (EOQ) model
2. Production order quantity model
3. Quantity discount model

The Basic Economic Order Quantity (EOQ) Model

Economic order quantity (EOQ) model

An inventory-control technique that minimizes the total of ordering and holding costs.

The economic order quantity (EOQ) model is one of the most commonly used inventory-control techniques. This technique is relatively easy to use but is based on several assumptions:

1. Demand for an item is known, reasonably constant, and independent of decisions for other items.
2. Lead time—that is, the time between placement and receipt of the order—is known and consistent.
3. Receipt of inventory is instantaneous and complete. In other words, the inventory from an order arrives in one batch at one time.
4. Quantity discounts are not possible.
5. The only variable costs are the cost of setting up or placing an order (setup or ordering cost) and the cost of holding or storing inventory over time (holding or carrying cost). These costs were discussed in the previous section.
6. Stockouts (shortages) can be completely avoided if orders are placed at the right time.

LO 12.3 *Explain* and use the EOQ model for independent inventory demand

With these assumptions, the graph of inventory usage over time has a sawtooth shape, as in Figure 12.3. In Figure 12.3, *Q* represents the amount that is ordered. If this amount is 500 dresses, all 500 dresses arrive at one time (when an order is received). Thus, the inventory

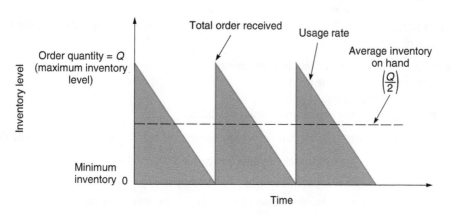

Figure **12.3**

Inventory Usage over Time

◆STUDENT TIP

If the maximum we can ever have is Q (say, 500 units) and the minimum is zero, then if inventory is used (or sold) at a fairly steady rate, the average $= (Q + 0)/2 = Q/2$.

level jumps from 0 to 500 dresses. In general, an inventory level increases from 0 to Q units when an order arrives.

Because demand is constant over time, inventory drops at a uniform rate over time. (Refer to the sloped lines in Figure 12.3.) Each time the inventory is received, the inventory level again jumps to Q units (represented by the vertical lines). This process continues indefinitely over time.

Minimizing Costs

The objective of most inventory models is to minimize total costs. With the assumptions just given, significant costs are setup (or ordering) cost and holding (or carrying) cost. All other costs, such as the cost of the inventory itself, are constant. Thus, if we minimize the sum of setup and holding costs, we will also be minimizing total costs. To help you visualize this, in Figure 12.4 we graph total costs as a function of the order quantity, Q. The optimal order size, Q^*, will be the quantity that minimizes the total costs. As the quantity ordered increases, the total number of orders placed per year will decrease. Thus, as the quantity ordered increases, the annual setup or ordering cost will decrease [Figure 12.4(a)]. But as the order quantity increases, the holding cost will increase due to the larger average inventories that are maintained [Figure 12.4(b)].

As we can see in Figure 12.4(c), a reduction in either holding or setup cost will reduce the total cost curve. A reduction in the setup cost curve also reduces the optimal order quantity (lot size). In addition, smaller lot sizes have a positive impact on quality and production flexibility. At Toshiba, the $77 billion Japanese conglomerate, workers can make as few as 10 laptop computers before changing models. This lot-size flexibility has allowed Toshiba to move toward a "build-to-order" mass customization system, an important ability in an industry that has product life cycles measured in months, not years.

You should note that in Figure 12.4(c), the optimal order quantity occurs at the point where the ordering-cost curve and the carrying-cost curve intersect. This was not by chance. With the EOQ model, the optimal order quantity will occur at a point where the total setup cost is equal

◆STUDENT TIP

Figure 12.4 is the heart of EOQ inventory modeling. We want to find the smallest total cost (top curve), which is the sum of the two curves below it.

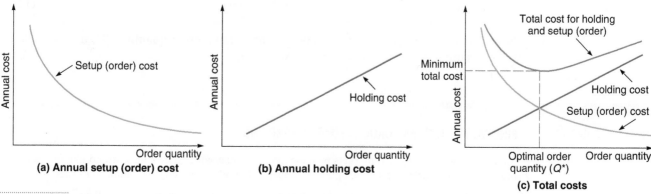

Figure **12.4**

Costs as a Function of Order Quantity

to the total holding cost.[2] We use this fact to develop equations that solve directly for Q^*. The necessary steps are:

1. Develop an expression for setup or ordering cost.
2. Develop an expression for holding cost.
3. Set setup (order) cost equal to holding cost.
4. Solve the equation for the optimal order quantity.

Using the following variables, we can determine setup and holding costs and solve for Q^*:

$$Q = \text{Number of units per order}$$
$$Q^* = \text{Optimum number of units per order (EOQ)}$$
$$D = \text{Annual demand in units for the inventory item}$$
$$S = \text{Setup or ordering cost for each order}$$
$$H = \text{Holding or carrying cost per unit per year}$$

1. Annual setup cost = (Number of orders placed per year) × (Setup or order cost per order)

$$= \left(\frac{\text{Annual demand}}{\text{Number of units in each order}} \right) (\text{Setup or order cost per order})$$

$$= \left(\frac{D}{Q} \right) (S) = \frac{D}{Q} S$$

2. Annual holding cost = (Average inventory level) × (Holding cost per unit per year)

$$= \left(\frac{\text{Order quantity}}{2} \right) (\text{Holding cost per unit per year})$$

$$= \left(\frac{Q}{2} \right) (H) = \frac{Q}{2} H$$

3. Optimal order quantity is found when annual setup (order) cost equals annual holding cost, namely:

$$\frac{D}{Q} S = \frac{Q}{2} H$$

4. To solve for Q^*, simply cross-multiply terms and isolate Q on the left of the equal sign:

$$2DS = Q^2 H$$

$$Q^2 = \frac{2DS}{H}$$

$$Q^* = \sqrt{\frac{2DS}{H}} \qquad\qquad (12\text{-}1)$$

Now that we have derived the equation for the optimal order quantity, Q^*, it is possible to solve inventory problems directly, as in Example 3.

Example 3 | **FINDING THE OPTIMAL ORDER SIZE AT SHARP, INC.**

Sharp, Inc., a company that markets painless hypodermic needles to hospitals, would like to reduce its inventory cost by determining the optimal number of hypodermic needles to obtain per order.

APPROACH ▶ The annual demand is 1,000 units; the setup or ordering cost is $10 per order; and the holding cost per unit per year is $.50.

SOLUTION ▶ Using these figures, we can calculate the optimal number of units per order:

$$Q^* = \sqrt{\frac{2DS}{H}}$$

$$Q^* = \sqrt{\frac{2(1,000)(10)}{0.50}} = \sqrt{40,000} = 200 \text{ units}$$

INSIGHT ▶ Sharp, Inc., now knows how many needles to order per order. The firm also has a basis for determining ordering and holding costs for this item, as well as the number of orders to be processed by the receiving and inventory departments.

LEARNING EXERCISE ▶ If D increases to 1,200 units, what is the new Q^*? [Answer: $Q^* = 219$ units.]

RELATED PROBLEMS ▶ 12.7, 12.8, 12.9, 12.10, 12.11, 12.14, 12.15, 12.17, 12.29 (12.31, 12.32, 12.33a, 12.35a are available in MyOMLab)

EXCEL **OM** Data File **Ch12Ex3.xls** can be found in MyOMLab.

ACTIVE **MODEL** 12.1 This example is further illustrated in Active Model 12.1 in MyOMLab.

We can also determine the expected number of orders placed during the year (N) and the expected time between orders (T), as follows:

$$\text{Expected number of orders} = N = \frac{\text{Demand}}{\text{Order quantity}} = \frac{D}{Q^*} \quad (12\text{-}2)$$

$$\text{Expected time between orders} = T = \frac{\text{Number of working days per year}}{N} \quad (12\text{-}3)$$

Example 4 illustrates this concept.

Example 4

COMPUTING NUMBER OF ORDERS AND TIME BETWEEN ORDERS AT SHARP, INC.

Sharp, Inc. (in Example 3) has a 250-day working year and wants to find the number of orders (N) and the expected time between orders (T).

APPROACH ▶ Using Equations (12-2) and (12-3), Sharp enters the data given in Example 3.

SOLUTION ▶

$$N = \frac{\text{Demand}}{\text{Order quantity}}$$
$$= \frac{1,000}{200} = 5 \text{ orders per year}$$
$$T = \frac{\text{Number of working days per year}}{\text{Expected number of orders}}$$
$$= \frac{250 \text{ working days per year}}{5 \text{ orders}} = 50 \text{ days between orders}$$

INSIGHT ▶ The company now knows not only how many needles to order per order but that the time between orders is 50 days and that there are five orders per year.

LEARNING EXERCISE ▶ If $D = 1,200$ units instead of 1,000, find N and T. [Answer: $N \approx 5.48$, $T = 45.62$.]

RELATED PROBLEMS ▶ 12.14, 12.15, 12.17 (12.35c,d are available in MyOMLab)

As mentioned earlier in this section, the total annual variable inventory cost is the sum of setup and holding costs:

$$\text{Total annual cost} = \text{Setup (order) cost} + \text{Holding cost} \quad (12\text{-}4)$$

In terms of the variables in the model, we can express the total cost TC as:

$$TC = \frac{D}{Q}S + \frac{Q}{2}H \quad (12\text{-}5)$$

Example 5 shows how to use this formula.

Example 5

COMPUTING COMBINED COST OF ORDERING AND HOLDING

Sharp, Inc. (from Examples 3 and 4) wants to determine the combined annual ordering and holding costs.

APPROACH ▶ Apply Equation (12-5), using the data in Example 3.

SOLUTION ▶

$$TC = \frac{D}{Q}S + \frac{Q}{2}H$$

$$= \frac{1,000}{200}(\$10) + \frac{200}{2}(\$.50)$$

$$= (5)(\$10) + (100)(\$.50)$$

$$= \$50 + \$50 = \$100$$

INSIGHT ▶ These are the annual setup and holding costs. The $100 total does not include the actual cost of goods. Notice that in the EOQ model, holding costs always equal setup (order) costs.

LEARNING EXERCISE ▶ Find the total annual cost if $D = 1,200$ units in Example 3. [Answer: $109.54.]

RELATED PROBLEMS ▶ 12.11, 12.14, 12.15, 12.16 (12.33b,c; 12.35e; 12.36a,b are available in MyOMLab)

Inventory costs may also be expressed to include the actual cost of the material purchased. If we assume that the annual demand and the price per hypodermic needle are known values (e.g., 1,000 hypodermics per year at $P = \$10$) and total annual cost should include purchase cost, then Equation (12-5) becomes:

$$TC = \frac{D}{Q}S + \frac{Q}{2}H + PD$$

Because material cost does not depend on the particular order policy, we still incur an annual material cost of $D \times P = (1,000)(\$10) = \$10,000$. (Later in this chapter we will discuss the case in which this may not be true—namely, when a quantity discount is available.)[3]

Robust

Giving satisfactory answers even with substantial variation in the parameters.

Robust Model A benefit of the EOQ model is that it is robust. By robust we mean that it gives satisfactory answers even with substantial variation in its parameters. As we have observed, determining accurate ordering costs and holding costs for inventory is often difficult. Consequently, a robust model is advantageous. The total cost of the EOQ changes little in the neighborhood of the minimum. The curve is very shallow. This means that variations in setup costs, holding costs, demand, or even EOQ make relatively modest differences in total cost. Example 6 shows the robustness of EOQ.

Example 6

EOQ IS A ROBUST MODEL

Management in the Sharp, Inc., examples underestimates total annual demand by 50% (say demand is actually 1,500 needles rather than 1,000 needles) while using the same Q. How will the annual inventory cost be impacted?

APPROACH ▶ We will solve for annual costs twice. First, we will apply the wrong EOQ; then we will recompute costs with the correct EOQ.

SOLUTION ▶ If demand in Example 5 is actually 1,500 needles rather than 1,000, but management uses an order quantity of $Q = 200$ (when it should be $Q = 244.9$ based on $D = 1,500$), the sum of holding and ordering cost increases to $125:

$$\text{Annual cost} = \frac{D}{Q}S + \frac{Q}{2}H$$

$$= \frac{1,500}{200}(\$10) + \frac{200}{2}(\$.50)$$

$$= \$75 + \$50 = \$125$$

However, had we known that the demand was for 1,500 with an EOQ of 244.9 units, we would have spent $122.47, as shown:

$$\text{Annual cost} = \frac{1,500}{244.9}(\$10) + \frac{244.9}{2}(\$.50)$$
$$= 6.125(\$10) + 122.45(\$.50)$$
$$= \$61.25 + \$61.22 = \$122.47$$

INSIGHT ▶ Note that the expenditure of $125.00, made with an estimate of demand that was substantially wrong, is only 2% ($2.52/$122.47) higher than we would have paid had we known the actual demand and ordered accordingly. Note also that were it not due to rounding, the annual holding costs and ordering costs would be exactly equal.

LEARNING EXERCISE ▶ Demand at Sharp remains at 1,000, H is still $.50, and we order 200 needles at a time (as in Example 5). But if the true order cost $= S = \$15$ (rather than $10), what is the annual cost? [Answer: Annual order cost increases to $75, and annual holding cost stays at $50. So the total cost = $125.]

RELATED PROBLEMS ▶ 12.10b, 12.16 (12.36a,b are available in MyOMLab)

We may conclude that the EOQ is indeed robust and that significant errors do not cost us very much. This attribute of the EOQ model is most convenient because our ability to accurately determine demand, holding cost, and ordering cost is limited.

Reorder Points

Now that we have decided *how much* to order, we will look at the second inventory question, *when* to order. Simple inventory models assume that receipt of an order is instantaneous. In other words, they assume (1) that a firm will place an order when the inventory level for that particular item reaches zero and (2) that it will receive the ordered items immediately. However, the time between placement and receipt of an order, called lead time, or delivery time, can be as short as a few hours or as long as months. Thus, the when-to-order decision is usually expressed in terms of a reorder point (ROP)—the inventory level at which an order should be placed (see Figure 12.5).

The reorder point (ROP) is given as:

ROP = Demand per day ×
      Lead time for a new order in days

$$\text{ROP} = d \times L \qquad (12\text{-}6)$$

This equation for ROP *assumes that demand during lead time and lead time itself are constant.* When this is not the case, extra stock, often called safety stock (*ss*), should be added. The reorder point with safety stock then becomes:

ROP = Expected demand during lead time +
      Safety stock

The demand per day, d, is found by dividing the annual demand, D, by the number of working days in a year:

$$d = \frac{D}{\text{Number of working days in a year}}$$

Lead time
In purchasing systems, the time between placing an order and receiving it; in production systems, the wait, move, queue, setup, and run times for each component produced.

Reorder point (ROP)
The inventory level (point) at which action is taken to replenish the stocked item.

Safety stock (*ss*)
Extra stock to allow for uneven demand; a buffer.

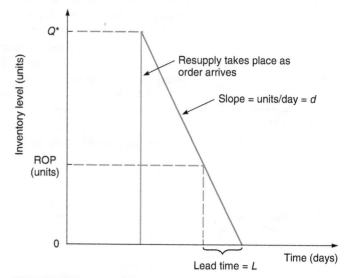

Figure **12.5**

The Reorder Point (ROP)

Q^* is the optimum order quantity, and lead time represents the time between placing and receiving an order.

Computing the reorder point is demonstrated in Example 7.

Example 7

COMPUTING REORDER POINTS (ROP) FOR IPHONES WITH AND WITHOUT SAFETY STOCK

An Apple store has a demand (D) for 8,000 iPhones per year. The firm operates a 250-day working year. On average, delivery of an order takes 3 working days, but has been known to take as long as 4 days. The store wants to calculate the reorder point without a safety stock and then with a one-day safety stock.

APPROACH ▶ First compute the daily demand and then apply Equation (12-6) for the ROP. Then compute the ROP with safety stock.

LO 12.4 *Compute* a reorder point and explain safety stock

SOLUTION ▶

$$d = \frac{D}{\text{Number of working days in a year}} = \frac{8,000}{250} = 32 \text{ units}$$

$$\text{ROP} = \text{Reorder point} = d \times L = 32 \text{ units per day} \times 3 \text{ days} = 96 \text{ units}$$

ROP with safety stock adds 1 day's demand (32 units) to the ROP (for 128 units).

INSIGHT ▶ When iPhone inventory stock drops to 96 units, an order should be placed. If the safety stock for a possible one-day delay in delivery is added, the ROP is 128 (= 96 + 32).

LEARNING EXERCISE ▶ If there are only 200 working days per year, what is the correct ROP, without safety stock and with safety stock? [Answer: 120 iPhones without safety stock and 160 with safety stock.]

RELATED PROBLEMS ▶ 12.11d, 12.12, 12.13, 12.15f (12.33d, 12.34, 12.35f, 12.36c are available in MyOMLab)

When demand is not constant or variability exists in the supply chain, safety stock can be critical. We discuss safety stock in more detail later in this chapter.

Production Order Quantity Model

In the previous inventory model, we assumed that the entire inventory order was received at one time. There are times, however, when the firm may receive its inventory over a period of time. Such cases require a different model, one that does not require the instantaneous-receipt assumption. This model is applicable under two situations: (1) when inventory continuously flows or builds up over a period of time after an order has been placed or (2) when units are produced and sold simultaneously. Under these circumstances, we take into account daily production (or inventory-flow) rate and daily demand rate. Figure 12.6 shows inventory levels as a function of time (and inventory dropping to zero between orders).

Production order quantity model

An economic order quantity technique applied to production orders.

Because this model is especially suitable for the production environment, it is commonly called the production order quantity model. It is useful when inventory continuously builds up over time, and traditional economic order quantity assumptions are valid. We derive this model by setting ordering or setup costs equal to holding costs and solving for optimal order size, Q^*. Using the following symbols, we can determine the expression for annual inventory holding cost for the production order quantity model:

Figure 12.6

Change in Inventory Levels over Time for the Production Model

Q = Number of units per order

H = Holding cost per unit per year

p = Daily production rate

d = Daily demand rate, or usage rate

t = Length of the production run in days

1. $\left(\begin{array}{c}\text{Annual inventory} \\ \text{holding cost}\end{array}\right) = (\text{Average inventory level}) \times \left(\begin{array}{c}\text{Holding cost} \\ \text{per unit per year}\end{array}\right)$

LO 12.5 *Apply* the production order quantity model

2. $(\text{Average inventory level}) = (\text{Maximum inventory level})/2$

3. $\left(\begin{array}{c}\text{Maximum} \\ \text{inventory level}\end{array}\right) = \left(\begin{array}{c}\text{Total production during} \\ \text{the production run}\end{array}\right) - \left(\begin{array}{c}\text{Total used during} \\ \text{the production run}\end{array}\right)$

$$= pt - dt$$

However, Q = total produced = pt, and thus $t = Q/p$. Therefore:

$$\text{Maximum inventory level} = p\left(\frac{Q}{p}\right) - d\left(\frac{Q}{p}\right) = Q - \frac{d}{p}Q$$

$$= Q\left(1 - \frac{d}{p}\right)$$

STUDENT TIP

Note in Figure 12.6 that inventory buildup is not instantaneous but gradual. So the formula reduces the average inventory and thus the holding cost by the ratio of that buildup.

4. Annual inventory holding cost (or simply holding cost) =

$$\frac{\text{Maximum inventory level}}{2}(H) = \frac{Q}{2}\left[1 - \left(\frac{d}{p}\right)\right]H$$

Using this expression for holding cost and the expression for setup cost developed in the basic EOQ model, we solve for the optimal number of pieces per order by equating setup cost and holding cost:

$$\text{Setup cost} = (D/Q)S \qquad\qquad \text{Holding cost} = \tfrac{1}{2}HQ[1 - (d/p)]$$

Set ordering cost equal to holding cost to obtain Q_p^*:

$$\frac{D}{Q}S = \tfrac{1}{2}HQ[1 - (d/p)]$$

$$Q^2 = \frac{2DS}{H[1 - (d/p)]}$$

$$Q_p^* = \sqrt{\frac{2DS}{H[1 - (d/p)]}} \qquad\qquad (12\text{-}7)$$

Dmitry Kalinovsky/Shutterstock

Each order may require a change in the way a machine or process is set up. Reducing setup time usually means a reduction in setup cost, and reductions in setup costs make smaller batches (lots) economical to produce. Increasingly, setup (and operation) is performed by computer-controlled machines, such as this one, operating from previously written programs.

In Example 8, we use the above equation, Q_p^*, to solve for the optimum order or production quantity when inventory is consumed as it is produced.

Example 8

A PRODUCTION ORDER QUANTITY MODEL

Nathan Manufacturing, Inc., makes and sells specialty hubcaps for the retail automobile aftermarket. Nathan's forecast for its wire-wheel hubcap is 1,000 units next year, with an average daily demand of 4 units. However, the production process is most efficient at 8 units per day. So the company produces 8 per day but uses only 4 per day. The company wants to solve for the optimum number of units per order. (*Note:* This plant schedules production of this hubcap only as needed, during the 250 days per year the shop operates.)

APPROACH ▶ Gather the cost data and apply Equation (12-7):

$$\text{Annual demand} = D = 1{,}000 \text{ units}$$
$$\text{Setup costs} = S = \$10$$
$$\text{Holding cost} = H = \$0.50 \text{ per unit per year}$$
$$\text{Daily production rate} = p = 8 \text{ units daily}$$
$$\text{Daily demand rate} = d = 4 \text{ units daily}$$

SOLUTION ▶

$$Q_p^* = \sqrt{\frac{2DS}{H[1 - (d/p)]}}$$

$$Q_p^* = \sqrt{\frac{2(1{,}000)(10)}{0.50[1 - (4/8)]}}$$

$$= \sqrt{\frac{20{,}000}{0.50(1/2)}} = \sqrt{80{,}000} = 282.8 \text{ hubcaps, or 283 hubcaps}$$

INSIGHT ▶ The difference between the production order quantity model and the basic EOQ model is that the effective annual holding cost per unit is reduced in the production order quantity model because the entire order does not arrive at once.

LEARNING EXERCISE ▶ If Nathan can increase its daily production rate from 8 to 10, how does Q_p^* change? [Answer: $Q_p^* = 258$.]

RELATED PROBLEMS ▶ 12.18, 12.19, 12.20, 12.30 (12.37 is available in MyOMLab)

EXCEL **OM** Data File **Ch12Ex8.xls** can be found in MyOMLab.

ACTIVE **MODEL** 12.2 This example is further illustrated in Active Model 12.2 in MyOMLab.

You may want to compare this solution with the answer in Example 3, which had identical D, S, and H values. Eliminating the instantaneous-receipt assumption, where $p = 8$ and $d = 4$, resulted in an increase in Q^* from 200 in Example 3 to 283 in Example 8. This increase in Q^* occurred because holding cost dropped from $.50 to [$.50 \times (1 - d/p)]$, making a larger order quantity optimal. Also note that:

$$d = 4 = \frac{D}{\text{Number of days the plant is in operation}} = \frac{1{,}000}{250}$$

We can also calculate Q_p^* when *annual* data are available. When annual data are used, we can express Q_p^* as:

$$Q_p^* = \sqrt{\frac{2DS}{H\left(1 - \dfrac{\text{Annual demand rate}}{\text{Annual production rate}}\right)}} \qquad (12\text{-}8)$$

Quantity Discount Models

Quantity discounts appear everywhere—you cannot go into a grocery store without seeing them on nearly every shelf. In fact, researchers have found that *most* companies either offer or receive quantity discounts for at least some of the products that they sell or purchase. A **quantity discount** is simply a reduced price (P) for an item when it is purchased in larger quantities. A typical quantity discount schedule appears in Table 12.2. As can be seen in the table, the normal price of the item is $100. When 120 to 1,499 units are ordered at one time, the price per unit drops to $98; when the quantity ordered at one time is 1,500 units or more, the price is $96 per unit. The 120 quantity and the 1,500 quantity are called *price-break quantities* because they represent the first order amount that would lead to a new lower price. As always, management must decide when and how much to order. However, given these quantity discounts, how does the operations manager make these decisions?

Quantity discount
A reduced price for items purchased in large quantities.

As with other inventory models, the objective is to minimize total cost. Because the unit cost for the second discount in Table 12.2 is the lowest, you may be tempted to order 1,500 units. Placing an order for that quantity, however, even with the greatest discount price, may not minimize total inventory cost. This is because holding cost increases. Thus, the major trade-off when considering quantity discounts is between *reduced product cost* and *increased holding cost*. When we include the cost of the product, the equation for the total annual inventory cost can be calculated as follows:

Total annual cost = Annual setup (ordering) cost + Annual holding cost
+ Annual product cost,

or

LO 12.6 *Explain* and use the quantity discount model

$$TC = \frac{D}{Q}S + \frac{Q}{2}IP + PD \qquad (12\text{-}9)$$

where Q = Quantity ordered
D = Annual demand in units
S = Setup or ordering cost per order
P = Price per unit
I = Holding cost per unit per year expressed as a percent of price P

Note that holding cost is IP instead of H as seen in the regular EOQ model. Because the price of the item is a factor in annual holding cost, we do not assume that the holding cost is a constant when the price per unit changes for each quantity discount. Thus, it is common to express the holding cost as a percent (I) of unit price (P) when evaluating costs of quantity discount schedules.

The EOQ formula (12-1) is modified for the quantity discount problem as follows:

$$Q^* = \sqrt{\frac{2DS}{IP}} \qquad (12\text{-}10)$$

The solution procedure uses the concept of a *feasible EOQ*. An EOQ is feasible if it lies in the quantity range that leads to the same price P used to compute it in Equation (12-10). For example, suppose that $D = 5,200$, $S = \$200$, and $I = 28\%$. Using Table 12.2 and Equation (12-10), the EOQ for the $96 price equals $\sqrt{2(5,200)(200)/[(.28)(96)]} = 278$ units. Because $278 < 1,500$ (the price-break quantity needed to receive the $96 price), the EOQ for the $96 price is *not feasible*. On the other hand, the EOQ for the $98 price equals 275 units. This amount is *feasible* because if 275 units were actually ordered, the firm would indeed receive the $98 purchase price.

TABLE 12.2	A Quantity Discount Schedule	
PRICE RANGE	QUANTITY ORDERED	PRICE PER UNIT P
Initial price	1–119	$100
Discount price 1	120–1,499	$ 98
Discount price 2	1,500 and over	$ 96

Figure 12.7

EOQs and Possible Best Order Quantities for the Quantity Discount Problem with Three Prices in Table 12.2

The solid black curves represent the realized total annual setup plus holding plus purchasing cost at the applicable order quantities. The black curve drops to the total cost curve for the next discount level when each price-break quantity is reached.

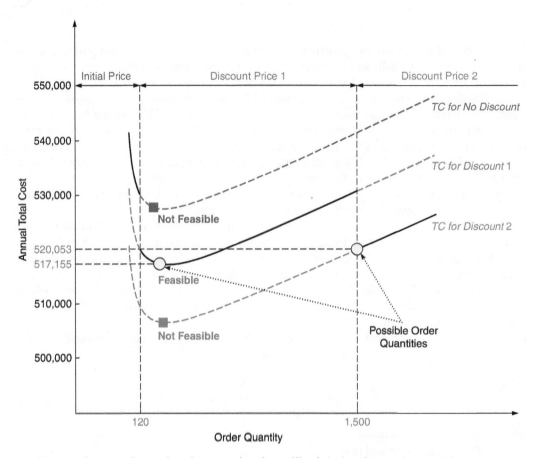

Now we have to determine the quantity that will minimize the total annual inventory cost. Because there are a few discounts, this process involves two steps. In Step 1, we identify all possible order quantities that could be the best solution. In Step 2, we calculate the total cost of all possible best order quantities, and the least expensive order quantity is selected.

Solution Procedure

STEP 1: Starting with the *lowest* possible purchase price in a quantity discount schedule and working toward the highest price, keep calculating Q^* from Equation (12-10) until the first feasible EOQ is found. The first feasible EOQ is a possible best order quantity, along with all price-break quantities for all *lower* prices.

STEP 2: Calculate the total annual cost TC using Equation (12-9) for each of the possible best order quantities determined in Step 1. Select the quantity that has the lowest total cost.

Note that no quantities need to be considered for any prices greater than the first feasible EOQ found in Step 1. This occurs because if an EOQ for a given price is feasible, then the EOQ for any *higher* price *cannot* lead to a lower cost (TC is guaranteed to be higher).

Figure 12.7 provides a graphical illustration of Step 1 using the three price ranges from Table 12.2. In that example, the EOQ for the lowest price is infeasible, but the EOQ for the second-lowest price is feasible. So the EOQ for the second-lowest price, along with the price-break quantity for the lowest price, are the possible best order quantities. Finally, the highest price (no discount) can be ignored because a feasible EOQ has already been found for a lower price.

Example 9 illustrates how the full solution procedure can be applied.

Example 9

QUANTITY DISCOUNT MODEL

Chris Beehner Electronics stocks toy remote control flying drones. Recently, the store has been offered a quantity discount schedule for these drones. This quantity schedule was shown in Table 12.2. Furthermore, setup cost is $200 per order, annual demand is 5,200 units, and annual inventory carrying charge as a percent of cost, I, is 28%. What order quantity will minimize the total inventory cost?

APPROACH ▶ We will follow the two steps just outlined for the quantity discount model.

SOLUTION ▶ First we calculate the Q^* for the lowest possible price of $96, as we did earlier:

$$Q^*_{\$96} = \sqrt{\frac{2(5,200)(\$200)}{(.28)(\$96)}} = 278 \text{ flying drones per order}$$

Because $278 < 1,500$, this EOQ is *infeasible* for the $96 price. So now we calculate Q^* for the next-higher price of $98:

$$Q^*_{\$98} = \sqrt{\frac{2(5,200)(\$200)}{(.28)(\$98)}} = 275 \text{ flying drones per order}$$

Because 275 is between 120 and 1,499 units, this EOQ is *feasible* for the $98 price. Thus, the possible best order quantities are 275 (the first feasible EOQ) and 1,500 (the price-break quantity for the lower price of $96). We need not bother to compute Q^* for the initial price of $100 because we found a feasible EOQ for a lower price.

Step 2 uses Equation (12-9) to compute the total cost for each of the possible best order quantities. This step is taken with the aid of Table 12.3.

TABLE 12.3	Total Cost Computations for Chris Beehner Electronics				
ORDER QUANTITY	UNIT PRICE	ANNUAL ORDERING COST	ANNUAL HOLDING COST	ANNUAL PRODUCT COST	TOTAL ANNUAL COST
275	$98	$3,782	$ 3,773	$509,600	$517,155
1,500	$96	$ 693	$20,160	$499,200	$520,053

Because the total annual cost for 275 units is lower, 275 units should be ordered. The costs for this example are shown in Figure 12.7.

INSIGHT ▶ Even though Beehner Electronics could save more than $10,000 in annual product costs, ordering 1,500 units (28.8% of annual demand) at a time would generate even more than that in increased holding costs. So in this example it is not in the store's best interest to order enough to attain the lowest possible purchase price per unit. On the other hand, if the price-break quantity for the $96 had been 1,000 units rather than 1,500 units, then total annual costs would have been $513,680, which would have been cheaper than ordering 275 units at $98.

LEARNING EXERCISE ▶ Resolve the problem with $D = 2,000$, $S = \$5$, $I = 50\%$, discount price $1 = \$99$, and discount price $2 = \$98$. [Answer: only 20 units should be ordered each time, which is the EOQ at the $100 price.]

RELATED PROBLEMS ▶ 12.21–12.28 (12.38–12.40 are available in MyOMLab)

EXCEL **OM** Data file **Ch12Ex9.xls** can be found in MyOMLab.

In this section we have studied the most popular form of single-purchase quantity discount called the *all-units discount*. In practice, quantity discounts appear in a variety of forms. For example, *incremental quantity discounts* apply only to those units purchased beyond the price-break quantities rather than to all units. *Fixed fees*, such as a fixed shipping and processing cost for a catalog order or a $5,000 tooling setup cost for any order placed with a manufacturer, encourage buyers to purchase more units at a time. Some discounts are *aggregated* over items or time. *Item aggregation* bases price breaks on total units or dollars purchased. *Time aggregation* applies to total items or dollars spent over a specific time period such as one year. *Truckload discounts*, *buy-one-get-one-free offers*, and *one-time-only sales* also represent types of quantity discounts in that they provide price incentives for buyers to purchase more units at one time. Most purchasing managers deal with some form of quantity discounts on a regular basis.

Probabilistic Models and Safety Stock

All the inventory models we have discussed so far make the assumption that demand for a product is constant and certain. We now relax this assumption. The following inventory models apply when product demand is not known but can be specified by means of a probability distribution. These types of models are called probabilistic models. Probabilistic models are a real-world adjustment because demand and lead time won't always be known and constant.

An important concern of management is maintaining an adequate service level in the face of uncertain demand. The service level is the *complement* of the probability of a stockout. For instance, if the probability of a stockout is 0.05, then the service level is .95. Uncertain demand raises the possibility of a stockout. One method of reducing stockouts is to hold extra units in inventory. As we noted earlier such inventory is referred to as safety stock. Safety stock involves adding a number of units as a buffer to the reorder point. As you recall:

$$\text{Reorder point} = \text{ROP} = d \times L$$

where d = Daily demand

L = Order lead time, or number of working days it takes to deliver an order

The inclusion of safety stock (ss) changed the expression to:

$$\text{ROP} = d \times L + ss \tag{12-11}$$

The amount of safety stock maintained depends on the cost of incurring a stockout and the cost of holding the extra inventory. Annual stockout cost is computed as follows:

$$\begin{aligned}\text{Annual stockout costs} = &\text{ The sum of the units short for each demand level}\\ &\times \text{ The probability of that demand level} \times \text{ The stockout cost/unit}\\ &\times \text{ The number of orders per year}\end{aligned} \tag{12-12}$$

Example 10 illustrates this concept.

Example 10

DETERMINING SAFETY STOCK WITH PROBABILISTIC DEMAND AND CONSTANT LEAD TIME

David Rivera Optical has determined that its reorder point for eyeglass frames is 50 ($d \times L$) units. Its carrying cost per frame per year is $5, and stockout (or lost sale) cost is $40 per frame. The store has experienced the following probability distribution for inventory demand during the lead time (reorder period). The optimum number of orders per year is six.

NUMBER OF UNITS	PROBABILITY
30	.2
40	.2
ROP → 50	.3
60	.2
70	.1
	$\overline{1.0}$

How much safety stock should David Rivera keep on hand?

APPROACH ▶   The objective is to find the amount of safety stock that minimizes the sum of the additional inventory holding costs and stockout costs. The annual holding cost is simply the holding cost per unit multiplied by the units added to the ROP. For example, a safety stock of 20 frames, which implies that the new ROP, with safety stock, is 70 (= 50 + 20), raises the annual carrying cost by $5(20) = $100.

However, computing annual stockout cost is more interesting. For any level of safety stock, stockout cost is the expected cost of stocking out. We can compute it, as in Equation (12-12), by multiplying the number of frames short (Demand − ROP) by the probability of demand at that level, by the stockout cost, by the number of times per year the stockout can occur (which in our case is the number of orders per year). Then we add stockout costs for each possible stockout level for a given ROP.[4]

SOLUTION ▶ We begin by looking at zero safety stock. For this safety stock, a shortage of 10 frames will occur if demand is 60, and a shortage of 20 frames will occur if the demand is 70. Thus the stockout costs for zero safety stock are:

$$(10 \text{ frames short})(.2)(\$40 \text{ per stockout})(6 \text{ possible stockouts per year})$$
$$+ (20 \text{ frames short})(.1)(\$40)(6) = \$960$$

The following table summarizes the total costs for each of the three alternatives:

SAFETY STOCK	ADDITIONAL HOLDING COST	STOCKOUT COST		TOTAL COST
20	(20)($5) = $100		$ 0	$100
10	(10)($5) = $ 50	(10) (.1) ($40) (6)	= $240	$290
0	$ 0	(10) (.2) ($40) (6) + (20) (.1) ($40) (6) = $960		$960

The safety stock with the lowest total cost is 20 frames. Therefore, this safety stock changes the reorder point to 50 + 20 = 70 frames.

INSIGHT ▶ The optical company now knows that a safety stock of 20 frames will be the most economical decision.

LEARNING EXERCISE ▶ David Rivera's holding cost per frame is now estimated to be $20, while the stockout cost is $30 per frame. Does the reorder point change? [Answer: Safety stock = 10 now, with a total cost of $380, which is the lowest of the three. ROP = 60 frames.]

RELATED PROBLEMS ▶ 12.43, 12.44, 12.45

When it is difficult or impossible to determine the cost of being out of stock, a manager may decide to follow a policy of keeping enough safety stock on hand to meet a prescribed customer service level. For instance, Figure 12.8 shows the use of safety stock when demand (for hospital resuscitation kits) is probabilistic. We see that the safety stock in Figure 12.8 is 16.5 units, and the reorder point is also increased by 16.5.

The manager may want to define the service level as meeting 95% of the demand (or, conversely, having stockouts only 5% of the time). Assuming that demand during lead time (the reorder period) follows a normal curve, only the mean and standard deviation are needed to define the inventory requirements for any given service level. Sales data are usually adequate for computing the mean and standard deviation. Example 11 uses a normal curve with a known mean (μ) and standard deviation (σ) to determine the reorder point and safety stock necessary

Figure 12.8

Probabilistic Demand for a Hospital Item

Expected number of kits needed during lead time is 350, but for a 95% service level, the reorder point should be raised to 366.5.

for a 95% service level. We use the following formula:

$$\text{ROP} = \text{Expected demand during lead time} + Z\sigma_{dLT} \qquad (12\text{-}13)$$

where $Z = \text{Number of standard deviations}$

$\sigma_{dLT} = \text{Standard deviation of demand during lead time}$

Example 11

SAFETY STOCK WITH PROBABILISTIC DEMAND

Memphis Regional Hospital stocks a "code blue" resuscitation kit that has a normally distributed demand during the reorder period. The mean (average) demand during the reorder period is 350 kits, and the standard deviation is 10 kits. The hospital administrator wants to follow a policy that results in stockouts only 5% of the time.

(a) What is the appropriate value of Z? (b) How much safety stock should the hospital maintain? (c) What reorder point should be used?

APPROACH ▶ The hospital determines how much inventory is needed to meet the demand 95% of the time. The figure in this example may help you visualize the approach. The data are as follows:

$$\mu = \text{Mean demand} = 350 \text{ kits}$$

$$\sigma_{dLT} = \text{Standard deviation of demand during lead time} = 10 \text{ kits}$$

$$Z = \text{Number of standard normal deviations}$$

STUDENT TIP ◆
Recall that the service level is
1 minus the risk of a stockout.

SOLUTION ▶

a) We use the properties of a standardized normal curve to get a Z-value for an area under the normal curve of .95 (or $1 - .05$). Using a normal table (see Appendix I) or the Excel formula $=\text{NORMSINV}(.95)$, we find a Z-value of 1.645 standard deviations from the mean.

b) Because: Safety stock $= x - \mu$

and: $$Z = \frac{x - \mu}{\sigma_{dLT}}$$

then: Safety stock $= Z\sigma_{dLT}$ (12-14)

Solving for safety stock, as in Equation (12-14), gives:

$$\text{Safety stock} = 1.645(10) = 16.5 \text{ kits}$$

This is the situation illustrated in Figure 12.8.

c) The reorder point is:

$$\text{ROP} = \text{Expected demand during lead time} + \text{Safety stock}$$

$$= 350 \text{ kits} + 16.5 \text{ kits of safety stock} = 366.5, \text{ or } 367 \text{ kits}$$

INSIGHT ▶ The cost of the inventory policy increases dramatically (exponentially) with an increase in service levels.

LEARNING EXERCISE ▶ What policy results in stockouts 10% of the time? [Answer: $Z = 1.28$; safety stock $= 12.8$; ROP $= 363$ kits.]

RELATED PROBLEMS ▶ 12.41, 12.42, 12.49 (12.50 is available in MyOMLab)

Other Probabilistic Models

Equations (12-13) and (12-14) assume that both an estimate of expected demand during lead times and its standard deviation are available. When data on lead time demand are *not* available, the preceding formulas cannot be applied. However, three other models are available. We need to determine which model to use for three situations:

1. Demand is variable and lead time is constant
2. Lead time is variable and demand is constant
3. Both demand and lead time are variable

All three models assume that demand and lead time are independent variables. Note that our examples use days, but weeks can also be used. Let us examine these three situations separately, because a different formula for the ROP is needed for each.

LO 12.7 *Understand service levels and probabilistic inventory models*

Demand Is Variable and Lead Time Is Constant   (See Example 12.) When *only the demand is variable*, then:[5]

$$\text{ROP} = (\textit{Average daily demand} \times \text{Lead time in days}) + Z\sigma_{dLT} \qquad (12\text{-}15)$$

where σ_{dLT} = Standard deviation of demand during lead time = $\sigma_d \sqrt{\text{Lead time}}$

and σ_d = Standard deviation of demand per day

Example 12

ROP FOR VARIABLE DEMAND AND CONSTANT LEAD TIME

The *average* daily demand for Lenovo laptop computers at a Circuit Town store is 15, with a standard deviation of 5 units. The lead time is constant at 2 days. Find the reorder point if management wants a 90% service level (i.e., risk stockouts only 10% of the time). How much of this is safety stock?

APPROACH ▶   Apply Equation (12-15) to the following data:

Average daily demand (normally distributed) = 15

Lead time in days (constant) = 2

Standard deviation of daily demand = σ_d = 5

Service level = 90%

SOLUTION ▶   From the normal table (Appendix I) or the Excel formula =NORMSINV(.90), we derive a Z-value for 90% of 1.28. Then:

$$\begin{aligned}
\text{ROP} &= (15 \text{ units} \times 2 \text{ days}) + Z\sigma_d\sqrt{\text{Lead time}} \\
&= 30 + 1.28(5)(\sqrt{2}) \\
&= 30 + 1.28(5)(1.41) = 30 + 9.02 = 39.02 \cong 39
\end{aligned}$$

Thus, safety stock is about 9 Lenovo computers.

INSIGHT ▶   The value of Z depends on the manager's stockout risk level. The smaller the risk, the higher the Z.

LEARNING EXERCISE ▶   If the Circuit Town manager wants a 95% service level, what is the new ROP? [Answer: ROP = 41.63, or 42.]

RELATED PROBLEM ▶   12.46

Lead Time Is Variable and Demand Is Constant   When the demand is constant and *only the lead time is variable*, then:

$$\text{ROP} = (\text{Daily demand} \times \textit{Average lead time in days}) + Z \times \text{Daily demand} \times \sigma_{LT} \qquad (12\text{-}16)$$

where σ_{LT} = Standard deviation of lead time in days

Example 13

ROP FOR CONSTANT DEMAND AND VARIABLE LEAD TIME

The Circuit Town store in Example 12 sells about 10 digital cameras a day (almost a constant quantity). Lead time for camera delivery is normally distributed with a mean time of 6 days and a standard deviation of 1 day. A 98% service level is set. Find the ROP.

APPROACH ▶ Apply Equation (12-16) to the following data:

Daily demand = 10

Average lead time = 6 days

Standard deviation of lead time = σ_{LT} = 1 day

Service level = 98%, so Z (from Appendix I or the Excel formula =NORMSINV(.98)) = 2.055

SOLUTION ▶ From the equation we get:

$$\text{ROP} = (10 \text{ units} \times 6 \text{ days}) + 2.055(10 \text{ units})(1)$$
$$= 60 + 20.55 = 80.55$$

The reorder point is about 81 cameras.

INSIGHT ▶ Note how the very high service level of 98% drives the ROP up.

LEARNING EXERCISE ▶ If a 90% service level is applied, what does the ROP drop to? [Answer: ROP = 60 + (1.28)(10)(1) = 60 + 12.8 = 72.8 because the Z-value is only 1.28.]

RELATED PROBLEM ▶ 12.47

Both Demand and Lead Time Are Variable When both the demand and lead time are variable, the formula for reorder point becomes more complex:[6]

$$\text{ROP} = (\text{Average daily demand} \times \text{Average lead time in days}) + Z\sigma_{dLT} \quad (12\text{-}17)$$

where

$$\sigma_d = \text{Standard deviation of demand per day}$$
$$\sigma_{LT} = \text{Standard deviation of lead time in days}$$

and $\sigma_{dLT} = \sqrt{(\text{Average lead time} \times \sigma_d^2) + (\text{Average daily demand})^2 \sigma_{LT}^2}$

Example 14

ROP FOR VARIABLE DEMAND AND VARIABLE LEAD TIME

The Circuit Town store's most popular item is six-packs of 9-volt batteries. About 150 packs are sold per day, following a normal distribution with a standard deviation of 16 packs. Batteries are ordered from an out-of-state distributor; lead time is normally distributed with an average of 5 days and a standard deviation of 1 day. To maintain a 95% service level, what **ROP** is appropriate?

APPROACH ▶ Determine a quantity at which to reorder by applying Equation (12-17) to the following data:

Average daily demand = 150 packs

Standard deviation of demand = σ_d = 16 packs

Average lead time = 5 days

Standard deviation of lead time = σ_{LT} = 1 day

Service level = 95%, so Z =1.645 (from Appendix I or the Excel formula =NORMSINV(.95))

SOLUTION ▶ From the equation we compute:

$$\text{ROP} = (150 \text{ packs} \times 5 \text{ days}) + 1.645\,\sigma_{dLT}$$

where
$$\sigma_{dLT} = \sqrt{(5 \text{ days} \times 16^2) + (150^2 \times 1^2)}$$
$$= \sqrt{(5 \times 256) + (22,500 \times 1)}$$
$$= \sqrt{1,280 + 22,500} = \sqrt{23,780} \cong 154$$

So ROP = $(150 \times 5) + 1.645(154) \cong 750 + 253 = 1,003$ packs

INSIGHT ▶ When both demand and lead time are variable, the formula looks quite complex. But it is just the result of squaring the standard deviations in Equations (12-15) and (12-16) to get their variances, then summing them, and finally taking the square root.

LEARNING EXERCISE ▶ For an 80% service level, what is the ROP? [Answer: $Z = .84$ and ROP = 879 packs.]

RELATED PROBLEM ▶ 12.48

Single-Period Model

Single-period inventory model
A system for ordering items that have little or no value at the end of a sales period (perishables).

A single-period inventory model describes a situation in which *one* order is placed for a product. At the end of the sales period, any remaining product has little or no value. This is a typical problem for Christmas trees, seasonal goods, bakery goods, newspapers, and magazines. (Indeed, this inventory issue is often called the "newsstand problem.") In other words, even though items at a newsstand are ordered weekly or daily, they cannot be held over and used as inventory in the next sales period. So our decision is how much to order at the beginning of the period.

Because the exact demand for such seasonal products is never known, we consider a probability distribution related to demand. If the normal distribution is assumed, and we stocked and sold an average (mean) of 100 Christmas trees each season, then there is a 50% chance we would stock out and a 50% chance we would have trees left over. To determine the optimal stocking policy for trees before the season begins, we also need to know the standard deviation and consider these two marginal costs:

C_s = Cost of shortage (we underestimated) = Sales price per unit − Cost per unit

C_o = Cost of overage (we overestimated) = Cost per unit − Salvage value per unit
(if there is any)

The service level, that is, the probability of *not* stocking out, is set at:

$$\text{Service level} = \frac{C_s}{C_s + C_o} \qquad (12\text{-}18)$$

Therefore, we should consider increasing our order quantity until the service level is equal to or more than the ratio of $[C_s/(C_s + C_o)]$.

This model, illustrated in Example 15, is used in many service industries, from hotels to airlines to bakeries to clothing retailers.

| Example 15 | **SINGLE-PERIOD INVENTORY DECISION** |

Chris Ellis's newsstand, just outside the Smithsonian subway station in Washington, DC, usually sells 120 copies of the *Washington Post* each day. Chris believes the sale of the *Post* is normally distributed, with a standard deviation of 15 papers. He pays 70 cents for each paper, which sells for $1.25. The *Post* gives him a 30-cent credit for each unsold paper. He wants to determine how many papers he should order each day and the stockout risk for that quantity.

APPROACH ▶ Chris's data are as follows:

$$C_s = \text{cost of shortage} = \$1.25 - \$.70 = \$.55$$
$$C_o = \text{cost of overage} = \$.70 - \$.30 \text{ (salvage value)} = \$.40$$

Chris will apply Equation (12-18) and the normal table, using $\mu = 120$ and $\sigma = 15$.

SOLUTION ▶

a) Service level $= \dfrac{C_s}{C_s + C_o} = \dfrac{.55}{.55 + .40} = \dfrac{.55}{.95} = .579$

b) Chris needs to find the Z score for his normal distribution that yields a probability of .579.

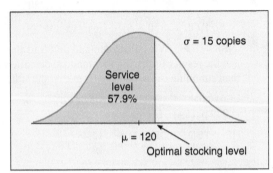

So 57.9% of the area under the normal curve must be to the left of the optimal stocking level.

c) Using Appendix I or the Excel formula $=\text{NORMSINV}(.578)$, for an area of .578, the Z value $\cong .195$.

Then, the optimal stocking level $= 120 \text{ copies} + (.195)(\sigma)$

$$= 120 + (.195)(15) = 120 + 3 = 123 \text{ papers}$$

The stockout risk if Chris orders 123 copies of the *Post* each day is $1 - \text{Service level} = 1 - .578 = .422 = 42.2\%$.

INSIGHT ▶ If the service level is ever under .50, Chris should order fewer than 120 copies per day.

LEARNING EXERCISE ▶ How does Chris's decision change if the *Post* changes its policy and offers *no credit* for unsold papers, a policy many publishers are adopting?

[Answer: Service level $= .44$, $Z = -.15$. Therefore, stock $120 + (-.15)(15) = 117.75$, or 118 papers.]

RELATED PROBLEMS ▶ 12.51, 12.52, 12.53

Fixed-quantity (Q) system
An ordering system with the same order amount each time.

Perpetual inventory system
A system that keeps track of each withdrawal or addition to inventory continuously, so records are always current.

Fixed-period (P) system
A system in which inventory orders are made at regular time intervals.

Fixed-Period (*P*) Systems

The inventory models that we have considered so far are fixed-quantity, or Q, systems. That is, the same fixed amount is added to inventory every time an order for an item is placed. We saw that orders are event triggered. When inventory decreases to the reorder point (ROP), a new order for Q units is placed.

To use the fixed-quantity model, inventory must be continuously monitored.[7] This requires a perpetual inventory system. Every time an item is added to or withdrawn from inventory, records must be updated to determine whether the ROP has been reached. In a fixed-period system (also called a periodic review, or P system), on the other hand, inventory is ordered at the end of a given period. Then, and only then, is on-hand inventory counted. Only the amount necessary to bring total inventory up to a prespecified target level (T) is ordered. Figure 12.9 illustrates this concept.

Fixed-period systems have several of the same assumptions as the basic EOQ fixed-quantity system:

- The only relevant costs are the ordering and holding costs.
- Lead times are known and constant.
- Items are independent of one another.

The downward-sloped lines in Figure 12.9 again represent on-hand inventory levels. But now, when the time between orders (P) passes, we place an order to raise inventory up to the target quantity (T).

Figure 12.9

Inventory Level in a Fixed-Period (*P*) System

Various amounts (Q_1, Q_2, Q_3, etc.) are ordered at regular time intervals (*P*) based on the quantity necessary to bring inventory up to the target quantity (*T*).

The amount ordered during the first period may be Q_1, the second period Q_2, and so on. The Q_i value is the difference between current on-hand inventory and the target inventory level.

● STUDENT TIP

A fixed-period model potentially orders a different quantity each time.

The advantage of the fixed-period system is that there is no physical count of inventory items after an item is withdrawn—this occurs only when the time for the next review comes up. This procedure is also convenient administratively.

A fixed-period (P) system is appropriate when vendors make routine (i.e., at fixed-time interval) visits to customers to take fresh orders or when purchasers want to combine orders to save ordering and transportation costs (therefore, they will have the same review period for similar inventory items). For example, a vending machine company may come to refill its machines every Tuesday. This is also the case at Anheuser-Busch, whose sales reps may visit a store every 5 days.

The disadvantage of the P system is that because there is no tally of inventory during the review period, there is the possibility of a stockout during this time. This scenario is possible if a large order draws the inventory level down to zero right after an order is placed. Therefore, a higher level of safety stock (as compared to a fixed-quantity system) needs to be maintained to provide protection against stockout during both the time between reviews and the lead time.

Summary

Inventory represents a major investment for many firms. This investment is often larger than it should be because firms find it easier to have "just-in-case" inventory rather than "just-in-time" inventory. Inventories are of four types:

1. Raw material and purchased components
2. Work-in-process
3. Maintenance, repair, and operating (MRO)

4. Finished goods

In this chapter, we discussed independent inventory, ABC analysis, record accuracy, cycle counting, and inventory models used to control independent demands. The EOQ model, production order quantity model, and quantity discount model can all be solved using Excel, Excel OM, or POM for Windows software.

Key Terms

Raw material inventory (p. 490)
Work-in-process (WIP) inventory (p. 490)
Maintenance/repair/operating (MRO) inventory (p. 490)
Finished-goods inventory (p. 491)
ABC analysis (p. 491)
Cycle counting (p. 493)
Shrinkage (p. 494)
Pilferage (p. 494)

Holding cost (p. 495)
Ordering cost (p. 495)
Setup cost (p. 496)
Setup time (p. 496)
Economic order quantity (EOQ) model (p. 496)
Robust (p. 500)
Lead time (p. 501)
Reorder point (ROP) (p. 501)

Safety stock (ss) (p. 501)
Production order quantity model (p. 502)
Quantity discount (p. 505)
Probabilistic model (p. 508)
Service level (p. 508)
Single-period inventory model (p. 513)
Fixed-quantity (Q) system (p. 514)
Perpetual inventory system (p. 514)
Fixed-period (P) system (p. 514)

Ethical Dilemma

Wayne Hills Hospital in tiny Wayne, Nebraska, faces a problem common to large, urban hospitals as well as to small, remote ones like itself. That problem is deciding how much of each type of whole blood to keep in stock. Because blood is expensive and has a limited shelf life (up to 5 weeks under 1–6°C refrigeration), Wayne Hills naturally wants to keep its stock as low as possible. Unfortunately, past disasters such as a major tornado and a train wreck demonstrated that lives would be lost when not enough blood was available to handle massive needs. The hospital administrator wants to set an 85% service level based on demand over the past decade. Discuss the implications of this decision. What is the hospital's responsibility with regard to stocking lifesaving medicines with short shelf lives? How would you set the inventory level for a commodity such as blood?

Discussion Questions

1. Describe the four types of inventory.
2. With the advent of low-cost computing, do you see alternatives to the popular ABC classifications?
3. What is the purpose of the ABC classification system?
4. Identify and explain the types of costs that are involved in an inventory system.

5. Explain the major assumptions of the basic EOQ model.
6. What is the relationship of the economic order quantity to demand? To the holding cost? To the setup cost?
7. Explain why it is not necessary to include product cost (price or price times quantity) in the EOQ model, but the quantity discount model requires this information.

8. What are the advantages of cycle counting?
9. What impact does a decrease in setup time have on EOQ?
10. When quantity discounts are offered, why is it not necessary to check discount points that are below the EOQ or points above the EOQ that are not discount points?
11. What is meant by "service level"?
12. Explain the following: All things being equal, the production order quantity will be larger than the economic order quantity.
13. Describe the difference between a fixed-quantity (Q) and a fixed-period (P) inventory system.

14. Explain what is meant by the expression "robust model." Specifically, what would you tell a manager who exclaimed, "Uh-oh, we're in trouble! The calculated EOQ is wrong; actual demand is 10% greater than estimated."
15. What is "safety stock"? What does safety stock provide safety against?
16. When demand is not constant, the reorder point is a function of what four parameters?
17. How are inventory levels monitored in retail stores?
18. State a major advantage, and a major disadvantage, of a fixed-period (P) system.

Using Software to Solve Inventory Problems

This section presents three ways to solve inventory problems with computer software. First, you can create your own Excel spreadsheets. Second, you can use the Excel OM software that comes free with this text. Third, POM for Windows, also free with this text, can solve all problems marked with a **P** .

CREATING YOUR OWN EXCEL SPREADSHEETS

Program 12.1 illustrates how you can make an Excel model to solve Example 8, which is a production order quantity model.

Program **12.1**

Using Excel for a Production Model, with Data from Example 8

Program 12.2 illustrates how you can make an Excel model to solve Example 15, which is a single-period inventory model.

Program **12.2**

Using Excel for a Single-Period Inventory Model, with Data from Example 15

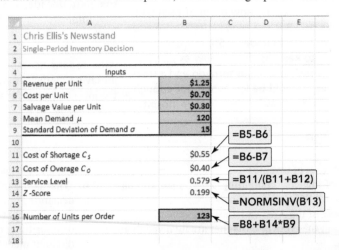

✗ USING EXCEL OM

Excel OM allows us to easily model inventory problems ranging from ABC analysis, to the basic EOQ model, to the production model, to quantity discount situations.

Program 12.3 shows the input data, selected formulas, and results for an ABC analysis, using data from Example 1. After the data are entered, we use the *Data* and *Sort* Excel commands to rank the items from largest to smallest dollar volumes.

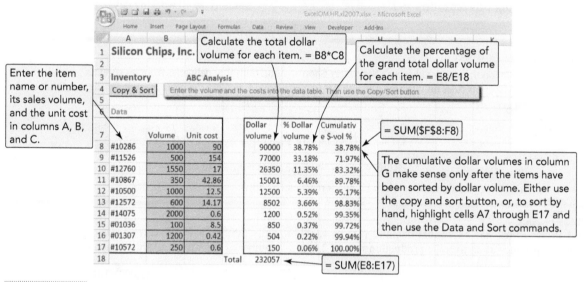

Program **12.3**

Using Excel OM for an ABC Analysis, with Data from Example 1

P USING POM FOR WINDOWS

The POM for Windows Inventory module can also solve the entire EOQ family of problems. Please refer to Appendix IV for further details.

Solved Problems   Virtual Office Hours help is available in MyOMLab.

SOLVED PROBLEM 12.1

David Alexander has compiled the following table of six items in inventory at Angelo Products, along with the unit cost and the annual demand in units:

IDENTIFICATION CODE	UNIT COST (S)	ANNUAL DEMAND (UNITS)
XX1	5.84	1,200
B66	5.40	1,110
3CPO	1.12	896
33CP	74.54	1,104
R2D2	2.00	1,110
RMS	2.08	961

Use ABC analysis to determine which item(s) should be carefully controlled using a quantitative inventory technique and which item(s) should not be closely controlled.

SOLUTION

The item that needs strict control is 33CP, so it is an A item. Items that do not need to be strictly controlled are 3CPO, R2D2, and RMS; these are C items. The B items will be XX1 and B66.

CODE	ANNUAL DOLLAR VOLUME = UNIT COST × DEMAND
XX1	$ 7,008.00
B66	$ 5,994.00
3CPO	$ 1,003.52
33CP	$82,292.16
R2D2	$ 2,220.00
RMS	$ 1,998.88

Total cost = $100,516.56
70% of total cost = $70,347.92

SOLVED PROBLEM 12.2

The Warren W. Fisher Computer Corporation purchases 8,000 transistors each year as components in minicomputers. The unit cost of each transistor is $10, and the cost of carrying one transistor in inventory for a year is $3. Ordering cost is $30 per order.

What are (a) the optimal order quantity, (b) the expected number of orders placed each year, and (c) the expected time between orders? Assume that Fisher operates on a 200-day working year.

SOLUTION

a) $Q^* = \sqrt{\dfrac{2DS}{H}} = \sqrt{\dfrac{2(8,000)(30)}{3}} = 400$ units

b) $N = \dfrac{D}{Q^*} = \dfrac{8,000}{400} = 20$ orders

c) Time between orders $= T = \dfrac{\text{Number of working days}}{N} = \dfrac{200}{20} = 10$ working days

With 20 orders placed each year, an order for 400 transistors is placed every 10 working days.

SOLVED PROBLEM 12.3

Annual demand for notebook binders at Meyer's Stationery Shop is 10,000 units. Brad Meyer operates his business 300 days per year and finds that deliveries from his supplier generally take 5 working days. Calculate the reorder point for the notebook binders.

SOLUTION

$$L = 5 \text{ days}$$

$$d = \dfrac{10,000}{300} = 33.3 \text{ units per day}$$

$$\text{ROP} = d \times L = (33.3 \text{ units per day})(5 \text{ days}) = 166.7 \text{ units}$$

Thus, Brad should reorder when his stock reaches 167 units.

SOLVED PROBLEM 12.4

Leonard Presby, Inc., has an annual demand rate of 1,000 units but can produce at an average production rate of 2,000 units. Setup cost is $10; carrying cost is $1. What is the optimal number of units to be produced each time?

SOLUTION

$$Q_p^* = \sqrt{\dfrac{2DS}{H\left(1 - \dfrac{\text{Annual demand rate}}{\text{Annual production rate}}\right)}} = \sqrt{\dfrac{2(1,000)(10)}{1[1 - (1,000/2,000)]}}$$

$$= \sqrt{\dfrac{20,000}{1/2}} = \sqrt{40,000} = 200 \text{ units}$$

SOLVED PROBLEM 12.5

Whole Nature Foods sells a gluten-free product for which the annual demand is 5,000 boxes. At the moment, it is paying $6.40 for each box; carrying cost is 25% of the unit cost; ordering costs are $25. A new supplier has offered to sell the same item for $6.00 if Whole Nature Foods buys at least 3,000 boxes per order. Should the firm stick with the old supplier, or take advantage of the new quantity discount?

SOLUTION

Step 1, under the lowest possible price of $6.00 per box:
  Economic order quantity, using Equation (12-10):

$$Q^*_{\$6.00} = \sqrt{\dfrac{2(5,000)(25)}{(0.25)(6.00)}}$$

$$= 408.25, \text{ or } 408 \text{ boxes}$$

Because 408 < 3,000, this EOQ is *infeasible* for the $6.00 price. So now we calculate Q^* for the next-higher price of $6.40, which equals 395 boxes (and is feasible). Thus, the best possible order quantities are 395 (the first feasible EOQ) and 3,000 (the price-break quantity for the lower price of $6.00).

Step 2 uses Equation (12-9) to compute the total cost for both of the possible best order quantities:

$$TC_{395} = \dfrac{5,000}{395}(\$25) + \dfrac{395}{2}(0.25)(\$6.40) + \$6.40(5,000)$$

$$= \$316 + \$316 + \$32,000$$

$$= \$32,632$$

And under the quantity discount price of $6.00 per box:

$$TC_{3,000} = \dfrac{5,000}{3,000}(\$25) + \dfrac{3,000}{2}(0.25)(\$6.00) + \$6.00(5,000)$$

$$= \$42 + \$2,250 + \$30,000$$

$$= \$32,292$$

Therefore, the new supplier with which Whole Nature Foods would incur a total cost of $32,292 is preferable, but not by a large amount. If buying 3,000 boxes at a time raises problems of storage or freshness, the company may very well wish to stay with the current supplier.

SOLVED PROBLEM 12.6

Children's art sets are ordered once each year by Ashok Kumar, Inc., and the reorder point, without safety stock (dL), is 100 art sets. Inventory carrying cost is $10 per set per year, and the cost of a stockout is $50 per set per year. Given the following demand probabilities during the lead time, how much safety stock should be carried?

DEMAND DURING LEAD TIME	PROBABILITY
0	.1
50	.2
ROP → 100	.4
150	.2
200	.1
	1.0

SOLUTION

		INCREMENTAL COSTS	
SAFETY STOCK	CARRYING COST	STOCKOUT COST	TOTAL COST
0	0	$50 \times (50 \times 0.2 + 100 \times 0.1) = 1,000$	$1,000
50	$50 \times 10 = 500$	$50 \times (0.1 \times 50) = 250$	750
100	$100 \times 10 = 1,000$	0	1,000

The safety stock that minimizes total incremental cost is 50 sets. The reorder point then becomes 100 sets + 50 sets, or 150 sets.

SOLVED PROBLEM 12.7

What safety stock should Ron Satterfield Corporation maintain if mean sales are 80 during the reorder period, the standard deviation is 7, and Ron can tolerate stockouts 10% of the time?

SOLUTION

From Appendix I, Z at an area of .9 (or $1 - .10$) = 1.28, and Equation (12-14):

$$\text{Safety stock} = Z\sigma_{dLT}$$
$$= 1.28(7) = 8.96 \text{ units, or 9 units}$$

SOLVED PROBLEM 12.8

The daily demand for 52" flat-screen TVs at Sarah's Discount Emporium is normally distributed, with an average of 5 and a standard deviation of 2 units. The lead time for receiving a shipment of new TVs is 10 days and is fairly constant. Determine the reorder point and safety stock for a 95% service level.

SOLUTION

The ROP for this variable demand and constant lead time model uses Equation (12-15):

$$\text{ROP} = (\text{Average daily demand} \times \text{Lead time in days}) + Z\sigma_{dLT}$$

where $\sigma_{dLT} = \sigma_d\sqrt{\text{Lead time}}$

So, with $Z = 1.645$,

$$\text{ROP} = (5 \times 10) + 1.645(2)\sqrt{10}$$
$$= 50 + 10.4 = 60.4 \cong 60 \text{ TVs, or rounded up to 61 TVs}$$

The safety stock is 10.4, which can be rounded up to 11 TVs.

SOLVED PROBLEM 12.9

The demand at Arnold Palmer Hospital for a specialized surgery pack is 60 per week, virtually every week. The lead time from McKesson, its main supplier, is normally distributed, with a mean of 6 weeks for this product and a standard deviation of 2 weeks. A 90% weekly service level is desired. Find the ROP.

SOLUTION

Here the demand is constant and lead time is variable, with data given in weeks, not days. We apply Equation (12-16):

$$\text{ROP} = (\text{Weekly demand} \times \text{Average lead time in weeks}) + Z(\text{Weekly demand})\sigma_{LT}$$

where σ_{LT} = standard deviation of lead time in weeks = 2

So, with $Z = 1.28$, for a 90% service level:

$$\text{ROP} = (60 \times 6) + 1.28(60)(2)$$
$$= 360 + 153.6 = 513.6 \cong 514 \text{ surgery packs}$$

Problems
Note: **Px** means the problem may be solved with POM for Windows and/or Excel OM.

Problems 12.1–12.6 relate to Managing Inventory

•• **12.1** L. Houts Plastics is a large manufacturer of injection-molded plastics in North Carolina. An investigation of the company's manufacturing facility in Charlotte yields the information presented in the table below. How would the plant classify these items according to an ABC classification system? **Px**

L. Houts Plastics' Charlotte Inventory Levels

ITEM CODE #	AVERAGE INVENTORY (UNITS)	VALUE ($/UNIT)
1289	400	3.75
2347	300	4.00
2349	120	2.50
2363	75	1.50
2394	60	1.75
2395	30	2.00
6782	20	1.15
7844	12	2.05
8210	8	1.80
8310	7	2.00
9111	6	3.00

•• **12.2** Boreki Enterprises has the following 10 items in inventory. Theodore Boreki asks you, a recent OM graduate, to divide these items into ABC classifications.

ITEM	ANNUAL DEMAND	COST/UNIT
A2	3,000	$ 50
B8	4,000	12
C7	1,500	45
D1	6,000	10
E9	1,000	20
F3	500	500
G2	300	1,500
H2	600	20
I5	1,750	10
J8	2,500	5

a) Develop an ABC classification system for the 10 items.
b) How can Boreki use this information?
c) Boreki reviews the classification and then places item A2 into the A category. Why might he do so? **Px**

•• **12.3** Jean-Marie Bourjolly's restaurant has the following inventory items that it orders on a weekly basis:

INVENTORY ITEM	$ VALUE/CASE	# ORDERED/WEEK
Ribeye steak	135	3
Lobster tail	245	3
Pasta	23	12
Salt	3	2
Napkins	12	2
Tomato sauce	23	11
French fries	43	32

cont'd

(cont'd)

INVENTORY ITEM	$ VALUE/CASE	# ORDERED/WEEK
Pepper	3	3
Garlic powder	11	3
Trash can liners	12	3
Table cloths	32	5
Fish filets	143	10
Prime rib roasts	166	6
Oil	28	2
Lettuce (case)	35	24
Chickens	75	14
Order pads	12	2
Eggs (case)	22	7
Bacon	56	5
Sugar	4	2

a) Which is the most expensive item, using annual dollar volume?
b) Which are C items?
c) What is the annual dollar volume for all 20 items? **Px**

• **12.4** Lindsay Electronics, a small manufacturer of electronic research equipment, has approximately 7,000 items in its inventory and has hired Joan Blasco-Paul to manage its inventory. Joan has determined that 10% of the items in inventory are A items, 35% are B items, and 55% are C items. She would like to set up a system in which all A items are counted monthly (every 20 working days), all B items are counted quarterly (every 60 working days), and all C items are counted semiannually (every 120 working days). How many items need to be counted each day?

> *Additional problems 12.5–12.6 are available in* MyOMLab.

Problems 12.7–12.40 relate to Inventory Models for Independent Demand

• **12.7** William Beville's computer training school, in Richmond, stocks workbooks with the following characteristics:

$$\text{Demand } D = 19,500 \text{ units/year}$$
$$\text{Ordering cost } S = \$25/\text{order}$$
$$\text{Holding cost } H = \$4/\text{unit/year}$$

a) Calculate the EOQ for the workbooks.
b) What are the annual holding costs for the workbooks?
c) What are the annual ordering costs? **Px**

• **12.8** If D = 8,000 per month, S = $45 per order, and H = $2 per unit per month,
a) What is the economic order quantity?
b) How does your answer change if the holding cost doubles?
c) What if the holding cost drops in half? **Px**

•• **12.9** Henry Crouch's law office has traditionally ordered ink refills 60 units at a time. The firm estimates that carrying cost is 40% of the $10 unit cost and that annual demand is about 240 units per year. The assumptions of the basic EOQ model are thought to apply.
a) For what value of ordering cost would its action be optimal?
b) If the true ordering cost turns out to be much greater than your answer to (a), what is the impact on the firm's ordering policy?

• **12.10** Matthew Liotine's Dream Store sells beds and assorted supplies. His best-selling bed has an annual demand of 400 units. Ordering cost is $40; holding cost is $5 per unit per year.

a) To minimize the total cost, how many units should be ordered each time an order is placed?

b) If the holding cost per unit was $6 instead of $5, what would be the optimal order quantity? **PX**

· **12.11**   Southeastern Bell stocks a certain switch connector at its central warehouse for supplying field service offices. The yearly demand for these connectors is 15,000 units. Southeastern estimates its annual holding cost for this item to be $25 per unit. The cost to place and process an order from the supplier is $75. The company operates 300 days per year, and the lead time to receive an order from the supplier is 2 working days.

a) Find the economic order quantity.

b) Find the annual holding costs.

c) Find the annual ordering costs.

d) What is the reorder point? **PX**

· **12.12**   Lead time for one of your fastest-moving products is 21 days. Demand during this period averages 100 units per day.

a) What would be an appropriate reorder point?

b) How does your answer change if demand during lead time doubles?

c) How does your answer change if demand during lead time drops in half?

· **12.13**   Annual demand for the notebook binders at Duncan's Stationery Shop is 10,000 units. Dana Duncan operates her business 300 days per year and finds that deliveries from her supplier generally take 5 working days.

a) Calculate the reorder point for the notebook binders that she stocks.

b) Why is this number important to Duncan?

·· **12.14**   Thomas Kratzer is the purchasing manager for the headquarters of a large insurance company chain with a central inventory operation. Thomas's fastest-moving inventory item has a demand of 6,000 units per year. The cost of each unit is $100, and the inventory carrying cost is $10 per unit per year. The average ordering cost is $30 per order. It takes about 5 days for an order to arrive, and the demand for 1 week is 120 units. (This is a corporate operation, and there are 250 working days per year.)

a) What is the EOQ?

b) What is the average inventory if the EOQ is used?

c) What is the optimal number of orders per year?

d) What is the optimal number of days in between any two orders?

e) What is the annual cost of ordering and holding inventory?

f) What is the total annual inventory cost, including the cost of the 6,000 units? **PX**

·· **12.15**   Joe Henry's machine shop uses 2,500 brackets during the course of a year. These brackets are purchased from a supplier 90 miles away. The following information is known about the brackets:

Annual demand:	2,500
Holding cost per bracket per year:	$1.50
Order cost per order:	$18.75
Lead time:	2 days
Working days per year:	250

a) Given the above information, what would be the economic order quantity (EOQ)?

b) Given the EOQ, what would be the average inventory? What would be the annual inventory holding cost?

c) Given the EOQ, how many orders would be made each year? What would be the annual order cost?

d) Given the EOQ, what is the total annual cost of managing the inventory?

e) What is the time between orders?

f) What is the reorder point (ROP)? **PX**

·· **12.16**   Abey Kuruvilla, of Parkside Plumbing, uses 1,200 of a certain spare part that costs $25 for each order, with an annual holding cost of $24.

a) Calculate the total cost for order sizes of 25, 40, 50, 60, and 100.

b) Identify the economic order quantity and consider the implications for making an error in calculating economic order quantity. **PX**

··· **12.17** M. Cotteleer Electronics supplies microcomputer circuitry to a company that incorporates microprocessors into refrigerators and other home appliances. One of the components has an annual demand of 250 units, and this is constant throughout the year. Carrying cost is estimated to be $1 per unit per year, and the ordering (setup) cost is $20 per order.

a) To minimize cost, how many units should be ordered each time an order is placed?

b) How many orders per year are needed with the optimal policy?

c) What is the average inventory if costs are minimized?

d) Suppose that the ordering (setup) cost is not $20, and Cotteleer has been ordering 150 units each time an order is placed. For this order policy (of $Q = 150$) to be optimal, determine what the ordering (setup) cost would have to be. **PX**

·· **12.18**   Race One Motors is an Indonesian car manufacturer. At its largest manufacturing facility, in Jakarta, the company produces subcomponents at a rate of 300 per day, and it uses these subcomponents at a rate of 12,500 per year (of 250 working days). Holding costs are $2 per item per year, and ordering (setup) costs are $30 per order.

a) What is the economic production quantity?

b) How many production runs per year will be made?

c) What will be the maximum inventory level?

d) What percentage of time will the facility be producing components?

e) What is the annual cost of ordering and holding inventory? **PX**

·· **12.19**   Radovilsky Manufacturing Company, in Hayward, California, makes flashing lights for toys. The company operates its production facility 300 days per year. It has orders for about 12,000 flashing lights per year and has the capability of producing 100 per day. Setting up the light production costs $50. The cost of each light is $1. The holding cost is $0.10 per light per year.

a) What is the optimal size of the production run?

b) What is the average holding cost per year?

c) What is the average setup cost per year?

d) What is the total cost per year, including the cost of the lights? **PX**

·· **12.20**   Arthur Meiners is the production manager of Wheel-Rite, a small producer of metal parts. Wheel-Rite supplies Cal-Tex, a larger assembly company, with 10,000 wheel bearings each year. This order has been stable for some time. Setup cost for Wheel-Rite is $40, and holding cost is $.60 per wheel bearing per year. Wheel-Rite can produce 500 wheel bearings per day. Cal-Tex is a just-in-time manufacturer and requires that 50 bearings be shipped to it each business day.

a) What is the optimum production quantity?

b) What is the maximum number of wheel bearings that will be in inventory at Wheel-Rite?

c) How many production runs of wheel bearings will Wheel-Rite have in a year?

d) What is the total setup + holding cost for Wheel-Rite? **Px**

•• **12.21** Cesar Rego Computers, a Mississippi chain of computer hardware and software retail outlets, supplies both educational and commercial customers with memory and storage devices. It currently faces the following ordering decision relating to purchases of very high-density disks:

$$D = 36{,}000 \text{ disks}$$
$$S = \$25$$
$$H = \$0.45$$
$$\text{Purchase price} = \$.85$$
$$\text{Discount price} = \$0.82$$

Quantity needed to qualify for the discount = 6,000 disks

Should the discount be taken? **Px**

•• **12.22** Bell Computers purchases integrated chips at $350 per chip. The holding cost is $35 per unit per year, the ordering cost is $120 per order, and sales are steady, at 400 per month. The company's supplier, Rich Blue Chip Manufacturing, Inc., decides to offer price concessions in order to attract larger orders. The price structure is shown below.

Rich Blue Chip's Price Structure

QUANTITY PURCHASED	PRICE/UNIT
1–99 units	$350
100–199 units	$325
200 or more units	$300

a) What is the optimal order quantity and the minimum annual cost for Bell Computers to order, purchase, and hold these integrated chips?

b) Bell Computers wishes to use a 10% holding cost rather than the fixed $35 holding cost in (a). What is the optimal order quantity, and what is the optimal annual cost? **Px**

•• **12.23** Wang Distributors has an annual demand for an airport metal detector of 1,400 units. The cost of a typical detector to Wang is $400. Carrying cost is estimated to be 20% of the unit cost, and the ordering cost is $25 per order. If Ping Wang, the owner, orders in quantities of 300 or more, he can get a 5% discount on the cost of the detectors. Should Wang take the quantity discount? **Px**

•• **12.24** The catering manager of La Vista Hotel, Lisa Ferguson, is disturbed by the amount of silverware she is losing every week. Last Friday night, when her crew tried to set up for a banquet for 500 people, they did not have enough knives. She decides she needs to order some more silverware, but wants to take advantage of any quantity discounts her vendor will offer.

For a small order (2,000 or fewer pieces), her vendor quotes a price of $1.80/piece.

If she orders 2,001–5,000 pieces, the price drops to $1.60/piece. 5,001–10,000 pieces brings the price to $1.40/piece, and 10,001 and above reduces the price to $1.25.

Lisa's order costs are $200 per order, her annual holding costs are 5%, and the annual demand is 45,000 pieces. For the best option:

a) What is the optimal order quantity?

b) What is the annual holding cost?

c) What is the annual ordering (setup) cost?

d) What are the annual costs of the silverware itself with an optimal order quantity?

e) What is the total annual cost, including ordering, holding, and purchasing the silverware? **Px**

•• **12.25** Rocky Mountain Tire Center sells 20,000 go-cart tires per year. The ordering cost for each order is $40, and the holding cost is 20% of the purchase price of the tires per year. The purchase price is $20 per tire if fewer than 500 tires are ordered, $18 per tire if 500 or more—but fewer than 1,000—tires are ordered, and $17 per tire if 1,000 or more tires are ordered.

a) How many tires should Rocky Mountain order each time it places an order?

b) What is the total cost of this policy? **Px**

•• **12.26** M. P. VanOyen Manufacturing has gone out on bid for a regulator component. Expected demand is 700 units per month. The item can be purchased from either Allen Manufacturing or Baker Manufacturing. Their price lists are shown in the table. Ordering cost is $50, and annual holding cost per unit is $5.

ALLEN MFG.		BAKER MFG.	
QUANTITY	UNIT PRICE	QUANTITY	UNIT PRICE
1–499	$16.00	1–399	$16.10
500–999	15.50	400–799	15.60
1,000+	15.00	800+	15.10

a) What is the economic order quantity?

b) Which supplier should be used? Why?

c) What is the optimal order quantity and total annual cost of ordering, purchasing, and holding the component? **Px**

••• **12.27** Chris Sandvig Irrigation, Inc., has summarized the price list from four potential suppliers of an underground control valve. See the accompanying table. Annual usage is 2,400 valves; order cost is $10 per order; and annual inventory holding costs are $3.33 per unit.

Which vendor should be selected and what order quantity is best if Sandvig Irrigation wants to minimize total cost? **Px**

VENDOR A		VENDOR B	
QUANTITY	PRICE	QUANTITY	PRICE
1–49	$35.00	1–74	$34.75
50–74	34.75	75–149	34.00
75–149	33.55	150–299	32.80
150–299	32.35	300–499	31.60
300–499	31.15	500+	30.50
500+	30.75		

VENDOR C		VENDOR D	
QUANTITY	PRICE	QUANTITY	PRICE
1–99	$34.50	1–199	$34.25
100–199	33.75	200–399	33.00
200–399	32.50	400+	31.00
400+	31.10		

••• **12.28** Emery Pharmaceutical uses an unstable chemical compound that must be kept in an environment where both temperature and humidity can be controlled. Emery uses 800 pounds per month of the chemical, estimates the holding cost to be 50% of the purchase price (because of spoilage), and estimates order costs to be $50 per order. The cost schedules of two suppliers are as follows:

VENDOR 1		VENDOR 2	
QUANTITY	PRICE/LB	QUANTITY	PRICE/LB
1–499	$17.00	1–399	$17.10
500–999	16.75	400–799	16.85
1,000+	16.50	800–1,199	16.60
		1,200+	16.25

a) What is the economic order quantity for each supplier?

b) What quantity should be ordered, and which supplier should be used?

c) What is the total cost for the most economic order size?

d) What factor(s) should be considered besides total cost? ▶x

••• **12.29** Kim Clark has asked you to help him determine the best ordering policy for a new product. The demand for the new product has been forecasted to be about 1,000 units annually. To help you get a handle on the carrying and ordering costs, Kim has given you the list of last year's costs. He thought that these costs might be appropriate for the new product.

COST FACTOR	COST ($)	COST FACTOR	COST ($)
Taxes for the warehouse	2,000	Warehouse supplies	280
Receiving and incoming inspection	1,500	Research and development	2,750
New product development	2,500	Purchasing salaries & wages	30,000
Acct. Dept. costs to pay invoices	500	Warehouse salaries & wages	12,800
Inventory insurance	600	Pilferage of inventory	800
Product advertising	800	Purchase order supplies	500
Spoilage	750	Inventory obsolescence	300
Sending purchasing orders	800	Purchasing Dept. overhead	1,000

He also told you that these data were compiled for 10,000 inventory items that were carried or held during the year. You have also determined that 200 orders were placed last year. Your job as a new operations management graduate is to help Kim determine the economic order quantity for the new product.

•••• **12.30** Emarpy Appliance is a company that produces all kinds of major appliances. Bud Banis, the president of Emarpy, is concerned about the production policy for the company's best-selling refrigerator. The annual demand has been about 8,000 units each year, and this demand has been constant throughout the year. The production capacity is 200 units per day. Each time production starts, it costs the company $120 to move materials into place, reset the assembly line, and clean the equipment. The holding cost of a refrigerator is $50 per year. The current production plan calls for 400 refrigerators to be produced in each production run. Assume there are 250 working days per year.

a) What is the daily demand of this product?

b) If the company were to continue to produce 400 units each time production starts, how many days would production continue?

c) Under the current policy, how many production runs per year would be required? What would the annual setup cost be?

d) If the current policy continues, how many refrigerators would be in inventory when production stops? What would the average inventory level be?

e) If the company produces 400 refrigerators at a time, what would the total annual setup cost and holding cost be?

f) If Bud Banis wants to minimize the total annual inventory cost, how many refrigerators should be produced in each production run? How much would this save the company in inventory costs compared to the current policy of producing 400 in each production run? ▶x

Additional problems **12.31–12.40** *are available in* MyOMLab.

Problems 12.41–12.50 relate to Probabilistic Models and Safety Stock

•• **12.41** Barbara Flynn is in charge of maintaining hospital supplies at General Hospital. During the past year, the mean lead time demand for bandage BX-5 was 60 (and was normally distributed). Furthermore, the standard deviation for BX-5 was 7. Ms. Flynn would like to maintain a 90% service level.

a) What safety stock level do you recommend for BX-5?

b) What is the appropriate reorder point? ▶x

•• **12.42** Based on available information, lead time demand for PC jump drives averages 50 units (normally distributed), with a standard deviation of 5 drives. Management wants a 97% service level.

a) What value of Z should be applied?

b) How many drives should be carried as safety stock?

c) What is the appropriate reorder point? ▶x

••• **12.43** Authentic Thai rattan chairs (shown in the photo) are delivered to Gary Schwartz's chain of retail stores, called The Kathmandu Shop, once a year. The reorder point, without safety stock, is 200 chairs. Carrying cost is $30 per unit per year, and the cost of a stockout is $70 per chair per year. Given the following demand probabilities during the lead time, how much safety stock should be carried?

Barry Render

DEMAND DURING LEAD TIME	PROBABILITY
0	0.2
100	0.2
200	0.2
300	0.2
400	0.2

•• **12.44** Tobacco is shipped from North Carolina to a cigarette manufacturer in Cambodia once a year. The reorder point, without safety stock, is 200 kilos. The carrying cost is $15 per kilo per year, and the cost of a stockout is $70 per kilo per year. Given the following demand probabilities during the lead time, how much safety stock should be carried?

DEMAND DURING LEAD TIME (KILOS)	PROBABILITY
0	0.1
100	0.1
200	0.2
300	0.4
400	0.2

••• **12.45** Mr. Beautiful, an organization that sells weight training sets, has an ordering cost of $40 for the BB-1 set. (BB-1 stands for Body Beautiful Number 1.) The carrying cost for BB-1 is $5 per set per year. To meet demand, Mr. Beautiful orders large quantities of BB-1 seven times a year. The stockout cost for BB-1 is estimated to be $50 per set. Over the past several years, Mr. Beautiful has observed the following demand during the lead time for BB-1:

DEMAND DURING LEAD TIME	PROBABILITY
40	.1
50	.2
60	.2
70	.2
80	.2
90	.1
	1.0

The reorder point for BB-1 is 60 sets. What level of safety stock should be maintained for BB-1? **Px**

•• **12.46** Chicago's Hard Rock Hotel distributes a mean of 1,000 bath towels per day to guests at the pool and in their rooms. This demand is normally distributed with a standard deviation of 100 towels per day, based on occupancy. The laundry firm that has the linens contract requires a 2-day lead time. The hotel expects a 98% service level to satisfy high guest expectations.
a) What is the safety stock?
b) What is the ROP? **Px**

•• **12.47** First Printing has contracts with legal firms in San Francisco to copy their court documents. Daily demand is almost constant at 12,500 pages of documents. The lead time for paper delivery is normally distributed with a mean of 4 days and a standard deviation of 1 day. A 97% service level is expected. Compute First's ROP. **Px**

•••• **12.48** Gainesville Cigar stocks Cuban cigars that have variable lead times because of the difficulty in importing the product: lead time is normally distributed with an average of 6 weeks and a standard deviation of 2 weeks. Demand is also a variable and normally distributed with a mean of 200 cigars per week and a standard deviation of 25 cigars.
a) For a 90% service level, what is the ROP?
b) What is the ROP for a 95% service level?

c) Explain what these two service levels mean. Which is preferable? **Px**

•••• **12.49** A gourmet coffee shop in downtown San Francisco is open 200 days a year and sells an average of 75 pounds of Kona coffee beans a day. (Demand can be assumed to be distributed normally, with a standard deviation of 15 pounds per day.) After ordering (fixed cost = $16 per order), beans are always shipped from Hawaii within exactly 4 days. Per-pound annual holding costs for the beans are $3.
a) What is the economic order quantity (EOQ) for Kona coffee beans?
b) What are the total annual holding costs of stock for Kona coffee beans?
c) What are the total annual ordering costs for Kona coffee beans?
d) Assume that management has specified that no more than a 1% risk during stockout is acceptable. What should the reorder point (ROP) be?
e) What is the safety stock needed to attain a 1% risk of stockout during lead time?
f) What is the annual holding cost of maintaining the level of safety stock needed to support a 1% risk?
g) If management specified that a 2% risk of stockout during lead time would be acceptable, would the safety stock holding costs decrease or increase?

Additional problem **12.50** is available in MyOMLab.

Problems 12.51–12.53 relate to Single-Period Model

•• **12.51** Cynthia Knott's oyster bar buys fresh Louisiana oysters for $5 per pound and sells them for $9 per pound. Any oysters not sold that day are sold to her cousin, who has a nearby grocery store, for $2 per pound. Cynthia believes that demand follows the normal distribution, with a mean of 100 pounds and a standard deviation of 15 pounds. How many pounds should she order each day?

•• **12.52** Henrique Correa's bakery prepares all its cakes between 4 A.M. and 6 A.M. so they will be fresh when customers arrive. Day-old cakes are virtually always sold, but at a 50% discount off the regular $10 price. The cost of baking a cake is $6, and demand is estimated to be normally distributed, with a mean of 25 and a standard deviation of 4. What is the optimal stocking level?

••• **12.53** University of Florida football programs are printed 1 week prior to each home game. Attendance averages 90,000 screaming and loyal Gators fans, of whom two-thirds usually buy the program, following a normal distribution, for $4 each. Unsold programs are sent to a recycling center that pays only 10 cents per program. The standard deviation is 5,000 programs, and the cost to print each program is $1.
a) What is the cost of underestimating demand for each program?
b) What is the overage cost per program?
c) How many programs should be ordered per game?
d) What is the stockout risk for this order size?

CASE STUDIES

Zhou Bicycle Company

Zhou Bicycle Company (ZBC), located in Seattle, is a wholesale distributor of bicycles and bicycle parts. Formed in 1981 by University of Washington Professor Yong-Pin Zhou, the firm's primary retail outlets are located within a 400-mile radius of the distribution center. These retail outlets receive the order from ZBC within 2 days after notifying the distribution center, provided that the stock is available. However, if an order is not fulfilled by the company, no backorder is placed; the retailers arrange to get their shipment from other distributors, and ZBC loses that amount of business.

The company distributes a wide variety of bicycles. The most popular model, and the major source of revenue to the company, is the AirWing. ZBC receives all the models from a single manufacturer in China, and shipment takes as long as 4 weeks from the time an order is placed. With the cost of communication, paperwork, and customs clearance included, ZBC estimates that each time an order is placed, it incurs a cost of $65. The purchase price paid by ZBC, per bicycle, is roughly 60% of the suggested retail price for all the styles available, and the inventory carrying cost is 1% per month (12% per year) of the purchase price paid by ZBC. The retail price (paid by the customers) for the AirWing is $170 per bicycle.

ZBC is interested in making an inventory plan for 2016. The firm wants to maintain a 95% service level with its customers to minimize the losses on the lost orders. The data collected for the past 2 years are summarized in the following table. A forecast for AirWing model sales in 2016 has been developed and will be used to make an inventory plan for ZBC.

Demands For Airwing Model

MONTH	2014	2015	FORECAST FOR 2016
January	6	7	8
February	12	14	15

MONTH	2014	2015	FORECAST FOR 2016
March	24	27	31
April	46	53	59
May	75	86	97
June	47	54	60
July	30	34	39
August	18	21	24
September	13	15	16
October	12	13	15
November	22	25	28
December	38	42	47
Total	343	391	439

Discussion Questions

1. Develop an inventory plan to help ZBC.
2. Discuss ROPs and total costs.
3. How can you address demand that is not at the level of the planning horizon?

Source: Professor Kala Chand Seal, Loyola Marymount University.

Parker Hi-Fi Systems

Parker Hi-Fi Systems, located in Wellesley, Massachusetts, a Boston suburb, assembles and sells the very finest home theater systems. The systems are assembled with components from the best manufacturers worldwide. Although most of the components are procured from wholesalers on the East Coast, some critical items, such as LCD screens, come directly from their manufacturer. For instance, the LCD screens are shipped via air from Foxy, Ltd., in Taiwan, to Boston's Logan airport, and the top-of-the-line speakers are purchased from the world-renowned U.S. manufacturer Boss.

Parker's purchasing agent, Raktim Pal, submits an order release for LCD screens once every 4 weeks. The company's annual requirements total 500 units (2 per working day), and Parker's per unit cost is $1,500. (Because of Parker's relatively low volume and the quality focus—rather than volume focus—of many of Parker's suppliers, Parker is seldom able to obtain quantity discounts.) Because Foxy promises delivery within 1 week following receipt of an order release, Parker has never had a shortage of LCDs. (Total time between date of the release and date of receipt is 1 week or 5 working days.)

Parker's activity-based costing system has generated the following inventory-related costs. Procurement costs, which amount to $500 per order, include the actual labor costs involved in ordering, customs inspection, arranging for airport pickup, delivery to the plant, maintaining inventory records, and arranging for the bank to issue a check. Parker's holding costs take into account storage, damage, insurance, taxes, and so forth on a square-foot basis. These costs equal $150 per LCD per year.

With added emphasis being placed on efficiencies in the supply chain, Parker's president has asked Raktim to seriously evaluate the purchase of the LCDs. One area to be closely scrutinized for possible cost savings is inventory procurement.

Discussion Questions

1. What is the optimal order number of LCDs that should be placed in each order?
2. What is the optimal reorder point (ROP) for LCDs?
3. What cost savings will Parker realize if it implements an order plan based on EOQ?

Managing Inventory at Frito-Lay

Video Case

Frito-Lay has flourished since its origin—the 1931 purchase of a small San Antonio firm for $100 that included a recipe, 19 retail accounts, and a hand-operated potato ricer. The multibillion-dollar company, headquartered in Dallas, now has 41 products—15 with sales of over $100 million per year and 7 at over $1 billion in sales. Production takes place in 36 product-focused plants in the U.S. and Canada, with 48,000 employees.

Inventory is a major investment and an expensive asset in most firms. Holding costs often exceed 25% of product value, but in Frito-Lay's prepared food industry, holding cost can be much higher because the raw materials are perishable. In the food industry, inventory spoils. So poor inventory management is not only expensive but can also yield an unsatisfactory product that in the extreme can also ruin market acceptance.

Major ingredients at Frito-Lay are corn meal, corn, potatoes, oil, and seasoning. Using potato chips to illustrate rapid inventory flow: potatoes are moved via truck from farm, to regional plants for processing, to warehouse, to the retail store. This happens in a matter of hours—not days or weeks. This keeps freshness high and holding costs low.

Frequent deliveries of the main ingredients at the Florida plant, for example, take several forms:

◆ Potatoes are delivered in 10 truckloads per day, with 150,000 lbs consumed in one shift: the entire potato storage area will only hold 7½ hours' worth of potatoes.
◆ Oil inventory arrives by rail car, which lasts only 4½ days.
◆ Corn meal arrives from various farms in the Midwest, and inventory typically averages 4 days' production.
◆ Seasoning inventory averages 7 days.
◆ Packaging inventory averages 8 to 10 days.

Frito-Lay's product-focused facility represents a major capital investment. That investment must achieve high utilization to be efficient. The capital cost must be spread over a substantial volume to drive down total cost of the snack foods produced. This demand for high utilization requires reliable equipment and tight schedules. Reliable machinery requires an inventory of critical components: this is known as MRO, or maintenance, repair, and operating supplies. MRO inventory of motors, switches, gears, bearings, and other critical specialized components can be costly but is necessary.

Frito-Lay's non-MRO inventory moves rapidly. Raw material quickly becomes work-in-process, moving through the system and out the door as a bag of chips in about $1\frac{1}{2}$ shifts. Packaged finished products move from production to the distribution chain in less than 1.4 days.

Discussion Questions*

1. How does the mix of Frito-Lay's inventory differ from those at a machine or cabinet shop (a process-focused facility)?
2. What are the major inventory items at Frito-Lay, and how rapidly do they move through the process?
3. What are the four types of inventory? Give an example of each at Frito-Lay.
4. How would you rank the dollar investment in each of the four types (from the most investment to the least investment)?
5. Why does inventory flow so quickly through a Frito-Lay plant?
6. Why does the company keep so many plants open?
7. Why doesn't Frito-Lay make all its 41 products at each of its plants?

*You may wish to view the video that accompanies this case before addressing these questions.

Inventory Control at Wheeled Coach

Video Case

Controlling inventory is one of Wheeled Coach's toughest problems. Operating according to a strategy of mass customization and responsiveness, management knows that success is dependent on tight inventory control. Anything else results in an inability to deliver promptly, chaos on the assembly line, and a huge inventory investment. Wheeled Coach finds that almost 50% of the cost of every ambulance it manufactures is purchased materials. A large proportion of that 50% is in chassis (purchased from Ford), aluminum (from Reynolds Metal), and plywood used for flooring and cabinetry construction (from local suppliers). Wheeled Coach tracks these A inventory items quite carefully, maintaining tight security/control and ordering carefully so as to maximize quantity discounts while minimizing on-hand stock. Because of long lead times and scheduling needs at Reynolds, aluminum must actually be ordered as much as 8 months in advance.

In a crowded ambulance industry in which it is the only giant, its 45 competitors don't have the purchasing power to draw the same discounts as Wheeled Coach. But this competitive cost advantage cannot be taken lightly, according to President Bob Collins. "Cycle counting in our stockrooms is critical. No part can leave the locked stockrooms without appearing on a bill of materials."

Accurate bills of material (BOM) are a requirement if products are going to be built on time. Additionally, because of the custom nature of each vehicle, most orders are won only after a bidding process. Accurate BOMs are critical to cost estimation and the resulting bid. For these reasons, Collins was emphatic that Wheeled Coach maintain outstanding inventory control. The *Global Company Profile* featuring Wheeled Coach (which opens Chapter 14) provides further details about the ambulance inventory control and production process.

Discussion Questions*

1. Explain how Wheeled Coach implements ABC analysis.
2. If you were to take over as inventory control manager at Wheeled Coach, what additional policies and techniques would you initiate to ensure accurate inventory records?
3. How would you go about implementing these suggestions?

*You may wish to view the video that accompanies this case before addressing these questions.

- **Additional Case Studies:** Visit MyOMLab for these free case studies:
  Southwestern University (F): The university must decide how many football day programs to order, and from whom.
  LaPlace Power and Light: This utility company is evaluating its current inventory policies.

Endnotes

1. See E. Malykhina, "Retailers Take Stock," *Information Week* (February 7, 2005): 20–22, and A. Raman, N. DeHoratius, and Z. Ton, "Execution: The Missing Link in Retail Operations," *California Management Review* 43, no. 3 (Spring 2001): 136–141.
2. This is the case when holding costs are linear and begin at the origin—that is, when inventory costs do not decline (or they increase) as inventory volume increases and all holding costs are in small increments. In addition, there is probably some learning each time a setup (or order) is executed—a fact that lowers subsequent setup costs. Consequently, the EOQ model is probably a special case. However, we abide by the conventional wisdom that this model is a reasonable approximation.
3. The formula for the economic order quantity (Q^*) can also be determined by finding where the total cost curve is at a minimum (i.e., where the slope of the total cost curve is zero). Using calculus, we set the derivative of the total cost with respect to Q^* equal to 0. The calculations for finding the minimum of

$$TC = \frac{D}{Q}S + \frac{Q}{2}H + PD$$

are $\dfrac{d(TC)}{dQ} = \left(\dfrac{-DS}{Q^2}\right) + \dfrac{H}{2} + 0 = 0$

Thus, $Q^* = \sqrt{\dfrac{2DS}{H}}$

4. The number of units short, Demand–ROP, is true only when Demand–ROP is non-negative.
5. Equations (12-15), (12-16), and (12-17) are expressed in days; however, they could equivalently be expressed in weeks, months, or even years. Just be consistent, and use the same time units for all terms in the equations.
6. Note that Equation (12-17) can also be expressed as:

   ROP = Average daily demand × Average lead time +

   $Z\sqrt{(\text{Average lead time} \times \sigma_d^2) + \overline{d}^2\sigma_{LT}^2}$.

7. OM managers also call these *continuous review systems*.

Chapter 12 *Rapid* Review

Main Heading	Review Material	MyOMLab
THE IMPORTANCE OF INVENTORY (pp. 490–491)	Inventory is one of the most expensive assets of many companies. *The objective of inventory management is to strike a balance between inventory investment and customer service.* The two basic inventory issues are how much to order and when to order. • **Raw material inventory**—Materials that are usually purchased but have yet to enter the manufacturing process. • **Work-in-process (WIP) inventory**—Products or components that are no longer raw materials but have yet to become finished products. • **MRO inventory**—Maintenance, repair, and operating materials. • **Finished-goods inventory**—An end item ready to be sold but still an asset on the company's books.	Concept Questions: 1.1–1.4 **VIDEO 12.1** Managing Inventory at Frito-Lay
MANAGING INVENTORY (pp. 491–495)	• **ABC analysis**—A method for dividing on-hand inventory into three classifications based on annual dollar volume. • **Cycle counting**—A continuing reconciliation of inventory with inventory records. • **Shrinkage**—Retail inventory that is unaccounted for between receipt and sale. • **Pilferage**—A small amount of theft.	Concept Questions: 2.1–2.4 Problems: 12.1–12.6 Virtual Office Hours for Solved Problem: 12.1
INVENTORY MODELS (pp. 495–496)	• **Holding cost**—The cost to keep or carry inventory in stock. • **Ordering cost**—The cost of the ordering process. • **Setup cost**—The cost to prepare a machine or process for production. • **Setup time**—The time required to prepare a machine or process for production.	Concept Questions: 3.1–3.4 **VIDEO 12.2** Inventory Control at Wheeled Coach Ambulance
INVENTORY MODELS FOR INDEPENDENT DEMAND (pp. 496–507)	• **Economic order quantity (EOQ) model**—An inventory-control technique that minimizes the total of ordering and holding costs: $$Q^* = \sqrt{\frac{2DS}{H}} \quad (12\text{-}1)$$ $$\text{Expected number of orders} = N = \frac{\text{Demand}}{\text{Order quantity}} = \frac{D}{Q^*} \quad (12\text{-}2)$$ $$\text{Expected time between orders} = T = \frac{\text{Number of working days per year}}{N} \quad (12\text{-}3)$$ $$\text{Total annual cost} = \text{Setup (order) cost} + \text{Holding cost} \quad (12\text{-}4)$$ $$TC = \frac{D}{Q}S + \frac{Q}{2}H \quad (12\text{-}5)$$ • **Robust**—Giving satisfactory answers even with substantial variation in the parameters. • **Lead time**—In purchasing systems, the time between placing an order and receiving it; in production systems, the wait, move, queue, setup, and run times for each component produced. • **Reorder point (ROP)**—The inventory level (point) at which action is taken to replenish the stocked item. *ROP for known demand:* $\text{ROP} = \text{Demand per day} \times \text{Lead time for a new order in days} = d \times L \quad (12\text{-}6)$ • **Safety stock (*ss*)**—Extra stock to allow for uneven demand; a buffer. • **Production order quantity model**—An economic order quantity technique applied to production orders: $$Q_p^* = \sqrt{\frac{2DS}{H[1-(d/p)]}} \quad (12\text{-}7)$$ $$Q_p^* = \sqrt{\frac{2DS}{H\left(1 - \dfrac{\text{Annual demand rate}}{\text{Annual production rate}}\right)}} \quad (12\text{-}8)$$ • **Quantity discount**—A reduced price for items purchased in large quantities: $$TC = \frac{D}{Q}S + \frac{Q}{2}H + PD \quad (12\text{-}9)$$ $$Q^* = \sqrt{\frac{2DS}{IP}} \quad (12\text{-}10)$$	Concept Questions: 4.1–4.4 Problems: 12.7–12.40 Virtual Office Hours for Solved Problems: 12.2–12.5 **ACTIVE MODELS 12.1, 12.2**

Main Heading	Review Material	MyOMLab
PROBABILISTIC MODELS AND SAFETY STOCK (pp. 508–513)	▪ **Probabilistic model**—A statistical model applicable when product demand or any other variable is not known but can be specified by means of a probability distribution. ▪ **Service level**—The complement of the probability of a stockout. *ROP for unknown demand:* $$ROP = d \times L + ss \qquad (12\text{-}11)$$ Annual stockout costs = The sum of the units short for each demand level $\times$ The probability of that demand level $\times$ The stockout cost/unit $\qquad$ (12-12) $\times$ The number of orders per year *ROP for unknown demand and given service level:* $$ROP = \text{Expected demand during lead time} + Z\sigma_{dLT} \qquad (12\text{-}13)$$ $$\text{Safety stock} = Z\sigma_{dLT} \qquad (12\text{-}14)$$ *ROP for variable demand and constant lead time:* $$ROP = (\text{Average daily demand} \times \text{Lead time in days}) + Z\sigma_{dLT} \quad (12\text{-}15)$$ *ROP for constant demand and variable lead time:* $$ROP = (\text{Daily demand} \times \text{Average lead time in days}) + Z \times \text{Daily demand} \times \sigma_{LT}$$ $$(12\text{-}16)$$ *ROP for variable demand and variable lead time:* $$ROP = (\text{Average daily demand} \times \text{Average lead time in days}) + Z\sigma_{dLT} \quad (12\text{-}17)$$ In each case, $\sigma_{dLT} = \sqrt{(\text{Average lead time} \times \sigma_d^2) + \bar{d}^2\sigma_{LT}^2}$ but under constant demand: $\sigma_d^2 = 0$, and under constant lead time: $\sigma_{LT}^2 = 0$.	Concept Questions: 5.1–5.4 Problems: 12.41–12.50 Virtual Office Hours for Solved Problems: 12.6–12.9
SINGLE-PERIOD MODEL (pp. 513–514)	▪ **Single-period inventory model**—A system for ordering items that have little or no value at the end of the sales period: $$\text{Service level} = \frac{C_s}{C_s + C_o} \qquad (12\text{-}18)$$	Concept Questions: 6.1–6.4 Problems: 12.51–12.53
FIXED-PERIOD (P) SYSTEMS (pp. 514–515)	▪ **Fixed-quantity (Q) system**—An ordering system with the same order amount each time. ▪ **Perpetual inventory system**—A system that keeps track of each withdrawal or addition to inventory continuously, so records are always current. ▪ **Fixed-period (P) system**—A system in which inventory orders are made at regular time intervals.	Concept Questions: 7.1–7.4

Self Test

▪ **Before taking the self-test,** refer to the learning objectives listed at the beginning of the chapter and the key terms listed at the end of the chapter.

LO 12.1 ABC analysis divides on-hand inventory into three classes, based on:
 a) unit price. b) the number of units on hand.
 c) annual demand. d) annual dollar values.

LO 12.2 Cycle counting:
 a) provides a measure of inventory turnover.
 b) assumes that all inventory records must be verified with the same frequency.
 c) is a process by which inventory records are periodically verified.
 d) all of the above.

LO 12.3 The two most important inventory-based questions answered by the typical inventory model are:
 a) when to place an order and the cost of the order.
 b) when to place an order and how much of an item to order.
 c) how much of an item to order and the cost of the order.
 d) how much of an item to order and with whom the order should be placed.

LO 12.4 Extra units in inventory to help reduce stockouts are called:
 a) reorder point. b) safety stock.
 c) just-in-time inventory. d) all of the above.

LO 12.5 The difference(s) between the basic EOQ model and the production order quantity model is(are) that:
 a) the production order quantity model does not require the assumption of known, constant demand.
 b) the EOQ model does not require the assumption of negligible lead time.
 c) the production order quantity model does not require the assumption of instantaneous delivery.
 d) all of the above.

LO 12.6 The EOQ model with quantity discounts attempts to determine:
 a) the lowest amount of inventory necessary to satisfy a certain service level.
 b) the lowest purchase price.
 c) whether to use a fixed-quantity or fixed-period order policy.
 d) how many units should be ordered.
 e) the shortest lead time.

LO 12.7 The appropriate level of safety stock is typically determined by:
 a) minimizing an expected stockout cost.
 b) choosing the level of safety stock that assures a given service level.
 c) carrying sufficient safety stock so as to eliminate all stockouts.
 d) annual demand.

Answers: LO 12.1. d; LO 12.2. c; LO 12.3. b; LO 12.4. b; LO 12.5. c; LO 12.6. d; LO 12.7. b.

Material Requirements Planning (MRP) and ERP

CHAPTER OUTLINE

Alaska Airlines

10 OM STRATEGY DECISIONS

- Design of Goods and Services
- Managing Quality
- Process Strategy
- Location Strategies
- Layout Strategies
- Human Resources
- Supply-Chain Management

- Inventory Management
  - Independent Demand (Ch. 12)
  - *Dependent Demand (Ch. 14)*
  - Lean Operations (Ch. 16)
- Scheduling
- Maintenance

MRP Provides a Competitive Advantage for Wheeled Coach

Wheeled Coach, headquartered in Winter Park, Florida, is the largest manufacturer of ambulances in the world. The $200 million firm is an international competitor that sells more than 25% of its vehicles to markets outside the U.S. Twelve major ambulance designs are produced on assembly lines (i.e., a repetitive process) at the Florida plant, using 18,000 different

This cutaway of one ambulance interior indicates the complexity of the product, which for some rural locations may be the equivalent of a hospital emergency room in miniature. To complicate production, virtually every ambulance is custom ordered. This customization necessitates precise orders, excellent bills of materials, exceptional inventory control from supplier to assembly, and an MRP system that works.

Wheeled Coach uses work cells to feed the assembly line. It maintains a complete carpentry shop (to provide interior cabinetry), a paint shop (to prepare, paint, and detail each vehicle), an electrical shop (to provide for the complex electronics in a modern ambulance), an upholstery shop (to make interior seats and benches), and as shown here, a metal fabrication shop (to construct the shell of the ambulance).

inventory items, of which 6,000 are manufactured and 12,000 purchased. Most of the product line is custom designed and assembled to meet the specific and often unique requirements demanded by the ambulance's application and customer preferences.

This variety of products and the nature of the process demand good material requirements planning (MRP). Effective use of an MRP system requires accurate bills of material and inventory records. The Wheeled Coach system provides daily updates and has reduced inventory by more than 30% in just two years.

Wheeled Coach insists that four key tasks be performed properly. First, the material plan must meet both the requirements of the master schedule and the capabilities of the production facility. Second, the plan must be executed as designed. Third, inventory investment must be minimized through effective "time-phased" material deliveries, consignment inventories, and a constant review of purchase methods. Finally, excellent record integrity must be maintained. Record accuracy is recognized as a fundamental ingredient of Wheeled Coach's successful MRP program. Its cycle counters are charged with material audits that not only correct errors but also investigate and correct problems.

Wheeled Coach Industries uses MRP as the catalyst for low inventory, high quality, tight schedules, and accurate records. Wheeled Coach has found competitive advantage via MRP.

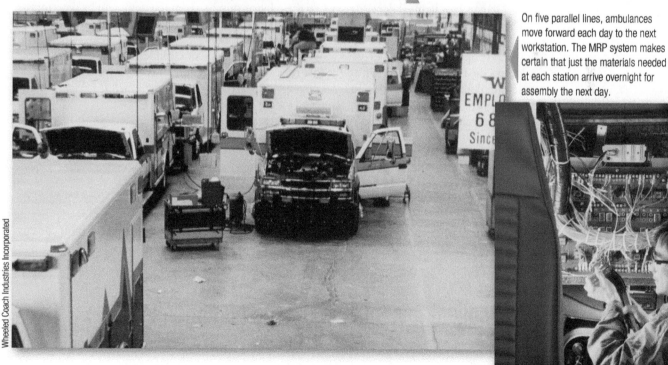

On five parallel lines, ambulances move forward each day to the next workstation. The MRP system makes certain that just the materials needed at each station arrive overnight for assembly the next day.

Here an employee is installing the wiring for an ambulance. There are an average of 15 miles of wire in a Wheeled Coach vehicle. This compares to 17 miles of wire in a sophisticated F-16 fighter jet.

Wheeled Coach Industries Incorporated

Wheeled Coach Industries Incorporated

Dependent Demand

STUDENT TIP ◆
"Dependent demand" means the demand for one item is related to the demand for another item.

Wheeled Coach, the subject of the *Global Company Profile*, and many other firms have found important benefits in material requirements planning (MRP). These benefits include (1) better response to customer orders as the result of improved adherence to schedules, (2) faster response to market changes, (3) improved utilization of facilities and labor, and (4) reduced inventory levels. Better response to customer orders and to the market wins orders and market share. Better utilization of facilities and labor yields higher productivity and return on investment. Less inventory frees up capital and floor space for other uses. These benefits are the result of a strategic decision to use a *dependent* inventory scheduling system. Demand for every component of an ambulance is dependent.

Demand for items is dependent when the relationship between the items can be determined. Therefore, once management receives an order or makes a forecast for the final product, quantities for all components can be computed. All components are dependent items. The Boeing Aircraft operations manager who schedules production of one plane per week, for example, knows the requirements down to the last rivet. For any product, all components of that product are dependent demand items. *More generally, for any product for which a schedule can be established, dependent techniques should be used.*

When the requirements of MRP are met, dependent models are preferable to the models for independent demand (EOQ) described in Chapter 12.[1] Dependent models are better not only for manufacturers and distributors but also for a wide variety of firms from restaurants to hospitals. The dependent technique used in a production environment is called material requirements planning (MRP).

Material requirements planning (MRP)

A dependent demand technique that uses a bill-of-material, inventory, expected receipts, and a master production schedule to determine material requirements.

Because MRP provides such a clean structure for dependent demand, it has evolved as the basis for Enterprise Resource Planning (ERP). ERP is an information system for identifying and planning the enterprise-wide resources needed to take, make, ship, and account for customer orders. We will discuss ERP in the latter part of this chapter.

Dependent Inventory Model Requirements

Effective use of dependent inventory models requires that the operations manager know the following:

1. Master production schedule (what is to be made and when)
2. Specifications or bill of material (materials and parts required to make the product)
3. Inventory availability (what is in stock)
4. Purchase orders outstanding (what is on order, also called expected receipts)
5. Lead times (how long it takes to get various components)

We now discuss each of these requirements in the context of material requirements planning.

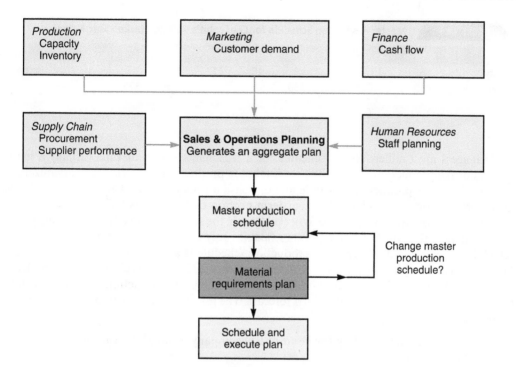

Figure **14.1**

The Planning Process

Master Production Schedule

A master production schedule (MPS) specifies what is to be made (e.g., the number of finished products or items) and when. The schedule must be in accordance with an aggregate plan. The aggregate plan sets the overall level of output in broad terms (e.g., product families, standard hours, or dollar volume). The plan, usually developed by the sales and operations planning team, includes a variety of inputs, including financial data, customer demand, engineering capabilities, labor availability, inventory fluctuations, supplier performance, and other considerations. Each of these inputs contributes in its own way to the aggregate plan, as shown in Figure 14.1.

As the planning process moves from the aggregate plan to execution, each of the lower-level plans must be feasible. When one is not, feedback to the next higher level is required to make the necessary adjustment. One of the major strengths of MRP is its ability to determine precisely the feasibility of a schedule within aggregate capacity constraints. This planning process can yield excellent results. The aggregate plan sets the upper and lower bounds on the master production schedule.

The master production schedule tells us how to satisfy demand by specifying what items to make and when. It *disaggregates* the aggregate plan. While the *aggregate plan* (as discussed in Chapter 13) is established in gross terms such as families of products or tons of steel, the *master production schedule* is established in terms of specific products. Figure 14.2 shows the master production schedules for three stereo models that flow from the aggregate plan for a family of stereo amplifiers.

Master production schedule (MPS)

A timetable that specifies what is to be made (usually finished goods) and when.

Aggregate Plan (Shows the total quantity of amplifiers)	Months				January				February		
					1,500				1,200		

Master Production Schedule (Shows the specific type and quantity of amplifier to be produced)	Weeks	1	2	3	4	5	6	7	8
	240-watt amplifier	100		100		100		100	
	150-watt amplifier		500		500		450		450
	75-watt amplifier			300				100	

Figure **14.2**

The Aggregate Plan Is the Basis for Development of the Master Production Schedule

TABLE 14.1	Master Production Schedule for Chef John's Buffalo Chicken Mac & Cheese

GROSS REQUIREMENTS FOR CHEF JOHN'S BUFFALO CHICKEN MAC & CHEESE									
Day	6	7	8	9	10	11	12	13	14	and so on
Quantity	450		200	350	525		235	375		

Managers must adhere to the schedule for a reasonable length of time (usually a major portion of the production cycle—the time it takes to produce a product). Many organizations establish a master production schedule and establish a policy of not changing ("fixing") the near-term portion of the plan. This near-term portion of the plan is then referred to as the "fixed," "firm," or "frozen" schedule. Wheeled Coach, the subject of the *Global Company Profile* for this chapter, fixes the last 14 days of its schedule. Only changes farther out, beyond the fixed schedule, are permitted. The master production schedule is a "rolling" production schedule. For example, a fixed 7-week plan has an additional week added to it as each week is completed, so a 7-week fixed schedule is maintained. Note that the master production schedule is a statement of *what is to be produced;* it is *not* a forecast. The master schedule can be expressed in the following terms:

- A *customer order* in a job shop (make-to-order) company (examples: print shops, machine shops, fine-dining restaurants)
- *Modules* in a repetitive (assemble-to-order or forecast) company (examples: Harley-Davidson motorcycles, TVs, fast-food restaurant)
- An *end item* in a continuous (stock-to-forecast) company (examples: steel, beer, bread, light bulbs, paper)

A master production schedule for Chef John's "Buffalo Chicken Mac & Cheese" at the Orlando Magic's Amway Center is shown in Table 14.1.

Bills of Material

Defining what goes into a product may seem simple, but it can be difficult in practice. As we noted in Chapter 5, to aid this process, manufactured items are defined via a bill of material. A bill of material (BOM) is a list of quantities of components, ingredients, and materials required to make a product. Individual drawings describe not only physical dimensions but also any special processing as well as the raw material from which each part is made. Chef John's recipe for Buffalo Chicken Mac & Cheese specifies ingredients and quantities, just as Wheeled Coach has a full set of drawings for an ambulance. Both are bills of material (although we call one a recipe, and they do vary somewhat in scope).

One way a bill of material defines a product is by providing a product structure. Example 1 shows how to develop the product structure and "explode" it to reveal the requirements for each component. A bill of material for item A in Example 1 consists of items B and C. Items above any level are called *parents*; items below any level are called *components* or *children*. By convention, the top level in a BOM is the 0 level.

VIDEO 14.1
When 18,500 Orlando Magic Fans Come to Dinner

Bill of material (BOM)
A listing of the components, their description, and the quantity of each required to make one unit of a product.

VIDEO 14.2
MRP at Wheeled Coach Ambulances

Example 1 | **DEVELOPING A PRODUCT STRUCTURE AND GROSS REQUIREMENTS**

Speaker Kits, Inc., packages high-fidelity components for mail order. Components for the top-of-the-line speaker kit, "Awesome" (A), include 2 Bs and 3 Cs.

Each B consists of 2 Ds and 2 Es. Each of the Cs has 2 Fs and 2 Es. Each F includes 2 Ds and 1 G. It is an *awesome* sound system. (Most purchasers require hearing aids within 3 years, and at least one court case is pending because of structural damage to a men's dormitory.) As we can see, the demand for B, C, D, E, F, and G is completely dependent on the master production schedule for A—the Awesome speaker kits.

LO 14.1 *Develop a product structure*

APPROACH ▶ Given the preceding information, we construct a product structure and "explode" the requirements.

SOLUTION ▶ This structure has four levels: 0, 1, 2, and 3. There are four parents: A, B, C, and F. Each parent item has at least one level below it. Items B, C, D, E, F, and G are components because each item has at least one level above it. In this structure, B, C, and F are both parents and components. The number in parentheses indicates how many units of that particular item are needed to make the item immediately above it. Thus, $B_{(2)}$ means that it takes two units of B for every unit of A, and $F_{(2)}$ means that it takes two units of F for every unit of C.

Level   Product structure for "Awesome" (A)

Once we have developed the product structure, we can determine the number of units of each item required to satisfy demand for a new order of 50 Awesome speaker kits. We "explode" the requirements as shown:

Part B:	2 × number of As =	(2)(50) =	100
Part C:	3 × number of As =	(3)(50) =	150
Part D:	2 × number of Bs + 2 × number of Fs =	(2)(100) + (2)(300) =	800
Part E:	2 × number of Bs + 2 × number of Cs =	(2)(100) + (2)(150) =	500
Part F:	2 × number of Cs =	(2)(150) =	300
Part G:	1 × number of Fs =	(1)(300) =	300

INSIGHT ▶ We now have a visual picture of the Awesome speaker kit requirements and knowledge of the quantities required. Thus, for 50 units of A, we will need 100 units of B, 150 units of C, 800 units of D, 500 units of E, 300 units of F, and 300 units of G.

LEARNING EXERCISE ▶ If there are 100 Fs in stock, how many Ds do you need? [Answer: 600.]

RELATED PROBLEMS ▶ 14.1–14.4, 14.5a,b, 14.13a,b, 14.17a,b (14.20a,b are available in MyOMLab)

Bills of material not only specify requirements but also are useful for costing, and they can serve as a list of items to be issued to production or assembly personnel. When bills of material are used in this way, they are usually called *pick lists*.

Modular Bills Bills of material may be organized around product modules (see Chapter 5). *Modules* are not final products to be sold, but are components that can be produced and assembled into units. They are often major components of the final product or product options. Bills of material for modules are called modular bills. Modular bills are convenient because production scheduling and production are often facilitated by organizing around relatively few modules rather than a multitude of final assemblies. For instance, a firm may make 138,000 different final products but may have only 40 modules that are mixed and matched to produce those 138,000 final products. The firm builds an aggregate production plan and prepares its master production schedule for the 40 modules, not the 138,000

Modular bills

Bills of material organized by major subassemblies or by product options.

configurations of the final product. This approach allows the MPS to be prepared for a reasonable number of items. The 40 modules can then be configured for specific orders at final assembly.

Planning Bills and Phantom Bills   Two other special kinds of bills of material are planning bills and phantom bills. Planning bills (sometimes called "pseudo" bills, or super bills) are created in order to assign an artificial parent to the bill of material. Such bills are used (1) when we want to group subassemblies so the number of items to be scheduled is reduced and (2) when we want to issue "kits" to the production department. For instance, it may not be efficient to issue inexpensive items such as washers and cotter pins with each of numerous subassemblies, so we call this a *kit* and generate a planning bill. The planning bill specifies the *kit* to be issued. Consequently, a planning bill may also be known as kitted material, or kit. Phantom bills of material are bills of material for components, usually subassemblies, that exist only temporarily. These components go directly into another assembly and are never inventoried. Therefore, components of phantom bills of material are coded to receive special treatment; lead times are zero, and they are handled as an integral part of their parent item. An example is a transmission shaft with gears and bearings assembly that is placed directly into a transmission.

Low-Level Coding   Low-level coding of an item in a BOM is necessary when identical items exist at various levels in the BOM. Low-level coding means that the item is coded at the lowest level at which it occurs. For example, item D in Example 1 is coded at the lowest level at which it is used. Item D could be coded as part of B and occur at level 2. However, because D is also part of F, and F is level 2, item D becomes a level-3 item. Low-level coding is a convention to allow easy computing of the requirements of an item.

Accurate Inventory Records

As we saw in Chapter 12, knowledge of what is in stock is the result of good inventory management. Good inventory management is an absolute necessity for an MRP system to work. If the firm does not exceed 99% record accuracy, then material requirements planning will not work.[2]

Purchase Orders Outstanding

Knowledge of outstanding orders exists as a by-product of well-managed purchasing and inventory-control departments. When purchase orders are executed, records of those orders and their scheduled delivery dates must be available to production personnel. Only with good purchasing data can managers prepare meaningful production plans and effectively execute an MRP system.

Lead Times for Components

Once managers determine when products are needed, they determine when to acquire them. The time required to acquire (that is, purchase, produce, or assemble) an item is known as lead time. Lead time for a manufactured item consists of *move, setup,* and *assembly* or *run times* for each component. For a purchased item, the lead time includes the time between recognition of need for an order and when it is available for production.

When the bill of material for Awesome speaker kits (As), in Example 1, is turned on its side and modified by adding lead times for each component (see Table 14.2), we then have a *time-phased product structure*. Time in this structure is shown on the horizontal axis of Figure 14.3 with item A due for completion in week 8. Each component is then offset to accommodate lead times.

Planning bills (or kits)
Material groupings created in order to assign an artificial parent to a bill of material; also called "pseudo" bills.

Phantom bills of material
Bills of material for components, usually assemblies, that exist only temporarily; they are never inventoried.

Low-level coding
A number that identifies items at the lowest level at which they occur.

Lead time
In purchasing systems, the time between recognition of the need for an order and receiving it; in production systems, it is the order, wait, move, queue, setup, and run times for each component.

TABLE 14.2

Lead Times for Awesome Speaker Kits (As)

COMPONENT	LEAD TIME
A	1 week
B	2 weeks
C	1 week
D	1 week
E	2 weeks
F	3 weeks
G	2 weeks

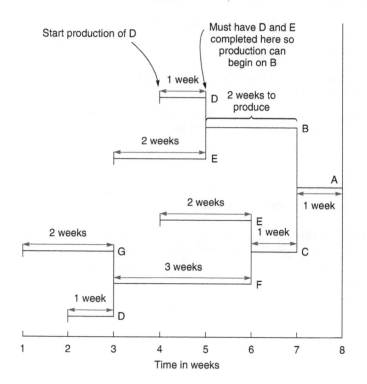

Figure **14.3**

Time-Phased Product Structure

◆ STUDENT TIP

This is a product structure on its side, with lead times.

MRP Structure

Although most MRP systems are computerized, the MRP procedure is straightforward, and we can illustrate a small one by hand. A master production schedule, a bill of material, inventory and purchase records, and lead times for each item are the ingredients of a material requirements planning system (see Figure 14.4).

Once these ingredients are available and accurate, the next step is to construct a gross material requirements plan. The gross material requirements plan is a schedule, as shown in Example 2. It combines a master production schedule (that requires one unit of A in week 8) and the time-phased schedule (Figure 14.3). It shows when an item must be ordered from suppliers if there is no inventory on hand or when the production of an item must be started to satisfy demand for the finished product by a particular date.

Gross material requirements plan

A schedule that shows the total demand for an item (prior to subtraction of on-hand inventory and scheduled receipts) and (1) when it must be ordered from suppliers, or (2) when production must be started to meet its demand by a particular date.

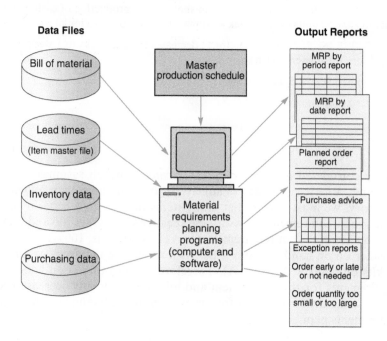

Figure **14.4**

Structure of the MRP System

◆ STUDENT TIP

MRP software programs are popular because manual approaches are slow and error prone.

Example 2

BUILDING A GROSS REQUIREMENTS PLAN

Each Awesome speaker kit (item A of Example 1) requires all the items in the product structure for A. Lead times are shown in Table 14.2.

APPROACH ▶ Using the information in Example 1 and Table 14.2, we construct the gross material requirements plan with a production schedule that will satisfy the demand of 50 units of A by week 8.

SOLUTION ▶ We prepare a schedule as shown in Table 14.3.

TABLE 14.3	Gross Material Requirements Plan for 50 Awesome Speaker Kits (As) with Order Release Dates Also Shown								
	WEEK								LEAD TIME
	1	2	3	4	5	6	7	8	
A. Required date								50	
Order release date							50		1 week
B. Required date							100		
Order release date					100				2 weeks
C. Required date							150		
Order release date						150			1 week
E. Required date					200	300			
Order release date			200	300					2 weeks
F. Required date						300			
Order release date			300						3 weeks
D. Required date			600	200					
Order release date		600		200					1 week
G. Required date			300						
Order release date	300								2 weeks

You can interpret the gross material requirements shown in Table 14.3 as follows: If you want 50 units of A at week 8, you must start assembling A in week 7. Thus, in week 7, you will need 100 units of B and 150 units of C. These two items take 2 weeks and 1 week, respectively, to produce. Production of B, therefore, should start in week 5, and production of C should start in week 6 (lead time subtracted from the required date for these items). Working backward, we can perform the same computations for all of the other items. Because D and E are used in two different places in Awesome speaker kits, there are two entries in each data record.

INSIGHT ▶ The gross material requirements plan shows when production of each item should begin and end in order to have 50 units of A at week 8. Management now has an initial plan.

LEARNING EXERCISE ▶ If the lead time for G decreases from 2 weeks to 1 week, what is the new order release date for G? [Answer: 300 in week 2.]

RELATED PROBLEMS ▶ 14.6, 14.8, 14.10a, 14.11a

EXCEL **OM** Data File **Ch14Ex2.xls** can be found in MyOMLab.

LO 14.2 *Build* a gross requirements plan

Net requirements plan
The result of adjusting gross requirements for inventory on hand and scheduled receipts.

So far, we have considered *gross material requirements*, which assumes that there is no inventory on hand. A net requirements plan adjusts for on-hand inventory. When considering on-hand inventory, we must realize that many items in inventory contain subassemblies or parts. If the gross requirement for Awesome speaker kits (As) is 100 and there are 20 of those speakers on hand, the net requirement for As is 80 (that is, 100 − 20). However, each Awesome speaker kit on hand contains 2 Bs. As a result, the requirement for Bs drops by 40 Bs (20 A kits on hand × 2 Bs per A). Therefore, if inventory is on hand for a parent item, the requirements for the parent item and all its components decrease because each Awesome kit contains the components for lower-level items. Example 3 shows how to create a net requirements plan.

Example 3

DETERMINING NET REQUIREMENTS

Speaker Kits, Inc., developed a product structure from a bill of material in Example 1. Example 2 developed a gross requirements plan. Given the following on-hand inventory, Speaker Kits, Inc., now wants to construct a net requirements plan. The gross requirement remains 50 units in week 8, and component requirements are as shown in the product structure in Example 1.

LO 14.3 *Build* a net requirements plan

ITEM	ON HAND	ITEM	ON HAND
A	10	E	10
B	15	F	5
C	20	G	0
D	10		

Net Material Requirements Plan for 50 Units of Product A in Week 8. *(The superscript is the source of the demand)*

Item A — Lot Size: Lot-for-Lot | Lead Time: 1 | On Hand: 10 | Safety Stock: — | Allocated: — | Low-Level Code: 0 | Item Identification: A

Row	On Hand	1	2	3	4	5	6	7	8
Gross Requirements									50
Scheduled Receipts									
Projected On Hand	10	10	10	10	10	10	10	10	10
Net Requirements									40
Planned Order Receipts									40
Planned Order Releases									40

Item B — Lot Size: Lot-for-Lot | Lead Time: 2 | On Hand: 15 | Safety Stock: — | Allocated: — | Low-Level Code: 1 | Item Identification: B *(2 × number of As = 80)*

Row	On Hand	1	2	3	4	5	6	7	8
Gross Requirements									80^A
Scheduled Receipts									
Projected On Hand	15	15	15	15	15	15	15	15	
Net Requirements									65
Planned Order Receipts									65
Planned Order Releases								65	

Item C — Lot Size: Lot-for-Lot | Lead Time: 1 | On Hand: 20 | Safety Stock: — | Allocated: — | Low-Level Code: 1 | Item Identification: C *(3 × number of As = 120)*

Row	On Hand	1	2	3	4	5	6	7	8
Gross Requirements									120^A
Scheduled Receipts									
Projected On Hand	20	20	20	20	20	20	20	20	
Net Requirements									100
Planned Order Receipts									100
Planned Order Releases								100	

Item E — Lot Size: Lot-for-Lot | Lead Time: 2 | On Hand: 10 | Safety Stock: — | Allocated: — | Low-Level Code: 2 | Item Identification: E *(2 × number of Bs = 130; 2 × number of Cs = 200)*

Row	On Hand	1	2	3	4	5	6	7	8
Gross Requirements							130^B	200^C	
Scheduled Receipts									
Projected On Hand	10	10	10	10	10	10			
Net Requirements							120	200	
Planned Order Receipts							120	200	
Planned Order Releases					120	200			

Item F — Lot Size: Lot-for-Lot | Lead Time: 3 | On Hand: 5 | Safety Stock: — | Allocated: — | Low-Level Code: 2 | Item Identification: F *(2 × number of Cs = 200)*

Row	On Hand	1	2	3	4	5	6	7	8
Gross Requirements								200^C	
Scheduled Receipts									
Projected On Hand	5	5	5	5	5	5	5		
Net Requirements								195	
Planned Order Receipts								195	
Planned Order Releases					195				

Item D — Lot Size: Lot-for-Lot | Lead Time: 1 | On Hand: 10 | Safety Stock: — | Allocated: — | Low-Level Code: 3 | Item Identification: D *(2 × number of Bs = 130; 2 × number of Fs = 390)*

Row	On Hand	1	2	3	4	5	6	7	8
Gross Requirements						390^F	130^B		
Scheduled Receipts									
Projected On Hand	10	10	10	10	10				
Net Requirements						380	130		
Planned Order Receipts						380	130		
Planned Order Releases					380	130			

Item G — Lot Size: Lot-for-Lot | Lead Time: 2 | On Hand: 0 | Safety Stock: — | Allocated: — | Low-Level Code: 3 | Item Identification: G *(1 × number of Fs = 195)*

Row	On Hand	1	2	3	4	5	6	7	8
Gross Requirements						195^F			
Scheduled Receipts									
Projected On Hand						0			
Net Requirements						195			
Planned Order Receipts						195			
Planned Order Releases				195					

Planned order receipt
The quantity planned to be received at a future date.

Planned order release
The scheduled date for an order to be released.

APPROACH ▶ A net material requirements plan includes gross requirements, on-hand inventory, net requirements, planned order receipt, and planned order release for each item. We begin with A and work backward through the components.

SOLUTION ▶ Shown in the MRP format on the previous page is the net material requirements plan for product A.

Constructing a net requirements plan is similar to constructing a gross requirements plan. Starting with item A, we work backward to determine net requirements for all items. To do these computations, we refer to the product structure, on-hand inventory, and lead times. The gross requirement for A is 50 units in week 8. Ten items are on hand; therefore, the net requirements and the scheduled planned order receipt are both 40 items in week 8. Because of the one-week lead time, the planned order release is 40 items in week 7 (see the arrow connecting the order receipt and order release). Referring to week 7 and the product structure in Example 1, we can see that 80 (2 × 40) items of B and 120 (3 × 40) items of C are required in week 7 to have a total for 50 items of A in week 8. The letter superscripted A to the right of the gross figure for items B and C was generated as a result of the demand for the parent, A. Performing the same type of analysis for B and C yields the net requirements for D, E, F, and G. Note the on-hand inventory in row E in week 6 is zero. It is zero because the on-hand inventory (10 units) was used to make B in week 5. By the same token, the inventory for D was used to make F in week 3.

INSIGHT ▶ Once a net requirement plan is completed, management knows the quantities needed, an ordering schedule, and a production schedule for each component.

LEARNING EXERCISE ▶ If the on-hand inventory quantity of component F is 95 rather than 5, how many units of G will need to be ordered in week 1? [Answer: 105 units.]

RELATED PROBLEMS ▶ 14.9, 14.10b, 14.11b, 14.12, 14.13c, 14.14b, 14.15a,b,c, 14.16a,b, 14.17c (14.18–14.21 are available in MyOMLab)

ACTIVE **MODEL** 14.1 This example is further illustrated in Active Model 14.1 in MyOMLab.

EXCEL **OM** Data File **Ch14Ex3.xls** can be found in MyOMLab.

STUDENT TIP ◆
MRP gross requirements can combine multiple products, spare parts, and items sold directly.

Examples 2 and 3 considered only product A, the Awesome speaker kit, and its completion only in week 8. Fifty units of A were required in week 8. Normally, however, there is a demand for many products over time. For each product, management must prepare a master production schedule (as we saw earlier, in Table 14.1). Scheduled production of each product is added to the master schedule and ultimately to the net material requirements plan. Figure 14.5 shows how several product schedules, including requirements for components sold directly, can contribute to one gross material requirements plan.

Most inventory systems also note the number of units in inventory that have been assigned to specific future production but not yet used or issued from the stockroom. Such items are often

Figure **14.5**

Several Schedules Contributing to a Gross Requirements Schedule for B

One B is in each A, and one B is in each S; in addition, 10 Bs sold directly are scheduled in week 1, and 10 more that are sold directly are scheduled in week 2.

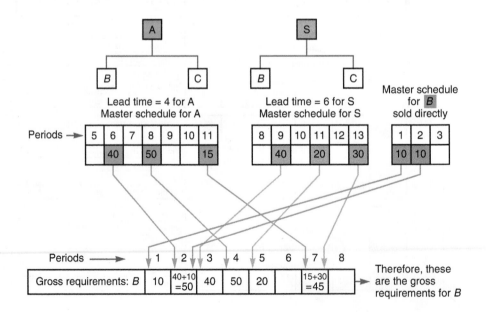

Lot Size	Lead Time	On Hand	Safety Stock	Allocated	Low-Level Code	Item ID		Period							
								1	2	3	4	5	6	7	8
Lot For Lot	1	0	0	10	0	Z	Gross Requirements								80 90
							Scheduled Receipts								0
							Projected On Hand 0	0	0	0	0	0	0	0	0
							Net Requirements								90
							Planned Order Receipts								90
							Planned Order Releases							90	

Figure **14.6**

Sample MRP Planning Sheet for Item Z

referred to as *allocated* items. Allocated items increase requirements as shown in Figure 14.6, where gross requirements have been increased from 80 to 90 to reflect the 10 allocated items.

Safety Stock The continuing task of operations managers is to remove variability. This is the case in MRP systems as in other operations systems. Realistically, however, managers need to realize that bills of material and inventory records, like purchase and production quantities, as well as lead times, may not be perfect. This means that some consideration of safety stock may be prudent. Because of the significant domino effect of any change in requirements, safety stock should be minimized, with a goal of ultimate elimination. When safety stock is deemed absolutely necessary, the usual policy is to build it into (increase) the inventory requirement of the MRP logic. Distortion can be minimized when safety stock is held at the finished goods or module level and at the purchased component or raw material level.

MRP Management

Now let's look at the dynamics and limitations of MRP.

MRP Dynamics

The inputs to MRP (the master schedule, BOM, lead times, purchasing, and inventory) frequently change. Conveniently, a central strength of MRP systems is timely and accurate replanning. However, many firms find they do not want to respond to minor scheduling or quantity changes even if they are aware of them. These frequent changes generate what is called system nervousness and can create havoc in purchasing and production departments if implemented. Consequently, OM personnel reduce such nervousness by evaluating the need and impact of changes prior to disseminating requests to other departments. Two tools are particularly helpful when trying to reduce MRP system nervousness.

The first is time fences. Time fences allow a segment of the master schedule to be designated as "not to be rescheduled." This segment of the master schedule is therefore not changed during the periodic regeneration of schedules. The second tool is pegging. Pegging means tracing upward in the BOM from the component to the parent item. By pegging upward, the production planner can determine the cause for the requirement and make a judgment about the necessity for a change in the schedule.

With MRP, the operations manager *can* react to the dynamics of the real world. If the nervousness is caused by legitimate changes, then the proper response may be to investigate the production environment—not adjust via MRP.

MRP Limitations

MRP does not do detailed scheduling—it plans. MRP is an excellent tool for product-focused and repetitive facilities, but it has limitations in process (make-to-order) environments. MRP will tell you that a job needs to be completed on a certain week or day but does not tell you

System nervousness
Frequent changes in an MRP system.

Time fences
A means for allowing a segment of the master schedule to be designated as "not to be rescheduled."

Pegging
In material requirements planning systems, tracing upward the bill of material from the component to the parent item.

that Job X needs to run on Machine A at 10:30 A.M. and be completed by 11:30 A.M. so that Job X can then run on Machine B. MRP is also a planning technique with *fixed* lead times that loads work into *infinite* size "buckets." The buckets are time units, usually one week. MRP puts work into these buckets without regard to capacity. Consequently, MRP is considered an *infinite* scheduling technique. Techniques for the alternative, *finite* scheduling, are discussed in Chapter 15.

Lot-Sizing Techniques

An MRP system is an excellent way to do production planning and determine net requirements. But net requirements still demand a decision about *how much and when* to order. This decision is called a lot-sizing decision. There are a variety of ways to determine lot sizes in an MRP system; commercial MRP software usually includes the choice of several lot-sizing techniques. We now review a few of them.

Lot-for-Lot   In Example 3, we used a lot-sizing technique known as lot-for-lot, which produced exactly what was required. This decision is consistent with the objective of an MRP system, which is to meet the requirements of *dependent* demand. Thus, an MRP system should produce units only as needed, with no safety stock and no anticipation of further orders. When frequent orders are economical (i.e., when setup costs are low) and just-in-time inventory techniques implemented, lot-for-lot can be very efficient. However, when setup costs are significant, lot-for-lot can be expensive. Example 4 uses the lot-for-lot criteria and determines cost for 10 weeks of demand.

Example 4

LOT SIZING WITH LOT-FOR-LOT

Speaker Kits, Inc., wants to compute its ordering and carrying cost of inventory on lot-for-lot criteria.

APPROACH ▶   With lot-for-lot, we order material only as it is needed. Once we have the cost of ordering (setting up), the cost of holding each unit for a given time period, and the production schedule, we can assign orders to our net requirements plan.

SOLUTION ▶   Speaker Kits has determined that, for **component B**, setup cost is $100 and holding cost is $1 per period. The production schedule, as reflected in net requirements for assemblies, is as follows:

MRP Lot Sizing: Lot-for-Lot Technique*

WEEK		1	2	3	4	5	6	7	8	9	10
Gross requirements		35	30	40	0	10	40	30	0	30	55
Scheduled receipts											
Projected on hand	35	35	0	0	0	0	0	0	0	0	0
Net requirements		0	30	40	0	10	40	30	0	30	55
Planned order receipts			30	40		10	40	30		30	55
Planned order releases		30	40		10	40	30		30	55	

*Holding costs = $1/unit/week; setup cost = $100; gross requirements average per week = 27; lead time = 1 week.

The lot-sizing solution using the lot-for-lot technique is shown in the table. The holding cost is zero as there is never any end-of-period inventory. (Inventory in the first period is used immediately and therefore has no holding cost.) But seven separate setups (one associated with each order) yield a total cost of $700. (Holding cost = 0 × 1 = 0; ordering cost = 7 × 100 = 700.)

INSIGHT ▶   When supply is reliable and frequent orders are inexpensive, but holding cost or obsolescence is high, lot-for-lot ordering can be very efficient.

LEARNING EXERCISE ▶   What is the impact on total cost if holding cost is $2 per period rather than $1? [Answer: Total holding cost remains zero, as no units are held from one period to the next with lot-for-lot.]

RELATED PROBLEMS ▶   14.22, 14.25, 14.26a, 14.27a (14.28b is available in MyOMLab)

This Nissan line in Smyrna, Tennessee, has little inventory because Nissan schedules to a razor's edge. At Nissan, MRP helps reduce inventory to world-class standards. World-class automobile assembly requires that purchased parts have a turnover of slightly more than once a day and that overall turnover approaches 150 times per year.

Economic Order Quantity (EOQ) We now extend our discussion of EOQ in Chapter 12 to use it as a lot-sizing technique for MRP systems. As we indicated there, EOQ is useful when we have relatively constant demand. However, demand may change every period in MRP systems. Therefore, EOQ lot sizing often does not perform well in MRP. Operations managers should take advantage of demand information when it is known, rather than assuming a constant demand. EOQ is used to do lot sizing in Example 5 for comparison purposes.

LO 14.4 *Determine* lot sizes for lot-for-lot, EOQ, and POQ

Example 5

LOT SIZING WITH EOQ

With a setup cost of $100 and a holding cost per week of $1, Speaker Kits, Inc., wants to examine its cost for **component B,** with lot sizes based on an EOQ criteria.

APPROACH ▶ Using the same cost and production schedule as in Example 4, we determine net requirements and EOQ lot sizes.

SOLUTION ▶ Ten-week usage equals a gross requirement of 270 units; therefore, weekly usage equals 27, and 52 weeks (annual usage) equals 1,404 units. From Chapter 12, the EOQ model is:

$$Q^* = \sqrt{\frac{2DS}{H}}$$

where
D = annual usage = 1,404
S = setup cost = $100
H = holding (carrying) cost, on an annual basis per unit
= $1 × 52 weeks = $52

$$Q^* = 73 \text{ units}$$

Therefore, place an order of 73 units, as necessary, to avoid a stockout.

MRP Lot Sizing: EOQ Technique*

WEEK		1	2	3	4	5	6	7	8	9	10
Gross requirements		35	30	40	0	10	40	30	0	30	55
Scheduled receipts											
Projected on hand	35	35	0	43	3	3	66	26	69	69	39
Net requirements		0	30	0	0	7	0	4	0	0	16
Planned order receipts			73			73		73			73
Planned order releases		73			73		73			73	

*Holding costs = $1/unit/week; setup cost = $100; gross requirements average per week = 27; lead time = 1 week.

For the 10-week planning period:

Holding cost = 375 units × $1 = $375 (includes 57 remaining at the end of week 10)

Ordering cost = 4 × $100 = $400

Total = $375 + $400 = $775

INSIGHT ▶ EOQ can be a reasonable lot-sizing technique when demand is relatively constant. However, notice that actual holding cost will vary substantially depending on the rate of actual usage. If any stockouts had occurred, these costs too would need to be added to our actual EOQ cost of $775.

LEARNING EXERCISE ▶ What is the impact on total cost if holding cost is $2 per period rather than $1? [Answer: The EOQ quantity becomes 52, the theoretical annual total cost becomes $5,404, and the 10-week cost is $1,039 ($5,404 × (10/52).]

RELATED PROBLEMS ▶ 14.23, 14.25, 14.26b, 14.27c (14.28a is available in MyOMLab)

Periodic order quantity (POQ)

An inventory ordering technique that issues orders on a predetermined time interval, with the order quantity covering the total of the interval's requirements.

Periodic Order Quantity Periodic order quantity (POQ) is a lot-sizing technique that orders the quantity needed during a predetermined time between orders, such as every 3 weeks. We define the *POQ interval* as the EOQ divided by the average demand per period (e.g., one week).[3] The POQ is the order quantity that covers the specific demand for that interval. *Each order quantity is recalculated at the time of the order release*, never leaving extra inventory. An application of POQ is shown in Example 6.

Example 6

LOT SIZING WITH POQ

With a setup cost of $100 and a holding cost per week of $1, Speaker Kits, Inc., wants to examine its cost for **component B,** with lot sizes based on POQ.

APPROACH ▶ Using the same cost and production schedule as in Example 5, we determine net requirements and POQ lot sizes.

SOLUTION ▶ Ten-week usage equals a gross requirement of 270 units; therefore, average weekly usage equals 27, and from Example 5, we know the EOQ is 73 units.

We set the *POQ interval* equal to the EOQ divided by the average weekly usage.

Therefore:

POQ interval = EOQ/Average weekly usage = 73/27 = 2.7, or 3 weeks.

The *POQ order size* will vary by the quantities required in the respective weeks, as shown in the following table, with first planned order release in week 1.

Note: Orders are postponed if no demand exists, which is why week 7's order is postponed until week 8.

MRP Lot Sizing: POQ Technique*

WEEK		1	2	3	4	5	6	7	8	9	10
Gross requirements		35	30	40	0	10	40	30	0	30	55
Scheduled receipts											
Projected on hand	35	35	0	40	0	0	70	30	0	0	55
Net requirements		0	30	0	0	10	0	0	0	55	0
Planned order receipts			70			80			0	85	0
Planned order releases		70			80				85		

*Holding costs = $1/unit/week; setup cost = $100; gross requirements average per week = 27; lead time = 1 week.

$$\text{Setups} = 3 \times \$100 = \$300$$
$$\text{Holding cost} = (40 + 70 + 30 + 55) \text{ units} \times \$1 \text{ each} = \$195$$
The POQ solution yields a computed 10-week cost of $300 + $195 = $495

INSIGHT ▶ Because POQ tends to produce a balance between holding and ordering costs with no excess inventory, POQ typically performs much better than EOQ. Notice that even with frequent recalculations, actual holding cost can vary substantially, depending on the demand fluctuations. We are assuming no stockouts. In this and similar examples, we are also assuming no safety stock; such costs would need to be added to our actual cost.

LEARNING EXERCISE ▶ What is the impact on total cost if holding cost is $2 per period rather than $1? [Answer: EOQ = 52; POQ interval = 52/27 = 1.93 ≈ 2 weeks; holding cost = $270; setups = $400. The POQ total cost becomes $670.]

RELATED PROBLEMS ▶ 14.24, 14.25, 14.26c, 14.27b (14.28c is available in MyOMLab)

Other lot-sizing techniques, known as *dynamic lot-sizing*, are similar to periodic order quantity as they attempt to balance the lot size against the setup cost. These are *part period balancing* (also called *least total cost*), *least unit cost*, and *least period cost* (also called *Silver-Meal*). Another technique, *Wagner-Whitin*, takes a different approach by using dynamic programming to optimize ordering over a finite time horizon.[4]

Lot-Sizing Summary In the three speaker kits lot-sizing examples, we found the following costs:

	COSTS		
	SETUP	HOLDING	TOTAL
Lot-for-lot	$700	$0	$700
Economic order quantity (EOQ)	$400	$375	$775
Periodic order quantity (POQ)	$300	$195	$495

These examples should not, however, lead operations personnel to hasty conclusions about the preferred lot-sizing technique. In theory, new lot sizes should be computed whenever there is a schedule or lot-size change anywhere in the MRP hierarchy. In practice, such changes cause the instability and system nervousness referred to earlier in this chapter. Consequently, such frequent changes are not made. This means that all lot sizes are wrong because the production system cannot and should not respond to frequent changes. Note that there are no "shortage" (out of stock) charges in any of these lot-sizing techniques. This limitation places added demands on accurate forecasts and "time fences."

In general, the lot-for-lot approach should be used whenever low-cost setup can be achieved. Lot-for-lot is the goal. Lots can be modified as necessary for scrap allowances, process constraints (for example, a heat-treating process may require a lot of a given size), or raw material purchase lots (for example, a truckload of chemicals may be available in only one lot size). However, caution should be exercised prior to any modification of lot size because the modification can cause substantial distortion of actual requirements at lower levels in the MRP hierarchy. When setup costs are significant and demand is reasonably smooth, POQ or even EOQ should provide satisfactory results. Too much concern with lot sizing yields false accuracy because of MRP dynamics. A correct lot size can be determined only after the fact, based on what actually happened in terms of requirements.

Extensions of MRP

In this section, we review three extensions of MRP.

Material Requirements Planning II (MRP II)

Material requirements
planning II (MRP II)

A system that allows, with MRP in place, inventory data to be augmented by other resource variables; in this case, MRP becomes *material resource planning.*

LO 14.5 *Describe* MRP II

Material requirements planning II is an extremely powerful technique. Once a firm has MRP in place, requirements data can be enriched by resources other than just components. When MRP is used this way, *resource* is usually substituted for *requirements,* and MRP becomes MRP II. It then stands for material resource planning.

So far in our discussion of MRP, we have scheduled products and their components. However, products require many resources, such as energy and money, beyond the product's tangible components. In addition to these resource inputs, *outputs* can be generated as well. Outputs can include such things as scrap, packaging waste, effluent, and carbon emissions. As OM becomes increasingly sensitive to environmental and sustainability issues, identifying and managing by-products takes on more significance. MRP II provides a vehicle for doing so. Table 14.4 provides an example of labor-hours, machine-hours, grams of greenhouse gas emissions, pounds of scrap, and cash, in the format of a gross requirements plan. With MRP II, management can identify both the inputs and outputs as well as the relevant schedule. MRP II provides another tool in OM's battle for sustainable operations.

Many MRP programs, such as *Resource Manager for Excel,* are commercially available. *Resource Manager's* initial menu screen is shown here.

A demo program is available for student use at **www.usersolutions.com.**

Jim Corwis, User Solutions, Inc.

TABLE 14.4	Material Resource Planning (MRP II)					
				Weeks		
	LEAD TIME	5	6	7	8	
Computer	1				100	
Labor-hours: .2 each					20	
Machine-hours: .2 each					20	
GHG Emissions: .25 each					25 grams	
Scrap: 1 ounce fiberglass each					6.25 lb	
Payables: $0					$0	
PC board (1 each)	2			100		
Labor-hours: .15 each				15		
Machine-hours: .1 each				10		
GHG Emissions: 2.5 each				250 grams		
Scrap: .5 ounces copper each				3.125 lb		
Payables: raw material at $5 each				$500		
Processors (5 each)	4	500				
Labor-hours: .2 each		100				
Machine-hours: .2 each		100				
GHG Emissions: .50 each		25,000 grams				
Scrap: .01 ounces of acid waste each		0.3125 lb				
Payables: processor components at $10 each		$5,000				

By utilizing the logic of MRP, resources such as labor, machine-hours, greenhouse gas emissions, scrap, and cost can be accurately determined and scheduled. Weekly demand for labor, machine-hours, greenhouse gas emissions, scrap, and payables for 100 computers are shown.

MRP II systems are seldom stand-alone programs. Most are tied into other computer software. Purchasing, production scheduling, capacity planning, inventory, and warehouse management systems are a few examples of this data integration.

Closed-Loop MRP

Closed-loop material requirements planning implies an MRP system that provides feedback to scheduling from the inventory control system. Specifically, a closed-loop MRP system provides information to the capacity plan, master production schedule, and ultimately to the production plan (as shown in Figure 14.7). Virtually all commercial MRP systems are closed-loop.

Closed-loop MRP system
A system that provides feedback to the capacity plan, master production schedule, and production plan so planning can be kept valid at all times.

Capacity Planning

In keeping with the definition of closed-loop MRP, feedback about workload is obtained from each work center. Load reports show the resource requirements in a work center for all work currently assigned to the work center, all work planned, and expected orders.

Load report
A report showing the resource requirements in a work center for all work currently assigned there as well as all planned and expected orders.

Figure **14.7**

Closed-Loop Material Requirements Planning

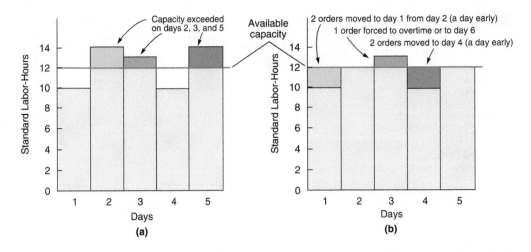

Figure 14.8

(a) Initial Resource Requirements Profile for a Work Center
(b) Smoothed Resource Requirements Profile for a Work Center

LO 14.6 *Describe closed-loop MRP*

Figure 14.8(a) shows that the initial load in the milling center exceeds capacity on days 2, 3, and 5. Closed-loop MRP systems allow production planners to move the work between time periods to smooth the load or at least bring it within capacity. (This is the "capacity planning" part of Figure 14.7.) The closed-loop MRP system can then reschedule all items in the net requirements plan (see Figure 14.8[b]).

Tactics for smoothing the load and minimizing the impact of changed lead time include the following:

1. *Overlapping,* which reduces the lead time, sends pieces to the second operation before the entire lot is completed on the first operation.
2. *Operations splitting* sends the lot to two different machines for the same operation. This involves an additional setup, but results in shorter throughput times because only part of the lot is processed on each machine.
3. *Order splitting,* or *lot splitting*, involves breaking up the order and running part of it earlier (or later) in the schedule.

Example 7 shows a brief detailed capacity scheduling example using order splitting to improve utilization.

Example 7 | **ORDER SPLITTING**

Kevin Watson, the production planner at Wiz Products, needs to develop a capacity plan for a work center. He has the production orders shown below for the next 5 days. There are 12 hours available in the work cell each day. The parts being produced require 1 hour each.

Day	1	2	3	4	5
Orders	10	14	13	10	14

APPROACH ▶ Compute the time available in the work center and the time necessary to complete the production requirements.

SOLUTION ▶

DAY	UNITS ORDERED	CAPACITY REQUIRED (HOURS)	CAPACITY AVAILABLE (HOURS)	UTILIZATION: OVER/ (UNDER) (HOURS)	PRODUCTION PLANNER'S ACTION	NEW PRODUCTION SCHEDULE
1	10	10	12	(2)		12
2	14	14	12	2	Split order: move 2 units to day 1	12
3	13	13	12	1	Split order: move 1 unit to day 6 or request overtime	13
4	10	10	12	(2)		12
5	14	14	12	2	Split order: move 2 units to day 4	12
	61					

> INSIGHT ▶ By moving orders, the production planner is able to utilize capacity more effectively and still meet the order requirements, with only 1 order produced on overtime in day 3.
>
> LEARNING EXERCISE ▶ If the units ordered for day 5 increase to 16, what are the production planner's options? [Answer: In addition to moving 2 units to day 4, move 2 units of production to day 6, or request overtime.]
>
> RELATED PROBLEMS ▶ 14.29, 14.30

When the workload consistently exceeds work-center capacity, the tactics just discussed are not adequate. This may mean adding capacity via personnel, machinery, overtime, or subcontracting.

MRP in Services

The demand for many services or service items is classified as dependent demand when it is directly related to or derived from the demand for other services. Such services often require product-structure trees, bills of material and labor, and scheduling. Variations of MRP systems can make a major contribution to operational performance in such services. Examples from restaurants, hospitals, and hotels follow.

Restaurants In restaurants, ingredients and side dishes (bread, vegetables, and condiments) are typically meal components. These components are dependent on the demand for meals. The meal is an end item in the master schedule. Figure 14.9 shows (a) a product-structure tree and

(a) PRODUCT STRUCTURE TREE

Figure 14.9

Product Structure Tree and Bill of Material for Chef John's Buffalo Chicken Mac & Cheese

(b) BILL OF MATERIALS

Production Specification	Buffalo Chicken Mac & Cheese (6 portions)				
Ingredients	*Quantity*	*Measure*	*Unit Cost*	*Total Cost*	*Labor Hrs.*
Elbow Macaroni (large, uncooked)	20.00	oz.	$ 0.09	$ 1.80	
Cheese—Pepper Jack (grated)	10.00	oz.	0.17	1.70	
Mac and Cheese Base (from refrigerator)	32.00	oz.	0.80	25.60	
Milk	4.00	oz.	0.03	0.12	
Smoked Pulled Chicken	2.00	lb.	2.90	5.80	
Buffalo Sauce	8.00	oz.	0.09	0.72	
Blue Cheese Crumbles	4.00	oz.	0.19	0.76	
Scallions	2.00	oz.	0.18	0.36	
Total Labor Hours					0.2 hrs

(b) bill of material (here called a *product specification*) for 6 portions of *Buffalo Chicken Mac & Cheese*, a popular dish prepared by Chef John for Orlando Magic fans at the Amway Center.

Hospitals MRP is also applied in hospitals, especially when dealing with surgeries that require known equipment, materials, and supplies. Houston's Park Plaza Hospital and many hospital suppliers, for example, use the technique to improve the scheduling and management of expensive surgical inventory.

Hotels Marriott develops a bill of material and a bill of labor when it renovates each of its hotel rooms. Marriott managers explode the BOM to compute requirements for materials, furniture, and decorations. MRP then provides net requirements and a schedule for use by purchasing and contractors.

Distribution Resource Planning (DRP)

> **Distribution resource planning (DRP)**
> A time-phased stock-replenishment plan for all levels of a distribution network.

When dependent techniques are used in the supply chain, they are called distribution resource planning (DRP). Distribution resource planning (DRP) is a time-phased stock-replenishment plan for all levels of the supply chain.

DRP procedures and logic are analogous to MRP. With DRP, expected demand becomes gross requirements. Net requirements are determined by allocating available inventory to gross requirements. The DRP procedure starts with the forecast at the retail level (or the most distant point of the distribution network being supplied). All other levels are computed. As is the case with MRP, inventory is then reviewed with an aim to satisfying demand. So that stock will arrive when it is needed, net requirements are offset by the necessary lead time. A planned order release quantity becomes the gross requirement at the next level down the distribution chain.

DRP *pulls* inventory through the system. Pulls are initiated when the retail level orders more stock. Allocations are made to the retail level from available inventory and production after being adjusted to obtain shipping economies. Effective use of DRP requires an integrated information system to rapidly convey planned order releases from one level to the next. The goal of the DRP system is small and frequent replenishment within the bounds of economical ordering and shipping.

Enterprise Resource Planning (ERP)

> **Enterprise resource planning (ERP)**
> An information system for identifying and planning the enterprise-wide resources needed to take, make, ship, and account for customer orders.

Advances in MRP II systems that tie customers and suppliers to MRP II have led to the development of enterprise resource planning (ERP) systems. Enterprise resource planning (ERP) is software that allows companies to (1) automate and integrate many of their business processes, (2) share a common database and business practices throughout the enterprise, and (3) produce information in real time. A schematic showing some of these relationships for a manufacturing firm appears in Figure 14.10.

The objective of an ERP system is to coordinate a firm's entire business, from supplier evaluation to customer invoicing. This objective is seldom achieved, but ERP systems are umbrella systems that tie together a variety of specialized systems. This is accomplished by using a centralized database to assist the flow of information among business functions. Exactly what is tied together, and how, varies on a case-by-case basis. In addition to the traditional components of MRP, ERP systems usually provide financial and human resource (HR) management information. ERP systems may also include:

> **LO 14.7** *Describe* ERP

- *Supply-chain management (SCM)* software to support sophisticated vendor communication, e-commerce, and those activities necessary for efficient warehousing and logistics. The idea is to tie operations (MRP) to procurement, to materials management, and to suppliers, providing the tools necessary for effective management of all four areas.
- *Customer relationship management (CRM)* software for the incoming side of the business. CRM is designed to aid analysis of sales, target the most profitable customers, and manage the sales force.
- *Sustainability* software to tie together sustainable workforce issues and provide transparency for supply-chain sustainability issues, as well as monitor health and safety activities, energy use and efficiency, emissions (carbon footprint, greenhouse gases), and environmental compliance.

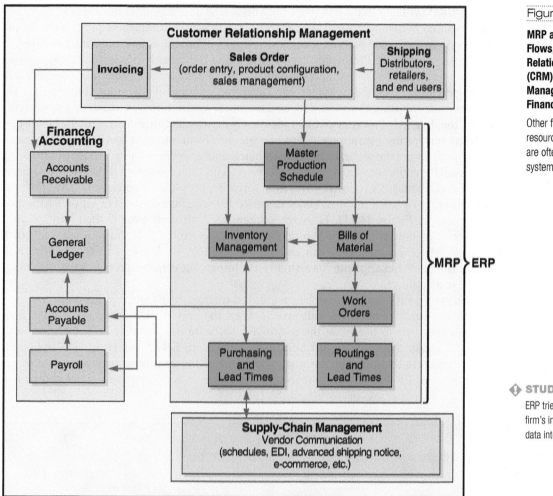

Figure **14.10**

MRP and ERP Information Flows, Showing Customer Relationship Management (CRM), Supply-Chain Management (SCM), and Finance/Accounting

Other functions such as human resources and sustainability are often also included in ERP systems.

STUDENT TIP
ERP tries to integrate all of a firm's information to ensure data integrity.

In addition to data integration, ERP software promises reduced transaction costs and fast, accurate information. A strategic emphasis on just-in-time systems and supply chain integration drives the desire for enterprise-wide software. The *OM in Action* box "Managing Benetton with ERP Software" provides an example of how ERP software helps integrate company operations.

OM in Action | Managing Benetton with ERP Software

Thanks to ERP, the Italian sportswear company Benetton can probably claim to have the world's fastest factory and the most efficient distribution in the garment industry. Located in Ponzano, Italy, Benetton makes and ships 50 million pieces of clothing each year. That is 30,000 boxes every day—boxes that must be filled with exactly the items ordered going to the correct store of the 5,000 Benetton outlets in 60 countries. This highly automated distribution center uses only 19 people. Without ERP, hundreds of people would be needed.

Here is how ERP software works:

1. *Ordering:* A salesperson in the south Boston store finds that she is running out of a best-selling blue sweater. Using a laptop PC, her local Benetton sales agent taps into the ERP sales module.
2. *Availability:* ERP's inventory software simultaneously forwards the order to the mainframe in Italy and finds that half the order can be filled immediately from the Italian warehouse. The rest will be manufactured and shipped in 4 weeks.

3. *Production:* Because the blue sweater was originally created by computer-aided design (CAD), ERP manufacturing software passes the specifications to a knitting machine. The knitting machine makes the sweaters.
4. *Warehousing:* The blue sweaters are boxed with a radio frequency ID (RFID) tag addressed to the Boston store and placed in one of the 300,000 slots in the Italian warehouse. A robot flies by, reading RFID tags, picks out any and all boxes ready for the Boston store, and loads them for shipment.
5. *Order tracking:* The Boston salesperson logs onto the ERP system through the Internet and sees that the sweater (and other items) are completed and being shipped.
6. *Planning:* Based on data from ERP's forecasting and financial modules, Benetton's chief buyer decides that blue sweaters are in high demand and quite profitable. She decides to add three new hues.

Sources: Forbes (December 2, 2011); *The Wall Street Journal* (April 10, 2007); *Information Week* (June 13, 2005); and *MIT Sloan Management Review* (Fall 2001).

In an ERP system, data are entered only once into a common, complete, and consistent database shared by all applications. For example, when a Nike salesperson enters an order into his ERP system for 20,000 pairs of sneakers for Foot Locker, the data are instantly available on the manufacturing floor. Production crews start filling the order if it is not in stock, accounting prints Foot Locker's invoice, and shipping notifies Foot Locker of the future delivery date. The salesperson, or even the customer, can check the progress of the order at any point. This is all accomplished using the same data and common applications. To reach this consistency, however, the data fields must be defined identically across the entire enterprise. In Nike's case, this means integrating operations at production sites from Vietnam to China to Mexico, at business units across the globe, in many currencies, and with reports in a variety of languages.

Each ERP vendor produces unique products. The major vendors, SAP AG (a German firm), BEA (Canada), SSAGlobal, American Software, PeopleSoft/Oracle, and CMS Software (all U.S. firms), sell software or modules designed for specific industries (a set of SAP's modules is shown in Figure 14.11). However, companies must determine if their way of doing business will fit the standard ERP module. If they determine that the product will not fit the standard ERP product, they can change the way they do business to accommodate the software. But such a change can have an adverse impact on their business process, reducing a competitive advantage.

Alternatively, ERP software can be customized to meet their specific process requirements. Although the vendors build the software to keep the customization process simple, many companies spend up to five times the cost of the software to customize it. In addition to the expense, the major downside of customization is that when ERP vendors provide an upgrade or enhancement to the software, the customized part of the code must be rewritten to fit into the new version. ERP programs cost from a minimum of $300,000 for a small company to

CASH TO CASH

Covers all financial related activity:

Accounts receivable — General ledger — Cash management
Accounts payable — Treasury — Asset management

PROMOTE TO DELIVER
Covers front-end customer-oriented activities:
Marketing
Quote and order processing
Transportation
Documentation and labeling
After sales service
Warranty and guarantees

DESIGN TO MANUFACTURE
Covers internal production activities:
Design engineering — Shop floor reporting
Production engineering — Contract/project management
Plant maintenance — Subcontractor management

RECRUIT TO RETIRE
Covers all HR- and payroll-oriented activity:
Time and attendance — Payroll
Travel and expenses

PROCURE TO PAY
Covers sourcing activities:
Vendor sourcing
Purchase requisitioning
Purchase ordering
Purchase contracts
Inbound logistics
Supplier invoicing/matching
Supplier payment/settlement
Supplier performance

DOCK TO DISPATCH
Covers internal inventory management:
Warehousing — Forecasting — Physical inventory
Distribution planning — Replenishment planning — Material handling

Figure **14.11**

SAP's Modules for ERP
Source: www.sap.com.

hundreds of millions of dollars for global giants like Ford and Coca-Cola. It is easy to see, then, that ERP systems are expensive, full of hidden issues, and time-consuming to install.

ERP in the Service Sector

ERP vendors have developed a series of service modules for such markets as health care, government, retail stores, and financial services. Springer-Miller Systems, for example, has created an ERP package for the hotel market with software that handles all front- and back-office functions. This system integrates tasks such as maintaining guest histories, booking room and dinner reservations, scheduling golf tee times, and managing multiple properties in a chain. PeopleSoft/Oracle combines ERP with supply chain management to coordinate airline meal preparation. In the grocery industry, these supply chain systems are known as *efficient consumer response* (ECR) systems. Efficient consumer response systems tie sales to buying, to inventory, to logistics, and to production.

> **Efficient consumer response (ECR)**
>
> Supply chain management systems in the grocery industry that tie sales to buying, to inventory, to logistics, and to production.

Summary

Material requirements planning (MRP) schedules production and inventory when demand is dependent. For MRP to work, management must have a master schedule, precise requirements for all components, accurate inventory and purchasing records, and accurate lead times.

When properly implemented, MRP can contribute in a major way to reduction in inventory while improving customer service levels. MRP techniques allow the operations manager to schedule and replenish stock on a "need-to-order" basis rather than simply a "time-to-order" basis.

Many firms using MRP systems find that lot-for-lot can be the low-cost lot-sizing option.

The continuing development of MRP systems has led to its use with lean manufacturing techniques. In addition, MRP can integrate production data with a variety of other activities, including the supply chain and sales. As a result, we now have integrated database-oriented enterprise resource planning (ERP) systems. These expensive and difficult-to-install ERP systems, when successful, support strategies of differentiation, response, and cost leadership.

Key Terms

Material requirements planning (MRP) (p. 566)
Master production schedule (MPS) (p. 567)
Bill of material (BOM) (p. 568)
Modular bills (p. 569)
Planning bills (or kits) (p. 570)
Phantom bills of material (p. 570)
Low-level coding (p. 570)
Lead time (p. 570)

Gross material requirements plan (p. 571)
Net requirements plan (p. 572)
Planned order receipt (p. 574)
Planned order release (p. 574)
System nervousness (p. 575)
Time fences (p. 575)
Pegging (p. 575)
Buckets (p. 576)
Lot-sizing decision (p. 576)
Lot-for-lot (p. 576)

Periodic order quantity (POQ) (p. 578)
Material requirements planning II (MRP II) (p. 580)
Closed-loop MRP system (p. 581)
Load report (p. 581)
Distribution resource planning (DRP) (p. 584)
Enterprise resource planning (ERP) (p. 584)
Efficient consumer response (ECR) (p. 587)

Ethical Dilemma

For many months your prospective ERP customer has been analyzing the hundreds of assumptions built into the $900,000 ERP software you are selling. So far, you have knocked yourself out to try to make this sale. If the sale goes through, you will reach your yearly quota and get a nice bonus. On the other hand, loss of this sale may mean you start looking for other employment.

The accounting, human resource, supply chain, and marketing teams put together by the client have reviewed the specifications and finally recommended purchase of the software. However, as you looked over their shoulders and helped them through the evaluation process, you began to realize that their purchasing procedures—with much of the purchasing being done at hundreds of regional stores—were not a good fit for the software. At the very least, the customizing will add $250,000 to the implementation and training cost. The team is not aware of the issue, and you know that the necessary $250,000 is not in the budget.

What do you do?

Discussion Questions

1. What is the difference between a *gross* requirements plan and a *net* requirements plan?
2. Once a material requirements plan (MRP) has been established, what other managerial applications might be found for the technique?
3. What are the similarities between MRP and DRP?
4. How does MRP II differ from MRP?
5. Which is the best lot-sizing policy for manufacturing organizations?
6. What impact does ignoring carrying cost in the allocation of stock in a DRP system have on lot sizes?
7. MRP is more than an inventory system; what additional capabilities does MRP possess?
8. What are the options for the production planner who has:
   a) scheduled more than capacity in a work center next week?
   b) a consistent lack of capacity in that work center?
9. Master schedules are expressed in three different ways depending on whether the process is continuous, a job shop, or repetitive. What are these three ways?
10. What functions of the firm affect an MRP system? How?
11. What is the rationale for (a) a phantom bill of material, (b) a planning bill of material, and (c) a pseudo bill of material?
12. Identify five specific requirements of an effective MRP system.
13. What are the typical benefits of ERP?
14. What are the distinctions between MRP, DRP, and ERP?
15. As an approach to inventory management, how does MRP differ from the approach taken in Chapter 12, dealing with economic order quantities (EOQ)?
16. What are the disadvantages of ERP?
17. Use the Web or other sources to:
    a) Find stories that highlight the advantages of an ERP system.
    b) Find stories that highlight the difficulties of purchasing, installing, or failure of an ERP system.
18. Use the Web or other sources to identify what an ERP vendor (SAP, PeopleSoft/Oracle, American Software, etc.) includes in these software modules:
    a) Customer relationship management.
    b) Supply-chain management.
    c) Product life cycle management.
19. The structure of MRP systems suggests "buckets" and infinite loading. What is meant by these two terms?

Using Software to Solve MRP Problems

There are many commercial MRP software packages, for companies of all sizes. MRP software for small and medium-size companies includes User Solutions, Inc., a demo of which is available at **www.usersolutions.com,** and MAX, from Exact Software North America, Inc. Software for larger systems is available from SAP, CMS, BEA, Oracle, i2 Technologies, and many others. The Excel OM software that accompanies this text includes an MRP module, as does POM for Windows. The use of both is explained in the following sections.

✖ USING EXCEL OM

Using Excel OM's MRP module requires the careful entry of several pieces of data. The initial MRP screen is where we enter (1) the total number of occurrences of items in the BOM (including the top item), (2) what we want the BOM items to be called (e.g., Item no., Part), (3) total number of periods to be scheduled, and (4) what we want the periods called (e.g., days, weeks).

Excel OM's second MRP screen provides the data entry for an indented bill of material. Here we enter (1) the name of each item in the BOM, (2) the quantity of that item in the assembly, and (3) the correct indent (e.g., parent/child relationship) for each item. The indentations are critical, as they provide the logic for the BOM explosion. The indentations should follow the logic of the product structure tree with indents for each assembly item in that assembly.

Excel OM's third MRP screen repeats the indented BOM and provides the standard MRP tableau for entries. This is shown in Program 14.1 using the data from Examples 1, 2, and 3.

P USING POM FOR WINDOWS

The POM for Windows MRP module can also solve Examples 1 to 3. Up to 18 periods can be analyzed. Here are the inputs required:

1. *Item names:* The item names are entered in the left column. The same item name will appear in more than one row if the item is used by two parent items. Each item must follow its parents.
2. *Item level:* The level in the indented BOM must be given here. The item *cannot* be placed at a level more than one below the item immediately above.
3. *Lead time:* The lead time for an item is entered here. The default is 1 week.
4. *Number per parent:* The number of units of this subassembly needed for its parent is entered here. The default is 1.
5. *On hand:* List current inventory on hand once, even if the subassembly is listed twice.
6. *Lot size:* The lot size can be specified here. A 0 or 1 will perform lot-for-lot ordering. If another number is placed here, then all orders for that item will be in integer multiples of that number.
7. *Demands:* The demands are entered in the end item row in the period in which the items are demanded.
8. *Scheduled receipts:* If units are scheduled to be received in the future, they should be listed in the appropriate time period (column) and item (row). (An entry here in level 1 is a demand; all other levels are receipts.)

Further details regarding POM for Windows are seen in Appendix IV.

Program **14.1**

Using Excel OM's MRP Module to Solve Examples 1, 2, and 3

The data in columns A, B, C, D (down to row 15) are entered on the second screen and automatically transferred here.

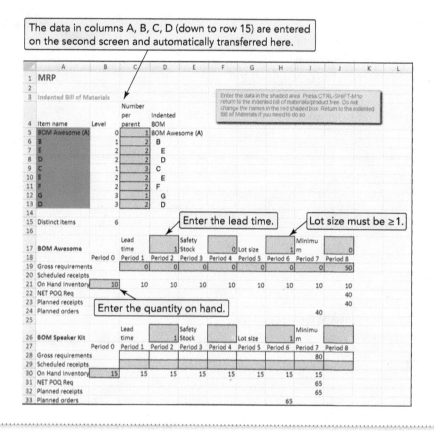

Enter the lead time.

Lot size must be ≥1.

Enter the quantity on hand.

Solved Problems

Virtual Office Hours help is available in MyOMLab.

SOLVED PROBLEM 14.1

Determine the low-level coding and the quantity of each component necessary to produce 10 units of an assembly we will call Alpha. The product structure and quantities of each component needed for each assembly are noted in parentheses.

SOLUTION

Redraw the product structure with low-level coding. Then multiply down the structure until the requirements of each branch are determined. Then add across the structure until the total for each is determined.

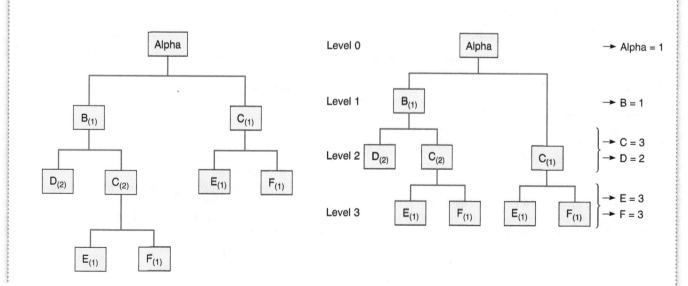

Es required for left branch:

$$(1_{\text{alpha}} \times 1_B \times 2_C \times 1_E) = 2 \text{ Es}$$

and Es required for right branch:

$$(1_{\text{alpha}} \times 1_C \times 1_E) = \underline{1 \text{ E}}$$
$$3 \text{ Es required in total}$$

Then "explode" the requirement by multiplying each by 10, as shown in the table to the right:

LEVEL	ITEM	QUANTITY PER UNIT	TOTAL REQUIREMENTS FOR 10 ALPHA
0	Alpha	1	10
1	B	1	10
2	C	3	30
2	D	2	20
3	E	3	30
3	F	3	30

SOLVED PROBLEM 14.2

Using the product structure for Alpha in Solved Problem 14.1, and the following lead times, quantity on hand, and master production schedule, prepare a net MRP table for Alphas.

ITEM	LEAD TIME	QUANTITY ON HAND
Alpha	1	10
B	2	20
C	3	0
D	1	100
E	1	10
F	1	50

Master Production Schedule for Alpha

PERIOD	6	7	8	9	10	11	12	13
Gross requirements			50			50		100

SOLUTION

See the chart on following page.

SOLVED PROBLEM 14.3

Hip Replacements, Inc., has a master production schedule for its newest model, as shown below, a setup cost of $50, a holding cost per week of $2, beginning inventory of 0, and lead time of 1 week. What are the costs of using lot-for-lot for this 10-week period?

SOLUTION

Holding cost = $0 (as there is never any end-of-period inventory)

Ordering costs = 4 orders × $50 = $200

Total cost for lot-for-lot = $0 + $200 = $200

WEEK		1	2	3	4	5	6	7	8	9	10
Gross requirements		0	0	50	0	0	35	15	0	100	0
Scheduled receipts											
Projected on hand	0	0	0	0	0	0	0	0	0	0	0
Net requirements		0	0	50	0	0	35	15	0	100	
Planned order receipts				50			35	15		100	
Planned order releases			50			35	15		100		

SOLVED PROBLEM 14.4

Hip Replacements, Inc., has a master production schedule for its newest model, as shown on page 592, a setup cost of $50, a holding cost per week of $2, beginning inventory of 0, and lead time of 1 week. What are the costs of using (a) EOQ and (b) POQ for this 10-week period?

SOLUTION

a) For the **EOQ** lot size, first determine the EOQ.
Annual usage = 200 units for 10 weeks; weekly usage = 200/10 weeks = 20 per week. Therefore, 20 units × 52 weeks

(annual demand) = 1,040 units. From Chapter 12, the EOQ model is:

$$Q^* = \sqrt{\frac{2DS}{H}}$$

where
D = annual demand = 1,040
S = Setup cost = $50
H = holding (carrying) cost, on an annual basis per unit = $2 × 52 = $104
Q^* = 31.62 ≈ 32 units (order the EOQ or in multiples of the EOQ)

(Continued on page 592)

Net Material Requirements Planning Sheet for Alpha for Solved Problem 14.2

The letter in parentheses (A) is the source of the demand.

Alpha (A) — Lot Size: Lot-for-Lot | Lead Time: 1 | On Hand: 10 | Safety Stock: — | Allocated: — | Low-Level Code: 0

Row	1	2	3	4	5	6	7	8	9	10	11	12	13
Gross Requirements								50			50		100
Scheduled Receipts													
Projected On Hand [10]								10					
Net Requirements								40			50		100
Planned Order Receipts								40			50		100
Planned Order Releases							40			50		100	

B — Lot Size: Lot-for-Lot | Lead Time: 2 | On Hand: 20 | Safety Stock: — | Allocated: — | Low-Level Code: 1

Row	1	2	3	4	5	6	7	8	9	10	11	12	13
Gross Requirements							40(A)			50(A)		100(A)	
Scheduled Receipts													
Projected On Hand [20]							20						
Net Requirements							20			50		100	
Planned Order Receipts							20			50		100	
Planned Order Releases					20			50		100			

C — Lot Size: Lot-for-Lot | Lead Time: 3 | On Hand: 0 | Safety Stock: — | Allocated: — | Low-Level Code: 2

Row	1	2	3	4	5	6	7	8	9	10	11	12	13
Gross Requirements					40(B)		40(A)	100(B)		200(B) + 50(A)		100(A)	
Scheduled Receipts													
Projected On Hand [0]													
Net Requirements					40		40	100		250		100	
Planned Order Receipts					40		40	100		250		100	
Planned Order Releases		40		40	100		250		100				

D — Lot Size: Lot-for-Lot | Lead Time: 1 | On Hand: 100 | Safety Stock: — | Allocated: — | Low-Level Code: 2

Row	1	2	3	4	5	6	7	8	9	10	11	12	13
Gross Requirements					40(B)			100(B)		200(B)			
Scheduled Receipts													
Projected On Hand [100]					60			0		0			
Net Requirements					0			40		200			
Planned Order Receipts					0			40		200			
Planned Order Releases							40		200				

E — Lot Size: Lot-for-Lot | Lead Time: 1 | On Hand: 10 | Safety Stock: — | Allocated: — | Low-Level Code: 3

Row	1	2	3	4	5	6	7	8	9	10	11	12	13
Gross Requirements		40(C)		40(C)	100(C)		250(C)		100(C)				
Scheduled Receipts													
Projected On Hand [10]		10											
Net Requirements		30		40	100		250		100				
Planned Order Receipts		30		40	100		250		100				
Planned Order Releases	30		40	100		250		100					

F — Lot Size: Lot-for-Lot | Lead Time: 1 | On Hand: 50 | Safety Stock: — | Allocated: — | Low-Level Code: 3

Row	1	2	3	4	5	6	7	8	9	10	11	12	13
Gross Requirements		40(C)		40(C)	100(C)		250(C)		100(C)				
Scheduled Receipts													
Projected On Hand [50]		10		0									
Net Requirements				30	100		250		100				
Planned Order Receipts				30	100		250		100				
Planned Order Releases			30	100		250		100					

WEEK		1	2	3	4	5	6	7	8	9	10
Gross requirements		0	0	50	0	0	35	15	0	100	0
Scheduled receipts											
Projected on hand	0	0	0	0	14	14	14	11	28	28	24	24
Net requirements		0	0	50	0	0	21	0	0	72	0
Planned order receipts				64			32	32		96	
Planned order releases			64				32	32		96	

Holding cost = 157 units × \$2 = \$314 (note the 24 units available in period 11, for which there
  is an inventory charge as they are in on-hand inventory at the end of period 10)

Ordering costs = 4 orders × \$50 = \$200

Total cost for EOQ lot sizing = \$314 + \$200 = \$514

b) For the **POQ** lot size we use the EOQ computed above to find the time period between orders:

Period interval = EOQ/average weekly usage = 32/20 = 1.6 ≈ 2 periods

POQ order size = Demand required in the 2 periods, postponing orders in periods with no demand.

WEEK		1	2	3	4	5	6	7	8	9	10
Gross requirements		0	0	50	0	0	35	15	0	100	0
Scheduled receipts											
Projected on hand	0	0	0	0	0	0	0	0	15	0	0
Net requirements		0	0	50	0	0	50	0	0	100	0
Planned order receipts				50			50			100	
Planned order releases			50			50			100		

Holding cost = 15 units × \$2 = \$30

Ordering costs = 3 orders × \$50 = \$150

Total cost for POQ lot sizing = \$30 + \$150 = \$180

Problems*

Note: **PX** means the problem may be solved with POM for Windows and/or Excel OM. Many of the exercises in this chapter (14.1 through 14.16 and 14.29 through 14.32) can be done on *Resource Manager for Excel*, a commercial system made available by User Solutions, Inc. Access to a trial version of the software and a set of notes for the user are available at **www.usersolutions.com.**

Problems 14.1–14.4 relate to Dependent Inventory Model Requirements

• **14.1** You have developed the following simple product structure of items needed for your gift bag for a rush party for prospective pledges in your organization. You forecast 200 attendees. Assume that there is no inventory on hand of any of the items. Explode the bill of material. (Subscripts indicate the number of units required.)

•• **14.2** You are expected to have the gift bags in Problem 14.1 ready at 5 P.M. However, you need to personalize the items (monogrammed pens, note pads, literature from the printer, etc.). The lead time is 1 hour to assemble 200 Js once the other items are prepared. The other items will take a while as well. Given the volunteers you have, the other time estimates are item K (2 hours), item L (1 hour), and item M (4 hours). Develop a time-phased assembly plan to prepare the gift bags.

•• **14.3** As the production planner for Xiangling Hu Products, Inc., you have been given a bill of material for a bracket that is made up of a base, two springs, and four clamps. The base is assembled from one clamp and two housings. Each clamp has one handle and one casting. Each housing has two bearings and one shaft. There is no inventory on hand.

a) Design a product structure noting the quantities for each item and show the low-level coding.

b) Determine the gross quantities needed of each item if you are to assemble 50 brackets.

c) Compute the net quantities needed if there are 25 of the base and 100 of the clamp in stock. **PX**

•• **14.4** Your boss at Xiangling Hu Products, Inc., has just provided you with the schedule and lead times for the bracket in Problem 14.3. The unit is to be prepared in week 10. The lead times for the components are bracket (1 week), base (1 week), spring (1 week), clamp (1 week), housing (2 weeks), handle (1 week), casting (3 weeks), bearing (1 week), and shaft (1 week).

a) Prepare the time-phased product structure for the bracket.

b) In what week do you need to start the castings? **PX**

Problems 14.5–14.21 relate to MRP Structure

•• **14.5** The demand for subassembly S is 100 units in week 7. Each unit of S requires 1 unit of T and 2 units of U. Each unit of T requires 1 unit of V, 2 units of W, and 1 unit of X. Finally, each unit of U requires 2 units of Y and 3 units of Z. One firm manufactures all items. It takes 2 weeks to make S, 1 week to make T,

2 weeks to make U, 2 weeks to make V, 3 weeks to make W, 1 week to make X, 2 weeks to make Y, and 1 week to make Z.
a) Construct a product structure. Identify all levels, parents, and components.
b) Prepare a time-phased product structure.

•• **14.6** Using the information in Problem 14.5, construct a gross material requirements plan. **Px**

•• **14.7** Using the information in Problem 14.5, construct a net material requirements plan using the following on-hand inventory.

ITEM	ON-HAND INVENTORY	ITEM	ON-HAND INVENTORY
S	20	W	30
T	20	X	25
U	40	Y	240
V	30	Z	40 **Px**

•• **14.8** Refer again to Problems 14.5 and 14.6. In addition to 100 units of S, there is also a demand for 20 units of U, which is a component of S. The 20 units of U are needed for maintenance purposes. These units are needed in week 6. Modify the *gross material requirements plan* to reflect this change. **Px**

•• **14.9** Refer again to Problems 14.5 and 14.7. In addition to 100 units of S, there is also a demand for 20 units of U, which is a component of S. The 20 units of U are needed for maintenance purposes. These units are needed in week 6. Modify the *net material requirements plan* to reflect this change. **Px**

•• **14.10**
a) Given the product structure and master production schedule (Figure 14.12 below), develop a gross requirements plan for all items.
b) Given the preceding product structure, master production schedule, and inventory status (Figure 14.12), develop a net materials requirements (planned order release) for all items. **Px**

••• **14.11** Given the product structure, master production schedule, and inventory status in Figure 14.13 on the next page and assuming the requirements for each BOM item is 1:
a) develop a gross requirements plan for Item C;
b) develop a net requirements plan for Item C. **Px**

•••• **14.12** Based on the data in Figure 14.13, complete a net material requirements schedule for:
a) All items (10 schedules in all), assuming the requirement for each BOM item is 1.
b) All 10 items, assuming the requirement for all items is 1, except B, C, and F, which require *2 each*. **Px**

••• **14.13** Electro Fans has just received an order for one thousand 20-inch fans due week 7. Each fan consists of a housing assembly, two grills, a fan assembly, and an electrical unit. The housing assembly consists of a frame, two supports, and a handle. The fan assembly consists of a hub and five blades. The electrical unit consists of a motor, a switch, and a knob. The following table gives lead times, on-hand inventory, and scheduled receipts.
a) Construct a product structure.
b) Construct a time-phased product structure.
c) Prepare a net material requirements plan. **Px**

Data Table for Problem 14.13

COMPONENT	LEAD TIME	ON-HAND INVENTORY	LOT SIZE*	SCHEDULED RECEIPT
20" Fan	1	100	—	
Housing	1	100	—	
Frame	2	—	—	
Supports (2)	1	50	100	
Handle	1	400	500	
Grills (2)	2	200	500	
Fan Assembly	3	150	—	
Hub	1	—	—	
Blades (5)	2	—	100	
Electrical Unit	1	—	—	
Motor	1	—	—	
Switch	1	20	12	
Knob	1	—	25	200 knobs in week 2

* Lot-for-lot unless otherwise noted.

•••• **14.14** A part structure, lead time (weeks), and on-hand quantities for product A are shown in Figure 14.14. From the information shown, generate:
a) An indented bill of material for product A (see Figure 5.9 in Chapter 5 as an example of a BOM).
b) Net requirements for each part to produce 10 As in week 8 using lot-for-lot. **Px**

•••• **14.15** You are product planner for product A (in Problem 14.14 and Figure 14.14). The field service manager, Al Trostel, has just called and told you that the requirements for B and F should each be increased by 10 units for his repair requirements in the field.
a) Prepare a list showing the quantity of each part required to produce the requirements for the service manager *and* the production request of 10 Bs and Fs.
b) Prepare a net requirement plan by date for the new requirements (for both production and field service), assuming that the field service manager wants his 10 units of B and F in week 6 and the 10 production units of A in week 8. **Px**

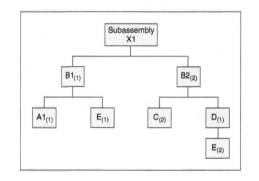

Master Production Schedule for X1

PERIOD	7	8	9	10	11	12
Gross requirements		50		20		100

ITEM	LEAD TIME	ON HAND	ITEM	LEAD TIME	ON HAND
X1	1	50	C	1	0
B1	2	20	D	1	0
B2	2	20	E	3	10
A1	1	5			

Figure **14.12**

Information for Problem 14.10

PERIOD			8	9	10	11	12
Gross requirements: A			100		50		150
Gross requirements: H				100		50	

ITEM	ON HAND	LEAD TIME	ITEM	ON HAND	LEAD TIME
A	0	1	F	75	2
B	100	2	G	75	1
C	50	2	H	0	1
D	50	1	J	100	2
E	75	2	K	100	2

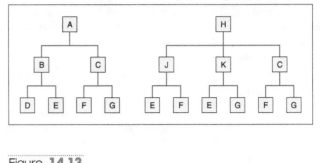

Figure **14.13**

Information for Problems 14.11 and 14.12

••• **14.16** You have just been notified via fax that the lead time for component G of product A (Problem 14.15 and Figure 14.14) has been increased to 4 weeks.
a) Which items have changed, and why?
b) What are the implications for the production plan?
c) As production planner, what can you do? **Px**

•• **14.17** Heather Adams, production manager for a Colorado exercise equipment manufacturer, needs to schedule an order for 50 UltimaSteppers, which are to be shipped in week 8. Subscripts indicate quantity required for each parent. Assume lot-for-lot ordering. Below is information about the steppers:

ITEM	LEAD TIME	ON-HAND INVENTORY	COMPONENTS
Stepper	2	20	$A_{(1)}$, $B_{(3)}$, $C_{(2)}$
A	1	10	$D_{(1)}$, $F_{(2)}$
B	2	30	$E_{(1)}$, $F_{(3)}$
C	3	10	$D_{(2)}$, $E_{(3)}$
D	1	15	
E	2	5	
F	2	20	

a) Develop a product structure for Heather.
b) Develop a time-phased structure.
c) Develop a net material requirements plan for F. **Px**

*Additional problems **14.18–14.21** are available in MyOMLab.*

Problems 14.22–14.28 relate to Lot-Sizing Techniques

Data Table for Problems 14.22 through 14.25*

PERIOD	1	2	3	4	5	6	7	8	9	10	11	12
Gross requirements	30		40		30	70	20		10	80		50

*Holding cost = $2.50/unit/week; setup cost = $150; lead time = 1 week; beginning inventory = 40; stockout cost = $10.

••• **14.22** Develop a lot-for-lot solution and calculate total relevant costs for the data in the preceding table. **Px**

••• **14.23** Develop an EOQ solution and calculate total relevant costs for the data in the preceding table. **Px**

••• **14.24** Develop a POQ solution and calculate total relevant costs for the data in the preceding table. **Px**

••• **14.25** Using your answers for the lot sizes computed in Problems 14.22, 14.23, and 14.24, which is the best technique and why?

•• **14.26** M. de Koster, of Rene Enterprises, has the master production plan shown below:

Period (weeks)	1	2	3	4	5	6	7	8	9
Gross requirements		15		20		10			25

Lead time = 1 period; setup cost = $200; holding cost = $10 per week; stockout cost = $10 per week. Your job is to develop an ordering plan and costs for:

a) Lot-for-lot.   b) EOQ.
c) POQ.   d) Which plan has the lowest cost? **Px**

•• **14.27** Grace Greenberg, production planner for Science and Technology Labs, in New Jersey, has the master production plan shown below:

Period (weeks)	1	2	3	4	5	6	7	8	9	10	11	12
Gross requirements		35		40		10			25	10		45

Lead time = 1 period; setup costs = $200; holding cost = $10 per week; stockout cost = $10 per week. Develop an ordering plan and costs for Grace, using these techniques:

a) Lot-for-lot.   b) EOQ.
c) POQ.   d) Which plan has the lowest cost? **Px**

Figure **14.14**

Information for Problems 14.14, 14.15, and 14.16

PART	INVENTORY ON HAND
A	0
B	2
C	10
D	5
E	4
F	5
G	1
H	10

PART STRUCTURE TREE

A LT = 1
LT = lead time in weeks
(1) = All quantities = 1

$B_{(1)}$ LT = 1 $F_{(1)}$ LT = 1

$C_{(1)}$ LT = 2 $D_{(1)}$ LT = 1 $G_{(1)}$ LT = 3 $H_{(1)}$ LT = 1

$E_{(1)}$ LT = 1 $E_{(1)}$ LT = 1 $C_{(1)}$ LT = 2

Additional problem **14.28** is available in MyOMLab.

Problems 14.29–14.32 relate to Extensions of MRP

••• **14.29** Karl Knapps, Inc., has received the following orders:

Period	1	2	3	4	5	6	7	8	9	10
Order size	0	40	30	40	10	70	40	10	30	60

The entire fabrication for these units is scheduled on one machine. There are 2,250 usable minutes in a week, and each unit will take 65 minutes to complete. Develop a capacity plan, using lot splitting, for the 10-week time period.

••• **14.30** Coleman Rich, Ltd., has received the following orders:

Period	1	2	3	4	5	6	7	8	9	10
Order size	60	30	10	40	70	10	40	30	40	0

The entire fabrication for these units is scheduled on one machine. There are 2,250 usable minutes in a week, and each unit will take 65 minutes to complete. Develop a capacity plan, using lot splitting, for the 10-week time period.

••• **14.31** Courtney Kamauf schedules production of a popular Rustic Coffee Table at Kamauf Enterprises, Inc. The table requires a top, four legs, $\frac{1}{8}$ gallon of stain, $\frac{1}{16}$ gallon of glue, 2 short braces between the legs and 2 long braces between the legs, and a brass cap that goes on the bottom of each leg. She has 100 gallons of glue in inventory, but none of the other components. All items except the brass caps, stain, and glue are ordered on a lot-for-lot basis. The caps are purchased in quantities of 1,000, stain and glue by the gallon. Lead time is 1 day for each item. Schedule the order releases necessary to produce 640 coffee tables on days 5 and 6, and 128 on days 7 and 8.

•••• **14.32** Using the data for the coffee table in Problem 14.31, build a labor schedule when the labor standard for each top is 2 labor-hours; each leg including brass cap installation requires $\frac{1}{4}$ hour, as does each pair of braces. Base assembly requires 1 labor-hour, and final assembly requires 2 labor-hours. What is the total number of labor-hours required each day, and how many employees are needed each day at 8 hours per day?

CASE STUDIES

When 18,500 Orlando Magic Fans Come to Dinner

Video Case 📷

With vast experience at venues such as the American Airlines Arena (in Miami), the Kentucky Derby, and Super Bowls, Chef John Nicely now also plans huge culinary events at Orlando's Amway Center, home of the Orlando Magic basketball team. With his unique talent and exceptional operations skills, Nicely serves tens of thousands of cheering fans at some of the world's largest events. And when more than 18,500 basketball fans show up for a game, expecting great food and great basketball, he puts his creative as well as operations talent to work.

Chef John must be prepared. This means determining not only a total demand for all 18,500 fans, but also translating that demand into specific menu items and beverages. He prepares a forecast from current ticket sales, history of similar events at other venues, and his own records, which reflect the demand with this particular opponent, night of week, time of year, and even time of day. He then breaks the demand for specific menu items and quantities into items to be available at each of the 22 concession stands, 7 restaurants, and 68 suites. He must also be prepared to accommodate individual requests from players on both teams.

Chef John frequently changes the menu to keep it interesting for the fans who attend many of the 41 regular season home games each season. Even the culinary preference of the opponent's fans who may be attending influences the menu. Additionally, when entertainment other than the Magic is using the Amway Center, the demographic mix is likely to be different, requiring additional tweaking of the menu. The size of the wait staff and the kitchen staff change to reflect the size of the crowd; Chef John may be supervising as many as 90 people working in the kitchen. Similarly, the concessions stands, 40% of which have their own grills and fryers, present another challenge, as they are managed by volunteers from nonprofit organizations. The use of these volunteers adds the need for special training and extra enforcement of strict quality standards.

Once deciding on the overall demand and the menu, Chef John must prepare the production specifications (a bill of material) for each item. For the evening game with the Celtics, Chef John is preparing his unique *Cheeto Crusted Mac & Cheese* dish. The ingredients, quantity, costs, and labor requirements are shown below:

Production Specifications

CHEETO CRUSTED MAC & CHEESE (6 PORTIONS)					
INGREDIENTS	QUANTITY	MEASURE	UNIT COST	TOTAL COST	LABOR-HOURS
Elbow macaroni (large, uncooked)	20.00	oz.	$0.09	$1.80	
Cheese—cheddar shredded	10.00	oz.	0.16	1.60	
Mac and cheese base (see recipe)	44.00	oz.	0.80	35.20	
Milk	4.00	oz.	0.03	0.12	
Cheetos, crushed	6.00	oz.	0.27	1.62	
Sliced green onion—garnish	0.50	oz.	0.18	0.09	
Whole Cheetos—garnish	2.00	oz.	0.27	0.54	
Total labor hours					0.2 hours

The yield on this dish is 6 portions, and labor cost is $15 per hour, with fringes. The entire quantity required for the evening is prepared prior to the game and kept in warming ovens until needed. Demand for each basketball game is divided into 5 periods: prior to the game, first quarter, second quarter, half-time, and second half. At the Magic vs. Celtics game next week, the demand (number of portions) in each period is 60, 36, 48, 60, and 12 for the Cheeto Crusted Mac & Cheese dish, respectively.

Discussion Questions*

1. Prepare a bill of material explosion and total cost for the 216 portions of Cheeto Crusted Mac & Cheese.

2. What is the cost per portion? How much less expensive is the Cheeto Crusted Mac & Cheese than Chef John's alternative creation, the Buffalo Chicken Mac & Cheese, shown in Figure 14.9 of this chapter?

3. Assuming that there is no beginning inventory of the Cheeto Crusted Mac & Cheese and cooking time for the entire 216 portions is 0.6 hours, when must preparation begin?

*You may wish to view the video that accompanies this case before answering the questions.

MRP at Wheeled Coach

Video Case

Wheeled Coach, the world's largest manufacturer of ambulances, builds thousands of different and constantly changing configurations of its products. The custom nature of its business means lots of options and special designs—and a potential scheduling and inventory nightmare. Wheeled Coach addressed such problems, and succeeded in solving a lot of them, with an MRP system (described in the *Global Company Profile* that opens this chapter). As with most MRP installations, however, solving one set of problems uncovers a new set.

One of the new issues that had to be addressed by plant manager Lynn Whalen was newly discovered excess inventory. Managers discovered a substantial amount of inventory that was not called for in any finished products. Excess inventory was evident because of the new level of inventory accuracy required by the MRP system. The other reason was a new series of inventory reports generated by the IBM MAPICS MRP system purchased by Wheeled Coach. One of those reports indicates where items are used and is known as the "Where Used" report. Interestingly, many inventory items were not called out on bills of material (BOMs) for any current products. In some cases, the reason some parts were in the stockroom remained a mystery.

The discovery of this excess inventory led to renewed efforts to ensure that the BOMs were accurate. With substantial work, BOM accuracy increased and the number of engineering change notices (ECNs) decreased. Similarly, purchase-order accuracy, with regard to both part numbers and quantities ordered, was improved. Additionally, receiving department and stockroom accuracy went up, all helping to maintain schedule, costs, and ultimately, shipping dates and quality.

Eventually, Lynn Whalen concluded that the residual amounts of excess inventory were the result, at least in part, of rapid changes in ambulance design and technology. Another source was customer changes made after specifications had been determined and materials ordered. This latter excess occurs because, even though Wheeled Coach's own throughput time is only 17 days, many of the items that it purchases require much longer lead times.

Discussion Questions*

1. Why is accurate inventory such an important issue at Wheeled Coach?

2. Why does Wheeled Coach have excess inventory, and what kind of a plan would you suggest for dealing with it?

3. Be specific in your suggestions for reducing inventory and how to implement them.

*You may wish to view the video that accompanies this case before answering the questions.

- **Additional Case Studies:** Visit MyOMLab for these free case studies:
  Ikon's attempt at ERP: The giant office technology firm faces hurdles with ERP implementation.
  Hill's Automotive, Inc.: An after-market producer and distributor of auto replacement parts has trouble making MRP work.

Endnotes

1. The inventory models (EOQ) discussed in Chapter 12 assumed that the demand for one item was independent of the demand for another item. For example, EOQ assumes the demand for refrigerator parts is *independent* of the demand for refrigerators and that demand for parts is constant. MRP makes neither of these assumptions.

2. Record accuracy of 99% may sound good, but note that even when each component has an availability of 99% and a product has only seven components, the likelihood of a product being completed is only .932 (because $.99^7 = .932$).

3. Using EOQ is a convenient approach for determining the time between orders, but other rules can be used.

4. *Part period balancing, Silver-Meal,* and *Wagner-Whitin* are included in the software POM for Windows and ExcelOM, available with this text.

Chapter 14 *Rapid* Review

Main Heading	Review Material	MyOMLab
DEPENDENT DEMAND (p. 566)	Demand for items is *dependent* when the relationship between the items can be determined. For any product, all components of that product are dependent demand items. ■ **Material requirements planning (MRP)**—A dependent demand technique that uses a bill-of-material, inventory, expected receipts, and a master production schedule to determine material requirements.	Concept Questions: 1.1–1.4
DEPENDENT INVENTORY MODEL REQUIREMENTS (pp. 566–571)	Dependent inventory models require that the operations manager know the: (1) Master production schedule; (2) Specifications or bill of material; (3) Inventory availability; (4) Purchase orders outstanding; and (5) Lead times. ■ **Master production schedule (MPS)**—A timetable that specifies what is to be made and when. The MPS is a statement of *what is to be produced*, not a forecast of demand. ■ **Bill of material (BOM)**—A listing of the components, their description, and the quantity of each required to make one unit of a product. Items above any level in a BOM are called *parents*; items below any level are called *components*, or *children*. The top level in a BOM is the 0 level. ■ **Modular bills**—Bills of material organized by major subassemblies or by product options. ■ **Planning bills (or kits)**—Material groupings created in order to assign an artificial parent to a bill of material; also called "pseudo" bills. ■ **Phantom bills of material**—Bills of material for components, usually subassemblies, that exist only temporarily; they are never inventoried. ■ **Low-level coding**—A number that identifies items at the lowest level at which they occur. ■ **Lead time**—In purchasing systems, the time between recognition of the need for an order and receiving it; in production systems, it is the order, wait, move, queue, setup, and run times for each component. When a bill of material is turned on its side and modified by adding lead times for each component, it is called a *time-phased product structure*.	Concept Questions: 2.1–2.4 Problems: 14.1–14.4 Virtual Office Hours for Solved Problem: 14.1 **VIDEO 14.1** When 18,500 Orlando Magic Fans Come to Dinner **VIDEO 14.2** MRP at Wheeled Coach Ambulances
MRP STRUCTURE (pp. 571–575)	■ **Gross material requirements plan**—A schedule that shows the total demand for an item (prior to subtraction of on-hand inventory and scheduled receipts) and (1) when it must be ordered from suppliers, or (2) when production must be started to meet its demand by a particular date. ■ **Net material requirements**—The result of adjusting gross requirements for inventory on hand and scheduled receipts. ■ **Planned order receipt**—The quantity planned to be received at a future date. ■ **Planned order release**—The scheduled date for an order to be released. Net requirements = Gross requirements + Allocations − (On hand + Scheduled receipts)	Concept Questions: 3.1–3.4 Problems: 14.5–14.9, 14.11, 14.16–14.21 Virtual Office Hours for Solved Problem: 14.2 **ACTIVE MODEL 14.1**
MRP MANAGEMENT (pp. 575–576)	■ **System nervousness**—Frequent changes in an MRP system. ■ **Time fences**—A means for allowing a segment of the master schedule to be designated as "not to be rescheduled." ■ **Pegging**—In material requirements planning systems, tracing upward the bill of material from the component to the parent item. Four approaches for integrating MRP and JIT are (1) finite capacity scheduling, (2) small buckets, (3) balanced flow, and (4) supermarkets. ■ **Buckets**—Time units in a material requirements planning system. Finite capacity scheduling (FCS) considers department and machine capacity. FCS provides the precise scheduling needed for rapid material movement.	Concept Questions: 4.1–4.4
LOT-SIZING TECHNIQUES (pp. 576–580)	■ **Lot-sizing decision**—The process of, or techniques used in, determining lot size. ■ **Lot-for-lot**—A lot-sizing technique that generates exactly what is required to meet the plan. ■ **Periodic order quantity (POQ)**—A lot-sizing technique that issues orders on a predetermined time interval with an order quantity equal to all of the interval's requirements. In general, the lot-for-lot approach should be used whenever low-cost deliveries setup can be achieved.	Concept Questions: 5.1–5.4 Problems: 14.22, 14.26, 14.28

MyOMLab

Main Heading	Review Material	
EXTENSIONS OF MRP (pp. 580–583)	■ **Material requirements planning II (MRP II)**—A system that allows, with MRP in place, inventory data to be augmented by other resource variables; in this case, MRP becomes *material resource planning*. ■ **Closed-loop MRP system**—A system that provides feedback to the capacity plan, master production schedule, and production plan so planning can be kept valid at all times. ■ **Load report**—A report for showing the resource requirements in a work center for all work currently assigned there as well as all planned and expected orders. Tactics for smoothing the load and minimizing the impact of changed lead time include: *overlapping, operations splitting,* and *order splitting,* or *lot splitting.*	Concept Questions: 6.1–6.4 Problem: 14.32
MRP IN SERVICES (pp. 583–584)	■ **Distribution resource planning (DRP)**—A time-phased stock-replenishment plan for all levels of a distribution network.	Concept Questions: 7.1–7.4
ENTERPRISE RESOURCE PLANNING (ERP) (pp. 584–587)	■ **Enterprise resource planning (ERP)**—An information system for identifying and planning the enterprise-wide resources needed to take, make, ship, and account for customer orders. In an ERP system, data are entered only once into a common, complete, and consistent database shared by all applications. ■ **Efficient consumer response (ECR)**—Supply-chain management systems in the grocery industry that tie sales to buying, to inventory, to logistics, and to production.	Concept Questions: 8.1–8.4

Self Test

■ **Before taking the self-test,** refer to the learning objectives listed at the beginning of the chapter and the key terms listed at the end of the chapter.

LO 14.1 In a product structure diagram:
a) parents are found only at the top level of the diagram.
b) parents are found at every level in the diagram.
c) children are found at every level of the diagram except the top level.
d) all items in the diagrams are both parents and children.
e) all of the above.

LO 14.2 The difference between a gross material requirements plan (gross MRP) and a net material requirements plan (net MRP) is:
a) the gross MRP may not be computerized, but the net MRP must be computerized.
b) the gross MRP includes consideration of the inventory on hand, whereas the net MRP doesn't include the inventory consideration.
c) the net MRP includes consideration of the inventory on hand, whereas the gross MRP doesn't include the inventory consideration.
d) the gross MRP doesn't take taxes into account, whereas the net MRP includes the tax considerations.
e) the net MRP is only an estimate, whereas the gross MRP is used for actual production scheduling.

LO 14.3 Net requirements =
a) Gross requirements + Allocations − On-hand inventory + Scheduled receipts.
b) Gross requirements − Allocations − On-hand inventory − Scheduled receipts.
c) Gross requirements − Allocations − On-hand inventory + Scheduled receipts.
d) Gross requirements + Allocations − On-hand inventory − Scheduled receipts.

LO 14.4 A lot-sizing procedure that orders on a predetermined time interval with the order quantity equal to the total of the interval's requirement is:
a) periodic order quantity.
b) part period balancing.
c) economic order quantity.
d) all of the above.

LO 14.5 MRP II stands for:
a) material resource planning.
b) management requirements planning.
c) management resource planning.
d) material revenue planning.
e) material risk planning.

LO 14.6 A(n) _____ MRP system provides information to the capacity plan, to the master production schedule, and ultimately to the production plan.
a) dynamic
b) closed-loop
c) continuous
d) retrospective
e) introspective

LO 14.7 Which system extends MRP II to tie in customers and suppliers?
a) MRP III
b) JIT
c) IRP
d) ERP
e) Enhanced MRP II

Answers: LO 14.1. c; LO 14.2. c; LO 14.3. d; LO 14.4. a; LO 14.5. a; LO 14.6. b; LO 14.7. d.

Lean Operations

Alaska Airlines

10 OM STRATEGY DECISIONS

- Design of Goods and Services
- Managing Quality
- Process Strategy
- Location Strategies
- Layout Strategies
- Human Resources
- Supply-Chain Management

- *Inventory Management*
  - Independent Demand (Ch. 12)
  - Dependent Demand (Ch. 14)
  - *Lean Operations (Ch. 16)*
- Scheduling
- Maintenance

Achieving Competitive Advantage with Lean Operations at Toyota Motor Corporation

oyota Motor Corporation, with $250 billion in annual sales of over 9 million cars and trucks, is one of the largest vehicle manufacturers in the world. Two Lean techniques, just-in-time (JIT) and the Toyota Production System (TPS), have been instrumental in its growth. Toyota, with a wide range of vehicles, competes head-to-head with successful, long-established companies in Europe and the U.S. Taiichi Ohno, a former vice president of Toyota, created the basic framework for two of the world's most discussed systems for improving productivity, JIT and TPS. These two concepts provide much of the foundation for Lean operations:

♦ Central to JIT is a philosophy of continuous problem solving. In practice, JIT means making only what is needed, when it is needed. JIT provides an excellent vehicle for finding and eliminating problems because problems are easy to find in a system that eliminates the slack that inventory generates. When excess inventory is eliminated, shortcomings related to quality, layout, scheduling, and supplier performance become immediately evident—as does excess production.

♦ Central to TPS is employee learning and a continuing effort to create and produce products under ideal conditions. Ideal conditions exist only when management

Railway lines bring in engines from a Toyota plant in Alabama, axles from a supplier in Arkansas, and ship out finished trucks.

Tundras go from main assembly complex to test track or to staging area where they are shipped by truck or rail.

Toyota Logistics Services coordinates the shipment of finished Tundras by truck or rail.

Completed trucks exit here

Main assembly complex
Tundras are built here.

Land available for Toyota expansion

Supplier buildings surround main assembly complex.

Reception entrance

Large supplier sites for future expansion.

1 **Metalsa**
Truck frames

2 **Kautex**
Fuel tanks

3 **Tenneco Automotive**
Exhaust systems

4 **Curtis-Maruyasu America Inc.**
Tubing

5 **Millenium Steel Service Texas LLC**
Steel processing

6 **Green Metals Inc.**
Scrap steel recycling

7 **Avanzar Interior Technologies**
Seats and interior parts

8 **Toyotetsu Texas**
Stamped parts

9 **Futaba Industrial Texas Corp.**
Stamped parts

10 **Toyoda-Gosei Texas LLC**
Interior/exterior parts

11 **Reyes-Amtex**
Interior parts

12 **Vutex Inc.**
Assembly services

13 **Takumi Stamping Texas Inc.**
Stamped parts

14 **MetoKote**
E-coater

14 Suppliers outside the main plant

Outside: Toyota has a 2,000-acre site with 14 of the 21 onsite suppliers, adjacent rail lines, and nearby interstate highway. The site provides expansion space for both Toyota and for its suppliers — and provides an environment for just-in-time.

Assembly Components
Placed in cab for easy access rather than on shelves adjacent to the assembly line.

Andon
Problem display board that communicates abnormalities.

Pull System
Units produced only when more production is needed.

Kanban
Signal that indicates production of small batches of components.

Respect for People
Employees treated as knowledge workers.

Empowered Employees
Can stop production, ideas solicited, quality circles, etc.

Standard Work Practices
Rigorous, agreed upon, documented procedures for production.

JIT
Parts and supplies delivered just as needed in the quantity needed.

Minimal Machines
Proprietary machines designed for specific Toyota applications.

Level Schedules
Models mixed on production lines to meet customer orders.

Kaizen Area
An area where suggestions are tested and evaluated.

Jidoka
Monitoring performance, making judgements, and even stopping the line as necessary.

1. **AGC Automotive Americas** Glass assemblies
2. **ARK Inc.** Industrial waste management, recycling
3. **HERO Assemblers LLP** Assembly of tire onto wheel
4. **HERO Logistics LLP** Logistics
5. **PPG Industries Inc.** Glass assemblies
6. **Reyes Automotive Group** Interior/exterior parts
7. **Tokai Rika** Functional parts

Seven suppliers inside the main plant

Toyota's San Antonio plant has about 2 million interior sq. ft., providing facilities within the final assembly building for 7 of the 21 onsite suppliers, and capacity to build 200,000 pick-up trucks annually. But most importantly, Toyota practices the world-class Toyota Production System and expects its suppliers to do the same thing, wherever they are.

brings facilities, machines, and people together to add value without waste. Waste undermines productivity by diverting resources to excess inventory, unnecessary processing, and poor quality. Respect for people, extensive training, cross-training, and standard work practices of empowered employees focusing on driving out waste are fundamental to TPS.

Toyota's implementation of TPS and JIT is present at its 2,000-acre San Antonio, Texas, facility, the largest Toyota land site for an automobile assembly plant in the U.S. Interestingly, despite its large site and annual production capability of 200,000, a throughput time of 20 ½ hours, and the output of a truck every 63 seconds, the building itself is one of the smallest in the industry. Modern automobiles have 30,000 parts, but at Toyota, independent suppliers combine many of these parts into subassemblies. Twenty-one of these suppliers are on site at the San Antonio facility and transfer components to the assembly line on a JIT basis.

Operations such as these taking place in the San Antonio plant are why Toyota continues to perform near the top in quality and maintain the lowest labor-hour assembly time in the industry. Lean operations *do* work—and they provide a competitive advantage for Toyota Motor Corporation.

Lean Operations

LO 16.1 *Define* Lean operations

Lean operations
Eliminates waste through continuous improvement and focus on exactly what the customer wants.

Just-in-time (JIT)
Continuous and forced problem solving via a focus on throughput and reduced inventory.

Toyota Production System (TPS)
Focus on continuous improvement, respect for people, and standard work practices.

As shown in the *Global Company Profile*, the Toyota Production System (TPS) contributes to a world-class operation at Toyota Motor Corporation. In this chapter, we discuss Lean operations, including JIT and TPS, as approaches to continuous improvement that lead to world-class operations.

Lean operations supply the customer with exactly what the customer wants when the customer wants it, without waste, through continuous improvement. Lean operations are driven by workflow initiated by the "pull" of the customer's order. Just-in-time (JIT) is an approach of continuous and forced problem solving via a focus on throughput and reduced inventory. The Toyota Production System (TPS), with its emphasis on continuous improvement, respect for people, and standard work practices, is particularly suited for assembly lines.

In this chapter we use the term *Lean operations* to encompass all the related approaches and techniques of both JIT and TPS. When implemented as a comprehensive operations strategy, Lean sustains competitive advantage and results in increased overall returns to stakeholders.

Regardless of the approach and label, operations managers address three issues that are fundamental to operations improvement: *eliminate waste, remove variability,* and *improve throughput.* We now introduce these three issues and then discuss the major attributes of Lean operations. Finally, we look at Lean applied to services.

Eliminate Waste

Lean producers set their sights on perfection: *no* bad parts, *no* inventory, *only* value-added activities, and *no* waste. Any activity that does not add value in the eyes of the customer is a waste. The customer defines product value. If the customer does not want to pay for it, it is a waste. Taiichi Ohno, noted for his work on the Toyota Production System, identified seven categories of waste. These categories have become popular in Lean organizations and cover many of the ways organizations waste or lose money. Ohno's seven wastes are:

Seven wastes
Overproduction
Queues
Transportation
Inventory
Motion
Overprocessing
Defective product

- ◆ *Overproduction:* Producing more than the customer orders or producing early (before it is demanded) is waste.
- ◆ *Queues:* Idle time, storage, and waiting are wastes (they add no value).
- ◆ *Transportation:* Moving material between plants or between work centers and handling it more than once is waste.
- ◆ *Inventory:* Unnecessary raw material, work-in-process (WIP), finished goods, and excess operating supplies add no value and are wastes.
- ◆ *Motion:* Movement of equipment or people that adds no value is waste.

LO 16.2 *Define* the seven wastes and the 5Ss

- ◆ *Overprocessing:* Work performed on the product that adds no value is waste.
- ◆ *Defective product:* Returns, warranty claims, rework, and scrap are wastes.

A broader perspective—one that goes beyond immediate production—suggests that other resources, such as energy, water, and air, are often wasted but should not be. Efficient, sustainable production minimizes inputs and maximizes outputs, wasting nothing.

For over a century, managers have pursued "housekeeping" for a neat, orderly, and efficient workplace and as a means of reducing waste. Operations managers have embellished "housekeeping" to include a checklist—now known as the 5Ss.[1] The Japanese developed the initial 5Ss. Not only are the 5Ss a good checklist for Lean operations, but they also provide an easy vehicle with which to assist the culture change that is often necessary to bring about Lean operations. The 5Ss follow:

In keeping with 5S, airports, like many other facilities, specify with painted guidelines exactly where tools and equipment such as this fuel pump are to be positioned.

- *Sort/segregate:* Keep what is needed and remove everything else from the work area; when in doubt, throw it out. Identify nonvalue items and remove them. Getting rid of these items makes space available and usually improves workflow.

- *Simplify/straighten:* Arrange and use methods analysis tools (see Chapter 7 and Chapter 10) to improve workflow and reduce wasted motion. Consider long-run and short-run ergonomic issues. Label and display for easy use only what is needed in the immediate work area. (For examples of visual displays, see Chapter 10, Figure 10.8 and the adjacent photo of equipment located within prescribed lines on the tarmac at Seattle's airport.)

- *Shine/sweep:* Clean daily; eliminate all forms of dirt, contamination, and clutter from the work area.

- *Standardize:* Remove variations from the process by developing standard operating procedures and checklists; good standards make the abnormal obvious. Standardize equipment and tooling so that cross-training time and cost are reduced. Train and retrain the work team so that when deviations occur, they are readily apparent to all.

- *Sustain/self-discipline:* Review periodically to recognize efforts and to motivate to sustain progress. Use visuals wherever possible to communicate and sustain progress.

5Ss

A Lean production checklist:
Sort
Simplify
Shine
Standardize
Sustain

U.S. managers often add two additional Ss that contribute to establishing and maintaining a Lean workplace:

- *Safety:* Build good safety practices into the preceding five activities.
- *Support/maintenance:* Reduce variability, unplanned downtime, and costs. Integrate daily *shine* tasks with preventive maintenance.

The Ss support continuous improvement and provide a vehicle with which employees can identify. Operations managers need think only of the examples set by a well-run hospital emergency room or the spit-and-polish of a fire department for a benchmark. Offices and retail stores, as well as manufacturers, have successfully used the 5Ss in their respective efforts to eliminate waste and move to Lean operations. A place for everything and everything in its place does make a difference in a well-run office. And retail stores successfully use the Ss to reduce misplaced merchandise and improve customer service. An orderly workplace reduces waste, releasing assets for other, more productive, purposes.

Remove Variability

Managers seek to remove variability caused by both internal and external factors. Variability is any deviation from the optimum process that delivers a perfect product on time, every time. Variability is a polite word for problems. The less variability in a system, the less waste in the system. Most variability is caused by tolerating waste or by poor management. Among the many sources of variability are:

Variability

Any deviation from the optimum process that delivers a perfect product on time, every time.

- Poor processes that allow employees and suppliers to produce improper quantities or nonconforming units
- Inadequate maintenance of facilities and processes
- Unknown and changing customer demands
- Incomplete or inaccurate drawings, specifications, and bills of material

Inventory reduction via JIT is an effective tool for identifying causes of variability. The precise timing of JIT makes variability evident, just as reducing inventory exposes variability. Defeating variability allows managers to move good materials on schedule, add value at each step of the process, drive down costs, and ultimately win orders.

Improve Throughput

Throughput
The rate at which units move through a process.

Manufacturing cycle time
The time between the arrival of raw materials and the shipping of finished products.

Pull system
A concept that results in material being produced only when requested and moved to where it is needed just as it is needed.

Throughput is the rate at which units move through a process. Each minute that products remain on the books, costs accumulate, and competitive advantage is lost. Time is money. The time that an order is in the shop is called manufacturing cycle time. This is the time between the arrival of raw materials and the shipping of finished product. For example, phone-system manufacturer Nortel had materials pulled directly from qualified suppliers to the assembly line. This effort reduced a segment of the manufacturing cycle time from 3 weeks to just 4 hours, the incoming inspection staff from 47 to 24, and problems on the shop floor caused by defective materials by 97%. Driving down manufacturing cycle time can make a major improvement in throughput.

A technique for increasing throughput is a pull system. A pull system *pulls* a unit to where it is needed just as it is needed. Pull systems are a standard tool of Lean. Pull systems use signals to request production and delivery from supplying stations to stations that have production capacity available. The pull concept is used both within the immediate production process and with suppliers. By *pulling* material through the system in very small lots—just as it is needed—waste and inventory are removed. As inventory is removed, clutter is reduced, problems become evident, and continuous improvement is emphasized. Removing the cushion of inventory also reduces both investment in inventory and manufacturing cycle time. A *push* system dumps orders on the next downstream workstation, regardless of timeliness and resource availability. Push systems are the antithesis of Lean. Pulling material through a production process as it is needed rather than in a "push" mode typically lowers cost and improves schedule performance, enhancing customer satisfaction.

Lean and Just-in-Time

STUDENT TIP ❶
JIT places added demands on performance, but that is why it pays off.

Just-in-time (JIT), with its focus on rapid throughput and reduced inventory, is a powerful component of Lean. With the inclusion of JIT in Lean, materials arrive *where* they are needed only *when* they are needed. When good units do not arrive just as needed, a "problem" has been identified. This is the reason this aspect of Lean is so powerful—it focuses attention on *problems*. By driving out waste and delay, JIT reduces inventory, cuts variability and waste, and improves throughput. Every moment material is held, an activity that adds value should be occurring. Consequently, as Figure 16.1 suggests, JIT often yields a competitive advantage.

A well-executed Lean program requires a meaningful buyer–supplier partnership.

Supplier Partnerships

Supplier partnerships
Partnerships of suppliers and purchasers that remove waste and drive down costs for mutual benefits.

Supplier partnerships exist when a supplier and a purchaser work together with open communication and a goal of removing waste and driving down costs. Trust and close collaboration are critical to

Many services have adopted Lean techniques as a normal part of their business. Restaurants like Olive Garden expect and receive JIT deliveries. Both buyer and supplier expect fresh, high-quality produce delivered without fail just when it is needed. The system doesn't work any other way.

Culinary Institute of America

JIT TECHNIQUES:

Figure 16.1

Lean Contributes to Competitive Advantage

Suppliers:	Few vendors; supportive supplier relationships; quality deliveries on time, directly to work areas
Layout:	Work cells; group technology; flexible machinery; organized workplace; reduced space for inventory
Inventory:	Small lot sizes; low setup time; specialized parts bins
Scheduling:	Zero deviation from schedules; level schedules; suppliers informed of schedules; kanban techniques
Preventive maintenance:	Scheduled; daily routine; operator involvement
Quality production:	Statistical process control; quality suppliers; quality within the firm
Employee empowerment:	Empowered and cross-trained employees; training support; few job classifications to ensure flexibility of employees
Commitment:	Support of management, employees, and suppliers

WHICH RESULTS IN:

Rapid throughput frees assets

Quality improvement reduces waste

Cost reduction adds pricing flexibility

Variability reduction

Rework reduction

WHICH WINS ORDERS BY:

Faster response to the customer at lower cost and higher quality—

A Competitive Advantage

the success of Lean. Figure 16.2 shows the characteristics of supplier partnerships. Some specific goals are:

- *Removal of unnecessary activities*, such as receiving, incoming inspection, and paperwork related to bidding, invoicing, and payment.
- *Removal of in-plant inventory* by delivery in small lots directly to the using department as needed.

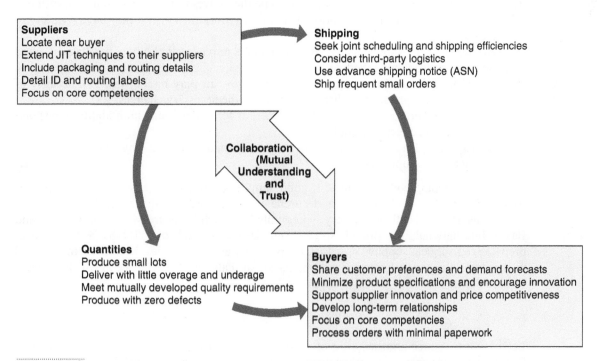

Suppliers
Locate near buyer
Extend JIT techniques to their suppliers
Include packaging and routing details
Detail ID and routing labels
Focus on core competencies

Shipping
Seek joint scheduling and shipping efficiencies
Consider third-party logistics
Use advance shipping notice (ASN)
Ship frequent small orders

**Collaboration
(Mutual
Understanding
and
Trust)**

Quantities
Produce small lots
Deliver with little overage and underage
Meet mutually developed quality requirements
Produce with zero defects

Buyers
Share customer preferences and demand forecasts
Minimize product specifications and encourage innovation
Support supplier innovation and price competitiveness
Develop long-term relationships
Focus on core competencies
Process orders with minimal paperwork

Figure 16.2

Characteristics of Supplier Partnerships

OM in Action — Lean Production at Cessna Aircraft Company

When Cessna Aircraft opened its new plant in Independence, Kansas, it saw the opportunity to switch from craftwork to a Lean manufacturing system. The initial idea was to focus on three Lean concepts: (1) vendor-managed inventory, (2) cross-training of employees, and (3) using technology and manufacturing cells to move away from batch processing.

After several years, with these goals accomplished, Cessna began working on the next phase of Lean. This phase focuses on *Team Build* and *Area Team Development*.

Team Build at Cessna empowers employees to expand their skills, sequence their own work, and then sign off on it. This reduces wait time, inventory, part shortages, rework, and scrap, all contributing to improved productivity.

Area Team Development (ATD) provides experts when a factory employee cannot complete his or her standard work in the time planned. Team members trained in the ATD process are called Skill Coaches. Skill Coaches provide support throughout each area to improve response time to problems. Andon boards and performance metrics are used for evaluating daily performance.

These commitments to Lean manufacturing are a major contributor to Cessna being the world's largest manufacturer of single-engine aircraft.

Sources: Interviews with Cessna executives, 2013.

Cessna Aircraft Company

Consignment inventory
An arrangement in which the supplier maintains title to the inventory until it is used.

♦ *Removal of in-transit inventory* by encouraging suppliers to locate nearby and provide frequent small shipments. The shorter the flow of material in the resource pipeline, the less inventory. Inventory can also be reduced through a technique known as *consignment*. Consignment inventory (see the *OM in Action* box, "Lean Production at Cessna Aircraft Company"), a variation of vendor-managed inventory (Chapter 11), means the supplier maintains the title to the inventory until it is used.

♦ *Obtain improved quality and reliability* through long-term commitments, communication, and cooperation.

Leading organizations view suppliers as extensions of their own organizations and expect suppliers to be fully committed to constant improvement. However, supplier concerns can be significant and must be addressed. These concerns include:

LO 16.3 *Identify* the concerns of suppliers when moving to supplier partnerships

1. *Diversification:* Suppliers may not want to tie themselves to long-term contracts with one customer. The suppliers' perception is that they reduce their risk if they have a variety of customers.
2. *Scheduling:* Many suppliers have little faith in the purchaser's ability to produce orders to a smooth, coordinated schedule.
3. *Lead time:* Engineering or specification changes can play havoc with JIT because of inadequate lead time for suppliers to implement the necessary changes.
4. *Quality:* Suppliers' capital budgets, processes, or technology may limit ability to respond to changes in product and quality.
5. *Lot sizes:* Suppliers may see frequent delivery in small lots as a way to transfer buyers' holding costs to suppliers.

As the foregoing concerns suggest, good supplier partnerships require a high degree of trust and respect by both supplier and purchaser—in a word, collaboration. Many firms establish this trust and collaborate very successfully. Two such firms are McKesson-General and Baxter International, who provide surgical supplies for hospitals on a JIT basis. They deliver prepackaged surgical supplies based on hospital operating schedules. Moreover, the surgical packages themselves are prepared so supplies are available in the sequence in which they will be used during surgery.

Lean Layout

Lean layouts reduce another kind of waste—movement. The movement of material on a factory floor (or paper in an office) does not add value. Consequently, managers want flexible layouts that reduce the movement of both people and material. Lean layouts place material directly in the location where needed. For instance, an assembly line should be designed with delivery points next to the line so material need not be delivered first to a receiving department and then moved again. Toyota has gone one step further and places components in the chassis of each vehicle moving down the assembly line. This is not only convenient, but it also allows Toyota to save space and opens areas adjacent to the assembly line previously occupied by shelves. When a layout reduces distance, firms often save labor and space and may have the added bonus of eliminating potential areas for accumulation of unwanted inventory. Table 16.1 provides a list of Lean layout tactics.

Distance Reduction Reducing distance is a major contribution of work cells, work centers, and focused factories (see Chapter 9). The days of long production lines and huge economic lots, with goods passing through monumental, single-operation machines, are gone. Now firms use work cells, often arranged in a U shape, containing several machines performing different operations. These work cells are often based on group technology codes (as discussed in Chapter 5). Group technology codes help identify components with similar characteristics so they can be grouped into families. Once families are identified, work cells are built for them. The result can be thought of as a small product-oriented facility where the "product" is actually a group of similar products—a family of products. The cells produce one good unit at a time, and ideally, they produce the units *only* after a customer orders them.

Increased Flexibility Modern work areas are designed so they can be easily rearranged to adapt to changes in volume and product changes. Almost nothing is bolted down. This concept of layout flexibility applies to both factory and office environments. Not only is furniture and equipment movable, but so are walls, computer connections, and telecommunications. Equipment is modular. Layout flexibility aids the changes that result from product *and* process improvements that are inevitable at a firm with a philosophy of continuous improvement.

Impact on Employees When layouts provide for sequential operations, feedback, including quality issues, can be immediate, allowing employees working together to tell each other about problems and opportunities for improvement. When workers produce units one at a time, they test each product or component at each subsequent production stage. Work processes with self-testing *poka-yoke* functions detect defects automatically. Before Lean, defective products were replaced from inventory. Because surplus inventory is not kept in Lean facilities, there are no such buffers. Employees learn that getting it right the first time is critical. Indeed, Lean layouts allow cross-trained employees to bring flexibility and efficiency to the work area, reducing defects. Defects are waste.

Reduced Space and Inventory Because Lean layouts reduce travel distance, they also reduce inventory. When there is little space, inventory travels less and must be moved in very small lots or even single units. Units are always moving because there is no storage. For instance, each month a Bank of America focused facility sorts 7 million checks, processes 5 million statements, and mails 190,000 customer statements. With a Lean layout, mail-processing time has been reduced by 33%, annual salary costs by tens of thousands of dollars, floor space by 50%, and in-process waiting lines by 75% to 90%. Storage, including shelves and drawers, has been removed.

Lean Inventory

Inventories in production and distribution systems often exist "just in case" something goes wrong. That is, they are used just in case some variation from the production plan occurs. The "extra" inventory is then used to cover variations or problems. Lean inventory tactics require "just in time," not "just in case." Lean inventory is the minimum inventory necessary to keep a perfect system running. With Lean inventory, the exact amount of goods arrives at the moment it is needed, not a minute before or a minute after. Some useful Lean inventory tactics are shown in Table 16.2 and discussed in more detail in the following sections.

Reduce Inventory and Variability Operations managers move toward Lean by first reducing inventory. The idea is to eliminate variability in the production system hidden by inventory. Reducing inventory uncovers the "rocks" in Figure 16.3(a) that represent the variability and problems currently being tolerated. With reduced inventory, management chips away at the exposed problems. After the lake is lowered, managers make additional cuts

TABLE 16.1
LEAN LAYOUT TACTICS
Build work cells for families of products
Include a large number of operations in a small area
Minimize distance
Design little space for inventory
Improve employee communication
Use *poka-yoke* devices
Build flexible or movable equipment
Cross-train workers to add flexibility

TABLE 16.2
LEAN INVENTORY TACTICS
Use a pull system to move inventory
Reduce lot size
Develop just-in-time delivery systems with suppliers
Deliver directly to the point of use
Perform to schedule
Reduce setup time
Use group technology

Lean inventory
The minimum inventory necessary to keep a perfect system running.

◆ STUDENT TIP

Accountants book inventory as an asset, but operations managers know it is a cost.

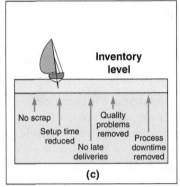

(a)   **(b)**   **(c)**

Figure **16.3**

High levels of inventory hide problems (a), but as we reduce inventory, problems are exposed (b), and finally after reducing inventory and removing problems, we have lower inventory, lower costs, and smooth sailing (c).

"Inventory is evil."
S. Shingo

in inventory and continue to chip away at the next level of exposed problems [see Figure 16.3(b, c)]. Ultimately, there will be little inventory and few problems (variability).

Firms with technology-sensitive products estimate that the rapid product innovations can cost as much as $\frac{1}{2}$% to 2% of the values of inventory *each week*. Shigeo Shingo, codeveloper of the Toyota JIT system, says, "Inventory is evil." He is not far from the truth. If inventory itself is not evil, it hides evil at great cost.

Reduce Lot Sizes   Lean also reduces waste by cutting the investment in inventory. A key to slashing inventory is to produce good product in small lot sizes. Reducing the size of batches can be a major help in reducing inventory and inventory costs. As we saw in Chapter 12, when inventory usage is constant, the average inventory level is the sum of the maximum inventory plus the minimum inventory divided by 2. Figure 16.4 shows that lowering the order size increases the number of orders, but drops inventory levels.

Ideally, in a Lean environment, order size is one and single units are being pulled from one adjacent process to another. More realistically, analysis of the process, transportation time, and physical attributes such as size of containers used for transport are considered when determining lot size. Such analysis typically results in a small lot size, but a lot size larger than one. Once a lot size has been determined, the EOQ production order quantity model can be modified to determine the desired setup time. We saw in Chapter 12 that the production order quantity model takes the form:

$$Q_p^* = \sqrt{\frac{2DS}{H[1 - (d/p)]}} \qquad (16\text{-}1)$$

where D = Annual demand d = Daily demand
            S = Setup cost p = Daily production
            H = Holding cost

Figure **16.4**

Frequent Orders Reduce Average Inventory

A lower order size increases the number of orders and total ordering cost but reduces average inventory and total holding cost.

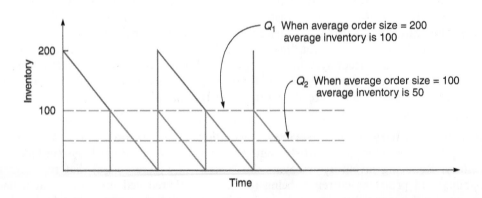

Q_1 When average order size = 200 average inventory is 100

Q_2 When average order size = 100 average inventory is 50

Example 1 shows how to determine the desired setup time.

<h1>Example 1</h1>

DETERMINING OPTIMAL SETUP TIME

Crate Furniture, Inc., a firm that produces rustic furniture, desires to move toward a reduced lot size. Crate Furniture's production analyst, Aleda Roth, determined that a 2-hour production cycle would be acceptable between two departments. Further, she concluded that a setup time that would accommodate the 2-hour cycle time should be achieved.

APPROACH ▶ Roth developed the following data and procedure to determine optimum setup time analytically:

D = Annual demand = 400,000 units
d = Daily demand = 400,000 per 250 days = 1,600 units per day
p = Daily production rate = 4,000 units per day
Q_p = EOQ desired = 400 (which is the 2-hour demand; that is, 1,600 per day per four 2-hour periods)
H = Holding cost = \$20 per unit per year
S = Setup cost (to be determined)

Hourly labor rate = \$30.00

LO 16.4 *Determine optimal setup time*

SOLUTION ▶ Roth determines that the cost and related time per setup should be:

$$Q_p = \sqrt{\frac{2DS}{H(1 - d/p)}}$$

$$Q_p^2 = \frac{2DS}{H(1 - d/p)}$$

$$S = \frac{(Q_p^2)(H)(1 - d/p)}{2D} \qquad (16\text{-}2)$$

$$= \frac{(400)^2(20)(1 - 1,600/4,000)}{2(400,000)} = \frac{(3,200,000)(0.6)}{800,000} = \$2.40$$

Setup time = \$2.40/(hourly labor rate)
= \$2.40/(\$30 per hour)
= 0.08 hour, or 4.8 minutes

INSIGHT ▶ Now, rather than produce components in large lots, Crate Furniture can produce in a 2-hour cycle with the advantage of an inventory turnover of four *per day*.

LEARNING EXERCISE ▶ If labor cost goes to \$40 per hour, what should be the setup time? [Answer: 0.06 hours, or 3.6 minutes.]

RELATED PROBLEMS ▶ 16.1, 16.2, 16.3

Only two changes need to be made for small-lot material flow to work. First, material handling and work flow need to be improved. With short production cycles, there can be very little wait time. Improving material handling is usually easy and straightforward. The second change is more challenging, and that is a radical reduction in setup times. We discuss setup reduction next.

Reduce Setup Costs Both the quantity of inventory and the cost of holding it go down as the inventory-reorder quantity and the maximum inventory level drop. However, because inventory requires incurring an ordering or setup cost that is applied to the units produced, managers tend to purchase (or produce) large orders; the larger the order the less the cost to be absorbed by each unit. Consequently, the way to drive down lot sizes *and* reduce inventory cost is to reduce setup cost, which in turn lowers the optimum order size.

The effect of reduced setup costs on total cost and lot size is shown in Figure 16.5. Moreover, smaller lot sizes hide fewer problems. In many environments, setup cost is highly correlated with setup time. In a manufacturing facility, setups usually require a substantial amount of preparation. Much of the preparation required by a setup can be done prior to shutting down

▶ STUDENT TIP
Reduced lot sizes must be accompanied by reduced setup times.

Figure **16.5**

Lower Setup Costs Will Lower Total Cost

More frequent orders require reducing setup costs; otherwise, inventory costs will rise. As the setup costs are lowered (from S_1 to S_2), total inventory costs also fall (from T_1 to T_2).

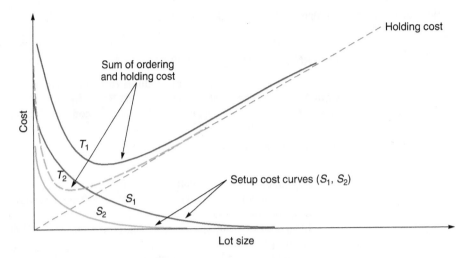

the machine or process. Setup times can be reduced substantially, as shown in Figure 16.6. For example in one Kodak plant in Mexico, the setup time to change a bearing was reduced from 12 hours to 6 minutes! This is the kind of progress that is typical of world-class manufacturers.

Just as setup costs can be reduced at a machine in a factory, setup time can also be reduced during the process of getting the order ready in the office. Driving down factory setup time from hours to minutes does little good if orders are going to take weeks to process or "set up" in the office. This is exactly what happens in organizations that forget that Lean concepts have applications in offices as well as in the factory. Reducing setup time (and cost) is an excellent way to reduce inventory investment, improve productivity, and speed throughput.

STUDENT TIP ◆

Effective scheduling is required for effective use of capital and personnel.

Lean Scheduling

Effective schedules, communicated to those within the organization as well as to outside suppliers, support Lean. Better scheduling also improves the ability to meet customer orders, drives down inventory by allowing smaller lot sizes, and reduces work-in-process. For instance, many companies, such as Ford, now tie suppliers to their final assembly schedule. Ford communicates its schedules to bumper manufacturer Polycon Industries from the Ford production control system. The scheduling system describes the style and color of the bumper needed for each vehicle moving down the final assembly line. The scheduling system transmits the information to portable terminals carried by Polycon warehouse personnel, who load the bumpers onto conveyors leading to the loading dock. The bumpers are then trucked 50 miles to the Ford plant. Total time is 4 hours. However, as we saw in our opening *Global Company Profile*, Toyota has moved its bumper supplier *inside* the new Tundra plant; techniques such as this drive down delivery time even further.

Table 16.3 suggests several items that can contribute to achieving these goals, but two techniques (in addition to communicating schedules) are paramount. They are *level schedules* and *kanban*.

Initial Setup Time

Step 1 — Separate setup into preparation and actual setup, doing as much as possible while the machine/process is operating (save 30 minutes) — 90 min

Step 2 — Move material closer and improve material handling (save 20 minutes) — 60 min

Step 3 — Standardize and improve tooling (save 15 minutes) — 40 min

Step 4 — Use one-touch system to eliminate adjustments (save 10 minutes) — 25 min

Step 5 — Train operators and standardize work procedures (save 2 minutes) — 15 min

Step 6 — Repeat cycle until subminute setup is achieved — 13 min

Figure **16.6**

Steps for Reducing Setup Times

Reduced setup times are a major component of Lean.

JIT Level Material-Use Approach

AA BBB C AA BBB C AA BBB C AA BBB C AA BBB C AA BBB C AA BBB C AA BBB C

Large-Lot Approach

AAAAAA BBBBBBBBB CCC AAAAAA BBBBBBBBB CCC AAAAAA BBBBBBBBB CCC

Time

Figure **16.7**

Scheduling Small Lots of Parts A, B, and C Increases Flexibility to Meet Customer Demand and Reduces Inventory

The Lean approach to scheduling, described as heijunka by the Japanese, produces just as many of each model per time period as the large-lot approach, provided setup times are lowered.

Level Schedules Level schedules process frequent small batches rather than a few large batches. Figure 16.7 contrasts a traditional large-lot approach using large batches with a level schedule using many small batches. The operations manager's task is to make and move small lots so the level schedule is economical. This requires success with the issues discussed in this chapter that allow small lots. As lots get smaller, the constraints may change and become increasingly challenging. At some point, processing a unit or two may not be feasible. The constraint may be the way units are sold and shipped (four to a carton), or an expensive paint changeover (on an automobile assembly line), or the proper number of units in a sterilizer (for a food-canning line).

The scheduler may find that *freezing*, that is holding a portion of the schedule near due dates constant, allows the production system to function and the schedule to be met. Operations managers expect the schedule to be achieved with no deviations.

Kanban One way to achieve small lot sizes is to move inventory through the shop only as needed rather than *pushing* it on to the next workstation whether or not the personnel there are ready for it. As noted earlier, when inventory is moved only as needed, it is referred to as a *pull* system, and the ideal lot size is one. The Japanese call this system *kanban*. Kanbans allow arrivals at a work center to match (or nearly match) the processing time.

Kanban is a Japanese word for *card*. In their effort to reduce inventory, the Japanese use systems that "pull" inventory through work centers. They often use a "card" to signal the need for another container of material—hence the name *kanban*. The card is the authorization for the next container of material to be produced. Typically, a kanban signal exists for each container of items to be obtained. An order for the container is then initiated by each kanban and "pulled" from the producing department or supplier. A sequence of kanbans "pulls" the material through the plant.

The system has been modified in many facilities so that even though it is called a *kanban*, the card itself does not exist. In some cases, an empty position on the floor is sufficient indication that the next container is needed. In other cases, some sort of signal, such as a flag or rag (Figure 16.8), alerts that it is time for the next container.

When there is visual contact between producer and user, the process works like this:

1. The user removes a standard-size container of parts from a small storage area, as shown in Figure 16.8.
2. The signal at the storage area is seen by the producing department as authorization to replenish the using department or storage area. Because there is an optimum lot size, the producing department may make several containers at a time.

A kanban system is similar to the resupply that occurs in your neighborhood supermarket: the customer buys; the stock clerk observes the shelf or receives notice from the end-of-day sales list and restocks. When the store's limited supply is depleted, a "pull" signal is sent to the warehouse, distributor, or manufacturer for resupply, usually that night. The complicating factor in a manufacturing firm is the time needed for actual manufacturing (production) to take place.

Level schedules

Scheduling products so that each day's production meets the demand for that day.

TABLE 16.3
LEAN SCHEDULING TACTICS
Make level schedules
Use kanbans
Communicate schedules to suppliers
Freeze part of the schedule
Perform to schedule
Seek one-piece-make and one-piece-move
Eliminate waste
Produce in small lots
Each operation produces a perfect part

Kanban

The Japanese word for *card*, which has come to mean "signal"; a kanban system moves parts through production via a "pull" from a signal.

LO 16.5 *Define* kanban

Signal marker hanging on post for part Z405 shows that production should start for that part. The post is located so that workers in normal locations can easily see it.

Signal marker on stack of boxes.

Part numbers mark location of specific part.

Figure **16.8**

Diagram of Storage Area with Warning-Signal Marker

A kanban need not be as formal as signal lights or empty carts. The cook in a fast-food restaurant knows that when six cars are in line, eight meat patties and six orders of french fries should be cooking.

Several additional points regarding kanbans may be helpful:

♦ When the producer and user are not in visual contact, a card can be used; otherwise, a light, flag, or empty spot on the floor may be adequate.

♦ Usually each card controls a specific quantity of parts, although multiple card systems are used if the work cell produces several components or if the lot size is different from the move size.

♦ The kanban cards provide a direct control (limit) on the amount of work-in-process between cells.

Determining the Number of Kanban Cards or Containers The number of kanban cards, or containers, sets the amount of authorized inventory. To determine the number of containers moving back and forth between the using area and the producing areas, management first sets the size of each container. This is done by computing the lot size, using a model such as the production order quantity model [discussed in Chapter 12 and shown again on page 644 in Equation (16-1)]. Setting the number of containers involves knowing: (1) lead time needed to produce a container of parts and (2) the amount of safety stock needed to account for variability or uncertainty in the system. The number of kanban cards is computed as follows:

LO 16.6 *Compute* the required number of kanbans

$$\text{Number of kanbans (containers)} = \frac{\text{Demand during lead time} + \text{Safety stock}}{\text{Size of container}} \qquad (16\text{-}3)$$

Example 2 illustrates how to calculate the number of kanbans needed.

Example 2 | **DETERMINING THE NUMBER OF KANBAN CONTAINERS**

Hobbs Bakery produces short runs of cakes that are shipped to grocery stores. The owner, Ken Hobbs, wants to try to reduce inventory by changing to a kanban system. He has developed the following data and asked you to finish the project.

$$\text{Production lead time} = \text{Wait time} + \text{Material handling time} + \text{Processing time} = 2 \text{ days}$$

$$\text{Daily demand} = 500 \text{ cakes}$$

$$\text{Safety stock} = \tfrac{1}{2} \text{ day}$$

$$\text{Container size (determined on a production order size EOQ basis)} = 250 \text{ cakes}$$

APPROACH ▶ Having determined that the EOQ size is 250, we then determine the number of kanbans (containers) needed.

SOLUTION ▶ Demand during lead time =

$$\text{Lead time} \times \text{Daily demand} = 2 \text{ days} \times 500 \text{ cakes} = 1,000$$

$$\text{Safety stock} = \tfrac{1}{2} \times \text{Daily demand} = 250$$

Number of kanbans (containers) needed =

$$\frac{\text{Demand during lead time} + \text{Safety stock}}{\text{Container size}} = \frac{1,000 + 250}{250} = 5$$

INSIGHT ▶ Once the reorder point is hit, five containers should be released.

LEARNING EXERCISE ▶ If lead time drops to 1 day, how many containers are needed? [Answer: 3.]

RELATED PROBLEMS ▶ 16.4, 16.5, 16.6, 16.7, 16.8, 16.9, 16.10 (16.11, 16.12 are available in MyOMLab)

Advantages of Kanban Containers are typically very small, usually a matter of a few hours' worth of production. Such a system requires tight schedules, with small quantities being produced several times a day. The process must run smoothly with little variability in quality or lead time because any shortage has an almost immediate impact on the entire system. Kanban places added emphasis on meeting schedules, reducing the time and cost required by setups, and economical material handling.

In-plant kanban systems often use standardized, reusable containers that protect the specific quantities to be moved. Such containers are also desirable in the supply chain. Standardized containers reduce weight and disposal costs, generate less wasted space, and require less labor to pack, unpack, and prepare items.

Lean Quality

STUDENT TIP
Good quality costs less.

There is no Lean without quality. And Lean's "pull" production, smaller batch sizes, and low inventory all enhance quality by exposing bad quality. Savings occur because scrap, rework, inventory investment, and poor product are no longer buried in inventory. This means fewer bad units are produced. In short, whereas inventory *hides* bad quality, Lean *exposes* it.

As Lean shrinks queues and lead time, it keeps evidence of errors fresh and limits the number of potential sources of error. In effect, Lean creates an early warning system for quality problems so that fewer bad units are produced and feedback is immediate. This advantage accrues both within the firm and with goods received from outside vendors.

In addition, better quality means fewer buffers are needed, and therefore, a better, easier-to-maintain inventory system can exist. Often the purpose of keeping inventory is to protect against unreliable quality. But, when consistent quality exists, Lean firms can reduce all costs associated with inventory. Table 16.4 suggests some tactics for quality in a Lean environment.

TABLE 16.4

LEAN QUALITY TACTICS
Use statistical process control
Empower employees
Build fail-safe methods (poka-yoke, checklists, etc.)
Expose poor quality with small lots
Provide immediate feedback

Lean and the Toyota Production System

Toyota Motor's Eiji Toyoda and Taiichi Ohno are given credit for the Toyota Production System (TPS; see the *Global Company Profile* that opens this chapter). Three components of TPS are *continuous improvement*, *respect for people*, and *standard work practice*, which are now considered an integral part of Lean.

Continuous Improvement

Continuous improvement under TPS means building an organizational culture and instilling in its people a value system stressing that processes can be improved—indeed, that improvement is an integral part of every employee's job. This process is formalized in TPS by kaizen, the Japanese word for change for the good, or what is more generally known as *continuous improvement*. Kaizen is often implemented by a kaizen event. A kaizen event occurs when members of a work cell group or team meet to develop innovative ways to immediately implement improvements in the work area or process. In application, kaizen means making a multitude of small or incremental changes as one seeks elusive perfection. (See the *OM in Action* box, "Toyota's New Challenge.") Instilling the mantra of continuous improvement begins at personnel recruiting and continues through extensive and continuing training. One of the reasons continuous improvement works at Toyota, we should note, is because of another core value at Toyota, Toyota's respect for people.

Kaizen
A focus on continuous improvement.

Kaizen event
Members of a work cell or team meet to develop improvements in the process.

Respect for People

Toyota, like other Lean organizations, recruits, trains, and treats people as knowledge workers. Aided by aggressive cross-training and few job classifications, Lean firms engage the mental as well as physical capacities of employees in the challenging task of improving operations. Employees are empowered. They are empowered not only to make improvements, but also to stop machines and processes when quality problems exist. Indeed, empowered employees are an integral part of Lean. This means that those tasks that have traditionally been assigned to staff are moved to employees. Toyota recognizes that employees know more about their jobs than anyone else. Lean firms respect employees by giving them the opportunity to enrich both their jobs and their lives.

STUDENT TIP
Respect for people brings the entire person to work.

OM in Action   Toyota's New Challenge

With the generally high value of the yen, making a profit on cars built in Japan but sold in foreign markets is a challenge. As a result, Honda and Nissan are moving plants overseas, closer to customers. But Toyota, despite marginal profit on cars produced for export, is maintaining its current Japanese capacity. Toyota, which led the way with JIT and the TPS, is doubling down on its manufacturing prowess and continuous improvement. For an organization that traditionally does things slowly and step-by-step, the changes are radical. With its first new plant in Japan in 18 years, Toyota believes it can once again set new production benchmarks. It is drastically reforming its production processes in a number of ways:

- The assembly line has cars sitting side-by-side, rather than bumper-to-bumper, shrinking the length of the line by 35% and requiring fewer steps by workers.
- Instead of having car chassis dangling from overhead conveyors, they are perched on raised platforms, reducing heating and cooling costs by 40%.

- Retooling permits faster changeovers, allowing for shorter product runs of components, supporting level scheduling.
- The assembly line uses quiet friction rollers with fewer moving parts, requiring less maintenance than conventional lines and reducing worker fatigue.

These TPS innovations, efficient production with small lot sizes, rapid change-over, level scheduling, half the workers, and half the square footage, are being duplicated in Toyota's new plant in Blue Springs, Mississippi.

Sources: Forbes (July 29, 2012); *Automotive News* (February, 2011); and *The Wall Street Journal* (November 29, 2011).

This Porsche assembly line, like most other Lean facilities, empowers employees so they can stop the entire production line, what the Japanese call *jidoka*, if any quality problems are spotted.

Bernd Weissbrod/dpa/picture-alliance/Newscom

Processes and Standard Work Practice

Building effective and efficient processes requires establishing what Toyota calls standard work practices. The underlying principles are:

- Work is completely specified as to content, sequence, timing, and outcome; this is fundamental to a good process.
- Supplier connections for both internal and external customers are direct, specifying personnel, methods, timing, and quantity.
- Material and service flows are simple and directed to a specific person or machine.
- Process improvements are made only after rigorous analysis at the lowest possible level in the organization.

Lean requires that activities, connections, and flows include built-in tests (or poka-yokes) to signal problems. When a problem or defect occurs, production is stopped. Japanese call the practice of stopping production because of a defect, *jidoka*. The dual focus on (1) education and training of employees and (2) the responsiveness of the system to problems make the seemingly rigid system flexible and adaptable. The result is continuous improvement.

Lean Organizations

Lean organizations understand the customer and the customer's expectations. Moreover, Lean organizations have functional areas that communicate and collaborate to verify that customer expectations are not only understood, but also met efficiently. This means identifying and delivering the customer's value expectation by implementing the tools of Lean throughout the organization.

STUDENT TIP ◆
Lean drives out non-value-added activities.

Building a Lean Organization

Building Lean organizations is difficult, requiring exceptional leadership. Such leaders imbue the organization not just with the tools of Lean, but with a *culture* of continuous improvement. Building such a culture requires open communication and destroying isolated functional disciplines that act as independent "silos." There is no substitute for open two-way communication that fosters effective and efficient processes. Such an organizational culture will have a demonstrated respect for people and a management willing to fully understand how and where the work is performed. Lean firms sometimes use the Japanese term Gemba or Gemba walk to refer to going to where the work is actually performed.

Gemba or Gemba walk
Going to where the work is actually performed.

Building organizational cultures that foster ongoing improvement and that accept the constant change and improvement that makes improvement habitual is a challenge. However, such organizations exist. They understand the customer and drive out activities that do not add value in the eyes of the customer. They include industry leaders such as United Parcel Service, Alaska Airlines, and, of course, Toyota. Even traditionally idiosyncratic organizations such as hospitals (see the *OM in Action* box, "Lean Delivers the Medicine") find improved productivity with Lean operations. Lean operations adopt a philosophy of minimizing waste by striving for perfection through continuous learning, creativity, and teamwork. They tend to share the following attributes:

VIDEO 16.1
Lean Operations at Alaska Airlines

- *Respect and develop employees* by improving job design, providing constant training, instilling commitment, and building teamwork.
- *Empower employees* with jobs that are made challenging by pushing responsibility to the lowest level possible.
- *Develop worker flexibility* through cross-training and reducing job classifications.
- *Build processes* that destroy variability by helping employees produce a perfect product every time.
- *Develop collaborative partnerships with suppliers*, helping them not only to understand the needs of the ultimate customer, but also to accept responsibility for satisfying those needs.
- *Eliminate waste by performing only value-added activities.* Material handling, inspection, inventory, travel time, wasted space, and rework are targets, as they do not add value.

LO 16.7 *Identify* six attributes of Lean organizations

Success requires leadership as well as the full commitment and involvement of managers, employees, and suppliers. The rewards that Lean producers reap are spectacular. Lean producers often become benchmark performers.

OM in Action   Lean Delivers the Medicine

Using kaizen techniques straight out of Lean, a team of employees at San Francisco General Hospital target and then analyze a particular area within the hospital for improvement. Hospitals today are focusing on throughput and quality in the belief that excelling on these measures will drive down costs and push up patient satisfaction. Doctors and nurses now work together in teams that immerse themselves in a weeklong kaizen event. These events generate plans that make specific improvements in flow, quality, costs, or the patients' experience.

One recent kaizen event focused on the number of minutes it takes from the moment a patient is wheeled into the operating room to when the first incision is made. A team spent a week coming up with ways to whittle 10 minutes off this "prep" time. Every minute saved reduces labor cost and opens up critical facilities. Another kaizen event targeted the Urgent Care Center, dropping the average wait from 5 hours down to 2.5, primarily by adding an on-site X-ray machine instead of requiring patients to walk 15 minutes to the main radiology department. Similarly, wait times in the Surgical Clinic dropped from 2.5 hours to 70 minutes. The operating room now uses a *5S* protocol and has implemented *Standard Work* for the preoperation process.

As hospitals focus on improving medical quality and patient satisfaction, they are exposed to some Japanese terms associated with Lean, many of which do not have a direct English translation: **Gemba,** the place where work is actually performed; **Hansei,** a period of critical self-reflection; **Heijunka,** a level production schedule that provides balance and smooths day-to-day

Franck Boston/Fotolia

variation; **Jidoka,** using both human intelligence and technology to stop a process at the first sign of a potential problem; **Kaizen,** continuous improvement; and **Muda,** anything that consumes resources, but provides no value.

Lean systems are increasingly being adopted by hospitals as they try to reduce costs while improving quality and increasing patient satisfaction—and as San Francisco General has demonstrated, Lean techniques are working.

Sources: San Francisco Chronicle (Oct. 14, 2013) and San Francisco General Hospital & Trauma Center Annual Report, 2012–2013.

Lean Sustainability

Lean and sustainability are two sides of the same coin. Both seek to maximize resource and economic efficiency. However, if Lean focuses on only the immediate process and system, then managers may miss the sustainability issues beyond the firm. As we discussed in Supplement 5, sustainability requires examining the systems in which the firm and its stakeholders operate. When this is done, both Lean and sustainability achieve higher levels of performance.

Lean drives out waste because waste adds nothing for the customer. Sustainability drives out waste because waste is both expensive and has an adverse effect on the environment. Driving out waste is the common ground of Lean sustainability.

STUDENT TIP ◆
Lean began in factories, but is now also used in services throughout the world.

Lean in Services

The features of Lean apply to services—from hospitals to amusement parks and airlines—directly influencing the customers' received value. The Lean attributes of respect for people, efficient processes with rigorous standard practices that drive out waste, and a focus on continuous improvement are pervasive vehicles for consistently generating value for all stakeholders. If there is any change in focus of Lean between manufacturing and services, it may be that the high level of customer interaction places added emphasis on enabling people through training, motivation, and empowerment to contribute to their fullest. However, in addition to the customer interaction aspect of services, here are some specific applications of Lean applied to suppliers, layout, inventory, and scheduling in the service sector.

LO 16.8 *Explain* how Lean applies to services

Suppliers   Virtually every restaurant deals with its suppliers on a JIT basis. Those that do not are usually unsuccessful. The waste is too evident—food spoils, and customers complain, get sick, and may die. Similarly, JIT is basic to the financial sector that processes your deposits, withdrawals, and brokerage activities on a JIT basis. That is the industry standard.

Layouts   Lean layouts are required in restaurant kitchens, where cold food must be served cold and hot food hot. McDonald's, for example, has reconfigured its kitchen layout, at great expense, to drive seconds out of the production process, thereby speeding delivery to customers. With the new process, McDonald's can produce made-to-order hamburgers in 45 seconds. Layouts also make a difference at Alaska Airline's baggage claim, where customers expect their bags in 20 minutes or less.

Inventory   Stockbrokers drive inventory down to nearly zero every day. Most sell and buy orders occur on an immediate basis because an unexecuted sell or buy order is not acceptable to the client. A broker may be in serious trouble if left holding an unexecuted trade. Similarly, McDonald's reduces inventory waste by maintaining a time-stamped finished-goods inventory of only a few minutes; after that, it is thrown away. Hospitals, such as Arnold Palmer (described in this chapter's *Video Case Study*), manage JIT inventory and low safety stocks for many items. For instance, critical supplies such as pharmaceuticals may be held to low levels by developing community networks as backup. In this manner, if one pharmacy runs out of a needed drug, another member of the network can supply it until the next day's shipment arrives.

VIDEO 16.2
JIT at Arnold Palmer Hospital

Scheduling   Airlines must adjust to fluctuations in customer demand. But rather than adjusting by changes in inventory, demand is satisfied by personnel availability. Through elaborate scheduling, personnel show up just in time to cover peaks in customer demand. In other words, rather than "things" being inventoried, personnel are scheduled. At a salon, the focus is only slightly different: prompt service is assured by scheduling both the *customer* and the staff. At McDonald's and Walmart, scheduling of personnel is down to 15-minute increments, based on precise forecasting of demand. Notice that in these organizations scheduling is a key ingredient of Lean. Excellent forecasts drive those schedules. Such forecasts may be very elaborate, with seasonal, daily, and even hourly components in the case of the airline ticket counter (holiday sales, flight time, etc.), seasonal and weekly components at the salon (holidays and Fridays create special problems), and down to a few minutes (to respond to the daily meal cycle) at McDonald's.

To deliver goods and services to customers under continuously changing demand, suppliers need to be reliable, inventories low, cycle times short, and schedules nimble. Lean engages and empowers employees to create and deliver the customer's perception of value, eliminating whatever does not contribute to this goal. Lean techniques are widely used in both goods-producing and service-producing firms; they just look different.

Summary

Lean operations, including JIT and TPS, focuses on continuous improvement to eliminate waste. Because waste is found in anything that does not add value, organizations that implement these techniques are adding value more efficiently than other firms. The expectation of lean firms is that empowered employees work with committed management to build systems that respond to customers with ever-increasing efficiency and higher quality.

Key Terms

Lean operations (p. 638)
Just-in-time (JIT) (p. 638)
Toyota Production System (TPS) (p. 638)
Seven wastes (p. 638)
5Ss (p. 639)
Variability (p. 639)

Throughput (p. 640)
Manufacturing cycle time (p. 640)
Pull system (p. 640)
Supplier partnerships (p. 640)
Consignment inventory (p. 642)
Lean inventory (p. 643)

Level schedules (p. 647)
Kanban (p. 647)
Kaizen (p. 649)
Kaizen event (p. 649)
Gemba or Gemba walk (p. 651)

Ethical Dilemma

In this Lean operations world, in an effort to lower handling costs, speed delivery, and reduce inventory, retailers are forcing their suppliers to do more and more in the way of preparing their merchandise for their cross-docking warehouses, shipment to specific stores, and shelf presentation. Your company, a small manufacturer of aquarium decorations, is in a tough position. First, Mega-Mart wanted you to develop bar-code technology, then special packaging, then small individual shipments bar coded for each store. (This way when the merchandise hits the warehouse, it is cross-docked immediately to the truck destined for that store, and upon arrival the merchandise is ready for shelf placement.) And now Mega-Mart wants you to develop RFID—immediately.

Mega-Mart has made it clear that suppliers that cannot keep up with the technology will be dropped.

Earlier, when you didn't have the expertise for bar codes, you had to borrow money and hire an outside firm to do the development, purchase the technology, and train your shipping clerk. Then, meeting the special packaging requirement drove you into a loss for several months, resulting in a loss for last year. Now it appears that the RFID request is impossible. Your business, under the best of conditions, is marginally profitable, and the bank may not be willing to bail you out again. Over the years, Mega-Mart has slowly become your major customer and without it, you are probably out of business. What are the ethical issues, and what do you do?

Discussion Questions

1. What is a Lean producer?
2. What is JIT?
3. What is TPS?
4. What is level scheduling?
5. JIT attempts to remove delays, which do not add value. How, then, does JIT cope with weather and its impact on crop harvest and transportation times?
6. What are three ways in which Lean and quality are related?
7. What is kaizen, and what is a kaizen event?
8. What are the characteristics of supplier partnerships with respect to suppliers?
9. Discuss how the Japanese word for *card* has application in the study of JIT.
10. Standardized, reusable containers have obvious benefits for shipping. What is the purpose of these devices within the plant?
11. Does Lean production work in the service sector? Provide an example.
12. Which Lean techniques work in both the manufacturing *and* service sectors?

Solved Problem   Virtual Office Hours help is available in MyOMLab.

SOLVED PROBLEM 16.1

Krupp Refrigeration, Inc., is trying to reduce inventory and wants you to install a kanban system for compressors on one of its assembly lines. Determine the size of the kanban and the number of kanbans (containers) needed.

Setup cost = $10
Annual holding cost per compressor = $100
Daily production = 200 compressors
Annual usage = 25,000 (50 weeks × 5 days each × daily usage of 100 compressors)
Lead time = 3 days
Safety stock = $\frac{1}{2}$ day's production of compressors

SOLUTION

First, we must determine kanban container size. To do this, we determine the production order quantity [see discussion in Chapter 12 or Equation (16-1)], which determines the kanban size:

$$Q_p^* = \sqrt{\frac{2DS}{H\left(1 - \frac{d}{p}\right)}} = \sqrt{\frac{2(25,000)(10)}{H\left(1 - \frac{d}{p}\right)}} = \sqrt{\frac{500,000}{100\left(1 - \frac{100}{200}\right)}} = \sqrt{\frac{500,000}{50}}$$

$$= \sqrt{10,000} = 100 \text{ compressors. So the production order size and the size of the kanban container} = 100.$$

Then we determine the number of kanbans:

$$\text{Demand during lead time} = 300 \ (= 3 \text{ days} \times \text{daily usage of } 100)$$

$$\text{Safety stock} = 100 \ (= \tfrac{1}{2} \times \text{daily production of } 200)$$

$$\text{Number of kanbans} = \frac{\text{Demand during lead time} + \text{Safety stock}}{\text{Size of container}}$$

$$= \frac{300 + 100}{100} = \frac{400}{100} = 4 \text{ containers}$$

Problems

Note: **PX** means the problem may be solved with POM for Windows and/or Excel OM.

Problems 16.1–16.12 relate to Lean and Just-in-Time

••• **16.1**   Carol Cagle has a repetitive manufacturing plant producing trailer hitches in Arlington, Texas. The plant has an average inventory turnover of only 12 times per year. She has therefore determined that she will reduce her component lot sizes. She has developed the following data for one component, the safety chain clip:

$$\text{Annual demand} = 31,200 \text{ units}$$
$$\text{Daily demand} = 120 \text{ units}$$
$$\text{Daily production (in 8 hours)} = 960 \text{ units}$$
$$\text{Desired lot size (1 hour of production)} = 120 \text{ units}$$
$$\text{Holding cost per unit per year} = \$12$$
$$\text{Setup labor cost per hour} = \$20$$

How many minutes of setup time should she have her plant manager aim for regarding this component?

••• **16.2**   Given the following information about a product at Michael Gibson's firm, what is the appropriate setup time?

$$\text{Annual demand} = 39,000 \text{ units}$$
$$\text{Daily demand} = 150 \text{ units}$$
$$\text{Daily production} = 1,000 \text{ units}$$
$$\text{Desired lot size} = 150 \text{ units}$$
$$\text{Holding cost per unit per year} = \$10$$
$$\text{Setup labor cost per hour} = \$40$$

••• **16.3**   Rick Wing has a repetitive manufacturing plant producing automobile steering wheels. Use the following data to prepare for a reduced lot size. The firm uses a work year of 305 days.

Annual demand for steering wheels	30,500
Daily demand	100
Daily production (8 hours)	800
Desired lot size (2 hours of production)	200
Holding cost per unit per year	$10

a) What is the setup cost, based on the desired lot size?
b) What is the setup time, based on $40 per hour setup labor?

• **16.4**   Hartley Electronics, Inc., in Nashville, produces short runs of custom airwave scanners for the defense industry. The owner, Janet Hartley, has asked you to reduce inventory by introducing a kanban system. After several hours of analysis, you develop the following data for scanner connectors used in one work cell. How many kanbans do you need for this connector?

Daily demand	1,000 connectors
Lead time	2 days
Safety stock	$\frac{1}{2}$ day
Kanban size	500 connectors

• **16.5**   Tej Dhakar's company wants to establish kanbans to feed a newly established work cell. The following data have been provided. How many kanbans are needed?

Daily demand	250 units
Lead time	$\frac{1}{2}$ day
Safety stock	$\frac{1}{4}$ day
Kanban size	50 units

•• **16.6**   Pauline Found Manufacturing, Inc., is moving to kanbans to support its telephone switching-board assembly lines. Determine the size of the kanban for subassemblies and the number of kanbans needed.

$$\text{Setup cost} = \$30$$
$$\text{Annual holding cost} = \$120 \text{ per subassembly}$$
$$\text{Daily production} = 20 \text{ subassemblies}$$
$$\text{Annual usage} = 2,500 \ (50 \text{ weeks} \times 5 \text{ days each}$$
$$\times \text{ daily usage of } 10 \text{ subassemblies})$$
$$\text{Lead time} = 16 \text{ days}$$
$$\text{Safety stock} = 4 \text{ days' production of subassemblies} \ \textbf{PX}$$

•• **16.7** Maggie Moylan Motorcycle Corp. uses kanbans to support its transmission assembly line. Determine the size of the kanban for the mainshaft assembly and the number of kanbans needed.

$$Setup\ cost = \$20$$

Annual holding cost

of mainshaft assembly = $250 per unit

Daily production = 300 mainshafts

Annual usage = 20,000 (= 50 weeks × 5 days each

× daily usage of 80 mainshafts)

Lead time = 3 days

Safety stock = $\frac{1}{2}$ day's production of mainshafts **Px**

• **16.8** Discount-Mart, a major East Coast retailer, wants to determine the economic order quantity (see Chapter 12 for EOQ formulas) for its halogen lamps. It currently buys all halogen lamps from Specialty Lighting Manufacturers in Atlanta. Annual demand is 2,000 lamps, ordering cost per order is $30, and annual carrying cost per lamp is $12.

a) What is the EOQ?
b) What are the total annual costs of holding and ordering (managing) this inventory?
c) How many orders should Discount-Mart place with Specialty Lighting per year? **Px**

••• **16.9** Discount-Mart (see Problem 16.8), as part of its new Lean program, has signed a long-term contract with Specialty Lighting and will place orders electronically for its halogen lamps. Ordering costs will drop to $.50 per order, but Discount-Mart also reassessed its carrying costs and raised them to $20 per lamp.

a) What is the new economic order quantity?
b) How many orders will now be placed?
c) What is the total annual cost of managing the inventory with this policy? **Px**

•• **16.10** How do your answers to Problems 16.8 and 16.9 provide insight into a collaborative purchasing strategy?

> *Additional problems* **16.11–16.12** *are available in* MyOMLab.

CASE STUDIES

Lean Operations at Alaska Airlines

Video Case

Alaska Airlines operates in a land of rugged beauty, crystal clear lakes, spectacular glaciers, majestic mountains, and bright blue skies. But equally awesome is its operating performance. Alaska Airlines consistently provides the industry's number one overall ranking and best on-time performance. A key ingredient of this excellent performance is Alaska Airlines' Lean initiative.

With an aggressive implementation of Lean, Ben Minicucci, Executive VP for Operations, is finding ever-increasing levels of performance. He pushes this initiative throughout the company with: (1) a focus on continuous improvement, (2) metrics that measure performance against targets, and (3) making performance relevant to Alaska Airlines' empowered employees.

With leadership training that includes a strong focus on participative management, Minicucci has created a seven-person Lean Department. The department provides extensive training in Lean via one-week courses, participative workshops, and two-week classes that train employees to become a Six Sigma Green Belt. Some employees even pursue the next step, Black Belt certification.

A huge part of any airline's operations is fuel cost, but capital utilization and much of the remaining cost is dependent upon ground equipment and crews that handle aircraft turnaround and maintenance, in-flight services, and customer service.

As John Ladner, Director of Seattle Airport Operations, has observed, "Lean eliminates waste, exposes non-standard work, and is forcing a focus on variations in documented best practices and work time."

Lean is now part of the Alaska Airlines corporate culture, with some 60 ongoing projects. Kaizen events (called "Accelerated Improvement Workshops" at Alaska Airlines), Gemba Walks (called "waste walks" by Alaska Airlines), and 5S are now a part of everyday conversation at Alaska Airlines. Lean projects have included:

♦ Applying 5S to identify aircraft ground equipment and its location on the tarmac.
♦ Improving preparation for and synchronization of the arrival and departure sequences; time to open the front door after arrival has been reduced from 4.5 to 1 min.
♦ Redefining the disconnect procedure for tow bars used to "push back" aircraft at departure time; planes now depart 2–3 minutes faster.
♦ Revising the deicing process, meaning less time for the plane to be on the tarmac.
♦ Improving pilot staffing, making Alaska's pilot productivity the highest in the industry. Every 1% improvement in productivity leads to a $5 million savings on a recurring basis. Alaska Airlines has achieved a 7% productivity improvement over the last five years.

Alaska Airlines

Another current Lean project is passenger unloading and loading. Lean instructor Allison Fletcher calls this "the most unique project I have worked on." One exciting aspect of deplaning is Alaska's solar-powered "switchback" staircase for unloading passengers through the rear door (see photo). Alaska is saving two minutes, or nearly 17%, off previous unloading time with this new process. Alaska Airlines' Lean culture has made it a leader in the industry.

Discussion Questions*

1. What are the key ingredients of Lean, as identified at Alaska Airlines?
2. As an initial phase of a kaizen event, discuss the many ways passengers can be loaded and unloaded from airplanes.
3. Document the research that is being done on the aircraft passenger-loading problem.

* You may wish to view the video that accompanies this case before addressing these questions.

JIT at Arnold Palmer Hospital

Video Case

Orlando's Arnold Palmer Hospital, founded in 1989, specializes in treatment of women and children and is renowned for its high-quality rankings (top 10% of 2000 benchmarked hospitals), its labor and delivery volume (more than 14,000 births per year), and its neonatal intensive care unit (one of the highest survival rates in the nation). But quality medical practices and high patient satisfaction require costly inventory—some $30 million per year and thousands of SKUs.* With pressure on medical care to manage and reduce costs, Arnold Palmer Hospital has turned toward controlling its inventory with just-in-time (JIT) techniques.

Within the hospital, for example, drugs are now distributed at the nursing stations via dispensing machines (almost like vending machines) that electronically track patient usage and post the related charge to each patient. Each night, based on patient demand and prescriptions written by doctors, the dispensing stations are refilled.

To address JIT issues externally, Arnold Palmer Hospital turned to a major distribution partner, McKesson General Medical, which as a first-tier supplier provides the hospital with about one-quarter of all its medical/surgical inventory. McKesson supplies sponges, basins, towels, Mayo stand covers, syringes, and hundreds of other medical/surgical items. To ensure coordinated daily delivery of inventory purchased from McKesson, an account executive has been assigned to the hospital on a full-time basis, as well as two other individuals who address customer service and product issues. The result has been a drop in Central Supply average daily inventory from $400,000 to $114,000 since JIT.

JIT success has also been achieved in the area of *custom surgical packs*. Custom surgical packs are the sterile coverings, disposable plastic trays, gauze, and the like, specialized to each type of surgical procedure. Arnold Palmer Hospital uses 10 different custom packs for various surgical procedures. "Over 50,000 packs are used each year, for a total cost of about $1.5 million," says George DeLong, head of Supply-Chain Management.

The packs are not only delivered in a JIT manner, but packed that way as well. That is, they are packed in the reverse order they are used so each item comes out of the pack in the sequence it is needed. The packs are bulky, are expensive, and must remain sterile. Reducing the inventory and handling while maintaining an ensured sterile supply for scheduled surgeries presents a challenge to hospitals.

Here is how the supply chain works: Custom packs are *assembled* by a packing company with *components supplied* primarily from manufacturers selected by the hospital, and *delivered* by McKesson from its local warehouse. Arnold Palmer Hospital works with its own surgical staff (through the Medical Economics Outcome Committee) to identify and standardize the custom packs to reduce the number of custom pack SKUs. With this integrated system, pack safety stock inventory has been cut to one day.

The procedure to drive the custom surgical pack JIT system begins with a "pull" from the doctors' daily surgical schedule. Then, Arnold Palmer Hospital initiates an electronic order to McKesson between 1:00 and 2:00 P.M. daily. At 4:00 A.M. the next day, McKesson delivers the packs. Hospital personnel arrive at 7:00 A.M. and stock the shelves for scheduled surgeries. McKesson then reorders from the packing company, which in turn "pulls" necessary inventory for the quantity of packs needed from the manufacturers.

Arnold Palmer Hospital's JIT system reduces inventory investment, expensive traditional ordering, and bulky storage and supports quality with a sterile delivery.

Discussion Questions**

1. What do you recommend be done when an error is found in a pack as it is opened for an operation?
2. How might the procedure for custom surgical packs described here be improved?
3. When discussing JIT in services, the text notes that suppliers, layout, inventory, and scheduling are all used. Provide an example of each of these at Arnold Palmer Hospital.
4. When a doctor proposes a new surgical procedure, how do you recommend the SKU for a new custom pack be entered into the hospital's supply-chain system?

**You may wish to view the video that accompanies this case before answering these questions.

*SKU = stock keeping unit

- **Additional Case Studies:** Visit MyOMLab for these case studies:
  JIT after a Catastrophe: How Caterpillar responded after a tornado tore apart its Oxford plant.
  Mutual Insurance Company of Iowa: Applying JIT in an insurance office.

Endnote

1. The term 5S comes from the Japanese words seiri (*sort* and clear out), seiton (*straighten* and configure), seiso (*scrub* and clean up), seiketsu (maintain *sanitation* and cleanliness of self and workplace), and shitsuke (*self-discipline and standardization* of these practices).

Chapter 16 *Rapid* Review

Main Heading	Review Material	MyOMLab
LEAN OPERATIONS (pp. 638–640)	▪ **Lean operations**—Eliminates waste through continuous improvement and focus on exactly what the customer wants. ▪ **Just-in-time (JIT)**—Continuous and forced problem solving via a focus on throughput and reduced inventory. ▪ **Toyota Production System (TPS)**—Focus on continuous improvement, respect for people, and standard work practices. *When implemented as a comprehensive manufacturing strategy, Lean, JIT, and TPS systems sustain competitive advantage and result in increased overall returns.* ▪ **Seven wastes**—Overproduction, queues, transportation, inventory, motion, overprocessing, and defective product. ▪ **5Ss**—A Lean production checklist: sort, simplify, shine, standardize, and sustain. U.S. managers often add two additional *Ss* to the 5 original ones: *safety* and *support/maintenance.* ▪ **Variability**—Any deviation from the optimum process that delivers perfect product on time, every time. Both JIT and inventory reduction are effective tools for identifying causes of variability. ▪ **Throughput**—The rate at which units move through a process. ▪ **Manufacturing cycle time**—The time between the arrival of raw materials and the shipping of finished products. ▪ **Pull system**—A concept that results in material being produced only when requested and moved to where it is needed just as it is needed. Pull systems use signals to request production and delivery from supplying stations to stations that have production capacity available.	Concept Questions: 1.1–1.4
LEAN AND JUST-IN-TIME (pp. 640–649)	▪ **Supplier partnerships**—Suppliers and purchasers work together to remove waste and drive down costs for mutual benefit. Some specific goals of supplier partnerships are *removal of unnecessary activities, removal of in-plant inventory, removal of in-transit inventory,* and *obtain improved quality and reliability.* ▪ **Consignment inventory**—An arrangement in which the supplier maintains title to the inventory until it is used. Concerns of suppliers in suppler partnerships include (1) *diversification*, (2) *scheduling*, (3) *lead time*, (4) *quality*, and (5) *lot sizes.* *Lean layout tactics* include building work cells for families of products, including a large number of operations in a small area, minimizing distance, designing little space for inventory, improving employee communication, using poka-yoke devices, building flexible or movable equipment, and cross-training workers to add flexibility. ▪ **Lean inventory**—The minimum inventory necessary to keep a perfect system running. The idea behind JIT is to eliminate inventory that hides variability in the production system. *Lean inventory tactics* include using a pull system to move inventory, reducing lot size, developing just-in-time delivery systems with suppliers, delivering directly to the point of use, performing to schedule, reducing setup time, and using group technology. $$Q_p^* = \sqrt{\frac{2DS}{H[1-(d/p)]}} \quad (16\text{-}1)$$ Using Equation (16-1), for a given desired lot size, Q, we can solve for the optimal setup cost, S: $$S = \frac{(Q^2)(H)(1-d/p)}{2D} \quad (16\text{-}2)$$ *Lean scheduling tactics* include communicate schedules to suppliers, make level schedules, freeze part of the schedule, perform to schedule, seek one-piece-make and one-piece-move, eliminate waste, produce in small lots, use kanbans, and make each operation produce a perfect part. ▪ **Level schedules**—Scheduling products so that each day's production meets the demand for that day. ▪ **Kanban**—The Japanese word for *card*, which has come to mean "signal"; a kanban system moves parts through production via a "pull" from a signal. $$\text{Number of kanbans (containers)} = \frac{\text{Demand during lead time} + \text{Safety stock}}{\text{Size of container}} \quad (16\text{-}3)$$ *Lean quality*—whereas inventory *hides* bad quality, Lean immediately *exposes* it. Lean quality tactics include using statistical process control, empowering employees, building fail-safe methods (poka-yoke, checklists, etc.), exposing poor quality with small lots, and providing immediate feedback.	Concept Questions: 2.1–2.4 Problems: 16.1–16.3 Problems: 16.4–16.9, 16.11, 16.12 Virtual Office Hours for Solved Problem: 16.1

Main Heading	Review Material	MyOMLab
LEAN AND THE TOYOTA PRODUCTION SYSTEM (pp. 649–650)	■ **Kaizen**—A focus on continuous improvement. ■ **Kaizen event**—Members of a work cell or team meet to develop improvements in the process. Toyota recruits, trains, and treats people as knowledge workers. They are empowered. TPS employs aggressive cross-training and few job classifications.	Concept Questions: 3.1–3.4
LEAN ORGANIZATIONS (pp. 650–652)	Lean operations tend to share the following attributes: *respect and develop employees* by improving job design, providing constant training, instilling commitment, and building teamwork; *empower employees* by pushing responsibility to the lowest level possible; *develop worker flexibility* through cross-training and reducing job classifications; *build processes* that destroy variability; *develop collaborative partnerships with suppliers* to help them accept responsibility for satisfying end customer needs; and *eliminate waste by performing only value-added activities*. ■ **Gemba** or **Gemba walk**—Going to where the work is actually performed.	Concept Questions: 4.1–4.4 **VIDEO 16.1** Lean Operations at Alaska Airlines
LEAN IN SERVICES (p. 652)	The features of Lean operations apply to services just as they do in other sectors. Forecasts in services may be very elaborate, with seasonal, daily, hourly, or even shorter components.	Concept Questions: 5.1–5.4 **VIDEO 16.2** JIT at Arnold Palmer Hospital

Self Test

■ **Before taking the self-test,** refer to the learning objectives listed at the beginning of the chapter and the key terms listed at the end of the chapter.

LO 16.1 Match Lean Operations, JIT, and TPS with the concepts shown below:
  a) Continuous improvement and a focus on exactly what the customer wants, and when.
  b) Supply the customer with exactly what the customer wants when the customer wants it, without waste, through continuous improvement.
  c) Emphasis on continuous improvement, respect for people, and standard work practices.

LO 16.2 Define the seven wastes and the 5Ss. The seven wastes are _____, _____, _____, _____, _____.
_____, and _____, and the 5Ss are _____, _____, _____, _____, and _____.

LO 16.3 Concerns of suppliers when moving to Supplier Partnerships include:
  a) small lots sometimes seeming economically prohibitive.
  b) realistic quality demands.
  c) changes without adequate lead time.
  d) erratic schedules.
  e) all of the above.

LO 16.4 What is the formula for optimal setup time?
  a) $\sqrt{2DQ/[H(1 - d/p)]}$
  b) $\sqrt{Q^2 H(1 - d/p)/(2D)}$
  c) $QH(1 - d/p)/(2D)$
  d) $Q^2 H(1 - d/p)/(2D)$
  e) $H(1 - d/p)$

LO 16.5 Kanban is the Japanese word for:
  a) car.
  b) pull.
  c) card.
  d) continuous improvement.
  e) level schedule.

LO 16.6 The required number of kanbans equals:
  a) 1.
  b) Demand during lead time / Q
  c) Size of container.
  d) Demand during lead time.
  e) Demand during lead time + Safety stock / Size of container

LO 16.7 The six attributes of Lean organizations are: _____, _____, _____, _____, _____, and _____.

LO 16.8 Lean applies to services:
  a) only in rare instances.
  b) except in terms of the supply chain.
  c) except in terms of employee issues.
  d) except in terms of both supply chain issues and employee issues.
  e) just as it applies to manufacturing.

Answers: LO 16.1. Lean = a, JIT = b, TPS = c; LO 16.2. overproduction, queues, transportation, inventory, motion, overprocessing, defective product; sort, simplify, shine, standardize, sustain; LO 16.3. e; LO 16.4. d; LO 16.5. c; LO 16.6. e; LO 16.7. respect and develop people, empower employees, develop worker flexibility, build excellent processes, develop collaborative partnerships with suppliers, eliminate waste; LO 16.8. e.

Decision-Making Tools

MODULE **A**

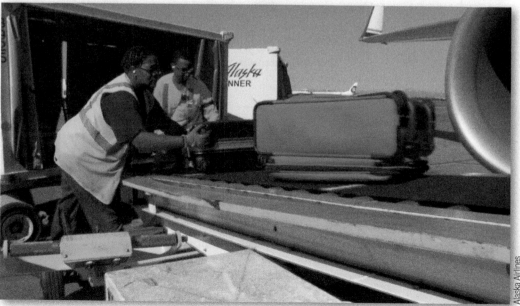

Alaska Airlines

Alaska Airlines

WOULD *YOU* GO ALL IN?

At the Legends of Poker tournament in Los Angeles, veteran T.J. Cloutier opens with a $60,000 bet. (Antes and required bets of $39,000 are already on the table.) Former Go2net CTO Paul Phillips ponders going "all in"—betting virtually all his chips. Using decision theory, here's how he decided.

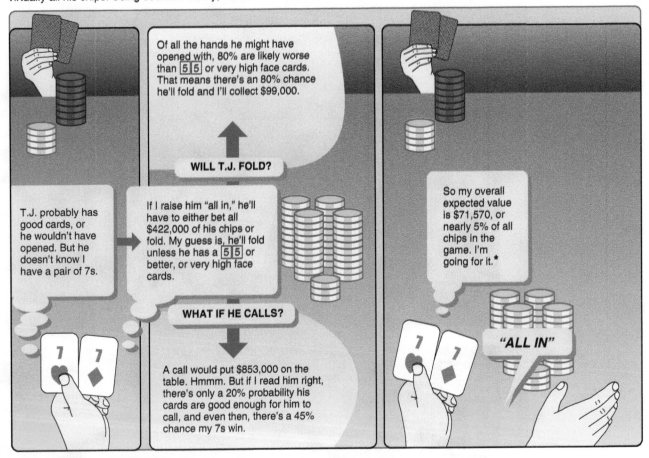

Source: Based on *Business 2.0* (November 2003): 128–134.

*To see the details of Phillips's decision, see Example A8.

The Decision Process in Operations

Operations managers are not gamblers. But they are decision makers. To achieve the goals of their organizations, managers must understand how decisions are made and know which decision-making tools to use. To a great extent, the success or failure of both people and companies depends on the quality of their decisions. Overcoming uncertainty is a manager's challenge.

What makes the difference between a good decision and a bad decision? A "good" decision—one that uses analytic decision making—is based on logic and considers all available data and possible alternatives. It also follows these six steps:

1. Clearly define the problem and the factors that influence it.
2. Develop specific and measurable objectives.
3. Develop a model—that is, a relationship between objectives and variables (which are measurable quantities).
4. Evaluate each alternative solution based on its merits and drawbacks.
5. Select the best alternative.
6. Implement and evaluate the decision and then set a timetable for completion.

So analytic decision making requires models, objectives, and quantifiable variables, often in the form of probabilities and payoffs. Such information is not always easy to obtain or derive from existing data. This challenge exists because of either a lack of data or an overabundance of data. However, because data are now easily generated and stored in digital form, we tend to have the latter—massive volumes of data. Data are collected automatically from production processes, as well as from websites, credit cards, point-of-sale records, and social media. Although this mass of data is a potential source of information, it requires sophistication in how it is stored, processed, and analyzed. Big data is the term used to describe this huge amount of data, which often cannot be efficiently processed by traditional data techniques.

Big data

The huge amount of economic, production, and consumer data now being collected in digital form.

Throughout this text, we have introduced a broad range of mathematical models and tools that help operations managers make better decisions. Because good decisions require data that can be analyzed and turned into information, decision makers appreciate the potential of big data. This module provides an introduction to the challenges facing managers by introducing two of the tools of decision making—decision tables and decision trees. These two tools are used in numerous OM situations, ranging from new-product analysis, to capacity planning, to location planning, to supply-chain disaster planning, to scheduling, and to maintenance planning.

Fundamentals of Decision Making

Regardless of the complexity of a decision or the sophistication of the technique used to analyze it, all decision makers are faced with alternatives and "states of nature." The following notation will be used in this module:

1. Terms:
   a. *Alternative*—A course of action or strategy that may be chosen by a decision maker (e.g., not carrying an umbrella tomorrow).
   b. *State of nature*—An occurrence or a situation over which the decision maker has little or no control (e.g., tomorrow's weather).
2. Symbols used in a decision tree:
   a. ▢—Decision node from which one of several alternatives may be selected.
   b. ◯—A state-of-nature node out of which one state of nature will occur.

To present a manager's decision alternatives, we can develop *decision trees* using the above symbols. When constructing a decision tree, we must be sure that all alternatives and states of nature are in their correct and logical places and that we include *all* possible alternatives and states of nature.

Example A1 | **A SIMPLE DECISION TREE**

Getz Products Company is investigating the possibility of producing and marketing backyard storage sheds. Undertaking this project would require the construction of either a large or a small manufacturing plant. The market for the product produced—storage sheds—could be either favorable or unfavorable. Getz, of course, has the option of not developing the new product line at all.

APPROACH ▶ Getz decides to build a decision tree.

SOLUTION ▶ Figure A.1 illustrates Getz's decision tree.

Figure **A.1**

Getz Products' Decision Tree

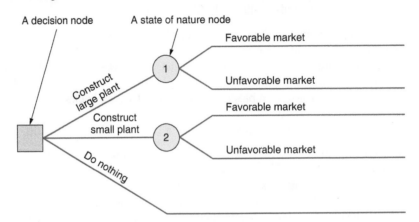

A decision node   A state of nature node

Construct large plant

Construct small plant

Do nothing

1 — Favorable market / Unfavorable market

2 — Favorable market / Unfavorable market

LO A.1 *Create* a simple decision tree

INSIGHT ▶ We never want to overlook the option of "doing nothing," as that is usually a possible decision.

LEARNING EXERCISE ▶ Getz now considers constructing a medium-sized plant as a fourth option. Redraw the tree in Figure A.1 to accommodate this. [Answer: Your tree will have a new node and branches between "Construct large plant" and "Construct small plant."]

RELATED PROBLEMS ▶ A.2e, A.8b, A.22–A.25

Decision Tables

Decision table

A tabular means of analyzing decision alternatives and states of nature.

We may also develop a decision or payoff table to help Getz Products define its alternatives. For any alternative and a particular state of nature, there is a *consequence* or *outcome*, which is usually expressed as a monetary value. This is called a *conditional value*. Note that all of the alternatives in Example A2 are listed down the left side of the table, that states of nature (outcomes) are listed across the top, and that conditional values (payoffs) are in the body of the decision table.

Example A2

A DECISION TABLE

Getz Products now wishes to organize the following information into a table. With a favorable market, a large facility will give Getz Products a net profit of $200,000. If the market is unfavorable, a $180,000 net loss will occur. A small plant will result in a net profit of $100,000 in a favorable market, but a net loss of $20,000 will be encountered if the market is unfavorable.

APPROACH ▶ These numbers become conditional values in the decision table. We list alternatives in the left column and states of nature across the top of the table.

LO A.2 *Build* a decision table

SOLUTION ▶ The completed table is shown in Table A.1.

TABLE A.1	Decision Table with Conditional Values for Getz Products	
	STATES OF NATURE	
ALTERNATIVES	FAVORABLE MARKET	UNFAVORABLE MARKET
Construct large plant	$200,000	−$180,000
Construct small plant	$100,000	−$ 20,000
Do nothing	$ 0	$ 0

STUDENT TIP ☝

Decision tables force logic into decision making.

INSIGHT ▶ The toughest part of decision tables is obtaining the data to analyze.

LEARNING EXERCISE ▶ In Examples A3 and A4, we see how to use decision tables to make decisions.

Types of Decision-Making Environments

The types of decisions people make depend on how much knowledge or information they have about the situation. There are three decision-making environments:

◆ Decision making under uncertainty
◆ Decision making under risk
◆ Decision making under certainty

LO A.3 *Explain* when to use each of the three types of decision-making environments

Decision Making Under Uncertainty

When there is complete *uncertainty* as to which state of nature in a decision environment may occur (i.e., when we cannot even assess probabilities for each possible outcome), we rely on three decision methods:

1. Maximax: This method finds an alternative that *max*imizes the *max*imum outcome for every alternative. First, we find the maximum outcome within every alternative, and then we pick the alternative with the maximum number. Because this decision criterion locates the alternative with the *highest* possible *gain*, it has been called an "optimistic" decision criterion.

2. Maximin: This method finds the alternative that *max*imizes the *min*imum outcome for every alternative. First, we find the minimum outcome within every alternative, and then we pick the alternative with the maximum number. Because this decision criterion locates the alternative that has the *least* possible *loss*, it has been called a "pessimistic" decision criterion.

3. Equally likely: This method finds the alternative with the highest average outcome. First, we calculate the average outcome for every alternative, which is the sum of all outcomes divided by the number of outcomes. We then pick the alternative with the maximum number. The equally likely approach assumes that each state of nature is equally likely to occur.

Maximax
A criterion that finds an alternative that maximizes the maximum outcome.

Maximin
A criterion that finds an alternative that maximizes the minimum outcome.

Equally likely
A criterion that assigns equal probability to each state of nature.

Example A3

A DECISION TABLE ANALYSIS UNDER UNCERTAINTY

Getz Products Company would like to apply each of these three approaches now.

APPROACH ▶ Given Getz's decision table from Example A2, he determines the maximax, maximin, and equally likely decision criteria.

SOLUTION ▶ Table A.2 provides the solution.

| TABLE A.2 | Decision Table for Decision Making Under Uncertainty |

ALTERNATIVES	STATES OF NATURE FAVORABLE MARKET	STATES OF NATURE UNFAVORABLE MARKET	MAXIMUM IN ROW	MINIMUM IN ROW	ROW AVERAGE
Construct large plant	$200,000	−$180,000	$200,000 ◀	−180,000	$10,000
Construct small plant	$100,000	−$ 20,000	$100,000	−$20,000	$40,000 ◀
Do nothing	$ 0	$ 0	$ 0	$ 0 ◀	$ 0
			Maximax	Maximin	Equally likely

1. The maximax choice is to construct a large plant. This is the *max*imum of the *max*imum number within each row, or alternative.

   2. The maximin choice is to do nothing. This is the *max*imum of the *min*imum number within each row, or alternative.
   3. The equally likely choice is to construct a small plant. This is the maximum of the average outcome of each alternative. This approach assumes that all outcomes for any alternative are *equally likely*.

   INSIGHT ▶ There are optimistic decision makers ("maximax") and pessimistic ones ("maximin"). Maximax and maximin present best case–worst case planning scenarios.

   LEARNING EXERCISE ▶ Getz reestimates the outcome for constructing a large plant when the market is favorable and raises it to $250,000. What numbers change in Table A.2? Do the decisions change? [Answer: The maximax is now $250,000, and the row average is $35,000 for large plant. No decision changes.]

   RELATED PROBLEMS ▶ A.1, A.2b–d, A.4, A.6 (A.15 is available in MyOMLab)

Decision Making Under Risk

Decision making under risk, a more common occurrence, relies on probabilities. Several possible states of nature may occur, each with an assumed probability. The states of nature must be mutually exclusive and collectively exhaustive and their probabilities must sum to 1.[1] Given a decision table with conditional values and probability assessments for all states of nature, we can determine the expected monetary value (EMV) for each alternative. This figure represents the expected value or *mean* return for each alternative *if we could repeat this decision (or similar types of decisions) a large number of times.*

   The EMV for an alternative is the sum of all possible payoffs from the alternative, each weighted by the probability of that payoff occurring:

Expected monetary value (EMV)

The expected payout or value of a variable that has different possible states of nature, each with an associated probability.

LO A.4 *Calculate* an expected monetary value (EMV)

$$\begin{aligned} \text{EMV (Alternative } i) = {} & (\text{Payoff of 1st state of nature}) \\ & \times (\text{Probability of 1st state of nature}) \\ & + (\text{Payoff of 2nd state of nature}) \\ & \times (\text{Probability of 2nd state of nature}) \\ & + \ldots + (\text{Payoff of last state of nature}) \\ & \times (\text{Probability of last state of nature}) \end{aligned}$$

Example A4 illustrates how to compute the maximum EMV.

Example A4

EXPECTED MONETARY VALUE

Getz would like to find the EMV for each alternative.

APPROACH ▶ Getz Products' operations manager believes that the probability of a favorable market is 0.6, and that of an unfavorable market is 0.4. He can now determine the EMV for each alternative (see Table A.3).

SOLUTION ▶

1. $\text{EMV }(A_1) = (0.6)(\$200,000) + (0.4)(-\$180,000) = \$48,000$
2. $\text{EMV }(A_2) = (0.6)(\$100,000) + (0.4)(-\$20,000) = \$52,000$
3. $\text{EMV }(A_3) = (0.6)(\$0) + (0.4)(\$0) = \$0$

TABLE A.3	Decision Table for Getz Products	
	STATES OF NATURE	
ALTERNATIVES	FAVORABLE MARKET	UNFAVORABLE MARKET
Construct large plant (A_1)	$200,000	–$180,000
Construct small plant (A_2)	$100,000	–$ 20,000
Do nothing (A_3)	$ 0	$ 0
Probabilities	0.6	0.4

INSIGHT ▶ The maximum EMV is seen in alternative A_2. Thus, according to the EMV decision criterion, Getz would build the small facility.

LEARNING EXERCISE ▶ What happens to the three EMVs if Getz increases the conditional value on the "large plant/favorable market" result to $250,000? [Answer: EMV ($A_1$) = $78,000. A_1 is now the preferable decision.]

RELATED PROBLEMS ▶ A.2e, A.3a, A.5a, A.7a, A.8, A.9a, A.10, A.11, A.12, A.13a, A.14, A.22b,c (A.16, A.17, A.18, A.19, A.20 are available in MyOMLab)

EXCEL **OM** Data File **ModAExA4.xls** can be found in MyOMLab.

Decision Making Under Certainty

Now suppose that the Getz operations manager has been approached by a marketing research firm that proposes to help him make the decision about whether to build the plant to produce storage sheds. The marketing researchers claim that their technical analysis will tell Getz with certainty whether the market is favorable for the proposed product. In other words, it will change Getz's environment from one of decision making *under risk* to one of decision making *under certainty*. This information could prevent Getz from making a very expensive mistake. The marketing research firm would charge Getz $65,000 for the information. What would you recommend? Should the operations manager hire the firm to make the study? Even if the information from the study is perfectly accurate, is it worth $65,000? What might it be worth? Although some of these questions are difficult to answer, determining the value of such *perfect information* can be very useful. It places an upper bound on what you would be willing to spend on information, such as that being sold by a marketing consultant. This is the concept of the expected value of perfect information (EVPI), which we now introduce.

Expected Value of Perfect Information (EVPI)

If a manager were able to determine which state of nature would occur, then he or she would know which decision to make. Once a manager knows which decision to make, the payoff increases because the payoff is now a certainty, not a probability. Because the payoff will increase with knowledge of which state of nature will occur, this knowledge has value. Therefore, we now look at how to determine the value of this information. We call this difference between the payoff under perfect information and the payoff under risk the expected value of perfect information (EVPI).

$$EVPI = \text{Expected value with perfect information} - \text{Maximum EMV}$$

To find the EVPI, we must first compute the expected value with perfect information (EVwPI), which is the expected (average) return if we have perfect information before a decision has to be made.

LO A.5 *Compute* the expected value of perfect information (EVPI)

Expected value of perfect information (EVPI)
The difference between the payoff under perfect information and the payoff under risk.

Expected value *with* perfect information (EVwPI)
The expected (average) return if perfect information is available.

To calculate this value, we choose the best alternative for each state of nature and multiply its payoff times the probability of occurrence of that state of nature:

Expected value *with*
perfect information (EVwPI) = (Best outcome or consequence for 1st state of nature)
$$\times \text{ (Probability of 1st state of nature)}$$
$$+ \text{ (Best outcome for 2nd state of nature)}$$
$$\times \text{ (Probability of 2nd state of nature)}$$
$$+ \ldots + \text{ (Best outcome for last state of nature)}$$
$$\times \text{ (Probability of last state of nature)}$$

In Example A5 we use the data and decision table from Example A4 to examine the expected value of perfect information.

Example A5

EXPECTED VALUE OF PERFECT INFORMATION

The Getz operations manager would like to calculate the maximum that he would pay for information—that is, the expected value of perfect information, or EVPI.

APPROACH ▶ Referring to Table A.3 in Example 4, he follows a two-stage process. First, the expected value *with* perfect information (EVwPI) is computed. Then, using this information, the EVPI is calculated.

SOLUTION ▶

1. The best outcome for the state of nature "favorable market" is "build a large facility" with a payoff of $200,000. The best outcome for the state of nature "unfavorable market" is "do nothing" with a payoff of $0. Expected value *with* perfect information = ($200,000)(0.6) + ($0)(0.4) = $120,000. Thus, if we had perfect information, we would expect (on the average) $120,000 if the decision could be repeated many times.
2. The maximum EMV is $52,000 for A_2, which is the expected outcome without perfect information. Thus:

$$\text{EVPI} = \text{EVwPI} - \text{Maximum EMV}$$
$$= \$120,000 - \$52,000 = \$68,000$$

INSIGHT ▶ The *most* Getz should be willing to pay for perfect information is $68,000. This conclusion, of course, is again based on the assumption that the probability of the first state of nature is 0.6 and the second is 0.4.

STUDENT TIP ◑
EVPI places an upper limit on what you should pay for information.

LEARNING EXERCISE ▶ How does the EVPI change if the "large plant/favorable market" conditional value is $250,000? [Answer: EVPI = $72,000.]

RELATED PROBLEMS ▶ A.3b, A.5b, A.7, A.9, A.13, A.22c

Decision Trees

STUDENT TIP ◑
Decision trees can become complex, so we illustrate two of them in this section.

Decision tree
A graphical means of analyzing decision alternatives and states of nature.

Decisions that lend themselves to display in a decision table also lend themselves to display in a decision tree. We will therefore analyze some decisions using decision trees. Although the use of a decision table is convenient in problems having one set of decisions and one set of states of nature, many problems include *sequential* decisions and states of nature.

When there are two or more sequential decisions, and later decisions are based on the outcome of prior ones, the decision tree approach becomes appropriate. A decision tree is a graphic display of the decision process that indicates decision alternatives, states of nature and their respective probabilities, and payoffs for each combination of decision alternative and state of nature.

Expected monetary value (EMV) is the most commonly used criterion for decision tree analysis. One of the first steps in such analysis is to graph the decision tree and to specify the monetary consequences of all outcomes for a particular problem.

When Tomco Oil had to decide which of its new Kentucky lease areas to drill for oil, it turned to decision tree analysis. The 74 different factors, including geological, engineering, economic, and political factors, became much clearer. Decision tree software such as DPL (shown here), Tree Plan, and Supertree allow decision problems to be analyzed with less effort and greater depth than ever before.

Analyzing problems with *decision trees* involves five steps:

1. Define the problem.
2. Structure or draw the decision tree.
3. Assign probabilities to the states of nature.
4. Estimate payoffs for each possible combination of decision alternatives and states of nature.
5. Solve the problem by computing the expected monetary values (EMV) for each state-of-nature node. This is done by working *backward*—that is, by starting at the right of the tree and working back to decision nodes on the left.

Example A6

SOLVING A TREE FOR EMV

Getz wants to develop a completed and solved decision tree.

APPROACH ▶ The payoffs are placed at the right-hand side of each of the tree's branches (see Figure A.2). The probabilities (first used by Getz in Example A4) are placed in parentheses next to each

Figure **A.2**

Completed and Solved Decision Tree for Getz Products

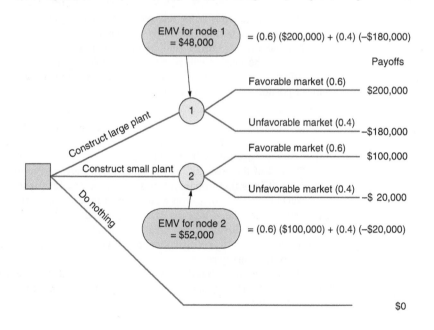

LO A.6 *Evaluate* the nodes in a decision tree

state of nature. The expected monetary values for each state-of-nature node are then calculated and placed by their respective nodes. The EMV of the first node is $48,000. This represents the branch from the decision node to "construct a large plant." The EMV for node 2, to "construct a small plant," is $52,000. The option of "doing nothing" has, of course, a payoff of $0.

SOLUTION ▶ The branch leaving the decision node leading to the state-of-nature node with the highest EMV will be chosen. In Getz's case, a small plant should be built.

INSIGHT ▶ This graphical approach is an excellent way for managers to understand all the options in making a major decision. Visual models are often preferred over tables.

LEARNING EXERCISE ▶ Correct Figure A.2 to reflect a $250,000 payoff for "construct large plant/favorable market." [Answer: Change one payoff and recompute the EMV for node 1.]

RELATED PROBLEMS ▶ A.2e, A.8b, A.22a,b, A.24, A.25

EXCEL **OM** Data File **ModAExA6.xls** can be found in MyOMLab.

A More Complex Decision Tree

When a *sequence* of decisions must be made, decision trees are much more powerful tools than are decision tables. Let's say that Getz Products has two decisions to make, with the second decision dependent on the outcome of the first. Before deciding about building a new plant, Getz has the option of conducting its own marketing research survey, at a cost of $10,000. The information from this survey could help it decide whether to build a large plant, to build a small plant, or not to build at all. Getz recognizes that although such a survey will not provide it with *perfect* information, it may be extremely helpful.

Getz's new decision tree is represented in Figure A.3 of Example A7. Take a careful look at this more complex tree. Note that *all possible outcomes and alternatives* are included in their logical sequence. This procedure is one of the strengths of using decision trees. The manager is forced to examine all possible outcomes, including unfavorable ones. He or she is also forced to make decisions in a logical, sequential manner.

Example A7

A DECISION TREE WITH SEQUENTIAL DECISIONS

Getz Products wishes to develop the new tree for this sequential decision.

APPROACH ▶ Examining the tree in Figure A.3, we see that Getz's first decision point is whether to conduct the $10,000 market survey. If it chooses not to do the study (the lower part of the tree), it can either build a large plant, a small plant, or no plant. This is Getz's second decision point. If the decision is to build, the market will be either favorable (0.6 probability) or unfavorable (0.4 probability). The payoffs for each of the possible consequences are listed along the right-hand side. As a matter of fact, this lower portion of Getz's tree is *identical* to the simpler decision tree shown in Figure A.2.

SOLUTION ▶ The upper part of Figure A.3 reflects the decision to conduct the market survey. State-of-nature node number 1 has 2 branches coming out of it. Let us say there is a 45% chance that the survey results will indicate a favorable market for the storage sheds. We also note that the probability is 0.55 that the survey results will be negative.

The rest of the probabilities shown in parentheses in Figure A.3 are all *conditional* probabilities. For example, 0.78 is the probability of a favorable market for the sheds given a favorable result from the market survey. Of course, you would expect to find a high probability of a favorable market given that the research indicated that the market was good. Don't forget, though: There is a chance that Getz's $10,000 market survey did not result in perfect or even reliable information. Any market research study is subject to error. In this case, there remains a 22% chance that the market for sheds will be unfavorable given positive survey results.

Likewise, we note that there is a 27% chance that the market for sheds will be favorable given negative survey results. The probability is much higher, 0.73, that the market will actually be unfavorable given a negative survey.

Figure A.3

Getz Products Decision Tree with Probabilities and EMVs Shown

LO A.7 *Create* a decision tree with sequential decisions

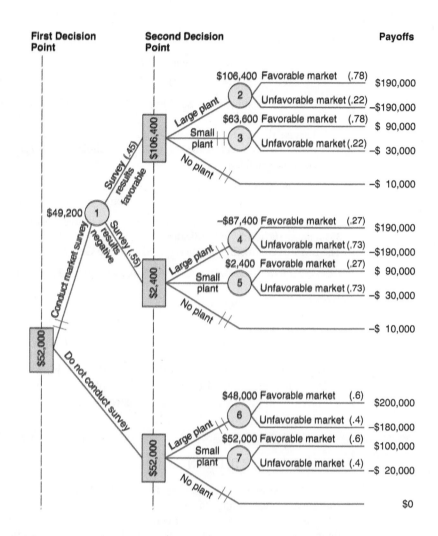

Finally, when we look to the payoff column in Figure A.3, we see that $10,000—the cost of the marketing study—has been subtracted from each of the top 10 tree branches. Thus, a large plant constructed in a favorable market would normally net a $200,000 profit. Yet because the market study was conducted, this figure is reduced by $10,000. In the unfavorable case, the loss of $180,000 would increase to $190,000. Similarly, conducting the survey and building *no plant* now results in a −$10,000 payoff.

With all probabilities and payoffs specified, we can start calculating the expected monetary value of each branch. We begin at the end or right-hand side of the decision tree and work back toward the origin. When we finish, the best decision will be known.

1. Given favorable survey results:

$$\text{EMV (node 2)} = (.78)(\$190,000) + (.22)(-\$190,000) = \$106,400$$
$$\text{EMV (node 3)} = (.78)(\$90,000) + (.22)(-\$30,000) = \$63,600$$

The EMV of no plant in this case is −$10,000. Thus, if the survey results are favorable, a large plant should be built.

2. Given negative survey results:

$$\text{EMV (node 4)} = (.27)(\$190,000) + (.73)(-\$190,000) = -\$87,400$$
$$\text{EMV (node 5)} = (.27)(\$90,000) + (.73)(-\$30,000) = \$2,400$$

The EMV of no plant is again −$10,000 for this branch. Thus, given a negative survey result, Getz should build a small plant with an expected value of $2,400.

3. Continuing on the upper part of the tree and moving backward, we compute the expected value of conducting the market survey:

$$\text{EMV (node 1)} = (.45)(\$106,400) + (.55)(\$2,400) = \$49,200$$

4. If the market survey is *not* conducted:

$$EMV \text{ (node 6)} = (.6)(\$200,000) + (.4)(-\$180,000) = \$48,000$$
$$EMV \text{ (node 7)} = (.6)(\$100,000) + (.4)(-\$20,000) = \$52,000$$

The EMV of no plant is $0. Thus, building a small plant is the best choice, given the marketing research is not performed.

5. Because the expected monetary value of not conducting the survey is $52,000—vs. an EMV of $49,200 for conducting the study—the best choice is to *not seek marketing information*. Getz should build the small plant.

INSIGHT ▶ You can reduce complexity in a large decision tree by viewing and solving a number of smaller trees—start at the end branches of a large one. Take one decision at a time.

LEARNING EXERCISE ▶ Getz estimates that if he conducts a market survey, there is really only a 35% chance the results will indicate a favorable market for the sheds. How does the tree change? [Answer: The EMV of conducting the survey = $38,800, so Getz should still not do it.]

RELATED PROBLEMS ▶ A.21, A.25–A.29 (A.31, A.32 are available in MyOMLab)

The Poker Decision Process

We opened Module A with ex-dot-commer Paul Phillips's decision to go "all in" at the Legends of Poker tournament in Los Angeles. Example A8 shows how he computed the expected value. Problem A.30 gives you a chance to create a decision tree for this process.

Example A8

PHILLIPS'S POKER DECISION

As on the first page in this module, Paul Phillips is deciding whether to bet all his chips against poker star T.J. Cloutier. Phillips holds a pair of 7s. Phillips reasons that T.J. will fold (with 80% probability) if he does not have a pair of 5s or better, or very high cards like a jack, queen, king, or ace. But he also figures that a call would put $853,000 into the pot and surmises that even then, there is 45% chance his pair of 7s will win.

APPROACH ▶ Phillips does an expected monetary analysis.

SOLUTION ▶ If T.J. folds,

$$EMV = (.80)(\$99,000)$$

— The amount of money already in the pot

$$= \$79,200$$

If T.J. calls,

$$EMV = .20[(.45)(\$853,000) - \text{Phillips's bet of } \$422,000]$$

— the chance T.J. will call

$$= .20[\$383,850 - \$422,000]$$
$$= .20[-\$38,150] = -\$7,630$$

Overall EMV = $79,200 − $7,630 = $71,570

INSIGHT ▶ The overall EMV of $71,570 indicates that if this decision were to be made many times, the average payoff would be large. So Phillips decides to bet almost all of his chips. As it turns out, T.J. was holding a pair of jacks. Even though Phillips's decision in this instance did not work out, his analysis and procedure was the correct one.

LEARNING EXERCISE ▶ What would happen if the amount of money already in the pot were only $39,000? [Answer: The overall EMV = $23,570.]

RELATED PROBLEM ▶ A.30

Summary

This module examines two of the most widely used decision techniques—decision tables and decision trees. These techniques are especially useful for making decisions under risk. Many decisions in research and development, plant and equipment, and even new buildings and structures can be analyzed with these decision models. Problems in inventory control, aggregate planning, maintenance, scheduling, and production control also lend themselves to decision table and decision tree applications.

Key Terms

Big data (p. 679)
Decision table (p. 680)
Maximax (p. 681)
Maximin (p. 681)

Equally likely (p. 681)
Expected monetary value (EMV) (p. 682)
Expected value of perfect information (EVPI) (p. 683)

Expected value *with* perfect information (EVwPI) (p. 683)
Decision tree (p. 684)

Discussion Questions

1. Identify the six steps in the decision process.
2. Give an example of a good decision you made that resulted in a bad outcome. Also give an example of a bad decision you made that had a good outcome. Why was each decision good or bad?
3. What is the *equally likely* decision model?
4. Discuss the differences between decision making under certainty, under risk, and under uncertainty.
5. What is a decision tree?
6. Explain how decision trees might be used in several of the 10 OM decisions.
7. What is the expected value of perfect information (EVPI)?
8. What is the expected value *with* perfect information (EVwPI)?
9. Identify the five steps in analyzing a problem using a decision tree.
10. Why are the maximax and maximin strategies considered to be optimistic and pessimistic, respectively?
11. The expected value criterion is considered to be the rational criterion on which to base a decision. Is this true? Is it rational to consider risk?
12. When are decision trees most useful?

Using Software for Decision Models

Analyzing decision tables is straightforward with Excel, Excel OM, and POM for Windows. When decision trees are involved, Excel OM or commercial packages such as DPL, Tree Plan, and Supertree provide flexibility, power, and ease. POM for Windows will also analyze trees but does not have graphic capabilities.

CREATING AN EXCEL SPREADSHEET TO EVALUATE A DECISION TABLE

In Program A.1, we illustrate how you can build your own Excel spreadsheet to analyze decision making under uncertainty and under risk. The data from Getz Products in Examples A3 and A4 are used. Maximax, maximin, equally likely, and EMV are computed, along with EVPI.

✖ USING EXCEL OM

Excel OM allows decision makers to evaluate decisions quickly and to perform sensitivity analysis on the results. Program A.2 uses Excel OM to create the decision tree for Getz Products shown earlier in Example A6. The tool to create the tree is seen in the window on the right.

℗ USING POM FOR WINDOWS

POM for Windows can be used to calculate all of the information described in the decision tables and decision trees in this module. For details on how to use this software, please refer to Appendix IV.

Program A.1

An Excel Spreadsheet for Analyzing Data in Examples A3 and A4 for Getz Products

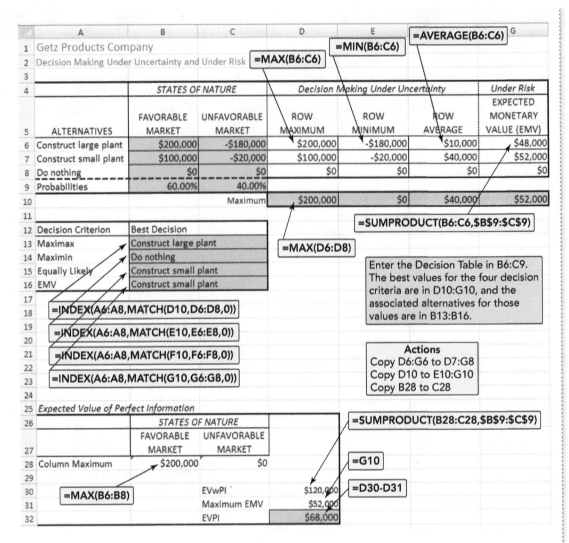

=MAX(B6:C6)

=MIN(B6:C6)

=AVERAGE(B6:C6)

	ALTERNATIVES	FAVORABLE MARKET	UNFAVORABLE MARKET	ROW MAXIMUM	ROW MINIMUM	ROW AVERAGE	EXPECTED MONETARY VALUE (EMV)
		STATES OF NATURE		Decision Making Under Uncertainty			Under Risk
6	Construct large plant	$200,000	-$180,000	$200,000	-$180,000	$10,000	$48,000
7	Construct small plant	$100,000	-$20,000	$100,000	-$20,000	$40,000	$52,000
8	Do nothing	$0	$0	$0	$0	$0	$0
9	Probabilities	60.00%	40.00%				
10			Maximum	$200,000	$0	$40,000	$52,000

=SUMPRODUCT(B6:C6,$B$9:$C$9)

=MAX(D6:D8)

Decision Criterion	Best Decision
Maximax	Construct large plant
Maximin	Do nothing
Equally Likely	Construct small plant
EMV	Construct small plant

=INDEX(A6:A8,MATCH(D10,D6:D8,0))

=INDEX(A6:A8,MATCH(E10,E6:E8,0))

=INDEX(A6:A8,MATCH(F10,F6:F8,0))

=INDEX(A6:A8,MATCH(G10,G6:G8,0))

Enter the Decision Table in B6:C9. The best values for the four decision criteria are in D10:G10, and the associated alternatives for those values are in B13:B16.

Actions
Copy D6:G6 to D7:G8
Copy D10 to E10:G10
Copy B28 to C28

Expected Value of Perfect Information

		FAVORABLE MARKET	UNFAVORABLE MARKET	
		STATES OF NATURE		
28	Column Maximum	$200,000	$0	
30			EVwPI	$120,000
31			Maximum EMV	$52,000
32			EVPI	$68,000

=SUMPRODUCT(B28:C28,$B$9:$C$9)

=G10

=D30-D31

=MAX(B6:B8)

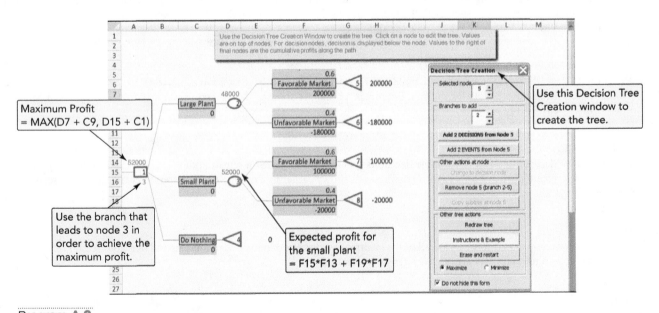

Maximum Profit = MAX(D7 + C9, D15 + C1)

Use the branch that leads to node 3 in order to achieve the maximum profit.

Expected profit for the small plant = F15*F13 + F19*F17

Use this Decision Tree Creation window to create the tree.

Program A.2

Getz Products' Decision Tree Using Excel OM

Solved Problems   Virtual Office Hours help is available in MyOMLab.

SOLVED PROBLEM A.1

Stella Yan Hua is considering the possibility of opening a small dress shop on Fairbanks Avenue, a few blocks from the university. She has located a good mall that attracts students. Her options are to open a small shop, a medium-sized shop, or no shop at all. The market for a dress shop can be good, average, or bad. The probabilities for these three possibilities are .2 for a good market, .5 for an average market, and .3 for a bad market. The net profit or loss for the medium-sized or small shops for the various market conditions are given in the adjacent table. Building no shop at all yields no loss and no gain. What do you recommend?

	STATES OF NATURE		
ALTERNATIVES	GOOD MARKET ($)	AVERAGE MARKET ($)	BAD MARKET ($)
Small shop	75,000	25,000	−40,000
Medium-sized shop	100,000	35,000	−60,000
No shop	0	0	0
Probabilities	.20	.50	.30

SOLUTION

The problem can be solved by computing the expected monetary value (EMV) for each alternative:

$$\text{EMV (Small shop)} = (.2)(\$75,000) + (.5)(\$25,000) + (.3)(-\$40,000) = \$15,500$$
$$\text{EMV (Medium-sized shop)} = (.2)(\$100,000) + (.5)(\$35,000) + (.3)(-\$60,000) = \$19,500$$
$$\text{EMV (No shop)} = (.2)(\$0) + (.5)(\$0) + (.3)(\$0) = \$0$$

As you can see, the best decision is to build the medium-sized shop. The EMV for this alternative is $19,500.

SOLVED PROBLEM A.2

T.S. Amer's Ski Shop in Nevada has a 100-day season. T.S. has established the probability of various store traffic, based on historical records of skiing conditions, as indicated in the table to the right. T.S. has four merchandising plans, each focusing on a popular name brand. Each plan yields a daily net profit as noted in the table. He also has a meteorologist friend who, for a small fee, will accurately tell tomorrow's weather so T.S. can implement one of his four merchandising plans.
a) What is the expected monetary value (EMV) under risk?
b) What is the expected value *with* perfect information (EVwPI)?
c) What is the expected value of perfect information (EVPI)?

DECISION ALTERNATIVES (MERCHANDISING PLAN FOCUSING ON:)	TRAFFIC IN STORE BECAUSE OF SKI CONDITIONS (STATES OF NATURE)			
	1	2	3	4
Patagonia	$40	92	20	48
North Face	50	84	10	52
Cloud Veil	35	80	40	64
Columbia	45	72	10	60
Probabilities	.20	.25	.30	.25

SOLUTION
a) The highest expected monetary value under risk is:

$$\text{EMV (Patagonia)} = .20(40) + .25(92) + .30(20) + .25(48) = \$49$$
$$\text{EMV (North Face)} = .20(50) + .25(84) + .30(10) + .25(52) = \$47$$
$$\text{EMV (Cloud Veil)} = .20(35) + .25(80) + .30(40) + .25(64) = \$55$$
$$\text{EMV (Columbia)} = .20(45) + .25(72) + .30(10) + .25(60) = \$45$$

So the maximum EMV = $55
b) The expected value *with* perfect information is:

$$\text{EVwPI} = .20(50) + .25(92) + .30(40) + .25(64)$$
$$= 10 + 23 + 12 + 16 = \$61$$

c) The expected value of perfect information is:

$$\text{EVPI} = \text{EVwPI} - \text{Maximum EMV} = 61 - 55 = \$6$$

SOLVED PROBLEM A.3

Daily demand for cases of Tidy Bowl cleaner at Ravinder Nath's Supermarket has always been 5, 6, or 7 cases. Develop a decision tree that illustrates her decision alternatives as to whether to stock 5, 6, or 7 cases.

SOLUTION

The decision tree is shown in Figure A.4.

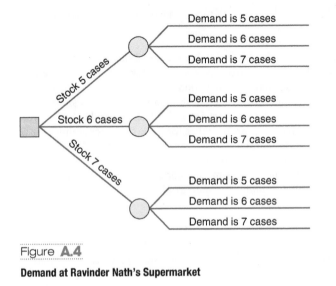

Figure **A.4**

Demand at Ravinder Nath's Supermarket

Problems   *Note:* **PX** *means the problem may be solved with POM for Windows and/or Excel OM.*

Problems A.1–A.20 relate to Types of Decision-Making Environments

•   **A.1**   Given the following conditional value table, determine the appropriate decision under uncertainty using:
a) Maximax
b) Maximin
c) Equally likely **PX**

	STATES OF NATURE		
ALTERNATIVES	VERY FAVORABLE MARKET	AVERAGE MARKET	UNFAVORABLE MARKET
Build new plant	$350,000	$240,000	−$300,000
Subcontract	$180,000	$ 90,000	−$ 20,000
Overtime	$110,000	$ 60,000	−$ 10,000
Do nothing	$ 0	$ 0	$ 0

• • • **A.2**   Even though independent gasoline stations have been having a difficult time, Ian Langella has been thinking about starting his own independent gasoline station. Ian's problem is to decide how large his station should be. The annual returns will depend on both the size of his station and a number of marketing factors related to the oil industry and demand for gasoline. After a careful analysis, Ian developed the following table:

SIZE OF FIRST STATION	GOOD MARKET ($)	FAIR MARKET ($)	POOR MARKET ($)
Small	50,000	20,000	−10,000
Medium	80,000	30,000	−20,000
Large	100,000	30,000	−40,000
Very large	300,000	25,000	−160,000

For example, if Ian constructs a small station and the market is good, he will realize a profit of $50,000.
a) Develop a decision table for this decision, like the one illustrated in Table A.2 earlier.
b) What is the maximax decision?
c) What is the maximin decision?

d) What is the equally likely decision?
e) Develop a decision tree. Assume each outcome is equally likely, then find the highest EMV. **PX**

•   **A.3**   Andrew Thomas, a sandwich vendor at Hard Rock Cafe's annual Rockfest, created a table of conditional values for the various alternatives (stocking decision) and states of nature (size of crowd):

	STATES OF NATURE (DEMAND)		
ALTERNATIVES	BIG	AVERAGE	SMALL
Large stock	$22,000	$12,000	−$2,000
Average stock	$14,000	$10,000	$6,000
Small stock	$ 9,000	$ 8,000	$4,000

The probabilities associated with the states of nature are 0.3 for a big demand, 0.5 for an average demand, and 0.2 for a small demand.
a) Determine the alternative that provides Andrew the greatest expected monetary value (EMV).
b) Compute the expected value of perfect information (EVPI).

• • **A.4**   Jeffrey Helm owns a health and fitness center called Bulk-Up in Harrisburg. He is considering adding more floor space to meet increasing demand. He will either add no floor space (N), a moderate area of floor space (M), a large area of floor space (L), or an area of floor space that doubles the size of the facility (D). Demand will either stay fixed, increase slightly, or increase greatly. The following are the changes in Bulk-Up's annual profits under each combination of expansion level and demand change level:

DEMAND CHANGE	EXPANSION LEVEL			
	N	M	L	D
Fixed	$ 0	−$4,000	−$10,000	−$50,000
Slight increase	$2,000	$8,000	$ 6,000	$ 4,000
Major increase	$3,000	$9,000	$20,000	$40,000

Jeffrey is risk averse and wishes to use the maximin criterion.

a) What are his decision alternatives and what are the states of nature?

b) What should he do? **Px**

• **A.5** Howard Weiss, Inc., is considering building a sensitive new radiation scanning device. His managers believe that there is a probability of 0.4 that the ATR Co. will come out with a competitive product. If Weiss adds an assembly line for the product and ATR Co. does not follow with a competitive product, Weiss's expected profit is $40,000; if Weiss adds an assembly line and ATR follows suit, Weiss still expects $10,000 profit. If Weiss adds a new plant addition and ATR does not produce a competitive product, Weiss expects a profit of $600,000; if ATR does compete for this market, Weiss expects a loss of $100,000.

a) Determine the EMV of each decision.

b) Compute the expected value of perfect information. **Px**

• • • **A.6** Jerry Bildery's factory is considering three approaches for meeting an expected increase in demand. These three approaches are increasing capacity, using overtime, and buying more equipment. Demand will increase either slightly (S), moderately (M), or greatly (G). The profits for each approach under each possible scenario are as follows:

APPROACH	DEMAND SCENARIO		
	S	M	G
Increasing capacity	$700,000	$700,000	$ 700,000
Using overtime	$500,000	$600,000	$1,000,000
Buying equipment	$600,000	$800,000	$ 800,000

Since the goal is to maximize, and Jerry is risk-neutral, he decides to use the *equally likely* decision criterion to make the decision as to which approach to use. According to this criterion, which approach should be used?

• **A.7** The following payoff table provides profits based on various possible decision alternatives and various levels of demand at Robert Klassan's print shop:

	DEMAND	
	LOW	HIGH
Alternative 1	$10,000	$30,000
Alternative 2	$ 5,000	$40,000
Alternative 3	–$ 2,000	$50,000

The probability of low demand is 0.4, whereas the probability of high demand is 0.6.

a) What is the highest possible expected monetary value?

b) What is the expected value *with* perfect information (EVwPI)?

c) Calculate the expected value of perfect information for this situation. **Px**

• **A.8** Leah Johnson, director of Urgent Care of Brookline, wants to increase capacity to provide low-cost flu shots but must decide whether to do so by hiring another full-time nurse or by using part-time nurses. The table below shows the expected *costs* of the two options for three possible demand levels:

ALTERNATIVES	STATES OF NATURE		
	LOW DEMAND	MEDIUM DEMAND	HIGH DEMAND
Hire full-time	$300	$500	$ 700
Hire part-time	$ 0	$350	$1,000
Probabilities	.2	.5	.3

a) Using expected value, what should Ms. Johnson do?

b) Draw an appropriate decision tree showing payoffs and probabilities. **Px**

• • **A.9** Zhu Manufacturing is considering the introduction of a family of new products. Long-term demand for the product group is somewhat predictable, so the manufacturer must be concerned with the risk of choosing a process that is inappropriate. Faye Zhu is VP of operations. She can choose among batch manufacturing or custom manufacturing, or she can invest in group technology. Faye won't be able to forecast demand accurately until after she makes the process choice. Demand will be classified into four compartments: poor, fair, good, and excellent. The table below indicates the payoffs (profits) associated with each process/demand combination, as well as the probabilities of each long-term demand level:

	POOR	FAIR	GOOD	EXCELLENT
Probability	.1	.4	.3	.2
Batch	–$ 200,000	$1,000,000	$1,200,000	$1,300,000
Custom	$ 100,000	$ 300,000	$ 700,000	$ 800,000
Group technology	–$1,000,000	–$ 500,000	$ 500,000	$2,000,000

a) Based on expected value, what choice offers the greatest gain?

b) What would Faye Zhu be willing to pay for a forecast that would accurately determine the level of demand in the future? **Px**

• • **A.10** Consider the following decision table, which Joe Blackburn has developed for Vanderbilt Enterprises:

DECISION ALTERNATIVES	STATES OF NATURE		
	LOW	MEDIUM	HIGH
A	$40	$100	$60
B	$85	$ 60	$70
C	$60	$ 70	$70
D	$65	$ 75	$70
E	$70	$ 65	$80
Probability	.40	.20	.40

Which decision alternative maximizes the expected value of the payoff? **Px**

• • **A.11** The University of Miami bookstore stocks textbooks in preparation for sales each semester. It normally relies on departmental forecasts and preregistration records to determine how many copies of a text are needed. Preregistration shows 90 operations management students enrolled, but bookstore manager Vaidy Jayaraman has second thoughts, based on his intuition and some historical evidence. Vaidy believes that the distribution of sales may range from 70 to 90 units, according to the following probability model:

Demand	70	75	80	85	90
Probability	.15	.30	.30	.20	.05

This textbook costs the bookstore $82 and sells for $112. Any unsold copies can be returned to the publisher, less a restocking fee and shipping, for a net refund of $36.

a) Construct the table of conditional profits.

b) How many copies should the bookstore stock to achieve highest expected value? **Px**

•• **A.12**   Palmer Jam Company is a small manufacturer of several different jam products. One product is an organic jam that has no preservatives, sold to retail outlets. Susan Palmer must decide how many cases of jam to manufacture each month. The probability that demand will be 6 cases is .1, for 7 cases it is .3, for 8 cases it is .5, and for 9 cases it is .1. The cost of every case is $45, and the price Susan gets for each case is $95. Unfortunately, any cases not sold by the end of the month are of no value as a result of spoilage. How many cases should Susan manufacture each month? **Px**

•• **A.13**   Deborah Hollwager, a concessionaire for the Amway Center in Orlando, has developed a table of conditional values for the various alternatives (stocking decisions) and states of nature (size of crowd):

	STATES OF NATURE (SIZE OF CROWD)		
ALTERNATIVES	LARGE	AVERAGE	SMALL
Large inventory	$20,000	$10,000	–$2,000
Average inventory	$15,000	$12,000	$6,000
Small inventory	$ 9,000	$ 6,000	$5,000

If the probabilities associated with the states of nature are 0.3 for a large crowd, 0.5 for an average crowd, and 0.2 for a small crowd, determine:
a) The alternative that provides the greatest expected monetary value (EMV).
b) The expected value of perfect information (EVPI). **Px**

•••• **A.14** The city of Belgrade, Serbia, is contemplating building a second airport to relieve congestion at the main airport and is considering two potential sites, X and Y. Hard Rock Hotels would like to purchase land to build a hotel at the new airport. The value of land has been rising in anticipation and is expected to skyrocket once the city decides between sites X and Y. Consequently, Hard Rock would like to purchase land now. Hard Rock will sell the land if the city chooses not to locate the airport nearby. Hard Rock has four choices: (1) buy land at X, (2) buy land at Y, (3) buy land at both X and Y, or (4) do nothing. Hard Rock has collected the following data (which are in millions of euros):

	SITE X	SITE Y
Current purchase price	27	15
Profits if airport and hotel built at this site*	45	30
Sale price if airport not built at this site	9	6

*The second row of the table represents net operating profits from the hotel, not including the upfront cost of land.

Hard Rock determines there is a 45% chance the airport will be built at X (hence, a 55% chance it will be built at Y).
a) Set up the decision table.
b) What should Hard Rock decide to do to maximize total net profit? **Px**

Additional problems **A.15–A.20** *are available in* MyOMLab.

Problems A.21–A.32 relate to Decision Trees

••• **A.21**   Ronald Lau, chief engineer at South Dakota Electronics, has to decide whether to build a new state-of-the-art processing facility. If the new facility works, the company could realize a profit of $200,000. If it fails, South Dakota Electronics could lose $180,000. At this time, Lau estimates a 60% chance that the new process will fail.

The other option is to build a pilot plant and then decide whether to build a complete facility. The pilot plant would cost $10,000 to build. Lau estimates a 50–50 chance that the pilot plant will work. If the pilot plant works, there is a 90% probability that the complete plant, if it is built, will also work. If the pilot plant does not work, there is only a 20% chance that the complete project (if it is constructed) will work. Lau faces a dilemma. Should he build the plant? Should he build the pilot project and then make a decision? Help Lau by analyzing this problem. **Px**

•• **A.22**   Dwayne Whitten, president of Whitten Industries, is considering whether to build a manufacturing plant in north Texas. His decision is summarized in the following table:

ALTERNATIVES	FAVORABLE MARKET	UNFAVORABLE MARKET
Build large plant	$400,000	–$300,000
Build small plant	$ 80,000	–$ 10,000
Don't build	$ 0	$ 0
Market probabilities	0.4	0.6

a) Construct a decision tree.
b) Determine the best strategy using expected monetary value (EMV).
c) What is the expected value of perfect information (EVPI)? **Px**

•• **A.23**   Deborah Kellogg buys Breathalyzer test sets for the Winter Park Police Department. The quality of the test sets from her two suppliers is indicated in the following table:

PERCENT DEFECTIVE	PROBABILITY FOR WINTER PARK TECHNOLOGY	PROBABILITY FOR DAYTON ENTERPRISES
1	.70	.30
3	.20	.30
5	.10	.40

For example, the probability of getting a batch of tests that are 1% defective from Winter Park Technology is .70. Because Kellogg orders 10,000 tests per order, this would mean that there is a .70 probability of getting 100 defective tests out of the 10,000 tests if Winter Park Technology is used to fill the order. A defective Breathalyzer test set can be repaired for $0.50. Although the quality of the test sets of the second supplier, Dayton Enterprises, is lower, it will sell an order of 10,000 test sets for $37 less than Winter Park.

Jabiru/Shutterstock

a) Develop a decision tree.
b) Which supplier should Kellogg use? **Px**

· **A.24**   Joseph Biggs owns his own ice cream truck and lives 30 miles from a Florida beach resort. The sale of his products is highly dependent on his location and on the weather. At the resort, his profit will be $120 per day in fair weather, $10 per day in bad weather. At home, his profit will be $70 in fair weather and $55 in bad weather. Assume that on any particular day, the weather service suggests a 40% chance of foul weather.

a) Construct Joseph's decision tree.

b) What decision is recommended by the expected value criterion? **Px**

·· **A.25**   Jonatan Jelen is considering opening a bicycle shop in New York City. Jonatan enjoys biking, but this is to be a business endeavor from which he expects to make a living. He can open a small shop, a large shop, or no shop at all. Because there will be a 5-year lease on the building that Jonatan is thinking about using, he wants to make sure he makes the correct decision. Jonatan is also thinking about hiring his old marketing professor to conduct a marketing research study to see if there is a market for his services. The results of such a study could be either favorable or unfavorable. Develop a decision tree for Jonatan. **Px**

·· **A.26**   F. J. Brewerton Retailers, Inc., must decide whether to build a small or a large facility at a new location in Omaha. Demand at the location will either be low or high, with probabilities 0.4 and 0.6, respectively. If Brewerton builds a small facility and demand proves to be high, he then has the option of expanding the facility. If a small facility is built and demand proves to be high, and then the retailer expands the facility, the payoff is $270,000. If a small facility is built and demand proves to be high, but Brewerton then decides not to expand the facility, the payoff is $223,000.

If a small facility is built and demand proves to be low, then there is no option to expand and the payoff is $200,000. If a large facility is built and demand proves to be low, Brewerton then has the option of stimulating demand through local advertising. If he does not exercise this option, then the payoff is $40,000. If he does exercise the advertising option, then the response to advertising will either be modest or sizable, with probabilities of 0.3 and 0.7, respectively. If the response is modest, the payoff is $20,000. If it is sizable, the payoff is $220,000. Finally, if a large facility is built and demand proves to be high, then no advertising is needed and the payoff is $800,000.

a) What should Brewerton do to maximize his expected payoff?

b) What is the value of this expected payoff?

··· **A.27**   Philip Musa can build either a large electronics section or a small one in his Birmingham drugstore. He can also gather additional information or simply do nothing. If he gathers additional information, the results could suggest either a favorable or an unfavorable market, but it would cost him $3,000 to gather the information. Musa believes that there is a 50–50 chance that the information will be favorable. If the market is favorable, Musa will earn $15,000 with a large section or $5,000 with a small one. With an unfavorable electronics market, however, Musa could lose $20,000 with a large section or $10,000 with a small section. Without gathering additional information, Musa estimates that the probability of a favorable market is .7. A favorable report from the study would increase the probability of a favorable market to .9. Furthermore, an unfavorable report from the additional information would decrease the probability of a favorable market to .4. Of course, Musa could ignore these numbers and do nothing. What is your advice to Musa?

···· **A.28** Jeff Kaufmann's machine shop sells a variety of machines for job shops. A customer wants to purchase a model XPO2 drilling machine from Jeff's store. The model XPO2 sells for $180,000, but Jeff is out of XPO2s. The customer says he will wait for Jeff to get a model XPO2 in stock. Jeff knows that there is a wholesale market for XPO2s from which he can purchase an XPO2. Jeff can buy an XPO2 today for $150,000, or he can wait a day and buy an XPO2 (if one is available) tomorrow for $125,000. If at least one XPO2 is still available tomorrow, Jeff can wait until the day after tomorrow and buy an XPO2 (if one is still available) for $110,000.

There is a 0.40 probability that there will be no model XPO2s available tomorrow. If there are model XPO2s available tomorrow, there is a 0.70 probability that by the day after tomorrow, there will be no model XPO2s available in the wholesale market. Three days from now, it is certain that no model XPO2s will be available on the wholesale market. What is the maximum expected profit that Jeff can achieve? What should Jeff do?

···· **A.29** Louisiana is busy designing new lottery scratch-off games. In the latest game, Bayou Boondoggle, the player is instructed to scratch off one spot: A, B, or C. A can reveal "Loser," "Win $1," or "Win $50." B can reveal "Loser" or "Take a Second Chance." C can reveal "Loser" or "Win $500." On the second chance, the player is instructed to scratch off D or E. D can reveal "Loser" or "Win $1." E can reveal "Loser" or "Win $10." The probabilities at A are .9, .09, and .01. The probabilities at B are .8 and .2. The probabilities at C are .999 and .001. The probabilities at D are .5 and .5. Finally, the probabilities at E are .95 and .05. Draw the decision tree that represents this scenario. Use proper symbols and label all branches clearly. Calculate the expected value of this game.

···· **A.30** On the opening page of Module A and in Example A8, we follow the poker decision made by Paul Phillips against veteran T.J. Cloutier. Create a decision tree that corresponds with the decision made by Phillips. **Px**

Additional problems **A.31–A.32** *are available in* MyOMLab.

CASE STUDY

Warehouse Tenting at the Port of Miami

The Collector's Choice Inc. (CCI), a luxury car import company, has an old warehouse at the Port of Miami, Florida, where it temporarily stores expensive sports cars and automotive parts that arrive from Europe. This summer, CCI has noticed that the termite infestation in the warehouse has escalated to a point where tenting cannot be postponed anymore. (Tenting is the process of wrapping a building inside a huge tent that is subsequently filled with a poisonous gas capable of killing most forms of life inside, including insects, plants, pets, and human beings.) CCI's pest control company's contract specifies a to-do list of pre-tenting tasks, which include:

◆ Turning off all air-conditioning units and opening all windows of the warehouse
◆ Turning off all internal and external lights, including those operating on a timer
◆ Pruning all outdoor vegetation at least 18″ away from the warehouse
◆ Soaking the soil around the warehouse on the first day of tenting

Halima Ahkdar/Shutterstock

The requirement of opening all windows is particularly worrisome to CCI because it means turning off the alarm system, leaving the warehouse vulnerable to burglary for 48 hours—the required amount of time for the poisonous gas to do its job. Therefore, Alex Ferrari, the warehouse manager, is thinking about hiring a security company to monitor the facility during that period. CCI's property insurance deductible is $25,000, and Alex is assuming that if thieves are willing to enter a building full of poisonous gas to steal something, they would certainly take more than $25,000 worth of parts—or even an entire car!

After making a few phone calls, Alex gets in touch with ProGuard, a trustworthy local security company that charges $150 per hour to have a security guard stationed outside their warehouse. The city of Miami police records indicate that about 30% of businesses that left their facilities unattended during tenting reported stolen property in the past 3 years. Although Alex thinks ProGuard's prices are reasonable, and having a guard outside the warehouse would certainly help, he is still not sure whether it is worth spending the extra money. After all, ProGuard's contract does not guarantee the protection it provides is infallible. In fact, an analysis of the company's records indicates that 3% of their clients were burglarized over the past 3 years. (Despite this figure, ProGuard is still the best security company in the area.)

Discussion Questions

1. Create a decision tree analysis to help decide whether Alex Ferrari should hire ProGuard's services.
2. Come up with a simple rule of thumb that can be applied to decisions of this nature, given any deductible amount d, extra surveillance cost c, and burglary probabilities p_1 (without surveillance) and p_2 (with surveillance).
3. Does your decision based on the tree guarantee success? Why or why not?

Source: Professor Tallys Yunes, University of Miami. Reprinted with permission.

● **Additional Case Studies:** Visit MyOMLab for these additional free case studies:
Arctic, Inc.: A refrigeration company has several major options with regard to capacity and expansion.
Ski Right Corp.: Which of four manufacturers should be selected to manufacture ski helmets?
Tom Tucker's Liver Transplant: An executive must decide whether or not to opt for a dangerous surgery.

Endnote

1. To review these other statistical terms, refer to Tutorial 1, "Statistical Review for Managers," in MyOMLab.

Module A *Rapid* Review

Main Heading	Review Material	MyOMLab
THE DECISION PROCESS IN OPERATIONS (pp. 678–679)	To achieve the goals of their organizations, managers must understand how decisions are made and know which decision-making tools to use. Overcoming uncertainty is a manager's mission. Decision tables and decision trees are used in a wide number of OM situations. ■ **Big data**—The huge amount of economic, production, and consumer data now being collected in digital form.	Concept Questions: 1.1–1.4
FUNDAMENTALS OF DECISION MAKING (pp. 679–680)	*Alternative*—A course of action or strategy that may be chosen by a decision maker. *State of nature*—An occurrence or a situation over which a decision maker has little or no control. Symbols used in a decision tree: 1. ☐—A decision node from which one of several alternatives may be selected. 2. ○—A state-of-nature node out of which one state of nature will occur. When constructing a decision tree, we must be sure that all alternatives and states of nature are in their correct and logical places and that we include *all* possible alternatives and states of nature, usually including the "do nothing" option.	Concept Questions: 2.1–2.4
DECISION TABLES (p. 680)	■ **Decision table**—A tabular means of analyzing decision alternatives and states of nature. A decision table is sometimes called a payoff table. For any alternative and a particular state of nature, there is a *consequence*, or an *outcome*, which is usually expressed as a monetary value; this is called the *conditional value*.	Concept Questions: 3.1–3.4
TYPES OF DECISION-MAKING ENVIRONMENTS (pp. 681–684)	There are three decision-making environments: (1) decision making under uncertainty, (2) decision making under risk, and (3) decision making under certainty. When there is complete *uncertainty* about which state of nature in a decision environment may occur (i.e., when we cannot even assess probabilities for each possible outcome), we rely on three decision methods: (1) maximax, (2) maximin, and (3) equally likely. ■ **Maximax**—A criterion that finds an alternative that maximizes the maximum outcome. ■ **Maximin**—A criterion that finds an alternative that maximizes the minimum outcome. ■ **Equally likely**—A criterion that assigns equal probability to each state of nature. Maximax is also called an "optimistic" decision criterion, while maximin is also called a "pessimistic" decision criterion. Maximax and maximin present best case/worst case planning scenarios. Decision making under risk relies on probabilities. The states of nature must be mutually exclusive and collectively exhaustive, and their probabilities must sum to 1. ■ **Expected monetary value (EMV)**—The expected payout or value of a variable that has different possible states of nature, each with an associated probability. The EMV represents the expected value or *mean* return for each alternative *if we could repeat this decision (or similar types of decisions) a large number of times*. The EMV for an alternative is the sum of all possible payoffs from the alternative, each weighted by the probability of that payoff occurring: EMV (Alternative i) = (Payoff of 1st state of nature) × (Probability of 1st of state of nature) + (Payoff of 2nd state of nature) × (Probability of 2nd state of nature) + ... + (Payoff of last state of nature) × (Probability of last state of nature) ■ **Expected value of perfect information (EVPI)**—The difference between the payoff under perfect information and the payoff under risk. ■ **Expected value *with* perfect information (EVwPI)**—The expected (average) return if perfect information is available. EVPI represents an upper bound on what you would be willing to spend on state-of-nature information: EVPI = EVwPI − Maximum EMV EVwPI = (Best outcome for 1st state of nature) × (Probability of 1st state of nature) + (Best outcome for 2nd state of nature) × (Probability of 2nd state of nature) + ... + (Best outcome for last state of nature) × (Probability of last state of nature)	Concept Questions: 4.1–4.4 Problems: A.1–A.20 Virtual Office Hours for Solved Problems: A.1, A.2

Main Heading	Review Material	MyOMLab
DECISION TREES (pp. 684–688)	When there are two or more sequential decisions, and later decisions are based on the outcome of prior ones, the decision tree (as opposed to decision table) approach becomes appropriate. ■ **Decision tree**—A graphical means of analyzing decision alternatives and states of nature. Analyzing problems with *decision trees* involves five steps: 1. Define the problem. 2. Structure or draw the decision tree. 3. Assign probabilities to the states of nature. 4. Estimate payoffs for each possible combination of decision alternatives and states of nature. 5. Solve the problem by computing the expected monetary values (EMV) for each state-of-nature node. This is done by working *backward*—that is, by starting at the right of the tree and working back to decision nodes on the left: Decision trees force managers to examine all possible outcomes, including unfavorable ones. A manager is also forced to make decisions in a logical, sequential manner. Short parallel lines on a decision tree mean "prune" that branch, as it is less favorable than another available option and may be dropped.	Concept Questions: 5.1–5.4 Problems: A.21–A.32 Virtual Office Hours for Solved Problem: A.3

Self Test

■ **Before taking the self-test,** refer to the learning objectives listed at the beginning of the module and the key terms listed at the end of the module.

LO A.1 On a decision tree, at each state-of-nature node:
a) the alternative with the greatest EMV is selected.
b) an EMV is calculated.
c) all probabilities are added together.
d) the branch with the highest probability is selected.

LO A.2 In decision table terminology, a course of action or a strategy that may be chosen by a decision maker is called a(n):
a) payoff.
b) alternative.
c) state of nature.
d) all of the above.

LO A.3 If probabilities are available to the decision maker, then the decision-making environment is called:
a) certainty.   b) uncertainty.
c) risk.   d) none of the above.

LO A.4 What is the EMV for Alternative 1 in the following decision table?

	STATE OF NATURE	
Alternative	S1	S2
A1	$15,000	$20,000
A2	$10,000	$30,000
Probability	0.30	0.70

a) $15,000   b) $17,000
c) $17,500   d) $18,500
e) $20,000

LO A.5 The most that a person should pay for perfect information is:
a) the EVPI.
b) the maximum EMV minus the minimum EMV.
c) the minimum EMV.
d) the maximum EMV.

LO A.6 On a decision tree, once the tree has been drawn and the payoffs and probabilities have been placed on the tree, the analysis (computing EMVs and selecting the best alternative):
a) is done by working backward (starting on the right and moving to the left).
b) is done by working forward (starting on the left and moving to the right).
c) is done by starting at the top of the tree and moving down.
d) is done by starting at the bottom of the tree and moving up.

LO A.7 A decision tree is preferable to a decision table when:
a) a number of sequential decisions are to be made.
b) probabilities are available.
c) the maximax criterion is used.
d) the objective is to maximize regret.

Answers: LO A.1. b; LO A.2. b; LO A.3. c; LO A.4. d; LO A.5. a; LO A.6. a; LO A.7. a.

Linear Programming

MODULE OUTLINE

Alaska Airlines

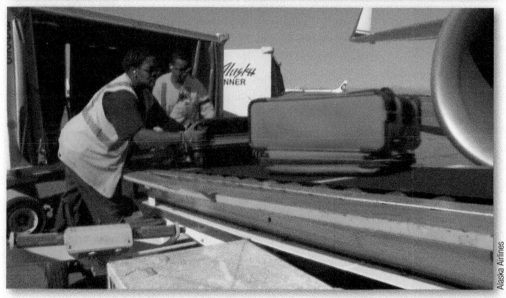

Alaska Airlines

The storm front closed in quickly on Boston's Logan Airport, shutting it down without warning. The heavy snowstorms and poor visibility sent airline passengers and ground crew scurrying. Because airlines use linear programming (LP) to schedule flights, hotels, crews, and refueling, LP has a direct impact on profitability. If an airline gets a major weather disruption at one of its hubs, a lot of flights may get canceled, which means a lot of crews and airplanes in the wrong places. LP is the tool that helps airlines unsnarl and cope with this weather mess.

Paul Italiano/Alamy

Why Use Linear Programming?

Many operations management decisions involve trying to make the most effective use of an organization's resources. Resources typically include machinery (such as planes, in the case of an airline), labor (such as pilots), money, time, and raw materials (such as jet fuel). These resources may be used to produce products (such as machines, furniture, food, or clothing) or services (such as airline schedules, advertising policies, or investment decisions). Linear programming (LP) is a widely used mathematical technique designed to help operations managers plan and make the decisions necessary to allocate resources.

A few examples of problems in which LP has been successfully applied in operations management are:

1. Scheduling school buses to *minimize* the total distance traveled when carrying students
2. Allocating police patrol units to high crime areas to *minimize* response time to 911 calls
3. Scheduling tellers at banks so that needs are met during each hour of the day while *minimizing* the total cost of labor
4. Selecting the product mix in a factory to make best use of machine- and labor-hours available while *maximizing* the firm's profit
5. Picking blends of raw materials in feed mills to produce finished feed combinations at *minimum* cost
6. Determining the distribution system that will *minimize* total shipping cost from several warehouses to various market locations
7. Developing a production schedule that will satisfy future demands for a firm's product and at the same time *minimize* total production and inventory costs
8. Allocating space for a tenant mix in a new shopping mall to *maximize* revenues to the leasing company

Linear programming (LP)
A mathematical technique designed to help operations managers plan and make decisions necessary to allocate resources.

VIDEO B.1
Scheduling Challenges at Alaska Airlines

Requirements of a Linear Programming Problem

All LP problems have four requirements: an objective, constraints, alternatives, and linearity:

1. LP problems seek to *maximize* or *minimize* some quantity (usually profit or cost). We refer to this property as the objective function of an LP problem. The major objective of a typical firm is to maximize dollar profits in the long run. In the case of a trucking or airline distribution system, the objective might be to minimize shipping costs.

2. The presence of restrictions, or constraints, limits the degree to which we can pursue our objective. For example, deciding how many units of each product in a firm's product line to manufacture is restricted by available labor and machinery. We want, therefore, to maximize or minimize a quantity (the objective function) subject to limited resources (the constraints).

3. There must be *alternative courses of action* to choose from. For example, if a company produces three different products, management may use LP to decide how to allocate among them its limited production resources (of labor, machinery, and so on). If there were no alternatives to select from, we would not need LP.

4. The objective and constraints in linear programming problems must be expressed in terms of *linear equations* or inequalities. Linearity implies proportionality and additivity. If x_1 and x_2 are decision variables, there can be no products (e.g., $x_1 x_2$) or powers (e.g., x_1^3) in the objective or constraints. For example, the expression $5x_1 + 8x_2 \leq 250$ is linear; however, the expression $5x_1 + 8x_2 - 2x_1 x_2 \leq 300$ is not linear.

Objective function
A mathematical expression in linear programming that maximizes or minimizes some quantity (often profit or cost, but any goal may be used).

Constraints
Restrictions that limit the degree to which a manager can pursue an objective.

Formulating Linear Programming Problems

One of the most common linear programming applications is the *product-mix problem*. Two or more products are usually produced using limited resources. The company would like to determine how many units of each product it should produce to maximize overall profit given its limited resources. Let's look at an example.

◆ **STUDENT TIP**
Here we set up an LP example that we will follow for most of this module.

Glickman Electronics Example

The Glickman Electronics Company in Washington, DC, produces two products: (1) the Glickman x-pod and (2) the Glickman BlueBerry. The production process for each product is similar in that both require a certain number of hours of electronic work and a certain number of labor-hours in the assembly department. Each x-pod takes 4 hours of electronic work and 2 hours in the assembly shop. Each BlueBerry requires 3 hours in electronics and 1 hour in assembly. During the current production period, 240 hours of electronic time are available, and 100 hours of assembly department time are available. Each x-pod sold yields a profit of $7; each BlueBerry produced may be sold for a $5 profit.

Glickman's problem is to determine the best possible combination of x-pods and BlueBerrys to manufacture to reach the maximum profit. This product-mix situation can be formulated as a linear programming problem.

We begin by summarizing the information needed to formulate and solve this problem (see Table B.1). Further, let's introduce some simple notation for use in the objective function and constraints. Let:

ACTIVE MODEL B.1
This example is further illustrated in Active Model B.1 in MyOMLab.

$$X_1 = \text{number of x-pods to be produced}$$
$$X_2 = \text{number of BlueBerrys to be produced}$$

TABLE B.1	Glickman Electronics Company Problem Data		
	HOURS REQUIRED TO PRODUCE ONE UNIT		
DEPARTMENT	X-PODS (X_1)	BLUEBERRYS (X_2)	AVAILABLE HOURS THIS WEEK
Electronic	4	3	240
Assembly	2	1	100
Profit per unit	$7	$5	

Now we can create the LP *objective function* in terms of X_1 and X_2:

$$\text{Maximize profit} = \$7X_1 + \$5X_2$$

Our next step is to develop mathematical relationships to describe the two constraints in this problem. One general relationship is that the amount of a resource used is to be less than or equal to ($\leq$) the amount of resource *available*.

LO B.1 *Formulate* linear programming models, including an objective function and constraints

First constraint: Electronic time used is $\leq$ Electronic time available.

$$4X_1 + 3X_2 \leq 240 \text{ (hours of electronic time)}$$

Second constraint: Assembly time used is $\leq$ Assembly time available.

$$2X_1 + 1X_2 \leq 100 \text{ (hours of assembly time)}$$

Both these constraints represent production capacity restrictions and, of course, affect the total profit. For example, Glickman Electronics cannot produce 70 x-pods during the production period because if $X_1 = 70$, both constraints will be violated. It also cannot make $X_1 = 50$ x-pods and $X_2 = 10$ BlueBerrys. This constraint brings out another important aspect of linear programming; that is, certain interactions will exist between variables. The more units of one product that a firm produces, the fewer it can make of other products.

Graphical Solution to a Linear Programming Problem

The easiest way to solve a small LP problem such as that of the Glickman Electronics Company is the graphical solution approach. The graphical procedure can be used only when there are two decision variables (such as number of x-pods to produce, X_1, and number of BlueBerrys to produce, X_2). When there are more than two variables, it is *not* possible to plot the solution on a two-dimensional graph; we then must turn to more complex approaches described later in this module.

Graphical solution approach

A means of plotting a solution to a two-variable problem on a graph.

Decision variables

Choices available to a decision maker.

Graphical Representation of Constraints

To find the optimal solution to a linear programming problem, we must first identify a set, or region, of feasible solutions. The first step in doing so is to plot the problem's constraints on a graph.

The variable X_1 (x-pods, in our example) is usually plotted as the horizontal axis of the graph, and the variable X_2 (BlueBerrys) is plotted as the vertical axis. The complete problem may be restated as:

$$\text{Maximize profit} = \$7X_1 + \$5X_2$$

Subject to the constraints:

$$4X_1 + 3X_2 \leq 240 \ (electronics \ constraint)$$
$$2X_1 + 1X_2 \leq 100 \ (assembly \ constraint)$$
$$X_1 \geq 0 \ (number \ of \ x\text{-}pods \ produced \ is \ greater \ than \ or \ equal \ to \ 0)$$
$$X_2 \geq 0 \ (number \ of \ BlueBerrys \ produced \ is \ greater \ than \ or \ equal \ to \ 0)$$

STUDENT TIP ◆

We named the decision variables X_1 and X_2 here, but any notations (e.g., *x-p* and B or *X* and *Y*) would do as well.

(These last two constraints are also called *nonnegativity constraints*.)

The first step in graphing the constraints of the problem is to convert the constraint *inequalities* into *equalities* (or equations):

$$\text{Constraint A:} \qquad 4X_1 + 3X_2 = 240$$
$$\text{Constraint B:} \qquad 2X_1 + 1X_2 = 100$$

The equation for constraint A is plotted in Figure B.1 and for constraint B in Figure B.2.

To plot the line in Figure B.1, all we need to do is to find the points at which the line $4X_1 + 3X_2 = 240$ intersects the X_1 and X_2 axes. When $X_1 = 0$ (the location where the line touches the X_2 axis), it implies that $3X_2 = 240$ and that $X_2 = 80$. Likewise, when $X_2 = 0$, we see that $4X_1 = 240$ and that $X_1 = 60$. Thus, constraint A is bounded by the line running from ($X_1 = 0$, $X_2 = 80$) to ($X_1 = 60$, $X_2 = 0$). The shaded area represents all points that satisfy the original *inequality*.

Constraint B is illustrated similarly in Figure B.2. When $X_1 = 0$, then $X_2 = 100$; and when $X_2 = 0$, then $X_1 = 50$. Constraint B, then, is bounded by the line between

Figure B.1

Constraint A

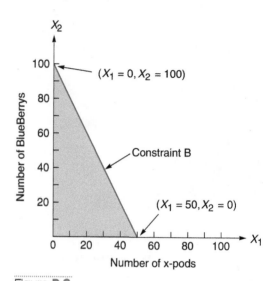

Figure B.2

Constraint B

$(X_1 = 0, X_2 = 100)$ and $(X_1 = 50, X_2 = 0)$. The shaded area represents the original inequality.

Figure B.3 shows both constraints together (along with the nonnegativity constraints). The shaded region is the part that satisfies all restrictions. The shaded region in Figure B.3 is called the *area of feasible solutions*, or simply the feasible region. This region must satisfy *all* conditions specified by the program's constraints and is thus the region where all constraints overlap. Any point in the region would be a *feasible solution* to the Glickman Electronics Company problem. Any point outside the shaded area would represent an *infeasible solution*. Hence, it would be feasible to manufacture 30 x-pods and 20 BlueBerrys $(X_1 = 30, X_2 = 20)$, but it would violate the constraints to produce 70 x-pods and 40 BlueBerrys. This can be seen by plotting these points on the graph of Figure B.3.

Feasible region
The set of all feasible combinations of decision variables.

Iso-Profit Line Solution Method

Now that the feasible region has been graphed, we can proceed to find the *optimal* solution to the problem. The optimal solution is the point lying in the feasible region that produces the highest profit.

Once the feasible region has been established, several approaches can be taken in solving for the optimal solution. The speediest one to apply is called the iso-profit line method.[1]

We start by letting profits equal some arbitrary but small dollar amount. For the Glickman Electronics problem, we may choose a profit of \$210. This is a profit level that can easily be obtained without violating either of the two constraints. The objective function can be written as $\$210 = 7X_1 + 5X_2$.

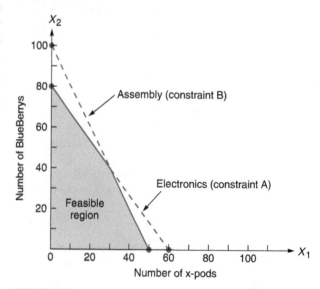

Figure B.3

Feasible Solution Region for the Glickman Electronics Company Problem

This expression is just the equation of a line; we call it an *iso-profit line*. It represents all combinations (of X_1, X_2) that will yield a total profit of \$210. To plot the profit line, we proceed exactly as we did to plot a constraint line. First, let $X_1 = 0$ and solve for the point at which the line crosses the X_2 axis:

Iso-profit line method
An approach to solving a linear programming maximization problem graphically.

$$\$210 = \$7(0) + \$5X_2$$
$$X_2 = 42 \text{ BlueBerrys}$$

Then let $X_2 = 0$ and solve for X_1:

$$\$210 = \$7X_1 + \$5(0)$$
$$X_1 = 30 \text{ x-pods}$$

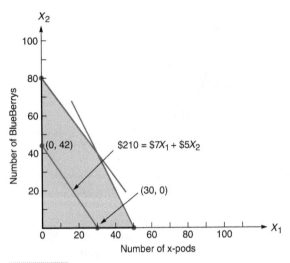

Figure **B.4**

A Profit Line of $210 Plotted for the Glickman Electronics Company

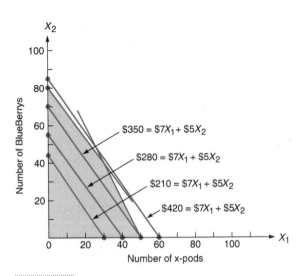

Figure **B.5**

Four Iso-Profit Lines Plotted for the Glickman Electronics Company

LO B.2 *Graphically solve an LP problem with the iso-profit line method*

We can now connect these two points with a straight line. This profit line is illustrated in Figure B.4. All points on the line represent feasible solutions that produce a profit of $210.

We see, however, that the iso-profit line for $210 does not produce the highest possible profit to the firm. In Figure B.5, we try graphing three more lines, each yielding a higher profit. The middle equation, $\$280 = \$7X_1 + \$5X_2$, was plotted in the same fashion as the lower line. When $X_1 = 0$:

$$\$280 = \$7(0) + \$5X_2$$
$$X_2 = 56 \text{ BlueBerrys}$$

When $X_2 = 0$:

$$\$280 = \$7X_1 + \$5(0)$$
$$X_1 = 40 \text{ x-pods}$$

Again, any combination of x-pods (X_1) and BlueBerrys (X_2) on this iso-profit line will produce a total profit of $280.

Note that the third line generates a profit of $350, even more of an improvement. The farther we move from the 0 origin, the higher our profit will be. Another important point to note is that these iso-profit lines are parallel. We now have two clues how to find the optimal solution to the original problem. We can draw a series of parallel profit lines (by carefully moving our ruler in a plane parallel to the first profit line). The highest profit line that still touches some point of the feasible region will pinpoint the optimal solution. Notice that the fourth line ($420) is too high to count because it does not touch the feasible region.

The highest possible iso-profit line is illustrated in Figure B.6. It touches the tip of the feasible region at the point where the two resource constraints intersect. To find its coordinates *accurately*, we will have to solve for the intersection of the two constraint lines. As you may recall from algebra, we can apply the method of *simultaneous equations* to the two constraint equations:

$$4X_1 + 3X_2 = 240 \quad (electronics\ time)$$
$$2X_1 + 1X_2 = 100 \quad (assembly\ time)$$

To solve these equations simultaneously, we multiply the second equation by -2:

$$-2(2X_1 + 1X_2 = 100) = -4X_1 - 2X_2 = -200$$

Figure **B.6**

Optimal Solution for the Glickman Electronics Problem

and then add it to the first equation:

$$+4X_1 + 3X_2 = 240$$
$$-4X_1 - 2X_2 = -200$$
$$\overline{ + 1X_2 = 40}$$

or:

$$X_2 = 40$$

Doing this has enabled us to eliminate one variable, X_1, and to solve for X_2. We can now substitute 40 for X_2 in either of the original constraint equations and solve for X_1. Let us use the first equation. When $X_2 = 40$, then:

$$4X_1 + 3(40) = 240$$
$$4X_1 + 120 = 240$$
$$4X_1 = 120$$
$$X_1 = 30$$

Thus, the optimal solution has the coordinates ($X_1 = 30$, $X_2 = 40$). The profit at this point is $7(30) + $5(40) = $410.

Corner-Point Solution Method

A second approach to solving linear programming problems employs the corner-point method. This technique is simpler in concept than the iso-profit line approach, but it involves looking at the profit at every corner point of the feasible region.

Corner-point method
A method for solving graphical linear programming problems.

The mathematical theory behind linear programming states that an optimal solution to any problem (that is, the values of X_1, X_2 that yield the maximum profit) will lie at a *corner point*, or *extreme point*, of the feasible region. Hence, it is necessary to find only the values of the variables at each corner; the maximum profit or optimal solution will lie at one (or more) of them.

Once again we can see (in Figure B.7) that the feasible region for the Glickman Electronics Company problem is a four-sided polygon with four corner, or extreme, points. These points are labeled ①, ②, ③, and ④ on the graph. To find the (X_1, X_2) values producing the maximum profit, we find out what the coordinates of each corner point are, then determine and compare their profit levels. (We showed how to find the coordinates for point ③ in the previous section describing the iso-profit line solution method.)

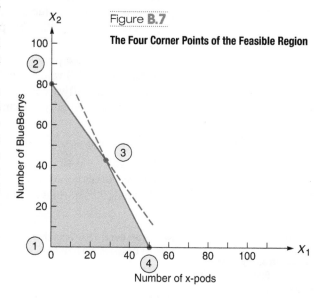

X_2

Figure **B.7**

The Four Corner Points of the Feasible Region

Number of BlueBerrys

Number of x-pods

X_1

Point ①: ($X_1 = 0$, $X_2 = 0$) Profit $7(0) + $5(0) = $0
Point ②: ($X_1 = 0$, $X_2 = 80$) Profit $7(0) + $5(80) = $400
Point ③: ($X_1 = 30$, $X_2 = 40$) Profit $7(30) + $5(40) = $410
Point ④: ($X_1 = 50$, $X_2 = 0$) Profit $7(50) + $5(0) = $350

Because point ③ produces the highest profit of any corner point, the product mix of $X_1 = 30$ x-pods and $X_2 = 40$ BlueBerrys is the optimal solution to the Glickman Electronics problem. This solution will yield a profit of $410 per production period; it is the same solution we obtained using the iso-profit line method.

LO B.3 *Graphically* solve an LP problem with the corner-point method

Sensitivity Analysis

Operations managers are usually interested in more than the optimal solution to an LP problem. In addition to knowing the value of each decision variable (the X_is) and the value of the objective function, they want to know how sensitive these answers are to input parameter changes. For example, what happens if the coefficients of the objective function are not exact, or if they change by 10% or 15%? What happens if the right-hand-side values of the constraints

Parameter
Numerical value that is given in a model.

Sensitivity analysis

An analysis that projects how much a solution may change if there are changes in the variables or input data.

change? Because solutions are based on the assumption that input parameters are constant, the subject of sensitivity analysis comes into play. Sensitivity analysis, or postoptimality analysis, is the study of how sensitive solutions are to parameter changes.

There are two approaches to determining just how sensitive an optimal solution is to changes. The first is simply a trial-and-error approach. This approach usually involves resolving the entire problem, preferably by computer, each time one input data item or parameter is changed. It can take a long time to test a series of possible changes in this way.

The approach we prefer is the analytic postoptimality method. After an LP problem has been solved, we determine a range of changes in problem parameters that will not affect the optimal solution or change the variables in the solution. This is done without resolving the whole problem. LP software, such as Excel's Solver or POM for Windows, has this capability. Let us examine several scenarios relating to the Glickman Electronics example.

STUDENT TIP

Here we look at the sensitivity of the final answers to changing inputs.

Program B.1 is part of the Excel Solver computer-generated output available to help a decision maker know whether a solution is relatively insensitive to reasonable changes in one or more of the parameters of the problem. (The complete computer run for these data, including input and full output, is illustrated in Programs B.3 and B.4 later in this module.)

LO B.4 *Interpret* sensitivity analysis and shadow prices

Sensitivity Report

The Excel *Sensitivity Report* for the Glickman Electronics example in Program B.1 has two distinct components: (1) a table titled Variable Cells and (2) a table titled Constraints. These tables permit us to answer several what-if questions regarding the problem solution.

It is important to note that while using the information in the sensitivity report to answer what-if questions, we assume that we are considering a change to only a *single* input data value at a time. That is, the sensitivity information does not always apply to simultaneous changes in several input data values.

The *Variable Cells* table presents information regarding the impact of changes to the objective function coefficients (i.e., the unit profits of $7 and $5) on the optimal solution. The *Constraints* table presents information related to the impact of changes in constraint right-hand-side (RHS) values (i.e., the 240 hours and 100 hours) on the optimal solution. Although different LP software packages may format and present these tables differently, the programs all provide essentially the same information.

Changes in the Resources or Right-Hand-Side Values

The right-hand-side values of the constraints often represent resources available to the firm. The resources could be labor-hours or machine time or perhaps money or production materials available. In the Glickman Electronics example, the two resources are hours available of

Program B.1

Sensitivity Analysis for Glickman Electronics, Using Excel's Solver

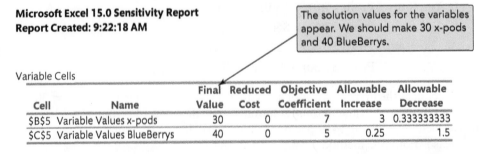

Microsoft Excel 15.0 Sensitivity Report
Report Created: 9:22:18 AM

> The solution values for the variables appear. We should make 30 x-pods and 40 BlueBerrys.

Variable Cells

Cell	Name	Final Value	Reduced Cost	Objective Coefficient	Allowable Increase	Allowable Decrease
$B$5	Variable Values x-pods	30	0	7	3	0.333333333
$C$5	Variable Values BlueBerrys	40	0	5	0.25	1.5

Constraints

Cell	Name	Final Value	Shadow Price	Constraint R.H. Side	Allowable Increase	Allowable Decrease
$D$8	Electronic Time Available	240	1.5	240	60	40
$D$9	Assembly Time Available	100	0.5	100	20	20

> We will use 240 hours and 100 hours of Electronics and Assembly time, respectively.

> If we use 1 more Electronics hour, our profit will increase by $1.50. This is true for up to 60 more hours. The profit will fall by $1.50 for each Electronics hour less than 240 hours, down to as low as 200 hours.

electronics time and hours of assembly time. If additional hours were available, a higher total profit could be realized. How much should the company be willing to pay for additional hours? Is it profitable to have some additional electronics hours? Should we be willing to pay for more assembly time? Sensitivity analysis about these resources will help us answer these questions.

If the right-hand side of a constraint is changed, the feasible region will change (unless the constraint is redundant), and often the optimal solution will change. In the Glickman example, there were 100 hours of assembly time available each week and the maximum possible profit was \$410. If the available assembly hours are *increased* to 110 hours, the new optimal solution seen in Figure B.8(a) is (45,20) and the profit is \$415. Thus, the extra 10 hours of time resulted in an increase in profit of \$5 or \$0.50 per hour. If the hours are *decreased* to 90 hours as shown in Figure B.8(b), the new optimal solution is (15,60) and the profit is \$405. Thus, reducing the hours by 10 results in a decrease in profit of \$5 or \$0.50 per hour. This \$0.50 per hour change in profit that resulted from a change in the hours available is called the shadow price, or dual value. The shadow price for a constraint is the improvement in the objective function value that results from a one-unit increase in the right-hand side of the constraint.

> **Shadow price (or dual value)**
> The value of one additional unit of a scarce resource in LP.

Validity Range for the Shadow Price   Given that Glickman Electronics' profit increases by \$0.50 for each additional hour of assembly time, does it mean that Glickman can do this indefinitely, essentially earning infinite profit? Clearly, this is illogical. How far can Glickman increase its assembly time availability and still earn an extra \$0.50 profit per hour? That is, for what level of increase in the RHS value of the assembly time constraint is the shadow price of \$0.50 valid?

The shadow price of \$0.50 is valid as long as the available assembly time stays in a range within which all current corner points continue to exist. The information to compute the upper and lower limits of this range is given by the entries labeled Allowable Increase and Allowable Decrease in the *Sensitivity Report* in Program B.1. In Glickman's case, these values show that the shadow price of \$0.50 for assembly time availability is valid for an increase of up to 20 hours from the current value and a decrease of up to 20 hours. That is, the available assembly time can range from a low of 80 (= 100 − 20) to a high of 120 (= 100 + 20) for the shadow price of \$0.50 to be valid. Note that the allowable decrease implies that for each hour of assembly time that Glickman loses (up to 20 hours), its profit decreases by \$0.50.

Changes in the Objective Function Coefficient

Let us now focus on the information provided in Program B.1 titled Variable Cells. Each row in the Variable Cells table contains information regarding a decision variable (i.e., x-pods or BlueBerrys) in the LP model.

Figure **B.8**

Glickman Electronics Sensitivity Analysis on the Right-Hand Side (RHS) of the Assembly Resource Constraint

Allowable Ranges for Objective Function Coefficients   As the unit profit contribution of either product changes, the slope of the iso-profit lines we saw earlier in Figure B.5 changes. The size of the feasible region, however, remains the same. That is, the locations of the corner points do not change.

The limits to which the profit coefficient of x-pods or BlueBerrys can be changed without affecting the optimality of the current solution is revealed by the values in the Allowable Increase and Allowable Decrease columns of the *Sensitivity Report* in Program B.1. The allowable increase in the objective function coefficient for BlueBerrys is only $0.25. In contrast, the allowable decrease is $1.50. Hence, if the unit profit of BlueBerrys drops to $4 (i.e., a decrease of $1 from the current value of $5), it is still optimal to produce 30 x-pods and 40 BlueBerrys. The total profit will drop to $370 (from $410) because each BlueBerry now yields less profit (of $1 per unit). However, if the unit profit drops below $3.50 per BlueBerry (i.e., a decrease of more than $1.50 from the current $5 profit), the current solution is no longer optimal. The LP problem will then have to be resolved using Solver, or other software, to find the new optimal corner point.

STUDENT TIP◆
LP problems can be structured
to minimize costs as well as
maximize profits.

Solving Minimization Problems

Many linear programming problems involve *minimizing* an objective such as cost instead of maximizing a profit function. A restaurant, for example, may wish to develop a work schedule to meet staffing needs while minimizing the total number of employees. Also, a manufacturer may seek to distribute its products from several factories to its many regional warehouses in a way that minimizes total shipping costs.

Iso-cost

An approach to solving a
linear programming minimization
problem graphically.

Minimization problems can be solved graphically by first setting up the feasible solution region and then using either the corner-point method or an iso-cost line approach (which is analogous to the iso-profit approach in maximization problems) to find the values of X_1 and X_2 that yield the minimum cost.

Example B1 shows how to solve a minimization problem.

Example B1

A MINIMIZATION PROBLEM WITH TWO VARIABLES

Cohen Chemicals, Inc., produces two types of photo-developing fluids. The first, a black-and-white picture chemical, costs Cohen $2,500 per ton to produce. The second, a color photo chemical, costs $3,000 per ton.

Based on an analysis of current inventory levels and outstanding orders, Cohen's production manager has specified that at least 30 tons of the black-and-white chemical and at least 20 tons of the color chemical must be produced during the next month. In addition, the manager notes that an existing inventory of a highly perishable raw material needed in both chemicals must be used within 30 days. To avoid wasting the expensive raw material, Cohen must produce a total of at least 60 tons of the photo chemicals in the next month.

APPROACH ▶   Formulate this information as a minimization LP problem.

Let:

X_1 = number of tons of black-and-white photo chemical produced
X_2 = number of tons of color photo chemical produced
Objective: Minimize cost = $2,500X_1 + \$3,000X_2$

Subject to:

$X_1 \geq 30$ tons of black-and-white chemical
$X_2 \geq 20$ tons of color chemical
$X_1 + X_2 \geq 60$ tons total
$X_1, X_2 \geq 0$ nonnegativity requirements

SOLUTION ▶   To solve the Cohen Chemicals problem graphically, we construct the problem's feasible region, shown in Figure B.9.

Figure **B.9**

Cohen Chemicals' Feasible Region

LO B.5 *Construct* and solve a minimization problem

Minimization problems are often unbounded outward (that is, on the right side and on the top), but this characteristic causes no problem in solving them. As long as they are bounded inward (on the left side and the bottom), we can establish corner points. The optimal solution will lie at one of the corners.

In this case, there are only two corner points, **a** and **b**, in Figure B.9. It is easy to determine that at point **a**, $X_1 = 40$ and $X_2 = 20$, and that at point **b**, $X_1 = 30$ and $X_2 = 30$. The optimal solution is found at the point yielding the lowest total cost.

Thus:

$$\text{Total cost at } \mathbf{a} = 2{,}500X_1 + 3{,}000X_2$$
$$= 2{,}500(40) + 3{,}000(20)$$
$$= \$160{,}000$$
$$\text{Total cost at } \mathbf{b} = 2{,}500X_1 + 3{,}000X_2$$
$$= 2{,}500(30) + 3{,}000(30)$$
$$= \$165{,}000$$

The lowest cost to Cohen Chemicals is at point **a**. Hence the operations manager should produce 40 tons of the black-and-white chemical and 20 tons of the color chemical.

INSIGHT ▶ The area is either not bounded to the right or above in a minimization problem (as it is in a maximization problem).

LEARNING EXERCISE ▶ Cohen's second constraint is recomputed and should be $X_2 \geq 15$. Does anything change in the answer? [Answer: Now $X_1 = 45$, $X_2 = 15$, and total cost = \$157,500.]

RELATED PROBLEMS ▶ B.25–B.31 (B.32, B.33 are available in MyOMLab)

EXCEL **OM** Data File **ModBExB1.xls** can be found in MyOMLab.

OM in Action LP at UPS

On an *average* day, the $58.2 billion shipping giant UPS delivers 18 million packages to 8.2 million customers in 220 countries. On a *really* busy day, say a few days before Christmas, it handles almost twice that number, or 300 packages per second. It does all this with a fleet of 600+ owned and chartered planes, making it one of the largest airline operators in the world.

When UPS decided it should use linear programming to map its entire operation—every pickup and delivery center and every sorting facility (now nearly 2,000 locations)—to find the best routes to move the millions of packages, it invested close to a decade in developing VOLCANO. This LP-based optimization system (which stands for *Volume, Location,* and *Aircraft Network Optimization)* is used to determine the least-cost set of routes, fleet assignments, and package flows. Constraints include the number of planes, airport restrictions, and plane aircraft speed, capacity, and range.

The VOLCANO system is credited with saving UPS hundreds of millions of dollars. But that's just the start. UPS is investing $600 million more to optimize the whole supply chain to include drivers—the employees closest to the customer—so they will be able to update schedules, priorities, and time conflicts on the fly.

The UPS "airline" is not alone. Southwest runs its massive LP model (called *ILOG Optimizer)* every day to schedule its thousands of flight legs. The program has 90,000 constraints and 2 million variables. United's LP program is called *OptSolver,* and Delta's is called *Coldstart.* Airlines, like many other firms, manage their millions of daily decisions with LP.

Sources: ups.com (June 2015); *Aviation Daily* (February 9, 2004); and *Interfaces* (January–February 2004).

Linear Programming Applications

The foregoing examples each contained just two variables (X_1 and X_2). Most real-world problems (as we saw in the UPS *OM in Action* box) contain many more variables, however. Let's use the principles already developed to formulate a few more-complex problems. The practice you will get by "paraphrasing" the following LP situations should help develop your skills for applying linear programming to other common operations situations.

Production-Mix Example

LO B.6 *Formulate production-mix, diet, and labor scheduling problems*

Example B2 involves another *production-mix* decision. Limited resources must be allocated among various products that a firm produces. The firm's overall objective is to manufacture the selected products in such quantities as to maximize total profits.

Example B2

A PRODUCTION-MIX PROBLEM

Failsafe Electronics Corporation primarily manufactures four highly technical products, which it supplies to aerospace firms that hold NASA contracts. Each of the products must pass through the following departments before they are shipped: wiring, drilling, assembly, and inspection. The time requirements in each department (in hours) for each unit produced and its corresponding profit value are summarized in this table:

	DEPARTMENT				
PRODUCT	WIRING	DRILLING	ASSEMBLY	INSPECTION	UNIT PROFIT
XJ201	.5	3	2	.5	$ 9
XM897	1.5	1	4	1.0	$12
TR29	1.5	2	1	.5	$15
BR788	1.0	3	2	.5	$11

The production time available in each department each month and the minimum monthly production requirement to fulfill contracts are as follows:

DEPARTMENT	CAPACITY (HOURS)	PRODUCT	MINIMUM PRODUCTION LEVEL
Wiring	1,500	XJ201	150
Drilling	2,350	XM897	100
Assembly	2,600	TR29	200
Inspection	1,200	BR788	400

APPROACH ▶ Formulate this production-mix situation as an LP problem. The production manager first specifies production levels for each product for the coming month. He lets:

$$X_1 = \text{number of units of XJ201 produced}$$
$$X_2 = \text{number of units of XM897 produced}$$
$$X_3 = \text{number of units of TR29 produced}$$
$$X_4 = \text{number of units of BR788 produced}$$

SOLUTION ▶ The LP formulation is:

Objective: Maximize profit $= 9X_1 + 12X_2 + 15X_3 + 11X_4$

subject to:

$$.5X_1 + 1.5X_2 + 1.5X_3 + 1X_4 \le 1{,}500 \text{ hours of wiring available}$$
$$3X_1 + 1X_2 + 2X_3 + 3X_4 \le 2{,}350 \text{ hours of drilling available}$$
$$2X_1 + 4X_2 + 1X_3 + 2X_4 \le 2{,}600 \text{ hours of assembly available}$$
$$.5X_1 + 1X_2 + .5X_3 + .5X_4 \le 1{,}200 \text{ hours of inspection}$$
$$X_1 \ge 150 \text{ units of XJ201}$$
$$X_2 \ge 100 \text{ units of XM897}$$
$$X_3 \ge 200 \text{ units of TR29}$$
$$X_4 \ge 400 \text{ units of BR788}$$
$$X_1, X_2, X_3, X_4 \ge 0$$

INSIGHT ▶ There can be numerous constraints in an LP problem. The constraint right-hand sides may be in different units, but the objective function uses one common unit—dollars of profit, in this case. Because there are more than two decision variables, this problem is not solved graphically.

LEARNING EXERCISE ▶ Solve this LP problem as formulated. What is the solution? [Answer: $X_1 = 150$, $X_2 = 300$, $X_3 = 200$, $X_4 = 400$.]

RELATED PROBLEMS ▶ B.5–B.8, B.10–B.14, B.37 (B.15, B.17, B.19, B.21, B.24 are available in MyOMLab)

Diet Problem Example

Example B3 illustrates the *diet problem*, which was originally used by hospitals to determine the most economical diet for patients. Known in agricultural applications as the *feed-mix problem*, the diet problem involves specifying a food or feed ingredient combination that will satisfy stated nutritional requirements at a minimum cost level.

Example B3 | A DIET PROBLEM

The Feed 'N Ship feedlot fattens cattle for local farmers and ships them to meat markets in Kansas City and Omaha. The owners of the feedlot seek to determine the amounts of cattle feed to buy to satisfy minimum nutritional standards and, at the same time, minimize total feed costs.

Each grain stock contains different amounts of four nutritional ingredients: A, B, C, and D. Here are the ingredient contents of each grain, in *ounces per pound of grain*:

	FEED		
INGREDIENT	STOCK X	STOCK Y	STOCK Z
A	3 oz	2 oz	4 oz
B	2 oz	3 oz	1 oz
C	1 oz	0 oz	2 oz
D	6 oz	8 oz	4 oz

The cost per pound of grains X, Y, and Z is $0.02, $0.04, and $0.025, respectively. The minimum requirement per cow per month is 64 ounces of ingredient A, 80 ounces of ingredient B, 16 ounces of ingredient C, and 128 ounces of ingredient D.

The feedlot faces one additional restriction—it can obtain only 500 pounds of stock Z per month from the feed supplier, regardless of its need. Because there are usually 100 cows at the Feed 'N Ship feedlot at any given time, this constraint limits the amount of stock Z for use in the feed of each cow to no more than 5 pounds, or 80 ounces, per month.

APPROACH ▶ Formulate this as a minimization LP problem.

Let: X_1 = number of pounds of stock X purchased per cow each month
X_2 = number of pounds of stock Y purchased per cow each month
X_3 = number of pounds of stock Z purchased per cow each month

SOLUTION ▶

Objective: Minimize cost = $.02X_1 + .04X_2 + .025X_3$

subject to:
Ingredient A requirement: $3X_1 + 2X_2 + 4X_3 \geq 64$
Ingredient B requirement: $2X_1 + 3X_2 + 1X_3 \geq 80$
Ingredient C requirement: $1X_1 + 0X_2 + 2X_3 \geq 16$
Ingredient D requirement: $6X_1 + 8X_2 + 4X_3 \geq 128$
Stock Z limitation: $X_3 \leq 5$
$X_1, X_2, X_3 \geq 0$

The cheapest solution is to purchase 40 pounds of grain X_1, at a cost of $0.80 per cow.

INSIGHT ▶ Because the cost per pound of stock X is so low, the optimal solution excludes grains Y and Z.

LEARNING EXERCISE ▶ The cost of a pound of stock X just increased by 50%. Does this affect the solution? [Answer: Yes, when the cost per pound of grain X is $0.03, $X_1 = 16$ pounds, $X_2 = 16$ pounds, $X_3 = 0$, and cost = $1.12 per cow.]

RELATED PROBLEMS ▶ B.27, B.28, B.40 (B.33 is available in MyOMLab)

Labor Scheduling Example

Labor scheduling problems address staffing needs over a specific time period. They are especially useful when managers have some flexibility in assigning workers to jobs that require overlapping or interchangeable talents. Large banks and hospitals frequently use LP to tackle their labor scheduling. Example B4 describes how one bank uses LP to schedule tellers.

| Example B4 | **SCHEDULING BANK TELLERS** |

Mexico City Bank of Commerce and Industry is a busy bank that has requirements for between 10 and 18 tellers depending on the time of day. Lunchtime, from noon to 2 P.M., is usually heaviest. The table below indicates the workers needed at various hours that the bank is open.

TIME PERIOD	NUMBER OF TELLERS REQUIRED	TIME PERIOD	NUMBER OF TELLERS REQUIRED
9 A.M.–10 A.M.	10	1 P.M.–2 P.M.	18
10 A.M.–11 A.M.	12	2 P.M.–3 P.M.	17
11 A.M.–Noon	14	3 P.M.–4 P.M.	15
Noon–1 P.M.	16	4 P.M.–5 P.M.	10

The bank now employs 12 full-time tellers, but many people are on its roster of available part-time employees. A part-time employee must put in exactly 4 hours per day but can start anytime between 9 A.M. and 1 P.M. Part-timers are a fairly inexpensive labor pool because no retirement or lunch benefits are provided them. Full-timers, on the other hand, work from 9 A.M. to 5 P.M. but are allowed 1 hour for lunch. (Half the full-timers eat at 11 A.M., the other half at noon.) Full-timers thus provide 35 hours per week of productive labor time.

By corporate policy, the bank limits part-time hours to a maximum of 50% of the day's total requirement.

Part-timers earn $6 per hour (or $24 per day) on average, whereas full-timers earn $75 per day in salary and benefits on average.

APPROACH ▶ The bank would like to set a schedule, using LP, that would minimize its total manpower costs. It will release 1 or more of its full-time tellers if it is profitable to do so.

We can let:

$$F = \text{full-time tellers}$$
$$P_1 = \text{part-timers starting at 9 A.M. (leaving at 1 P.M.)}$$
$$P_2 = \text{part-timers starting at 10 A.M. (leaving at 2 P.M.)}$$
$$P_3 = \text{part-timers starting at 11 A.M. (leaving at 3 P.M.)}$$
$$P_4 = \text{part-timers starting at noon (leaving at 4 P.M.)}$$
$$P_5 = \text{part-timers starting at 1 P.M. (leaving at 5 P.M.)}$$

SOLUTION ▶ Objective function:

$$\text{Minimize total daily manpower cost} = \$75F + \$24(P_1 + P_2 + P_3 + P_4 + P_5)$$

Constraints: For each hour, the available labor-hours must be at least equal to the required labor-hours:

$$
\begin{aligned}
F + P_1 &\ge 10 && (\textit{9 A.M. to 10 A.M. needs}) \\
F + P_1 + P_2 &\ge 12 && (\textit{10 A.M. to 11 A.M. needs}) \\
\tfrac{1}{2}F + P_1 + P_2 + P_3 &\ge 14 && (\textit{11 A.M. to noon needs}) \\
\tfrac{1}{2}F + P_1 + P_2 + P_3 + P_4 &\ge 16 && (\textit{noon to 1 P.M. needs}) \\
F + P_2 + P_3 + P_4 + P_5 &\ge 18 && (\textit{1 P.M. to 2 P.M. needs}) \\
F + P_3 + P_4 + P_5 &\ge 17 && (\textit{2 P.M. to 3 P.M. needs}) \\
F + P_4 + P_5 &\ge 15 && (\textit{3 P.M. to 4 P.M. needs}) \\
F + P_5 &\ge 10 && (\textit{4 P.M. to 5 P.M. needs})
\end{aligned}
$$

Only 12 full-time tellers are available, so:

$$F \le 12$$

Part-time worker-hours cannot exceed 50% of total hours required each day, which is the sum of the tellers needed each hour:

$$4(P_1 + P_2 + P_3 + P_4 + P_5) \le .50(10 + 12 + 14 + 16 + 18 + 17 + 15 + 10)$$

or:

$$4P_1 + 4P_2 + 4P_3 + 4P_4 + 4P_5 \leq 0.50(112)$$
$$F, P_1, P_2, P_3, P_4, P_5 \geq 0$$

There are two alternative optimal schedules that Mexico City Bank can follow. The first is to employ only 10 full-time tellers ($F = 10$) and to start 7 part-timers at 10 A.M. ($P_2 = 7$), 2 part-timers at 11 A.M. and noon ($P_3 = 2$ and $P_4 = 2$), and 3 part-timers at 1 P.M. ($P_5 = 3$). No part-timers would begin at 9 A.M.

The second solution also employs 10 full-time tellers, but starts 6 part-timers at 9 A.M. ($P_1 = 6$), 1 part-timer at 10 A.M. ($P_2 = 1$), 2 part-timers at 11 A.M. and noon ($P_3 = 2$ and $P_4 = 2$), and 3 part-timers at 1 P.M. ($P_5 = 3$). The cost of either of these two policies is $1,086 per day.

INSIGHT ▶ It is not unusual for multiple optimal solutions to exist in large LP problems. In this case, it gives management the option of selecting, at the same cost, between schedules. To find an alternate optimal solution, you may have to enter the constraints in a different sequence.

LEARNING EXERCISE ▶ The bank decides to give part-time employees a raise to $7 per hour. Does the solution change? [Answer: Yes, cost = $1,142, $F = 10$, $P_1 = 6$, $P_2 = 1$, $P_3 = 2$, $P_4 = 5$, $P_5 = 0$.]

RELATED PROBLEMS ▶ B.36

The Simplex Method of LP

Simplex method

An algorithm for solving linear programming problems of all sizes.

Most real-world linear programming problems have more than two variables and thus are too complex for graphical solution. A procedure called the simplex method may be used to find the optimal solution to such problems. The simplex method is actually an algorithm (or a set of instructions) with which we examine corner points in a methodical fashion until we arrive at the best solution—highest profit or lowest cost. Computer programs (such as Excel OM and POM for Windows) and Excel spreadsheets are available to solve linear programming problems via the simplex method.

For details regarding the algebraic steps of the simplex algorithm, see Tutorial 3 at our text student download site or in MyOMLab, or refer to a management science textbook.[2]

Integer and Binary Variables

Binary variables

Decision variables that can only take on the value of 0 or 1.

All the examples we have seen in this module so far have produced integer solutions. But it is very common to see LP solutions where the decision variables are not whole numbers. Computer software provides a simple way to guarantee only integer solutions. In addition, computers allow us to create special decision variables called binary variables that can only take on the values of 0 or 1. Binary variables allow us to introduce "yes-or-no" decisions into our linear programs and to introduce special logical conditions.

Creating Integer and Binary Variables

If we wish to ensure that decision variable values are integers rather than fractions, it is generally *not* good practice to simply round the solutions to the nearest integer values. The rounded solutions may not be optimal and, in fact, may not even be feasible. Fortunately, all LP software programs have simple ways to add constraints that enforce some or all of the decision variables to be either integer or binary. The main disadvantage of introducing such constraints is that larger programs may take longer to solve. The same LP that may take 3 seconds to solve on a computer could take several hours or more to solve if many of its variables are forced to be integer or binary. For relatively small programs, though, the difference may be unnoticeable.

Using Excel's Solver (see *Using Software to Solve LP Problems* later in this module), integer and binary constraints can be added by clicking Add from the main Solver dialog box. Using the Add Constraint dialog box (see Program B.2), highlight the decision variables themselves under Cell Reference:. Then select int or bin to ensure that those variables are integer or binary, respectively, in the optimal solution.

Linear Programming Applications with Binary Variables

In the written formulation of a linear program, binary variables are usually defined using the following form:

$$Y = \begin{cases} 1 & \text{if some condition holds} \\ 0 & \text{otherwise} \end{cases}$$

Sometimes we designate decision variables as binary if we are making a yes-or-no decision; for example, "Should we undertake this particular project?" "Should we buy that machine?" or "Should we locate a facility in Arkansas?" Other times, we create binary variables to introduce additional logic into our programs.

Limiting the Number of Alternatives Selected One common use of 0-1 variables involves limiting the number of projects or items that are selected from a group. Suppose a firm is required to select no more than two of three potential projects. This could be modeled with the following constraint:

$$Y_1 + Y_2 + Y_3 \le 2$$

If we wished to force the selection of *exactly* two of the three projects for funding, the following constraint should be used:

$$Y_1 + Y_2 + Y_3 = 2$$

This forces exactly two of the variables to have values of 1, whereas the other variable must have a value of 0.

Dependent Selections At times the selection of one project depends in some way on the selection of another project. This situation can be modeled with the use of 0-1 variables. Suppose G.E.'s new catalytic converter could be purchased ($Y_1 = 1$) only if the software was also purchased ($Y_2 = 1$). The following constraint would force this to occur:

$$Y_1 \le Y_2$$

or, equivalently,

$$Y_1 - Y_2 \le 0$$

Thus, if the software is not purchased, the value of Y_2 is 0, and the value of Y_1 must also be 0 because of this constraint. However, if the software is purchased ($Y_2 = 1$), then it is possible that the catalytic converter could also be purchased ($Y_1 = 1$), although this is not required.

If we wished for the catalytic converter and the software projects to either both be selected or both not be selected, we should use the following constraint:

$$Y_1 = Y_2$$

or, equivalently,

$$Y_1 - Y_2 = 0$$

Thus, if either of these variables is equal to 0, the other must also be 0. If either of these is equal to 1, the other must also be 1.

A Fixed-Charge Integer Programming Problem

Often businesses are faced with decisions involving a fixed charge that will affect the cost of future operations. Building a new factory or entering into a long-term lease on an existing facility would involve a fixed cost that might vary depending on the size of the facility and the location. Once a factory is built, the variable production costs will be affected by the labor cost in the particular city where it is located. Example B5 provides an illustration.

Example B5

A FIXED-CHARGE PROBLEM USING BINARY VARIABLES

Sitka Manufacturing is planning to build at least one new plant, and three cities are being considered: Baytown, Texas; Lake Charles, Louisiana; and Mobile, Alabama. Once the plant or plants have been constructed, the company wishes to have sufficient capacity to produce at least 38,000 units each year. The costs associated with the possible locations are given in the following table.

SITE	ANNUAL FIXED COST	VARIABLE COST PER UNIT	ANNUAL CAPACITY
Baytown, TX	$340,000	$32	21,000
Lake Charles, LA	$270,000	$33	20,000
Mobile, AL	$290,000	$30	19,000

APPROACH ▶ In modeling this as an integer program, the objective function is to minimize the total of the fixed costs and the variable costs. The constraints are: (1) total production capacity is at least 38,000; (2) the number of units produced at the Baytown plant is 0 if the plant is not built, and it is no more than 21,000 if the plant is built; (3) the number of units produced at the Lake Charles plant is 0 if the plant is not built, and it is no more than 20,000 if the plant is built; and (4) the number of units produced at the Mobile plant is 0 if the plant is not built, and it is no more than 19,000 if the plant is built.

Then, we define the decision variables as

$$Y_1 = \begin{cases} 1 & \text{if factory is built in Baytown} \\ 0 & \text{otherwise} \end{cases}$$

$$Y_2 = \begin{cases} 1 & \text{if factory is built in Lake Charles} \\ 0 & \text{otherwise} \end{cases}$$

$$Y_3 = \begin{cases} 1 & \text{if factory is built in Mobile} \\ 0 & \text{otherwise} \end{cases}$$

X_1 = number of units produced at the Baytown plant

X_2 = number of units produced at the Lake Charles plant

X_3 = number of units produced at the Mobile plant

SOLUTION ▶ The integer programming problem formulation becomes

Objective: Minimize cost = $340{,}000\,Y_1 + 270{,}000\,Y_2 + 290{,}000\,Y_3 + 32X_1 + 33X_2 + 30X_3$

subject to: $X_1 + X_2 + X_3 \geq 38{,}000$

$X_1 \leq 21{,}000\,Y_1$

$X_2 \leq 20{,}000\,Y_2$

$X_3 \leq 19{,}000\,Y_3$

$X_1, X_2, X_3 \geq 0$ and integer

$Y_1, Y_2, Y_3 = 0$ or 1

INSIGHT ▶ Examining the second constraint, the objective function will try to set the binary variable Y_1 equal to 0 because it wants to minimize cost. However, if $Y_1 = 0$, then the constraint will force X_1 to equal 0, in which case no units will be produced, and the plant will not be opened. Alternatively, if the rest of the program deems it worthwhile or necessary to produce some units of X_1, then Y_1 will have to equal 1 for the constraint to hold. And when $Y_1 = 1$, the firm will be charged the fixed cost of $340,000, and production will be limited to the capacity of 21,000 units. The same logic applies for constraints 3 and 4.

LEARNING EXERCISE ▶ Solve this integer program as formulated. What is the solution? [Answer: $Y_1 = 0$, $Y_2 = 1$, $Y_3 = 1$, $X_1 = 0$, $X_2 = 19{,}000$, $X_3 = 19{,}000$; Total Cost = $1,757,000.]

RELATED PROBLEMS ▶ B.41, B.42

Summary

This module introduces a special kind of model, linear programming. LP has proven to be especially useful when trying to make the most effective use of an organization's resources.

The first step in dealing with LP models is problem formulation, which involves identifying and creating an objective function and constraints. The second step is to solve the problem. If there are only two decision variables, the problem can be solved graphically, using the corner-point method or the iso-profit/iso-cost line method. With either approach, we first identify the feasible region, then find the corner point yielding the greatest profit or least cost. LP is used in a wide variety of business applications, as the examples and homework problems in this module reveal.

Key Terms

Linear programming (LP) (p. 700)
Objective function (p. 701)
Constraints (p. 701)
Graphical solution approach (p. 702)
Decision variables (p. 702)

Feasible region (p. 703)
Iso-profit line method (p. 703)
Corner-point method (p. 705)
Parameter (p. 705)
Sensitivity analysis (p. 706)

Shadow price (or dual value) (p. 707)
Iso-cost (p. 708)
Simplex method (p. 713)
Binary variables (p. 713)

Discussion Questions

1. List at least four applications of linear programming problems.
2. What is a "corner point"? Explain why solutions to linear programming problems focus on corner points.
3. Define the feasible region of a graphical LP problem. What is a feasible solution?
4. Each linear programming problem that has a feasible region has an infinite number of solutions. Explain.
5. Under what circumstances is the objective function more important than the constraints in a linear programming model?
6. Under what circumstances are the constraints more important than the objective function in a linear programming model?
7. Why is the diet problem, in practice, applicable for animals but not particularly for people?
8. How many feasible solutions are there in a linear program? Which ones do we need to examine to find the optimal solution?

9. Define shadow price (or dual value).
10. Explain how to use the iso-cost line in a graphical minimization problem.
11. Compare how the corner-point and iso-profit line methods work for solving graphical problems.
12. Where a constraint crosses the vertical or horizontal axis, the quantity is fairly obvious. How does one go about finding the quantity coordinates where two constraints cross, not at an axis?
13. Suppose a linear programming (maximation) problem has been solved and that the optimal value of the objective function is $300. Suppose an additional constraint is added to this problem. Explain how this might affect each of the following:
    a) The feasible region.
    b) The optimal value of the objective function.

Using Software to Solve LP Problems

All LP problems can be solved with the simplex method, using software such as Excel, Excel OM, or POM for Windows.

✗ CREATING YOUR OWN EXCEL SPREADSHEETS

Excel offers the ability to analyze linear programming problems using built-in problem-solving tools. Excel's tool is named *Solver*. We use Excel to set up the Glickman Electronics problem in Program B.3. The objective and constraints are repeated here:

Objective function: Maximize profit = $7(No. of x-pods) + $5(No. of BlueBerrys)

Subject to: 4(x-pods) + 3(BlueBerrys) ≤ 240

2(x-pods) + 1(BlueBerry) ≤ 100

Program B.3

Using Excel to Formulate the Glickman Electronics Problem

Action
Copy D6 to D8:D9

To ensure that Solver always loads when Excel is loaded, click on FILE, then Options, then Add-Ins. Next to Manage: at the bottom, make sure that Excel Add-Ins is selected, and click on the Go... button. Check Solver Add-In, and click OK. Once in Excel, the Solver dialog box will appear by clicking on: Data, then Analysis: Solver. (Or if using Excel for Mac, select Tools, Solver.) Program B.4 shows how to use Solver to find the optimal (very best) solution to the Glickman Electronics problem. Click on Solve, and the solution will automatically appear in the spreadsheet in the green and blue cells.

Program **B.4**

Solver Dialog Boxes for the Glickman Electronics Problem

The Excel screen in Program B.5 shows Solver's solution to the Glickman Electronics Company problem. Note that the optimal solution is now shown in cells B5 and C5, which serve as the variables. The Reports selections perform more extensive analysis of the solution and its environment. Excel's sensitivity analysis capability was illustrated earlier in Program B.1.

	A	B	C	D	E	F
1	Glickman Electronics					
2	Using Linear Programming to Solve a Product Mix Problem					
3						
4		x-pods	BlueBerrys			
5	Variable Values	30	40			
6	Objective Function	$7.00	$5.00	$410.00	Max	RHS
7	Subject to:					
8	Electronic Time Available	4	3	240	<=	240
9	Assembly Time Available	2	1	100	<=	100

Program **B.5**

Excel Solution to Glickman Electronics LP Problem

Px USING EXCEL OM AND POM FOR WINDOWS

Excel OM and POM for Windows can handle relatively large LP problems. As output, the software provides optimal values for the variables, optimal profit or cost, and sensitivity analysis. In addition, POM for Windows provides graphical output for problems with only two variables.

Solved Problems   Virtual Office Hours help is available in MyOMLab.

SOLVED PROBLEM B.1

Smith's, a Niagara, New York, clothing manufacturer that produces men's shirts and pajamas, has two primary resources available: sewing-machine time (in the sewing department) and cutting-machine time (in the cutting department). Over the next month, owner Barbara Smith can schedule up to 280 hours of work on sewing machines and up to 450 hours of work on cutting machines. Each shirt produced requires

1.00 hour of sewing time and 1.50 hours of cutting time. Producing each pair of pajamas requires .75 hours of sewing time and 2 hours of cutting time.

To express the LP constraints for this problem mathematically, we let:

$$X_1 = \text{number of shirts produced}$$
$$X_2 = \text{number of pajamas produced}$$

SOLUTION

First constraint: $1X_1 + .75X_2 \le 280$ hours of sewing-machine time available—our first scarce resource

Second constraint: $1.5X_1 + 2X_2 \le 450$ hours of cutting-machine time available—our second scarce resource

Note: This means that each pair of pajamas takes 2 hours of the cutting resource. Smith's accounting department analyzes cost and sales figures and states that each shirt produced will yield a $4 contribution to profit and that each pair of pajamas will yield a $3 contribution to profit.

This information can be used to create the LP *objective function* for this problem:

Objective function: Maximize total contribution to profit $= \$4X_1 + \$3X_2$

SOLVED PROBLEM B.2

We want to solve the following LP problem for Kevin Caskey Wholesale Inc. using the corner-point method:

Objective: Maximize profit $= \$9X_1 + \$7X_2$

Constraints: $2X_1 + 1X_2 \le 40$
$X_1 + 3X_2 \le 30$
$X_1, X_2 \ge 0$

SOLUTION

Figure B.10 illustrates these constraints:

Corner-point **a**: $(X_1 = 0, X_2 = 0)$ Profit $= 0$

Corner-point **b**: $(X_1 = 0, X_2 = 10)$ Profit $= 9(0) + 7(10) = \$70$

Corner-point **d**: $(X_1 = 20, X_2 = 0)$ Profit $= 9(20) + 7(0) = \$180$

Corner-point **c** is obtained by solving equations $2X_1 + 1X_2 = 40$ and $X_1 + 3X_2 = 30$ simultaneously. Multiply the second equation by -2 and add it to the first.

$$2X_1 + 1X_2 = 40$$
$$-2X_1 - 6X_2 = -60$$
$$\overline{ -5X_2 = -20}$$
$$\text{Thus } X_2 = 4$$

And $X_1 + 3(4) = 30$ or $X_1 + 12 = 30$ or $X_1 = 18$
Corner-point **c**: $(X_1 = 18, X_2 = 4)$ Profit $= 9(18) + 7(4) = \$190$
Hence the optimal solution is:
$(x_1 = 18, x_2 = 4)$ Profit $= \$190$

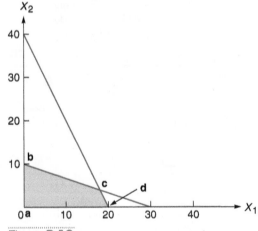

Figure B.10

K. Caskey Wholesale Inc.'s Feasible Region

SOLVED PROBLEM B.3

Holiday Meal Turkey Ranch is considering buying two different types of turkey feed. Each feed contains, in varying proportions, some or all of the three nutritional ingredients essential for fattening turkeys. Brand Y feed costs the ranch $.02 per pound. Brand Z costs $.03 per pound. The rancher would like to determine the lowest-cost diet that meets the minimum monthly intake requirement for each nutritional ingredient.

The following table contains relevant information about the composition of brand Y and brand Z feeds, as well as the minimum monthly requirement for each nutritional ingredient per turkey.

COMPOSITION OF EACH POUND OF FEED			
INGREDIENT	BRAND Y FEED	BRAND Z FEED	MINIMUM MONTHLY REQUIREMENT
A	5 oz	10 oz	90 oz
B	4 oz	3 oz	48 oz
C	.5 oz	0	1.5 oz
Cost/lb	$.02	$.03	

SOLUTION

If we let:

X_1 = number of pounds of brand Y feed purchased
X_2 = number of pounds of brand Z feed purchased

then we may proceed to formulate this linear programming problem as follows:

Objective: Minimize cost (in cents) = $2X_1 + 3X_2$

subject to these constraints:

$$5X_1 + 10X_2 \geq 90 \text{ oz} \quad \text{(ingredient A constraint)}$$
$$4X_1 + 3X_2 \geq 48 \text{ oz} \quad \text{(ingredient B constraint)}$$
$$\tfrac{1}{2}X_1 \geq 1\tfrac{1}{2} \text{ oz} \quad \text{(ingredient C constraint)}$$

Figure B.11 illustrates these constraints.

The iso-cost line approach may be used to solve LP minimization problems such as that of the Holiday Meal Turkey Ranch. As with iso-profit lines, we need not compute the cost at each corner point, but instead draw a series of parallel cost lines. The last cost point to touch the feasible region provides us with the optimal solution corner.

For example, we start in Figure B.12 by drawing a 54¢ cost line, namely, $54 = 2X_1 + 3X_2$. Obviously, there are many points in the feasible region that would yield a lower total cost. We proceed to move our iso-cost line toward the lower left, in a plane parallel to the 54¢ solution line. The last point we touch while still in contact with the feasible region is the same as corner point **b** of Figure B.11. It has the coordinates ($X_1 = 8.4, X_2 = 4.8$) and an associated cost of 31.2 cents.

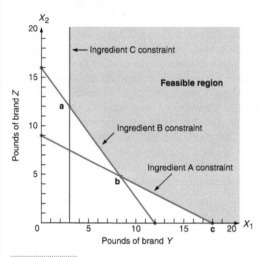

Figure **B.11**

Feasible Region for the Holiday Meal Turkey Ranch Problem

STUDENT TIP ⊕

Note that the last line parallel to the 54¢ iso-cost line that touches the feasible region indicates the optimal corner point.

Figure **B.12**

Graphical Solution to the Holiday Meal Turkey Ranch Problem Using the Iso-Cost Line

Problems   *Note:* **PX** means the problem may be solved with POM for Windows and/or Excel OM.

· **B.1**   The LP relationships that follow were formulated by Richard Martin at the Long Beach Chemical Company. Which ones are invalid for use in a linear programming problem, and why?

$$\text{Maximize} = 6X_1 + \tfrac{1}{2}X_1X_2 + 5X_3$$
$$\text{Subject to:}\quad 4X_1X_2 + 2X_3 \le 70$$
$$7.9X_1 - 4X_2 \ge 15.6$$
$$3X_1 + 3X_2 + 3X_3 \ge 21$$
$$19X_2 - \tfrac{1}{3}X_3 = 17$$
$$-X_1 - X_2 + 4X_3 = 5$$
$$4X_1 + 2X_2 + 3\sqrt{X_3} \le 80$$

· **B.2**   Solve the following linear programming problem graphically:

$$\text{Maximize profit} = 4X + 6Y$$
$$\text{Subject to:}\qquad X + 2Y \le 8$$
$$5X + 4Y \le 20$$
$$X, Y \ge 0 \quad \text{PX}$$

· **B.3**   Solve the following linear programming problem graphically:

$$\text{Maximize profit} = X + 10Y$$
$$\text{Subject to:}\qquad 4X + 3Y \le 36$$
$$2X + 4Y \le 40$$
$$Y \ge 3$$
$$X, Y \ge 0 \quad \text{PX}$$

·· **B.4**   Consider the following linear programming problem:

$$\text{Maximize profit} = 30X_1 + 10X_2$$
$$\text{Subject to:}\qquad 3X_1 + X_2 \le 300$$
$$X_1 + X_2 \le 200$$
$$X_1 \le 100$$
$$X_2 \ge 50$$
$$X_1 - X_2 \le 0$$
$$X_1, X_2 \ge 0$$

a) Solve the problem graphically.
b) Is there more than one optimal solution? Explain. **PX**

· **B.5**   The Attaran Corporation manufactures two electrical products: portable air conditioners and portable heaters. The assembly process for each is similar in that both require a certain amount of wiring and drilling. Each air conditioner takes 3 hours of wiring and 2 hours of drilling. Each heater must go through 2 hours of wiring and 1 hour of drilling. During the next production period, 240 hours of wiring time are available and up to 140 hours of drilling time may be used. Each air conditioner sold yields a profit of $25. Each heater assembled may be sold for a $15 profit.

Formulate and solve this LP production-mix situation, and find the best combination of air conditioners and heaters that yields the highest profit. **PX**

· **B.6**   The Chris Beehner Company manufactures two lines of designer yard gates, called model A and model B. Every gate requires blending a certain amount of steel and zinc; the company has available a total of 25,000 lb of steel and 6,000 lb of zinc. Each model A gate requires a mixture of 125 lb of steel and 20 lb of zinc, and each yields a profit of $90. Each model B gate requires 100 lb of steel and 30 lb of zinc and can be sold for a profit of $70.

Find by graphical linear programming the best production mix of yard gates. **PX**

·· **B.7**   Green Vehicle Inc. manufactures electric cars and small delivery trucks. It has just opened a new factory where the C1 car and the T1 truck can both be manufactured. To make either vehicle, processing in the assembly shop and in the paint shop are required. It takes 1/40 of a day and 1/60 of a day to paint a truck of type T1 and a car of type C1 in the paint shop, respectively. It takes 1/50 of a day to assemble either type of vehicle in the assembly shop.

A T1 truck and a C1 car yield profits of $300 and $220, respectively, per vehicle sold.
a) Define the objective function and constraint equations.
b) Graph the feasible region.
c) What is a maximum-profit daily production plan at the new factory?
d) How much profit will such a plan yield, assuming whatever is produced is sold? **PX**

· **B.8**   The Lifang Wu Corporation manufactures two models of industrial robots, the Alpha 1 and the Beta 2. The firm employs 5 technicians, working 160 hours each per month, on its assembly line. Management insists that full employment (that is, *all* 160 hours of time) be maintained for each worker during next month's operations. It requires 20 labor-hours to assemble each Alpha 1 robot and 25 labor-hours to assemble each Beta 2 model. Wu wants to see at least 10 Alpha 1s and at least 15 Beta 2s produced during the production period. Alpha 1s generate a $1,200 profit per unit, and Beta 2s yield $1,800 each.

Determine the most profitable number of each model of robot to produce during the coming month. **PX**

·· **B.9**   Consider the following LP problem developed at Zafar Malik's Carbondale, Illinois, optical scanning firm:

$$\text{Maximize profit} = \$1X_1 + \$1X_2$$
$$\text{Subject to:}\qquad 2X_1 + 1X_2 \le 100$$
$$1X_1 + 2X_2 \le 100$$

a) What is the optimal solution to this problem? Solve it graphically.
b) If a technical breakthrough occurred that raised the profit per unit of X_1 to $3, would this affect the optimal solution?
c) Instead of an increase in the profit coefficient X_1 to $3, suppose that profit was overestimated and should only have been $1.25. Does this change the optimal solution? **PX**

· **B.10**   A craftsman named William Barnes builds two kinds of birdhouses, one for wrens and a second for bluebirds. Each wren birdhouse takes 4 hours of labor and 4 units of lumber. Each bluebird house requires 2 hours of labor and 12 units of lumber. The craftsman has available 60 hours of labor and 120 units of lumber. Wren houses yield a profit of $6 each, and bluebird houses yield a profit of $15 each.
a) Write out the objective and constraints.
b) Solve graphically. **PX**

•• **B.11**   Each coffee table produced by Kevin Watson Designers nets the firm a profit of $9. Each bookcase yields a $12 profit. Watson's firm is small and its resources limited. During any given production period (of 1 week), 10 gallons of varnish and 12 lengths of high-quality redwood are available. Each coffee table requires approximately 1 gallon of varnish and 1 length of redwood. Each bookcase takes 1 gallon of varnish and 2 lengths of wood.

Formulate Watson's production-mix decision as a linear programming problem, and solve. How many tables and bookcases should be produced each week? What will the maximum profit be? **Px**

• **B.12**   Par, Inc., produces a standard golf bag and a deluxe golf bag on a weekly basis. Each golf bag requires time for cutting and dyeing and time for sewing and finishing, as shown in the following table:

	HOURS REQUIRED PER BAG	
PRODUCT	CUTTING AND DYEING	SEWING AND FINISHING
Standard bag	1/2	1
Deluxe bag	1	2/3

The profits per bag and weekly hours available for cutting and dyeing and for sewing and finishing are as follows:

PRODUCT	PROFIT PER UNIT ($)
Standard bag	10
Deluxe bag	8

ACTIVITY	WEEKLY HOURS AVAILABLE
Cutting and dyeing	300
Sewing and finishing	360

Par, Inc., will sell whatever quantities it produces of these two products.
a) Find the mix of standard and deluxe golf bags to produce per week that maximizes weekly profit from these activities.
b) What is the value of the profit? **Px**

•• **B.13**   The Denver advertising agency promoting the new Breem dishwashing detergent wants to get the best exposure possible for the product within the $100,000 advertising budget ceiling placed on it. To do so, the agency needs to decide how much of the budget to spend on each of its two most effective media: (1) television spots during the afternoon hours and (2) large ads in the city's Sunday newspaper. Each television spot costs $3,000; each Sunday newspaper ad costs $1,250. The expected exposure, based on industry ratings, is 35,000 viewers for each TV commercial and 20,000 readers for each newspaper advertisement. The agency director, Deborah Kellogg, knows from experience that it is important to use both media in order to reach the broadest spectrum of potential Breem customers. She decides that at least 5 but no more than 25 television spots should be ordered, and that at least 10 newspaper ads should be contracted. How many times should each of the two media be used to obtain maximum exposure while staying within the budget? Use the graphical method to solve. **Px**

•••• **B.14**   Baton Rouge's Mt. Cedar Hospital is a large, private, 600-bed facility complete with laboratories, operating rooms, and X-ray equipment. In seeking to increase revenues, Mt. Cedar's administration has decided to make a 90-bed addition on a portion of adjacent land currently used for staff parking. The administrators feel that the labs, operating rooms, and X-ray department are not being fully utilized at present and do not need to be expanded to handle additional patients. The addition of 90 beds, however, involves deciding how many beds should be allocated to the medical staff (for medical patients) and how many to the surgical staff (for surgical patients).

The hospital's accounting and medical records departments have provided the following pertinent information: The average hospital stay for a medical patient is 8 days, and the average medical patient generates $2,280 in revenues. The average surgical patient is in the hospital 5 days and generates $1,515 in revenues. The laboratory is capable of handling 15,000 tests per year more than it *was* handling. The average medical patient requires 3.1 lab tests, the average surgical patient 2.6 lab tests. Furthermore, the average medical patient uses 1 X-ray, the average surgical patient 2 X-rays. If the hospital were expanded by 90 beds, the X-ray department could handle up to 7,000 X-rays without significant additional cost. Finally, the administration estimates that up to 2,800 additional operations could be performed in existing operating-room facilities. Medical patients, of course, require no surgery, whereas each surgical patient generally has one surgery performed.

Formulate this problem so as to determine how many medical beds and how many surgical beds should be added to maximize revenues. Assume that the hospital is open 365 days per year. **Px**

Additional problems **B.15–B.21** *are available in* MyOMLab.

Problems B.22–B.24 relate to Sensitivity Analysis

•• **B.22**   Kalyan Singhal Corp. makes three products, and it has three machines available as resources as given in the following LP problem:

Maximize contribution = $4X_1 + 4X_2 + 7X_3$
Subject to: $1X_1 + 7X_2 + 4X_3 \leq 100$ (hours on machine 1)
$\qquad\qquad 2X_1 + 1X_2 + 7X_3 \leq 110$ (hours on machine 2)
$\qquad\qquad 8X_1 + 4X_2 + 1X_3 \leq 100$ (hours on machine 3)

a) Determine the optimal solution using LP software.
b) Is there unused time available on any of the machines with the optimal solution?
c) What would it be worth to the firm to make an additional hour of time available on the third machine?
d) How much would the firm's profit increase if an extra 10 hours of time were made available on the second machine at no extra cost? **Px**

•••• **B.23** A fertilizer manufacturer has to fulfill supply contracts to its two main customers (650 tons to Customer A and 800 tons to Customer B). It can meet this demand by shipping existing inventory from any of its three warehouses. Warehouse 1 (W1) has 400 tons of inventory on hand, Warehouse 2 (W2) has 500 tons, and Warehouse 3 (W3) has 600 tons. The company would like to arrange the shipping for the lowest cost possible, where the per-ton transit costs are as follows:

	W1	W2	W3
Customer A	$7.50	$6.25	$6.50
Customer B	$6.75	$7.00	$8.00

a) Explain what each of the six decision variables (V) is: (*Hint:* Look at the Solver report below.)

V A1: _____

V A2: _____

V A3: _____

V B1: _____

V B2: _____

V B3: _____

b) Write out the objective function in terms of the variables (V A1, V A2, etc.) and the objective coefficients.

c) Aside from nonnegativity of the variables, what are the five constraints? Write a short description for each constraint, and write out the formula (and circle the type of equality/inequality).

	Description	Variables and Coefficients	What Type?	RHS
C1:	_____	Formula: _____	(= > | = | = <)	_____
C2:	_____	Formula: _____	(= > | = | = <)	_____
C3:	_____	Formula: _____	(= > | = | = <)	_____
C4:	_____	Formula: _____	(= > | = | = <)	_____
C5:	_____	Formula: _____	(= > | = | = <)	_____

After you formulate and enter the linear program for Problem B.23 in Excel, the Solver gives you the following sensitivity report:

Variable Cells

CELL	NAME	FINAL VALUE	REDUCED COST	OBJECTIVE COEFFICIENT	ALLOWABLE INCREASE	ALLOWABLE DECREASE
$B$6	V A1	0	1.5	7.5	1E+30	1.5
$C$6	V A2	100	0	6.25	0.25	0.75
$D$6	V A3	550	0	6.5	0.75	0.25
$E$6	V B1	400	0	6.75	0.5	1E+30
$F$6	V B2	400	0	7	0.75	0.5
$G$6	V B3	0	0.75	8	1E+30	0.75

Constraints

CELL	NAME	FINAL VALUE	SHADOW PRICE	CONSTRAINT R.H. SIDE	ALLOWABLE INCREASE	ALLOWABLE DECREASE
$H$7	C1	650	6.5	650	50	550
$H$8	C2	800	7.25	800	50	400
$H$9	C3	400	−0.5	400	400	50
$H$10	C4	500	−0.25	500	550	50
$H$11	C5	550	0	600	1E+30	50

d) How many of the constraints are binding?

e) What is the range of optimality on variable V A3?

f) If we could ship 10 tons less to Customer A, how much money *might* we be able to save? If we could choose to short *either* Customer A or Customer B by 10 tons, which would we prefer to short? Why? **Px**

Additional problem **B.24** is available in MyOMLab.

Problems B.25–B.33 relate to Solving Minimization Problems

• **B.25**   Solve the following linear program graphically:

Minimize cost $= X_1 + X_2$

$$8X_1 + 16X_2 \geq 64$$
$$X_1 \geq 0$$
$$X_2 \geq -2 \textbf{ Px}$$

(*Note:* X_2 values can be negative in this problem.)

• **B.26**   Solve the following LP problem graphically:

Minimize cost $= 24X + 15Y$

Subject to: $7X + 11Y \geq 77$

$$16X + 4Y \geq 80$$
$$X, Y \geq 0$$

•• **B.27**   Doug Turner Food Processors wishes to introduce a new brand of dog biscuits composed of chicken- and liver-flavored biscuits that meet certain nutritional requirements. The liver-flavored biscuits contain 1 unit of nutrient A and 2 units of nutrient B; the chicken-flavored biscuits contain 1 unit of nutrient A and 4 units of nutrient B. According to federal requirements, there must be at least 40 units of nutrient A and 60 units of nutrient B in a package of the new mix. In addition, the company has decided that there can be no more than 15 liver-flavored biscuits in a package. If it costs 1¢ to make 1 liver-flavored biscuit and 2¢ to make 1 chicken-flavored, what is the optimal product mix for a package of the biscuits to minimize the firm's cost?

a) Formulate this as a linear programming problem.

b) Solve this problem graphically, giving the optimal values of all variables.

c) What is the total cost of a package of dog biscuits using the optimal mix? **Px**

· **B.28**   The Sweet Smell Fertilizer Company markets bags of manure labeled "not less than 60 lb dry weight." The packaged manure is a combination of compost and sewage wastes. To provide good-quality fertilizer, each bag should contain at least 30 lb of compost but no more than 40 lb of sewage. Each pound of compost costs Sweet Smell 5¢ and each pound of sewage costs 4¢. Use a graphical LP method to determine the least-cost blend of compost and sewage in each bag. **Px**

· **B.29**   Consider Paul Jordan's following linear programming formulation:

$$\text{Minimize cost} = \$1X_1 + \$2X_2$$
$$\text{Subject to:} \quad X_1 + 3X_2 \geq 90$$
$$8X_1 + 2X_2 \geq 160$$
$$3X_1 + 2X_2 \geq 120$$
$$X_2 \leq 70$$

a) Graphically illustrate the feasible region to indicate to Jordan which corner point produces the optimal solution.

b) What is the cost of this solution? **Px**

· **B.30**   Solve the following linear programming problem graphically:

$$\text{Minimize cost} = 4X_1 + 5X_2$$
$$\text{Subject to:} \quad X_1 + 2X_2 \geq 80$$
$$3X_1 + X_2 \geq 75$$
$$X_1, X_2 \geq 0 \text{ **Px**}$$

·· **B.31**   How many corner points are there in the feasible region of the following problem?

$$\text{Minimize cost} = X - Y$$
$$\text{Subject to:} \quad X \leq 4$$
$$-X \leq 2$$
$$X + 2Y \leq 6$$
$$-X + 2Y \leq 8$$
$$Y \geq 0$$

(*Note: X* values can be negative in this problem.)

Additional problems **B.32–B.33** *are available in* MyOMLab.

Problems B.34–B.40 relate to Linear Programming Applications

··· **B.34**   The Hills County, Michigan, superintendent of education is responsible for assigning students to the three high schools in his county. He recognizes the need to bus a certain number of students, because several sectors, A–E, of the county are beyond walking distance to a school. The superintendent partitions the county into five geographic sectors as he attempts to establish a plan that will minimize the total number of student miles traveled by bus. He also recognizes that if a student happens to live in a certain sector and is assigned to the high school in that sector, there is no need to bus him because he can walk to school. The three schools are located in sectors B, C, and E.

Hans Magelssen/Shutterstock

The accompanying table reflects the number of high-school-age students living in each sector and the distance in miles from each sector to each school:

	DISTANCE TO SCHOOL			
SECTOR	SCHOOL IN SECTOR B	SCHOOL IN SECTOR C	SCHOOL IN SECTOR E	NUMBER OF STUDENTS
A	5	8	6	700
B	0	4	12	500
C	4	0	7	100
D	7	2	5	800
E	12	7	0	400
				2,500

Each high school has a capacity of 900 students.

a) Set up the objective function and constraints of this problem using linear programming so that the total number of student miles traveled by bus is minimized.

b) Solve the problem. **Px**

·· **B.35**   The Rio Credit Union has $250,000 available to invest in a 12-month commitment. The money can be placed in Brazilian treasury notes yielding an 8% return or in riskier high-yield bonds at an average rate of return of 9%. Credit union regulations require diversification to the extent that at least 50% of the investment be placed in Treasury notes. It is also decided that no more than 40% of the investment be placed in bonds. How much should the Rio Credit Union invest in each security so as to maximize its return on investment? **Px**

·· **B.36**   Wichita's famous Sethi Restaurant is open 24 hours a day. Servers report for duty at 3 A.M., 7 A.M., 11 A.M., 3 P.M., 7 P.M., or 11 P.M., and each works an 8-hour shift. The following table shows the minimum number of workers needed during the 6 periods into which the day is divided:

PERIOD	TIME	NUMBER OF SERVERS REQUIRED
1	3 A.M.–7 A.M.	3
2	7 A.M.–11 A.M.	12
3	11 A.M.–3 P.M.	16
4	3 P.M.–7 P.M.	9
5	7 P.M.–11 P.M.	11
6	11 P.M.–3 A.M.	4

Owner Avanti Sethi's scheduling problem is to determine how many servers should report for work at the start of each time period in order to minimize the total staff required for one day's operation. (*Hint:* Let X_i equal the number of servers beginning work in time period i, where $i = 1, 2, 3, 4, 5, 6$.) **Px**

•• **B.37** Leach Distributors packages and distributes industrial supplies. A standard shipment can be packaged in a class A container, a class K container, or a class T container. A single class A container yields a profit of $9; a class K container, a profit of $7; and a class T container, a profit of $15. Each shipment prepared requires a certain amount of packing material and a certain amount of time.

RESOURCES NEEDED PER STANDARD SHIPMENT		
CLASS OF CONTAINER	PACKING MATERIAL (POUNDS)	PACKING TIME (HOURS)
A	2	2
K	1	6
T	3	4

Total resource available each week: 130 pounds   240 hours

Hugh Leach, head of the firm, must decide the optimal number of each class of container to pack each week. He is bound by the previously mentioned resource restrictions but also decides that he must keep his 6 full-time packers employed all 240 hours (6 workers × 40 hours) each week.
     Formulate and solve this problem using LP software. **Px**

•••**B.38** Tri-State Manufacturing has three factories (1, 2, and 3) and three warehouses (A, B, and C). The following table shows the shipping costs between each factory and warehouse, the factory manufacturing capabilities (in thousands), and the warehouse capacities (in thousands). Management would like to keep the warehouses filled to capacity in order to generate demand.

TO / FROM	WAREHOUSE A	WAREHOUSE B	WAREHOUSE C	PRODUCTION CAPABILITY
Factory 1	$ 6	$ 5	$ 3	6
Factory 2	$ 8	$10	$ 8	8
Factory 3	$11	$14	$18	10
Capacity	7	12	5	

a) Write the objective function and the constraint equations. Let X_{1A} = 1,000s of units shipped from factory 1 to warehouse A, and so on.
b) Solve by computer. **Px**

•••• **B.39** Bowman Builders manufactures steel storage sheds for commercial use. Joe Bowman, president of Bowman Builders, is contemplating producing sheds for home use. The activities necessary to build an experimental model and related data are given in Table B.2.
a) What is the project normal time completion date? (See Chapter 3 for a review of project management.)
b) Formulate an LP problem to crash this project to 10 weeks.

TABLE B.2   **Data for Problem B.39**

ACTIVITY	NORMAL TIME	CRASH TIME	NORMAL COST ($)	CRASH COST ($)	IMMEDIATE PREDECESSORS
A	3	2	1,000	1,600	—
B	2	1	2,000	2,700	—
C	1	1	300	300	—
D	7	3	1,300	1,600	A
E	6	3	850	1,000	B
F	2	1	4,000	5,000	C
G	4	2	1,500	2,000	D, E

•••• **B.40** You have just been hired as a planner for the municipal school system, and your first assignment is to redesign the subsidized lunch program. In particular, you are to formulate the least expensive lunch menu that will still meet all state and federal nutritional guidelines.
     The guidelines are as follows: A meal must be between 500 and 800 calories. It must contain at least 200 calories of protein, at least 200 calories of carbohydrates, and no more than 400 calories of fat. It also needs to have at least 200 calories of a food classified as a fruit or vegetable.
     Table B.3 provides a list of the foods you can consider as possible menu items, with contract-determined prices and nutritional information. Note that all percentages sum to 100% per food—as all calories are protein, carbohydrate, or fat calories. For example, a serving of applesauce has 100 calories, all of which are carbohydrates, and it counts as a fruit/veg food. You are allowed to use fractional servings, such as 2.25 servings of turkey breast and a 0.33 portion of salad. Costs and nutritional attributes scale likewise: e.g., a 0.33 portion of salad costs $.30 and has 33 calories.

TABLE B.3	Data for Problem B.40					
FOOD	COST/SERVING	CALORIES/SERVING	% PROTEIN	% CARBS	% FAT	FRUIT/VEG
Applesauce	$0.30	100	0%	100%	0%	Y
Canned corn	$0.40	150	20%	80%	0%	Y
Fried chicken	$0.90	250	55%	5%	40%	N
French fries	$0.20	400	5%	35%	60%	N
Mac and cheese	$0.50	430	20%	30%	50%	N
Turkey breast	$1.50	300	67%	0%	33%	N
Garden salad	$0.90	100	15%	40%	45%	Y

Formulate and solve as a linear problem. Print out your formulation in Excel showing the objective function coefficients and constraint matrix in standard form.

- ◆ Display, on a separate page, the full *Answer Report* as generated by Excel Solver.
- ◆ Highlight *and label as Z* the objective value for the optimal solution on the Answer Report.
- ◆ Highlight the nonzero decision variables for the optimal solution on the Answer Report.
- ◆ Display, on a separate page, the full *Sensitivity Report* as generated by Excel Solver. **Px**

Problems B.41–B.42 relate to Integer and Binary Variables

•• B.41 Rollins Publishing needs to decide what textbooks from the following table to publish.

TEXT-BOOK	DEMAND	FIXED COST	VARIABLE COST	SELLING PRICE
Book 1	9,000	$12,000	$19	$40
Book 2	8,000	$21,000	$28	$60
Book 3	5,000	$15,000	$30	$52
Book 4	6,000	$10,000	$20	$34
Book 5	7,000	$18,000	$20	$45

For each book, the maximum demand, fixed cost of publishing, variable cost, and selling price are provided. Rollins has the capacity to publish a total of 20,000 books.

a) Formulate this problem to determine which books should be selected and how many of each should be published to maximize profit.

b) Solve using computer software. **Px**

•• B.42 Porter Investments needs to develop an investment portfolio for Mrs. Singh from the following list of possible investments:

INVESTMENT	COST	EXPECTED RETURN
A	$10,000	$ 700
B	$12,000	$1,000
C	$ 3,500	$ 390
D	$ 5,000	$ 500
E	$ 8,500	$ 750
F	$ 8,000	$ 640
G	$ 4,000	$ 300

Mrs. Singh has a total of $60,000 to invest. The following conditions must be met: (1) If investment F is chosen, then investment G must also be part of the portfolio, (2) at least four investments should be chosen, and (3) of investments A and B, exactly one must be included. Formulate and solve this problem using LP software to determine which stocks should be included in Mrs. Singh's portfolio. **Px**

CASE STUDIES

Quain Lawn and Garden, Inc.

Bill and Jeanne Quain spent a career as a husband-and-wife real estate investment partnership in Atlantic City, New Jersey. When they finally retired to a 25-acre farm in nearby Cape May County, they became ardent amateur gardeners. Bill planted shrubs and fruit trees, and Jeanne spent her hours potting all sizes of plants. When the volume of shrubs and plants reached the point that the Quains began to think of their hobby in a serious vein, they built a greenhouse adjacent to their home and installed heating and watering systems.

By 2012, the Quains realized their retirement from real estate had really only led to a second career—in the plant and shrub business—and they filed for a New Jersey business license. Within

a matter of months, they asked their attorney to file incorporation documents and formed the firm Quain Lawn and Garden, Inc.

Early in the new business's existence, Bill Quain recognized the need for a high-quality commercial fertilizer that he could blend himself, both for sale and for his own nursery. His goal was to keep his costs to a minimum while producing a top-notch product that was especially suited to the New Jersey climate.

Working with chemists at Rutgers University, Quain blended "Quain-Grow." It consists of four chemical compounds, C-30, C-92, D-21, and E-11. The cost per pound for each compound is indicated in the table on the next page:

CHEMICAL COMPOUND	COST PER POUND
C-30	$.12
C-92	.09
D-21	.11
E-11	.04

The specifications for Quain-Grow are established as:

a) Chemical E-11 must constitute at least 15% of the blend.

b) C-92 and C-30 must together constitute at least 45% of the blend.

c) D-21 and C-92 can together constitute no more than 30% of the blend.

d) Quain-Grow is packaged and sold in 50-lb bags.

Discussion Questions

1. Formulate an LP problem to determine what blend of the four chemicals will allow Quain to minimize the cost of a 50-lb bag of the fertilizer.

2. Solve to find the best solution.

Scheduling Challenges at Alaska Airlines

Video Case

Good airline scheduling is essential to delivering outstanding customer service with high plane utilization rates. Airlines must schedule pilots, flight attendants, aircraft, baggage handlers, customer service agents, and ramp crews. At Alaska Airlines, it all begins with seasonal flight schedules that are developed 330 days in advance.

Revenue and marketing goals drive the potential routing decisions, but thousands of constraints impact these schedules. Using SABRE scheduling optimizer software, Alaska considers the number of planes available, seat capacity, ranges, crew availability, union contracts that dictate hours that crews can fly, and maintenance regulations that regularly take planes out of service, just to name a few. Alaska's scheduling department sends preliminary schedules to the human resources, maintenance, operations, customer service, marketing, and other departments for feedback before finalizing flight schedules.

Alaska Airlines' historic mission is to serve its extremely loyal customer base in the remote and unreachable small towns in Alaska. Serving many airports in Alaska is especially complex because the airline requires its pilots to have special skills to deal with extremely adverse weather, tight mountain passes, and short runways. Some airports lack full-time TSA agents or strong ground support and may not even be open 24 hours per day. In some cases, runways are not plowed because the village plow is busy clearing the roads for school buses. Navigational technology developed by Alaska Airlines has significantly reduced weather-related cancelled flights as Alaska can now land where many other carriers cannot.

After the SABRE optimizer schedules thousands of flights, scheduling activity turns to the next step: crew optimizing. The crew optimizer (Alaska uses Jeppersen software developed by Boeing and based on linear programming) attempts to eliminate unnecessary layovers and crew idle time while adhering to FAA and union restrictions. Alaska leads the industry in pilot "hard time" (i.e., the amount of time a pilot is being paid when passengers are actually being moved). After the crew requirements for every flight are determined, the 3,000 flight attendants and 1,500 pilots rank their preferred routings on a monthly basis. Personnel are assigned to each flight using seniority and feasibility.

Interestingly, not every pilot or flight attendant always bids on the Hawaii routes (about 20% of all flights), the long-haul East Coast routes, or the Mexico flights. Some prefer the flying challenge of the "milk run" flights to Ketchikan, Sitka, Juneau, Fairbanks, Anchorage, and back to Seattle, which are in keeping with the culture and contact with local residents.

As an airline that accentuates risk taking and empowers employees to think "out of the box," Alaska recently decided to experiment with a schedule change on its Seattle-to-Chicago route. Given crew restrictions on flying hours per day, the flight had previously included a crew layover in Chicago. When a company analyst documented the feasibility of running the same crew on the two 4-hour legs of the round trip (which implied an *extremely* tight turnaround schedule in Chicago), his data indicated that on 98.7% of the round trip flights, the crew would not "time out." His boss gave the go-ahead.

Discussion Questions*

1. Why is scheduling for Alaska more complex than for other airlines?

2. What operational considerations may prohibit Alaska from adding flights and more cities to its network?

3. What were the risks of keeping the same crew on the Seattle—Chicago—Seattle route?

4. Estimate the direct costs to the airline should the crew "time out" and not be able to fly its Boeing 737 back to Seattle from Chicago on the same day. These direct variable costs should include moving and parking the plane overnight along with hotel and meal costs for the crew and passengers. Do you think this is more advantageous than keeping a spare crew in Chicago?

*You may wish to view the video that accompanies this case before addressing these questions.

• **Additional Case Studies:** Visit MyOMLab for these free case studies:

Chase Manhattan Bank: This scheduling case involves finding the optimal number of full-time versus part-time employees at a bank.

Coastal States Chemical: The company must prepare for a shortage of natural gas.

Endnotes

1. *Iso* means "equal" or "similar." Thus, an iso-profit line represents a line with all profits the same, in this case $210.

2. See, for example, Barry Render, Ralph M. Stair, Michael Hanna, and T. Hale, *Quantitative Analysis for Management*, 12th ed. (Pearson Education, Inc., Upper Saddle River, NJ, 2013): Chapters 7–9; or Raju Balakrishnan, Barry Render, and Ralph M. Stair, *Managerial Decision Modeling with Spreadsheets*, 3rd ed. (Pearson Education, Inc., Upper Saddle River, NJ, 2012): Chapters 2–4.

Module B *Rapid* Review

Main Heading	Review Material	MyOMLab
WHY USE LINEAR PROGRAMMING? (p. 700)	■ **Linear programming (LP)**—A mathematical technique designed to help operations managers plan and make decisions relative to allocation of resources.	Concept Questions: 1.1–1.4 **VIDEO B.1** Scheduling Challenges at Alaska Airlines
REQUIREMENTS OF A LINEAR PROGRAMMING PROBLEM (p. 701)	■ **Objective function**—A mathematical expression in linear programming that maximizes or minimizes some quantity (often profit or cost, but any goal may be used). ■ **Constraints**—Restrictions that limit the degree to which a manager can pursue an objective. All LP problems have four properties in common: 1. LP problems seek to *maximize* or *minimize* some quantity. We refer to this property as the *objective function* of an LP problem. 2. The presence of restrictions, or *constraints*, limits the degree to which we can pursue our objective. We want, therefore, to maximize or minimize a quantity (the objective function) subject to limited resources (the constraints). 3. There must be *alternative courses of action* to choose from. 4. The objective and constraints in linear programming problems must be expressed in terms of *linear equations* or inequalities.	Concept Questions: 2.1–2.4 Problem: B.1
FORMULATING LINEAR PROGRAMMING PROBLEMS (pp. 701–702)	One of the most common linear programming applications is the *product-mix problem*. Two or more products are usually produced using limited resources. For example, a company might like to determine how many units of each product it should produce to maximize overall profit, given its limited resources. An important aspect of linear programming is that certain interactions will exist between variables. The more units of one product that a firm produces, the fewer it can make of other products.	Concept Questions: 3.1–3.4 Virtual Office Hours for Solved Problem: B.1 ACTIVE MODEL B.1
GRAPHICAL SOLUTION TO A LINEAR PROGRAMMING PROBLEM (pp. 702–705)	■ **Graphical solution approach**—A means of plotting a solution to a two-variable problem on a graph. ■ **Decision variables**—Choices available to a decision maker. Constraints of the form $X \geq 0$ are called *nonnegativity constraints*. ■ **Feasible region**—The set of all feasible combinations of decision variables. Any point inside the feasible region represents a *feasible solution*, while any point outside the feasible region represents an *infeasible solution*. ■ **Iso-profit line method**—An approach to identifying the optimum point in a graphic linear programming problem. The line that touches a particular point of the feasible region will pinpoint the optimal solution. ■ **Corner-point method**—Another method for solving graphical linear programming problems. The mathematical theory behind linear programming states that an optimal solution to any problem will lie at a *corner point*, or an *extreme point*, of the feasible region. Hence, it is necessary to find only the values of the variables at each corner; the optimal solution will lie at one (or more) of them. This is the corner-point method.	Concept Questions: 4.1–4.4 Problems: B.2–B.21 Virtual Office Hours for Solved Problem: B.2
SENSITIVITY ANALYSIS (pp. 705–708)	■ **Parameter**—A numerical value that is given in a model. ■ **Sensitivity analysis**—An analysis that projects how much a solution may change if there are changes in the variables or input data. Sensitivity analysis is also called *postoptimality analysis*. There are two approaches to determining just how sensitive an optimal solution is to changes: (1) a trial-and-error approach and (2) the analytic postoptimality method.	Concept Questions: 5.1–5.4 Problems: B.22–B.24

Main Heading	Review Material	MyOMLab
	To use the analytic postoptimality method, after an LP problem has been solved, we determine a range of changes in problem parameters that will not affect the optimal solution or change the variables in the solution. LP software has this capability. While using the information in a sensitivity report to answer what-if questions, we assume that we are considering a change to only a *single* input data value at a time. That is, the sensitivity information does not generally apply to simultaneous changes in several input data values. ■ **Shadow price** (or **dual value**)—The value of one additional unit of a scarce resource in LP. The shadow price is valid as long as the right-hand side of the constraint stays in a range within which all current corner points continue to exist. The information to compute the upper and lower limits of this range is given by the entries labeled Allowable Increase and Allowable Decrease in the sensitivity report.	
SOLVING MINIMIZATION PROBLEMS (pp. 708–709)	■ **Iso-cost**—An approach to solving a linear programming minimization problem graphically. The iso-cost line approach to solving minimization problems is analogous to the iso-profit approach for maximization problems, but successive iso-cost lines are drawn *inward* instead of outward.	Concept Questions: 6.1–6.3 Problems: B.25–B.33 Virtual Office Hours for Solved Problem: B.3
LINEAR PROGRAM-MING APPLICATIONS (pp. 710–713)	The *diet problem*, known in agricultural applications as the *feed-mix problem*, involves specifying a food or feed ingredient combination that will satisfy stated nutritional requirements at a minimum cost level. *Labor scheduling problems* address staffing needs over a specific time period. They are especially useful when managers have some flexibility in assigning workers to jobs that require overlapping or interchangeable talents.	Concept Questions: 7.1–7.3 Problems: B.34–B.40
THE SIMPLEX METHOD OF LP (p. 713)	■ **Simplex method**—An algorithm for solving linear programming problems of all sizes. The simplex method is actually a set of instructions with which we examine corner points in a methodical fashion until we arrive at the best solution—highest profit or lowest cost. Computer programs (such as Excel OM and POM for Windows) and Excel's Solver add-in are available to solve linear programming problems via the simplex method.	Concept Questions: 8.1–8.2 Virtual Office Hours for Solved Problem: C.1 (note that this Module C video is an LP application of the transportation problem)
INTEGER AND BINARY VARIABLES (pp. 713–715)	■ **Binary variables**—Decision variables that can only take on the value of 0 or 1. Using computer software, decision variables for linear programs can be forced to be integer or even binary. Binary variables extend the flexibility of linear programs to include such options as mutually exclusive alternatives, either-or constraints, contingent decisions, fixed-charge problems, and threshold levels.	Concept Questions: 9.1–9.4 Problems: B.41–B.42

Self Test

■ **Before taking the self-test,** refer to the learning objectives listed at the beginning of the module and the key terms listed at the end of the module.

LO B.1 Which of the following is *not* a valid LP constraint formulation?
a) $3X + 4Y \leq 12$ b) $2X \times 2Y \leq 12$
c) $3Y + 2Z = 18$ d) $100 \geq X + Y$
e) $2.5X + 1.5Z = 30.6$

LO B.2 Using a *graphical solution procedure* to solve a maximization problem requires that we:
a) move the iso-profit line up until it no longer intersects with any constraint equation.
b) move the iso-profit line down until it no longer intersects with any constraint equation.
c) apply the method of simultaneous equations to solve for the intersections of constraints.
d) find the value of the objective function at the origin.

LO B.3 Consider the following linear programming problem:
Maximize $4X + 10Y$
Subject to: $3X + 4Y \leq 480$
$4X + 2Y \leq 360$
$X, Y \geq 0$
The feasible corner points are (48,84), (0,120), (0,0), and (90,0). What is the maximum possible value for the objective function?
a) 1,032 b) 1,200 c) 360 d) 1,600 e) 840

LO B.4 A zero shadow price for a resource ordinarily means that:
a) the resource is scarce.
b) the resource constraint was redundant.
c) the resource has not been used up.
d) something is wrong with the problem formulation.
e) none of the above.

LO B.5 For these two constraints, which point is in the feasible region of this minimization problem?
$$14x + 6y \geq 42 \quad \text{and} \quad x + y \geq 3$$
a) $x = -1, y = 1$ b) $x = 0, y = 4$
c) $x = 2, y = 1$ d) $x = 5, y = 1$
e) $x = 2, y = 0$

LO B.6 When applying LP to diet problems, the objective function is usually designed to:
a) maximize profits from blends of nutrients.
b) maximize ingredient blends.
c) minimize production losses.
d) maximize the number of products to be produced.
e) minimize the costs of nutrient blends.

Answers: LO B.1. b; LO B.2. a; LO B.3. b; LO B.4. c; LO B.5. d; LO B.6. e.

Transportation Models

Alaska Airlines

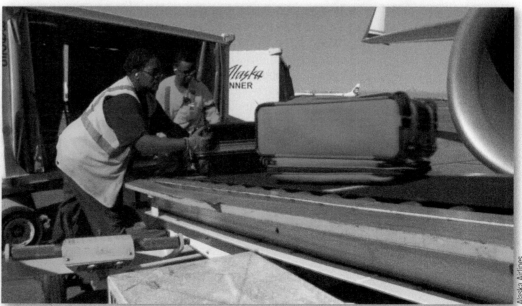

Alaska Airlines

The problem facing rental companies like Avis, Hertz, and National is cross-country travel. Lots of it. Cars rented in New York end up in Chicago, cars from L.A. come to Philadelphia, and cars from Boston come to Miami. The scene is repeated in over 100 cities around the U.S. As a result, there are too many cars in some cities and too few in others. Operations managers have to decide how many of these rentals should be trucked (by costly auto carriers) from each city with excess capacity to each city that needs more rentals. The process requires quick action for the most economical routing, so rental car companies turn to transportation modeling.

Vibrant Image Studio/Shutterstock

Transportation Modeling

Because location of a new factory, warehouse, or distribution center is a strategic issue with substantial cost implications, most companies consider and evaluate several locations. With a wide variety of objective and subjective factors to be considered, rational decisions are aided by a number of techniques. One of those techniques is transportation modeling.

The transportation models described in this module prove useful when considering alternative facility locations *within the framework of an existing distribution system*. Each new potential plant, warehouse, or distribution center will require a different allocation of shipments, depending on its own production and shipping costs and the costs of each existing facility. The choice of a new location depends on which will yield the minimum cost *for the entire system*.

Transportation modeling

An iterative procedure for solving problems that involves minimizing the cost of shipping products from a series of sources to a series of destinations.

Transportation modeling finds the least-cost means of shipping supplies from several origins to several destinations. *Origin points* (or *sources*) can be factories, warehouses, car rental agencies like Avis, or any other points from which goods are shipped. *Destinations* are any points that receive goods. To use the transportation model, we need to know the following:

1. The origin points and the capacity or supply per period at each.
2. The destination points and the demand per period at each.
3. The cost of shipping one unit from each origin to each destination.

The transportation model is one form of the linear programming models discussed in Business Analytics Module B. Software is available to solve both transportation problems and the more general class of linear programming problems. To fully use such programs, though, you need to understand the assumptions that underlie the model. To illustrate the transportation problem, we now look at a company called Arizona Plumbing, which makes, among other products,

TABLE C.1	Transportation Costs Per Bathtub for Arizona Plumbing		
FROM \ **TO**	**ALBUQUERQUE**	**BOSTON**	**CLEVELAND**
Des Moines	$5	$4	$3
Evansville	$8	$4	$3
Fort Lauderdale	$9	$7	$5

a full line of bathtubs. In our example, the firm must decide which of its factories should supply which of its warehouses. Relevant data for Arizona Plumbing are presented in Table C.1 and Figure C.1. Table C.1 shows, for example, that it costs Arizona Plumbing $5 to ship one bathtub from its Des Moines factory to its Albuquerque warehouse, $4 to Boston, and $3 to Cleveland.

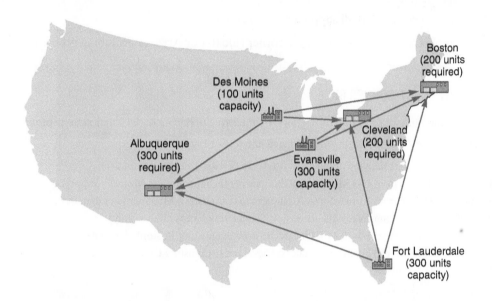

Figure **C.1**

Transportation Problem

Likewise, we see in Figure C.1 that the 300 units required by Arizona Plumbing's Albuquerque warehouse may be shipped in various combinations from its Des Moines, Evansville, and Fort Lauderdale factories.

The first step in the modeling process is to set up a *transportation matrix*. Its purpose is to summarize all relevant data and to keep track of algorithm computations. Using the information displayed in Figure C.1 and Table C.1, we can construct a transportation matrix as shown in Figure C.2.

From \ **To**	Albuquerque	Boston	Cleveland	Factory capacity
Des Moines	$5	$4	$3	100
Evansville	$8	$4	$3	300
Fort Lauderdale	$9	$7	$5	300
Warehouse requirement	300	200	200	700

Des Moines capacity constraint

Cell representing a possible source-to-destination shipping assignment (Evansville to Cleveland)

Cost of shipping 1 unit from Fort Lauderdale factory to Boston warehouse

Cleveland warehouse demand

Total demand and total supply

Figure **C.2**

Transportation Matrix for Arizona Plumbing

Developing an Initial Solution

Once the data are arranged in tabular form, we must establish an initial feasible solution to the problem. A number of different methods have been developed for this step. We now discuss two of them, the northwest-corner rule and the intuitive lowest-cost method.

The Northwest-Corner Rule

Northwest-corner rule

A procedure in the transportation model where one starts at the upper-left-hand cell of a table (the northwest corner) and systematically allocates units to shipping routes.

The northwest-corner rule requires that we start in the upper-left-hand cell (or northwest corner) of the table and allocate units to shipping routes as follows:

1. Exhaust the supply (factory capacity) of each row (e.g., Des Moines: 100) before moving down to the next row.
2. Exhaust the (warehouse) requirements of each column (e.g., Albuquerque: 300) before moving to the next column on the right.
3. Check to ensure that all supplies and demands are met.

Example C1 applies the northwest-corner rule to our Arizona Plumbing problem.

Example C1

THE NORTHWEST-CORNER RULE

Arizona Plumbing wants to use the northwest-corner rule to find an initial solution to its problem.

APPROACH ▶ Follow the three steps listed above. See Figure C.3.

SOLUTION ▶ To make the initial solution, these five assignments are made:

1. Assign 100 tubs from Des Moines to Albuquerque (exhausting Des Moines's supply).
2. Assign 200 tubs from Evansville to Albuquerque (exhausting Albuquerque's demand).
3. Assign 100 tubs from Evansville to Boston (exhausting Evansville's supply).
4. Assign 100 tubs from Fort Lauderdale to Boston (exhausting Boston's demand).
5. Assign 200 tubs from Fort Lauderdale to Cleveland (exhausting Cleveland's demand and Fort Lauderdale's supply).

Figure C.3

Northwest-Corner Solution to Arizona Plumbing Problem

To \ From	(A) Albuquerque	(B) Boston	(C) Cleveland	Factory capacity
(D) Des Moines	$5 — 100	$4	$3	100
(E) Evansville	$8 — 200	$4 — 100	$3	300
(F) Fort Lauderdale	$9	$7 — (100)	$5 — 200	300
Warehouse requirement	300	200	200	700

Means that the firm is shipping 100 bathtubs from Fort Lauderdale to Boston

The total cost of this shipping assignment is $4,200 (see Table C.2).

TABLE C.2   Computed Shipping Cost

ROUTE		TUBS SHIPPED	COST PER UNIT	TOTAL COST
FROM	TO			
D	A	100	$5	$ 500
E	A	200	8	1,600
E	B	100	4	400
F	B	100	7	700
F	C	200	5	$1,000
				Total: $4,200

INSIGHTS ▶ The solution given is feasible because it satisfies all demand and supply constraints. The northwest-corner rule is easy to use, but it totally ignores costs, and therefore should only be considered as a starting position.

LEARNING EXERCISE ▶ Does the shipping assignment change if the cost from Des Moines to Albuquerque increases from $5 per unit to $10 per unit? Does the total cost change? [Answer: The initial assignment is the same, but cost = $4,700.]

RELATED PROBLEMS ▶ C.1a, C.3a, C.15

The Intuitive Lowest-Cost Method

The intuitive method makes initial allocations based on lowest cost. This straightforward approach uses the following steps:

Intuitive method
A cost-based approach to finding an initial solution to a transportation problem.

1. Identify the cell with the lowest cost. Break any ties for the lowest cost arbitrarily.
2. Allocate as many units as possible to that cell without exceeding the supply or demand. Then cross out that row or column (or both) that is exhausted by this assignment.
3. Find the cell with the lowest cost from the remaining (not crossed out) cells.
4. Repeat Steps 2 and 3 until all units have been allocated.

Example C2 | THE INTUITIVE LOWEST-COST APPROACH

Arizona Plumbing now wants to apply the intuitive lowest-cost approach.

APPROACH ▶ Apply the 4 steps listed above to the data in Figure C.2.

SOLUTION ▶ When the firm uses the intuitive approach on the data (rather than the northwest-corner rule) for its starting position, it obtains the solution seen in Figure C.4.

The total cost of this approach = $3(100) + $3(100) + $4(200) + $9(300) = $4,100.
(D to C)   (E to C)   (E to B)   (F to A)

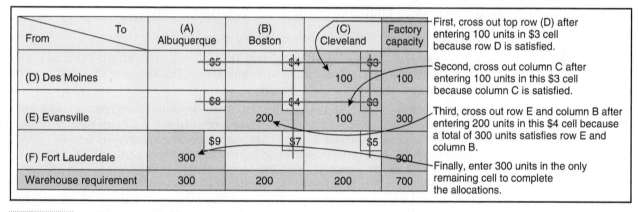

Figure **C.4**

Intuitive Lowest-Cost Solution to Arizona Plumbing Problem

INSIGHT ▶ This method's name is appropriate as most people find it intuitively correct to include costs when making an initial assignment.

LEARNING EXERCISE ▶ If the cost per unit from Des Moines to Cleveland is not $3, but rather $6, does this initial solution change? [Answer: Yes, now D − B = 100, D − C = 0, E − B = 100, E − C = 200, F − A = 300. Others unchanged at zero. Total cost stays the same.]

RELATED PROBLEMS ▶ C.1b, C.2, C.3b

Although the likelihood of a minimum-cost solution *does* improve with the intuitive method, we would have been fortunate if the intuitive solution yielded the minimum cost. In this case, as in the northwest-corner solution, it did not. Because the northwest-corner and the intuitive lowest-cost approaches are meant only to provide us with a starting point, we often will have to employ an additional procedure to reach an *optimal* solution.

The Stepping-Stone Method

Stepping-stone method

An iterative technique for moving from an initial feasible solution to an optimal solution in the transportation method.

LO C.2 *Solve* a problem with the stepping-stone method

The stepping-stone method will help us move from an initial feasible solution to an optimal solution. It is used to evaluate the cost effectiveness of shipping goods via transportation routes not currently in the solution. When applying it, we test each unused cell, or square, in the transportation table by asking: What would happen to total shipping costs if one unit of the product (for example, one bathtub) was tentatively shipped on an unused route? We conduct the test as follows:

1. Select any unused square to evaluate.
2. Beginning at this square, trace a closed path back to the original square via squares that are currently being used (only horizontal and vertical moves are permissible). You may, however, step over either an empty or an occupied square.
3. Beginning with a plus (+) sign at the unused square, place alternating minus signs and plus signs on each corner square of the closed path just traced.
4. Calculate an improvement index by first adding the unit-cost figures found in each square containing a plus sign and then by subtracting the unit costs in each square containing a minus sign.
5. Repeat Steps 1 through 4 until you have calculated an improvement index for all unused squares. If all indices computed are *greater than or equal to zero*, you have reached an optimal solution. If not, the current solution can be improved further to decrease total shipping costs.

Example C3 illustrates how to use the stepping-stone method to move toward an optimal solution. We begin with the northwest-corner initial solution developed in Example C1.

Example C3

CHECKING UNUSED ROUTES WITH THE STEPPING-STONE METHOD

Arizona Plumbing wants to evaluate unused shipping routes.

APPROACH ▶ Start with Example C1's Figure C.3 and follow the 5 steps listed above. As you can see, the four currently unassigned routes are Des Moines to Boston, Des Moines to Cleveland, Evansville to Cleveland, and Fort Lauderdale to Albuquerque.

SOLUTION ▶ **Steps 1 and 2.** Beginning with the Des Moines–Boston route, trace a closed path *using only currently occupied squares* (see Figure C.5). Place alternating plus and minus signs in the corners of this path. In the upper-left square, for example, we place a minus sign because we have *subtracted* 1 unit from the original 100. Note that we can use only squares currently used for shipping to turn the corners of the route we are tracing. Hence, the path Des Moines–Boston to Des Moines–Albuquerque to Fort Lauderdale–Albuquerque to Fort Lauderdale–Boston to Des Moines–Boston would not be acceptable because the Fort Lauderdale–Albuquerque square is empty. It turns out that *only one closed route exists for each empty square*. Once this one closed path is identified, we can begin assigning plus and minus signs to these squares in the path.

   Step 3. How do we decide which squares get plus signs and which squares get minus signs? The answer is simple. Because we are testing the cost-effectiveness of the Des Moines–Boston shipping route, we try shipping 1 bathtub from Des Moines to Boston. This is 1 *more* unit than we *were* sending between the two cities, so place a plus sign in the box. However, if we ship 1 more unit than before from Des Moines to Boston, we end up sending 101 bathtubs out of the Des Moines factory. Because the Des Moines factory's capacity is only 100 units, we must ship 1 bathtub less from Des Moines to Albuquerque. This change prevents us from violating the capacity constraint.

   To indicate that we have reduced the Des Moines–Albuquerque shipment, place a minus sign in its box. As you continue along the closed path, notice that we are no longer meeting our Albuquerque warehouse requirement for 300 units. In fact, if we reduce the Des Moines–Albuquerque shipment to 99 units, we must increase the Evansville–Albuquerque load by 1 unit, to 201 bathtubs. Therefore, place a plus sign in that box to indicate the increase. You may also observe that those squares in which we turn a corner (and only those squares) will have plus or minus signs.

Finally, note that if we assign 201 bathtubs to the Evansville–Albuquerque route, then we must reduce the Evansville–Boston route by 1 unit, to 99 bathtubs, to maintain the Evansville factory's capacity constraint of 300 units. To account for this reduction, we thus insert a minus sign in the Evansville–Boston box. By so doing, we have balanced supply limitations among all four routes on the closed path.

Step 4. Compute an improvement index for the Des Moines–Boston route by adding unit costs in squares with plus signs and subtracting costs in squares with minus signs.

$$\text{Des Moines–Boston index} = \$4 - \$5 + \$8 - \$4 = +\$3$$

This means that for every bathtub shipped via the Des Moines–Boston route, total transportation costs will increase by $3 over their current level.

Let us now examine the unused Des Moines–Cleveland route, which is slightly more difficult to trace with a closed path (see Figure C.6). Again, notice that we turn each corner along the path only at squares on the existing route. Our path, for example, can go through the Evansville–Cleveland box but cannot turn a corner; thus we cannot place a plus or minus sign there. We may use occupied squares only as stepping-stones:

$$\text{Des Moines–Cleveland index} = \$3 - \$5 + \$8 - \$4 + \$7 - \$5 = +\$4$$

Figure **C.6**

Testing Des Moines to Cleveland

From \ To	(A) Albuquerque	(B) Boston	(C) Cleveland	Factory capacity
(D) Des Moines	$5 100	$4	Start $3	100
(E) Evansville	$8 200+	$4 – 100	$3	300
(F) Fort Lauderdale	$9	$7 + 100	$5 – 200	300
Warehouse requirement	300	200	200	700

Again, opening this route fails to lower our total shipping costs.

Two other routes can be evaluated in a similar fashion:

$$\text{Evansville–Cleveland index} = \$3 - \$4 + \$7 - \$5 = +\$1$$

$$(\text{Closed path} = EC - EB + FB - FC)$$

$$\text{Fort Lauderdale–Albuquerque index} = \$9 - \$7 + \$4 - \$8 = -\$2$$

$$(\text{Closed path} = FA - FB + EB - EA)$$

INSIGHT ▶ Because this last index is negative, we can realize cost savings by using the (currently unused) Fort Lauderdale–Albuquerque route.

LEARNING EXERCISE ▶ What would happen to total cost if Arizona used the shipping route from Des Moines to Cleveland? [Answer: Total cost of the current solution would increase by $400.]

RELATED PROBLEMS ▶ C.1c, C.3c, C.4–C.11 (C.12, C.13 are available in MyOMLab)

EXCEL **OM** Data File **ModCExC3.xls** can be found in MyOMLab.

In Example C3, we see that a better solution is indeed possible because we can calculate a negative improvement index on one of our unused routes. *Each negative index represents the amount by which total transportation costs could be decreased if one unit was shipped by the source–destination combination.* The next step, then, is to choose that route (unused square) with the *largest* negative improvement index. We can then ship the maximum allowable number of units on that route and reduce the total cost accordingly.

What is the maximum quantity that can be shipped on our new money-saving route? That quantity is found by referring to the closed path of plus signs and minus signs drawn for the route and then selecting the *smallest number found in the squares containing minus signs*. To obtain a new solution, we add this number to all squares on the closed path with plus signs and subtract it from all squares on the path to which we have assigned minus signs.

One iteration of the stepping-stone method is now complete. Again, of course, we must test to see if the solution is optimal or whether we can make any further improvements. We do this by evaluating each unused square, as previously described. Example C4 continues our effort to help Arizona Plumbing arrive at a final solution.

Example C4

IMPROVEMENT INDICES

Arizona Plumbing wants to continue solving the problem.

APPROACH ▶ Use the improvement indices calculated in Example C3. We found in Example C3 that the largest (and only) negative index is on the Fort Lauderdale–Albuquerque route (which is the route depicted in Figure C.7).

SOLUTION ▶ The maximum quantity that may be shipped on the newly opened route, Fort Lauderdale–Albuquerque (FA), is the smallest number found in squares containing minus signs—in this case, 100 units. Why 100 units? Because the total cost decreases by $2 per unit shipped, we know we would like to ship the maximum possible number of units. Previous stepping-stone calculations indicate that each unit shipped over the FA route results in an increase of 1 unit shipped from Evansville (E) to Boston (B) and a decrease of 1 unit in amounts shipped both from F to B (now 100 units) and from E to A (now 200 units). Hence, the maximum we can ship over the FA route is 100 units. This solution results in zero units being shipped from F to B. Now we take the following four steps:

1. Add 100 units (to the zero currently being shipped) on route FA.
2. Subtract 100 from route FB, leaving zero in that square (though still balancing the row total for F).
3. Add 100 to route EB, yielding 200.
4. Finally, subtract 100 from route EA, leaving 100 units shipped.

Note that the new numbers still produce the correct row and column totals as required. The new solution is shown in Figure C.8.

Total shipping cost has been reduced by (100 units) × ($2 saved per unit) = $200 and is now $4,000. This cost figure, of course, can also be derived by multiplying the cost of

Figure **C.7**

**Transportation Table:
Route FA**

From \ To	(A) Albuquerque	(B) Boston	(C) Cleveland	Factory capacity
(D) Des Moines	$5 100	$4	$3	100
(E) Evansville	$8 200	$4 100	$3	300
(F) Fort Lauderdale	$9	$7 100	$5 200	300
Warehouse demand	300	200	200	700

STUDENT TIP ◆
FA has a negative index:
FA (+9) to FB (−7) to EB (+4)
to EA (−8) = −$2

Figure **C.8**

**Solution at Next Iteration
(Still Not Optimal)**

From \ To	(A) Albuquerque	(B) Boston	(C) Cleveland	Factory capacity
(D) Des Moines	$5 100	$4	$3	100
(E) Evansville	$8 100	$4 200	$3	300
(F) Fort Lauderdale	$9 100	$7	$5 200	300
Warehouse demand	300	200	200	700

shipping each unit by the number of units transported on its respective route, namely: $100(\$5) + 100(\$8) + 200(\$4) + 100(\$9) + 200(\$5) = \$4,000$.

INSIGHT ▶ Looking carefully at Figure C.8, however, you can see that it, too, is not yet optimal. Route EC (Evansville–Cleveland) has a negative cost improvement index of –$1. Closed path = EC − EA + FA − FC.

LEARNING EXERCISE ▶ Find the final solution for this route on your own. [Answer: Programs C.1 and C.2, at the end of this module, provide an Excel OM solution.]

RELATED PROBLEMS ▶ C.4–C.11 (C.12–C.13 are available in MyOMLab)

Special Issues in Modeling

Demand Not Equal to Supply

A common situation in real-world problems is the case in which total demand is not equal to total supply. We can easily handle these so-called unbalanced problems with the solution procedures that we have just discussed by introducing *dummy sources* or *dummy destinations*. If total supply is greater than total demand, we make demand exactly equal the surplus by creating a dummy destination. Conversely, if total demand is greater than total supply, we introduce a dummy source (factory) with a supply equal to the excess of demand. Because these units will not in fact be shipped, we assign cost coefficients of zero to each square on the dummy location. In each case, then, the cost is zero.

LO C.3 *Balance* a transportation problem

Degeneracy

To apply the stepping-stone method to a transportation problem, we must observe a rule about the number of shipping routes being used: *The number of occupied squares in any solution (initial or later) must be equal to the number of rows in the table plus the number of columns minus 1.* Solutions that do not satisfy this rule are called *degenerate*.

LO C.4 *Deal* with a problem that has degeneracy

Degeneracy

An occurrence in transportation models in which too few squares or shipping routes are being used, so that tracing a closed path for each unused square becomes impossible.

Degeneracy occurs when too few squares or shipping routes are being used. As a result, it becomes impossible to trace a closed path for one or more unused squares. The Arizona Plumbing problem we just examined was *not* degenerate, as it had 5 assigned routes (3 rows or factories + 3 columns or warehouses − 1).

To handle degenerate problems, we must artificially create an occupied cell: That is, we place a zero or a *very* small amount (representing a fake shipment) in one of the unused squares and *then treat that square as if it were occupied.* The chosen square must be in such a position as to allow all stepping-stone paths to be closed.

Summary

The transportation model, a form of linear programming, is used to help find the least-cost solutions to system-wide shipping problems. The northwest-corner method (which begins in the upper-left corner of the transportation table) or the intuitive lowest-cost method may be used for finding an initial feasible solution. The stepping-stone algorithm is then used for finding optimal solutions. Unbalanced problems are those in which the total demand and total supply are not equal. Degeneracy refers to the case in which the number of rows + the number of columns −1 is not equal to the number of occupied squares. The transportation model approach is one of the four location models described earlier in Chapter 8 and is one of the two aggregate planning models discussed in Chapter 13. Additional solution techniques are presented in Tutorial 4 in MyOMLab.

Key Terms

Transportation modeling (p. 730)
Northwest-corner rule (p. 732)

Intuitive method (p. 733)
Stepping-stone method (p. 734)

Degeneracy (p. 738)

Discussion Questions

1. What are the three information needs of the transportation model?
2. What are the steps in the intuitive lowest-cost method?
3. Identify the three "steps" in the northwest-corner rule.
4. How do you know when an optimal solution has been reached?
5. Which starting technique generally gives a better initial solution, and why?
6. The more sources and destinations there are for a transportation problem, the smaller the percentage of all cells that will be used in the optimal solution. Explain.
7. All of the transportation examples appear to apply to long distances. Is it possible for the transportation model to apply

on a much smaller scale, for example, within the departments of a store or the offices of a building? Discuss.
8. Develop a *northeast*-corner rule and explain how it would work. Set up an initial solution for the Arizona Plumbing problem analyzed in Example C1.
9. What is meant by an unbalanced transportation problem, and how would you balance it?
10. How many occupied cells must all solutions use?
11. Explain the significance of a negative improvement index in a transportation-minimizing problem.
12. How can the transportation method address production costs in addition to transportation costs?
13. Explain what is meant by the term *degeneracy* within the context of transportation modeling.

Using Software to Solve Transportation Problems

Excel, Excel OM, and POM for Windows may all be used to solve transportation problems. Excel uses Solver, which requires that you enter your own constraints. Excel OM also uses Solver but is prestructured so that you need enter only the actual data. POM for Windows similarly requires that only demand data, supply data, and shipping costs be entered.

✖ USING EXCEL OM

Excel OM's Transportation module uses Excel's built-in Solver routine to find optimal solutions to transportation problems. Program C.1 illustrates the input data (from Arizona Plumbing) and total-cost formulas. In Excel 2007, 2010, and 2013 Solver is in the Analysis section of the Data tab. Be certain that the solving method is "Simplex LP." The output appears in Program C.2.

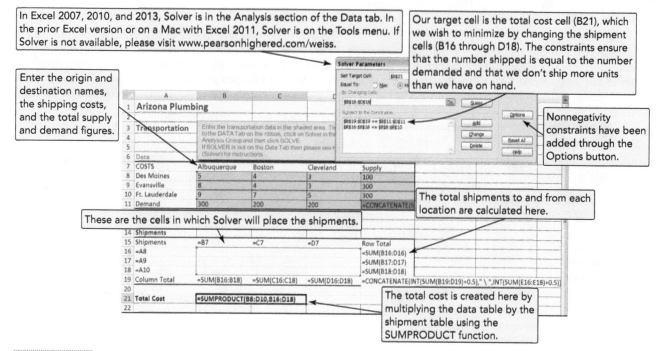

Program **C.1**

Excel OM Input Screen and Formulas, Using Arizona Plumbing Data

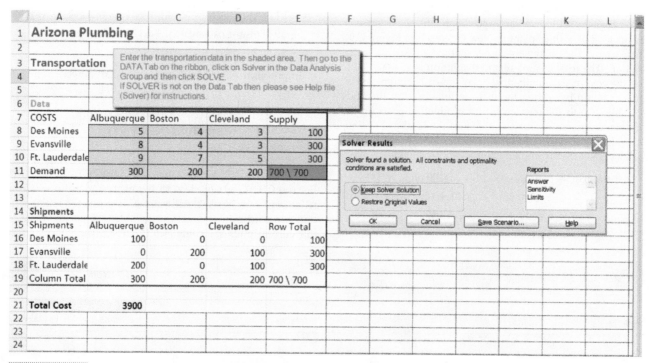

Program **C.2**

Output from Excel OM with Optimal Solution to Arizona Plumbing Problem

P USING POM FOR WINDOWS

The POM for Windows Transportation module can solve both maximization and minimization problems by a variety of methods. Input data are the demand data, supply data, and unit shipping costs. See Appendix IV for further details.

Solved Problems   Virtual Office Hours help is available in MyOMLab.

SOLVED PROBLEM C.1

Williams Auto Top Carriers currently maintains plants in Atlanta and Tulsa to supply auto top carriers to distribution centers in Los Angeles and New York. Because of expanding demand, Williams has decided to open a third plant and has narrowed the choice to one of two cities—New Orleans and Houston. Table C.3 provides pertinent production and distribution costs as well as plant capacities and distribution demands.

Which of the new locations, in combination with the existing plants and distribution centers, yields a lower cost for the firm?

TABLE C.3	Production Costs, Distribution Costs, Plant Capabilities, and Market Demands for Williams Auto Top Carriers			
	TO DISTRIBUTION CENTERS			
FROM PLANTS	**LOS ANGELES**	**NEW YORK**	**NORMAL PRODUCTION**	**UNIT PRODUCTION COST**
Existing plants				
Atlanta	$8	$5	600	$6
Tulsa	$4	$7	900	$5
Proposed locations				
New Orleans	$5	$6	500	$4 (anticipated)
Houston	$4	$6ª	500	$3 (anticipated)
Forecast demand	800	1,200	2,000	

ªIndicates distribution cost (shipping, handling, storage) will be $6 per carrier between Houston and New York.

SOLUTION

To answer this question, we must solve two transportation problems, one for each combination. We will recommend the location that yields a lower total cost of distribution and production in combination with the existing system.

We begin by setting up a transportation table that represents the opening of a third plant in New Orleans (see Figure C.9). Then we use the northwest-corner method to find an initial solution. The total cost of this first solution is $23,600. Note that the cost of each individual "plant-to-distribution-center" route is found by adding the distribution costs (in the body of Table C.3) to the respective unit production costs (in the right-hand column of Table C.3). Thus, the total production-plus-shipping cost of one auto top carrier from Atlanta to Los Angeles is $14 ($8 for shipping plus $6 for production).

$$\text{Total cost} = (600 \text{ units} \times \$14) + (200 \text{ units} \times \$9)$$
$$+ (700 \text{ units} \times \$12) + (500 \text{ units} \times \$10)$$
$$= \$8,400 + \$1,800 + \$8,400 + \$5,000$$
$$= \$23,600$$

Is this initial solution (in Figure C.9) optimal? We can use the stepping-stone method to test it and compute improvement indices for unused routes:

Improvement index for Atlanta–New York route:

$$= +\$11 \text{ (Atlanta–New York)} - \$14 \text{ (Atlanta–Los Angeles)}$$
$$+\$9 \text{ (Tulsa–Los Angeles)} - \$12 \text{ (Tulsa–New York)}$$
$$= -\$6$$

Improvement index for New Orleans–Los Angeles route:

$$= +\$9 \text{ (New Orleans–Los Angeles)}$$
$$-\$10 \text{ (New Orleans–New York)}$$
$$+\$12 \text{ (Tulsa–New York)}$$
$$-\$9 \text{ (Tulsa–Los Angeles)}$$
$$= \$2$$

Because the firm can save $6 for every unit shipped from Atlanta to New York, it will want to improve the initial solution and send as many units as possible (600, in this case) on this currently unused route (see Figure C.10). You may also

From \ To	Los Angeles	New York	Production capacity
Atlanta	$14	$11	600
	600		
Tulsa	$9	$12	900
	200	700	
New Orleans	$9	$10	500
		500	
Demand	800	1,200	2,000

Figure C.9

Initial Williams Transportation Table for New Orleans

From \ To	Los Angeles	New York	Production capacity
Atlanta	$14	$11	600
		600	
Tulsa	$9	$12	900
	800	100	
New Orleans	$9	$10	500
		500	
Demand	800	1,200	2,000

Figure C.10

Improved Transportation Table for Williams

want to confirm that the total cost is now $20,000, a savings of $3,600 over the initial solution.

Next, we must test the two unused routes to see if their improvement indices are also negative numbers:

Index for Atlanta–Los Angeles:

$$= \$14 - \$11 + \$12 - \$9 = \$6$$

Index for New Orleans–Los Angeles:

$$= \$9 - \$10 + \$12 - \$9 = \$2$$

Because both indices are greater than zero, we have already reached our optimal solution for the New Orleans location. If Williams elects to open the New Orleans plant, the firm's total production and distribution cost will be $20,000.

This analysis, however, provides only half the answer to Williams's problem. The same procedure must still be followed to determine the minimum cost if the new plant is built in Houston. Determining this cost is left as a homework problem. You can help provide complete information and recommend a solution by solving Problem C.7 (on p. 742).

SOLVED PROBLEM C.2

In Solved Problem C.1, we examined the Williams Auto Top Carriers problem by using a transportation table. An alternative approach is to structure the same decision analysis using linear programming (LP), which we explained in detail in Business Analytics Module B.

SOLUTION

Using the data in Figure C.9 (p. 740), we write the objective function and constraints as follows:

$$\text{Minimize total cost} = \$14X_{Atl,LA} + \$11X_{Atl,NY} + \$9X_{Tul,LA} + \$12X_{Tul,NY} + \$9X_{NO,LA} + \$10X_{NO,NY}$$

$$\begin{aligned}
\text{Subject to:} \quad & X_{Atl,LA} + X_{Atl,NY} && \leq 600 && \text{(production capacity at Atlanta)} \\
& X_{Tul,LA} + X_{Tul,NY} && \leq 900 && \text{(production capacity at Tulsa)} \\
& X_{NO,LA} + X_{NO,NY} && \leq 500 && \text{(production capacity at New Orleans)} \\
& X_{Atl,LA} + X_{Tul,LA} + X_{NO,LA} && \geq 800 && \text{(Los Angeles demand constraint)} \\
& X_{Atl,NY} + X_{Tul,NY} + X_{NO,NY} && \geq 1200 && \text{(New York demand constraint)}
\end{aligned}$$

Problems

Note: ▶️ means the problem may be solved with POM for Windows and/or Excel OM.

Problems C.1–C.3 relate to Developing an Initial Solution

• **C.1** Find an initial solution to the following transportation problem.

FROM	LOS ANGELES	CALGARY	PANAMA CITY	SUPPLY
Mexico City	$ 6	$18	$ 8	100
Detroit	$17	$13	$19	60
Ottawa	$20	$10	$24	40
Demand	50	80	70	

a) Use the northwest-corner method. What is its total cost?
b) Use the intuitive lowest-cost approach. What is its total cost?
c) Using the stepping-stone method, find the optimal solution. Compute the total cost. ▶️

• **C.2** Consider the transportation table at right. Unit costs for each shipping route are in dollars. What is the total cost of the basic feasible solution that the intuitive lowest-cost method would find for this problem? ▶️

Destination

Source	A	B	C	D	E	Supply
1	12	8	5	10	4	18
2	6	11	3	7	9	14
Demand	6	8	12	4	2	

• **C.3** Refer to the table that follows.
a) Use the northwest-corner method to find an initial feasible solution. What must you do before beginning the solution steps?
b) Use the intuitive lowest-cost approach to find an initial feasible solution. Is this approach better than the northwest-corner method?
c) Find the optimal solution using the stepping-stone method.

FROM	TO			SUPPLY
	A	B	C	
X	$10	$18	$12	100
Y	$17	$13	$ 9	50
Z	$20	$18	$14	75
Demand	50	80	70	

Problems C.4–C.13 relate to The Stepping-Stone Method

· C.4   Consider the transportation table below. The solution displayed was obtained by performing some iterations of the transportation method on this problem. What is the total cost of the shipping plan that would be obtained by performing *one more iteration* of the stepping-stone method on this problem?

Destination

Source	Denver	Yuma	Miami	Supply
Houston	$2 / 10	$8	$1	10
St. Louis	$4 / 10	$5 / 10	$6	20
Chicago	$6	$3 / 10	$2 / 20	30
Demand	20	20	20	

·· C.5   The following table is the result of one or more iterations.

From\To	1	2	3	Capacity
A	30 / 40	30	5 / 10	50
B	10	10 / 30	10	30
C	20	10 / 30	25 / 45	75
Demand	40	60	55	155

a) Complete the next iteration using the stepping-stone method.
b) Calculate the "total cost" incurred if your results were to be accepted as the final solution. **Px**

·· C.6   The three blood banks in Seminole County, Florida, are coordinated through a central office that facilitates blood delivery to four hospitals in the region. The cost to ship a standard container of blood from each bank to each hospital is shown in the table below. Also given are the biweekly number of containers available at each bank and the biweekly number of containers of blood needed at each hospital. How many shipments should be made biweekly from each blood bank to each hospital so that total shipment costs are minimized?

Minerva Studio/Fotolia

FROM	TO				SUPPLY
	HOSP. 1	HOSP. 2	HOSP. 3	HOSP. 4	
Bank 1	$ 8	$ 9	$11	$16	50
Bank 2	$12	$ 7	$ 5	$ 8	80
Bank 3	$14	$10	$ 6	$ 7	120
Demand	90	70	40	50	250

Px

·· C.7   In Solved Problem C.1 (page 740), Williams Auto Top Carriers proposed opening a new plant in either New Orleans or Houston. Management found that the total system cost (of production plus distribution) would be $20,000 for the New Orleans site. What would be the total cost if Williams opened a plant in Houston? At which of the two proposed locations (New Orleans or Houston) should Williams open the new facility? **Px**

·· C.8   The Donna Mosier Clothing Group owns factories in three towns (W, Y, and Z), which distribute to three retail dress shops in three other cities (A, B, and C). The following table summarizes factory availabilities, projected store demands, and unit shipping costs:

From\To	Dress Shop A	Dress Shop B	Dress Shop C	Factory availability
Factory W	$4	$3	$3	35
Factory Y	$6	$7	$6	50
Factory Z	$8	$2	$5	50
Store demand	30	65	40	135

a) Complete the analysis, determining the optimal solution for shipping at the Mosier Clothing Group.
b) How do you know whether it is optimal or not? **Px**

··· C.9   Captain Borders Corp. manufacturers fishing equipment. Currently, the company has a plant in Los Angeles and a plant in New Orleans. William Borders, the firm's owner, is deciding where to build a new plant—Philadelphia or Seattle. Use the following table to find the total shipping costs for each potential site. Which should Borders select?

PLANT	WAREHOUSE			
	PITTSBURGH	ST. LOUIS	DENVER	CAPACITY
Los Angeles	$100	$75	$50	150
New Orleans	$ 80	$60	$90	225
Philadelphia	$ 40	$50	$90	350
Seattle	$110	$70	$30	350
Demand	200	100	400	

Px

•• **C.10**   Dana Johnson Corp. is considering adding a fourth plant to its three existing facilities in Decatur, Minneapolis, and Carbondale. Both St. Louis and East St. Louis are being considered. Evaluating only the transportation costs per unit as shown in the table, decide which site is best.

TO	FROM EXISTING PLANTS			
	DECATUR	MINNEAPOLIS	CARBONDALE	DEMAND
Blue Earth	$20	$17	$21	250
Ciro	$25	$27	$20	200
Des Moines	$22	$25	$22	350
Capacity	300	200	150	

TO	FROM PROPOSED PLANTS	
	EAST ST. LOUIS	ST. LOUIS
Blue Earth	$29	$27
Ciro	$30	$28
Des Moines	$30	$31
Capacity	150	150

Px

•• **C.11**   Using the data from Problem C.10 and the unit production costs in the following table, show which locations yield the lowest cost.

LOCATION	PRODUCTION COSTS ($)
Decatur	$50
Minneapolis	60
Carbondale	70
East St. Louis	40
St. Louis	50

Px

Additional problems **C.12–C.13** *are available in* MyOMLab.

Problems C.14–C.18 relate to Special Issues in Modeling

•• **C.14**   Allen Air Conditioning manufactures room air conditioners at plants in Houston, Phoenix, and Memphis. These are sent to regional distributors in Dallas, Atlanta, and Denver. The shipping costs vary, and the company would like to find the least-cost way to meet the demands at each of the distribution centers. Dallas needs to receive 800 air conditioners per month, Atlanta needs 600, and Denver needs 200. Houston has 850 air conditioners available each month, Phoenix has 650, and Memphis has 300. The shipping cost per unit from Houston to Dallas is $8, to Atlanta $12, and to Denver $10. The cost per unit from Phoenix to Dallas is $10, to Atlanta $14, and to Denver $9. The cost per unit from Memphis to Dallas is $11, to Atlanta $8, and to Denver $12. How many units should owner Stephen Allen ship from each plant to each regional distribution center? What is the total transportation cost? (Note that a "dummy" destination is needed to balance the problem.) **Px**

•• **C.15**   For the following Gregory Bier Corp. data, find the starting solution and initial cost using the northwest-corner method. What must you do to balance this problem?

FROM	TO				
	W	X	Y	Z	SUPPLY
A	$132	$116	$250	$110	220
B	$220	$230	$180	$178	300
C	$152	$173	$196	$164	435
Demand	160	120	200	230	

Px

Additional problems **C.16–C.18** *are available in* MyOMLab.

CASE STUDY

Custom Vans, Inc.

Custom Vans, Inc., specializes in converting standard vans into campers. Depending on the amount of work and customizing to be done, the customizing can cost from less than $1,000 to more than $5,000. In less than 4 years, Tony Rizzo was able to expand his small operation in Gary, Indiana, to other major outlets in Chicago, Milwaukee, Minneapolis, and Detroit.

Innovation was the major factor in Tony's success in converting a small van shop into one of the largest and most profitable custom van operations in the Midwest. Tony seemed to have a special ability to design and develop unique features and devices that were always in high demand by van owners. An example was Shower-Rific, which was developed by Tony only 6 months after Custom Vans, Inc., was started. These small showers were completely self-contained, and they could be placed in almost any type of van and in a number of different locations within a van. Shower-Rific was made of fiberglass, and contained towel racks,

built-in soap and shampoo holders, and a unique plastic door. Each Shower-Rific took 2 gallons of fiberglass and 3 hours of labor to manufacture.

Most of the Shower-Rifics were manufactured in Gary in the same warehouse where Custom Vans, Inc., was founded. The manufacturing plant in Gary could produce 300 Shower-Rifics in a month, but this capacity never seemed to be enough. Custom Van shops in all locations were complaining about not getting enough Shower-Rifics, and because Minneapolis was farther away from Gary than the other locations, Tony was always inclined to ship Shower-Rifics to the other locations before Minneapolis. This infuriated the manager of Custom Vans at Minneapolis, and after many heated discussions, Tony decided to start another manufacturing plant for Shower-Rifics at Fort Wayne, Indiana. The manufacturing plant at Fort Wayne could produce 150 Shower-Rifics per month.

The manufacturing plant at Fort Wayne was still not able to meet current demand for Shower-Rifics, and Tony knew that the demand for his unique camper shower would grow rapidly in the next year. After consulting with his lawyer and banker, Tony concluded that he should open two new manufacturing plants as soon as possible. Each plant would have the same capacity as the Fort Wayne manufacturing plant. An initial investigation into possible manufacturing locations was made, and Tony decided that the two new plants should be located in Detroit, Michigan; Rockford, Illinois; or Madison, Wisconsin. Tony knew that selecting the best location for the two new manufacturing plants would be difficult. Transportation costs and demands for the various locations would be important considerations.

The Chicago shop was managed by Bill Burch. This shop was one of the first established by Tony, and it continued to outperform the other locations. The manufacturing plant at Gary was supplying 200 Shower-Rifics each month, although Bill knew that the demand for the showers in Chicago was 300 units. The transportation cost per unit from Gary was $10, and although the transportation cost from Fort Wayne was double that amount, Bill was always pleading with Tony to get an additional 50 units from the Fort Wayne manufacturer. The two additional manufacturing plants would certainly be able to supply Bill with the additional 100 showers he needed. The transportation costs would, of course, vary, depending on which two locations Tony picked. The transportation cost per shower would be $30 from Detroit, $5 from Rockford, and $10 from Madison.

Wilma Jackson, manager of the Custom Van shop in Milwaukee, was the most upset about not getting an adequate supply of showers. She had a demand for 100 units, and at the present time, she was only getting half of this demand from the Fort Wayne manufacturing plant. She could not understand why Tony didn't ship her all 100 units from Gary. The transportation cost per unit from Gary was only $20, while the transportation cost from Fort Wayne was $30. Wilma was hoping that Tony would select Madison for one of the manufacturing locations. She would be able to get all the showers needed, and the transportation cost per unit would only be $5. If not in Madison, a new plant in Rockford would be able to supply her total needs, but the transportation cost per unit would be twice as much as it would be from Madison. Because the transportation cost per unit from Detroit would be $40, Wilma speculated that even if Detroit became one of the new plants, she would not be getting any units from Detroit.

Custom Vans, Inc., of Minneapolis was managed by Tom Poanski. He was getting 100 showers from the Gary plant. Demand was 150 units. Tom faced the highest transportation costs of all locations. The transportation cost from Gary was $40 per unit. It would cost $10 more if showers were sent from the Fort Wayne location. Tom was hoping that Detroit would not be one of the new plants, as the transportation cost would be $60 per unit. Rockford and Madison would have a cost of $30 and $25, respectively, to ship one shower to Minneapolis.

The Detroit shop's position was similar to Milwaukee's—only getting half of the demand each month. The 100 units that Detroit did receive came directly from the Fort Wayne plant. The transportation cost was only $15 per unit from Fort Wayne, while it was

$25 from Gary. Dick Lopez, manager of Custom Vans, Inc., of Detroit, placed the probability of having one of the new plants in Detroit fairly high. The factory would be located across town, and the transportation cost would be only $5 per unit. He could get 150 showers from the new plant in Detroit and the other 50 showers from Fort Wayne. Even if Detroit was not selected, the other two locations were not intolerable. Rockford had a transportation cost per unit of $35, and Madison had a transportation cost of $40.

Tony pondered the dilemma of locating the two new plants for several weeks before deciding to call a meeting of all the managers of the van shops. The decision was complicated, but the objective was clear—to minimize total costs. The meeting was held in Gary, and everyone was present except Wilma.

Tony: Thank you for coming. As you know, I have decided to open two new plants at Rockford, Madison, or Detroit. The two locations, of course, will change our shipping practices, and I sincerely hope that they will supply you with the Shower-Rifics that you have been wanting. I know you could have sold more units, and I want you to know that I am sorry for this situation.

Dick: Tony, I have given this situation a lot of consideration, and I feel strongly that at least one of the new plants should be located in Detroit. As you know, I am now only getting half of the showers that I need. My brother, Leon, is very interested in running the plant, and I know he would do a good job.

Tom: Dick, I am sure that Leon could do a good job, and I know how difficult it has been since the recent layoffs by the auto industry. Nevertheless, we should be considering total costs and not personalities. I believe that the new plants should be located in Madison and Rockford. I am farther away from the other plants than any other shop, and these locations would significantly reduce transportation costs.

Dick: That may be true, but there are other factors. Detroit has one of the largest suppliers of fiberglass, and I have checked prices. A new plant in Detroit would be able to purchase fiberglass for $2 per gallon less than any of the other existing or proposed plants.

Tom: At Madison, we have an excellent labor force. This is due primarily to the large number of students attending the University of Wisconsin. These students are hard workers, and they will work for $1 less per hour than the other locations that we are considering.

Bill: Calm down, you two. It is obvious that we will not be able to satisfy everyone in locating the new plants. Therefore, I would like to suggest that we vote on the two best locations.

Tony: I don't think that voting would be a good idea. Wilma was not able to attend, and we should be looking at all of these factors together in some type of logical fashion.

Discussion Question

Where would you locate the two new plants? Why?

Source: From *Quantitative Analysis for Management*, B. Render, R. M. Stair, M. Hanna, and T. Hale. 12th ed. Copyright © 2015. Reprinted by permission of Pearson Publishing, Upper Saddle River, NJ.

- **Additional Case Study:** Visit MyOMLab for this free case study:
  Consolidated Bottling (B): This case involves determining where to add bottling capacity.

Module C *Rapid* Review

Main Heading	Review Material	MyOMLab
TRANSPORTATION MODELING (pp. 730–731)	The transportation models described in this module prove useful when considering alternative facility locations *within the framework of an existing distribution system.* The choice of a new location depends on which will yield the minimum cost for the entire system.	Concept Questions: 1.1–1.4

TRANSPORTATION MODELING (pp. 730–731)

The transportation models described in this module prove useful when considering alternative facility locations *within the framework of an existing distribution system.* The choice of a new location depends on which will yield the minimum cost for the entire system.

- **Transportation modeling**—An iterative procedure for solving problems that involves minimizing the cost of shipping products from a series of sources to a series of destinations.

Origin points (or *sources*) can be factories, warehouses, car rental agencies, or any other points from which goods are shipped.

Destinations are any points that receive goods.

To use the transportation model, we need to know the following:

1. The origin points and the capacity or supply per period at each.
2. The destination points and the demand per period at each.
3. The cost of shipping one unit from each origin to each destination.

The transportation model is a type of linear programming model.

A *transportation matrix* summarizes all relevant data and keeps track of algorithm computations. Shipping costs from each origin to each destination are contained in the appropriate cross-referenced box.

FROM \ TO	DESTINATION 1	DESTINATION 2	DESTINATION 3	CAPACITY
Source A				
Source B				
Source C				
Demand				

Concept Questions: 1.1–1.4

DEVELOPING AN INITIAL SOLUTION (pp. 732–734)

Two methods for establishing an initial feasible solution to the problem are the northwest-corner rule and the intuitive lowest-cost method.

- **Northwest-corner rule**—A procedure in the transportation model where one starts at the upper-left-hand cell of a table (the northwest corner) and systematically allocates units to shipping routes.

The northwest-corner rule requires that we:

1. Exhaust the supply (origin capacity) of each row before moving down to the next row.
2. Exhaust the demand requirements of each column before moving to the next column to the right.
3. Check to ensure that all supplies and demands are met.

The northwest-corner rule is easy to use and generates a feasible solution, but it totally ignores costs and therefore should be considered only as a starting position.

- **Intuitive method**—A cost-based approach to finding an initial solution to a transportation problem.

The intuitive method uses the following steps:

1. Identify the cell with the lowest cost. Break any ties for the lowest cost arbitrarily.
2. Allocate as many units as possible to that cell, without exceeding the supply or demand. Then cross out that row or column (or both) that is exhausted by this assignment.
3. Find the cell with the lowest cost from the remaining (not crossed out) cells.
4. Repeat Steps 2 and 3 until all units have been allocated.

Concept Questions: 2.1–2.4

Problems: C.1–C.3, C.15

THE STEPPING-STONE METHOD (pp. 734–737)

- **Stepping-stone method**—An iterative technique for moving from an initial feasible solution to an optimal solution in the transportation method.

The stepping-stone method is used to evaluate the cost-effectiveness of shipping goods via transportation routes not currently in the solution. When applying it, we test each unused cell, or square, in the transportation table by asking: What would happen to total shipping costs if one unit of the product were tentatively shipped on an unused route? We conduct the test as follows:

1. Select any unused square to evaluate.
2. Beginning at this square, trace a closed path back to the original square via squares that are currently being used (only horizontal and vertical moves are permissible). You may, however, step over either an empty or an occupied square.

Concept Questions: 3.1–3.4

Problems: C.4–C.13

Virtual Office Hours for Solved Problem: C.1

Main Heading	Review Material	MyOMLab
	3. Beginning with a plus (+) sign at the unused square, place alternative minus signs and plus signs on each corner square of the closed path just traced. 4. Calculate an improvement index by first adding the unit-cost figures found in each square containing a plus sign and then subtracting the unit costs in each square containing a minus sign. 5. Repeat Steps 1 through 4 until you have calculated an improvement index for all unused squares. If all indices computed are *greater than or equal to zero*, you have reached an optimal solution. If not, the current solution can be improved further to decrease total shipping costs. *Each negative index represents the amount by which total transportation costs could be decreased if one unit was shipped by the source–destination combination.* The next step, then, is to choose that route (unused square) with the *largest* negative improvement index. We can then ship the maximum allowable number of units on that route and reduce the total cost accordingly. That maximum quantity is found by referring to the closed path of plus signs and minus signs drawn for the route and then selecting the *smallest number found in the squares containing minus signs*. To obtain a new solution, we add this number to all squares on the closed path with plus signs and subtract it from all squares on the path to which we have assigned minus signs. From this new solution, a new test of unused squares needs to be conducted to see if the new solution is optimal or whether we can make further improvements.	
SPECIAL ISSUES IN MODELING (pp. 737–738)	*Dummy sources*—Artificial shipping source points created when total demand is greater than total supply to effect a supply equal to the excess of demand over supply. *Dummy destinations*—Artificial destination points created when the total supply is greater than the total demand; they serve to equalize the total demand and supply. Because units from dummy sources or to dummy destinations will not in fact be shipped, we assign cost coefficients of zero to each square on the dummy location. If you are solving a transportation problem by hand, be careful to decide first whether a dummy source (row) or a dummy destination (column) is needed. When applying the stepping-stone method, *the number of occupied squares in any solution (initial or later) must be equal to the number of rows in the table plus the number of columns minus 1.* Solutions that do not satisfy this rule are called *degenerate*. ■ **Degeneracy**—An occurrence in transportation models in which too few squares or shipping routes are being used, so that tracing a closed path for each unused square becomes impossible. To handle degenerate problems, we must artificially create an occupied cell: That is, we place a zero (representing a fake shipment) into one of the unused squares and *then treat that square as if it were occupied*. Remember that the chosen square must be in such a position as to allow all stepping-stone paths to be closed.	Concept Questions: 4.1–4.4 Problems: C.14–C.18 Virtual Office Hours for Solved Problem: C.2

Self Test

■ **Before taking the self-test,** refer to the learning objectives listed at the beginning of the module and the key terms listed at the end of the module.

LO C.1 With the transportation technique, the initial solution can be generated in any fashion one chooses. The only restriction(s) is that:
 a) the solution be optimal.
 b) one use the northwest-corner method.
 c) the edge constraints for supply and demand be satisfied.
 d) the solution not be degenerate.
 e) all of the above.

LO C.2 The purpose of the stepping-stone method is to:
 a) develop the initial solution to a transportation problem.
 b) identify the relevant costs in a transportation problem.
 c) determine whether a given solution is feasible.
 d) assist one in moving from an initial feasible solution to the optimal solution.
 e) overcome the problem of degeneracy.

LO C.3 The purpose of a *dummy source* or a *dummy destination* in a transportation problem is to:
 a) provide a means of representing a dummy problem.
 b) obtain a balance between total supply and total demand.
 c) prevent the solution from becoming degenerate.
 d) make certain that the total cost does not exceed some specified figure.
 e) change a problem from maximization to minimization.

LO C.4 If a solution to a transportation problem is degenerate, then:
 a) it will be impossible to evaluate all empty cells without removing the degeneracy.
 b) a dummy row or column must be added.
 c) there will be more than one optimal solution.
 d) the problem has no feasible solution.
 e) increase the cost of each cell by 1.

Answers: LO C.1. c; LO C.2. d; LO C.3. b; LO C.4. a.

Waiting-Line Models

MODULE OUTLINE

Alaska Airlines

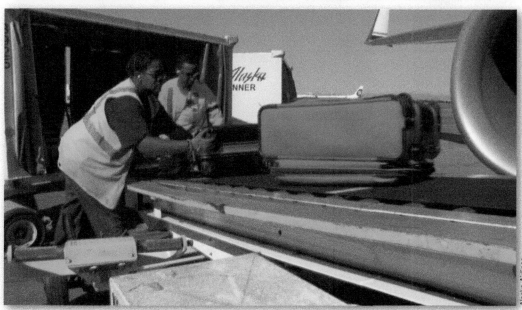

Alaska Airlines

Paris's EuroDisney, Tokyo's Disney Japan, and the U.S.'s Disney World and Disneyland all have one feature in common—long lines and seemingly endless waits. However, Disney is one of the world's leading companies in the scientific analysis of queuing theory. It analyzes queuing behaviors and can predict which rides will draw what length crowds. To keep visitors happy, Disney makes lines appear to be constantly moving forward, entertains people while they wait, and posts signs telling visitors how many minutes until they reach each ride.

Joshua Sudock/ZUMA Press/Corbis

Queuing Theory

Queuing theory
A body of knowledge about waiting lines.

Waiting line (queue)
Items or people in a line awaiting service.

The body of knowledge about waiting lines, often called queuing theory, is an important part of operations and a valuable tool for the operations manager. Waiting lines are a common situation—they may, for example, take the form of cars waiting for repair at a Midas Muffler Shop, copying jobs waiting to be completed at a FedEx office, or vacationers waiting to enter a ride at Disney. Table D.1 lists just a few OM uses of waiting-line models.

Waiting-line models are useful in both manufacturing and service areas. Analysis of queues in terms of waiting-line length, average waiting time, and other factors helps us to understand service systems (such as bank teller stations), maintenance activities (that might repair broken machinery), and shop-floor control activities. Indeed, patients waiting in a doctor's office and broken drill presses waiting in a repair facility have a lot in common from an OM perspective.

TABLE D.1	Common Queuing Situations	
SITUATION	**ARRIVALS IN QUEUE**	**SERVICE PROCESS**
Supermarket	Grocery shoppers	Checkout clerks at cash register
Highway toll booth	Automobiles	Collection of tolls at booth
Doctor's office	Patients	Treatment by doctors and nurses
Computer system	Programs to be run	Computer processes jobs
Telephone company	Callers	Switching equipment forwards calls
Bank	Customers	Transactions handled by teller
Machine maintenance	Broken machines	Repair people fix machines
Harbor	Ships and barges	Dock workers load and unload

Both use human and equipment resources to restore valuable production assets (people and machines) to good condition.

Characteristics of a Waiting-Line System

In this section, we take a look at the three parts of a waiting-line, or queuing, system (as shown in Figure D.1):

1. *Arrivals or inputs to the system:* These have characteristics such as population size, behavior, and a statistical distribution.
2. *Queue discipline, or the waiting line itself:* Characteristics of the queue include whether it is limited or unlimited in length and the discipline of people or items in it.
3. *The service facility:* Its characteristics include its design and the statistical distribution of service times.

We now examine each of these three parts.

LO D.1 *Describe* the characteristics of arrivals, waiting lines, and service systems

Arrival Characteristics

The input source that generates arrivals or customers for a service system has three major characteristics:

1. *Size* of the arrival population
2. *Behavior* of arrivals
3. *Pattern* of arrivals (statistical distribution)

Size of the Arrival (Source) Population Population sizes are considered either unlimited (essentially infinite) or limited (finite). When the number of customers or arrivals on hand at any given moment is just a small portion of all potential arrivals, the arrival population is considered unlimited, or infinite. Examples of unlimited populations include cars arriving at a big-city car wash, shoppers arriving at a supermarket, and students arriving to register for classes at a large university. Most queuing models assume such an infinite arrival population. An example of a limited, or finite, population is found in a copying shop that has, say, eight copying machines. Each of the copiers is a potential "customer" that may break down and require service.

Pattern of Arrivals at the System Customers arrive at a service facility either according to some known schedule (for example, one patient every 15 minutes or one student every half hour) or else they arrive *randomly*. Arrivals are considered random when they are

Unlimited, or infinite, population
A queue in which a virtually unlimited number of people or items could request the services, or in which the number of customers or arrivals on hand at any given moment is a very small portion of potential arrivals.

Limited, or finite, population
A queue in which there are only a limited number of potential users of the service.

Arrival Characteristics
• Size of arrival population
• Behavior of arrivals
• Statistical distribution of arrivals

Waiting-Line Characteristics
• Limited vs. unlimited
• Queue discipline

Service Characteristics
• Service design
• Statistical distribution of service

Figure **D.1**

Three Parts of a Waiting Line, or Queuing System, at Dave's Car Wash

independent of one another and their occurrence cannot be predicted exactly. Frequently in queuing problems, the number of arrivals per unit of time can be estimated by a probability distribution known as the Poisson distribution.[1] For any given arrival time (such as 2 customers per hour or 4 trucks per minute), a discrete Poisson distribution can be established by using the formula:

Poisson distribution

A discrete probability distribution that often describes the arrival rate in queuing theory.

$$P(x) = \frac{e^{-\lambda}\lambda^x}{x!} \quad \text{for } x = 0, 1, 2, 3, 4, \ldots \tag{D-1}$$

where $P(x)$ = probability of x arrivals
   x = number of arrivals per unit of time
   λ = average arrival rate
   e = 2.7183 (which is the base of the natural logarithms)

With the help of the table in Appendix II, which gives the value of $e^{-\lambda}$ for use in the Poisson distribution, these values are easy to compute. Figure D.2 illustrates the Poisson distribution for $\lambda = 2$ and $\lambda = 4$. This means that if the average arrival rate is $\lambda = 2$ customers per hour, the probability of 0 customers arriving in any random hour is about 0.13 (13%), probability of 1 customer is about 27%, 2 customers about 27%, 3 customers about 18%, 4 customers about 9%, and so on. The chances that 9 or more will arrive are virtually nil. Arrivals, of course, are not always Poisson distributed (they may follow some other distribution). Patterns, therefore, should be examined to make certain that they are well approximated by Poisson before that distribution is applied.

Behavior of Arrivals

Most queuing models assume that an arriving customer is a patient customer. Patient customers are people or machines that wait in the queue until they are served and do not switch between lines. Unfortunately, life is complicated by the fact that people have been known to balk or to renege. Customers who *balk* refuse to join the waiting line because it is too long to suit their needs or interests. *Reneging* customers are those who enter the queue but then become impatient and leave without completing their transaction. Actually, both of these situations just serve to highlight the need for queuing theory and waiting-line analysis.

Waiting-Line Characteristics

The waiting line itself is the second component of a queuing system. The length of a line can be either limited or unlimited. A queue is *limited* when it cannot, either by law or because of physical restrictions, increase to an infinite length. A small barbershop, for example, will have only a limited number of waiting chairs. Queuing models are treated in this module under an assumption of *unlimited* queue length. A queue is *unlimited* when its size is unrestricted, as in the case of the toll booth serving arriving automobiles.

A second waiting-line characteristic deals with *queue discipline*. This refers to the rule by which customers in the line are to receive service. Most systems use a queue discipline known

Figure D.2

Two Examples of the Poisson Distribution for Arrival Times

STUDENT TIP ◆

Notice that even though the mean arrival rate might be $\lambda = 2$ per hour, there is still a small chance that as many as 9 customers arrive in an hour.

Probability = $P(x) = \frac{e^{-\lambda}\lambda^x}{x!}$

Distribution for $\lambda = 2$

Distribution for $\lambda = 4$

as the first-in, first-out (FIFO) rule. In a hospital emergency room or an express checkout line at a supermarket, however, various assigned priorities may preempt FIFO. Patients who are critically injured will move ahead in treatment priority over patients with broken fingers or noses. Shoppers with fewer than 10 items may be allowed to enter the express checkout queue (but are *then* treated as first-come, first-served). Computer-programming runs also operate under priority scheduling. In most large companies, when computer-produced paychecks are due on a specific date, the payroll program gets highest priority.[2]

First-in, first-out (FIFO) rule
A queue discipline in which the first customers in line receive the first service.

Service Characteristics

The third part of any queuing system is the service characteristics. Two basic properties are important: (1) design of the service system and (2) the distribution of service times.

Basic Queuing System Designs   Service systems are usually classified in terms of their number of *servers* (number of channels) and number of *phases* (number of service stops that must be made). See Figure D.3. A single-server (or single-channel) queuing system, with one server, is typified by the drive-in bank with only one open teller. If, on the other hand, the

Single-server queuing system
A service system with one line and one server.

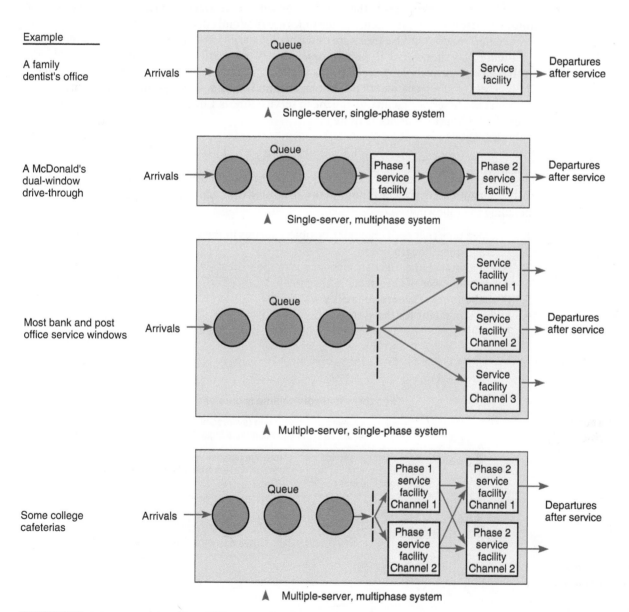

Figure **D.3**

Basic Queuing System Designs

Multiple-server queuing system

A service system with one waiting line but with several servers.

Single-phase system

A system in which the customer receives service from only one station and then exits the system.

Multiphase system

A system in which the customer receives services from several stations before exiting the system.

Negative exponential probability distribution

A continuous probability distribution often used to describe the service time in a queuing system.

bank has several tellers on duty, with each customer waiting in one common line for the first available teller, then we would have a multiple-server (or multiple channel) queuing system. Most banks today are multiple-server systems, as are most large barbershops, airline ticket counters, and post offices.

In a single-phase system, the customer receives service from only one station and then exits the system. A fast-food restaurant in which the person who takes your order also brings your food and takes your money is a single-phase system. So is a driver's license agency in which the person taking your application also grades your test and collects your license fee. However, say the restaurant requires you to place your order at one station, pay at a second, and pick up your food at a third. In this case, it is a multiphase system. Likewise, if the driver's license agency is large or busy, you will probably have to wait in one line to complete your application (the first service stop), queue again to have your test graded, and finally go to a third counter to pay your fee. To help you relate the concepts of servers and phases, Figure D.3 presents these four possible configurations.

Service Time Distribution Service patterns are like arrival patterns in that they may be either constant or random. If service time is constant, it takes the same amount of time to take care of each customer. This is the case in a machine-performed service operation such as an automatic car wash. More often, service times are randomly distributed. In many cases, we can assume that random service times are described by the negative exponential probability distribution.

Figure D.4 shows that if *service times* follow a negative exponential distribution, the probability of any very long service time is low. For example, when an average service time is 20 minutes (or three customers per hour), seldom if ever will a customer require more than 1.5 hours in the service facility. If the mean service time is 1 hour, the probability of spending more than 3 hours in service is quite low.

Measuring a Queue's Performance

Queuing models help managers make decisions that balance service costs with waiting-line costs. Queuing analysis can obtain many measures of a waiting-line system's performance, including the following:

1. Average time that each customer or object spends in the queue
2. Average queue length
3. Average time that each customer spends in the system (waiting time plus service time)
4. Average number of customers in the system
5. Probability that the service facility will be idle
6. Utilization factor for the system
7. Probability of a specific number of customers in the system

Figure D.4

Two Examples of the Negative Exponential Distribution for Service Times

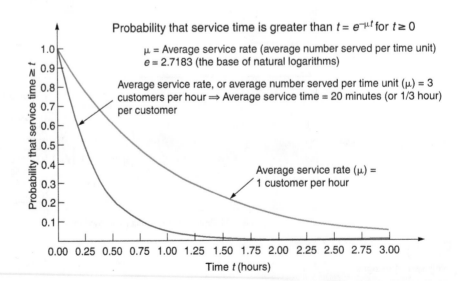

Probability that service time is greater than $t = e^{-\mu t}$ for $t \geq 0$

μ = Average service rate (average number served per time unit)
e = 2.7183 (the base of natural logarithms)

Average service rate, or average number served per time unit (μ) = 3 customers per hour $\Rightarrow$ Average service time = 20 minutes (or 1/3 hour) per customer

Average service rate (μ) = 1 customer per hour

OM in Action | Zero Wait Time Guarantee at This Michigan Hospital's ER

Other hospitals smirked a few years ago when Michigan's Oakwood Healthcare chain rolled out an emergency room (ER) guarantee that promised a written apology and movie tickets to patients not seen by a doctor within 30 minutes. Even employees cringed at what sounded like a cheap marketing ploy.

But if you have visited an ER lately and watched some patients wait for hours on end—the *official* average wait is 47 minutes—you can understand why Oakwood's patient satisfaction levels have soared. The 30-minute guarantee was such a huge success that fewer than 1% of the 191,000 ER patients asked for free tickets. The following year, Oakwood upped the stakes again, offering a 15-minute guarantee. Then Oakwood started its Zero Wait Program in the ERs. Patients who enter any Oakwood emergency department are *immediately* cared for by a healthcare professional.

Oakwood's CEO even extended the ER guarantee to on-time surgery, 45-minute meal service orders, and other custom room services. "Medicine is a service business," says Larry Alexander, the head of an ER in Sanford, Florida. "And people are in the mindset of the fast-food industry."

How did Oakwood make good on its promise to eliminate the ER queue? It first studied queuing theory, then reengineered its billing, records, and lab operations to drive down service time. Then, to improve service capability, Oakwood upgraded its technical staff. Finally, it replaced its ER physicians with a crew willing to work longer hours.

Sources: Wall Street Journal (October 19, 2010); *Time* (January 26, 2011); and **unitiv.com** (February 27, 2014).

Ric Feld/AP Images

Queuing Costs

As described in the *OM in Action* box "Zero Wait Time Guarantee at This Michigan Hospital's ER," operations managers must recognize the trade-off that takes place between two costs: the cost of providing good service and the cost of customer or machine waiting time. Managers want queues that are short enough so that customers do not become unhappy and either leave without buying, or buy, but never return. However, managers may be willing to allow some waiting if it is balanced by a significant savings in service costs.

One means of evaluating a service facility is to look at total expected cost. Total cost is the sum of expected service costs plus expected waiting costs.

As you can see in Figure D.5, service costs increase as a firm attempts to raise its level of service. Managers in *some* service centers can vary capacity by having standby personnel and machines that they can assign to specific service stations to prevent or shorten excessively long lines. In grocery stores, for example, managers and stock clerks can open extra checkout counters. In banks and airport check-in points, part-time workers may be called in to help. As the level of service improves (that is, speeds up), however, the cost of time spent

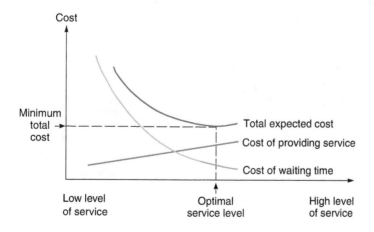

Figure D.5

The Trade-off Between Waiting Costs and Service Costs

waiting in lines decreases. (Refer to Figure D.5.) Waiting cost may reflect lost productivity of workers while tools or machines await repairs or may simply be an estimate of the cost of customers lost because of poor service and long queues. In some service systems (for example, an emergency ambulance service), the cost of long waiting lines may be intolerably high.

The Variety of Queuing Models

A wide variety of queuing models may be applied in operations management. We will introduce you to four of the most widely used models. These are outlined in Table D.2, and examples of each follow in the next few sections. More complex models are described in queuing theory textbooks or can be developed through the use of simulation (the topic of Module F). Note that all four queuing models listed in Table D.2 have three characteristics in common. They all assume:

STUDENT TIP ◆
This is the main section of Module D. We illustrate four important queuing models.

1. Poisson distribution arrivals
2. FIFO discipline
3. A single-service phase

In addition, they all describe service systems that operate under steady, ongoing conditions. This means that arrival and service rates remain stable during the analysis.

Model A (M/M/1): Single-Server Queuing Model with Poisson Arrivals and Exponential Service Times

LO D.2 *Apply* the single-server queuing model equations

The most common case of queuing problems involves the *single-server* (also called single-channel) waiting line. In this situation, arrivals form a single line to be serviced by a single station (see Figure D.3 on p. 751). We assume that the following conditions exist in this type of system:

1. Arrivals are served on a first-in, first-out (FIFO) basis, and every arrival waits to be served, regardless of the length of the line or queue.
2. Arrivals are independent of preceding arrivals, but the average number of arrivals (*arrival rate*) does not change over time.
3. Arrivals are described by a Poisson probability distribution and come from an infinite (or very, very large) population.

TABLE D.2	Queuing Models Described in This Chapter							
MODEL	NAME (TECHNICAL NAME IN PARENTHESES)	EXAMPLE	NUMBER OF SERVERS (CHANNELS)	NUMBER OF PHASES	ARRIVAL RATE PATTERN	SERVICE TIME PATTERN	POPULATION SIZE	QUEUE DISCIPLINE
A	Single-server system (M/M/1)	Information counter at department store	Single	Single	Poisson	Negative exponential	Unlimited	FIFO
B	Multiple-server (M/M/S)	Airline ticket counter	Multi-server	Single	Poisson	Negative exponential	Unlimited	FIFO
C	Constant service (M/D/1)	Automated car wash	Single	Single	Poisson	Constant	Unlimited	FIFO
D	Finite population (M/M/1 with finite source)	Shop with only a dozen machines that might break	Single	Single	Poisson	Negative exponential	Limited	FIFO

The giant Moscow McDonald's boasts 900 seats, 800 workers, and $80 million in annual sales (vs. less than $2 million in a U.S. outlet). Americans would balk at the average waiting time of 45 minutes, but Russians are used to such long lines. McDonald's represents good service in Moscow. Some people have even had their wedding receptions there.

4. Service times vary from one customer to the next and are independent of one another, but their average rate is known and follows the negative exponential distribution.
5. Service times occur according to the negative exponential probability distribution.
6. The service rate is faster than the arrival rate.

When these conditions are met, the series of equations shown in Table D.3 can be developed. Examples D1 and D2 illustrate how Model A (which in technical journals is known as the M/M/1 model) may be used.[3]

TABLE D.3	Queuing Formulas for Model A: Single-Server System, also Called M/M/1

λ = average number of arrivals per time period

μ = average number of people or items served per time period (average service rate)

L_s = average number of units (customers) in the system (waiting and being served)

$$= \frac{\lambda}{\mu - \lambda}$$

W_s = average time a unit spends in the system (waiting time plus service time)

$$= \frac{1}{\mu - \lambda}$$

L_q = average number of units waiting in the queue

$$= \frac{\lambda^2}{\mu(\mu - \lambda)}$$

W_q = average time a unit spends waiting in the queue

$$= \frac{\lambda}{\mu(\mu - \lambda)} = \frac{L_q}{\lambda}$$

ρ = utilization factor for the system

$$= \frac{\lambda}{\mu}$$

P_0 = probability of 0 units in the system (that is, the service unit is idle)

$$= 1 - \frac{\lambda}{\mu}$$

$P_{n>k}$ = probability of more than k units in the system, where n is the number of units in the system

$$= \left(\frac{\lambda}{\mu}\right)^{k+1}$$

Example D1

A SINGLE-SERVER QUEUE

Tom Jones, the mechanic at Golden Muffler Shop, is able to install new mufflers at an average rate of 3 per hour (or about 1 every 20 minutes), according to a negative exponential distribution. Customers seeking this service arrive at the shop on the average of 2 per hour, following a Poisson distribution. They are served on a first-in, first-out basis and come from a very large (almost infinite) population of possible buyers.

We would like to obtain the operating characteristics of Golden Muffler's queuing system.

APPROACH ▶ This is a single-server (M/M/1) system, and we apply the formulas in Table D.3.

SOLUTION ▶

$$\lambda = 2 \text{ cars arriving per hour}$$
$$\mu = 3 \text{ cars serviced per hour}$$
$$L_s = \frac{\lambda}{\mu - \lambda} = \frac{2}{3 - 2} = \frac{2}{1}$$
$$= 2 \text{ cars in the system, on average}$$
$$W_s = \frac{1}{\mu - \lambda} = \frac{1}{3 - 2} = 1$$
$$= 1\text{-hour average time in the system}$$
$$L_q = \frac{\lambda^2}{\mu(\mu - \lambda)} = \frac{2^2}{3(3 - 2)} = \frac{4}{3(1)} = \frac{4}{3}$$
$$= 1.33 \text{ cars waiting in line, on average}$$
$$W_q = \frac{\lambda}{\mu(\mu - \lambda)} = \frac{2}{3(3 - 2)} = \frac{2}{3} \text{ hour}$$
$$= 40\text{-minute average waiting time per car}$$
$$\rho = \frac{\lambda}{\mu} = \frac{2}{3}$$
$$= 66.6\% \text{ of time mechanic is busy}$$
$$P_0 = 1 - \frac{\lambda}{\mu} = 1 - \frac{2}{3}$$
$$= .33 \text{ probability there are 0 cars in the system}$$

Probability of More Than *K* Cars in The system

K	$P_{n>k} = (2/3)^{k+1}$
0	.667 ← Note that this is equal to $1 - P_0 = 1 - .33 = .667$.
1	.444
2	.296
3	.198 ← Implies that there is a 19.8% chance that more than 3 cars are in the system.
4	.132
5	.088
6	.058
7	.039

INSIGHT ▶ Recognize that arrival and service times are converted to the same rate. For example, a service time of 20 minutes is stated as an average *rate* of 3 mufflers *per hour*. It's also important to differentiate between time in the *queue* and time in the *system*.

LEARNING EXERCISE ▶ If $\mu = 4$ cars/hour instead of the current 3 arrivals, what are the new values of L_s, W_s, L_q, W_q, and P_0? [Answer: 1 car, 30 min., .5 cars, 15 min., 50%, .50.]

RELATED PROBLEMS ▶ D.1–D.4, D.6–D.8, D.9a–e, D.10, D.11a–c, D.12a–d (D.31–D.33, D.34a–e, D.35a–e, D.36, D.38, D.39 are available in MyOMLab)

EXCEL **OM** Data File **ModDExD1.xls** can be found in MyOMLab.

ACTIVE **MODEL** D.1 This example is further illustrated in Active Model D.1 in MyOMLab.

Once we have computed the operating characteristics of a queuing system, it is often important to do an economic analysis of their impact. Although the waiting-line model just described is valuable in predicting potential waiting times, queue lengths, idle times, and so on, it does not identify optimal decisions or consider cost factors. As we saw earlier, the solution to a queuing problem may require management to make a trade-off between the increased cost of providing better service and the decreased waiting costs derived from providing that service.

Example D2 examines the costs involved in Example D1.

Example D2

ECONOMIC ANALYSIS OF EXAMPLE D1

LO D.3 *Conduct* a cost analysis for a waiting line

Golden Muffler Shop's owner is interested in cost factors as well as the queuing parameters computed in Example D1. He estimates that the cost of customer waiting time, in terms of customer dissatisfaction and lost goodwill, is $15 per hour spent *waiting* in line. Jones, the mechanic, is paid $11 per hour.

APPROACH ▶ First compute the average daily customer waiting time, then the daily salary for Jones, and finally the total expected cost.

SOLUTION ▶ Because the average car has a $\frac{2}{3}$-hour wait (W_q) and because there are approximately 16 cars serviced per day (2 arrivals per hour times 8 working hours per day), the total number of hours that customers spend waiting each day for mufflers to be installed is:

$$\frac{2}{3}(16) = \frac{32}{3} = 10\frac{2}{3} \text{ hour}$$

Hence, in this case:

$$\text{Customer waiting-time cost} = \$15\left(10\frac{2}{3}\right) = \$160 \text{ per day}$$

The only other major cost that Golden's owner can identify in the queuing situation is the salary of Jones, the mechanic, who earns $11 per hour, or $88 per day. Thus:

$$\text{Total expected costs} = \$160 + \$88$$
$$= \$248 \text{ per day}$$

This approach will be useful in Solved Problem D.2 on page 767.

INSIGHT ▶ L_q and W_q are the two most important queuing parameters when it comes to cost analysis. Calculating customer wait times, we note, is based on average time waiting in the queue (W_q) times the number of arrivals per hour (λ) times the number of hours per day. This is because this example is set on a daily basis. This is the same as using L_q because $L_q = W_q\lambda$.

LEARNING EXERCISE ▶ If the customer waiting time is actually $20 per hour and Jones gets a salary increase to $15 per hour, what are the total daily expected costs? [Answer: $333.33.]

RELATED PROBLEMS ▶ D.12e–f, D.13, D.22, D.23, D.24 (D.37 is available in MyOMLab)

Model B (M/M/S): Multiple-Server Queuing Model

Now let's turn to a multiple-server (multiple-channel) queuing system in which two or more servers are available to handle arriving customers. We still assume that customers awaiting service form one single line and then proceed to the first available server. Multiple-server, single-phase waiting lines are found in many banks today: a common line is formed, and the customer at the head of the line proceeds to the first free teller. (Refer to Figure D.3 on p. 751 for a typical multiple-server configuration.)

LO D.4 *Apply* the multiple-server queuing model formulas

The multiple-server system presented in Example D3 again assumes that arrivals follow a Poisson probability distribution and that service times are negative exponentially distributed. Service is first-come, first-served, and all servers are assumed to perform at the same rate. Other assumptions listed earlier for the single-server model also apply.

The queuing equations for Model B (which also has the technical name M/M/S) are shown in Table D.4. These equations are obviously more complex than those used in the single-server model, yet they are used in exactly the same fashion and provide the same type of information as the simpler model. (*Note:* The POM for Windows and Excel OM software described later in this chapter can prove very useful in solving multiple-server and other queuing problems.)

To shorten lines (or wait times), each Costco register is staffed with two employees. This approach has improved efficiency by 20–30%.

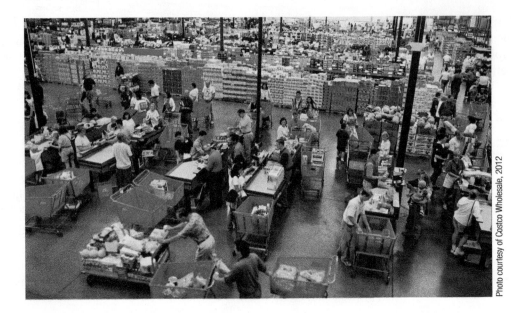

Photo courtesy of Costco Wholesale, 2012

TABLE D.4	Queuing Formulas for Model B: Multiple-Server System, also Called M/M/S

M = number of servers (channels) open
λ = average number of arrivals per time period (average arrival rate)
μ = average service rate at each server (channel)

The probability that there are zero people or units in the system is:

$$P_0 = \frac{1}{\left[\sum_{n=0}^{M-1} \frac{1}{n!}\left(\frac{\lambda}{\mu}\right)^n\right] + \frac{1}{M!}\left(\frac{\lambda}{\mu}\right)^M \frac{M\mu}{M\mu - \lambda}} \quad \text{for } M\mu > \lambda$$

The average number of people or units in the system is:

$$L_s = \frac{\lambda\mu(\lambda/\mu)^M}{(M-1)!(M\mu - \lambda)^2} P_0 + \frac{\lambda}{\mu}$$

The average time a unit spends in the waiting line and being serviced (namely, in the system) is:

$$W_s = \frac{\mu(\lambda/\mu)^M}{(M-1)!(M\mu - \lambda)^2} P_0 + \frac{1}{\mu} = \frac{L_s}{\lambda}$$

The average number of people or units in line waiting for service is:

$$L_q = L_s - \frac{\lambda}{\mu}$$

The average time a person or unit spends in the queue waiting for service is:

$$W_q = W_s - \frac{1}{\mu} = \frac{L_q}{\lambda}$$

Example D3

A MULTIPLE-SERVER QUEUE

The Golden Muffler Shop has decided to open a second garage bay and hire a second mechanic to handle installations. Customers, who arrive at the rate of about $\lambda = 2$ per hour, will wait in a single line until 1 of the 2 mechanics is free. Each mechanic installs mufflers at the rate of about $\mu = 3$ per hour.

The company wants to find out how this system compares with the old single-server waiting-line system.

APPROACH ▶ Compute several operating characteristics for the $M = 2$ server system, using the equations in Table D.4, and compare the results with those found in Example D1.

SOLUTION ▶

$$P_0 = \cfrac{1}{\left[\displaystyle\sum_{n=0}^{1}\frac{1}{n!}\left(\frac{2}{3}\right)^n\right] + \frac{1}{2!}\left(\frac{2}{3}\right)^2\frac{2(3)}{2(3)-2}}$$

$$= \cfrac{1}{1 + \frac{2}{3} + \frac{1}{2}\left(\frac{4}{9}\right)\left(\frac{6}{6-2}\right)} = \cfrac{1}{1 + \frac{2}{3} + \frac{1}{3}} = \frac{1}{2}$$

= .5 probability of zero cars in the system

Then:

$$L_s = \frac{(2)(3)(2/3)^2}{1![2(3)-2]^2}\left(\frac{1}{2}\right) + \frac{2}{3} = \frac{8/3}{16}\left(\frac{1}{2}\right) + \frac{2}{3} = \frac{3}{4}$$

= .75 average number of cars in the system

$$W_s = \frac{L_s}{\lambda} = \frac{3/4}{2} = \frac{3}{8} \text{ hour}$$

= 22.5 minutes average time a car spends in the system

$$L_q = L_s - \frac{\lambda}{\mu} = \frac{3}{4} - \frac{2}{3} = \frac{9}{12} - \frac{8}{12} = \frac{1}{12}$$

= .083 average number of cars in the queue (waiting)

$$W_q = \frac{L_q}{\lambda} = \frac{.083}{2} = .0415 \text{ hour}$$

= 2.5 minutes average time a car spends in the queue (waiting)

INSIGHT ▶ It is very interesting to see the big differences in service performance when an additional server is added.

LEARNING EXERCISE ▶ If $\mu = 4$ per hour, instead of $\mu = 3$, what are the new values for P_0, L_s, W_s, L_q, and W_q? [Answers: 0.6, .53 cars, 16 min, .033 cars, 1 min.]

RELATED PROBLEMS ▶ D.7h, D.9f, D.11d, D.15, D.20 (D.35f, D.36 are available in MyOMLab)

EXCEL **OM** Data File **ModDEx.xls** can be found in MyOMLab.

ACTIVE **MODEL** D.2 This example is further illustrated in Active Model D.2 in MyOMLab.

We can summarize the characteristics of the two-server model in Example D3 and compare them to those of the single-server model in Example D1 as follows:

MEASURE		SINGLE SERVER	TWO SERVERS (CHANNELS)
Probability of 0 units in the system	P_0	.33	.5
Number of units in the system	L_s	2 cars	.75 car
Average time in the system	W_s	60 minutes	22.5 minutes
Average number in the queue	L_q	1.33 cars	.083 car
Average time in the queue	W_q	40 minutes	2.5 minutes

The increased service has a dramatic effect on almost all characteristics. For instance, note that the time spent waiting in line drops from 40 minutes to only 2.5 minutes.

Use of Waiting-Line Tables Imagine the work a manager would face in dealing with $M = 3$-, 4-, or 5- server waiting-line models if a computer was not readily available. The arithmetic becomes increasingly troublesome. Fortunately, much of the burden of manually examining multiple-server queues can be avoided by using Table D.5. This table, the result of hundreds of computations, represents the relationship between three things: (1) a ratio, λ/μ, (2) number of servers open, and (3) the average number of customers in the queue, L_q (which is what we'd like to find). For any combination of the ratio λ/μ and $M = 1, 2, 3, 4,$ or 5 servers, you can quickly look in the body of the table to read off the appropriate value for L_q.

| TABLE D.5 | Values of L_q for M = 1–5 Servers (channels) and Selected Values of λ/μ |

| | POISSON ARRIVALS, EXPONENTIAL SERVICE TIMES | | | | |
| | NUMBER OF SERVERS (CHANNELS), M | | | | |
λ/μ	1	2	3	4	5
.10	.0111				
.15	.0264	.0008			
.20	.0500	.0020			
.25	.0833	.0039			
.30	.1285	.0069			
.35	.1884	.0110			
.40	.2666	.0166			
.45	.3681	.0239	.0019		
.50	.5000	.0333	.0030		
.55	.6722	.0449	.0043		
.60	.9000	.0593	.0061		
.65	1.2071	.0767	.0084		
.70	1.6333	.0976	.0112		
.75	2.2500	.1227	.0147		
.80	3.2000	.1523	.0189		
.85	4.8166	.1873	.0239	.0031	
.90	8.1000	.2285	.0300	.0041	
.95	18.0500	.2767	.0371	.0053	
1.0		.3333	.0454	.0067	
1.2		.6748	.0904	.0158	
1.4		1.3449	.1778	.0324	.0059
1.6		2.8444	.3128	.0604	.0121
1.8		7.6734	.5320	.1051	.0227
2.0			.8888	.1739	.0398
2.2			1.4907	.2770	.0659
2.4			2.1261	.4305	.1047
2.6			4.9322	.6581	.1609
2.8			12.2724	1.0000	.2411
3.0				1.5282	.3541
3.2				2.3856	.5128
3.4				3.9060	.7365
3.6				7.0893	1.0550
3.8				16.9366	1.5184
4.0					2.2164
4.2					3.3269
4.4					5.2675
4.6					9.2885
4.8					21.6384

Example D4 illustrates the use of Table D.5.

Example D4 | USE OF WAITING-LINE TABLES

Alaska National Bank is trying to decide how many drive-in teller windows to open on a busy Saturday. CEO Ted Eschenbach estimates that customers arrive at a rate of about $\lambda = 18$ per hour, and that each teller can service about $\mu = 20$ customers per hour.

APPROACH ▶ Ted decides to use Table D.5 to compute L_q and W_q.

SOLUTION ▶ The ratio is $\lambda/\mu = \frac{18}{20} = .90$. Turning to the table, under $\lambda/\mu = .90$, Ted sees that if only $M = 1$ service window is open, the average number of customers in line will be 8.1. If two windows are open, L_q drops to .2285 customers, to .03 for $M = 3$ tellers, and to .0041 for $M = 4$ tellers. Adding more open windows at this point will result in an average queue length of 0.

It is also a simple matter to compute the average waiting time in the queue, W_q, since $W_q = L_q/\lambda$. When one service window is open, $W_q = 8.1$ customers/(18 customers per hour) $= .45$ hours $= 27$ minutes waiting time; when two tellers are open, $W_q = .2285$ customers/(18 customers per hour) $= .0127$ hours $\cong \frac{3}{4}$ minute; and so on.

INSIGHT ▶ If a computer is not readily available, Table D.5 makes it easy to find L_q and to then compute W_q. Table D.5 is especially handy to compare L_q for different numbers of servers (M).

LEARNING EXERCISE ▶ The number of customers arriving on a Thursday afternoon at Alaska National is 15/hour. The service rate is still 20 customers/hour. How many people are in the queue if there are 1, 2, or 3 servers? [Answer: 2.25, .1227, .0147.]

RELATED PROBLEM ▶ D.5

You might also wish to check the calculations in Example D3 against tabled values just to practice the use of Table D.5. You may need to interpolate if your exact value is not found in the first column. Other common operating characteristics besides L_q are published in tabular form in queuing theory textbooks.

Long check-in lines (left photo) such as at Los Angeles International (LAX) are a common airport sight. This is an M/M/S model—passengers wait in a single queue for one of several agents. But at Anchorage International Airport (right photo), Alaska Air has jettisoned the traditional wall of ticket counters. Instead, 1.2 million passengers per year use self-service check-in machines and staffed "bag drop" stations. Looking nothing like a typical airport, the new system doubled the airline's check-in capacity and cut staff needs in half, all while speeding travelers through in less than 15 minutes, even during peak hours.

Model C (M/D/1): Constant-Service-Time Model

Some service systems have constant, instead of exponentially distributed, service times. When customers or equipment are processed according to a fixed cycle, as in the case of an automatic car wash or an amusement park ride, constant service times are appropriate. Because constant rates are certain, the values for L_q, W_q, L_s, and W_s are always less than they would be in Model A, which has variable service rates. As a matter of fact, both the average queue length and the average waiting time in the queue are halved with Model C. Constant-service-model formulas are given in Table D.6. Model C also has the technical name M/D/1 in the literature of queuing theory.

TABLE D.6	Queuing Formulas for Model C: Constant Service, also Called M/D/1

Average length of queue: $L_q = \dfrac{\lambda^2}{2\mu(\mu - \lambda)}$

Average waiting time in queue: $W_q = \dfrac{\lambda}{2\mu(\mu - \lambda)}$

Average number of customers in system: $L_s = L_q + \dfrac{\lambda}{\mu}$

Average time in system: $W_s = W_q + \dfrac{1}{\mu}$

Example D5 gives a constant-service-time analysis.

Example D5

A CONSTANT-SERVICE-TIME MODEL

Inman Recycling, Inc., collects and compacts aluminum cans and glass bottles in Reston, Louisiana. Its truck drivers currently wait an average of 15 minutes before emptying their loads for recycling. The cost of driver and truck time while they are in queues is valued at $60 per hour. A new automated compactor can be purchased to process truckloads at a *constant* rate of 12 trucks per hour (that is, 5 minutes per truck). Trucks arrive according to a Poisson distribution at an average rate of 8 per hour. If the new compactor is put in use, the cost will be amortized at a rate of $3 per truck unloaded.

APPROACH ► CEO Tony Inman hires a summer college intern to conduct an analysis to evaluate the costs versus benefits of the purchase. The intern uses the equation for W_q in Table D.6.

SOLUTION ►

Current waiting cost/trip = (1/4 hr waiting now)($60/hr cost) = $15/trip

New system: λ = 8 trucks/hr arriving μ = 12 trucks/hr served

Average waiting time in queue = $W_q = \dfrac{\lambda}{2\mu(\mu - \lambda)} = \dfrac{8}{2(12)(12 - 8)} = \dfrac{1}{12}$ hr

Waiting cost/trip with new compactor = (1/12 hr wait)($60/hr cost) = $5/trip

Savings with new equipment = $15(current system) – $5(new system) = $10/trip

Cost of new equipment amortized: = $ 3/trip

Net savings   = $ 7/trip

INSIGHT ► Constant service times, usually attained through automation, help control the variability inherent in service systems. This can lower average queue length and average waiting time. Note the 2 in the denominator of the equations for L_q and W_q in Table D.6.

LEARNING EXERCISE ► With the new constant-service-time system, what are the average waiting time in the queue, average number of trucks in the system, and average waiting time in the system? [Answer: 0.0833 hours, 1.33 trucks, 0.1667 hours.]

RELATED PROBLEMS ► D.14, D.16, D.21 (D.34f is found in MyOMLab)

EXCEL **OM** Data File **ModDExD5.xls** can be found in MyOMLab.

ACTIVE **MODEL** D.3 This example is further illustrated in Active Model D.3 in MyOMLab.

Little's Law

A practical and useful relationship in queuing for any system in a *steady state* is called Little's Law. A steady state exists when a queuing system is in its normal operating condition (e.g., after customers waiting at the door when a business opens in the morning are taken care of). Little's Law can be written as either:

$$L_s = \lambda W_s \text{ (which is the same as } W_s = L_s/\lambda) \qquad \text{(D-2)}$$

or:

$$L_q = \lambda W_q \text{ (which is the same as } W_q = L_q/\lambda) \qquad \text{(D-3)}$$

The advantage of these formulas is that once two of the parameters are known, the other one can easily be found. This is important because in certain waiting-line situations, one of these might be easier to determine than the other.

Example D6 | **LITTLE'S LAW**

Customers walk into the local U.S. Post Office at an average rate of 20 per hour. On average, there are 5 people waiting in line to be served. The probability distributions that describe arrival and service times are unknown. The manager, Vicky Luo, wishes to determine how long customers are waiting in line.

APPROACH ▶ Even though the probability distributions and even the number of servers are unknown, Vicky can use Little's Law to quickly determine the average waiting time.

SOLUTION ▶ $\lambda = 20$ customers per hour

$L_q = 5$ customers

Using Equation (D-3), $W_q = L_q/\lambda$

$$= 5/20 = 0.25 \text{ hours}$$

And (0.25 hours)(60 minutes/hour) = 15 minutes

INSIGHT ▶ It can be relatively easy to count the number of arriving customers per hour, and the average number of customers in line can be estimated by counting the line length throughout the day and taking the average of those lengths. However, it would take more effort to keep track of the time that the customers enter the facility and the time that they begin being served. Little's Law eliminates the need to track actual waiting times.

LEARNING EXERCISE ▶ Vicky believes that 15 minutes is an unreasonable waiting time. She adds a server to help during busy times, and the average number of customers in line reduces to 1.2 customers. Now how long do customers wait? [Answer: 3.6 minutes.]

RELATED PROBLEMS ▶ D.25–D.30

Little's Law is also important because it makes no assumptions about the probability distributions for arrivals and service times, the number of servers, or service priority rules. The law applies to all the queuing systems discussed in this module, except the finite-population model, which we discuss next.

Model D (M/M/1 with Finite Source): Finite-Population Model

When there is a limited (or finite) population of potential customers for a service facility, we must consider a different queuing model. This model would be used, for example, if we were considering equipment repairs in a factory that has 5 machines, if we were in charge of maintenance for a fleet of 10 commuter airplanes, or if we ran a hospital ward that has 20 beds. The finite-population model allows any number of repair people (servers) to be considered.

This model differs from the three earlier queuing models because there is now a *dependent* relationship between the length of the queue and the arrival rate. Let's illustrate the extreme situation: If your factory had five machines and all were broken and awaiting repair, the arrival rate would drop to zero. In general, then, as the *waiting line* becomes longer in the finite population model, the *arrival rate* of customers or machines drops.

LO D.6 *Perform* a finite-population model analysis

The finite calling population model has the following assumptions:

1. There is only one server.
2. The population of units seeking service is finite.[4]
3. Arrivals follow a Poisson distribution, and service times are negative exponentially distributed.
4. Customers are served on a first-come, first-served basis.

Table D.7 displays the queuing formulas for the finite-population model.

TABLE D.7	**Queuing Formulas for Model D: Finite-Population, also called M/M/1 with Finite Source**

λ = average arrival rate μ = average service rate N = size of the population	Average waiting time in the queue: $$W_q = \frac{L_q}{(N - L_s)\lambda}$$
Probability that the system is empty: $$P_0 = \frac{1}{\displaystyle\sum_{n=0}^{N} \frac{N!}{(N - n)!}\left(\frac{\lambda}{\mu}\right)^n}$$	Average time in the system: $$W_s = W_q + \frac{1}{\mu}$$
Average length of the queue: $$L_q = N - \left(\frac{\lambda + \mu}{\lambda}\right)(1 - P_0)$$	Probability of n units in the system: $$P_n = \frac{N!}{(N - n)!}\left(\frac{\lambda}{\mu}\right)^n P_0 \text{ for } n = 0, 1, ..., N$$
Average number of customers (units) in the system: $$L_s = L_q + (1 - P_0)$$	

Example D7 illustrates Model D.

Example D7 | A FINITE-POPULATION MODEL

Past records indicate that each of the 5 massive laser computer printers at the U.S. Department of Energy (DOE), in Washington, DC, needs repair after about 20 hours of use. Breakdowns have been determined to be Poisson distributed. The one technician on duty can service a printer in an average of 2 hours, following an exponential distribution. Printer downtime costs $120 per hour. The technician is paid $25 per hour.

APPROACH ▶ To compute the system's operation characteristics we note that the mean arrival rate is $\lambda = 1/20 = 0.05$ printers/hour. The mean service rate is $\mu = 1/2 = 0.50$ printers/hour.

SOLUTION ▶

1. $P_0 = \dfrac{1}{\displaystyle\sum_{n=0}^{5} \frac{5!}{(5 - n)!}\left(\frac{0.05}{0.5}\right)^n} = 0.564$ (we leave these calculations for you to confirm)

2. $L_q = 5 - \left(\dfrac{0.05 + 0.5}{0.05}\right)(1 - P_0) = 5 - (11)(1 - 0.564) = 5 - 4.8 = 0.2$ printers

3. $L_s = 0.2 + (1 - 0.564) = 0.64$ printers

4. $W_q = \dfrac{0.2}{(5 - 0.64)(0.05)} = \dfrac{0.2}{0.22} = 0.91$ hours

5. $W_s = 0.91 + \dfrac{1}{0.50} = 2.91$ hours

We can also compute the total cost per hour:

Total hourly cost = (Average number of printers down) (Cost per downtime hour)
+ Cost per technician hour

= (0.64)($120) + $25 = $76.80 + $25.00 = $101.80

INSIGHT ▶ Management can now determine whether these costs and wait times are acceptable. Perhaps it is time to add a second technician.

Other Queuing Approaches

Many practical waiting-line problems that occur in service systems have characteristics like those of the four mathematical models already described. Often, however, *variations* of these specific cases are present in an analysis. Service times in an automobile repair shop, for example, tend to follow the normal probability distribution instead of the exponential. A college registration system in which seniors have first choice of courses and hours over other students is an example of a first-come, first-served model with a preemptive priority queue discipline. A physical examination for military recruits is an example of a multiphase system, one that differs from the single-phase models discussed earlier in this module. A recruit first lines up to have blood drawn at one station, then waits for an eye exam at the next station, talks to a psychiatrist at the third, and is examined by a doctor for medical problems at the fourth. At each phase, the recruit must enter another queue and wait his or her turn. Many models, some very complex, have been developed to deal with situations such as these.

◆ **STUDENT TIP**
When the assumptions of the 4 models we just introduced do not hold true, there are other approaches still available to us.

Summary

Queues are an important part of the world of operations management. In this module, we describe several common queuing systems and present mathematical models for analyzing them.

The most widely used queuing models include Model A (M/M/1), the basic single-server, single-phase system with Poisson arrivals and negative exponential service times; Model B (M/M/S), the multiple-server equivalent of Model A; Model C (M/D/1), a constant-service-rate model; and Model D, a finite-population system (M/M/1 with finite source). All four models allow for Poisson arrivals; first-in, first-out service; and a single-service phase. Typical operating characteristics we examine include average time spent waiting in the queue and system, average number of customers in the queue and system, idle time, and utilization rate.

A variety of queuing models exists for which all the assumptions of the traditional models need not be met. In these cases, we use more complex mathematical models or turn to a technique called *simulation*. The application of simulation to problems of queuing systems is addressed in Module F.

Key Terms

Queuing theory (p. 748)
Waiting line (queue) (p. 748)
Unlimited, or infinite, population (p. 749)
Limited, or finite, population (p. 749)
Poisson distribution (p. 750)
First-in, first-out (FIFO) rule (p. 751)
Single-server queuing system (p. 751)
Multiple-server queuing system (p. 752)
Single-phase system (p. 752)
Multiphase system (p. 752)
Negative exponential probability distribution (p. 752)

Discussion Questions

1. Name the three parts of a typical queuing system.
2. When designing a waiting line system, what "qualitative" concerns need to be considered?
3. Name the three factors that govern the structure of "arrivals" in a queuing system.
4. State the seven common measures of queuing system performance.
5. State the assumptions of the "basic" single-server queuing model (Model A, or M/M/1).
6. Is it good or bad to operate a supermarket bakery system on a strict first-come, first-served basis? Why?
7. Describe what is meant by the waiting-line terms *balk* and *renege*. Provide an example of each.
8. Which is larger, W_s or W_q? Explain.
9. Briefly describe three situations in which the first-in, first-out (FIFO) discipline rule is not applicable in queuing analysis.
10. Describe the behavior of a waiting line where $\lambda > \mu$. Use both analysis and intuition.
11. Discuss the likely outcome of a waiting line system where $\mu > \lambda$ but only by a tiny amount (e.g., $\mu = 4.1$, $\lambda = 4$).

12. Provide examples of four situations in which there is a limited, or finite, waiting line.
13. What are the components of the following queuing systems? Draw and explain the configuration of each.
    a) Barbershop
    b) Car wash
    c) Laundromat
    d) Small grocery store
14. Do doctors' offices generally have random arrival rates for patients? Are service times random? Under what circumstances might service times be constant?

15. What happens if two single-server systems have the same mean arrival and service rates, but the service time is constant in one and exponential in the other?
16. What dollar value do you place on yourself per hour that you spend waiting in lines? What value do your classmates place on themselves? Why do the values differ?
17. Why is Little's Law a useful queuing concept?

Using Software to Solve Queuing Problems

Both Excel OM and POM for Windows may be used to analyze all but the last two homework problems in this module.

✗ USING EXCEL OM

Excel OM's Waiting-Line program handles all four of the models developed in this module. Program D.1 illustrates our first model, the M/M/1 system, using the data from Example D1.

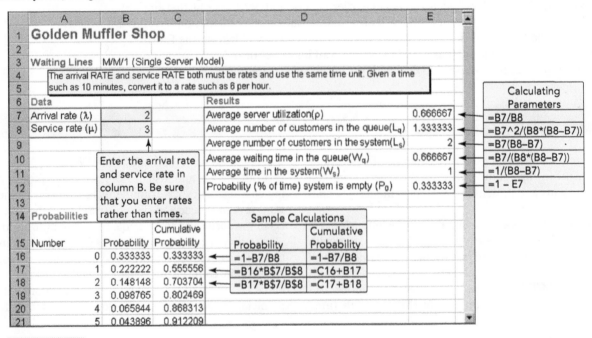

Program **D.1**

Using Excel OM for Queuing

Example D1's (Golden Muffler Shop) data are illustrated in the M/M/1 model.

P USING POM FOR WINDOWS

There are several POM for Windows queuing models from which to select in that program's Waiting-Line module. The program can include an economic analysis of cost data, and, as an option, you may display probabilities of various numbers of people/items in the system. See Appendix IV for further details.

Solved Problems   Virtual Office Hours help is available in MyOMLab.

SOLVED PROBLEM D.1

Sid Das Brick Distributors in Jamaica currently employs 1 worker whose job is to load bricks on outgoing company trucks. An average of 24 trucks per day, or 3 per hour, arrive at the loading platform, according to a Poisson distribution. The worker loads them at a rate of 4 trucks per hour, following approximately the exponential distribution in his service times.

Das believes that adding an additional brick loader will substantially improve the firm's productivity. He estimates that a 2-person crew loading each truck will double the loading rate (μ) from 4 trucks per hour to 8 trucks per hour. Analyze the effect on the queue of such a change, and compare the results to those achieved with one worker. What is the probability that there will be more than 3 trucks either being loaded or waiting?

SOLUTION

	NUMBER OF BRICK LOADERS	
	1	2
Truck arrival rate (λ)	3/hr	3/hr
Loading rate (μ)	4/hr	8/hr
Average number in system (L_s)	3 trucks	.6 truck
Average time in system (W_s)	1 hr	.2 hr
Average number in queue (L_q)	2.25 trucks	.225 truck
Average time in queue (W_q)	.75 hr	.075 hr
Utilization rate (ρ)	.75	.375
Probability system empty (P_0)	.25	.625

Probability of More than k Trucks in System

	PROBABILITY N > K	
K	1 LOADER	2 LOADERS
0	.75	.375
1	.56	.141
2	.42	.053
3	.32	.020

These results indicate that when only one loader is employed, the average truck must wait three-quarters of an hour before it is loaded. Furthermore, there is an average of 2.25 trucks waiting in line to be loaded. This situation may be unacceptable to management. Note also the decline in queue size after the addition of a second loader.

SOLVED PROBLEM D.2

Truck drivers working for Sid Das (see Solved Problem D.1) earn an average of $10 per hour. Brick loaders receive about $6 per hour. Truck drivers waiting *in the queue or at the loading platform* are drawing a salary but are productively idle and unable to generate revenue during that time. What would be the *hourly* cost savings to the firm if it employed 2 loaders instead of 1?

Referring to the data in Solved Problem D.1, we note that the average number of trucks *in the system* is 3 when there is only 1 loader and .6 when there are 2 loaders.

SOLUTION

	NUMBER OF LOADERS	
	1	2
Truck driver idle time costs [(Average number of trucks) × (Hourly rate)] = (3)($10) =	$30	$ 6 = (.6)($10)
Loading costs	6	12 = (2)($6)
Total expected cost per hour	$36	$18

The firm will save $18 per hour by adding another loader.

SOLVED PROBLEM D.3

Sid Das is considering building a second platform or gate to speed the process of loading trucks. This system, he thinks, will be even more efficient than simply hiring another loader to help out on the first platform (as in Solved Problem D.1).

Assume that the worker at each platform will be able to load 4 trucks per hour each and that trucks will continue to arrive at the rate of 3 per hour. Then apply the appropriate equations to find the waiting line's new operating conditions. Is this new approach indeed speedier than hiring a second loader, as Das has considered in the Solved Problems above?

SOLUTION

$$P_0 = \cfrac{1}{\left[\sum_{n=0}^{1} \frac{1}{n!}\left(\frac{3}{4}\right)^n\right] + \frac{1}{2!}\left(\frac{3}{4}\right)^2 \frac{2(4)}{2(4)-3}}$$

$$= \cfrac{1}{1 + \frac{3}{4} + \frac{1}{2}\left(\frac{3}{4}\right)^2\left(\frac{8}{8-3}\right)} = .4545$$

$$L_s = \frac{3(4)(3/4)^2}{(1)!(8-3)^2}(.4545) + \frac{3}{4} = .873$$

$$W_s = \frac{.873}{3} = .291 \text{ hr}$$

$$L_q = .873 - 3/4 = .123$$

$$W_q = \frac{.123}{3} = .041 \text{ hr}$$

Looking back at Solved Problem D.1, we see that although length of the *queue* and average time in the queue are lowest when a second platform is open, the average number of trucks in the *system* and average time spent waiting in the system are smallest when two workers are employed at a *single* platform. Thus, we would probably recommend not building a second platform.

SOLVED PROBLEM D.4

Mount Sinai Hospital's orthopedic care unit has 5 beds, which are virtually always occupied by patients who have just undergone orthopedic surgery. One registered nurse is on duty in the unit in each of the three 8-hour shifts. About every 2 hours (following a Poisson distribution), one of the patients requires a nurse's attention. The nurse will then spend an average of 30 minutes (negative exponentially distributed) assisting the patient and updating medical records regarding the problem and care provided.

Because immediate service is critical to the 5 patients, two important questions are: What is the average number of patients either waiting for or being attended by the nurse? What is the average time that a patient spends waiting for the nurse to arrive?

SOLUTION

$$\lambda = .5 \text{ arrivals/hour}$$
$$\mu = 2 \text{ served/hour}$$
$$N = 5 \text{ patients}$$

$$P_0 = \frac{1}{\sum_{n=0}^{5} \frac{5!}{(5-n)!}\left(\frac{.5}{2}\right)^n} = 0.20$$

$$L_q = 5 - \left(\frac{.5+2}{.5}\right)(1 - 0.20) = 1 \text{ patient}$$

$$L_s = 1 + (1 - 0.20) = 1.8 \text{ patients}$$

$$W_q = \frac{1}{(5 - 1.8)(.5)} = .62 \text{ hours} = 37.28 \text{ min.}$$

$$W_s = .62 + \frac{1}{2} = 1.12 \text{ hours} = 67.28 \text{ min}$$

So the average number of patients in the system = 1.8
Average wait time in the queue = .62 hours = 37.28 minutes

Problems

Note: **Px** means the problem may be solved with POM for Windows and/or Excel OM.

Problems D.1–D.39 relate to The Variety of Queuing Models

• **D.1** Customers arrive at Rich Dunn's Styling Shop at a rate of 3 per hour, distributed in a Poisson fashion. Rich's service times follow a negative exponential distribution, and Rich can complete an average of 5 haircuts per hour.
a) Find the average number of customers waiting for haircuts.
b) Find the average number of customers in the shop.
c) Find the average time a customer waits until it is his or her turn.
d) Find the average time a customer spends in the shop.
e) Find the percentage of time that Rich is busy. **Px**

• **D.2** There is only one copying machine in the student lounge of the business school. Students arrive at the rate of λ = 40 per hour (according to a Poisson distribution). Copying takes an average of 40 seconds, or μ = 90 per hour (according to a negative exponential distribution). Compute the following:
a) The percentage of time that the machine is used.
b) The average length of the queue.
c) The average number of students in the system.
d) The average time spent waiting in the queue.
e) The average time in the system. **Px**

• **D.3** Paul Fenster owns and manages a chili-dog and soft-drink stand near the Kean U. campus. While Paul can service 30 customers per hour on the average (μ), he gets only 20 customers per hour (λ). Because Paul could wait on 50% more customers than actually visit his stand, it doesn't make sense to him that he should have any waiting lines.

Paul hires you to examine the situation and to determine some characteristics of his queue. After looking into the problem, you find it follows the six conditions for a single-server waiting line (as seen in Model A). What are your findings? **Px**

• **D.4** Dr. Tarun Gupta, a Michigan vet, is running a rabies vaccination clinic for dogs at the local grade school. Tarun can "shoot" a dog every 3 minutes. It is estimated that the dogs will arrive independently and randomly throughout the day at a rate of one dog every 6 minutes according to a Poisson distribution. Also assume that Tarun's shooting times are negative exponentially distributed. Compute the following:
a) The probability that Tarun is idle.
b) The proportion of the time that Tarun is busy.
c) The average number of dogs being vaccinated and waiting to be vaccinated.
d) The average number of dogs waiting to be vaccinated.
e) The average time a dog waits before getting vaccinated.

f) The average amount of time a dog spends waiting in line and being vaccinated. **Px**

•• **D.5** The pharmacist at Arnold Palmer Hospital, Wende Huehn-Brown, receives 12 requests for prescriptions each hour, Poisson distributed. It takes her a mean time of 4 minutes to fill each, following a negative exponential distribution. Use the waiting-line table, Table D.5, and $W_q = L_q/\lambda$, to answer these questions.
a) What is the average number of prescriptions in the queue?
b) How long will the average prescription spend in the queue?
c) Wende decides to hire a second pharmacist, Ajay Aggerwal, with whom she went to school and who operates at the same speed in filling prescriptions. How will the answers to parts (a) and (b) change? **Px**

• **D.6** Calls arrive at Lynn Ann Fish's hotel switchboard at a rate of 2 per minute. The average time to handle each is 20 seconds. There is only one switchboard operator at the current time. The Poisson and negative exponential distributions appear to be relevant in this situation.
a) What is the probability that the operator is busy?
b) What is the average time that a customer must wait before reaching the operator?
c) What is the average number of calls waiting to be answered? **Px**

•• **D.7** Automobiles arrive at the drive-through window at the downtown Baton Rouge, Louisiana, post office at the rate of 4 every 10 minutes. The average service time is 2 minutes. The Poisson distribution is appropriate for the arrival rate and service times are negative exponentially distributed.
a) What is the average time a car is in the system?
b) What is the average number of cars in the system?
c) What is the average number of cars waiting to receive service?
d) What is the average time a car is in the queue?
e) What is the probability that there are no cars at the window?
f) What percentage of the time is the postal clerk busy?
g) What is the probability that there are exactly 2 cars in the system?
h) By how much would your answer to part (a) be reduced if a second drive-through window, with its own server, were added? **Px**

• **D.8** Virginia's Ron McPherson Electronics Corporation retains a service crew to repair machine breakdowns that occur on average λ = 3 per 8-hour workday (approximately Poisson in nature). The crew can service an average of μ = 8 machines per workday, with a repair time distribution that resembles the negative exponential distribution.
a) What is the utilization rate of this service system?
b) What is the average downtime for a broken machine?

c) How many machines are waiting to be serviced at any given time?

d) What is the probability that more than 1 machine is in the system? The probability that more than 2 are broken and waiting to be repaired or being serviced? More than 3? More than 4? **Px**

•• **D.9**   Neve Commercial Bank is the only bank in the town of York, Pennsylvania. On a typical Friday, an average of 10 customers per hour arrive at the bank to transact business. There is currently one teller at the bank, and the average time required to transact business is 4 minutes. It is assumed that service times may be described by the negative exponential distribution. If a single teller is used, find:

a) The average time in the line.

b) The average number in the line.

c) The average time in the system.

d) The average number in the system.

e) The probability that the bank is empty.

f) CEO Benjamin Neve is considering adding a second teller (who would work at the same rate as the first) to reduce the waiting time for customers. A single line would be used, and the customer at the front of the line would go to the first available bank teller. He assumes that this will cut the waiting time in half. If a second teller is added, find the new answers to parts (a) to (e). **Px**

•• **D.10**   Beate Klingenberg manages a Poughkeepsie, New York, movie theater complex called Cinema 8. Each of the eight auditoriums plays a different film; the schedule staggers starting times to avoid the large crowds that would occur if all four movies started at the same time. The theater has a single ticket booth and a cashier who can maintain an average service rate of 280 patrons per hour. Service times are assumed to follow a negative exponential distribution. Arrivals on a normally active day are Poisson distributed and average 210 per hour.

To determine the efficiency of the current ticket operation, Beate wishes to examine several queue-operating characteristics.

a) Find the average number of moviegoers waiting in line to purchase a ticket.

b) What percentage of the time is the cashier busy?

c) What is the average time that a customer spends in the system?

d) What is the average time spent waiting in line to get to the ticket window?

e) What is the probability that there are more than two people in the system? More than three people? More than four? **Px**

•• **D.11**   Bill Youngdahl has been collecting data at the TU student grill. He has found that, between 5:00 P.M. and 7:00 P.M., students arrive at the grill at a rate of 25 per hour (Poisson distributed) and service time takes an average of 2 minutes (negative exponential distribution). There is only 1 server, who can work on only 1 order at a time.

a) What is the average number of students in line?

b) What is the average time a student is in the grill area?

c) Suppose that a second server can be added to team up with the first (and, in effect, act as 1 faster server). This would reduce the average service time to 90 seconds. How would this affect the average time a student is in the grill area?

d) Suppose a second server is added and the 2 servers act independently, with *each* taking an average of 2 minutes. What would be the average time a student is in the system?

••• **D.12**   The wheat harvesting season in the American Midwest is short, and farmers deliver their truckloads of wheat to a giant central storage bin within a 2-week span. Because of this, wheat-filled trucks waiting to unload and return to the fields have been known to back up for a block at the receiving bin. The central bin is owned cooperatively, and it is to every farmer's benefit to make the unloading/storage process as efficient as possible. The cost of grain deterioration caused by unloading delays and the cost of truck rental and idle driver time are significant concerns to the cooperative members. Although farmers have difficulty quantifying crop damage, it is easy to assign a waiting and unloading cost for truck and driver of $18 per hour. During the 2-week harvest season, the storage bin is open and operated 16 hours per day, 7 days per week, and can unload 35 trucks per hour according to a negative exponential distribution. Full trucks arrive all day long (during the hours the bin is open) at a rate of about 30 per hour, following a Poisson pattern.

To help the cooperative get a handle on the problem of lost time while trucks are waiting in line or unloading at the bin, find the following:

a) The average number of trucks in the unloading system

b) The average time per truck in the system

c) The utilization rate for the bin area

d) The probability that there are more than three trucks in the system at any given time

e) The total daily cost to the farmers of having their trucks tied up in the unloading process

f) As mentioned, the cooperative uses the storage bin heavily only 2 weeks per year. Farmers estimate that enlarging the bin would cut unloading costs by 50% next year. It will cost $9,000 to do so during the off-season. Would it be worth the expense to enlarge the storage area? **Px**

••• **D.13**   Janson's Department Store in Stark, Ohio, maintains a successful catalog sales department in which a clerk takes orders by telephone. If the clerk is occupied on one line, incoming phone calls to the catalog department are answered automatically by a recording machine and asked to wait. As soon as the clerk is free, the party who has waited the longest is transferred and serviced first. Calls come in at a rate of about 12 per hour. The clerk can take an order in an average of 4 minutes. Calls tend to follow a Poisson distribution, and service times tend to be negative exponential.

The cost of the clerk is $10 per hour, but because of lost goodwill and sales, Janson's loses about $25 per hour of customer time spent waiting for the clerk to take an order.

a) What is the average time that catalog customers must wait before their calls are transferred to the order clerk?

b) What is the average number of customers waiting to place an order?

c) Pamela Janson is considering adding a second clerk to take calls. The store's cost would be the same $10 per hour. Should she hire another clerk? Explain your decision. **Px**

• **D.14**   Altug's Coffee Shop decides to install an automatic coffee vending machine outside one of its stores to reduce the number of people standing in line inside. Mehmet Altug charges $3.50 per cup. However, it takes too long for people to make change. The service time is a constant 3 minutes, and the arrival rate is 15 per hour (Poisson distributed).

a) What is the average wait in line?

b) What is the average number of people in line?

c) Mehmet raises the price to $5 per cup and takes 60 seconds off the service time. However, because the coffee is now so expensive, the arrival rate drops to 10 per hour. Now what are the average wait time and the average number of people in the queue (waiting)? **Px**

••• **D.15**   The typical subway station in Washington, DC, has six turnstiles, each of which can be controlled by the station manager to be used for either entrance or exit control—but never for both. The manager must decide at different times of the day how many turnstiles to use for entering passengers and how many to use for exiting passengers.

At the George Washington University (GWU) Station, passengers enter the station at a rate of about 84 per minute between the hours of 7 A.M. and 9 A.M. Passengers exiting trains at the stop reach the exit turnstile area at a rate of about 48 per minute during the same morning rush hours. Each turnstile can allow an average of 30 passengers per minute to enter or exit. Arrival and service times have been thought to follow Poisson and negative exponential distributions, respectively. Assume riders form a common queue at both entry and exit turnstile areas and proceed to the first empty turnstile.

The GWU station manager, Gerald Aase, does not want the average passenger at his station to have to wait in a turnstile line for more than 6 seconds, nor does he want more than 8 people in any queue at any average time.
a) How many turnstiles should be opened in each direction every morning?
b) Discuss the assumptions underlying the solution of this problem using queuing theory. **Px**

• • **D.16** Renuka Jain's Car Wash takes a constant time of 4.5 minutes in its automated car wash cycle. Autos arrive following a Poisson distribution at the rate of 10 per hour. Renuka wants to know:
a) The average waiting time in line.
b) The average length of the line.

• • • **D.17** Debra Bishop's cabinet-making shop, in Des Moines, has five tools that automate the drilling of holes for the installation of hinges. Each machine needs an average of 3 "resettings" every 8-hour day, following the Poisson distribution. There is a single technician for setting these machines. Her service times are negative exponential, averaging 2 hours each.
a) What is the probability this system is empty?
b) What is the average number of machines in the system (i.e., being reset or waiting to be reset)?
c) What is the average waiting time in the queue? **Px**

• • • **D.18** A technician monitors a group of 5 computers that run an automated manufacturing facility. It takes an average of 15 minutes (negative exponentially distributed) to adjust a computer that develops a problem. On average, one of the computers requires adjustment every 85 minutes. Determine the following:
a) The average number of computers waiting for adjustment (i.e., in the queue)
b) The average number in the system
c) The probability no computer needs adjustment **Px**

• • • **D.19** One mechanic services 5 drilling machines for a steel plate manufacturer. Machines break down on an average of once every 6 working days, and breakdowns tend to follow a Poisson distribution. The mechanic can handle an average of one repair job per day. Repairs follow a negative exponential distribution.

a) On the average, how many machines are waiting for service?
b) On the average, what is the *waiting* time to be serviced? **Px**

• • • **D.20** Ted Glickman, the administrator at D.C. General Hospital emergency room, faces the problem of providing treatment for patients who arrive at different rates during the day. There are four doctors available to treat patients when needed. If not needed, they can be assigned other responsibilities (such as doing lab tests, reports, X-ray diagnoses) or else rescheduled to work at other hours.

It is important to provide quick and responsive treatment, and Ted thinks that, on the average, patients should not have to sit in the waiting area for more than 5 minutes before being seen by a doctor. Patients are treated on a first-come, first-served basis and see the first available doctor after waiting in the queue. The arrival pattern for a typical day is as follows:

TIME	ARRIVAL RATE
9 A.M.–3 P.M.	6 patients/hour
3 P.M.–8 P.M.	4 patients/hour
8 P.M.–midnight	12 patients/hour

Arrivals follow a Poisson distribution, and treatment times, 12 minutes on the average, follow the negative exponential pattern.
a) How many doctors should be on duty during each period to maintain the level of patient care expected?
b) What condition would exist if only one doctor were on duty between 9 A.M. and 3 P.M.? **Px**

• • • **D.21** The Pontchartrain Bridge is a 16-mile toll bridge that crosses Lake Pontchartrain in New Orleans. Currently, there are 7 toll booths, each staffed by an employee. Since Hurricane Katrina, the Port Authority has been considering replacing the employees with machines. Many factors must be considered because the employees are unionized. However, one of the Port Authority's concerns is the effect that replacing the employees with machines will have on the times that drivers spend in the system. Customers arrive to any one toll booth at a rate of 10 per minute. In the exact change lanes with employees, the service time is essentially constant at 5 seconds for each driver. With machines, the average service time would still be 5 seconds, but it would be negative exponential rather than constant, because it takes time for the coins to rattle around in the machine. Contrast the two systems for a single lane. **Px**

• • • **D.22** The registration area has just opened at a large convention of dentists in Tallahassee, Florida. There are 200 people arriving per hour (Poisson distributed), and the cost of their waiting time in the queue is valued at $100 per person per hour. The Tallahassee Convention Center provides servers to register guests at a fee of $15 per person per hour. It takes about one minute to register an attendee (negative exponentially distributed). A single waiting line, with multiple servers, is set up.
a) What is the minimum number of servers for this system?
b) What is the optimal number of servers for this system?
c) What is the cost for the system, per hour, at the optimum number of servers?
d) What is the server utilization rate with the minimum number of servers? **Px**

• • **D.23** Refer to Problem D.22. A new registration manager, Dwayne Cole, is hired who initiates a program to entertain the people in line with a juggler whom he pays $15/hour. This reduces the waiting costs to $50 per hour.
a) What is the optimal number of servers?
b) What is the cost for the system, per hour, at the optimal service level?

•••• **D.24** The Chattanooga Furniture store gets an average of 50 customers per shift. Marilyn Helms, the manager, wants to calculate whether she should hire 1, 2, 3, or 4 salespeople. She has determined that average waiting times will be 7 minutes with one salesperson, 4 minutes with two salespeople, 3 minutes with three salespeople, and 2 minutes with four salespeople. She has estimated the cost per minute that customers wait at $1. The cost per salesperson per shift (including fringe benefits) is $70.

How many salespeople should be hired?

•• **D.25** During the afternoon peak hours the First Bank of Dubuque has an average of 40 customers arriving every hour. There is also an average of 8 customers at First Bank at any time. The probability of the arrival distribution is unknown. How long does the average customer spend in the bank?

•• **D.26** An average of 9 cars can be seen in the system (both the drive-through line and the drive-through window) at Burger Universe. Approximately every 20 seconds, a car attempts to enter the drive-through line; however, 40% of cars simply leave the restaurant because they're discouraged by the length of the line. On average, how long does a car spend going through the drive-through at Burger Universe?

•• **D.27** Lobster World stores approximately 1,000 pounds of fish on average. In a typical day, the busy restaurant cooks and sells 360 (raw) pounds of fish. How long do the fish stay in storage on average?

•• **D.28** Gamma Bank processes a typical loan application in 2.4 weeks. Customers fill out 30 loan applications per week. On average how many loan applications are being processed somewhere in the system at Gamma Bank?

•• **D.29** Fisher's Furniture Store sells $800,000 worth of furniture to customers on credit each month. The Accounts Receivable balance in the accounting books averages $2 million. On average, how long are customers taking to pay their bills?

•• **D.30** Vacation Inns, a chain of hotels operating in the southeastern region of the U.S., uses a toll-free telephone number to take reservations for all of its hotels. An average of 12 calls are received per hour. The probability distribution that describes the arrivals is unknown. Over a period of time, it is determined that the average caller spends 6 minutes on hold waiting for service. Find the average number of callers in the queue by using Little's Law.

Additional problems **D.31–D.39** *are available in* MyOMLab.

CASE STUDIES

New England Foundry

For more than 75 years, New England Foundry, Inc. (NEFI), has manufactured wood stoves for home use. In recent years, with increasing energy prices, president George Mathison has seen sales triple. This dramatic increase has made it difficult for George to maintain quality in all his wood stoves and related products.

Unlike other companies manufacturing wood stoves, NEFI is in the business of making *only* stoves and stove-related products. Its major products are the Warmglo I, the Warmglo II, the Warmglo III, and the Warmglo IV. The Warmglo I is the smallest wood stove, with a heat output of 30,000 BTUs, and the Warmglo IV is the largest, with a heat output of 60,000 BTUs.

The Warmglo III outsold all other models by a wide margin. Its heat output and available accessories were ideal for the typical home. The Warmglo III also had a number of other outstanding features that made it one of the most attractive and heat-efficient stoves on the market. These features, along with the accessories, resulted in expanding sales and prompted George to build a new factory to manufacture the Warmglo III model. An overview diagram of the factory is shown in Figure D.6.

The new foundry used the latest equipment, including a new Disamatic that helped in manufacturing stove parts. Regardless of new equipment or procedures, casting operations have remained basically unchanged for hundreds of years. To begin with, a wooden pattern is made for every cast-iron piece in the stove. The wooden pattern is an exact duplicate of the cast-iron piece that is to be manufactured. All NEFI patterns are made by Precision Patterns, Inc. and are stored in the pattern shop and maintenance room. Next, a specially formulated sand is molded around the wooden pattern. There can be two or more sand molds for each pattern. The sand is mixed and the molds are made in the molding room. When the wooden pattern is removed, the resulting sand molds form a negative image of the desired casting. Next, molds are transported to the casting room, where molten iron is poured into them and allowed to cool. When the iron has solidified, the

molds are moved into the cleaning, grinding, and preparation room, where they are dumped into large vibrators that shake most of the sand from the casting. The rough castings are then subjected to both sandblasting to remove the rest of the sand and grinding to finish some of their surfaces. Castings are then painted with a special heat-resistant paint, assembled into workable stoves, and inspected for manufacturing defects that may have gone undetected. Finally, finished stoves are moved to storage and shipping, where they are packaged and transported to the appropriate locations.

At present, the pattern shop and the maintenance department are located in the same room. One large counter is used by both maintenance personnel, who store tools and parts (which are mainly used by the casting department), and sand molders, who need various patterns for the molding operation. Pete Nawler and Bob Dillman, who work behind the counter, can service a total of 10 people per hour (about 5 per hour each). On average, 4 people from casting and 3 from molding arrive at the counter each hour. People from molding and casting departments arrive randomly, and to be served, they form a single line.

Pete and Bob have always had a policy of first come, first served. Because of the location of the pattern shop and maintenance department, it takes an average of 3 minutes for an individual from the casting department to walk to the pattern and maintenance room, and it takes about 1 minute for an individual to walk from the molding department to the pattern and maintenance room.

After observing the operation of the pattern shop and maintenance room for several weeks, George decided to make some changes to the factory layout. An overview of these changes appears in Figure D.7.

Separating the maintenance shop from the pattern shop would have a number of advantages. It would take people from the casting department only 1 minute instead of 3 to get to the

Figure **D.6**

Overview of Factory

Figure **D.7**

Overview of Factory after Changes

new maintenance room. The time from molding to the pattern shop would be unchanged. Using motion and time studies, George was also able to determine that improving the layout of the maintenance room would allow Bob to serve 6 people from the casting department per hour; improving the layout of the pattern department would allow Pete to serve 7 people from the molding shop per hour.

Discussion Questions

1. How much time would the new layout save?
2. If casting personnel were paid $9.50 per hour and molding personnel were paid $11.75 per hour, how much could be saved per hour with the new factory layout?
3. Should George have made the change in layout?

The Winter Park Hotel

Lori Cook, manager of the Winter Park Hotel, is considering how to restructure the front desk to reach an optimum level of staff efficiency and guest service. At present, the hotel has five clerks on duty, each with a separate waiting line, during peak check-in time of 3:00 P.M. to 5:00 P.M. Observation of arrivals during this period shows that an average of 90 guests arrive each hour (although there is no upward limit on the number that could arrive at any given time). It takes an average of 3 minutes for the front-desk clerk to register each guest.

Ms. Cook is considering three plans for improving guest service by reducing the length of time that guests spend waiting in line. The first proposal would designate one employee as a quick-service clerk for guests registering under corporate accounts, a market segment that fills about 30% of all occupied rooms. Because corporate guests are preregistered, their registration takes just 2 minutes. With these guests separated from the rest of the clientele, the average time for registering a typical guest would climb to 3.4 minutes. Under this plan, noncorporate guests would choose any of the remaining four lines.

The second plan is to implement a single-line system. All guests could form a single waiting line to be served by whichever of five clerks became available. This option would require sufficient lobby space for what could be a substantial queue.

The use of an automatic teller machine (ATM) for check-ins is the basis of the third proposal. This ATM would provide about the same service rate as would a clerk. Because initial use of this technology might be minimal, Cook estimates that 20% of customers, primarily frequent guests, would be willing to use the machines. (This might be a conservative estimate if guests perceive direct benefits from using the ATM, as bank customers do. Citibank reports that some 95% of its Manhattan customers use its ATMs.) Ms. Cook would set up a single queue for customers who prefer human check-in clerks. This line would be served by the five clerks, although Cook is hopeful that the ATM will allow a reduction to four.

Discussion Questions

1. Determine the average amount of time that a guest spends checking in. How would this change under each of the stated options?
2. Which option do you recommend?

- **Additional Case Study:** Visit MyOMLab for this additional free case study:
  Pantry Shopper: The case requires the redesign of a checkout system for a supermarket.

Endnotes

1. When the arrival rates follow a Poisson process with mean arrival rate, λ, the time between arrivals follows a negative exponential distribution with mean time between arrivals of $1/\lambda$. The negative exponential distribution, then, is also representative of a Poisson process but describes the time between arrivals and specifies that these time intervals are completely random.
2. The term *FIFS* (first-in, first-served) is often used in place of FIFO. Another discipline, LIFS (last-in, first-served), also called last-in, first-out (LIFO), is common when material is stacked or piled so that the items on top are used first.

3. In queuing notation, the first letter refers to the arrivals (where M stands for Poisson distribution); the second letter refers to service (where M is again a Poisson distribution, which is the same as an exponential rate for service—and D is a constant service rate); the third symbol refers to the number of servers. So an M/D/1 system (our Model C) has Poisson arrivals, constant service, and one server.
4. Although there is no definite number that we can use to divide finite from infinite populations, the general rule of thumb is this: If the number in the queue is a significant proportion of the calling population, use a finite queuing model.

Module D *Rapid* Review

Main Heading	Review Material	MyOMLab
QUEUING THEORY (pp. 748–749)	■ **Queuing theory**—A body of knowledge about waiting lines. ■ **Waiting line (queue)**—Items or people in a line awaiting service.	Concept Questions: 1.1–1.3
CHARACTERISTICS OF A WAITING-LINE SYSTEM (pp. 749–752)	The three parts of a waiting-line, or queuing, system are: *Arrivals or inputs to the system; queue discipline, or the waiting line itself;* and *the service facility.* ■ **Unlimited,** or **infinite, population**—A queue in which a virtually unlimited number of people or items could request the services, or in which the number of customers or arrivals on hand at any given moment is a very small portion of potential arrivals. ■ **Limited, or finite, population**—A queue in which there are only a limited number of potential users of the service. ■ **Poisson distribution**—A discrete probability distribution that often describes the arrival rate in queuing theory: $$P(x) = \frac{e^{-\lambda}\lambda^x}{x!} \text{ for } x = 0, 1, 2, 3, 4, \dots \qquad \text{(D-1)}$$ A queue is *limited* when it cannot, either by law or because of physical restrictions, increase to an infinite length. A queue is *unlimited* when its size is unrestricted. *Queue discipline* refers to the rule by which customers in the line are to receive service: ■ **First-in, first-out (FIFO) rule**—A queue discipline in which the first customers in line receive the first service. ■ **Single-server (single-channel) queuing system**—A service system with one line and one server. ■ **Multiple-server (multiple-channel) queuing system**—A service system with one waiting line but with more than one server (channel). ■ **Single-phase system**—A system in which the customer receives service from only one station and then exits the system. ■ **Multiphase system**—A system in which the customer receives services from several stations before exiting the system. ■ **Negative exponential probability distribution**—A continuous probability distribution often used to describe the service time in a queuing system.	Concept Questions: 2.1–2.4
QUEUING COSTS (pp. 753–754)	Operations managers must recognize the trade-off that takes place between two costs: the cost of providing good service and the cost of customer or machine waiting time.	Concept Questions: 3.1–3.4
THE VARIETY OF QUEUING MODELS (pp. 754–765)	***Model A:*** *Single-Server System (M/M/1):* *Queuing Formulas:* λ = mean number of arrivals per time period μ = mean number of people or items served per time period L_s = average number of units in the system = $\lambda/(\mu - \lambda)$ W_s = average time a unit spends in the system = $1/(\mu - \lambda)$ L_q = average number of units waiting in the queue = $\lambda^2/[\mu(\mu - \lambda)]$ W_q = average time a unit spends waiting in the queue = $\lambda/[\mu(\mu - \lambda)] = L_q/\lambda$ ρ = utilization factor for the system = λ/μ P_0 = probability of 0 units in the system (i.e., the service unit is idle) = $1 - (\lambda/\mu)$ $P_{n>k}$ = probability of $> k$ units in the system = $(\lambda/\mu)^{k+1}$ ***Model B:*** *Multiple-Server System (M/M/S):* $$P_0 = \frac{1}{\left[\sum_{n=0}^{M-1} \frac{1}{n!}\left(\frac{\lambda}{\mu}\right)^n\right] + \frac{1}{M!}\left(\frac{\lambda}{\mu}\right)^M \frac{M\mu}{M\mu - \lambda}} \text{ for } M\mu > \lambda$$ $$L_s = \frac{\lambda\mu(\lambda/\mu)^M}{(M - 1)!(M\mu - \lambda)^2} P_0 + \frac{\lambda}{\mu}$$ $$W_s = L_s/\lambda \quad L_q = L_s - (\lambda/\mu) \quad W_q = L_q/\lambda$$ ***Model C:*** *Constant Service (M/D/1):* $$L_q = \lambda^2/[2\mu(\mu - \lambda)] \qquad W_q = \lambda/[2\mu(\mu - \lambda)]$$ $$L_s = L_q + (\lambda/\mu) \qquad W_s = W_q + (1/\mu)$$	Concept Questions: 4.1–4.4 Problems: D.1–D.14, D.16–D.21, D.24–D.39 Virtual Office Hours for Solved Problems: D.1–D.4 **ACTIVE MODELS** D.1, D.2, D.3

Main Heading	Review Material	

Little's Law
A useful relationship in queuing for any system in a steady state is called Little's Law:

$$L_s = \lambda W_s \text{ (which is the same as } W_s = L_s/\lambda) \qquad \text{(D-2)}$$

$$L_q = \lambda W_q \text{ (which is the same as } W_q = L_q/\lambda) \qquad \text{(D-3)}$$

Model D: *Finite Population (M/M/1 with finite source)*
With a limited, or finite, population, there is a *dependent* relationship between the length of the queue and the arrival rate. As the *waiting* line becomes longer, the *arrival rate* drops.

N = size of the population

$$P_0 = \frac{1}{\sum_{n=0}^{N} \frac{N!}{(N-n)!}\left(\frac{\lambda}{\mu}\right)^n}$$

$$L_q = N - \left(\frac{\lambda + \mu}{\lambda}\right)(1 - P_0)$$

$$L_s = L_q + (1 - P_0)$$

$$W_q = \frac{L_q}{(N - L_s)\lambda}$$

$$W_s = W_q + \frac{1}{\mu}$$

$$P_n = \frac{N!}{(N-n)!}\left(\frac{\lambda}{\mu}\right)^n P_0 \quad \text{for } n = 0, 1, ..., N$$

| OTHER QUEUING APPROACHES (p. 765) | Often, *variations* of the four basic queuing models are present in an analysis. Many models, some very complex, have been developed to deal with such variations. | Concept Question: 5.1 |

Self Test

■ **Before taking the self-test,** refer to the learning objectives listed at the beginning of the module and the key terms listed at the end of the module.

LO D.1 Which of the following is *not* a key operating characteristic for a queuing system?
a) Utilization rate
b) Percent idle time
c) Average time spent waiting in the system and in the queue
d) Average number of customers in the system and in the queue
e) Average number of customers who renege

LO D.2 Customers enter the waiting line at a cafeteria's only cash register on a first-come, first-served basis. The arrival rate follows a Poisson distribution, while service times follow an exponential distribution. If the average number of arrivals is 6 per minute and the average service rate of a single server is 10 per minute, what is the average number of customers in the system?
a) 0.6   b) 0.9
c) 1.5   d) 0.25
e) 1.0

LO D.3 In performing a cost analysis of a queuing system, the waiting time cost is sometimes based on the time in the queue and sometimes based on the time in the system. The waiting cost should be based on time in the system for which of the following situations?
a) Waiting in line to ride an amusement park ride
b) Waiting to discuss a medical problem with a doctor
c) Waiting for a picture and an autograph from a rock star
d) Waiting for a computer to be fixed so it can be placed back in service

LO D.4 Which of the following is *not* an assumption in a multiple-server queuing model?
a) Arrivals come from an infinite, or very large, population.
b) Arrivals are Poisson distributed.
c) Arrivals are treated on a first-in, first-out basis and do not balk or renege.
d) Service times follow the exponential distribution.
e) Servers each perform at their own individual speeds.

LO D.5 If everything else remains the same, including the mean arrival rate and service rate, except that the service time becomes constant instead of exponential:
a) the average queue length will be halved.
b) the average waiting time will be doubled.
c) the average queue length will increase.
d) we cannot tell from the information provided.

LO D.6 A company has one computer technician who is responsible for repairs on the company's 20 computers. As a computer breaks, the technician is called to make the repair. If the repairperson is busy, the machine must wait to be repaired. This is an example of:
a) a multiple-server system.
b) a finite population system.
c) a constant service rate system.
d) a multiphase system.
e) all of the above.

Answers: LO D.1. e; LO D.2. c; LO D.3. d; LO D.4. e; LO D.5. a; LO D.6. b.

Learning Curves

E MODULE

Alaska Airlines

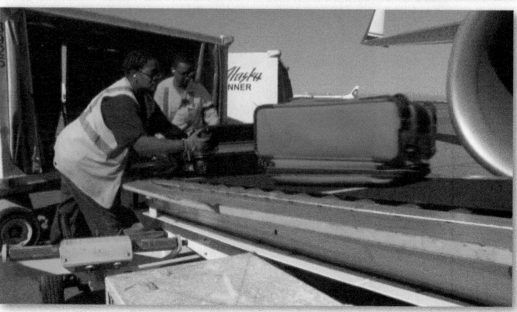

Alaska Airlines

775

Medical procedures such as heart surgery follow a learning curve. Research indicates that the death rate from heart transplants drops at a 79% learning curve, a learning rate not unlike that in many industrial settings. It appears that as doctors and medical teams improve with experience, so do your odds as a patient. If the death rate is halved every three operations, practice may indeed make perfect.

Derege/Fotolia

What Is a Learning Curve?

Most organizations learn and improve over time. As firms and employees perform a task over and over, they learn how to perform more efficiently. This means that task times and costs decrease.

Learning curves

The premise that people and organizations get better at their tasks as the tasks are repeated; sometimes called experience curves.

Learning curves are based on the premise that people and organizations become better at their tasks as the tasks are repeated. A learning curve graph (illustrated in Figure E.1) displays cost (or time) per unit versus the cumulative number of units produced. From it we see that the time needed to produce a unit decreases, usually following a negative exponential curve (part a), as the person or company produces more units. In other words, *it takes less time to complete each additional unit a firm produces*. However, we also see in Figure E.1 that the time *savings* in completing each subsequent unit *decreases*. These are the major attributes of the learning curve.

Learning curves were first applied to industry in a report by T. P. Wright of Curtis-Wright Corp. in 1936.[1] Wright described how direct labor costs of making a particular airplane decreased with learning, a theory since confirmed by other aircraft manufacturers. Regardless of the time needed to produce the first plane, learning curves are found to apply to various categories of air frames (e.g., jet fighters versus passenger planes versus bombers). Learning curves have since been applied not only to labor but also to a wide variety of other costs, including material and purchased components. The power of the learning curve is so significant that it plays a major role in many strategic decisions related to employment levels, costs, capacity, and pricing.

LO E.1 *Define* learning curve

(a)
Exponential graph of learning

(b)
Log-log graph of learning

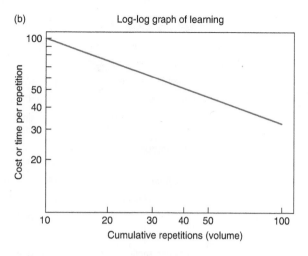

Figure **E.1**

The Learning-Curve Effect States That Time per Repetition Decreases as the Number of Repetitions Increases

Both curves show that the labor-hours to build an airplane decline by 20% each time the production volume doubles. The left graph (a) shows the exponential decline. The log-log graph (b) yields a straight line that is easier to extrapolate.

The learning curve is based on a *doubling* of production: That is, when production doubles, the decrease in time per unit affects the rate of the learning curve. So, if the learning curve is an 80% rate, the second unit takes 80% of the time of the first unit, the fourth unit takes 80% of the time of the second unit, the eighth unit takes 80% of the time of the fourth unit, and so forth. This principle is shown as:

$$T \times L^n = \text{Time required for the } n\text{th unit} \qquad (\text{E-1})$$

where T = unit cost or unit time of the first unit
               L = learning curve rate
               n = number of times T is doubled

If the first unit of a particular product took 10 labor-hours, and if a 70% learning curve is present, the hours the fourth unit will take require doubling twice—from 1 to 2 to 4. Therefore, the formula is:

$$\text{Hours required for unit 4} = 10 \times (.7)^2 = 4.9 \text{ hours}$$

Learning Curves in Services and Manufacturing

Different organizations—indeed, different products—have different learning curves. The rate of learning varies depending on the quality of management and the potential of the process and product. *Any change in process, product, or personnel disrupts the learning curve.* Therefore, caution should be exercised in assuming that a learning curve is continuing and permanent.

As you can see in Table E.1, industry learning curves vary widely. The lower the number (say, 70% compared to 90%), the steeper the slope and the faster the drop in costs. By tradition, learning curves are defined in terms of the *complements* of their improvement rates. For example, a 70% learning curve implies a 30% decrease in time each time the number of repetitions is doubled. A 90% curve means there is a corresponding 10% rate of improvement.

Stable, standardized products and processes tend to have costs that decline more steeply than others. Between 1920 and 1955, for instance, the steel industry was able to reduce labor-hours per unit to 79% each time cumulative production doubled.

Learning curves have application in services as well as industry. As was noted in the caption for the opening photograph, 1-year death rates of heart transplant patients at Temple

TABLE E.1	Examples of Learning-Curve Effects		
EXAMPLE	IMPROVING PARAMETER	CUMULATIVE PARAMETER	LEARNING-CURVE SLOPE (%)
1. Model-T Ford production	Price	Units produced	86
2. Aircraft assembly	Direct labor-hours per unit	Units produced	80
3. Equipment maintenance at GE	Average time to replace a group of parts	Number of replacements	76
4. Steel production	Production worker labor-hours per unit produced	Units produced	79
5. Integrated circuits	Average price per unit	Units produced	72[a]
6. Handheld calculator	Average factory selling price	Units produced	74
7. Disk memory drives	Average price per bit	Number of bits	76
8. Heart transplants	1-year death rates	Transplants completed	79
9. Cesarean section baby deliveries	Average operation time	Number of surgeries	93

[a]Constant dollars.

University Hospital follow a 79% learning curve. The results of that hospital's 3-year study of 62 patients receiving transplants found that every three operations resulted in a halving of the 1-year death rate. As more hospitals face pressure from both insurance companies and the government to enter fixed-price negotiations for their services, their ability to learn from experience becomes increasingly critical. In addition to having applications in both services and industry, learning curves are useful for a variety of purposes. These include:

1. **Internal:** Labor forecasting, scheduling, establishing costs and budgets.
2. **External:** Supply-chain negotiations (see the SMT case study at the end of this module).
3. **Strategic:** Evaluation of company and industry performance, including costs and pricing.

The consequences of learning curves can be far-reaching. For instance, for Boeing's 787 (the world's fastest-selling commercial jet) to reach break-even at 1,000 planes, the unit cost must drop to $113 million, down from the $184 million it cost to make the 45th unit. This can be accomplished only with a very aggressive learning curve rate of 76%. If Boeing follows the 84% learning curve seen for its jumbo 777 model, losses will be in the billions. In addition, there may be major problems in scheduling if the learning improvement is not considered: labor and plants may sit idle a portion of the time. Firms may also refuse more work because they ignore their own efficiency improvements.

Applying the Learning Curve

STUDENT TIP ◊
Here are the three ways of solving learning curve problems.

A mathematical relationship enables us to express the time required to produce a certain unit. This relationship is a function of how many units have been produced before the unit in question and how long it took to produce them. To gain a mastery of this relationship, we will work through learning curve scenarios using three different methods: the doubling approach, formula approach, and learning curve table approach.

Doubling Approach

LO E.2 *Use the doubling concept to estimate times*

The doubling approach is the simplest approach to learning-curve problems. As noted earlier, each time production doubles, labor per unit declines by a constant factor, known as the learning curve rate. So, if we know that the learning curve rate is 80% and that the first unit produced took 100 hours, the hours required to produce the 2nd, 4th, 8th, and 16th units are as follows:

NTH UNIT PRODUCED	HOURS FOR NTH UNIT
1	100.0
2	$80.0 = (.8 \times 100)$
4	$64.0 = (.8 \times 80)$
8	$51.2 = (.8 \times 64)$
16	$41.0 = (.8 \times 51.2)$

As long as we wish to find the hours required to produce N units and N is one of the doubled values, then this approach works. The doubling approach does not tell us how many hours will be needed to produce other units. For this flexibility, we turn to the formula approach.

Formula Approach

The formula approach allows us to determine labor for *any* unit, T_N, by the formula:

$$T_N = T_1(N^b) \qquad \text{(E-2)}$$

where $\quad T_N$ = time for the Nth unit

$\qquad T_1$ = time to produce the first unit

$\qquad b$ = (log of the learning rate)/(log 2) = slope of the learning curve

Some of the values for b are presented in Table E.2. Example E1 shows how this formula works.

TABLE E.2

Learning-Curve Values of b

LEARNING RATE (%)	b
70	−.515
75	−.415
80	−.322
85	−.234
90	−.152

Example E1 | USING LOGS TO COMPUTE LEARNING CURVES

The learning-curve rate for a typical CPA to conduct a dental practice audit is 80%. Greg Lattier, a new graduate of Lee College, completed his first audit in 100 hours. If the dental offices he audits are about the same, how long should he take to finish his third job?

APPROACH ▶ We will use the formula approach in Equation (E-2).

SOLUTION ▶ $\quad T_N = T_1(N^b)$

$\qquad T_3 = (100 \text{ hours})(3^b)$

$\qquad = (100)(3^{\log .8/\log 2})$

$\qquad = (100)(3^{-.322}) = 70.2 \text{ labor-hours}$

INSIGHT ▶ Greg improved quickly from his first to his third audit. An 80% learning-curve rate means that from just the first to second jobs, his time decreased by 20%.

LEARNING EXERCISE ▶ If Greg's learning-curve rate were only 90%, how long would the third audit take? [Answer: 84.621 hours.]

RELATED PROBLEMS ▶ E.1, E.2, E.9, E.10, E.11, E.16

EXCEL **OM** Data File **ModEExE1.xls** can be found in MyOMLab.

The formula approach allows us to determine the hours required for *any* unit produced, but there *is* a simpler method.

LO E.3 *Compute learning-curve effects with the formula and learning-curve table approaches*

Learning-Curve Table Approach

The learning-curve table technique uses Table E.3 (to provide the coefficient C) and the following equation:

$$T_N = T_1 C \qquad \text{(E-3)}$$

where $\quad T_N$ = number of labor-hours required to produce the Nth unit

$\qquad T_1$ = number of labor-hours required to produce the first unit

$\qquad C$ = learning-curve coefficient found in Table E.3

The learning-curve coefficient, C, depends on both the learning curve rate (70%, 75%, 80%, and so on) and the unit number of interest.

Example E2 uses the preceding equation and Table E.3 to calculate learning-curve effects.

Example E2 | USING LEARNING-CURVE COEFFICIENTS

It took a Korean shipyard 125,000 labor-hours to produce the first of several tugboats that you expect to purchase for your shipping company, Great Lakes, Inc. Boats 2 and 3 have been produced by the Koreans with a learning factor of 85%. At $40 per hour, what should you, as purchasing agent, expect to pay for the fourth unit?

APPROACH ▶ First, search Table E.3 for the fourth unit and a learning-curve rate of 85%. The learning-curve coefficient, C, is .723.

SOLUTION ▶ To produce the fourth unit, then, takes:

$$T_N = T_1 C$$
$$T_4 = (125,000 \text{ hours})(.723)$$
$$= 90,375 \text{ hours}$$

To find the cost, multiply by $40:

$$90,375 \text{ hours} \times \$40 \text{ per hour} = \$3,615,000$$

INSIGHT ▶ The learning-curve table approach is very easy to apply. If we had not factored learning into our cost estimates, the price would have been 125,000 hours × $40 per hour (same as the first boat) = $6,000,000.

LEARNING EXERCISE ▶ If the learning factor improved to 80%, how would the cost change? [Answer: It would drop to $3,200,000.]

RELATED PROBLEMS ▶ E.1, E.2, E.3a, E.5a,c, E.6a,b, E.9, E.10, E.11, E.14, E.16, E.22 (E.26, E.27, E.28, E.30, E.31 are available in MyOMLab)

EXCEL **OM** Data File **ModEExE2.xls** can be found in MyOMLab.

ACTIVE **MODEL** E.1 This example is further illustrated in Active Model E.1 in MyOMLab.

Table E.3 also shows *cumulative values*. These allow us to compute the total number of hours needed to complete a specified number of units. Again, the computation is straightforward. Just multiply the table coefficient value by the time required for the first unit. Example E3 illustrates this concept.

Example E3 | USING CUMULATIVE COEFFICIENTS

Example E2 computed the time to complete the fourth tugboat that Great Lakes plans to buy. How long will *all four* boats require?

APPROACH ▶ We look at the "Total Time Coefficient" column in Table E.3 and find that the cumulative coefficient for 4 boats with an 85% learning-curve factor is 3.345.

SOLUTION ▶ The time required is:

$$T_N = T_1 C$$
$$T_4 = (125,000)(3.345) = 418,125 \text{ hours in total for all 4 boats}$$

INSIGHT ▶ For an illustration of how Excel OM can be used to solve Examples E2 and E3, see Program E.1 at the end of this module.

LEARNING EXERCISE ▶ What is the value of T_4 if the learning-curve factor is 80% instead of 85%? [Answer: 392,750 hours.]

RELATED PROBLEMS ▶ E.3b, E.4, E.5b,c, E.6c, E.7, E.15, E.19, E.20a

| TABLE E.3 | | Learning-Curve Coefficients, Where Coefficient $C = N^{(\text{LOG OF LEARNING RATE/LOG 2})}$ | | | | | | | | | |

	70%		75%		80%		85%		90%	
UNIT NUMBER (N)	UNIT TIME CO-EFFICIENT	TOTAL TIME CO-EFFICIENT	UNIT TIME CO-EFFICIENT	TOTAL TIME CO-EFFICIENT	UNIT TIME CO-EFFICIENT	TOTAL TIME CO-EFFICIENT	UNIT TIME CO-EFFICIENT	TOTAL TIME CO-EFFICIENT	UNIT TIME CO-EFFICIENT	TOTAL TIME CO-EFFICIENT
1	1.000	1.000	1.000	1.000	1.000	1.000	1.000	1.000	1.000	1.000
2	.700	1.700	.750	1.750	.800	1.800	.850	1.850	.900	1.900
3	.568	2.268	.634	2.384	.702	2.502	.773	2.623	.846	2.746
4	.490	2.758	.562	2.946	.640	3.142	.723	3.345	.810	3.556
5	.437	3.195	.513	3.459	.596	3.738	.686	4.031	.783	4.339
6	.398	3.593	.475	3.934	.562	4.299	.657	4.688	.762	5.101
7	.367	3.960	.446	4.380	.534	4.834	.634	5.322	.744	5.845
8	.343	4.303	.422	4.802	.512	5.346	.614	5.936	.729	6.574
9	.323	4.626	.402	5.204	.493	5.839	.597	6.533	.716	7.290
10	.306	4.932	.385	5.589	.477	6.315	.583	7.116	.705	7.994
11	.291	5.223	.370	5.958	.462	6.777	.570	7.686	.695	8.689
12	.278	5.501	.357	6.315	.449	7.227	.558	8.244	.685	9.374
13	.267	5.769	.345	6.660	.438	7.665	.548	8.792	.677	10.052
14	.257	6.026	.334	6.994	.428	8.092	.539	9.331	.670	10.721
15	.248	6.274	.325	7.319	.418	8.511	.530	9.861	.663	11.384
16	.240	6.514	.316	7.635	.410	8.920	.522	10.383	.656	12.040
17	.233	6.747	.309	7.944	.402	9.322	.515	10.898	.650	12.690
18	.226	6.973	.301	8.245	.394	9.716	.508	11.405	.644	13.334
19	.220	7.192	.295	8.540	.388	10.104	.501	11.907	.639	13.974
20	.214	7.407	.288	8.828	.381	10.485	.495	12.402	.634	14.608
25	.191	8.404	.263	10.191	.355	12.309	.470	14.801	.613	17.713
30	.174	9.305	.244	11.446	.335	14.020	.450	17.091	.596	20.727
35	.160	10.133	.229	12.618	.318	15.643	.434	19.294	.583	23.666
40	.150	10.902	.216	13.723	.305	17.193	.421	21.425	.571	26.543
45	.141	11.625	.206	14.773	.294	18.684	.410	23.500	.561	29.366
50	.134	12.307	.197	15.776	.284	20.122	.400	25.513	.552	32.142

Using Table E.3 requires that we know how long it takes to complete the first unit. Yet, what happens if our most recent or most reliable information available pertains to some other unit? The answer is that we must use these data to find a revised estimate for the first unit and then apply the table coefficient to that number. Example E4 illustrates this concept.

Example E4

REVISING LEARNING-CURVE ESTIMATES

Great Lakes, Inc., believes that unusual circumstances in producing the first boat (see Example E2) imply that the time estimate of 125,000 hours is not as valid a base as the time required to produce the third boat. Boat number 3 was completed in 100,000 hours. It wants to solve for the revised estimate for boat number 1.

APPROACH ▶ We return to Table E.3, with a unit value of $N = 3$ and a learning-curve coefficient of $C = .773$ in the 85% column.

SOLUTION ▶ To find the revised estimate, divide the actual time for boat number 3, 100,000 hours, by $C = .773$:

$$\frac{100,000}{.773} = 129,366 \text{ hours}$$

So 129,366 hours is the new (revised) estimate for boat 1.

INSIGHT ▶ Any change in product, process, or personnel will change the learning curve. The new estimate for boat 1 suggests that related cost and volume estimates need to be revised.

LEARNING EXERCISE ▶ Boat 4 was just completed in 90,000 hours. Great Lakes thinks the 85% learning-curve rate is valid but isn't sure about the 125,000 hours for the first boat. Find a revised estimate for boat 1. [Answer: 124,481, suggesting that boat 1's time was fairly accurate after all.]

RELATED PROBLEMS ▶ E.8, E.12, E.13, E.17, E.18, E.20b, E.21, E.23

EXCEL OM Data File **ModEExE4.xls** can be found in MyOMLab.

Examples E1 through E4 all assume that the learning curve rate is known. For a new product, this can be a major assumption. If a firm has observed the cost or time of any two products already produced, it's easy to work backward from Equation (E-3) and Table E.3 to impute the actual learning curve *rate*. Example E5 illustrates this concept.

Example E5

COMPUTING THE LEARNING-CURVE RATE FROM OBSERVED PRODUCTION

In 2012, Boeing completed production on its forty-fifth 787 airliner, at a cost of $184 million. The first plane off the assembly line, in 2010, cost $448 million. What is Boeing's learning-curve rate for this model?

APPROACH ▶ We use Equation (E-3), with costs for T_1 and T_{45} known, and then find the learning-curve coefficient (C) in Table E.3.

SOLUTION ▶ Equation (E-3) is $T_N = T_1 C$. We solve for $C = \dfrac{T_N}{T_1}$.

$$C = \frac{184}{448} = .41$$

In Table E.3, we follow the "Unit Number" row for $N = 45$, and we see that .41 falls under the 85% learning-curve rate for unit times (or costs, in this case).

INSIGHT ▶ Boeing's goal is to reach a 76% learning-curve rate, so OM must begin to lower costs dramatically. Progress should be checked with each plane from this point on.

LEARNING EXERCISE ▶ Let's say Boeing's fifth 787 cost $350 million. What was the learning-curve rate at that time relative to plane number 1? [Answer: C = $350 million/$448 million = .78. This suggests a 90% learning-curve rate, so Boeing's performance has deteriorated.]

RELATED PROBLEMS ▶ E.20, E.26 (E.29, E.32 are available in MyOMLab)

LO E.4 *Describe* the strategic implications of learning curves

Strategic Implications of Learning Curves

So far, we have shown how operations managers can forecast labor-hour requirements for a product. We have also shown how purchasing agents can determine a supplier's cost, knowledge that can help in price negotiations. Another important application of learning curves concerns strategic planning.

An example of a company cost line and industry price line are so labeled in Figure E.2. These learning curves are straight because both scales are log scales. When the *rate* of change is constant, a log-log graph yields a straight line. If an organization believes its cost line to be the "company cost" line, and the industry price is indicated by the dashed horizontal line, then the company must have costs at the points below the dashed line (for example, point *a* or *b*) or else operate at a loss (point *c*).

STUDENT TIP

Both the vertical and horizontal axes of this figure are log scales in this log-log graph.

Figure **E.2**

Industry Learning Curve for Price Compared with Company Learning Curve for Cost

Lower costs are not automatic; they must be managed down. When a firm's strategy is to pursue a learning curve steeper than the industry average (the company cost line in Figure E.2), it does this by:

1. Following an aggressive pricing policy
2. Focusing on continuing cost reduction and productivity improvement
3. Building on shared experience
4. Keeping capacity growing ahead of demand

Costs may drop as a firm pursues the learning curve, but volume must increase for the learning curve to exist. Moreover, managers must understand competitors before embarking on a learning-curve strategy. Weak competitors are undercapitalized, stuck with high costs, or do not understand the logic of learning curves. However, strong and dangerous competitors control their costs, have solid financial positions for the large investments needed, and have a track record of using an aggressive learning-curve strategy. Taking on such a competitor in a price war may help only the consumer.

Limitations of Learning Curves

Before using learning curves, some cautions are in order:

- Because learning curves differ from company to company, as well as industry to industry, estimates for each organization should be developed rather than applying someone else's.
- Learning curves are often based on the time necessary to complete the early units; therefore, those times must be accurate. As current information becomes available, reevaluation is appropriate.
- Any changes in personnel, design, or procedure can be expected to alter the learning curve, causing the curve to spike up for a short time, even if it is going to drop in the long run.
- While workers and processes may improve, the same learning curves do not always apply to indirect labor and material.
- The culture of the workplace, as well as resource availability and changes in the process, may alter the learning curve. For instance, as a project nears its end, worker interest and effort may drop, curtailing progress down the curve.

◆ STUDENT TIP
Determining accurate rates of learning requires careful analysis.

Summary

The learning curve is a powerful tool for an operations manager. This tool can assist operations managers in determining future cost standards for items produced as well as purchased. In addition, the learning curve can provide understanding about company and industry performance. We saw three approaches to learning curves: the doubling approach, formula approach, and learning-curve table approach. Software can also help analyze learning curves.

Key Term

Learning curves (p. 776)

Discussion Questions

1. What are some of the limitations of learning curves?
2. Identify three applications of the learning curve.
3. What are the approaches to solving learning-curve problems?
4. Refer to Example E2. What are the implications for Great Lakes, Inc., if the engineering department wants to change the engine in the third and subsequent tugboats that the firm purchases?
5. Why isn't the learning-curve concept as applicable in a high-volume assembly line as it is in most other human activities?
6. What are the elements that can disrupt the learning curve?
7. Explain the concept of the doubling effect in learning curves.
8. What techniques can a firm use to move to a steeper learning curve?

Using Software for Learning Curves

Excel, Excel OM, and POM for Windows may all be used in analyzing learning curves. You can use the ideas in the following section on Excel OM to build your own Excel spreadsheet if you wish.

✖ USING EXCEL OM

Program E.1 shows how Excel OM develops a spreadsheet for learning-curve calculations. The input data come from Examples E2 and E3. In cell B7, we enter the unit number for the base unit (which does not have to be 1), and in B8 we enter the time for this unit. Learning-curve rates can also be developed from observed times or costs, as illustrated in Example E5.

These are used for computations. Do not touch these cells. In cell B11, the time for the first unit is computed, allowing us to use initial units other than unit 1. In cell B12, the power to be raised to is computed, making the formulas in the rest of column B much simpler.

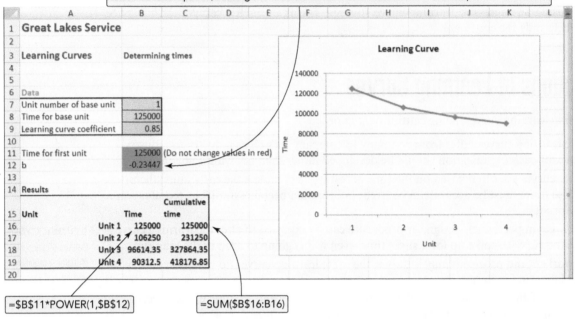

=$B$11*POWER(1,$B$12)

=SUM($B$16:B16)

Program **E.1**

Excel OM's Learning Curve Module, Using Data from Examples E2 and E3

℗ USING POM FOR WINDOWS

The POM for Windows Learning Curve module computes the length of time that future units will take, given the time required for the base unit and the learning rate (expressed as a number between 0 and 1). As an option, if the times required for the first and Nth units are already known, the learning *rate* can be computed. See Appendix IV for further details.

Solved Problems   Virtual Office Hours help is available in MyOMLab.

SOLVED PROBLEM E.1

Digicomp produces a new telephone system with built-in TV screens. Its learning-curve rate is 80%.

a) If the first one took 56 hours, how long will it take Digicomp to make the eleventh system?

b) How long will the first 11 systems take in total?

c) As a purchasing agent, you expect to buy units 12 through 15 of the new phone system. What would be your expected cost for the units if Digicomp charges $30 for each labor-hour?

SOLUTION

a) $T_N = T_1 C$ ⎯ from Table E.3, coefficient for 80% unit time
$T_{11} = (56 \text{ hours})(.462) = 25.9 \text{ hours}$

b) Total time for the first 11 units = $(56 \text{ hours})(6.777) = 379.5 \text{ hours}$

from Table E.3, coefficient for 80% total time

c) To find the time for units 12 through 15, we take the total cumulative time for units 1 to 15 and subtract the total time for units 1 to 11, which was computed in part (b). Total time for the first 15 units = (56 hours)(8.511) = 476.6 hours. So the time for units 12 through 15 is 476.6 − 379.5 = 97.1 hours. (This figure could also be confirmed by computing the times for units 12, 13, 14, and 15 separately using the unit-time coefficient column and then adding them.) Expected cost for units 12 through 15 = (97.1 hours)($30 per hour) = $2,913.

SOLVED PROBLEM E.2

If the first time you performed a job took 60 minutes, how long will the eighth job take if you are on an 80% learning curve?

SOLUTION

Three doublings from 1 to 2 to 4 to 8 implies $.8^3$. Therefore, we have:

$$60 \times (.8)^3 = 60 \times .512 = 30.72 \text{ minutes}$$

or, using Table E.3, we have $C = .512$. Therefore:

$$60 \times .512 = 30.72 \text{ minutes}$$

Problems   *Note:* **Px** means the problem may be solved with POM for Windows and/or Excel OM.

Problems E.1–E.32 relate to Applying the Learning Curve

• **E.1** Susan Sherer, an IRS auditor, took 45 minutes to process her first tax return. The IRS uses an 85% learning curve. How long will the:
a) 2nd return take?
b) 4th return take?
c) 8th return take? **Px**

• **E.2** Temple Trucking Co. just hired Ed Rosenthal to verify daily invoices and accounts payable. He took 9 hours and 23 minutes to complete his task on the first day. Prior employees in this job have tended to follow a 90% learning curve. How long will the task take at the end of:
a) the 2nd day?
b) the 4th day?
c) the 8th day?
d) the 16th day? **Px**

• **E.3** If Professor Laurie Macdonald takes 15 minutes to grade the first exam and follows an 80% learning curve, how long will it take her:
a) to grade the 25th exam?
b) to grade the first 10 exams? **Px**

• **E.4** If it took 563 minutes to complete a hospital's first cornea transplant, and the hospital uses a 90% learning rate, what is the cumulative time to complete:
a) the first 3 transplants?
b) the first 6 transplants?
c) the first 8 transplants?
d) the first 16 transplants? **Px**

•• **E.5** Beth Zion Hospital has received initial certification from the state of California to become a center for liver transplants. The hospital, however, must complete its first 18 transplants under great scrutiny and at no cost to the patients. The very first transplant, just completed, required 30 hours. On the basis of research at the hospital, Beth Zion estimates that it will have an 80% learning curve. Estimate the time it will take to complete:
a) the 5th liver transplant.
b) all of the first 5 transplants.
c) the 18th transplant.
d) all 18 transplants. **Px**

•• **E.6** Refer to Problem E.5. Beth Zion Hospital has just been informed that only the first 10 transplants must be performed at the hospital's expense. The cost per hour of surgery is estimated to be $5,000. Again, the learning rate is 80% and the first surgery took 30 hours.
a) How long will the 10th surgery take?
b) How much will the 10th surgery cost?
c) How much will all 10 cost the hospital? **Px**

• **E.7** Manceville Air has just produced the first unit of a large industrial compressor that incorporated new technology in the control circuits and a new internal venting system. The first unit took 112 hours of labor to manufacture. The company knows from past experience that this labor content will decrease significantly as more units are produced. In reviewing past production data, it appears that the company has experienced a 90% learning curve when producing similar designs. The company is interested in estimating the total time to complete the next 7 units. Your job as the production cost estimator is to prepare the estimate. **Px**

• **E.8** Elizabeth Perry, a student at SUNY, bought 6 bookcases for her dorm room. Each required unpacking of parts and assembly, which included some nailing and bolting.

doble.d/Fotolia

Elizabeth completed the first bookcase in 5 hours and the second in 4 hours.
a) What is her learning rate?
b) Assuming that the same rate continues, how long will the 3rd bookcase take?
c) The 4th, 5th, and 6th cases?
d) All 6 cases? **PX**

•• **E.9** Professor Mary Beth Marrs took 6 hours to prepare the first lecture in a new course. Traditionally, she has experienced a 90% learning curve. How much time should it take her to prepare the 15th lecture? **PX**

• **E.10** The first vending machine that William Kine, Inc., assembled took 80 labor-hours. Estimate how long the fourth machine will require for each of the following learning rates:
a) 95%
b) 87%
c) 72% **PX**

• **E.11** D. Shimshak Systems is installing networks for Advantage Insurance. The first installation took 46 labor-hours to complete. Estimate how long the 4th and the 8th installations will take for each of the following learning rates:
a) 92%
b) 84%
c) 77% **PX**

••• **E.12** Providence Assessment Center screens and trains employees for a computer assembly firm in Boston. The progress of all trainees is tracked, and those not showing the proper progress are moved to less demanding programs. By the tenth repetition trainees must be able to complete the assembly task in 1 hour or less. Susan Sweaney has just spent 5 hours on the fourth unit and 4 hours completing her eighth unit, while another trainee, Julie Burgmeier, took 4 hours on the third and 3 hours on the sixth unit. Should you encourage either or both of the trainees to continue? Why? **PX**

•• **E.13** The better students at Providence Assessment Center (see Problem E.12) have an 80% learning curve and can do a task in 20 minutes after just six times. You would like to weed out the weak students sooner and decide to evaluate them after the third unit. How long should the third unit take? **PX**

•• **E.14** Suad Alwan, the purchasing agent for Dubai Airlines, is interested in determining what he can expect to pay for airplane number 4 if the third plane took 20,000 hours to produce. What would Alwan expect to pay for plane number 5? Number 6? Use an 85% learning curve and a $40-per-hour labor charge. **PX**

•• **E.15** Using the data from Problem E.14, how long will it take to complete the 12th plane? The 15th plane? How long will it take to complete planes 12 through 15 inclusive? At $40 per hour, what can Alwan, as purchasing agent, expect to pay for planes 12 through 15? **PX**

•• **E.16** Central Electronics Corp. produces semiconductors and has a learning curve of .7. The price per bit is 100 millicents when the volume is $.7 \times 10^{12}$ bits. What is the expected price at 1.4×10^{12} bits? What is the expected price at 89.6×10^{12} bits? **PX**

•• **E.17** Regional Power owns 25 small power generating plants. It has contracted with Genco Services to overhaul the power turbines of each of the plants. The number of hours that Genco billed Regional to complete the third turbine was 460. Regional pays Genco $60 per hour for its services. As the maintenance manager for Regional, you are trying to estimate the cost of overhauling the fourth turbine. How much would you expect to pay for the overhaul of number 5 and number 6? All the turbines are similar, and an 80% learning curve is appropriate. **PX**

•• **E.18** If it took Boeing 28,718 hours to produce the eighth 787 jet and the learning-curve factor is 80%, how long did it take to produce the tenth 787? **PX**

•• **E.19** Richard Dulski's firm is about to bid on a new radar system. Although the product uses new technology, Dulski believes that a learning rate of 75% is appropriate. The first unit is expected to take 700 hours, and the contract is for 40 units. **PX**
a) What is the total amount of hours to build the 40 units?
b) What is the average time to build each of the 40 units?
c) Assume that a worker works 2,080 hours per year. How many workers should be assigned to this contract to complete it in a year? **PX**

••• **E.20** As the estimator for Rajendra Tibrewala Enterprises, your job is to prepare an estimate for a potential customer service contract. The contract is for the service of diesel locomotive cylinder heads. The shop has done some of these in the past on a sporadic basis. The time required to service the first cylinder head in each job has been exactly 4 hours, and similar work has been accomplished at an 85% learning curve. The customer wants you to quote the total time in batches of 12 and 20.
a) Prepare the quote.
b) After preparing the quote, you find a labor ticket for this customer for five locomotive cylinder heads. From the notations on the labor ticket, you conclude that the fifth unit took 2.5 hours. What do you conclude about the learning curve and your quote? **PX**

•• **E.21** Girish Shambu and William Reisel are teammates at a discount store; their new job is assembling bicycles for customers. Assembly of a bike has a learning rate of 90%. They forgot to time their effort on the first bike, but spent 4 hours on the second set. They have 6 more bikes to do. Determine approximately how much time will be (was) required for:
a) the 1st unit
b) the 8th unit
c) all 8 units **PX**

•• **E.22** Kelly-Lambing, Inc., a builder of government-contracted small ships, has a steady work force of 10 very skilled craftspeople. These workers can supply 2,500 labor-hours each per year. Kelly-Lambing is about to undertake a new contract, building a new style of boat. The first boat is expected to take 6,000 hours to complete. The firm thinks that 90% is the expected learning rate.
a) What is the firm's "capacity" to make these boats—that is, how many units can the firm make in 1 year?
b) If the operations manager can increase the learning rate to 85% instead of 90%, how many units can the firm make?

··· **E.23**   The service times for a new data entry clerk have been measured and sequentially recorded as shown below:

REPORT	TIME (MINUTES)
1	66
2	56
3	53
4	48
5	47
6	45
7	44
8	41

a) What is the learning curve rate, based on this information?
b) Using an 85% learning curve rate and the above times, estimate the length of time the clerk will take to complete the 48th report. **Px**

·· **E.24**   If the first unit of a production run takes 1 hour and the firm is on an 80% learning curve, how long will unit 100 take? (*Hint:* Apply the coefficient in Table E.3 twice.) **Px**

··· **E.25**   Boeing spent $270 million to make the eleventh 787 in its production line. The first 787 cost $448 million. What was the learning curve rate at this point?

> *Additional problems* **E.26–E.32** *are available in* MyOMLab.

Problem E.33 relates to Strategic Implications of Learning Curves

···· **E.33**   Using the accompanying log-log graph, answer the following questions:

a) What are the implications for management if it has forecast its cost on the optimum line?
b) What could be causing the fluctuations above the optimum line?
c) If management forecasted the 10th unit on the optimum line, what was that forecast in hours?
d) If management built the 10th unit as indicated by the actual line, how many hours did it take?

CASE STUDY

SMT's Negotiation with IBM

IBM asked SMT and one other, much larger company to bid on 80 more units of a particular computer product. The RFQ (request for quote) asked that the overall bid be broken down to show the hourly rate, the parts and materials component in the price, and any charges for subcontracted services. SMT quoted $1.62 million and supplied the cost breakdown as requested. The second company submitted only one total figure, $5 million, with no cost breakdown. The decision was made to negotiate with SMT.

The IBM negotiating team included two purchasing managers and two cost engineers. One cost engineer had developed manufacturing cost estimates for every component, working from engineering drawings and cost-data books that he had built up from previous experience and that contained time factors, both setup and run times, for a large variety of operations. He estimated material costs by working both from data supplied by the IBM corporate purchasing staff and from purchasing journals. He visited SMT facilities to see the tooling available so that he would know what processes were being used. He assumed that there would be perfect conditions and trained operators, and he developed cost estimates for the 158th unit (previous orders were for 25, 15, and 38 units). He added 5% for scrap-and-flow loss; 2% for the use of temporary tools, jigs, and fixtures; 5% for quality

control; and 9% for purchasing burden. Then, using an 85% learning curve, he backed up his costs to get an estimate for the first unit. He next checked the data on hours and materials for the 25, 15, and 38 units already made and found that his estimate for the first unit was within 4% of actual cost. His check, however, had indicated a 90% learning-curve effect on hours per unit.

In the negotiations, SMT was represented by one of the two owners of the business, two engineers, and one cost estimator. The sessions opened with a discussion of learning curves. The IBM cost estimator demonstrated that SMT had in fact been operating on a 90% learning curve. But, he argued, it should be possible to move to an 85% curve, given the longer runs, reduced setup time, and increased continuity of workers on the job that would be possible with an order for 80 units. The owner agreed with this analysis and was willing to reduce his price by 4%.

However, as each operation in the manufacturing process was discussed, it became clear that some IBM cost estimates were too low because certain crating and shipping expenses had been overlooked. These oversights were minor, however, and in the following discussions, the two parties arrived at a common understanding of specifications and reached agreements on the costs of each manufacturing operation.

At this point, SMT representatives expressed great concern about the possibility of inflation in material costs. The IBM negotiators volunteered to include a form of price escalation in the contract, as previously agreed among themselves. IBM representatives suggested that if overall material costs changed by more than 10%, the price could be adjusted accordingly. However, if one party took the initiative to have the price revised, the other could require an analysis of *all* parts and materials invoices in arriving at the new price.

Another concern of the SMT representatives was that a large amount of overtime and subcontracting would be required to meet IBM's specified delivery schedule. IBM negotiators thought that a relaxation in the delivery schedule might be possible if a price concession could be obtained. In response, the SMT team offered a 5% discount, and this was accepted. As a result of these negotiations, the SMT price was reduced almost 20% below its original bid price.

In a subsequent meeting called to negotiate the prices of certain pipes to be used in the system, it became apparent to an IBM cost estimator that SMT representatives had seriously underestimated their costs. He pointed out this apparent error because he could not understand why SMT had quoted such a low figure. He wanted to be sure that SMT was using the correct manufacturing process. In any case, if SMT estimators had made a mistake, it should be noted. It was IBM's policy to seek a fair price both for itself and for its suppliers. IBM procurement managers believed that if a vendor was losing money on a job, there would be a tendency to cut corners. In addition, the IBM negotiator felt that by pointing out the error, he generated some goodwill that would help in future sessions.

Discussion Questions

1. What are the advantages and disadvantages to IBM and SMT from this approach?
2. How does SMT's proposed learning rate compare with that of other industries?
3. What are the limitations of the learning curve in this case?

Source: Based on E. Raymond Corey, *Procurement Management: Strategy, Organization, and Decision Making* (New York: Van Nostrand Reinhold).

Endnote

1. T. P. Wright, "Factors Affecting the Cost of Airplanes," *Journal of the Aeronautical Sciences* (February 1936).

Module E *Rapid* Review

E

Rapid Review

Main Heading	Review Material	MyOMLab

WHAT IS A LEARNING CURVE? (pp. 776–777)	■ **Learning curves**—The premise that people and organizations get better at their tasks as the tasks are repeated; sometimes called experience curves.
	
	Learning usually follows a negative exponential curve.
	
	It takes less time to complete each additional unit a firm produces; however, the time *savings* in completing each subsequent unit *decreases*.
	
	Learning curves were first applied to industry in a report by T. P. Wright of Curtis-Wright Corp. in 1936. Wright described how direct labor costs of making a particular airplane decreased with learning.
	
	Learning curves have been applied not only to labor but also to a wide variety of other costs, including material and purchased components.
	
	The power of the learning curve is so significant that it plays a major role in many strategic decisions related to employment levels, costs, capacity, and pricing.
	
	The learning curve is based on a *doubling* of production: That is, when production doubles, the decrease in time per unit affects the rate of the learning curve.
	
	$$T \times L^n = \text{Time required for the } n\text{th unit} \qquad \text{(E-1)}$$
	
	where T = unit cost or time of the first unit
	               L = learning curve rate
	               n = number of times T is doubled
		Concept Questions: 1.1–1.4

LEARNING CURVES IN SERVICES AND MANUFACTURING (pp. 777–778)	Different organizations—indeed, different products—have different learning curves. The rate of learning varies, depending on the quality of management and the potential of the process and product. *Any change in process, product, or personnel disrupts the learning curve.* Therefore, caution should be exercised in assuming that a learning curve is continuing and permanent. The steeper the slope of the learning curve, the faster the drop in costs. By tradition, learning curves are defined in terms of the *complements* of their improvement rates (i.e., a 75% learning rate is better than an 85% learning rate). Stable, standardized products and processes tend to have costs that decline more steeply than others. Learning curves are useful for a variety of purposes, including: 1. *Internal:* Labor forecasting, scheduling, establishing costs and budgets 2. *External:* Supply-chain negotiations 3. *Strategic:* Evaluation of company and industry performance, including costs and pricing	Concept Questions: 2.1–2.4

APPLYING THE LEARNING CURVE (pp. 778–782)	If learning curve improvement is ignored, potential problems could arise, such as scheduling mismatches, leading to idle labor and productive facilities, refusal to accept new orders because capacity is assumed to be full, or missing an opportunity to negotiate with suppliers for lower purchase prices as a result of large orders.
	
	Three ways to approach the mathematics of learning curves are (1) doubling approach, (2) formula approach, and (3) learning-curve table approach.
	
	The doubling approach uses the production doubling Equation (E-1).
	
	The formula approach allows us to determine labor for *any* unit, T_N, by the formula:
	
	$$T_N = T_1(N^b) \qquad \text{(E-2)}$$
	
	where T_N = time for the Nth unit
	           T_1 = time to produce the first unit
	           b = (log of the learning rate)/(log 2) = slope of the learning curve
	
	The learning-curve table approach makes use of Table E.3 and uses the formula:
	
	$$T_N = T_1 C \qquad \text{(E-3)}$$
	
	where T_N = number of labor-hours required to produce the Nth unit
	           T_1 = number of labor-hours required to produce the first unit
	           C = learning-curve coefficient found in Table E.3
	
	The learning-curve coefficient, C, depends on both the learning rate and the unit number of interest.
		Concept Questions: 3.1–3.4
		
		Problems: E.1–E.32
		
		Virtual Office Hours for Solved Problems: E.1, E.2
		
		ACTIVE MODEL E.1

Main Heading	Review Material	MyOMLab
	Formula (E-3) can also use the "Total Time Coefficient" columns of Table E.3 to provide the total cumulative number of hours needed to complete the specified number of units. If the most recent or most reliable information available pertains to some unit other than the first, these data should be used to find a revised estimate for the first unit, and then the applicable formulas should be applied to that revised number.	
STRATEGIC IMPLICATIONS OF LEARNING CURVES (pp. 782–783)	When a firm's strategy is to pursue a learning cost curve steeper than the industry average, it can do this by: 1. Following an aggressive pricing policy 2. Focusing on continuing cost reduction and productivity improvement 3. Building on shared experience 4. Keeping capacity growing ahead of demand Managers must understand competitors before embarking on a learning-curve strategy. For example, taking on a strong competitor in a price war may help only the consumer.	Concept Questions: 4.1–4.3 Problem: E.33
LIMITATIONS OF LEARNING CURVES (p. 783)	Before using learning curves, some cautions are in order: ■ Because learning curves differ from company to company, as well as industry to industry, estimates for each organization should be developed rather than applying someone else's. ■ Learning curves are often based on the time necessary to complete the early units; therefore, those times must be accurate. As current information becomes available, reevaluation is appropriate. ■ Any changes in personnel, design, or procedure can be expected to alter the learning curve, causing the curve to spike up for a short time, even if it is going to drop in the long run. ■ While workers and process may improve, the same learning curves do not always apply to indirect labor and material. ■ The culture of the workplace, as well as resource availability and changes in the process, may alter the learning curve. For instance, as a project nears its end, worker interest and effort may drop, curtailing progress down the curve.	Concept Questions: 5.1–5.4

Self Test

■ **Before taking the self-test,** refer to the learning objectives listed at the beginning of the module and the key term listed at the end of the module.

LO E.1 A learning curve describes:
- a) the rate at which an organization acquires new data.
- b) the amount of production time per unit as the total number of units produced increases.
- c) the increase in production time per unit as the total number of units produced increases.
- d) the increase in number of units produced per unit time as the total number of units produced increases.

LO E.2 A surgical procedure with a 90% learning curve required 20 hours for the initial patient. The fourth patient should require approximately how many hours?
- a) 18
- b) 16.2
- c) 28
- d) 30
- e) 54.2

LO E.3 The first transmission took 50 hours to rebuild at Bob's Auto Repair, and the learning rate is 80%. How long will it take to rebuild the third unit? (Use at least three decimals in the exponent if you use the formula approach.)
- a) under 30 hours
- b) about 32 hours
- c) about 35 hours
- d) about 60 hours
- e) about 45 hours

LO E.4 Which one of the following courses of action would *not* be taken by a firm wanting to pursue a learning curve steeper than the industry average?
- a) Following an aggressive pricing policy
- b) Focusing on continuing cost reduction
- c) Keeping capacity equal to demand to control costs
- d) Focusing on productivity improvement
- e) Building on shared experience

Answers: LO E.1. b; LO E.2. b; LO E.3. c; LO E.4. c.

Simulation

MODULE OUTLINE

Alaska Airlines

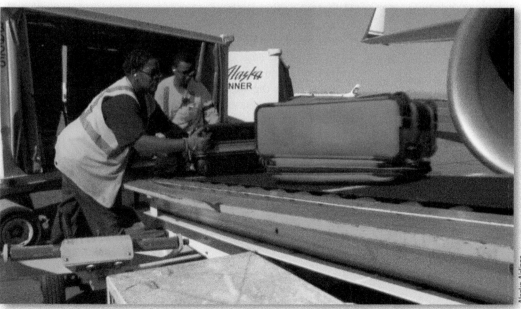

Alaska Airlines

LEARNING OBJECTIVES

LO F.1 *List* the advantages and disadvantages of modeling with simulation 793

LO F.2 *Perform* the five steps in a Monte Carlo simulation 794

LO F.3 *Simulate* an inventory problem 798

LO F.4 *Use* Excel spreadsheets to create a simulation 800

Minor Treatment Rooms

Dr. Station

To Hospital ➡

EKG

Registration

LAB

Nurses Station

X-RAY

Major Treatment Rooms

Micro Saint® Sharp image used with permission of Alion Science and Technology Corp.

Kaiser/Agencja Fotograficzna Caro/Alamy

When Bay Medical Center faced severe overcrowding at its outpatient clinic, it turned to computer simulation to try to reduce bottlenecks and improve patient flow. A simulation language called Micro Saint analyzed current data relating to patient service times between clinic rooms. By simulating different numbers of doctors and staff, simulating the use of another clinic for overflow, and simulating a redesign of the existing clinic, Bay Medical Center was able to make decisions based on an understanding of both costs and benefits. This resulted in better patient service at lower cost.

Source: Micro Analysis and Design Simulation Software, Inc., Boulder, CO.

What Is Simulation?

Simulation models abound in our world. The city of Atlanta, for example, uses them to control traffic. Europe's Airbus Industries uses them to test the aerodynamics of proposed jets. The U.S. Army simulates war games on computers. Business students use management gaming to simulate realistic business competition. And thousands of organizations like Bay Medical Center develop simulation models to help make operations decisions.

Most of the large companies in the world use simulation models. Table F.1 lists just a few areas in which simulation is now being applied.

Simulation is the attempt to duplicate the features, appearance, and characteristics of a real system. In this module, we will show how to simulate part of an operations management system by building a mathematical model that comes as close as possible to representing the reality

Simulation

The attempt to duplicate the features, appearance, and characteristics of a real system, usually via a computerized model.

TABLE F.1	Some Applications of Simulation
Ambulance location and dispatching	Bus scheduling
Assembly-line balancing	Design of library operations
Parking lot and harbor design	Taxi, truck, and railroad dispatching
Distribution system design	Production facility scheduling
Scheduling aircraft	Plant layout
Labor-hiring decisions	Capital investments
Personnel scheduling	Production scheduling
Traffic-light timing	Sales forecasting
Voting pattern prediction	Inventory planning and control

of the system. The model will then be used to estimate the effects of various actions. The idea behind simulation is threefold:

1. To imitate a real-world situation mathematically
2. Then to study its properties and operating characteristics
3. Finally, to draw conclusions and make action decisions based on the results of the simulation

In this way, a real-life system need not be touched until the advantages and disadvantages of a major policy decision are first measured on the model.

To use simulation, an OM manager should:

1. Define the problem.
2. Introduce the important variables associated with the problem.
3. Construct a numerical model.
4. Set up possible courses of action for testing by specifying values of variables.
5. Run the experiment.
6. Consider the results (possibly modifying the model or changing data inputs).
7. Decide what course of action to take.

These steps are illustrated in Figure F.1.

The problems tackled by simulation may range from very simple to extremely complex, from bank-teller lines to an analysis of the U.S. economy. Although small simulations can be conducted by hand, effective use of the technique requires a computer. Large-scale models, simulating perhaps years of business decisions, are virtually all handled by computer.

In this module, we examine the basic principles of simulation and then tackle some problems in the areas of waiting-line analysis and inventory control. Why do we use simulation in these areas when mathematical models described in other chapters can solve similar problems? The answer is that simulation provides an alternative approach for problems that are very complex mathematically. It can handle, for example, inventory problems in which demand or lead time is not constant.

Figure **F.1**

The Process of Simulation

Advantages and Disadvantages of Simulation

Simulation is a tool that has become widely accepted by managers for several reasons. The main *advantages* of simulation are as follows:

1. It can be used to analyze large and complex real-world situations that cannot be solved by conventional operations management models.
2. Real-world complications can be included that most OM models cannot permit. For example, simulation can use *any* probability distribution the user defines; it does not require standard distributions.
3. "Time compression" is possible. The effects of OM policies over many months or years can be obtained by computer simulation in a short time.
4. Simulation allows "what-if?" types of questions. Managers like to know in advance what options will be most attractive. With a computerized model, a manager can try out several policy decisions within a matter of minutes.
5. Simulations do not interfere with real-world systems. It may be too disruptive, for example, to experiment physically with new policies or ideas in a hospital or manufacturing plant.

The main *disadvantages* of simulation are as follows:

1. Good simulation models can take a long time to develop.
2. It is a repetitive approach that may produce different solutions in repeated runs. It does not generate optimal solutions to problems (as does linear programming).
3. Managers must generate all of the conditions and constraints for solutions that they want to examine. The simulation model does not produce answers without adequate, realistic input.
4. Each simulation model is unique. Its solutions and inferences are not usually transferable to other problems.

◆ **STUDENT TIP**
There are many reasons it's better to simulate a real-world system than to experiment with it.

LO F.1 *List* the advantages and disadvantages of modeling with simulation

Computer simulation models have been developed to address a variety of productivity issues at fast-food restaurants such as Burger King. In one, the ideal distance between the drive-through order station and the pickup window was simulated. For example, because a longer distance reduced waiting time, 12 to 13 additional customers could be served per hour—a benefit of about $20,000 in extra sales per restaurant per year. In another simulation, a second drive-through window was considered. This model predicted a sales increase of 15%.

Monte Carlo Simulation

Monte Carlo method

A simulation technique that uses random elements when chance exists in their behavior.

LO F.2 *Perform* the five steps in a Monte Carlo simulation

When a system contains elements that exhibit *chance* in their behavior, the Monte Carlo method of simulation may be applied. The basis of Monte Carlo simulation is experimentation on chance (or *probabilistic*) elements by means of random sampling.

The technique breaks down into five simple steps:

1. Setting up a probability distribution for important variables.
2. Building a cumulative probability distribution for each variable.
3. Establishing an interval of random numbers for each variable.
4. Generating random numbers.
5. Actually simulating a series of trials.

Let's examine these steps in turn.

Step 1. Establishing Probability Distributions. The basic idea in the Monte Carlo simulation is to generate values for the variables making up the model under study. In real-world systems, a lot of variables are probabilistic in nature. To name just a few: inventory demand; lead time for orders to arrive; times between machine breakdowns; times between customer arrivals at a service facility; service times; times required to complete project activities; and number of employees absent from work each day.

One common way to establish a *probability distribution* for a given variable is to examine historical outcomes. We can find the probability, or relative frequency, for each possible outcome of a variable by dividing the frequency of observation by the total number of observations. Here's an example.

The daily demand for radial tires at Barry's Auto Tire over the past 200 days is shown in columns 1 and 2 of Table F.2. Assuming that past arrival rates will hold in the future, we can convert this demand to a probability distribution by dividing each demand frequency by the total demand, 200. The results are shown in column 3.

Cumulative probability distribution

The accumulation of individual probabilities of a distribution.

Step 2. Building a Cumulative Probability Distribution for Each Variable. The conversion from a regular probability distribution, such as in column 3 of Table F.2, to a cumulative probability distribution is an easy job. In column 4, we see that the cumulative probability for each level of demand is the sum of the number in the probability column (column 3) added to the previous cumulative probability.

STUDENT TIP ◀
To establish a probability distribution for tires, we assume that historical demand is a good indicator of future demand.

TABLE F.2	Demand for Barry's Auto Tire		
(1) **DEMAND FOR TIRES**	**(2)** **FREQUENCY**	**(3)** **PROBABILITY OF** **OCCURRENCE**	**(4)** **CUMULATIVE** **PROBABILITY**
0	10	10/200 = .05	.05
1	20	20/200 = .10	.15
2	40	40/200 = .20	.35
3	60	60/200 = .30	.65
4	40	40/200 = .20	.85
5	30	30/200 = .15	1.00
	200 days	200/200 = 1.00	

TABLE F.3	The Assignment of Random-Number Intervals for Barry's Auto Tire		
DAILY DEMAND	PROBABILITY	CUMULATIVE PROBABILITY	INTERVAL OF RANDOM NUMBERS
0	.05	.05	01 through 05
1	.10	.15	06 through 15
2	.20	.35	16 through 35
3	.30	.65	36 through 65
4	.20	.85	66 through 85
5	.15	1.00	86 through 00

Step 3. Setting Random-Number Intervals. Once we have established a cumulative probability distribution for each variable in the simulation, we must assign a set of numbers to represent each possible value or outcome. These are referred to as random-number intervals. Basically, a random number is a series of digits (say, two digits from 01, 02, . . . , 98, 99, 00) that have been selected by a totally random process—a process in which each random number has an equal chance of being selected.

If, for example, there is a 5% chance that demand for Barry's radial tires will be 0 units per day, then we will want 5% of the random numbers available to correspond to a demand of 0 units. If a total of 100 two-digit numbers is used in the simulation, we could assign a demand of 0 units to the first 5 random numbers: 01, 02, 03, 04, and 05.[1] Then a simulated demand for 0 units would be created every time one of the numbers 01 to 05 was drawn. If there is also a 10% chance that demand for the same product will be 1 unit per day, we could let the next 10 random numbers (06, 07, 08, 09, 10, 11, 12, 13, 14, and 15) represent that demand—and so on for other demand levels.

Similarly, we can see in Table F.3 that the length of each interval on the right corresponds to the probability of 1 of each of the possible daily demands. Thus, in assigning random numbers

STUDENT TIP

You may start random-number intervals at either 01 or 00, but the text starts at 01 so that the top of each range is the cumulative probability.

Random-number intervals

A set of numbers to represent each possible value or outcome in a computer simulation.

Random number

A series of digits that have been selected by a totally random process.

TABLE F.4	Table of 2-Digit Random Numbers																
52	06	50	88	53	30	10	47	99	37	66	91	35	32	00	84	57	07
37	63	28	02	74	35	24	03	29	60	74	85	90	73	59	55	17	60
82	57	68	28	05	94	03	11	27	79	90	87	92	41	09	25	36	77
69	02	36	49	71	99	32	10	75	21	95	90	94	38	97	71	72	49
98	94	90	36	06	78	23	67	89	85	29	21	25	73	69	34	85	76
96	52	62	87	49	56	59	23	78	71	72	90	57	01	98	57	31	95
33	69	27	21	11	60	95	89	68	48	17	89	34	09	93	50	44	51
50	33	50	95	13	44	34	62	64	39	55	29	30	64	49	44	30	16
88	32	18	50	62	57	34	56	62	31	15	40	90	34	51	95	26	14
90	30	36	24	69	82	51	74	30	35	36	85	01	55	92	64	09	85
50	48	61	18	85	23	08	54	17	12	80	69	24	84	92	16	49	59
27	88	21	62	69	64	48	31	12	73	02	68	00	16	16	46	13	85
45	14	46	32	13	49	66	62	74	41	86	98	92	98	84	54	33	40
81	02	01	78	82	74	97	37	45	31	94	99	42	49	27	64	89	42
66	83	14	74	27	76	03	33	11	97	59	81	72	00	64	61	13	52
74	05	81	82	93	09	96	33	52	78	13	06	28	30	94	23	37	39
30	34	87	01	74	11	46	82	59	94	25	34	32	23	17	01	58	73
59	55	72	33	62	13	74	68	22	44	42	09	32	46	71	79	45	89
67	09	80	98	99	25	77	50	03	32	36	63	65	75	94	19	95	88
60	77	46	63	71	69	44	22	03	85	14	48	69	13	30	50	33	24
60	08	19	29	36	72	30	27	50	64	85	72	75	29	87	05	75	01
80	45	86	99	02	34	87	08	86	84	49	76	24	08	01	86	29	11
53	84	49	63	26	65	72	84	85	63	26	02	75	26	92	62	40	67
69	84	12	94	51	36	17	02	15	29	16	52	56	43	26	22	08	62
37	77	13	10	02	18	31	19	32	85	31	94	81	43	31	58	33	51

Source: Adapted from *A Million Random Digits with 100,000 Normal Deviates.* New York: The Free Press, 1995. Used by permission.

to the daily demand for 3 radial tires, the range of the random-number interval (36 through 65) corresponds *exactly* to the probability (or proportion) of that outcome. A daily demand for 3 radial tires occurs 30% of the time. All of the 30 random numbers greater than 35 up to and including 65 are assigned to that event.

Step 4. Generating Random Numbers. Random numbers may be generated for simulation problems in two ways. If the problem is large and the process under study involves many simulation trials, computer programs are available to generate the needed random numbers. If the simulation is being done by hand, the numbers may be selected from a table of random digits.

Step 5. Simulating the Experiment. We may simulate outcomes of an experiment by simply selecting random numbers from Table F.4. Beginning anywhere in the table, we note the interval in Table F.3 into which each number falls. For example, if the random number chosen is 81 and the interval 66 through 85 represents a daily demand for 4 tires, then we select a demand of 4 tires. Example F1 carries the simulation further.

Example F1

SIMULATING DEMAND

Barry's Auto Tire wants to simulate 10 days of demand for radial tires.

APPROACH ▶ Earlier, we went through Steps 1 and 2 in the Monte Carlo method (in Table F.2) and Step 3 (in Table F.3). Now we need to generate random numbers (Step 4) and simulate demand (Step 5).

SOLUTION ▶ We select the random numbers needed from Table F.4, starting in the upper-left-hand corner and continuing down the first column, and record the corresponding daily demand:

DAY NUMBER	RANDOM NUMBER	SIMULATED DAILY DEMAND
1	52	3
2	37	3
3	82	4
4	69	4
5	98	5
6	96	5
7	33	2
8	50	3
9	88	5
10	90	5
		39 Total 10-day demand
		39/10 = 3.9 = tires average daily demand

INSIGHT ▶ It is interesting to note that the average demand of 3.9 tires in this 10-day simulation differs substantially from the *expected* daily demand, which we may calculate from the data in Table F.3:

$$\text{Expected demand} = \sum_{i=0}^{5}(\text{probability of } i \text{ units}) \times (\text{demand of } i \text{ units})$$
$$= (.05)(0) + (.10)(1) + (.20)(2) + (.30)(3) + (.20)(4) + (.15)(5)$$
$$= 0 + .1 + .4 + .9 + .8 + .75$$
$$= 2.95 \text{ tires}$$

However, if this simulation was repeated hundreds or thousands of times, the average *simulated* demand would be nearly the same as the *expected* demand.

LEARNING EXERCISE ▶ Resimulate the 10 days, this time with random numbers from column 2 of Table F.4. What is the average daily demand? [Answer: 2.5.]

RELATED PROBLEMS ▶ F.1–F.12 (F.13–F.15 are available in MyOMLab)

OM in Action | Simulation Takes the Kinks out of Starbucks' Lines

The animation on the computer screen is not encouraging. Starbucks is running a digital simulation of customers ordering new warm sandwiches and pastries at a "virtual" store.

At first, things seem to go well, as animated workers rush around, preparing orders. But then they can't keep up. Soon the customers are stacking up in line, and the goal of serving each person in less than 3 minutes is blown. The line quickly reaches the point at which customers decide the snack or drink isn't worth the wait—called the "balking point" in queuing theory.

Fortunately for Starbucks, the customers departing without their Frappuccinos and decaf slim lattes are digital. The simulation helps operations managers find out what caused the backup before the scene repeats itself in the real world.

Simulation software is also used to find the point where capital expenditures will pay off. In large chains such as Starbucks, adding even a minor piece of equipment can add up. A $200 blender in each of Starbucks' more than 22,000 stores in 65 countries can cost the firm millons.

Sources: **www.news.starbucks.com/news**; *The Wall Street Journal* (August 4, 2009); and **slideshare.net** (April 25, 2015).

Naturally, it would be risky to draw any hard and fast conclusions about the operation of a firm from only a short simulation like Example F1. Seldom would anyone actually want to go to the effort of simulating such a simple model containing only one variable. Simulating by hand does, however, demonstrate the important principles involved and may be useful in small-scale studies.

Simulation with Two Decision Variables: An Inventory Example

Often, there is more than one variable to be simulated. In Example F1 it was demand for tires. But many OM decisions have multiple variables. In a queuing situation, it may be arrival times and service times. In an inventory problem, as we saw in Chapter 12, both demand and lead time might be variable (not constant).

In this section, we present an inventory problem with two decision variables and two probabilistic components. The owner of the hardware store in Example F2 would like to establish *order quantity* and *reorder point* decisions for a particular product that has probabilistic (uncertain) daily demand and reorder lead time. He wants to make a series of simulation runs, trying out various order quantities and reorder points, to minimize his total inventory cost for the item. Inventory costs in this case will include ordering, holding, and stockout costs.

> **◆ STUDENT TIP**
> Most real-world inventory systems have probabilistic events and benefit from a simulation approach.

Example F2 | AN INVENTORY SIMULATION WITH TWO VARIABLES

Simkin's Hardware Store, in Reno, sells the Ace model electric drill. Daily demand for this particular product is relatively low but subject to some variability. Lead times tend to be variable as well. Mark Simkin wants to develop a simulation to test an inventory policy of ordering 10 drills, with a reorder point of 5. In other words, every time the on-hand inventory level at the end of the day is 5 or less, Simkin will call his supplier that evening and place an order for 10 more drills. Simkin notes that if the lead time is 1 day, the order will not arrive the next morning but rather at the beginning of the following workday. Stockouts become lost sales, not backorders.

APPROACH ▶ Simkin wants to follow the 5 steps in the Monte Carlo simulation process.

SOLUTION ▶ Over the past 300 days, Simkin has observed the sales shown in column 2 of Table F.5. He converts this historical frequency into a probability distribution for the variable daily demand (column 3). A cumulative probability distribution is formed in column 4 of Table F.5. Finally, Simkin establishes an interval of random numbers to represent each possible daily demand (column 5).

When Simkin places an order to replenish his inventory of drills, there is a delivery lag of from 1 to 3 days. This means that lead time may also be considered a probabilistic variable. The number of days

TABLE F.5	Probabilities and Random-Number Intervals for Daily Ace Drill Demand			
(1) DEMAND FOR ACE DRILL	(2) FREQUENCY	(3) PROBABILITY	(4) CUMULATIVE PROBABILITY	(5) INTERVAL OF RANDOM NUMBERS
0	15	.05	.05	01 through 05
1	30	.10	.15	06 through 15
2	60	.20	.35	16 through 35
3	120	.40	.75	36 through 75
4	45	.15	.90	76 through 90
5	30	.10	1.00	91 through 00
	300 days	1.00		

LO F.3 *Simulate* an inventory problem

that it took to receive the past 50 orders is presented in Table F.6. In a fashion similar to the creation of the demand variable, Simkin establishes a probability distribution for the lead time variable (column 3 of Table F.6), computes the cumulative distribution (column 4), and assigns random-number intervals for each possible time (column 5).

TABLE F.6	Probabilities and Random-Number Intervals for Reorder Lead Time			
(1) LEAD TIME (DAYS)	(2) FREQUENCY	(3) PROBABILITY	(4) CUMULATIVE PROBABILITY	(5) RANDOM-NUMBER INTERVAL
1	10	.20	.20	01 through 20
2	25	.50	.70	21 through 70
3	15	.30	1.00	71 through 00
	50 orders	1.00		

The entire process is simulated in Table F.7 for a 10-day period. We assume that beginning inventory (column 3) is 10 units on day 1. We took the random numbers (column 4) from column 2 of Table F.4.

TABLE F.7	Simkin Hardware's First Inventory Simulation. Order Quantity = 10 Units; Reorder Point = 5 Units								
(1) DAY	(2) UNITS RECEIVED	(3) BEGINNING INVENTORY	(4) RANDOM NUMBER	(5) DEMAND	(6) ENDING INVENTORY	(7) LOST SALES	(8) ORDER?	(9) RANDOM NUMBER	(10) LEAD TIME
1		10	06	1	9	0	No		
2	0	9	63	3	6	0	No		
3	0	6	57	3	③[a]	0	Yes	⓪2[b]	1
4	0	3	94[c]	5	0	2	No[d]		
5	⑩[e]	10	52	3	7	0	No		
6	0	7	69	3	4	0	Yes	33	2
7	0	4	32	2	2	0	No		
8	0	2	30	2	0	0	No		
9	⑩[f]	10	48	3	7	0	No		
10	0	7	88	4	3	0	Yes	14	1
					Totals: 41	2			

[a]This is the first time inventory dropped to the reorder point of five drills. Because no prior order was outstanding, an order is placed.

[b]The random number 02 is generated to represent the first lead time. It was drawn from column 2 of Table F.4 as the next number in the list being used. A separate column could have been used from which to draw lead-time random numbers if we had wanted to do so, but in this example, we did not do so.

[c]Again, notice that the random digits 02 were used for lead time (see footnote b). So the next number in the column is 94.

[d]No order is placed on day 4 because there is an order outstanding from the previous day that has not yet arrived.

[e]The lead time for the first order placed is 1 day, but as noted in the text, an order does not arrive the next morning but rather the beginning of the following day. Thus, the first order arrives at the start of day 5.

[f]This is the arrival of the order placed at the close of business on day 6. Fortunately for Simkin, no lost sales occurred during the 2-day lead time before the order arrived.

Table F.7 was filled in by proceeding 1 day (or line) at a time, working from left to right. It is a four-step process:

1. Begin each simulated day by checking to see whether any ordered inventory has just arrived. If it has, increase current inventory by the quantity ordered (10 units, in this case).
2. Generate a daily demand from the demand probability distribution for the selected random number.
3. Compute: Ending inventory = Beginning inventory minus Demand. If on-hand inventory is insufficient to meet the day's demand, satisfy as much demand as possible and note the number of lost sales.
4. Determine whether the day's ending inventory has reached the reorder point (5 units). If it has, and if there are no outstanding orders, place an order. Lead time for a new order is simulated for the selected random number corresponding to the distribution in Table F.6.

INSIGHTS ▶ Simkin's inventory simulation yields some interesting results. The average daily ending inventory is:

$$\text{Average ending inventory} = \frac{41 \text{ total units}}{10 \text{ days}} = 4.1 \text{ units/day}$$

We also note the average lost sales and number of orders placed per day:

$$\text{Average lost sales} = \frac{2 \text{ sales lost}}{10 \text{ days}} = .2 \text{ units/day}$$

$$\text{Average number of orders placed} = \frac{3 \text{ orders}}{10 \text{ days}} = .3 \text{ orders/day}$$

LEARNING EXERCISE ▶ How would these 3 averages change if the random numbers for day 10 were 04 and 93 instead of 88 and 14? [Answer: 4.4, .2 (no change), and .2.]

RELATED PROBLEMS ▶ F.16–F.21 (F.22–F.25 are available in MyOMLab)

Now that we have worked through Example F2 we want to emphasize something very important: This simulation should be extended many more days before we draw any conclusions as to the cost of the order policy being tested. If a hand simulation is being conducted, 100 days would provide a better representation. If a computer is doing the calculations, 1,000 days would be helpful in reaching accurate cost estimates. (Moreover, remember that even with a 1,000-day simulation, the generated distribution should be compared with the desired distribution to ensure valid results.)

Summary

Simulation involves building mathematical models that attempt to act like real operating systems. In this way, a real-world situation can be studied without imposing on the actual system. Although simulation models can be developed manually, simulation by computer is generally more desirable. The Monte Carlo approach uses random numbers to represent variables, such as inventory demand or people waiting in line, which are then simulated in a series of trials. Simulation is widely used as an operations tool because its advantages usually outweigh its disadvantages.

Key Terms

Simulation (p. 792)
Monte Carlo method (p. 794)

Cumulative probability distribution (p. 794)
Random-number intervals (p. 795)

Random number (p. 795)

Discussion Questions

1. State the seven steps, beginning with "Defining the Problem," that an operations manager should perform when using simulation to analyze a problem.
2. List the advantages of simulation.
3. List the disadvantages of simulation.
4. Explain the difference between *simulated* average demand and *expected* average demand.
5. What is the role of random numbers in a Monte Carlo simulation?
6. Why might the results of a simulation differ each time you make a run?
7. What is Monte Carlo simulation? What principles underlie its use, and what steps are followed in applying it?
8. List six ways that simulation can be used in business.

9. Why is simulation such a widely used technique?
10. What are the advantages of special-purpose simulation languages (see below)?
11. In the simulation of an order policy for drills at Simkin's hardware (Example F2, pp. 797–799), would the results (of Table F.7) change significantly if a longer period were simulated? Why is the 10-day simulation valid or invalid?

12. Why is a computer necessary in conducting a real-world simulation?
13. Why might a manager be forced to use simulation instead of an analytical model in dealing with a problem of:
    a) inventory order policy?
    b) ships docking in a port to unload?
    c) bank-teller service windows?
    d) the U.S. economy?

Using Software in Simulation

Computers are critical in simulating complex tasks. They can generate random numbers, simulate thousands of time periods in a matter of seconds or minutes, and provide management with reports that improve decision making. A computer approach is almost a necessity in order to draw valid conclusions from a simulation.

Computer programming languages can help the simulation process. *General-purpose languages*, such as BASIC or C++, constitute one approach. *Special-purpose simulation languages*, such as GPSS and SIMSCRIPT, have a few advantages: (1) they require less programming time for large simulations, (2) they are usually more efficient and easier to check for errors, and (3) random-number generators are already built in as subroutines.

Commercial, easy-to-use prewritten simulation programs are also available. Some are generalized to handle a wide variety of situations ranging from queuing to inventory. These include programs such as Extend, Modsim, Witness, MAP/1, Enterprise Dynamics, Simfactory, ProModel, Micro Saint, and ARENA.

Spreadsheet software such as Excel can also be used to develop simulations quickly and easily. Such packages have built-in random-number generators and develop outputs through "data-fill" table commands.

✖ USING EXCEL SPREADSHEETS

The ability to generate random numbers and then "look up" these numbers in a table to associate them with a specific event makes spreadsheets excellent tools for conducting simulations. Program F.1 illustrates an Excel simulation for Example F1.

Notice that the cumulative probabilities are calculated in column E of Program F.1. This procedure reduces the chance of error and is useful in larger simulations involving more levels of demand.

The **VLOOKUP** function in column I looks up the random number (generated in column H) in the leftmost column of the defined lookup table. The **VLOOKUP** function moves downward through this column until it finds a cell that is bigger than the random number. It then goes to the previous row and gets the value from column B of the table.

LO F.4 *Use* Excel spreadsheets to create a simulation

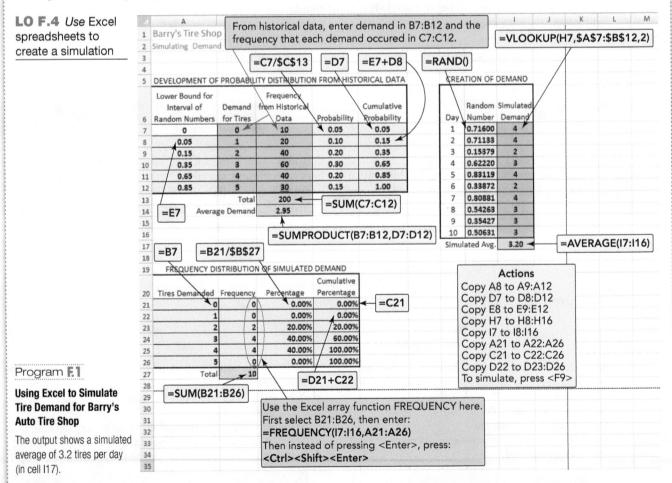

Program F.1

Using Excel to Simulate Tire Demand for Barry's Auto Tire Shop

The output shows a simulated average of 3.2 tires per day (in cell I17).

In column H, for example, the first random number shown is .716. Excel looked down the left-hand column of the lookup table ($A$7:$B$12) of Program F.1 until it found .85. From the previous row it retrieved the value in column B which is 4. Pressing the F9 function key recalculates the random numbers and the simulation.

▶X USING POM FOR WINDOWS AND EXCEL OM

POM for Windows and Excel OM are capable of handling any simulation that contains only one random variable, such as Example F1. For further details, please refer to Appendix IV.

Solved Problems   Virtual Office Hours help is available in MyOMLab.

SOLVED PROBLEM F.1

Higgins Plumbing and Heating maintains a stock of 30-gallon water heaters that it sells to homeowners and installs for them. Owner Jim Higgins likes the idea of having a large supply on hand to meet any customer demand. However, he also recognizes that it is expensive to do so. He examines water heater sales over the past 50 weeks and notes the following:

WATER HEATER SALES PER WEEK	NUMBER OF WEEKS THIS NUMBER WAS SOLD
4	6
5	5
6	9
7	12
8	8
9	7
10	3
	50 weeks total data

a) If Higgins maintains a constant supply of 8 water heaters in any given week, how many times will he stockout during a 20-week simulation? We use random numbers from the 7th column of Table F.4 (on p. 795), beginning with the random digit 10.

b) What is the average number of sales per week over the 20-week period?

c) Using an analytic nonsimulation technique, determine the expected number of sales per week. How does this compare with the answer in part (b)?

SOLUTION

HEATER SALES	PROBABILITY	CUMULATIVE PROBABILITY	RANDOM-NUMBER INTERVALS
4	.12	.12	01 through 12
5	.10	.22	13 through 22
6	.18	.40	23 through 40
7	.24	.64	41 through 64
8	.16	.80	65 through 80
9	.14	.94	81 through 94
10	.06	1.00	95 through 00
	1.00		

a)

WEEK	RANDOM NUMBER	SIMULATED SALES	WEEK	RANDOM NUMBER	SIMULATED SALES
1	10	4	11	08	4
2	24	6	12	48	7
3	03	4	13	66	8
4	32	6	14	97	10
5	23	6	15	03	4
6	59	7	16	96	10
7	95	10	17	46	7
8	34	6	18	74	8
9	34	6	19	77	8
10	51	7	20	44	7

With a supply of 8 heaters, Higgins will stock out three times during the 20-week period (in weeks 7, 14, and 16).

b) Average sales by simulation = total sales/20 weeks = 135/20 = 6.75 per week

c) Using expected values, we obtain:

E (sales) = .12(4 heaters) + .10(5) + .18(6) + .24(7) + .16(8) + .14(9) + .06(10) = 6.88 heaters

With a longer simulation, these two approaches will lead to even closer values.

SOLVED PROBLEM F.2

Random numbers may be used to simulate continuous distributions. As a simple example, assume that fixed cost equals $300, profit contribution equals $10 per item sold, and you expect an equally likely chance of 0 to 99 units to be sold. That is, profit equals $-\$300 + \$10X$, where X is the number sold. The mean amount you expect to sell is 49.5 units.

a) Calculate the expected value.
b) Simulate the sale of 5 items, using the following double-digit randomly-selected numbers of items sold:

37 77 13 10 85

c) Calculate the expected value of (b) and compare with the results of (a).

SOLUTION

a) Expected value $= -300 + 10(49.5) = \$195$

b) $-300 + \$10(37) = \$70$
   $-300 + \$10(77) = \$470$
   $-300 + \$10(13) = -\$170$
   $-300 + \$10(10) = -\$200$
   $-300 + \$10(85) = \$550$

c) The mean of these simulated sales is $144. If the sample size were larger, we would expect the two values to be closer.

Problems   Note: PX means the problem may be solved with POM for Windows and/or Excel OM or Excel.

The problems that follow involve simulations that can be done by hand. However, to obtain accurate and meaningful results, long periods must be simulated. This task is usually handled by a computer. If you are able to program some of the problems in Excel or a computer language with which you are familiar, we suggest you try to do so. If not, the hand simulations will still help you understand the simulation process.

Problems F.1–F.15 relate to Monte Carlo Simulation

· **F.1** The daily demand for tuna sandwiches at an Ohio University cafeteria vending machine is 8, 9, 10, or 11, with probabilities 0.4, 0.3, 0.2, or 0.1, respectively. Assume the following random numbers have been generated: 09, 55, 73, 67, 53, 59, 04, 23, 88, and 84. Using these numbers, generate daily sandwich sales for 10 days. PX

· **F.2** The number of machine breakdowns per day at Yuwen Chen's factory is 0, 1, or 2, with probabilities 0.5, 0.3, or 0.2, respectively. The following random numbers have been generated: 13, 14, 02, 18, 31, 19, 32, 85, 31, and 94. Use these numbers to generate the number of breakdowns for 10 consecutive days. What proportion of these days had at least one breakdown? PX

· **F.3** The table below shows the partial results of a Monte Carlo simulation. Assume that the simulation began at 8:00 A.M., and there is only one server.

CUSTOMER NUMBER	ARRIVAL TIME	SERVICE TIME
1	8:01	6
2	8:06	7
3	8:09	8
4	8:15	6
5	8:20	6

a) When does service begin for customer number 3?
b) When will customer number 5 leave?
c) What is the average waiting time in line?
d) What is the average time in the system?

· **F.4** Barbara Flynn sells papers at a newspaper stand for $.35. The papers cost her $.25, giving her a $.10 profit on each one she sells. From past experience Barbara knows that:
a) 20% of the time she sells 100 papers.
b) 20% of the time she sells 150 papers.
c) 30% of the time she sells 200 papers.
d) 30% of the time she sells 250 papers.

Assuming that Barbara believes the cost of a lost sale to be $.05 and any unsold papers cost her $.25, simulate her profit outlook over 5 days if she orders 200 papers for each of the 5 days. Use the following random numbers: 52, 06, 50, 88, and 53. PX

·· **F.5** Arnold Palmer Hospital is studying the number of emergency surgery kits that it uses on weekends. Over the past 40 weekends, the number of kits used was as follows:

NUMBER OF KITS	FREQUENCY
4	4
5	6
6	10
7	12
8	8

The following random numbers have been generated: 11, 52, 59, 22, 03, 03, 50, 86, 85, 15, 32, 47. Simulate 12 weekends of emergency kit usage. What is the average number of kits used during these 12 weekends? PX

· **F.6** Susan Sherer's grocery store has noted the following figures with regard to the number of people who arrive at the store's three checkout stands and the time it takes to check them out:

ARRIVALS/MINUTE	FREQUENCY
0	.3
1	.5
2	.2

SERVICE TIME/MINUTE	FREQUENCY
1	.1
2	.3
3	.4
4	.2

Simulate the utilization of the three checkout stands over 5 minutes, using the following random numbers: 07, 60, 77, 49, 76, 95, 51, 16, and 14. Record the results at the end of the 5-minute period. Start at time = 0. PX

· **F.7** A warehouse manager at Mary Beth Marrs Corp. needs to simulate the demand placed on a product that does not fit standard models. The concept being measured is "demand during lead time," where both lead time and daily demand are variable. The historical record for this product, along with the cumulative distribution, appear in the table. Random numbers have been generated to simulate the next 5 order cycles; they are 91, 45, 37, 65, and 51. What are the five demand values? What is their average?

DEMAND DURING LEAD TIME	PROBABILITY	CUMULATIVE PROBABILITY
100	.01	.01
120	.15	.16
140	.30	.46
160	.15	.61
180	.04	.65
200	.10	.75
220	.25	1.00

Px

F.8 Phantom Controls monitors and repairs control circuit boxes on elevators installed in multistory buildings in downtown Chicago. The company has the contract for 108 buildings. When a box malfunctions, Phantom installs a new one and rebuilds the failed unit in its repair facility in Gary, Indiana. The data for failed boxes over the last 2 years is shown in the following table:

NUMBER OF FAILED BOXES PER MONTH	PROBABILITY
0	.10
1	.14
2	.26
3	.20
4	.18
5	.12

Simulate 2 years (24 months) of operation for Phantom and determine the average number of failed boxes per month from the simulation. Was it common to have fewer than 7 failures over 3 months of operation? (Start your simulation at the top of the 10th column of Table F.4 on page 795, $RN = 37$, and go down in the table.) Px

F.9 The number of cars arriving at Patti Miles's Car Wash, in Orono, Maine, during the last 200 hours of operation is observed to be the following:

NUMBER OF CARS ARRIVING	FREQUENCY
3 or fewer	0
4	20
5	30
6	50
7	60
8	40
9 or more	0
	200

a) Set up a probability and cumulative-probability distribution for the variable of car arrivals.
b) Establish random-number intervals for the variable.
c) Simulate 15 hours of car arrivals and compute the average number of arrivals per hour. Select the random numbers needed from column 1, Table F.4, beginning with the digits 52. Px

F.10 Leonard Presby's newsstand uses naive forecasting to order tomorrow's papers. The number of newspapers ordered corresponds to the previous day's demands. Today's demand for papers was 22. Presby buys the newspapers for $.20 and sells them for $.50. Whenever there is unsatisfied demand, Presby estimates the lost goodwill cost at $.10. Complete the accompanying table, and answer the questions that follow.

DEMAND	PROBABILITY
21	.25
22	.15
23	.10
24	.20
25	.30

DAY	PAPERS ORDERED	RANDOM NUMBER	DEMAND	REVENUE	COST	GOODWILL COST	NET PROFIT
1	22	37					
2		19					
3		52					
4		8					
5		22					
6		61					

a) What is the demand on day 3?
b) What is the total net profit at the end of the 6 days?
c) What is the lost goodwill on day 6?
d) What is the net profit on day 2?
e) How many papers has Presby ordered for day 5? Px

F.11 Every home football game for the past 8 years at Southwestern University has been sold out. The revenues from ticket sales are significant, but the sale of food, beverages, and souvenirs has contributed greatly to the overall profitability of the football program. One particular souvenir is the football program for each game. The number of programs sold at each game is described by the probability distribution given in the following table.

NUMBERS OF PROGRAMS SOLD	PROBABILITY
2,300	0.15
2,400	0.22
2,500	0.24
2,600	0.21
2,700	0.18

Each program costs $.80 to produce and sells for $2.00. Any programs that are not sold are donated to a recycling center and do not produce any revenue.
a) Simulate the sales of programs at 10 football games. Use the last column in the random-number table (Table F.4 on p. 795) and begin at the top of the column.
b) If the university decided to print 2,500 programs for each game, what would the average profits be for the 10 games that were simulated?
c) If the university decided to print 2,600 programs for each game, what would the average profits be for the 10 games that were simulated? Px

F.12 Refer to the data in Solved Problem F.1, on page 801, which deals with Higgins Plumbing and Heating. Higgins has now collected 100 weeks of data and finds the following distribution for sales:

WATER HEATER SALES PER WEEK	NUMBER OF WEEKS THIS NUMBER WAS SOLD	WATER HEATER SALES PER WEEK	NUMBER OF WEEKS THIS NUMBER WAS SOLD
3	2	8	12
4	9	9	12
5	10	10	10
6	15	11	5
7	25		100

a) Assuming that Higgins maintains a constant supply of 8 heaters, simulate the number of stockouts incurred over a 20-week period (using the seventh column of Table F.4).
b) Conduct this 20-week simulation two more times and compare your answers with those in (a). Did they change significantly? Why or why not?
c) What is the new expected number of sales per week? **Px**

> *Additional problems* **F.13–F.15** *are available in* MyOMLab.

Problems F.16–F.25 relate to Simulation with Two Decision Variables: An Inventory Example

•• **F.16**   The time between arrivals at the drive-through window of Barry Harmon's fast-food restaurant follows the distribution given in the table. The service-time distribution is also given. Use the random numbers provided to simulate the activity of the first 4 arrivals. Assume that the window opens at 11:00 A.M. and that the first arrival occurs afterward, based on the first interarrival time generated.

TIME BETWEEN ARRIVALS	PROBABILITY	SERVICE TIME	PROBABILITY
1	.2	1	.3
2	.3	2	.5
3	.3	3	.2
4	.2		

Random numbers for arrivals: 14, 74, 27, 03
Random numbers for service times: 88, 32, 36, 24
At what time does the fourth customer leave the system? **Px**

••• **F.17**   Central Hospital in York, Pennsylvania, has an emergency room that is divided into six departments: (1) an initial exam station to treat minor problems or to make a diagnosis; (2) an X-ray department; (3) an operating room; (4) a cast-fitting room; (5) an observation room (for recovery and general observation before final diagnosis or release); and (6) an outprocessing department (where clerks check out patients and arrange for payment or insurance forms).

The probabilities that a patient will go from one department to another are presented in the following table:

FROM	TO	PROBABILITY
Initial exam at emergency room entrance	X-ray department	.45
	Operating room	.15
	Observation room	.10
	Outprocessing clerk	.30
X-ray department	Operating room	.10
	Cast-fitting room	.25
	Observation room	.35
	Outprocessing clerk	.30
Operating room	Cast-fitting room	.25
	Observation room	.70
	Outprocessing clerk	.05
Cast-fitting room	Observation room	.55
	X-ray department	.05
	Outprocessing clerk	.40
Observation room	Operating room	.15
	X-ray department	.15
	Outprocessing clerk	.70

a) Simulate the trail followed by 10 emergency room patients. Proceed, one patient at a time, from each one's entry at the initial exam station until he or she leaves through outprocessing. You should be aware that a patient can enter the same department more than once.
b) Using your simulation data, determine the chances that a patient enters the X-ray department twice.

••• **F.18**   Connecticut Tanning has two tanning beds. One bed serves the company's regular members exclusively. The second bed serves strictly walk-in customers (those without appointments) on a first-come, first-served basis. Orv Karan, the store manager, has noticed on several occasions during the busy 5 hours of the day (2:00 P.M. until 7:00 P.M.) that potential walk-in customers will most often walk away from the store if they see one person already waiting for the second bed. He wonders if capturing this lost demand would justify adding a third bed. Leasing and maintaining a tanning bed costs Connecticut Tanning $600 per month. The price paid per customer varies according to the time in the bed, but Orv has calculated the average net income for every 10 minutes of tanning time to be $2. A study of the pattern of arrivals during the busy hours and the time spent tanning has revealed the following:

TIME BETWEEN ARRIVALS (MINUTES)	PROBABILITY	TIME IN TANNING BED (MINUTES)	PROBABILITY
5	0.30	10	0.20
10	0.25	15	0.30
15	0.20	20	0.40
20	0.15	25	0.10
25	0.10		

a) Simulate 4 hours of operation (arrivals over 4 hours). Use the 14th column of Table F.4 (p. 795) for arrival times and the 8th column for tanning times. Assume there is one person who has just entered the bed at 2:00 P.M. for a 20-minute tan. Indicate which customers balk at waiting for the bed to become available. How many customers were lost over the 4 hours (the simulation ends at 6:00 P.M.)?
b) If the store is open an average of 24 days a month, will capturing all lost sales justify adding a new tanning bed?

••• **F.19**   Kathryn Marley owns and operates the largest Mercedes-Benz auto dealership in Pittsburgh. In the past 36 months, her sales have ranged from a low of 6 new cars to a high of 12 new cars, as reflected in the following table:

SALES OF NEW CARS/MONTH	FREQUENCY
6	3
7	4
8	6
9	12
10	9
11	1
12	1
	36 months

Marley believes that sales will continue during the next 24 months at about the same historical rates, and that delivery times will also continue to follow the following pace (stated in probability form):

DELIVERY TIME (MONTHS)*	PROBABILITY
1	.44
2	.33
3	.16
4	.07
	1.00

*With cars arriving at the end of the month (i.e., orders placed at the end of the 1st month, with a lead time of 2 months, will arrive at the end of the 3rd month, too late for sales in the 3rd month).

Marley's current policy is to order 14 cars at a time (two full truckloads, with 7 autos on each truck), and to place a new order whenever the stock on hand reaches 12 autos.

a) What are the results of this policy when simulated over the next 2 years?

b) Marley establishes the following relevant costs: (1) carrying cost per Mercedes per month is $600; (2) cost of a lost sale averages $4,350; and (3) cost of placing an order is $570. What is the total inventory cost of this policy?

•• F.20   Dumoor Appliance Center sells and services several brands of major appliances. Past sales for a particular model of refrigerator have resulted in the following probability distribution for demand:

Demand per week	0	1	2	3	4
Probability	0.20	0.40	0.20	0.15	0.05

The lead-time in weeks is described by the following distribution:

Lead time (weeks)	1	2	3
Probability	0.15	0.35	0.50

Based on cost considerations as well as storage space, the company has decided to order 10 of these each time an order is placed. The holding cost is $1 per week for each unit that is left in inventory at the end of the week. The stockout cost has been set at $40 per stockout. The company has decided to place an order whenever there are only two refrigerators left at the end of the week. Simulate 10 weeks of operation for Dumoor Appliance, assuming that there are currently 5 units in inventory. Determine what the weekly stockout cost and weekly holding cost would be for the problem. Use the random numbers in the first column of Table F.4 for demand and the second column for lead time.

•• F.21   Repeat the simulation in Problem F.20, assuming that the reorder point is 4 units rather than 2. Compare the costs for these two situations. Use the same random numbers as in Problem F.20.

Additional problems **F.22–F.25** are available in MyOMLab.

CASE STUDY

Alabama Airlines' Call Center

Alabama Airlines opened its doors in December 2015 as a commuter service with its headquarters and hub located in Birmingham. The airline was started and managed by two former pilots, David Douglas and George Devenney. It acquired a fleet of 12 used prop-jet planes and the airport gates vacated by Delta Air Lines in 2014.

TABLE F.8	Incoming Call Distribution

TIME BETWEEN CALLS (MINUTES)	PROBABILITY
1	.11
2	.21
3	.22
4	.20
5	.16
6	.10

With business growing quickly, Douglas turned his attention to Alabama Air's "800" reservations system. Between midnight and 6:00 A.M., only one telephone reservations agent had been on duty. The time between incoming calls during this period is distributed as shown in Table F.8. Carefully observing and timing the agent, Douglas estimated that the time required to process passenger inquiries is distributed as shown in Table F.9.

TABLE F.9	Service-Time Distribution

TIME TO PROCESS CUSTOMER INQUIRIES (MINUTES)	PROBABILITY
1	.20
2	.19
3	.18
4	.17
5	.13
6	.10
7	.03

All customers calling Alabama Air go "on hold" and are served in the order of the calls received unless the reservations agent is available for immediate service. Douglas is deciding whether a second agent should be on duty to cope with customer demand. To maintain customer satisfaction, Alabama Air wants a customer to be "on hold" for no more than 3 to 4 minutes; it also wants to maintain a "high" operator utilization.

Furthermore, the airline is planning a new TV advertising campaign. As a result, it expects an increase in "800" line phone inquiries. Based on similar campaigns in the past, the incoming call distribution from midnight to 6:00 A.M. is expected to be as shown in Table F.10. (The same service-time distribution will apply.)

TABLE F.10	Incoming Call Distribution
TIME BETWEEN CALLS (MINUTES)	PROBABILITY
1	.22
2	.25
3	.19
4	.15
5	.12
6	.07

Discussion Questions

1. Given the original call distribution, what would you advise Alabama Air to do for the current reservation system? Create a simulation model to investigate the scenario. Describe the model carefully, and justify the duration of the simulation, assumptions, and measures of performance.

2. What are your recommendations regarding operator utilization and customer satisfaction if the airline proceeds with the advertising campaign?

Source: Professor Zbigniew H. Przasnyski, Loyola Marymount University. Reprinted by permission.

- **Additional Case Study:** Visit MyOMLab for this free case study:
  Saigon Transport: This Vietnamese shipping company is trying to determine the ideal truck fleet size.

Endnote

1. Alternatively, we could have assigned the random numbers 00, 01, 02, 03, and 04 to represent a demand of 0 units. The 2 digits 00 can be thought of as either 0 or 100. As long as 5 numbers out of 100 are assigned to the 0 demand, it does not make any difference which 5 they are.

Module F *Rapid* Review

Main Heading	Review Material	MyOMLab

WHAT IS SIMULATION?
(pp. 792–793)

Most of the large companies in the world use simulation models.

- **Simulation**—The attempt to duplicate the features, appearance, and characteristics of a real system, usually via a computerized model.

The idea behind simulation is threefold:

1. To imitate a real-world situation mathematically
2. Then to study its properties and operating characteristics
3. Finally, to draw conclusions and make action decisions based on the results of the simulation

In this way, a real-life system need not be touched until the advantages and disadvantages of a major policy decision are first measured on the model.

To use simulation, an OM manager should:

1. Define the problem.
2. Introduce the important variables associated with the problem.
3. Construct a numerical model.
4. Set up possible courses of action for testing by specifying values of variables.
5. Run the experiment.
6. Consider the results (possibly modifying the model or changing data inputs).
7. Decide what course of action to take.

Figure F.1

The Process of Simulation

Concept Questions: 1.1–1.4

ADVANTAGES AND DISADVANTAGES OF SIMULATION
(p. 793)

The main *advantages* of simulation are:

1. It can be used to analyze large and complex real-world situations that cannot be solved using conventional operations management models.
2. Real-world complications can be included that most OM models cannot permit. For example, simulation can use any probability distribution the user defines; it does not require standard distributions.
3. "Time compression" is possible. The effects of OM policies over many months or years can be obtained by computer simulation in a short time.
4. Simulation allows "what-if?" types of questions. Managers like to know in advance what options will be most attractive. With a computerized model, a manager can try out several policy decisions within a matter of minutes.
5. Simulations do not interfere with real-world systems. It may be too disruptive, for example, to experiment physically with new policies or ideas.

The main *disadvantages* of simulation are:

1. Good simulation models can be very expensive; they may take many months to develop.
2. It is a repetitive approach that may produce different solutions in repeated runs. It does not generate optimal solutions to problems.

Concept Questions: 2.1–2.4

Main Heading	Review Material	MyOMLab
	3. Managers must generate all of the conditions and constraints for solutions that they want to examine. The simulation model does not produce answers without adequate, realistic input. 4. Each simulation model is unique. Its solutions and inferences are not usually transferable to other problems.	
MONTE CARLO SIMULATION (pp. 794–797)	■ **Monte Carlo method**—A simulation technique that selects random numbers assigned to a distribution. The Monte Carlo method breaks down into five simple steps: 1. Setting up a probability distribution for important variables 2. Building a cumulative probability distribution for each variable 3. Establishing an interval of random numbers for each variable 4. Generating random numbers 5. Actually simulating a series of trials One common way to establish a *probability distribution* for a given variable is to examine historical outcomes. We can find the probability, or relative frequency, for each possible outcome of a variable by dividing the frequency of observation by the total number of observations. ■ **Cumulative probability distribution**—The accumulation (summary) of probabilities of a distribution. ■ **Random-number intervals**—A set of numbers to represent each possible value or outcome in a computer simulation. ■ **Random number**—A series of digits that have been selected using a totally random process. Random numbers may be generated for simulation problems in two ways: (1) If the problem is large and the process under study involves many simulation trials, computer programs are available to generate the needed random numbers; or (2) if the simulation is being done by hand, the numbers may be selected from a table of random digits.	Concept Questions: 3.1–3.4 Problems: F.1–F.15 Virtual Office Hours for Solved Problems: F.1, F.2
SIMULATION WITH TWO DECISION VARIABLES: AN INVENTORY EXAMPLE (pp. 797–799)	The commonly used EOQ models are based on the assumption that both product demand and reorder lead time are known, constant values. In most real-world inventory situations, though, demand and lead time are variables, so accurate analysis becomes extremely difficult to handle by any means other than simulation.	Concept Questions: 4.1–4.4 Problems: F.16–F.25

Self Test

■ **Before taking the self-test,** refer to the learning objectives listed at the beginning of the module and the key terms listed at the end of the module.

LO F.1 Which of the following is *not* an advantage of simulation?
a) Simulation is relatively straightforward and flexible.
b) Good simulation models are usually inexpensive to develop.
c) "Time compression" is possible.
d) Simulation can study the interactive effects of individual variables.
e) Simulations do not interfere with real-world systems.

LO F.2 The five steps required to implement the Monte Carlo simulation technique are _____, _____, _____, _____, and _____.

LO F.3 Two particularly good candidates to be probabilistic components in the simulation of an inventory problem are:
a) order quantity and reorder point.
b) setup cost and holding cost.

c) daily demand and reorder lead time.
d) order quantity and reorder lead time.
e) reorder point and reorder lead time.

LO F.4 One important reason that spreadsheets are excellent tools for conducting simulations is that they can:
a) generate random numbers.
b) easily provide animation of the simulation.
c) provide more security than manual simulations.
d) prohibit "time compression" from corrupting the results.
e) be easily programmed.

Answers: LO F.1. b; LO F.2. set up a probability distribution for each of the important variables, build a cumulative probability distribution for each of the important variables, establish an interval of random numbers for each variable, generate sets of random numbers, actually simulate a set of trials; LO F.3. c; LO F.4. a.

Appendixes

APPENDIX I
Normal Curve Areas

APPENDIX II
Values of $e^{-\lambda}$ for Use in the Poisson Distribution

APPENDIX III
Table of Random Numbers

APPENDIX IV
Using Excel OM and POM for Windows

APPENDIX I

NORMAL CURVE AREAS

To find the area under the normal curve, you can apply either Table I.1 or Table I.2. In Table I.1, you must know how many standard deviations that point is to the right of the mean. Then, the area under the normal curve can be read directly from the normal table. For example, the total area under the normal curve for a point that is 1.55 standard deviations to the right of the mean is .93943.

TABLE I.1

z	.00	.01	.02	.03	.04	.05	.06	.07	.08	.09
.0	.50000	.50399	.50798	.51197	.51595	.51994	.52392	.52790	.53188	.53586
.1	.53983	.54380	.54776	.55172	.55567	.55962	.56356	.56749	.57142	.57535
.2	.57926	.58317	.58706	.59095	.59483	.59871	.60257	.60642	.61026	.61409
.3	.61791	.62172	.62552	.62930	.63307	.63683	.64058	.64431	.64803	.65173
.4	.65542	.65910	.66276	.66640	.67003	.67364	.67724	.68082	.68439	.68793
.5	.69146	.69497	.69847	.70194	.70540	.70884	.71226	.71566	.71904	.72240
.6	.72575	.72907	.73237	.73565	.73891	.74215	.74537	.74857	.75175	.75490
.7	.75804	.76115	.76424	.76730	.77035	.77337	.77637	.77935	.78230	.78524
.8	.78814	.79103	.79389	.79673	.79955	.80234	.80511	.80785	.81057	.81327
.9	.81594	.81859	.82121	.82381	.82639	.82894	.83147	.83398	.83646	.83891
1.0	.84134	.84375	.84614	.84849	.85083	.85314	.85543	.85769	.85993	.86214
1.1	.86433	.86650	.86864	.87076	.87286	.87493	.87698	.87900	.88100	.88298
1.2	.88493	.88686	.88877	.89065	.89251	.89435	.89617	.89796	.89973	.90147
1.3	.90320	.90490	.90658	.90824	.90988	.91149	.91309	.91466	.91621	.91774
1.4	.91924	.92073	.92220	.92364	.92507	.92647	.92785	.92922	.93056	.93189
1.5	.93319	.93448	.93574	.93699	.93822	.93943	.94062	.94179	.94295	.94408
1.6	.94520	.94630	.94738	.94845	.94950	.95053	.95154	.95254	.95352	.95449
1.7	.95543	.95637	.95728	.95818	.95907	.95994	.96080	.96164	.96246	.96327
1.8	.96407	.96485	.96562	.96638	.96712	.96784	.96856	.96926	.96995	.97062
1.9	.97128	.97193	.97257	.97320	.97381	.97441	.97500	.97558	.97615	.97670
2.0	.97725	.97784	.97831	.97882	.97932	.97982	.98030	.98077	.98124	.98169
2.1	.98214	.98257	.98300	.98341	.98382	.98422	.98461	.98500	.98537	.98574
2.2	.98610	.98645	.98679	.98713	.98745	.98778	.98809	.98840	.98870	.98899
2.3	.98928	.98956	.98983	.99010	.99036	.99061	.99086	.99111	.99134	.99158
2.4	.99180	.99202	.99224	.99245	.99266	.99286	.99305	.99324	.99343	.99361
2.5	.99379	.99396	.99413	.99430	.99446	.99461	.99477	.99492	.99506	.99520
2.6	.99534	.99547	.99560	.99573	.99585	.99598	.99609	.99621	.99632	.99643
2.7	.99653	.99664	.99674	.99683	.99693	.99702	.99711	.99720	.99728	.99736
2.8	.99744	.99752	.99760	.99767	.99774	.99781	.99788	.99795	.99801	.99807
2.9	.99813	.99819	.99825	.99831	.99836	.99841	.99846	.99851	.99856	.99861
3.0	.99865	.99869	.99874	.99878	.99882	.99886	.99889	.99893	.99896	.99900
3.1	.99903	.99906	.99910	.99913	.99916	.99918	.99921	.99924	.99926	.99929
3.2	.99931	.99934	.99936	.99938	.99940	.99942	.99944	.99946	.99948	.99950
3.3	.99952	.99953	.99955	.99957	.99958	.99960	.99961	.99962	.99964	.99965
3.4	.99966	.99968	.99969	.99970	.99971	.99972	.99973	.99974	.99975	.99976
3.5	.99977	.99978	.99978	.99979	.99980	.99981	.99981	.99982	.99983	.99983
3.6	.99984	.99985	.99985	.99986	.99986	.99987	.99987	.99988	.99988	.99989
3.7	.99989	.99990	.99990	.99990	.99991	.99991	.99992	.99992	.99992	.99992
3.8	.99993	.99993	.99993	.99994	.99994	.99994	.99994	.99995	.99995	.99995
3.9	.99995	.99995	.99996	.99996	.99996	.99996	.99996	.99996	.99997	.99997

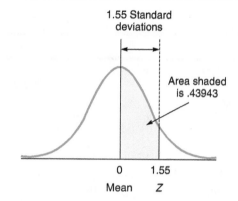

1.55 Standard deviations

Area shaded is .43943

0   1.55

Mean   Z

As an alternative to Table I.1, the numbers in Table I.2 represent the proportion of the total area away from the mean, μ, to one side. For example, the area between the mean and a point that is 1.55 standard deviations to its right is .43943.

TABLE I.2

Z	.00	.01	.02	.03	.04	.05	.06	.07	.08	.09
0.0	.00000	.00399	.00798	.01197	.01595	.01994	.02392	.02790	.03188	.03586
0.1	.03983	.04380	.04776	.05172	.05567	.05962	.06356	.06749	.07142	.07535
0.2	.07926	.08317	.08706	.09095	.09483	.09871	.10257	.10642	.11026	.11409
0.3	.11791	.12172	.12552	.12930	.13307	.13683	.14058	.14431	.14803	.15173
0.4	.15542	.15910	.16276	.16640	.17003	.17364	.17724	.18082	.18439	.18793
0.5	.19146	.19497	.19847	.20194	.20540	.20884	.21226	.21566	.21904	.22240
0.6	.22575	.22907	.23237	.23565	.23891	.24215	.24537	.24857	.25175	.25490
0.7	.25804	.26115	.26424	.26730	.27035	.27337	.27637	.27935	.28230	.28524
0.8	.28814	.29103	.29389	.29673	.29955	.30234	.30511	.30785	.31057	.31327
0.9	.31594	.31859	.32121	.32381	.32639	.32894	.33147	.33398	.33646	.33891
1.0	.34134	.34375	.34614	.34850	.35083	.35314	.35543	.35769	.35993	.36214
1.1	.36433	.36650	.36864	.37076	.37286	.37493	.37698	.37900	.38100	.38298
1.2	.38493	.38686	.38877	.39065	.39251	.39435	.39617	.39796	.39973	.40147
1.3	.40320	.40490	.40658	.40824	.40988	.41149	.41309	.41466	.41621	.41174
1.4	.41924	.42073	.42220	.42364	.42507	.42647	.42786	.42922	.43056	.43189
1.5	.43319	.43448	.43574	.43699	.43822	.43943	.44062	.44179	.44295	.44408
1.6	.44520	.44630	.44738	.44845	.44950	.45053	.45154	.45254	.45352	.45449
1.7	.45543	.45637	.45728	.45818	.45907	.45994	.46080	.46164	.46246	.46327
1.8	.46407	.46485	.46562	.46638	.46712	.46784	.46856	.46926	.46995	.47062
1.9	.47128	.47193	.47257	.47320	.47381	.47441	.47500	.47558	.47615	.47670
2.0	.47725	.47778	.47831	.47882	.47932	.47982	.48030	.48077	.48124	.48169
2.1	.48214	.48257	.48300	.48341	.48382	.48422	.48461	.48500	.48537	.48574
2.2	.48610	.48645	.48679	.48713	.48745	.48778	.48809	.48840	.48870	.48899
2.3	.48928	.48956	.48983	.49010	.49036	.49061	.49086	.49111	.49134	.49158
2.4	.49180	.49202	.49224	.49245	.49266	.49286	.49305	.49324	.49343	.49361
2.5	.49379	.49396	.49413	.49430	.49446	.49461	.49477	.49492	.49506	.49520
2.6	.49534	.49547	.49560	.49573	.49585	.49598	.49609	.49621	.49632	.49643
2.7	.49653	.49664	.49674	.49683	.49693	.49702	.49711	.49720	.49728	.49736
2.8	.49744	.49752	.49760	.49767	.49774	.49781	.49788	.49795	.49801	.49807
2.9	.49813	.49819	.49825	.49831	.49836	.49841	.49846	.49851	.49856	.49861
3.0	.49865	.49869	.49874	.49878	.49882	.49886	.49889	.49893	.49897	.49900
3.1	.49903	.49906	.49910	.49913	.49916	.49918	.49921	.49924	.49926	.49929

APPENDIX II

VALUES OF $e^{-\lambda}$ FOR USE IN THE POISSON DISTRIBUTION

				Values of $e^{-\lambda}$				
λ	$e^{-\lambda}$	λ	$e^{-\lambda}$	λ	$e^{-\lambda}$	λ	$e^{-\lambda}$
.0	1.0000	1.6	.2019	3.1	.0450	4.6	.0101
.1	.9048	1.7	.1827	3.2	.0408	4.7	.0091
.2	.8187	1.8	.1653	3.3	.0369	4.8	.0082
.3	.7408	1.9	.1496	3.4	.0334	4.9	.0074
.4	.6703	2.0	.1353	3.5	.0302	5.0	.0067
.5	.6065	2.1	.1225	3.6	.0273	5.1	.0061
.6	.5488	2.2	.1108	3.7	.0247	5.2	.0055
.7	.4966	2.3	.1003	3.8	.0224	5.3	.0050
.8	.4493	2.4	.0907	3.9	.0202	5.4	.0045
.9	.4066	2.5	.0821	4.0	.0183	5.5	.0041
1.0	.3679	2.6	.0743	4.1	.0166	5.6	.0037
1.1	.3329	2.7	.0672	4.2	.0150	5.7	.0033
1.2	.3012	2.8	.0608	4.3	.0136	5.8	.0030
1.3	.2725	2.9	.0550	4.4	.0123	5.9	.0027
1.4	.2466	3.0	.0498	4.5	.0111	6.0	.0025
1.5	.2231						

APPENDIX III

TABLE OF RANDOM NUMBERS

52	06	50	88	53	30	10	47	99	37	66	91	35	32	00	84	57	07
37	63	28	02	74	35	24	03	29	60	74	85	90	73	59	55	17	60
82	57	68	28	05	94	03	11	27	79	90	87	92	41	09	25	36	77
69	02	36	49	71	99	32	10	75	21	95	90	94	38	97	71	72	49
98	94	90	36	06	78	23	67	89	85	29	21	25	73	69	34	85	76
96	52	62	87	49	56	59	23	78	71	72	90	57	01	98	57	31	95
33	69	27	21	11	60	95	89	68	48	17	89	34	09	93	50	44	51
50	33	50	95	13	44	34	62	64	39	55	29	30	64	49	44	30	16
88	32	18	50	62	57	34	56	62	31	15	40	90	34	51	95	26	14
90	30	36	24	69	82	51	74	30	35	36	85	01	55	92	64	09	85
50	48	61	18	85	23	08	54	17	12	80	69	24	84	92	16	49	59
27	88	21	62	69	64	48	31	12	73	02	68	00	16	16	46	13	85
45	14	46	32	13	49	66	62	74	41	86	98	92	98	84	54	33	40
81	02	01	78	82	74	97	37	45	31	94	99	42	49	27	64	89	42
66	83	14	74	27	76	03	33	11	97	59	81	72	00	64	61	13	52
74	05	81	82	93	09	96	33	52	78	13	06	28	30	94	23	37	39
30	34	87	01	74	11	46	82	59	94	25	34	32	23	17	01	58	73
59	55	72	33	62	13	74	68	22	44	42	09	32	46	71	79	45	89
67	09	80	98	99	25	77	50	03	32	36	63	65	75	94	19	95	88
60	77	46	63	71	69	44	22	03	85	14	48	69	13	30	50	33	24
60	08	19	29	36	72	30	27	50	64	85	72	75	29	87	05	75	01
80	45	86	99	02	34	87	08	86	84	49	76	24	08	01	86	29	11
53	84	49	63	26	65	72	84	85	63	26	02	75	26	92	62	40	67
69	84	12	94	51	36	17	02	15	29	16	52	56	43	26	22	08	62
37	77	13	10	02	18	31	19	32	85	31	94	81	43	31	58	33	51

Source: Excerpted from *A Million Random Digits with 100,000 Normal Deviates*, The Free Press (1955): 7, with permission of the RAND Corporation.

APPENDIX IV

USING EXCEL OM AND POM FOR WINDOWS

Two approaches to computer-aided decision making are provided with this text: **Excel OM** and **POM** (Production and Operations Management) **for Windows**. These are the two most user-friendly software packages available to help you learn and understand operations management. Both programs can be used either to solve homework problems identified with an icon or to check answers you have developed by hand. Both software packages use the standard Windows interface and run on any IBM-compatible PC operating Windows XP or newer. Excel OM is also available for the Mac.

EXCEL OM

Excel OM has been designed to help you to better learn and understand both OM and Excel. Even though the software contains 24 modules and more than 60 submodules, the screens for every module are consistent and easy to use. The Chapter menu (Excel 2007 and later for PCs) or the Heizer menu (Excel 2011 for Macs) lists the modules in *chapter* order, as illustrated for Excel 2007 and later for PCs in Program IV.1(a). The Alphabetical menu (Excel 2007 and later for PCs) or Excel OM menu (Excel 2011 for Macs) lists the modules in alphabetical order, as illustrated for Excel OM for Macs in Program IV.1(b). The menu for Excel 2016 for Macs is slightly different and not displayed here. This software is provided at no cost to users of MyOMLab or purchasers of a new copy of this textbook. The software can also be purchased at www.pearsonhighered.com/heizer. Excel 2007 or newer must be on your PC or Excel 2011 or greater must be on your Mac.

To install Excel OM, click on the Download Center on the left side of your MyOMLab course, and follow the instructions. Default values have been assigned in the setup program, but you may change them if you like. For Windows, the default folder into which a program will be installed is

▼ **PROGRAM IV.1(a)**   **Excel OM Modules Menu in Excel OM Tab in Excel 2007 and later for PCs**

▲ **PROGRAM IV.1(b)** **Excel OM Modules Menu in OM for Macs 2011**

named C:\Program Files(x86)\ExcelomQMv4. Generally speaking, it is simply necessary to click *Next* each time the installation asks a question. For Macs, simply unzip the zip file that is provided.

Starting the Program To start Excel OM using Windows, double-click on the Excel OM V4 shortcut placed on the desktop during installation. The Excel OM menu will appear in an Excel OM tab that will be added to the Excel ribbon, as displayed in Program IV.1(a). To start Excel OM on the Mac, open the file excelomqmv4.xla. Be certain that you open the file from the folder that has the excelomqmv4 .lic file. On the Mac under Excel 2011, the Excel OM menu will appear in the main menu of Excel, as displayed in Program IV.1(b).

If you have Excel 2007 or later and do not see an Excel OM tab on the Ribbon, then your Excel security settings need to be revised to enable Excel OM V4. Please consult the Excel instructions at the support site, www.pearsonhighered.com/weiss, or see the document Excel.Security.pdf that has been installed in the default directory.

Excel OM serves two purposes in the learning process. First, it helps you solve problems. You enter the appropriate data, and the program provides numerical solutions. POM for Windows operates on the same principle. However, Excel OM allows for a second approach: the Excel *formulas* used to develop solutions can be modified to deal with a wider variety of problems. This "open" approach enables you to observe, understand, and even change the formulas underlying the Excel calculations—conveying Excel's power as an OM analysis tool.

POM FOR WINDOWS

POM for Windows is decision support software that is also offered free to students who use MyOMLab or who purchased this as a new text. It can also be purchased at our Web site www.pearsonhighered .com/heizer. Program IV.2 shows a list of the 25 OM modules that can be accessed from the menu tree on the left. The modules can also be accessed from the MODULE menu where they are in alphabetical order or the HEIZER menu where they are in chapter order. Once you follow the standard setup instructions, a POM for Windows program icon will be added to your desktop, and a program group will be added to your Start, All Programs menu. The program may be accessed by double-clicking on the desktop icon.

▲ **PROGRAM IV.2**   **POM for Windows Module List**

USING EXCEL OM AND POM FOR WINDOWS WITH MYOMLAB

Both Excel OM and POM for Windows have MyOMLab toolbars that make it very easy to copy from or paste to MyOMLab and very easy to set the specific number of decimals for which MyOMLab asks for any problem. To copy data from MyOMLab: after creating a model in Excel OM or POM, go to MyOMLab and click on the Copy icon. Then, in POM or in Excel OM, click on the **Paste from MyOMLab** icon on the toolbar or in the right-click menu.

Updates to POM for Windows and Excel OM are available on the Internet through the Downloads and Support links at *www.pearsonhighered.com/weiss*.

Bibliography

Chapter 1

Broedner, P., S. Kinkel, and G. Lay. "Productivity Effects of Outsourcing." *International Journal of Operations and Production Management* 29, no. 2 (2009): 127.

Hounshell, D. A. *From the American System to Mass Production 1800–1932: The Development of Manufacturing.* Baltimore: Johns Hopkins University Press, 1985.

Lewis, William W. *The Power of Productivity.* Chicago: University of Chicago Press, 2005.

Malone, T. W., R J. Laubacher, and T. Johns, "The Age of Hyperspecialization." *Harvard Business* 89, no. 7 (July–August 2011): 56–65.

Maroto, A., and L. Rubalcaba. "Services Productivity Revisited." *The Service Industries Journal* 28, no. 3 (April 2008): 337.

McLaughlin, Patrick. "Measuring Productivity." *Management Services* 58, no. 4 (Winter 2014): 31–37.

Sahay, B. S. "Multi-factor Productivity Measurement Model for Service Organization." *International Journal of Productivity and Performance Management* 54, no. 1–2 (2005): 7–23.

San, G., T. Huang, and L. Huang. "Does Labor Quality Matter on Productivity Growth?" *Total Quality Management and Business Excellence* 19, no. 10 (October 2008): 1043.

Sprague, Linda G. "Evolution of the Field of Operations Management." *Journal of Operations Management* 25, no. 2 (March 2007): 219–238.

Tangen, S. "Demystifying Productivity and Performance." *International Journal of Productivity and Performance Measurement* 54, no. 1–2 (2005): 34–47.

Taylor, F. W. *The Principles of Scientific Management.* New York: Harper & Brothers, 1911.

van Biema, Michael, and Bruce Greenwald. "Managing Our Way to Higher Service-Sector Productivity." *Harvard Business Review* 75, no. 4 (July–August 1997): 87–95.

Wren, Daniel A. *The Evolution of Management Thought.* New York: Wiley, 1994.

Chapter 2

Beckman, S. L., and D. B. Rosenfield. *Operations Strategy: Competing in the 21st Century.* New York: McGraw-Hill, 2008.

Bravard, J., and R. Morgan. *Smarter Outsourcing.* Upper Saddle River, NJ: Pearson, 2006.

Crotts, J. C., D. R. Dickson, and R. C. Ford. "Aligning Organizational Processes with Mission." *Academy of Management Executive* 19, no. 3 (August 2005): 54–68.

Flynn, B. B., R. G. Schroeder, and E. J. Flynn. "World Class Manufacturing." *Journal of Operations Management* 17, no. 3 (March 1999): 249–269.

Greenwald, Bruce C., and Judd Kahn. *Globalization: The Irrational Fear That Someone in China Will Take Your Job.* New York: Wiley, 2009.

Gordon, John Steel. *An Empire of Wealth: the Epic History of American Economic Power.* New York: HarperCollins, 2005.

Hirschheim, R., A. Heinzl, and J. Dibbern. *Information Systems Outsourcing.* Secaucus, NJ: Springer, 2009.

Lee, Hau L., and Chung-Yee Lee. *Building Supply Chain Excellence in Emerging Economies.* Secaucus, NJ: Springer, 2007.

Kaplan, Robert S., and David P. Norton. *Strategy Maps.* Boston: Harvard Business School Publishing, 2003.

Kathuria, R., M. P. Joshi, and S. Dellande. "International Growth Strategies of Service and Manufacturing Firms." *International Journal of Operations and Production Management* 28, no. 10 (2008): 968.

Midler, Paul. *Poorly Made in China: An Insider's Account of the Tactics Behind China's Production Game.* New York: Wiley, 2009.

Porter, Michael, and Nicolaj Siggelkow. "Contextuality within Activity Systems and Sustainability of Competitive Advantage." *Academy of Management Perspectives* 22, no. 2 (May 2008): 34–36.

Rothfeder, Jeffry. *Driving Honda: Inside the World's Most Innovative Car Company.* New York: Penguin Group, 2014.

Rudberg, Martin, and B. M. West. "Global Operations Strategy." *Omega* 36, no. 1 (February 2008): 91.

Skinner, Wickham. "Manufacturing Strategy: The Story of Its Evolution." *Journal of Operations Management* 25, no. 2 (March 2007): 328–334.

Slack, Nigel, and Mike Lewis. *Operation Strategy*, 3rd ed. Upper Saddle River, NJ: Prentice Hall, 2011.

Wolf, Martin. *Why Globalization Works.* London: Yale University Press, 2004.

Chapter 3

Balakrishnan, R., B. Render, and R. M. Stair. *Managerial Decision Modeling with Spreadsheets*, 3rd ed. Upper Saddle River, NJ: Prentice Hall, 2012.

Cleland, D. L., and L. R. Ireland. *Project Management*, 6th ed. New York: McGraw-Hill/Irwin, 2010.

Gray, C. L., and E. W. Larson. *Project Management with MS Project.* New York: McGraw-Hill/Irwin, 2008.

Helgadottir, Hilder. "The Ethical Dimension of Project Management." *International Journal of Project Management* 26, no. 7 (October 2008): 743.

Karlos, A., et al. "Foundations of Project Management." *International Journal of Project Management* 27, no. 1 (January 2009): 1.

Kerzner, H. *Project Management Case Studies*, 3rd ed. New York: Wiley, 2009.

Matta, N. F., and R. N. Ashkenas. "Why Good Projects Fail Anyway." *Harvard Business Review* 85, no. 5 (September 2003): 109–114.

Maylor, Harvey. *Project Management*, 5th ed. Upper Saddle River, NJ: Prentice Hall, 2011.

Meredith, J. R., and S. Mantel. *Project Management*, 8th ed. New York: Wiley, 2011.

Oates, David. "Understanding and Solving the Causes of Project Failure." *Knowledge Management Review* 9, no. 5 (May–June 2006): 5.

Render, B., R. M. Stair, and M. Hanna. *Quantitative Analysis for Management*, 11th ed. Upper Saddle River, NJ: Prentice Hall, 2012.

Verzuh, Eric. *The Fast Forward MBA in Project Management.* New York: Wiley, 2008.

Wysocki, R. K. *Effective Project Management,* 6th ed. New York: Wiley, 2012.

Chapter 4

Balakrishnan, R., B. Render, and R. M. Stair. *Managerial Decision Modeling with Spreadsheets*, 3rd ed. Upper Saddle River, NJ: Prentice Hall, 2012.

Berenson, Mark, Tim Krehbiel, and David Levine. *Basic Business Statistics*, 12th ed. Upper Saddle River, NJ: Prentice Hall, 2012.

Campbell, Omar. "Forecasting in Direct Selling Business: Tupperware's Experience." *The Journal of Business Forecasting* 27, no. 2 (Summer 2008): 18–19.

Diebold, F. X. *Elements of Forecasting*, 6th ed. Cincinnati: South-Western College Publishing, 2013.

Fildes, Robert, and Paul Goodwin. "Against Your Better Judgment? How Organizations Can Improve Their Use of Management Judgment in Forecasting." *Decision Sciences* 37, no. 6 (November–December 2007): 570–576.

Georgoff, D. M., and R. G. Murdick. "Manager's Guide to Forecasting." *Harvard Business Review* 64 (January–February 1986): 110–120.

Gilliland, M., and M. Leonard. "Forecasting Software—The Past and the Future." *The Journal of Business Forecasting* 25, no. 1 (Spring 2006): 33–36.

Hanke, J. E. and D. W. Wichern. *Business Forecasting*, 10th ed. Upper Saddle River, NJ: Prentice Hall, 2012.

Jain, Chaman L. "Benchmarking Forecasting Software and Systems." *The Journal of Business Forecasting* 26, no. 4 (Winter 2007/2008): 30–34.

Onkal, D., M. S. Gonul, and M. Lawrence. "Judgmental Adjustments of Previously Adjusted Forecasts." *Decision Sciences* 39, no. 2 (May 2008): 213–238.

Render, B., R. M. Stair, and M. Hanna. *Quantitative Analysis for Management*, 11th ed. Upper Saddle River, NJ: Prentice Hall, 2012.

Shah, Piyush. "Techniques to Support Better Forecasting." *APICS Magazine* (November/December 2008): 49–50.

Urs, Rajiv. "How to Use a Demand Planning System for Best Forecasting and Planning Results." *The Journal of Business Forecasting* 27, no. 2 (Summer 2008): 22–25.

Wilson, J. H., B. Keating, and J. Galt. *Business Forecasting*, 7th ed. New York: McGraw-Hill, 2012.

Yurklewicz, Jack. "Forecasting an Upward Trend." *OR/MS Today* (June 2012): 52–61.

Chapter 5

Alexy Oliver, P. Criscuelo, and A. Salter. "Managing Unsolicited Ideas for R&D." *California Management Review* 54, no. 3 (Spring 2012): 116–139.

Brown, Bruce, and S.D. Anthony; "How P&G Tripled Its Innovation Success Rate." *Harvard Business Review* 89, no. 6 (June 2011): 64–72.

Buckley, Peter J., and Roger Strange. "The Governance of the Global Factory: Location and Control of World Economic Activity." *Academy of Management Perspectives* 29, no. 2 (May 2015): 237–249.

Camevalli, J. A., and P. A. C. Miguel. "Review, Analysis, and Classification of the Literature on QFD." *International Journal of Production Economics* 114, no. 2 (August 2008): 737.

Ernst, David, and James Bamford. "Your Alliances Are too Stable." *Harvard Business Review* 83, no. 5 (June 2005): 133–141.

Gerwin, Donald. "Coordinating New Product Development in Strategic Alliances." *The Academy of Management Review* 29, no. 2 (April 2004): 241–257.

Gwynne, Peter. "Measuring R&D Productivity." *Research Technology Management* 58, no. 1 (Jan/Feb. 2015): 19–22.

Haines, Steven. *Managing Product Management*. New York; McGraw-Hill, 2012.

Krishnan, V., and Karl T. Ulrich. "Product Development Decisions: A Review of the Literature." *Management Science* 47, no. 1 (January 2001): 1–21.

Loch, C. H., and C. Terwiesch. "Rush and Be Wrong or Wait and Be Late?" *Production and Operations Management* 14, no. 3 (Fall 2005): 331–343.

Miguel, P. A. C., and J. A. Camevalli. "Benchmarking Practices of Quality Function Deployment." *Benchmarking* 15, no. 6 (2008): 657.

Phyper, J. D., and D. MacLean. *Good to Green: Managers' Business Risks and Opportunities in an Age of Environmental Awareness*. New York: Wiley, 2009.

Pisano, Gary P., and Roberto Verganti. "Which Kind of Collaboration Is Right for You?" *Harvard Business Review* 86, no. 12 (December 2008):78–86.

Reeves, Martin, and Mike Deimler. "Adaptability: The New Competitive Advantage." *Harvard Business Review* 90, no. 7 (July–August 2011): 135–141.

Saaksvuori, A., and A. Immonen. *Product Lifecycle Management*. Berlin: Springer-Verlag, 2004.

Seider, Warren D., et al. *Product and Process Design Principles*, 3rd. ed. New York: Wiley, 2008.

Ulrich, K., and S. Eppinger. *Product Design and Development*, 4th ed. New York: McGraw-Hill, 2008.

Supplement 5

Ambec, Stefan, and Paul Lanoie. "Does It Pay to Be Green? A Systematic Overview." *Academy of Management Perspectives* 22, no. 4 (November 2008): 13–20.

Banerjee, S. B. "Embedding Sustainability Across the Organization: A Critical Perspective." *Academy of Management, Learning & Education* 10, no. 4 (December 2011): 719–731.

Epstein, Marc J. *Making Sustainability Work*. San Francisco: Berrett-Koehler Publisher, 2008.

Haugh, Helen M., and A. Talwar. "How Do Corporations Embed Sustainability Across the Organization?" *Academy of Management, Learning & Education* 9, no. 3 (September 2010): 384–396.

Laszlo, Chris. *Sustainable Value*. Stanford, CA: Stanford University Press, 2008.

Laszlo, Chris, and N. Zhexembayeva. *Embedded Sustainability*. Stanford, CA: Stanford University Press, 2011.

Nidumolu, Ram, C. K. Prahalad, and M. R. Rangaswami. "Why Sustainability Is Now the Key Driver of Innovation." *Harvard Business Review* 87, no. 9 (September 2009): 56–64.

Stoner, J. A. F., and C. Wankel (Ed). *Global Sustainability Initiatives*. Charlotte, NC: Information Age Publishing, 2008.

Chapter 6

Besterfield, Dale H. *Quality Control*, 8th ed. Upper Saddle River, NJ: Prentice Hall, 2009.

Brown, Mark G. *Baldrige Award Winning Quality*, 19th ed. University Park, IL: Productivity Press, 2010.

Crosby, P. B. *Quality Is Still Free*. New York: McGraw-Hill, 1996.

Evans, J. R., and W. M. Lindsay. *Managing for Quality and Performance Excellence*, 8th ed. Mason, OH: Thomson-South-Western, 2012.

Feigenbaum, A. V. "Raising the Bar." *Quality Progress* 41, no. 7 (July 2008): 22–28.

Foster, Thomas. *Managing Quality*, 4th ed. Upper Saddle River, NJ: Pearson/Prentice Hall, 2010.

Gitlow, Howard S. *A Guide to Lean Six Sigma Management Skills*. University Park, IL: Productivity Press, 2009.

Gonzalez-Benito, J., and O. Gonzalez-Benito. "Operations Management Practices Linked to the Adoption of ISO 14001." *International Journal of Production Economics* 113, no. 1 (May 2008): 60.

Gray, John V., Gopesh Anand, and Aleda V. Roth. "The Influence of ISO 9000 Certification on Process Compliance." *Production and Operations Management* 24, no. 3 (March 2015): 369–382.

Gryna, F. M., R. C. H. Chua, and J. A. DeFeo. *Juran's Quality Planning and Analysis for Enterprise Quality*, 5th ed. New York: McGraw-Hill, 2007.

Mitra, Amit. *Fundamentals of Quality Control and Improvement*. New York: Wiley, 2009.

Pande, P. S., R. P. Neuman, R. R. Cavanagh. *What Is Design for Six Sigma?* New York: McGraw-Hill, 2005.

Petroski, Henry. *To Forgive Design: Understanding Failure*. Cambridge, MA: Belknap, 2012.

Schroeder, Roger G., et al. "Six Sigma: Definition and Underlying Theory." *Journal of Operations Management* 26, no. 4 (2008): 536–554.

Stewart, D. M. "Piecing Together Service Quality: A Framework for Robust Service." *Production and Operations Management* (Summer 2003): 246–265.

Summers, Donna. *Quality Management*, 2nd ed. Upper Saddle River, NJ: Prentice Hall, 2009.

Yan, Xinghao, Hui Zhao, and Kwei Tang. "Requirement or Promise? An Analysis of the First-Mover Advantage in Quality Contracting." *Production and Operations Management* 24, no. 6 (June 2015): 917–933.

Supplement 6

Bakir, S. T. "A Quality Control Chart for Work Performance Appraisal." *Quality Engineering* 17, no. 3 (2005): 429.

Besterfield, Dale H. *Quality Control*, 8th ed. Upper Saddle River, NJ: Prentice Hall, 2009.

Elg, M., J. Olsson, and J. J. Dahlgaard. "Implementing Statistical Process Control." *The International Journal of Quality and Reliability Management* 25, no. 6 (2008): 545.

Goetsch, David L., and Stanley B. Davis. *Quality Management*, 6th ed. Upper Saddle River, NJ: Prentice Hall, 2009.

Gryna, F. M., R. C. H. Chua, and J. A. DeFeo. *Juran's Quality Planning and Analysis*, 5th ed. New York: McGraw-Hill, 2007.

Lin, H., and G. Sheen. "Practical Implementation of the Capability Index C$_{pk}$ Based on Control Chart Data." *Quality Engineering* 17, no. 3 (2005): 371.

Matthes, N., et al. "Statistical Process Control for Hospitals." *Quality Management in Health Care* 16, no. 3 (July–September 2007): 205.

Mitra, Amit. *Fundamentals of Quality Control and Improvement*, 3rd ed. New York: Wiley, 2008.

Montgomery, D. C., C. L. Jennings, and M. E. Pfund. *Managing, Controlling, and Improving Quality*. New York: Wiley, 2011.

Roth, H. P. "How SPC Can Help Cut Costs." *Journal of Corporate Accounting and Finance* 16, no. 3 (March–April 2005): 21–30.

Sower, V. E. *Essentials of Quality*. New York: Wiley, 2011.

Summers, Donna. *Quality Management*, 2nd ed. Upper Saddle River, NJ: Prentice Hall, 2009.

Chapter 7

Davenport, T. H. "The Coming Commoditization of Processes." *Harvard Business Review* 83, no. 6 (June 2005): 101–108.

Debo, L. G., L. B. Toktay, and L. N. Van Wassenhove. "Market Segmentation and Product Technology Selection for Remanufacturable Products." *Management Science* 51, no. 8 (August 2005): 1193–1205.

Duray, R., P. T. Ward, G. W. Milligan, and W. L. Berry. "Approaches to Mass Customization: Configurations and Empirical Validation." *Journal of Operations Management* 18, no. 6 (November 2000): 605–625.

Duray, R. "Mass Customization Origins: Mass or Custom Manufacturing." *International Journal of Operations and Production Management* 22, no. 3 (2002): 314–328.

Hall, Joseph M., and M. Eric Johnson. "When Should a Process Be Art, Not Science?" *Harvard Business Review* 87, no. 3 (March 2009): 58–65.

Hegde, V. G., et al. "Customization: Impact on Product and Process Performance." *Production and Operations Management* 14, no. 4 (Winter 2005): 388–399.

Inderfurth, Karl, I. M. Langella. "An Approach for Solving Disassembly-to-order Problems under Stochastic Yields." In *Logistik Management*. Heidelberg: Physica, 2004: 309–331.

Moultrie, James, and Anja M. Maier. "A Simplified Approach to Design for Assembly." *Journal of Engineering Design* 25, no. 1–3 (March 2014): 44–63.

Rugtusanatham, M. Johnny, and Fabrizio Salvador. "From Mass Production to Mass Customization." *Production and Operations Management* 17, no. 3 (May–June 2008): 385–396.

Swamidass, Paul M. *Innovations in Competitive Manufacturing*. Dordrecht, NL: Kluwer, 2000.

Welborn, Cliff. "Mass Customization." *OR/MS Today* (December 2007): 38–42.

Zhang, M., Y. Qi, and X. Zhao. "The Impact of Mass Customization Practices on Performance." *International Journal of Mass Customization* 4, no. 1–2 (2011): 44–66.

Zipkin, Paul. "The Limits of Mass Customization." *MIT Sloan Management Review* 40, no. 1 (Spring 2001): 81–88.

Supplement 7

Anderson, Edward James, and Shu-Jung Sunny Yang. "The Timing of Capacity Investment with Lead Times: When Do Firms Act in Unison?" *Production and Operations Management* 24, no. 1 (January 2015): 21–41.

Anupindi, Ravi, S. Deshmukh, and S. Chopra. *Managing Business Process Flows*, 2nd ed. Upper Saddle River, NJ: Prentice Hall (2007).

Bowers, John, et al. "Modeling Outpatient Capacity for a Diagnosis and Treatment Center." *Health Care Management Science* 8, no. 3 (August 2005): 205.

Chambers, Chester, Eli M. Snir, and Asad Ata. "The Use of Flexible Manufacturing Capacity in Pharmaceutical Product Introductions." *Decision Sciences* 40, no. 2 (May 2009): 243–268.

Chen, Wen-Chih, and C. Chien. "Evaluating Capacity Pooling Strategy in Semiconductor Manufacturing: A Productivity Perspective Study." *International Journal of Production Research* 49, no 12 (June 2011): 3635–3652.

Goldratt, Eliyahu. *The Choice*. Great Barrington, MA: North River Press (2009).

Goodale, John C., Rohit Verma, and Madeleine E. Pullman. "A Market Utility-Based Model for Capacity Scheduling in Mass Services." *Production and Operations Management* 12, no. 2 (Summer 2003): 165–185.

Gupta, M. C., and L. H. Boyd. "Theory of Constraints: A Theory for Operations Management." *International Journal of Operations Management* 28, no. 10 (2008): 991.

Jonsson, Patrik, and Stig-Arne Mattsson. "Use and Applicability of Capacity Planning Methods." *Production and Inventory Management Journal* (3rd/4th Quarter 2002): 89–95.

Lee, Eva K., et al. "Transforming Hospital Emergency Department Workflow and Patient Care." *Interfaces* 45, no. 1 (January–February 2015): 58–82.

Li, Shanling, and L. Wang. "Outsourcing and Capacity Planning in an Uncertain Global Environment." *European Journal of Operational Research* 207, no. 1 (November 2010): 131–141.

May, Jerrold H., W. E. Spangler, D. P. Strum, and L. G. Vargas. "The Surgical Scheduling Problem: Current Research and Future Opportunities." *Production & Operations Management* 20, no. 3 (May–June 2011): 392–405.

Mincsovics, G. Z., and N. P. Dellaert. "Workload-Dependent Capacity Control in Production-to-Order Systems." *IIE Transactions,* 41, no. 10 (October 2009): 853–865.

Roy, Anjan. "Strategic Positioning and Capacity Utilization: Factors in Planning for Profitable Growth in Banking." *Journal of Performance Management* 23, no. 3 (November 2010): 23.

Tanrisever, Fehmi, D. Morrice, and D. Morton. "Managing Capacity Flexibility in Make-to-Order Production Environments." *European Journal of Operational Research* 216, no. 2 (January 2012): 334–345.

Tibben-Lembke, Ronald S. "Theory of Constraints at UniCo." *International Journal of Production Research* 47, no. 7 (January 2009): 1815.

Watson, Kevin J., John H. Blackstone, and Stanley C. Gardiner. "The Evolution of a Management Philosophy: The Theory of Constraints." *Journal of Operations Management* 25, no. 2 (March 2007): 387–402.

Chapter 8

Ballou, Ronald H. *Business Logistics Management*, 5th ed. Upper Saddle River, NJ: Prentice Hall, 2004.

Bartness, A. D. "The Plant Location Puzzle." *Harvard Business Review* 72, no. 2 (March–April 1994).

Denton, B. "Decision Analysis, Location Models, and Scheduling Problems." *Interfaces* 30, no. 3 (May–June 2005): 262–263.

Drezner, Z. *Facility Location: Applications and Theory*. Berlin: Springer-Verlag, 2002.

Florida, R. *The Flight of the Creative Class: The New Global Competition for Talent*. New York: HarperCollins, 2005.

Klamroth, K. *Single Facility Location Problems*. Berlin: Springer-Verlag, 2002.

Kennedy, M. *Introducing Geographic Information Systems with ArcGIS*. New York: Wiley, 2006.

Mentzer, John T. "Seven Keys to Facility Location." *Supply Chain Management Review* 12, no. 5 (May 2008): 25.

Partovi, F. Y. "An Analytic Model for Locating Facilities Strategically." *Omega* 34, no. 1 (January 2006): 41.

Porter, Michael E., and Scott Stern. "Innovation: Location Matters." *MIT Sloan Management Review* (Summer 2001): 28–36.

Render, B., R. M. Stair, and M. Hanna. *Quantitative Analysis for Management*, 11th ed. Upper Saddle River, NJ: Prentice Hall, 2012.

Snyder, L. V. "Facility Location Under Uncertainty." *IIE Transactions* 38, no. 7 (July 2006): 547.

Tallman, Stephen, et al. "Knowledge, Clusters, and Competitive Advantage." *The Academy of Management Review* 29, no. 2 (April 2004): 258–271.

White, G. "Location, Location, Location." *Nation's Restaurant News* 42, no. 27 (July 14, 2008): S10–S11.

Chapter 9

Aghazadeh, S. M., S. Hafeznezami, L. Najjar, and Z. Hug. "The Influence of Work-Cells and Facility Layout on Manufacturing Efficiency." *Journal of Facilities Management* 9, no. 3 (2011): 213–224.

Birchfield, J. C., and J. Birchfield. *Design and Layout of Foodservice Facilities*, 3rd ed. New York, Wiley & Sons, 2007.

Francis, R. L., L. F. McGinnis, and J. A. White. *Facility Layout and Location*, 3rd ed. Upper Saddle River, NJ: Prentice Hall, 1998.

Heragu, S. S. *Facilities Design*, 3rd ed. New York: CRC Press, 2008.

Heyer, N., and U. Wemmerlöv. *Reorganizing the Factory: Competing through Cellular Manufacturing*. Portland, OR: Productivity Press, 2002.

Johnson, Alan. "Getting the Right Factory Layout." *Manufacturer's Monthly* (July 2008): 16.

Kator, C. "Crossdocking on the Rise." *Modern Materials Handling* 63, no. 6 (June 2008): 15.

Larson, S. "Extreme Makover—OR Edition." *Nursing Management* (November 2005): 26.

Quillien, Jenny. *Clever Digs: How Workspaces Can Enable Thought*. Ames, Iowa: Culicidae Press, LLC., 2012.

Roodbergen, K. J., and I. F. A. Vis. "A Model for Warehouse Layout." *IIE Transactions* 38, no. 10 (October 2006): 799–811.

Stanowy, A. "Evolutionary Strategy for Manufacturing Cell Design." *Omega* 34, no. 1 (January 2006): 1.

Taghavi, A., and A. Murat. "A Heuristic Procedure for the Integrated Facility Layout Design and Flow Assignment Problem." *Computers & Industrial Engineering* 61, no. 1 (August 2011): 55–63.

Tompkins, James A. *Facility Planning*, 4th ed. New York: Wiley, 2009.

Upton, David. "What Really Makes Factories Flexible?" *Harvard Business Review* 73, no. 4 (July–August 1995): 74–84.

Zhao, T., and C. L. Tseng. "Flexible Facility Interior Layout." *The Journal of the Operational Research Society* 58, no. 6 (June 2007): 729–740.

Chapter 10

Aft, Larry, and Neil Schmeidler. "Work Measurement Practices." *Industrial Engineer* 35, no. 11 (November 2003): 44.

Barnes, R. M. *Motion and Time Study, Design and Measurement of Work*, 7th ed. New York: Wiley, 1980.

Bridger, R. S. *Introduction to Ergonomics*, 3rd ed. New York: CRC Press, 2008.

De Jong, A., K. De Ruyter, and J. Lemmink. "Service Climate in Self-Managing Teams." *The Journal of Management Studies* 42, no. 8 (December 2005): 1593.

Freivalds, Andris, and B. W. Niebel. *Methods, Standards, and Work Design*, 12th ed. New York: Irwin/McGraw-Hill, 2009.

Huselid, Mark A., Richard W. Beatty, and Brian E. Becker. "'A Players' or 'A Positions'? The Strategic Logic of Workforce Management." *Harvard Business Review* (December 2005): 110–117.

Konz, S., and Steven Johnson. *Work Design: Industrial Ergonomics*, 7th ed. Scottsdale, AZ: Holcomb Hathaway, 2007.

Muthusamy, S. K., J. V. Wheeler, and B. L. Simmons. "Self-Managing Work Teams." *Organization Development Journal* 23, no. 3 (Fall 2005): 53–66.

Pfeffer, Jeffrey. "Producing Sustainable Competitive Advantage Through the Effective Management of People." *Academy of Management Executive* 19, no. 4 (2005): 95.

Salvendy, G., ed. *Handbook of Human Factors and Ergonomics*, 3rd ed. New York: Wiley, 2006.

Shahrokh, Shahraki, and N. A. Bakar. "Relationship Between Human Factors Engineering and Productivity." *Interdisciplinary Journal of Contemporary Research in Business* 3, no. 3 (July 2011): 706–712.

Sonne, Michael, D. L. Villalta, and D. M. Andrews. "Development and Evaluation of an Office Ergonomic Risk Check List." *Applied Ergonomics* 43, no. 1 (January 2012): 98–100.

Tolo, B. "21st-Century Stopwatch." *Industrial Engineer* 37, no. 7 (July 2005): 34–37.

Village, Judy, Patrick W. Neumann. "Designing for Human Factors." *Industrial Engineer: IE* 46, no. 11 (November 2014): 36–41.

Walsh, Ellen. "Get Results with Workload Management." *Nursing Management* (October 2003): 16.

White, Catherine M. "Proactive Ergonomics." *Professional Safety* 60, no. 6 (June 2015): 69–73.

Chapter 11

Autry, Chad W., Thomas J. Goldsby, and John E. Bell. *Global Macrotrends and Their Impact on Supply Chain Management*. Upper Saddle River, NJ: FT Press, 2013.

Blackburn, Joseph, and Gary Scudder. "Supply Chain Strategies for Perishable Products." *Production and Operations Management* 18, no. 2 (March–April 2009): 129–137.

Boyer, Kenneth K., and G. Tomas M. Hult. "Extending the Supply Chain: Integrating Operations and Marketing in the Online Grocery Industry." *Journal of Operations Management* 23, no. 6 (September 2005): 642–661.

Chopra, Sunil, and Peter Meindl. *Supply Chain Management*, 4th ed. Upper Saddle River, NJ: Prentice Hall (2010).

Crandall, Richard E. "The Next Wave of Sourcing." *APICS* 24, no. 3 (May/June 2014): 26–28.

Crook, T. Russell, and James G. Combs. "Sources and Consequences of Bargaining Power in Supply Chains." *Journal of Operations Management* 25, no. 2 (March 2007): 546–555.

Hu, J., and C. L. Munson. "Speed versus Reliability Trade-offs in Supplier Selection." *International Journal Procurement Management* 1, no. 1/2 (2007): 238–259.

Kersten, Wolfgang, and Thorsten Blecker (eds.). *Managing Risk in Supply Chains*. Berlin: Erich Schmidt Verlag GmbH & Co. (2006).

Kreipl, Stephan, and Michael Pinedo. "Planning and Scheduling in Supply Chains." *Production and Operations Management* 13, no. 1 (Spring 2004): 77–92.

Linton, J. D., R. Klassen, and V. Jayaraman. "Sustainable Supply Chains: An Introduction." *Journal of Operations Management* 25, no. 6 (November, 2007): 1075–1082.

Monczka, R. M., R. B. Handfield, L. C. Gianipero, and J. L. Patterson. *Purchasing and Supply Chain Management*, 5th ed. Mason, OH: Cengage, 2012.

Munson, Chuck (ed.). *The Supply Chain Management Casebook: Comprehensive Coverage and Best Practices in SCM*. Upper Saddle River, NJ: FT Press, 2013.

Narayanan, Sriram, Ann S. Marucheck, and Robert B. Handfield. "Electronic Data Interchange: Research Review and Future Directions." *Decisions Sciences* 40, no. 1 (February 2009): 121–163.

Paine, Lincoln. *The Sea and Civilization*. New York: Knopf, 2013.

Pisano, Gary P., and Roberto Verganti. "Which Kind of Collaboration Is Right for You?" *Harvard Business Review* 86, no. 12 (December, 2008): 78–86.

Sinha, K. K., and E. J. Kohnke. "Health Care Supply Chain Design." *Decision Sciences* 40, no. 2 (May 2009): 197–212.

Stanley, L. L., and V. R. Singhal. "Service Quality Along the Supply Chain." *Journal of Operations Management* 19, no. 3 (May 2001): 287–306.

Wisner, Joel, K. Tan, and G. Keong Leong. *Principles of Supply Chain Management*, 4th ed., Mason, OH: Cengage, 2012.

Yang, Shilei, Charles L. Munson, Bintong Chen, and Chunming Shi. "Coordinated Contracts for Supply Chains that Market with Mail-In Rebates and Retailer Promotions." *Journal of the Operational Research Society* (2015), DOI: JORS.2014.127.

Supplement 11

Berger, Paul D., Arthur Gerstenfeld, and Amy Z. Zeng. "How Many Suppliers Are Best? A Decision-Analysis Approach." *Omega* 32, no. 1 (February 2004): 9–15.

Chopra, Sunil, and Peter Meindl. *Supply Chain Management*, 4th ed. Upper Saddle River, NJ: Prentice Hall, 2010.

Disney, Stephen M., and Marc R. Lambrecht. "On Replenishment Rules, Forecasting, and the Bullwhip Effect in Supply Chains." *Foundations and Trends in Technology, Information and Operations Management* 2, no. 1 (2007), 1–80.

Lee, Chieh, and Charles L. Munson. "A Predictive Global Sensitivity Analysis Approach to Monitoring and Modifying Operational Hedging Positions." *International Journal of Integrated Supply Management* 9, no. 3 (2015): 178–201.

Roodbergen, Kees Jan, Iris FA Vis, and G. Don Taylor Jr. "Simultaneous Determination of Warehouse Layout and Control Policies." *International Journal of Production Research* 53, no. 11 (2015): 3306–3326.

Wang, Phanich P., S. Kara, and B. Kayis. "Analysis of the Bullwhip Effect in Multi-product, Multi-stage Supply Chain Systems—A Simulation Approach." *International Journal of Production Research* 48, no. 15 (August 2010): 4501–4517.

Chapter 12

Abernathy, Frederick H., et al. "Control Your Inventory in a World of Lean Retailing." *Harvard Business Review* 78, no. 6 (November–December 2000): 169–176.

Arnold, J. R., S. N. Chapman, and L. M. Clive. *Introduction to Materials Management*, 6th ed. Upper Saddle River, NJ: Prentice Hall, 2008.

Baron, Opher, O. Derman, and D. Perry. "Shelf Space Management When Demand Depends on the Inventory Level." *Production and Operations Management* 20, no. 5 (September–October 2011): 714–726.

Burt, D. N., S. Petcavage, and R. Pinkerton. *Supply Management*, 8th ed. Burr Ridge, IL: Irwin/McGraw, 2010.

Chapman, Stephen. *Fundamentals of Production Planning and Control*. Upper Saddle River, NJ: Prentice Hall, 2006.

Chopra, Sunil, Gilles Reinhardt, and Maqbool Dada. "The Effect of Lead Time Uncertainty on Safety Stocks." *Decision Sciences* 35, no. 1 (Winter 2004): 1–24.

Doğru, Mustafa K., and Ulaş Özen. "Tactical Inventory Planning at Alcatel-Lucent's Repair and Exchange Services." *Interfaces* 45, no. 3 (May–June 2015): 228–242.

Geismar, H. N., M. Dawande, and C. Sriskandarajah. "Pool-Point Distribution of Zero-Inventory Products." *Production and Operations Management* 20, no. 5 (September–October 2011): 737–753.

Harris, Chris and Thomas Parker. "Portion Control." *APICS* 24, no. 5 (September/October 2014): 26–28.

Keren, Baruch. "The Single Period Inventory Model." *Omega* 37, no. 4 (August 2009): 801.

Lee, H., and O. Ozer. "Unlocking the Value of RFID." *Production and Operations Management* 16, no. 1 (2007): 40–64.

Liu, X., and Z. Lian. "Cost-effective Inventory Control in a Value-added Manufacturing System." *European Journal of Operational Research* 196, no. 2 (July 2009): 534.

McDonald, Stan C. *Materials Management*. New York: Wiley, 2009.

Munson, Charles L., and Jonathan Jackson. "Quantity Discounts: An Overview and Practical Guide for Buyers and Sellers." *Foundations and Trends in Technology, Information and Operations Management* 8, nos. 1–2 (2014): 1–130.

Render, B., R. M. Stair, and M. Hanna. *Quantitative Analysis for Management*, 11th ed. Upper Saddle River, NJ: Prentice Hall, 2012.

Rubin, Paul A., and W. C. Benton. "A Generalized Framework for Quantity Discount Pricing Schedules." *Decision Sciences* 34, no. 1 (Winter 2003): 173–188.

Sethi, Suresh P. "i3: Incomplete Inventory Models." *Decision Line* (October 2010): 16–19.

Stein, Andrew C. "Warehouse Measurement and Control." *APICS* 24, no. 3 (May/June 2014): 42–45.

Teunter, Ruud H., M. Z. Babai, and A. A. Syntetos. "ABC Classification: Service Levels and Inventory Cost." *Production and Operations Management* 19, no. 3 (May–June 2010): 343–352.

Vollmann, T. E., W. L. Berry, D. C. Whybark, and F. R. Jacobs. *Manufacturing Planning and Control for Supply Chain Management*, 5th ed. Burr Ridge, IL: Irwin/McGraw, 2005.

Witt, Clyde E. "Mobile Warehouse Supplies U.S. Marines in Iraq." *Material Handling Management* 60, no. 8 (August 2005): 24–25.

Chapter 13

APICS. *2011 Sales and Operations Planning Practices and Challenges.* Chicago: APICS, 2011.

Bilginer, Özlem, and Feryal Erhun. "Production and Sales Planning in Capacitated New Product Introductions." *Production and Operations Management* 24, no. 1 (January 2015): 42–53.

Buxey, G. "Aggregate Planning for Seasonal Demand." *International Journal of Operations & Production Management* 25, no. 11 (2005): 1083–1100.

Chen, Fangruo. "Salesforce Initiative, Market Information, and Production/Inventory Planning." *Management Science* 51, no. 1 (January 2005): 60–75.

Chen, Ming, and Zhi-Long Chen. "Recent Developments in Dynamic Pricing Research: Multiple Products, Competition, and Limited Demand Information." *Production and Operations Management* 24, no. 5 (May 2015): 704–731.

Jacobs, F. R., W. L. Berry, D. C. Whybark, and T. E. Vollmann. *Manufacturing Planning and Control for Supply Chain Management*, 6th ed. Burr Ridge, IL: Irwin, 2011.

Kin, S., and S. Yoo. "The Combined Manpower Planning Strategies by Aggregate Planning for the Service Division of Vending Machines." *Journal of the Operational Research Society* 62 (November 2011).

Kimes, S. E., and G. M. Thompson. "Restaurant Revenue Management at Chevy's." *Decision Sciences* 35, no. 3 (Summer 2004): 371–393.

Metters, R., K. King-Metters, M. Pullman, and S. Walton. *Successful Service Operations Management*. 2nd ed. Mason, OH: Thomson-South-Western, 2006.

Metters, Richard, et al. "The 'Killer Application' of Revenue Management: Harrah's Cherokee Casino and Hotel." *Interfaces* 38, no. 3 (May–June 2008): 161–178.

Mukhopadhyay, S., S. Samaddar, and G. Colville. "Improving Revenue Management Decision Making for Airlines." *Decision Science* 38, no. 2 (May 2007): 309–327.

Sillekens, Thomas, A. Koberstein, and L. Suhl, "Aggregate Production Planning in the Automotive Industry with Special Consideration of Workforce Flexibility." *International Journal of Production Research* 49, no. 17 (September 2011): 5055–5078.

Silver, E. A., D. F. Pyke, and R. Peterson. *Inventory Management and Production Planning and Scheduling*. New York: Wiley, 1998.

Chapter 14

Barba-Gutierrez, Y., B. Adenso-Diaz, and S. M. Gupta. "Lot Sizing in Reverse MRP for Scheduling Disassembly." *International Journal of Production Economics* 111, no. 2 (February 2008): 741.

Bell, Steve. "Time Fence Secrets." *APICS* 16, no. 4 (April 2006): 44–48.

Bolander, Steven, and Sam G. Taylor. "Scheduling Techniques: A Comparison of Logic." *Production and Inventory Management Journal* 41, no. 1 (1st Quarter 2000): 1–5.

Crandall, Richard E. "The Epic Life of ERP." *APICS* 16, no. 2 (February 2006): 17–19.

De Mathis J. J. "An Economic Lot-Sizing Technique: The Part-Period Algorithms." *IBM Systems Jonmal* 7 (1968): 30–38.

Diehl Gregory W., and A. J. Armstrong "Making MRP Work." *Industrial Engineer* 43, no. 11 (November 2011): 35–40.

Kanet, J., and V. Sridharan. "The Value of Using Scheduling Information in Planning Material Requirements." *Decision Sciences* 29, no. 2 (Spring 1998): 479–498.

Krupp, James A. G. "Integrating Kanban and MRP to Reduce Lead Time." *Production and Inventory Management Journal* 43, no. 3–4 (3rd/4th quarter 2002): 78–82.

Louly, Mohamed-Aly, and A. Dolgui. "Optimal Time Phasing and Periodicity for MRP with POQ Policy." *International Journal of Production Economics* 131, no. 1 (May 2011): 76.

Norris, G. *E-Business & ERP*. New York: Wiley, 2005.

O' Sullivan, Jill, and Gene Caiola. *Enterprise Resource Planning*, 2nd ed. New York: McGraw-Hill, 2008.

Segerstedt, A. "Master Production Scheduling and a Comparison of MRP and Cover-Time Planning." *International Journal of Production Research* 44, no. 18–19 (September 2006): 3585.

Steger-Jensen, Kenn, H. Hvolby, P. Nielsen, and I. Nielson. "Advanced Planning and Scheduling Technology." *Production Planning and Control* 22, no. 8 (December 2011): 800–808.

Summer, M. *Enterprise Resource Planning*. Upper Saddle River, NJ: Prentice Hall, 2005.

Tian, Feng, and Sean Xin Xu. "How do Enterprise Resource Planning Systems Affect Firm Risk? Post-Implementation Impact." *MIS Quarterly* 39, no. 1 (March 2015): 39–60.

Turbide, Dave. "New-Fashioned MRP." *APICS* 24, no. 3 (July/August 2015): 40–44.

Wagner, H. M., and T. M. Whitin. "Dynamic Version of the Economic Lot Size Model." *Management Science* 5, no. 1 (1958): 89–96.

Wu, Jen-Hur, et al. "Using Multiple Variables Decision-Making Analysis for ERP Selection." *International Journal of Manufacturing Technology and Management* 18, no. 2 (2009): 228.

Chapter 15

Baker, Kenneth A., and Dan Trietsch. *Principles of Sequencing and Scheduling.* New York: Wiley, 2009.

Cayirli, Tugba, and Emre Veral. "Outpatient Scheduling in Health Care: A Review of Literature." *Production and Operations Management* 12, no. 4 (Winter 2003): 519–549.

Chapman, Stephen. *Fundamentals of Production Planning and Control.* Upper Saddle River, NJ: Prentice Hall, 2006.

Deng, Honghui, Q. Wang, G. K. Leong, and S. X. Sun. "Usage of Opportunity Cost to Maximize Performance in Revenue Management." *Decision Sciences* 38, no. 4 (November 2008): 737–758.

Dietrich, Brenda, G. A. Paleologo, and L. Wynter. "Revenue Management in Business Services." *Production and Operations Management* 17, no. 4 (July–August 2008): 475–480.

Farmer, Adam, Jeffrey S. Smith, and Luke T. Miller. "Scheduling Umpire Crews for Professional Tennis Tournaments." *Interfaces* 37, no. 2 (March–April 2007): 187–196.

Kellogg, Deborah L., and Steven Walczak. "Nurse Scheduling." *Interfaces* 37, no. 4 (July–August 2007): 355–369.

Lopez, P., and F. Roubellat. *Production Scheduling.* New York: Wiley, 2008.

Mondschein, S. V., and G. Y. Weintraub. "Appointment Policies in Service Operations." *Production and Operations Management* 12, no. 2 (Summer 2003): 266–286.

Morton, Thomas E., and David W. Pentico. *Heuristic Scheduling Systems.* New York: Wiley, 1993.

Pinedo, M. *Scheduling: Theory, Algorithms, and Systems,* 2nd ed. Upper Saddle River, N.J.: Prentice Hall, 2002.

Plenert, Gerhard, and Bill Kirchmier. *Finite Capacity Scheduling.* New York: Wiley, 2000.

Render, B., R. M. Stair, and M. Hanna. *Quantitative Analysis for Management,* 11th ed. Upper Saddle River, NJ: Prentice Hall, 2012.

Robidoux, L., and P. Donnelly. "Automated Employee Scheduling." *Nursing Management* 42, no. 12 (December 2011): 41–43.

Veeraraghavan, S., and R. Vaidyanathan. "Measuring Seat Value in Stadiums and Theatres." *Production and Operations Management* 21, no. 1 (January–February 2012): 49–68.

Chapter 16

Black, I. T., and D. T. Phillips. "The Lean to Green Evolution." *Industrial Engineer* 42, no. 6 (June 2010): 46–51.

Flinchbauh, Jamie. *The Hitchhiker's Guide to Lean.* Dearborn, MI: Society of Manufacturing Engineers, 2006.

Graban, Mark. *Lean Hospitals.* 2nd ed. New York: CRC Press, 2012.

Hall, Robert W. "'Lean' and the Toyota Production System." *Target* 20, no. 3 (3rd Issue 2004): 22–27.

Keyte, Beau, and Drew Locher. *The Complete Lean Enterprise.* University Park, IL: Productivity Press, 2004.

Morgan, James M., and Jeffrey K. Liker. *The Toyota Product Development System.* New York: Productivity Press, 2007.

Nelson-Peterson, Dana L., and Carol J. Leppa, "Creating an Environment of Caring Using Lean Principles of the Virginia Mason Production System." *Journal of Nursing Administration* 37 (2007): 289.

Parks, Charles M. "The Bare Necessities of Lean." *Industrial Engineer* 35, no. 8 (August 2003): 39.

Radnor, Zoe J., M. Holweg, and J. Waring, "Lean in Healthcare: The Unfilled Promise?" *Social Science & Medicine* 74, no. 3 (February 2012): 364–371.

Sayre, Kim. "A Lean Introduction to Sustainability." *Industrial Engineer* 40, no. 9 (September 2008): 34.

Schonberger, Richard J. "Lean Extended." *Industrial Engineer* (December 2005): 26–31.

van Veen-Dirks, Paula. "Management Control and the Production Environment." *International Journal of Production Economics* 93 (January 8, 2005): 263.

Womack, James P., and Daniel T. Jones. "Lean Consumption." *Harvard Business Review* 83 (March 2005): 58–68.

Womack, James P., and Daniel T. Jones. *Lean Solutions: How Companies and Customers Can Create Value and Wealth Together.* New York: The Free Press, 2005.

Chapter 17

Ait-Kadi, D., J. B. Menge, and H. Kane. "Resource Assignment Model in Maintenance Activities Scheduling." *International Journal of Production Research* 49, no. 22 (November 2011): 6677–6689.

Bauer, Eric, X. Zhang, and D. A. Kimber. *Practical System Reliability.* New York: Wiley, 2009.

Blank, Ronald. *The Basics of Reliability.* University Park, IL: Productivity Press, 2004.

Finigen, Tim, and Jim Humphries. "Maintenance Gets Lean." *IE Industrial Systems* 38, no. 10 (October 2006): 26–31.

Phillippi, Brian, "3 Keys to Predictive Maintenance Success." *Flow Control* 21, no. 5 (May 2015): 7–8.

Rahman, Anisur, "Maintenance Contract Model for Complex Asset/Equipment." *International Journal of Reliability, Quality, & Safety Engineering* 21, no. 1 (February 2014): 1–11.

Stephens, M. P. *Productivity and Reliability-Based Maintenance Management.* Upper Saddle River, NJ: Prentice Hall, 2004.

Weil, Marty. "Beyond Preventive Maintenance." *APICS* 16, no. 4 (April 2006): 40–43.

Module A

Balakrishnan, R., B. Render, and R. M. Stair Jr. *Managerial Decision Modeling with Spreadsheets,* 3rd ed. Upper Saddle River, NJ: Prentice Hall, 2012.

Buchannan, Leigh, and Andrew O'Connell. "A Brief History of Decision Making." *Harvard Business Review* 84, no. 1 (January, 2006): 32–41.

Hammond, J. S., R. L. Kenney, and H. Raiffa. "The Hidden Traps in Decision Making." *Harvard Business Review* 84, no. 1 (January 2006): 118–126.

Keefer, Donald L. "Balancing Drug Safety and Efficacy for a Go/No-Go Decision." *Interfaces* 34, no. 2 (March–April 2004): 113–116.

Miller, C. C., and R. D. Ireland. "Intuition in Strategic Decision Making." *Academy of Management Executive* 19, no. 1 (February 2005): 19.

Parmigiani, G., and L. Inoue. *Decision Theory: Principles and Approaches.* New York: Wiley, 2010.

Raiffa, H., and R. Schlaifer. *Applied Statistical Decision Theory.* New York: Wiley, 2000.

Render, B., R. M. Stair Jr., and M. Hanna. *Quantitative Analysis for Management,* 11th ed. Upper Saddle River, NJ: Prentice Hall, 2012.

Module B

Anderson, Ross, et al. "Kidney Exchange and the Alliance for Paired Donation: Operations Research Changes the Way Kidneys Are Transplanted." *Interfaces* 45, no. 1 (January–February 2015), 26–42.

Balakrishman, R., B. Render, and R. M. Stair. *Managerial Decision Modeling with Spreadsheets,* 3rd ed. Upper Saddle River, NJ: Prentice Hall, 2012.

Denton, Brian T. "AusWest Timbers Uses an Optimization Model to Improve Its Manufacturing Process." *Interfaces* 38, no. 4 (July–August 2008): 341–344.

Duran, G., et al. "Scheduling the Chilean Soccer League by Integer Programming." *Interfaces* 37, no. 6 (November–December 2007): 539–555.

Harrod, Steven. "A Spreadsheet-Based, Matrix Formulation Linear Programming Lesson." *Decision Sciences Journal of Innovative Education* 7, no. 1 (January 2009): 249.

Martin, C. H. "Ohio University's College of Business Uses Integer Programming to Schedule Classes." *Interfaces* 34 (November–December 2004): 460–465.

Matthews, C. H. "Using Linear Programming to Minimize the Cost of Nurse Personnel." *Journal of Health Care Finance* (September 2005).

Pasupathy, K., and A. Medina-Borja. "Integrating Excel, Access, and Visual Basic to Deploy Performance Measurement and Evaluation at the American Red Cross." *Interfaces* 38, no. 4 (July–August 2008): 324–340.

Render, B., R. M. Stair, and Michael Hanna. *Quantitative Analysis for Management,* 11th ed. Upper Saddle River, NJ: Prentice Hall, 2012.

Sodhi, M. S., and S. Norri. "A Fast and Optimal Modeling Approach Applied to Crew Rostering at London Underground." *Annals of OR* 127 (March 2004): 259.

Taylor, Bernard. *Introduction to Management Science*, 10th ed. Upper Saddle River, NJ: Prentice Hall, 2011.

Tian, Zhili, Panos Kouvelis, and Charles L. Munson. "Understanding and Managing Product Line Complexity: Applying Sensitivity Analysis to a Large-Scale MILP Model to Price and Schedule New Customer Orders." *IIE Transactions* 47, no. 4 (2015), 307–328.

Module C

Balakrishnan, R., B. Render, and R. M. Stair. *Managerial Decision Modeling with Spreadsheets*, 3rd. ed. Upper Saddle River, NJ: Prentice Hall, 2012.

Drezner, Z. *Facility Location: A Survey of Applications and Methods.* Secaucus, NJ: Springer-Verlag, 1995.

Koksalan, M., and H. Sural. "Efes Beverage Group Makes Location and Distribution Decisions for Its Malt Plants." *Interfaces* 29 (March–April 1999): 89–103.

Ping, J., and K. F. Chu. "A Dual-Matrix Approach to the Transportation Problem." *Asia-Pacific Journal of Operations Research* 19 (May 2002): 35–46.

Render, B., R. M. Stair, and M. Hanna. *Quantitative Analysis for Management*, 11th ed. Upper Saddle River, NJ: Prentice Hall, 2012.

Schmenner, R. W. "Look Beyond the Obvious in Plant Location." *Harvard Business Review* 57, no. 1 (January–February 1979): 126–132.

Taylor, B. *Introduction to Management Science*, 10th ed., Upper Saddle River, NJ: Prentice Hall, 2011.

Module D

Balakrishnan, R., B. Render, and R. M. Stair. *Managerial Decision Modeling with Spreadsheets*, 3rd ed. Upper Saddle River, NJ: Prentice Hall, 2012.

Canonaco, P., et al. "A Queuing Network Model for the Management of Berth Crane Operations." *Computers & Operations Research* 35, no. 8 (August 2008): 2432.

Cochran, J. K., and K. Roche. "A Queueing-Based Decision Support Methodology to Estimate Hospital Inpatient Bed Demand." *Journal of the Operational Research Society* 59, no. 11 (November 2008): 1471–1483.

Gross, Donald, John F. Shortle, James M. Thompson, and Carl M. Harris. *Fundamentals of Queuing Theory*, 4th ed. New York: Wiley, 2008.

Parlar, M., and M. Sharafali. "Dynamic Allocation of Airline Check-In Counters: A Queueing Optimization Problem." *Management Science* 54, no. 8 (August 2008): 1410–1425.

Prabhu, N. U. *Foundations of Queuing Theory.* Dordecht, Netherlands: Kluwer Academic Publishers, 1997.

Render, B., R. M. Stair, and M. Hanna. *Quantitative Analysis for Management*, 11th ed. Upper Saddle River, NJ: Prentice Hall, 2012.

Stanford, D. A., E. Renouf, and V. C. McAlister. "Waiting for Liver Transplantation in Canada." *Health Care Management Science* 11, no. 2 (June 2008): 196–208.

Yan Kovic, N., and L. V. Green. "Identifying Good Nursing Levels: A Queuing Approach." *Operations Research* 59, no. 4 (July/August 2011): 942–955.

Module E

Boh, W. F., S. A. Slaughter, and J. A. Espinosa. "Learning from Experience in Software Development." *Management Science* 53, no. 8 (August 2007): 1315–1332.

Couto, J. P., and J. C. Teixeira. "Using a Linear Model for Learning Curve Effect on Highrise Floor Construction." *Construction Management & Economics* 23 (May 2005): 355.

McDonald, A., and L. Schrattenholzer. "Learning Curves and Technology Assessment." *International Journal of Technology Management* 23 (2002): 718.

Morrison, J. Bradley. "Putting the Learning Curve into Context." *Journal of Business Research* 61, no. 1 (November 2008): 1182.

Ngwenyama, O., A. Guergachi, and T. McLaren. "Using the Learning Curve to Maximize IT Productivity." *International Journal of Production Economics* 105, no. 2 (February 2007): 524.

Smunt, T. L., and C. A. Watts. "Improving Operations Planning with Learning Curves." *Journal of Operations Management* 21 (January 2003): 93.

Weston, M. *Learning Curves.* New York: Crown Publishing, 2000.

Module F

Balakrishnan, R., B. Render, and R. M. Stair. *Managerial Decision Modeling with Spreadsheets*, 3rd ed. Upper Saddle River, NJ: Prentice Hall, 2012.

Banks, Jerry, and Randall R. Gibson. "The ABC's of Simulation Practice." *Analytics* (Spring 2009): 16–23.

Banks, J., J. S. Carson, B. L. Nelson, and D. M. Nicol. *Discrete-Event System Simulation*, 5th ed. Upper Saddle River, NJ: Prentice Hall, 2010.

Huang, H. C., et al. "Sim Man—A Simulation Model for Workforce Capacity Planning." *Computers & Operations Research* 196, no. 3 (August 1, 2009): 1147.

Kelton, W. D., R. P. Sadowski, and N. B. Swets, *Simulation with Arena*, 5th ed. New York: McGraw-Hill, 2010.

Klassen, K., and R. Yoogalingam. "Improving Performance in Outpatient Appointment Services with a Simulation Optimization Approach." *Production and Operations Management* 18, no. 4 (2009): 447–458.

Render, B., R. M. Stair, and M. Hanna. *Quantitative Analysis for Management*, 11th ed. Upper Saddle River, NJ: Prentice Hall, 2012.

Rossetti, Manuel D. *Simulation Modeling and ARENA.* New York: Wiley, 2009.

Saltzman, Robert M., and Vijay Mehrotra. "A Call Center Uses Simulation to Drive Strategic Change." *Interfaces* 31, no. 3 (May–June 2001): 87–101.

Sud, V. P., et al. "Reducing Flight Delays Through Better Traffic Management." *Interfaces* 39, no. 1 (January/February 2009): 35–51.

Taylor, S. J .E., et al. "Simulation Modelling Is 50." *The Journal of the Operational Research Society* 60, no. S1 (May 2009): S69–S13.

Zhang, Aheng, and Xiaolan Xie. "Simulation-based Optimization for Surgery Appointment Scheduling of Multiple Operating Rooms." *IIE Transactions* 47, no. 9 (September 2015): 998–1012.

General Index

Note: Page numbers beginning with a T refer to the Online Tutorial chapters that appear on our web site **www.pearsonhighered.com/heizer.**